enVisionmath 2.0

SCOTT FORESMAN · ADDISON WESLEY

Volume 1 Topics 1–8

Authors

Randall I. Charles
Professor Emeritus
Department of Mathematics
San Jose State University
San Jose, California

Jennifer Bay-Williams
Professor of Mathematics Education
College of Education and Human Development
University of Louisville
Louisville, Kentucky

Robert Q. Berry, III
Associate Professor of Mathematics Education
Department of Curriculum, Instruction and Special Education
University of Virginia
Charlottesville, Virginia

Janet H. Caldwell
Professor of Mathematics
Rowan University
Glassboro, New Jersey

Zachary Champagne
Assistant in Research
Florida Center for Research in Science, Technology, Engineering, and Mathematics (FCR-STEM)
Jacksonville, Florida

Juanita Copley
Professor Emerita, College of Education
University of Houston
Houston, Texas

Warren Crown
Professor Emeritus of Mathematics Education
Graduate School of Education
Rutgers University
New Brunswick, New Jersey

Francis (Skip) Fennell
L. Stanley Bowlsbey Professor of Education and Graduate and Professional Studies
McDaniel College
Westminster, Maryland

Karen Karp
Professor of Mathematics Education
Department of Early Childhood and Elementary Education
University of Louisville
Louisville, Kentucky

Stuart J. Murphy
Visual Learning Specialist
Boston, Massachusetts

Jane F. Schielack
Professor of Mathematics
Associate Dean for Assessment and Pre K–12 Education, College of Science
Texas A&M University
College Station, Texas

Jennifer M. Suh
Associate Professor for Mathematics Education
George Mason University
Fairfax, Virginia

Jonathan A. Wray
Mathematics Instructional Facilitator
Howard County Public Schools
Ellicott City, Maryland

PEARSON

Glenview, Illinois Boston, Massachusetts Chandler, Arizona Hoboken, New Jersey

Mathematicians

Roger Howe
Professor of Mathematics
Yale University
New Haven, Connecticut

Gary Lippman
Professor of Mathematics and Computer Science
California State University, East Bay
Hayward, California

ELL Consultants

Janice R. Corona
Independent Education Consultant
Dallas, Texas

Jim Cummins
Professor
The University of Toronto
Toronto, Canada

Reviewers

Debbie Crisco
Math Coach
Beebe Public Schools
Beebe, Arkansas

Kathleen A. Cuff
Teacher
Kings Park Central School District
Kings Park, New York

Erika Doyle
Math and Science Coordinator
Richland School District
Richland, Washington

Susan Jarvis
Math and Science Curriculum Coordinator
Ocean Springs Schools
Ocean Springs, Mississippi

PEARSON

ISBN-13: 978-0-328-88707-1
ISBN-10: 0-328-88707-2
7 18

Digital Resources

Go to PearsonRealize.com

MP

Math Practices Animations to play anytime

Glossary

Animated Glossary in English and Spanish

Help

Another Look Homework Video for extra help

ACTIVe-book

Student Edition online for showing your work

Solve

Solve & Share problems plus math tools

Tools

Math Tools to help you understand

Games

Math Games to help you learn

Learn

Visual Learning Animation Plus with animation, interaction, and math tools

Assessment

Quick Check for each lesson

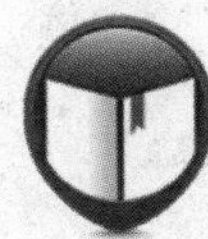

eText

Student Edition online

PEARSON realize™ Everything you need for math anytime, anywhere

Hi, we're here to help you.
Let's have a great year!

Contents

KEY

- Numbers: Concepts and Counting
- Operations and Algebra
- Numbers and Computation
- Measurement and Data
- Geometry

Digital Resources at PearsonRealize.com

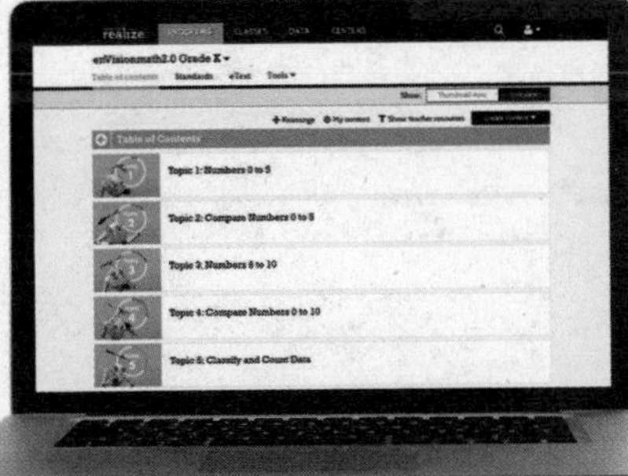

And remember your eText is available at PearsonRealize.com!

TOPICS

PearsonRealize.com

TOPIC 1
Numbers 0 to 5

TOPIC 2
Compare Numbers 0 to 5

TOPIC 3
Numbers 6 to 10

TOPIC 4
Compare Numbers 0 to 10

PearsonRealize.com

TOPIC 5
Classify and Count Data

TOPIC 6
Understand Addition

PearsonRealize.com

TOPIC 7
Understand Subtraction

TOPIC 8
More Addition and Subtraction

PearsonRealize.com

TOPIC 9 in Volume 2
Count Numbers to 20

TOPIC 10 in Volume 2

Compose and Decompose Numbers 11 to 19

PearsonRealize.com

TOPIC 11 in Volume 2

Count Numbers to 100

1	2	3	4	5	6	7	8	9	10
11	12	13	14	15	16	17	18	19	20
21	22	23	24	25	26	27	28	29	30

TOPIC 12 in Volume 2

Identify and Describe Shapes

PearsonRealize.com

TOPIC 13 in Volume 2

Analyze, Compare, and Create Shapes

TOPIC 14 in Volume 2
Describe and Compare Measurable Attributes

PearsonRealize.com

STEP UP to Grade 1 in Volume 2

Problem Solving Handbook

Problem Solving Handbook

Math Practices

1. Make sense of problems and persevere in solving them.
2. Reason abstractly and quantitatively.
3. Construct viable arguments and critique the reasoning of others.
4. Model with mathematics.
5. Use appropriate tools strategically.
6. Attend to precision.
7. Look for and make use of structure.
8. Look for and express regularity in repeated reasoning.

There are good Thinking Habits for each of these math practices.

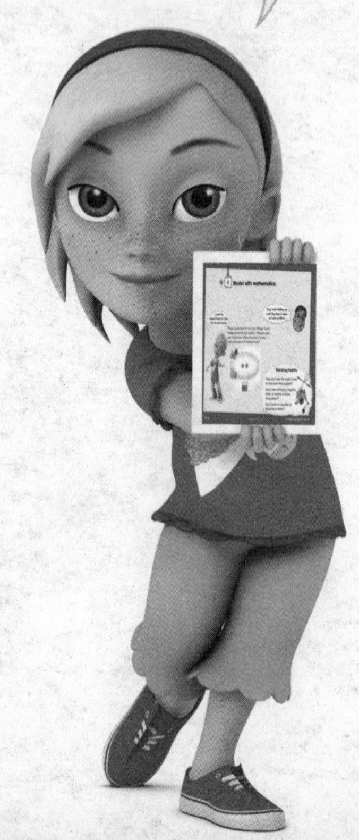

Make sense of problems and persevere in solving them.

Good math thinkers know what the problem is about. They have a plan to solve it. They keep trying if they get stuck.

My plan was to count the bees. The last number I counted was the total number of bees.

How many bees are there in all? How do you know?

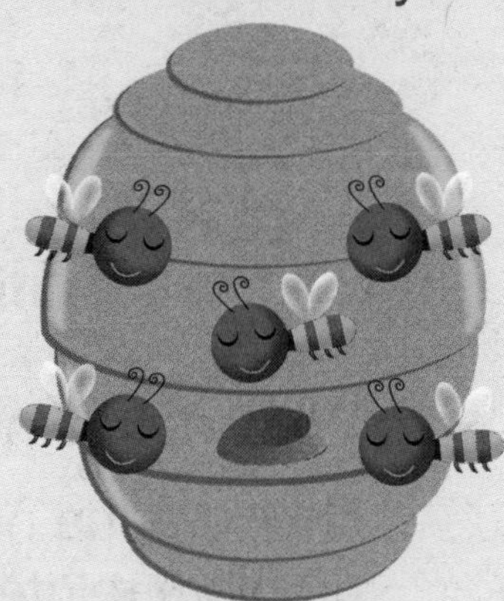

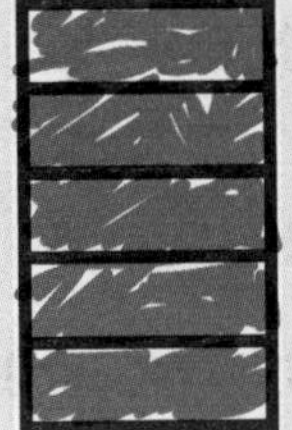

Thinking Habits

What do I need to find?

What do I know?

What's my plan for solving the problem?

What else can I try if I get stuck?

How can I check that my solution make sense?

Reason abstractly and quantitatively.

This problem is about the number 4. I can show 4 in a different way to solve the problem.

Good math thinkers know how to think about words and numbers to solve problems.

Daniel sees 4 frogs. He wants to draw 4 dragonflies in a different arrangement. What other way can he show the number 4?

4

4

Thinking Habits

What do the numbers stand for?

How are the numbers in the problem related?

How can I show a word problem using pictures or numbers?

How can I use a word problem to show what an equation means?

Construct viable arguments and critique the reasoning of others.

How is the second box like the first box? Explain your answer.

I counted the stars. I counted the counters. Both boxes have 3 things.

Thinking Habits

How can I use math to explain my work?

Am I using numbers and symbols correctly?

Is my explanation clear?

What questions can I ask to understand other people's thinking?

Are there mistakes in other people's thinking?

Can I improve other people's thinking?

Model with mathematics.

Good math thinkers use math they know to show and solve problems.

I used the colored boxes to show the correct answer.

Place 2 counters in the nest. Peeps found these worms for her babies. How can you use the model below the nest to show how many worms Peeps found?

Thinking Habits

How can I use the math I know to help solve this problem?

Can I use a drawing, diagram, table, or objects to show the problem?

Can I write an equation to show the problem?

Use appropriate tools strategically.

How many leaves are there in all? Use counters, connecting cubes, or other objects to show how many, and then write the number to tell how many.

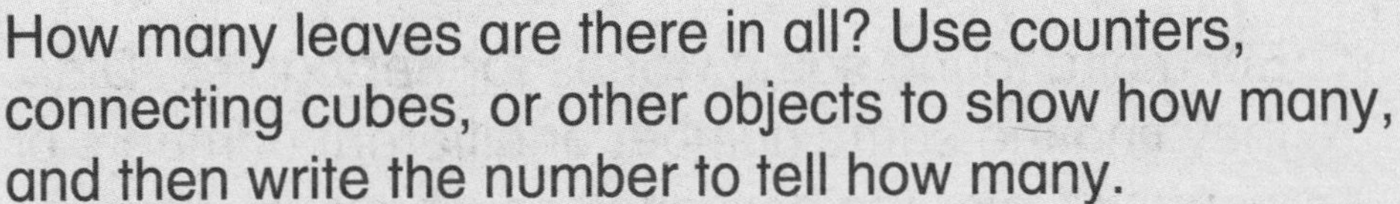

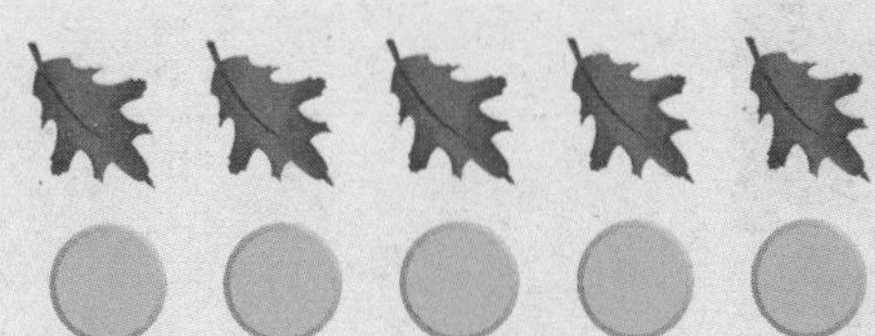

Thinking Habits

Which tools can I use?

Is there a different tool I could use?

Am I using the tool correctly?

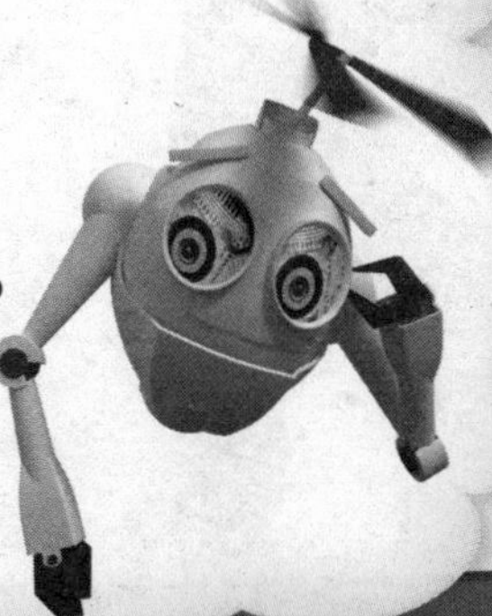

Attend to precision.

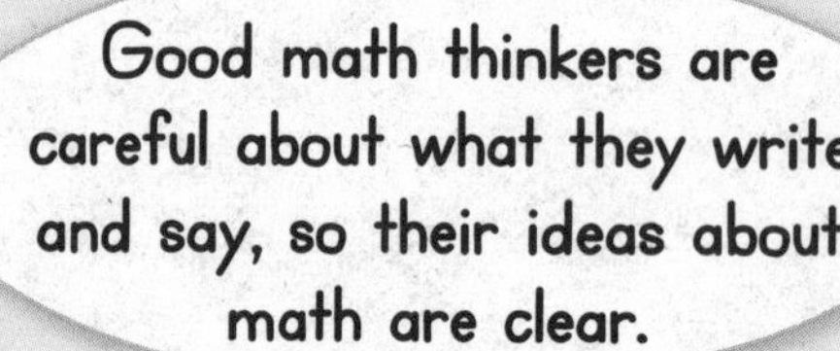

I was careful when I counted and colored.

Each bird found some worms for her babies. Did they find the same number or different numbers of worms? Color the boxes to show how you know.

Thinking Habits

Am I using numbers, units, and symbols correctly?

Am I using the correct definitions?

Is my answer clear?

Look for and make use of structure.

Good math thinkers look for patterns in math to help solve problems.

How can you tell how many objects you see without counting first? Explain how you know you are right.

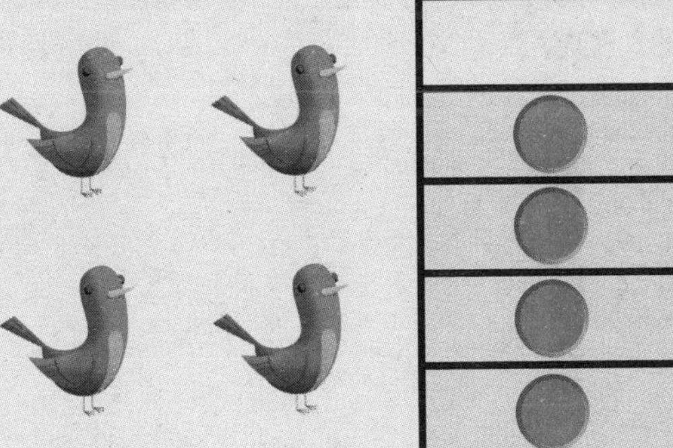

Thinking Habits

Is there a pattern?

How can I describe the pattern?

Can I break the problem into simpler parts?

Look for and express regularity in repeated reasoning.

I know that the 1 more repeats. That helped me solve the problem.

Good math thinkers look for things that repeat in a problem. They use what they learn from one problem to help them solve other problems.

The first row has 1 counter colored. Each row has 1 more counter than the row before. How many counters will be in the last row?

1

2

Thinking Habits

Does something repeat in the problem?

How can the solution help me solve another problem?

Problem Solving Guide

Make Sense of the Problem

Reason

- What do I need to find?
- What given information can I use?
- How are the quantities related?

Think About Similar Problems

- Have I solved problems like this before?

Persevere in Solving the Problem

Model with Math

- How can I use the math I know?
- How can I show the problem?
- Is there a pattern I can use?

Use Appropriate Tools

- What math tools could I use?
- How can I use those tools?

Check the Answer

Make Sense of the Answer

- Is my answer reasonable?

Check for Precision

- Did I check my work?
- Is my answer clear?
- Is my explanation clear?

Some Ways to Show Problems

- Draw a Picture
- Write an Equation

Some Math Tools

- Objects
- Technology
- Paper and Pencil

Problem Solving Recording Sheet

Name Gretchen

Teaching Tool 1

Problem Solving Recording Sheet

Problem:
5 birds are on a fence.
2 birds fly away.
How many birds are left?

MAKE SENSE OF THE PROBLEM

Need to Find	Given
I need to find how many birds are left.	5 birds are on a fence. 2 birds fly away.

PERSEVERE IN SOLVING THE PROBLEM

Some Ways to Represent Problems
- ☑ Draw a Picture
- ☑ Write an Equation

Some Math Tools
- ☐ Objects
- ☐ Technology
- ☑ Paper and Pencil

Solution and Answer

3 birds
5 − 2 = 3

CHECK THE ANSWER

I listened to the problem again. I checked my picture and counted the birds that were left, 3 birds. My answer is correct.

TOPIC 1

Numbers 0 to 5

Essential Question: How can numbers from 0 to 5 be counted, read, and written?

Math and Science Project: Weather Changes

Directions Read the character speech bubbles to students. **Find Out!** Have students pay attention to the daily weather changes. Say: *The weather changes from day to day. Talk to friends and relatives about the weather. Ask them to help you record the number of sunny days and rainy days from Monday to Friday.* **Journal: Make a Poster** Have students make a poster of the weather information they collected. Have them draw suns for the number of sunny days and clouds with raindrops for the number of rainy days. Then have students write the numbers to tell how many.

Name ______________________________

Review What You Know

4

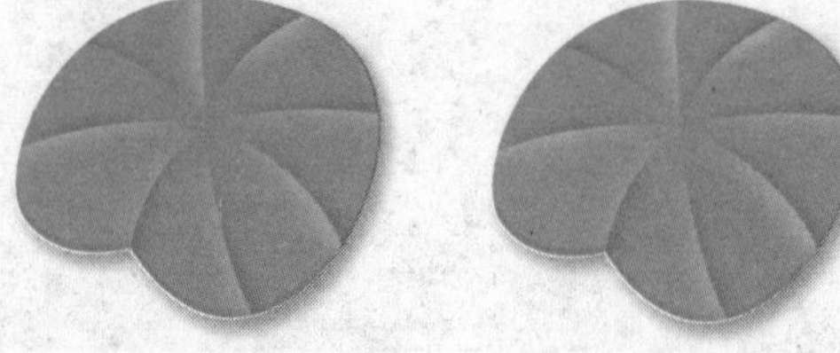

5

6

Directions Have students: 1 draw a circle around the animal that is on the right; 2 draw a circle around the animal that is on the left; 3 draw a circle around the animal that is green; 4–6 draw a line from each object in the top row to an object in the bottom row.

My Word Cards

Directions Have students cut out the vocabulary cards. Read the front of the card, and then ask them to explain what the word or phrase means.

count

one

two

three

number

four

My Word Cards

Directions Review the definitions and have students study the cards. Extend learning by having students draw pictures for each word on a separate piece of paper.

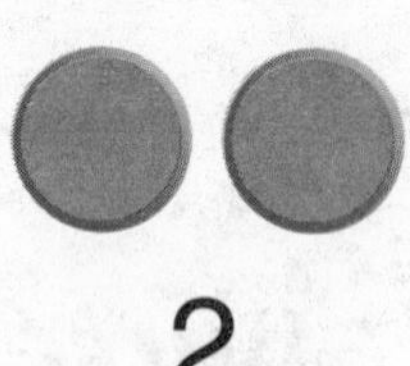

2

Point to the group of counters.
Say: *There are* ***two*** *counters.*

1

Point to the counter.
Say: *There is* ***one*** *counter.*

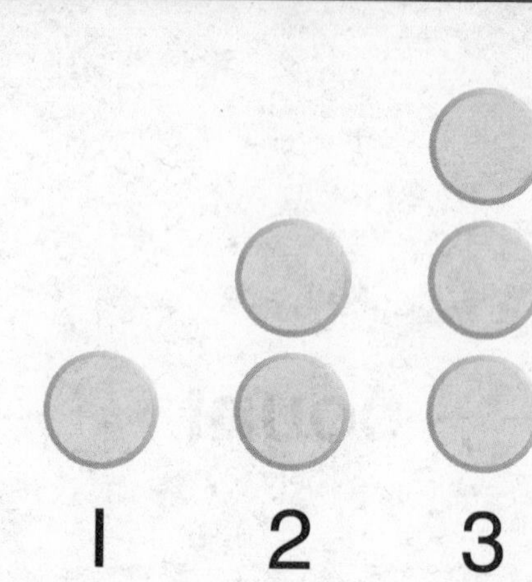

1 2 3

Point to each column of counters.
Say: *When I* ***count****, I say 1, 2, 3 . . .*

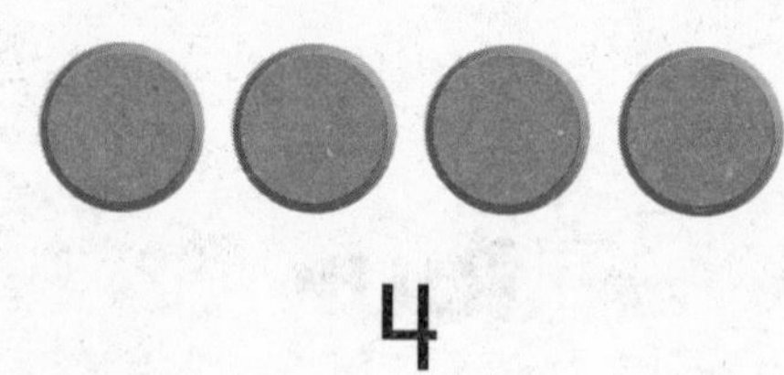

4

Point to the group of counters.
Say: *There are* ***four*** *counters.*

0 1 2 3 4 5

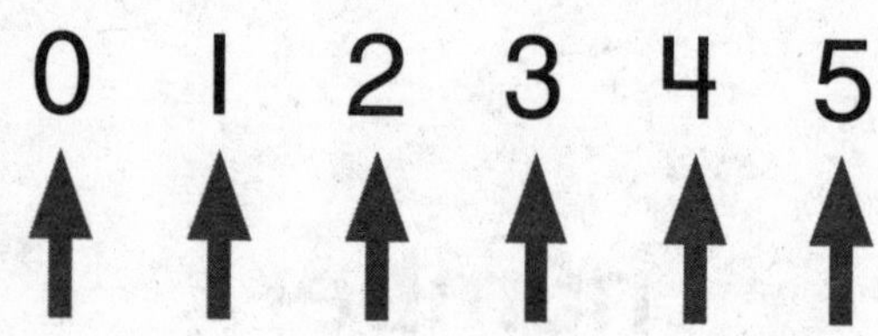

Point to each arrow.
Say: *Each arrow points to a* ***number****.*

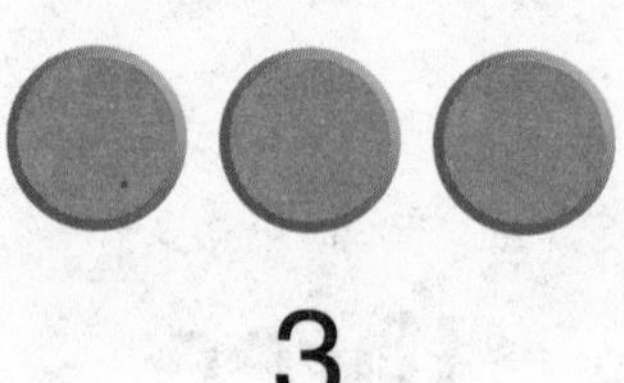

3

Point to the group of counters.
Say: *There are* ***three*** *counters.*

A-Z Glossary

My Word Cards

Directions Have students cut out the vocabulary cards. Read the front of the card, and then ask them to explain what the word or phrase means.

five	zero	none
whole	part	order

My Word Cards

Directions Review the definitions and have students study the cards. Extend learning by having students draw pictures for each word on a separate piece of paper.

0

Point to the 0.
Say: *Another word for 0 is **none**.*

0

Point to the 0.
Say: *This number is **zero**.*

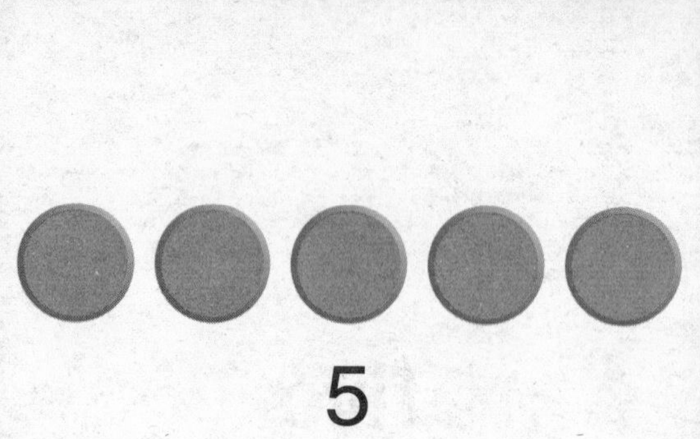

5

Point to the group of counters.
Say: *There are **five** counters.*

0 → 1 → 2 → 3 → 4 → 5

Point to the picture.
Say: *These numbers are in **order** from 0 to 5.*

Point to the bananas in the circle.
Say: *The 3 bananas are **part** of this group of 5 fruits.*

Point to the group of fruits.
Say: *The group of 5 fruits is the **whole** group.*

Solve & Share

Name ______________________________

Solve

Lesson 1-1
Count 1, 2, and 3

Directions Have students place 2 counters in the nest on the workmat. Say: *Peeps the bird found these worms for her babies. Draw a circle around the colored box that shows how many worms Peeps found. Tell how you know you are correct.*

I can ...
count 1, 2, and 3 objects.

I can also model with math.

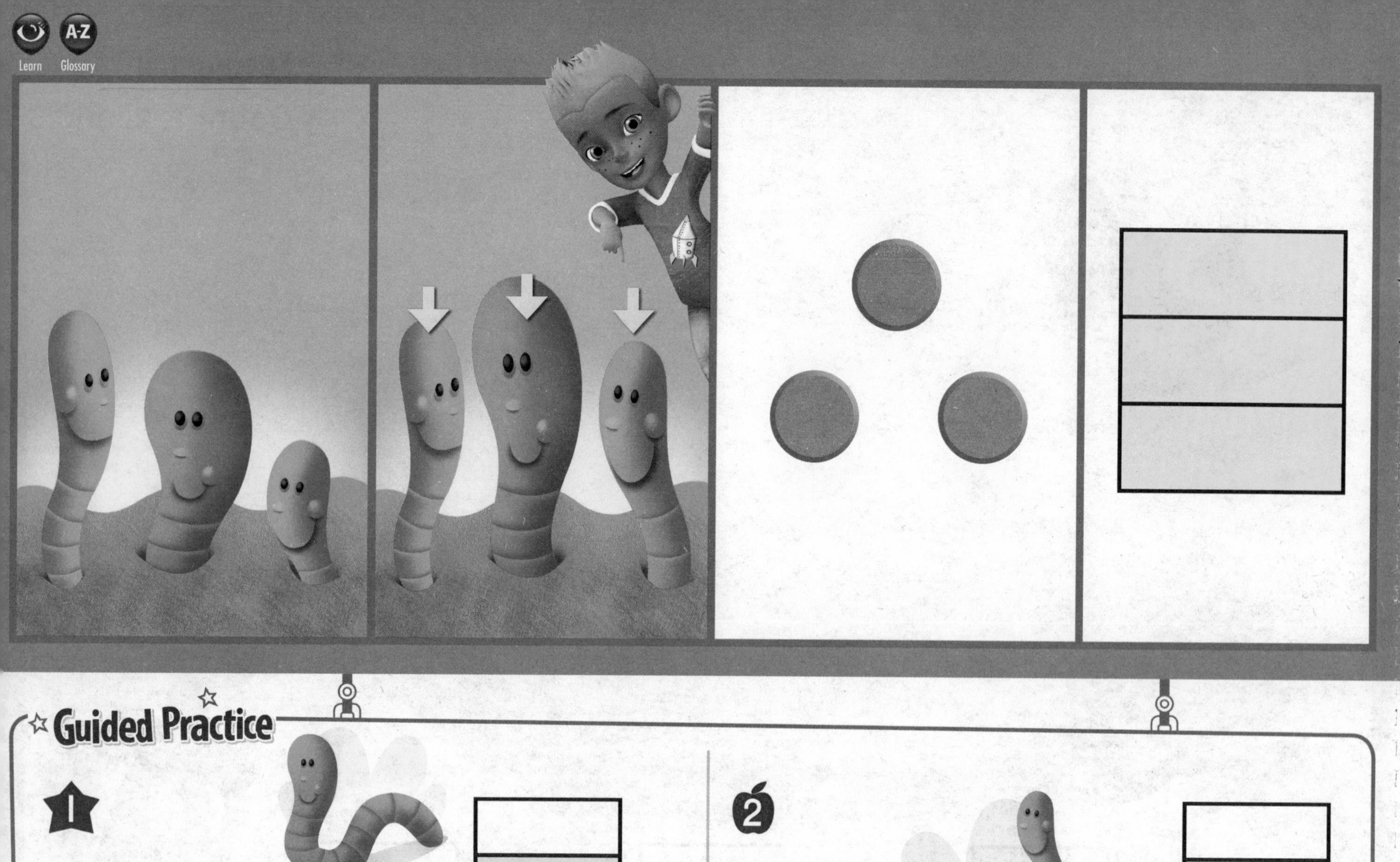

Guided Practice

1

2

Directions 1 and 2 Have students color a box as they count each worm to show how many.

Name

3

4

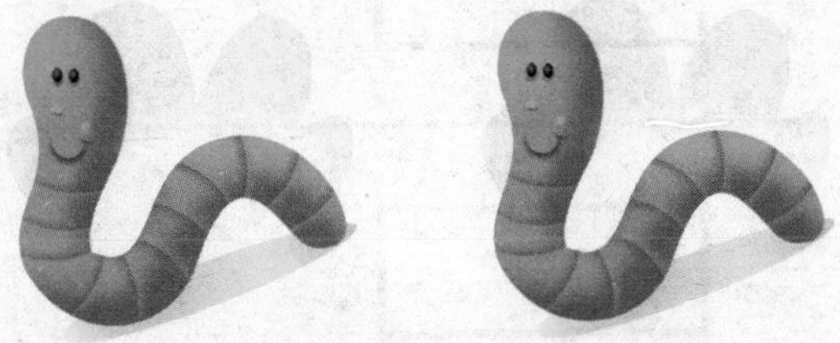

5

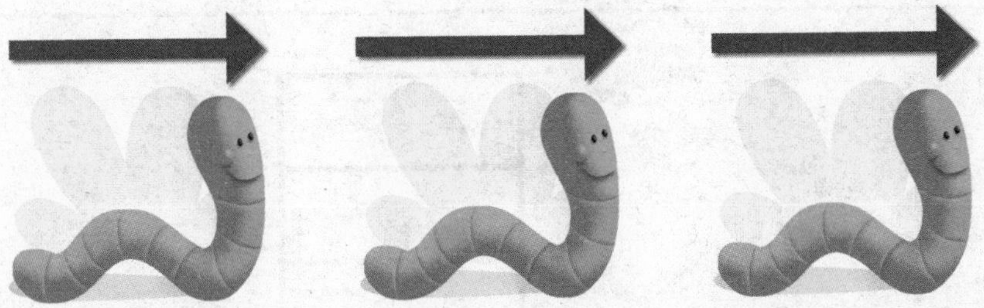

Directions 3 and 4 Have students color a box as they count each worm to show how many. 5 **Vocabulary** Have students **count** the worms, and color a box as they count each worm aloud.

Independent Practice

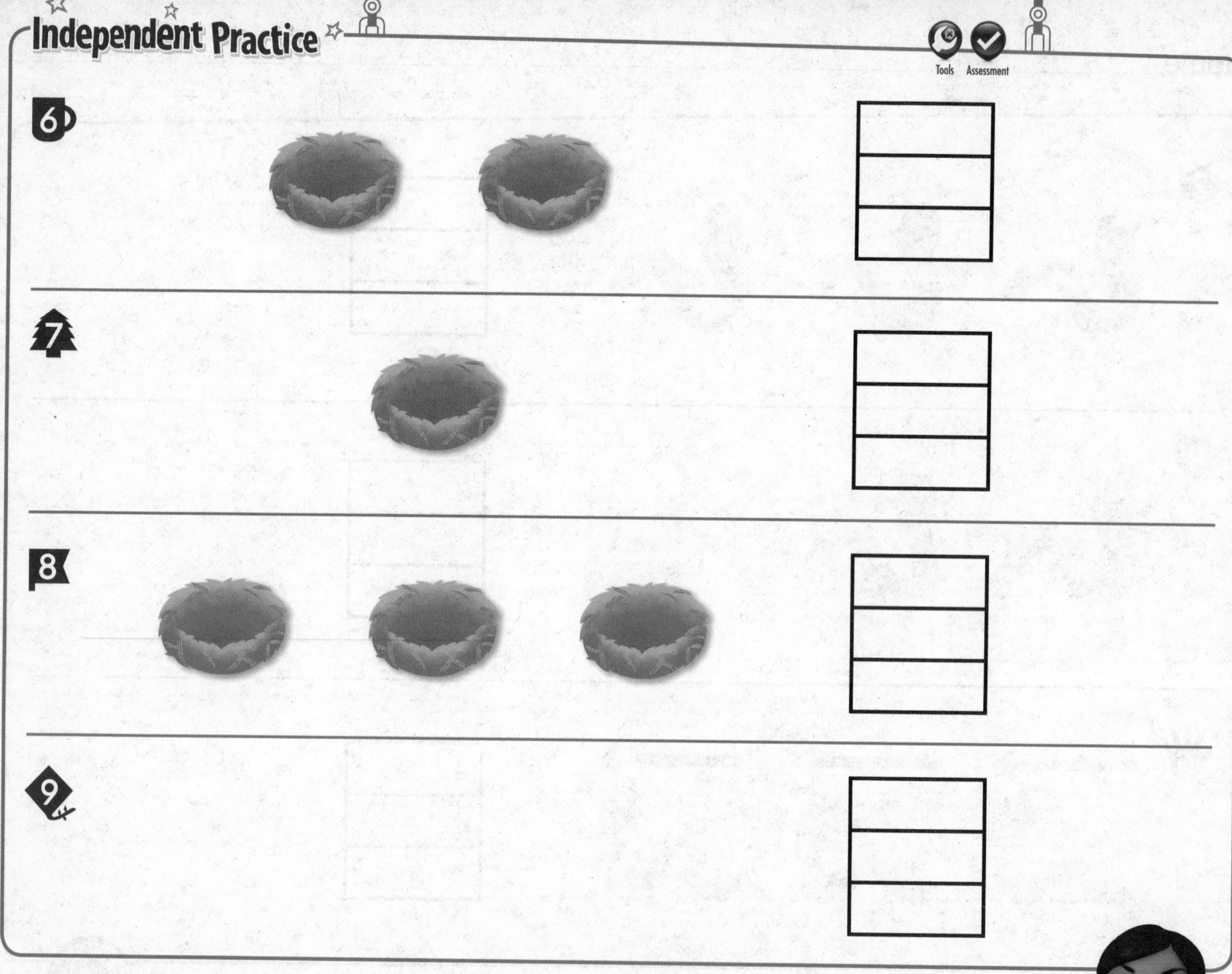

Directions 6–8 Have students color a box as they count each nest to show how many. 9 **Higher Order Thinking** Have students draw 1, 2, or 3 nests, and then color a box as they draw each nest to show how many.

Name ______________________

Homework & Practice 1-1

Count 1, 2, and 3

HOME ACTIVITY Have your child count groups of 1, 2, and 3 objects.

Another Look!

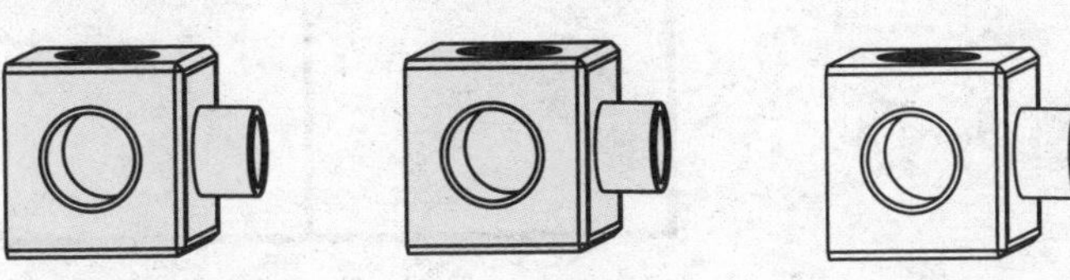

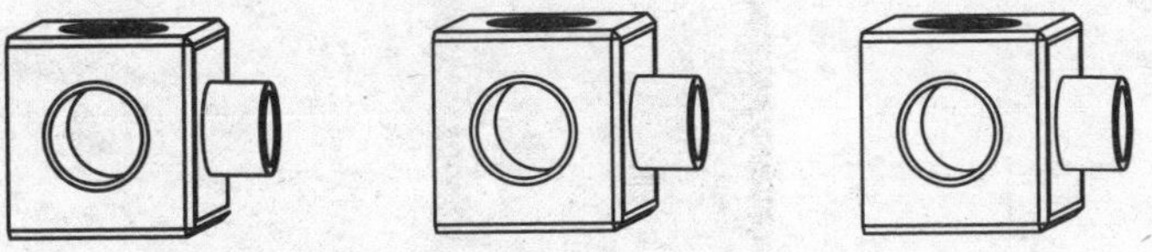

Directions Say: *Use connecting cubes or other objects to model making 2, and then color a cube for each cube you count.* Give students 3 cubes or other small counting objects. Have students: 1 choose 2 cubes or objects, and then color a cube as they count each cube to show how many; 2 choose 1 cube or object, and then color a cube as they count each cube to show how many; 3 choose 3 cubes or objects, and then color a cube as they count each cube to show how many.

6

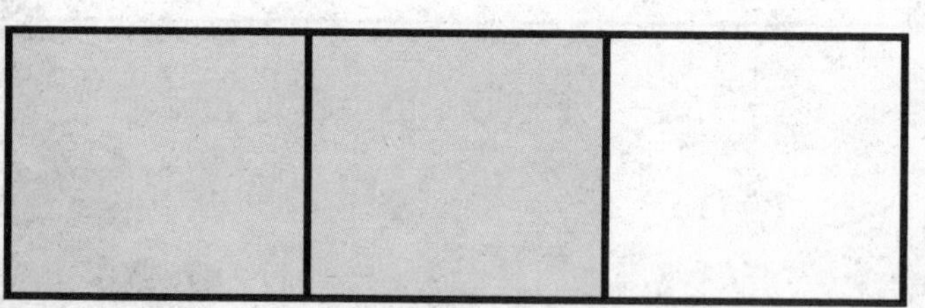

7

Directions 4 and 5 Have students color a box as they count each animal to show how many. 6 **Higher Order Thinking** Have students draw a bird as they count each colored box that shows how many. 7 **Higher Order Thinking** Have students draw 1 plant, 2 fish, and 3 rocks in the tank.

Lesson 1-2

Recognize 1, 2, and 3 in Different Arrangements

Directions Have students place counters in the empty circles on the workmat to show how many worms each bird found. Say: *Each bird found some worms for her babies. Did they find the same number or different numbers of worms? Color the boxes to show how you know.*

I can ...
count groups of 1, 2, and 3 objects shown in different ways.

I can also reason about math.

Guided Practice

1

2

Directions 1 and 2 Have students count each bird, and then color the boxes to show how many.

Name

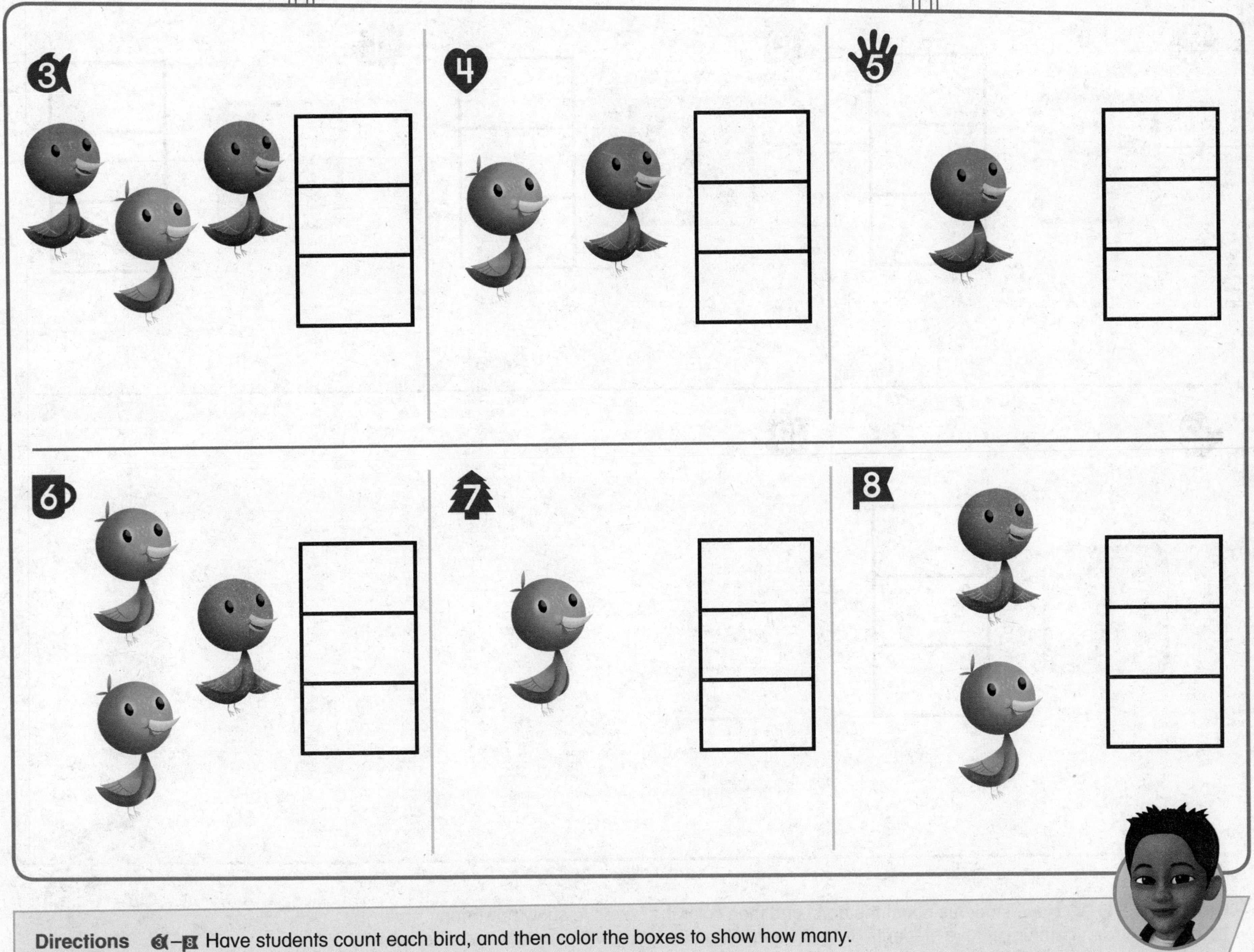

3

4

5

6

7

8

Directions 3–8 Have students count each bird, and then color the boxes to show how many.

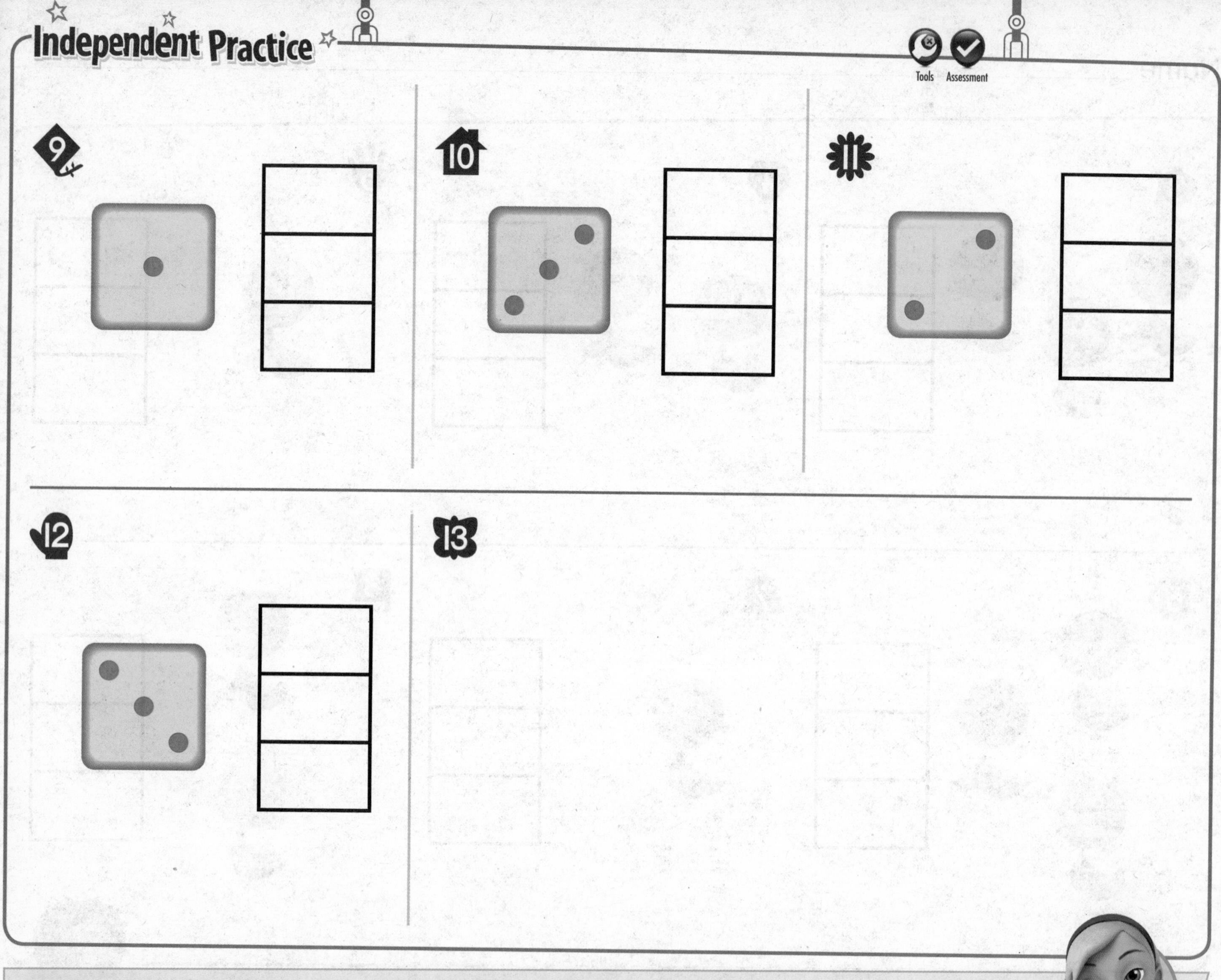

Directions 9–12 Have students count the dots, and then color the boxes to show how many.
13 **Higher Order Thinking** Have students draw 2 counters, and then draw 2 counters in a different way.

Name ______________________________

Help Tools Games

Homework & Practice 1-2

Recognize 1, 2, and 3 in Different Arrangements

HOME ACTIVITY Have your child recognize and count 1, 2, and 3 objects in different arrangements.

Another Look!

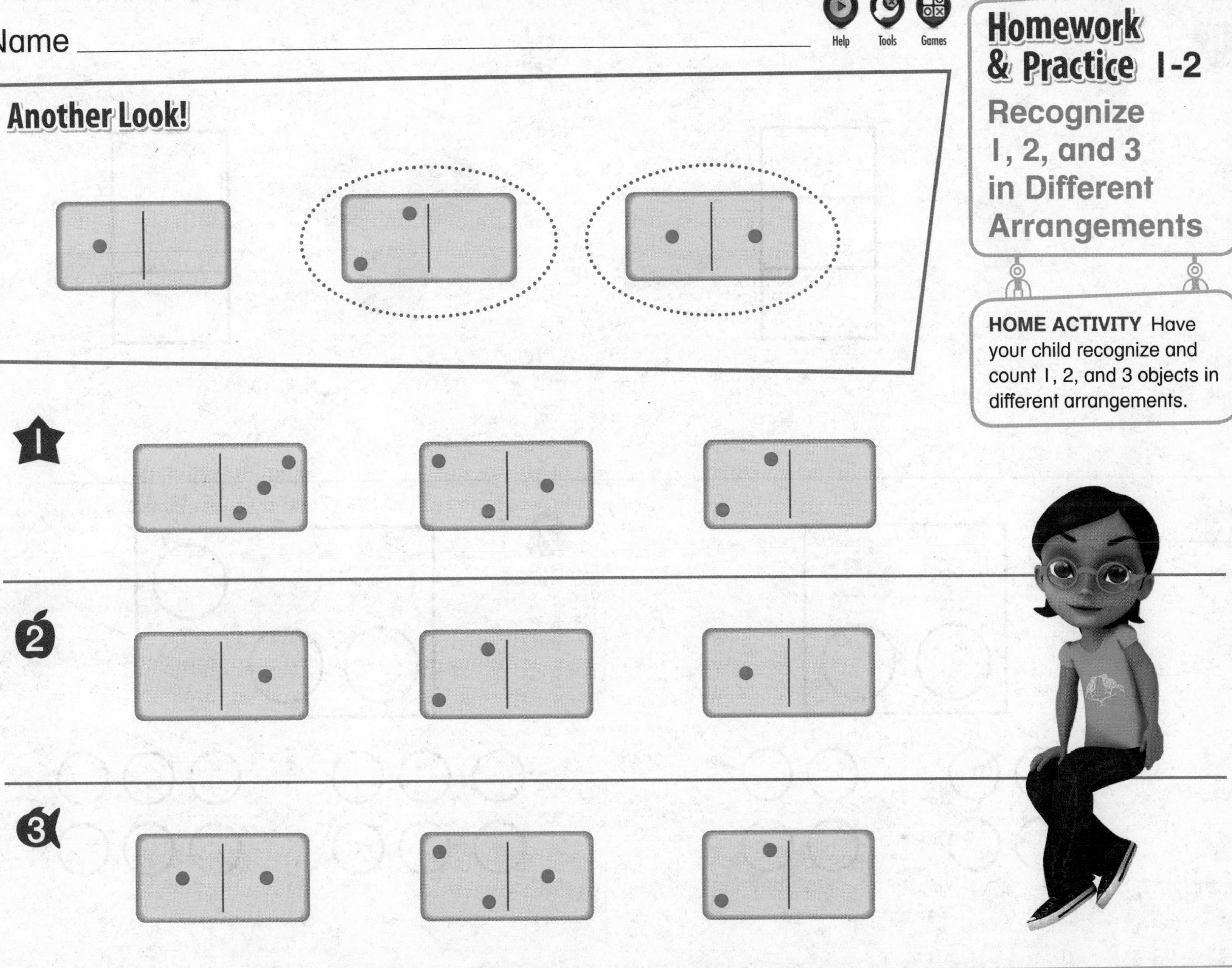

Directions Say: *Count the dots on each dot tile, and then draw a circle around the dot tiles with 2 dots.* Have students: 1 draw a circle around the dot tiles with 3 dots; 2 draw a circle around the dot tiles with 1 dot; 3 draw a circle around the dot tiles with 2 dots.

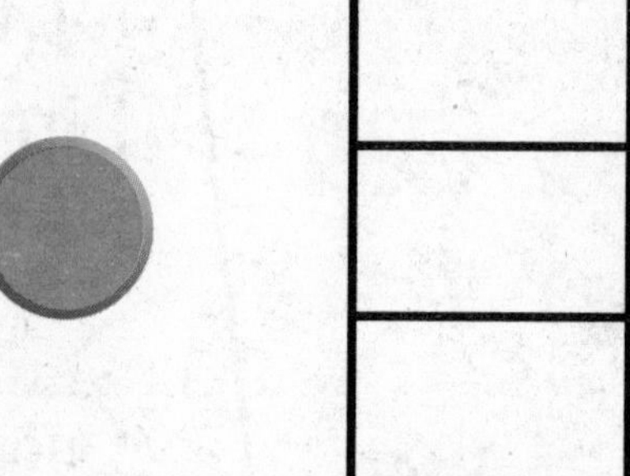

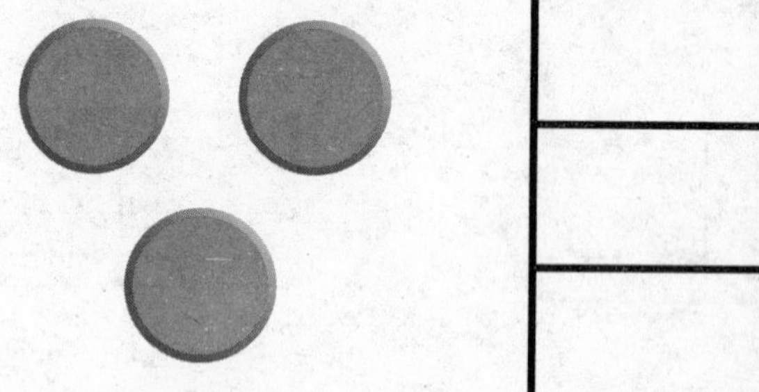

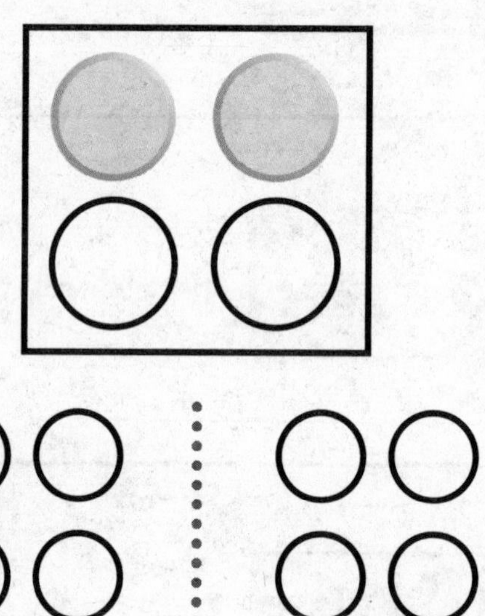

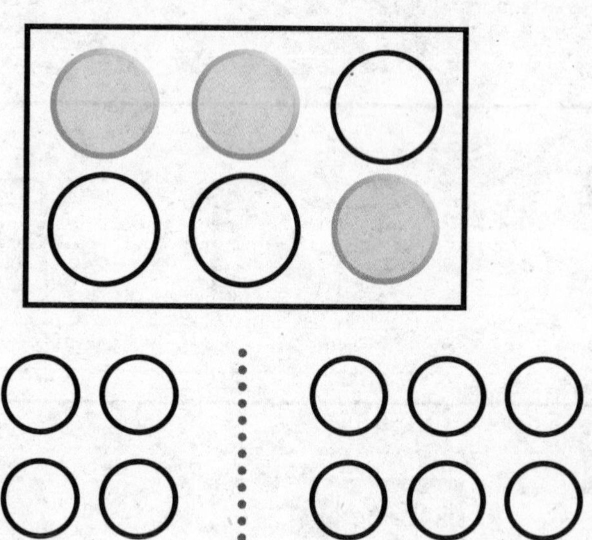

Directions 4 and 5 Have students count the counters, and then color the boxes to show how many. 6 and 7 **Higher Order Thinking** Have students count the number of yellow counters in the box, and then color the same number of counters in two different ways.

Name ______________________________

Solve

Lesson 1-3

Read and Write 1, 2, and 3

Directions Have students place 2 counters in the large cloud on the left side of the workmat. Say: *Alex sees 2 stars in the sky. He draws 2 stars in a cloud. How can he show how many stars in another way? Draw the other way in the small, empty cloud.*

I can ...
read and write the numbers 1, 2, and 3.

I can also reason about math.

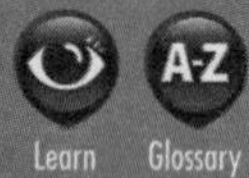

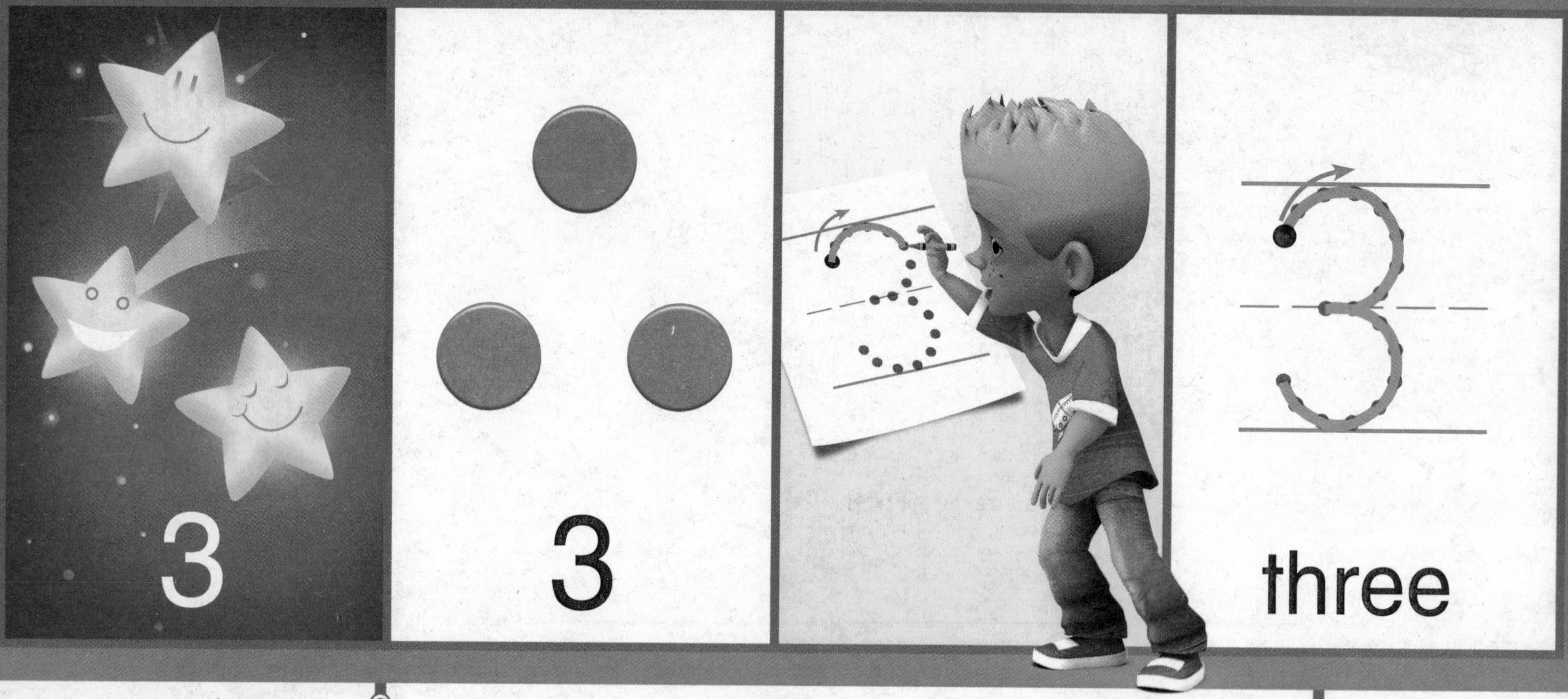

3

3

three

Guided Practice

Directions 1–3 Have students count the stars, and then write the number to tell how many.

Name ______________________________

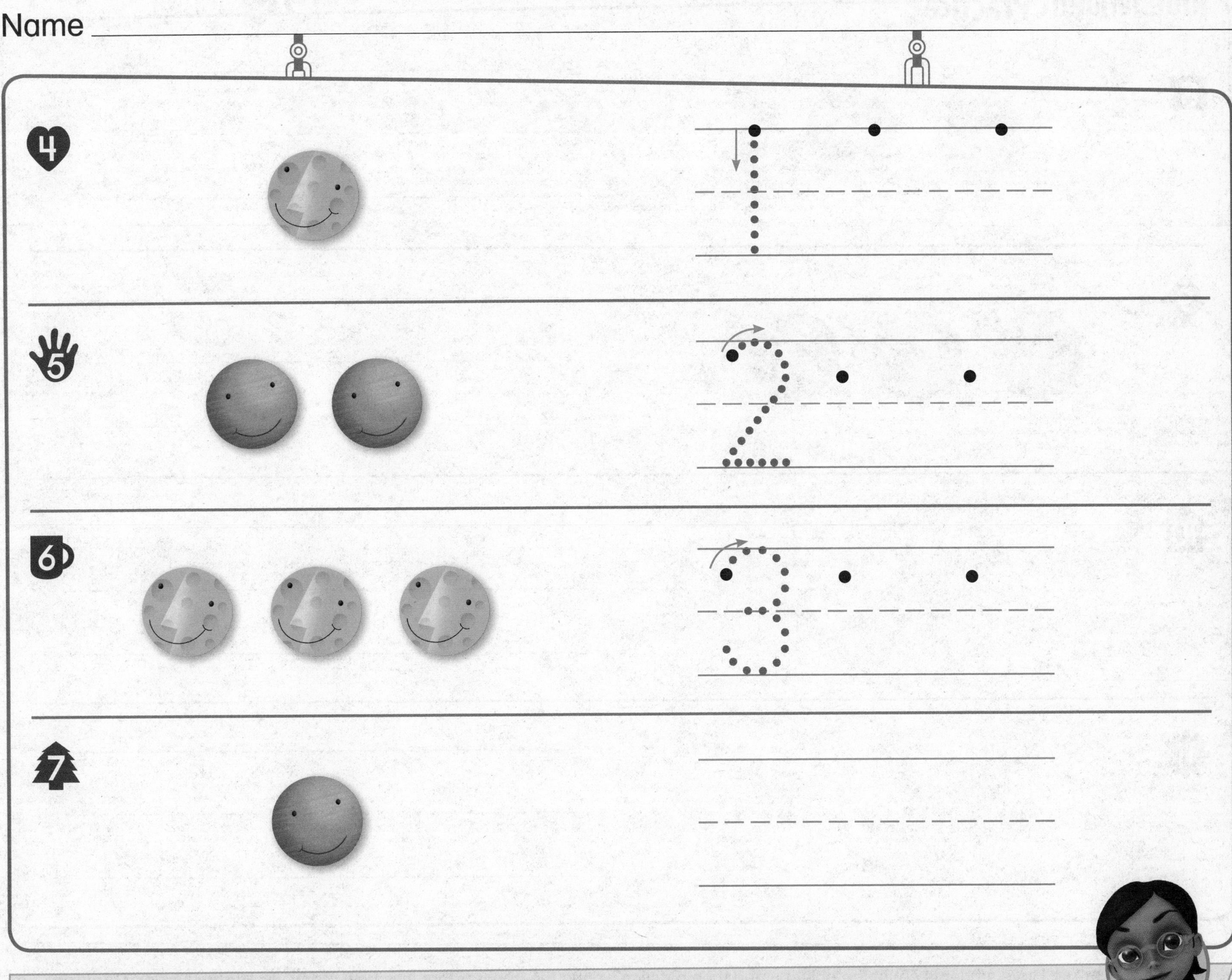

Directions 4–7 Have students count the objects, and then practice writing the number that tells how many.

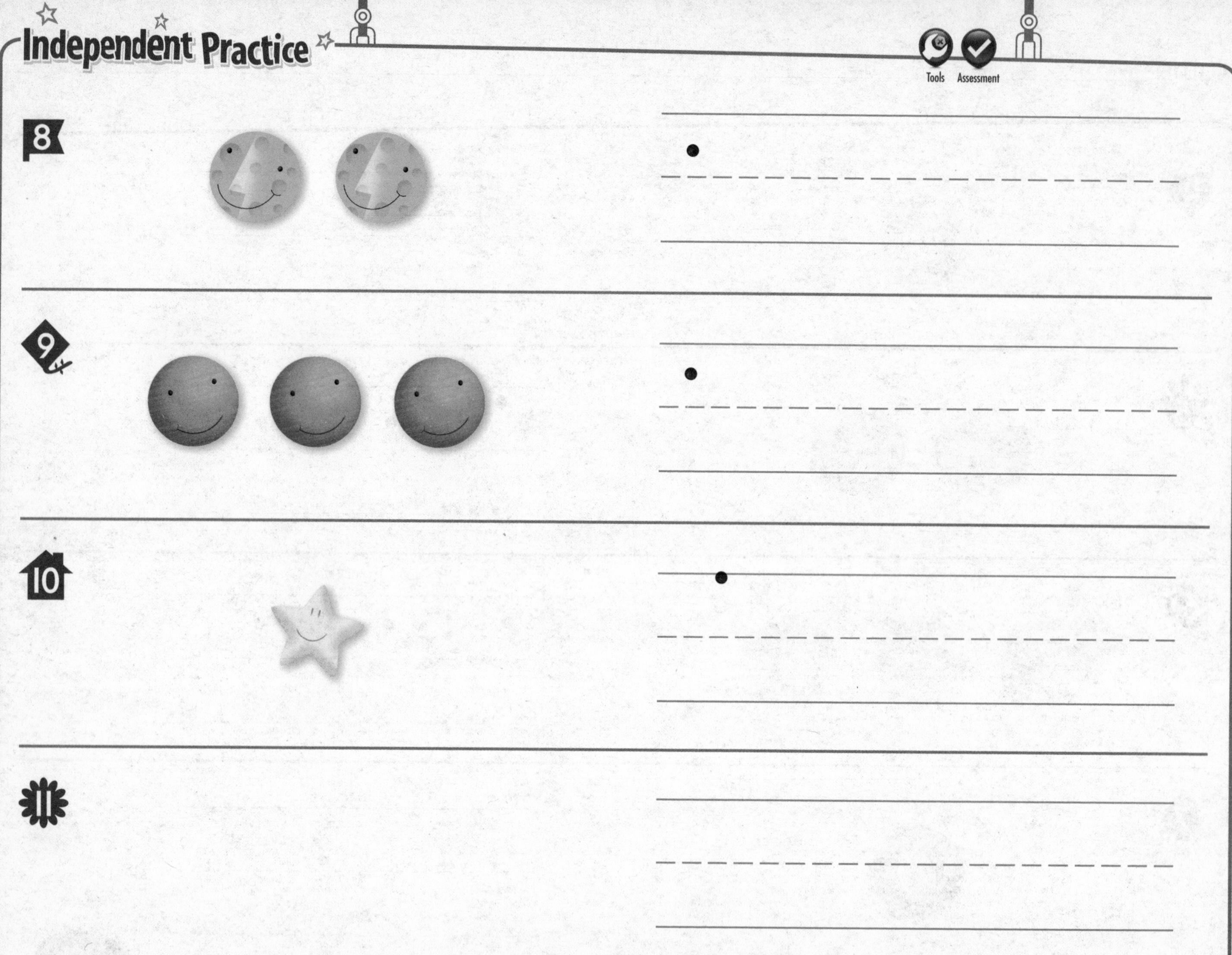

Directions 8–10 Have students count the objects, and then practice writing the number that tells how many. 11 **Higher Order Thinking** Have students draw 1, 2, or 3 stars, and then practice writing the number that tells how many.

Name ______________________

Homework & Practice 1-3

Read and Write 1, 2, and 3

HOME ACTIVITY Draw groups of 1, 2, and 3 circles on 3 index cards. Have your child write the correct number on the back of each card. Then use the cards to practice counting and reading the numbers 1, 2, and 3.

Another Look!

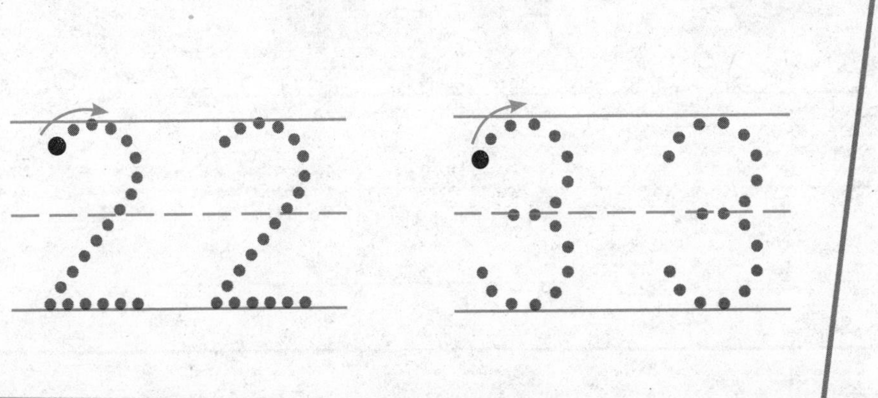

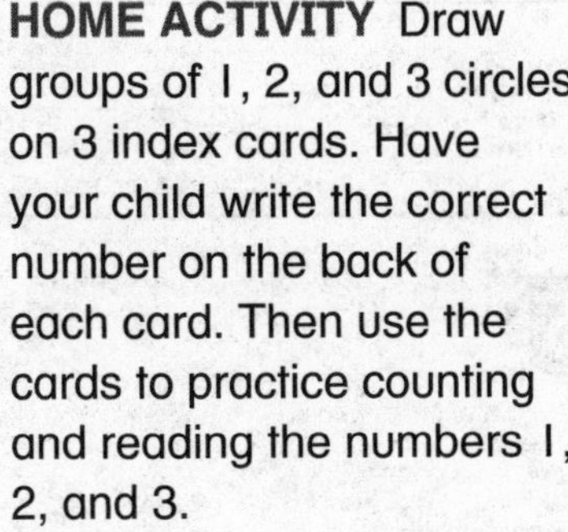

Directions Say: *Practice writing the numbers 1, 2, and 3.* Then have students: 1 count the moons, and then write the number of moons under each picture; 2 count the stars, and then write the number of stars under each picture.

3

4

5

6

2

7

Directions 3–5 Have students count the objects, and then practice writing the number that tells how many.
6 **Higher Order Thinking** Have students look at the number, and then draw moons to show how many.
7 **Higher Order Thinking** Have students draw 1, 2, or 3 rockets, and then practice writing the number that tells how many.

Solve & Share

Name ______________________

Solve

Lesson 1-4
Count 4 and 5

Directions Have students place 5 counters in the tree on the workmat. Then say: *Chips the chipmunk found these nuts. Draw a circle around the colored box that shows how many nuts Chips found. Tell how you know you are correct.*

I can ...
count 4 and 5 objects.

I can also model with math.

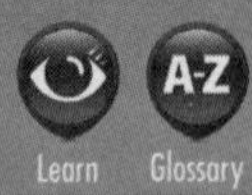

Guided Practice

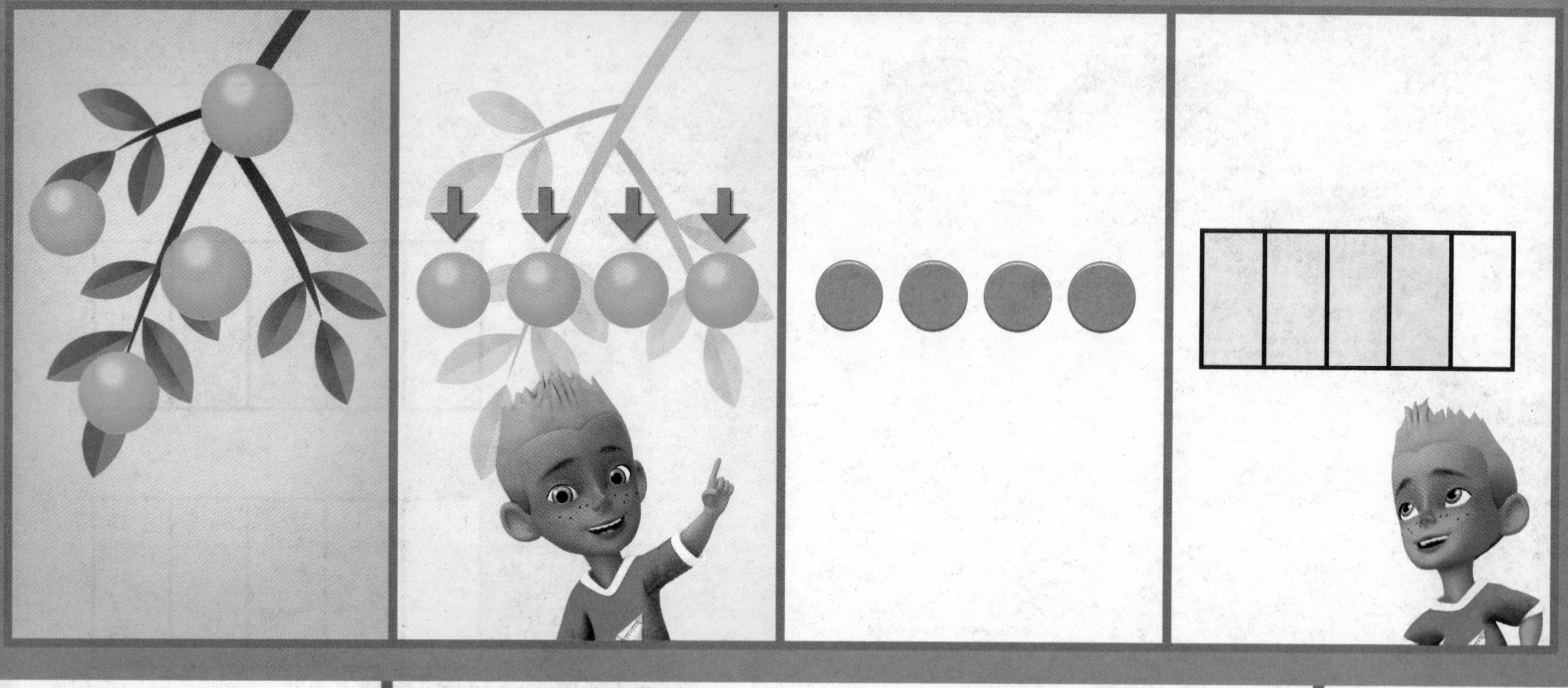

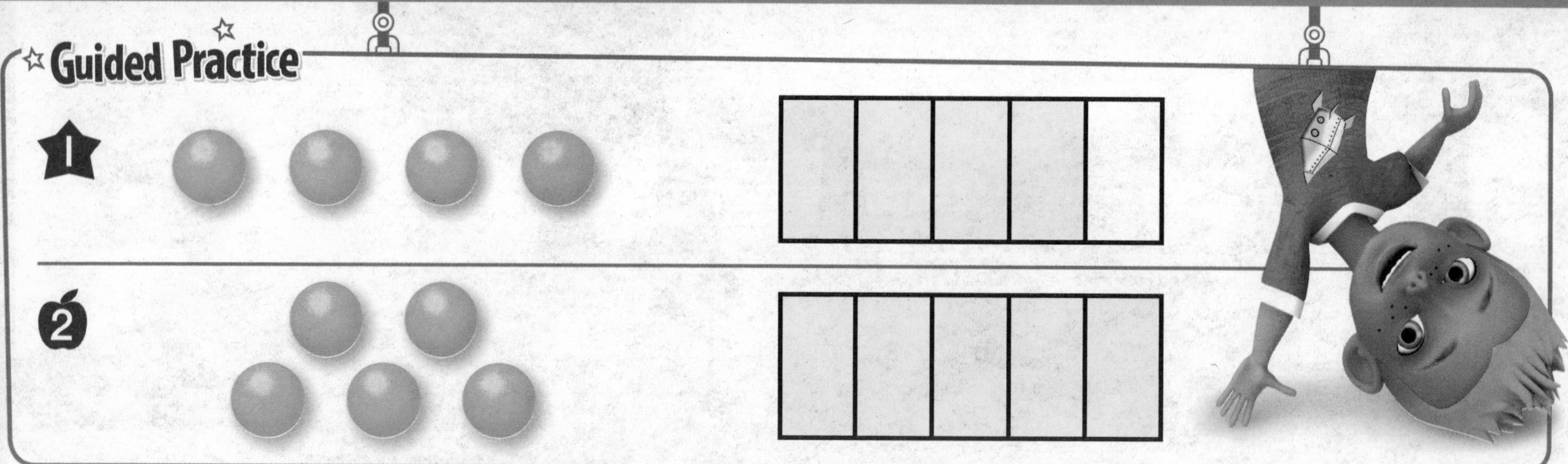

Directions 1 and 2 Have students color a box as they count each orange to show how many.

Name ______________________________

3

4

5

6

Directions 3–6 Have students color a box as they count each piece of fruit to show how many.

Independent Practice

Tools Assessment

7

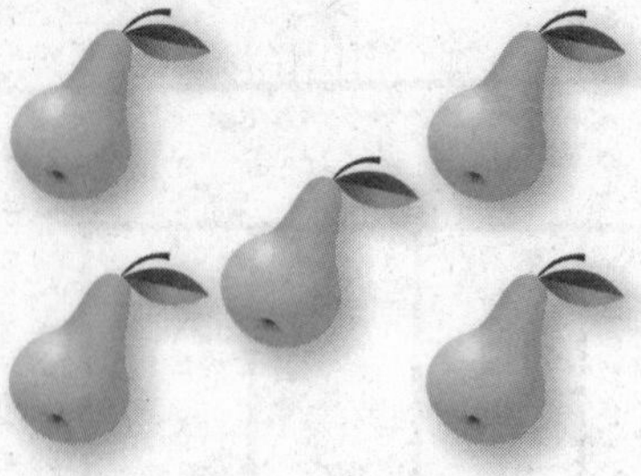

8

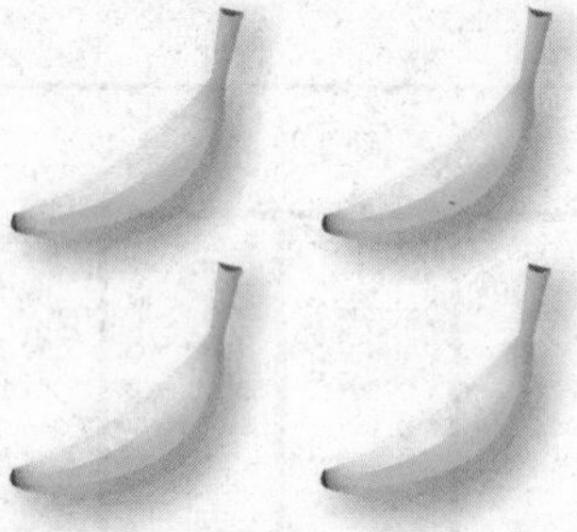

9

10

Directions 7–9 Have students color a box as they count each piece of fruit to show how many. 10 **Higher Order Thinking** Have students draw 4 or 5 oranges, and then color a box as they draw each orange to show how many.

Name ______________________________

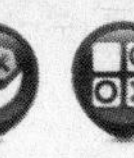
Help Tools Games

Homework & Practice 1-4

Count 4 and 5

HOME ACTIVITY Have your child count groups of 4 objects. Then have him or her draw pictures of 4 objects. Repeat using the number 5.

Another Look!

1

2

3

Directions Say: *Count the dots in the blue box. Draw a counter for each dot you count.* 1–3 Have students draw a counter for each dot they count, and then use counters or objects to show that number.

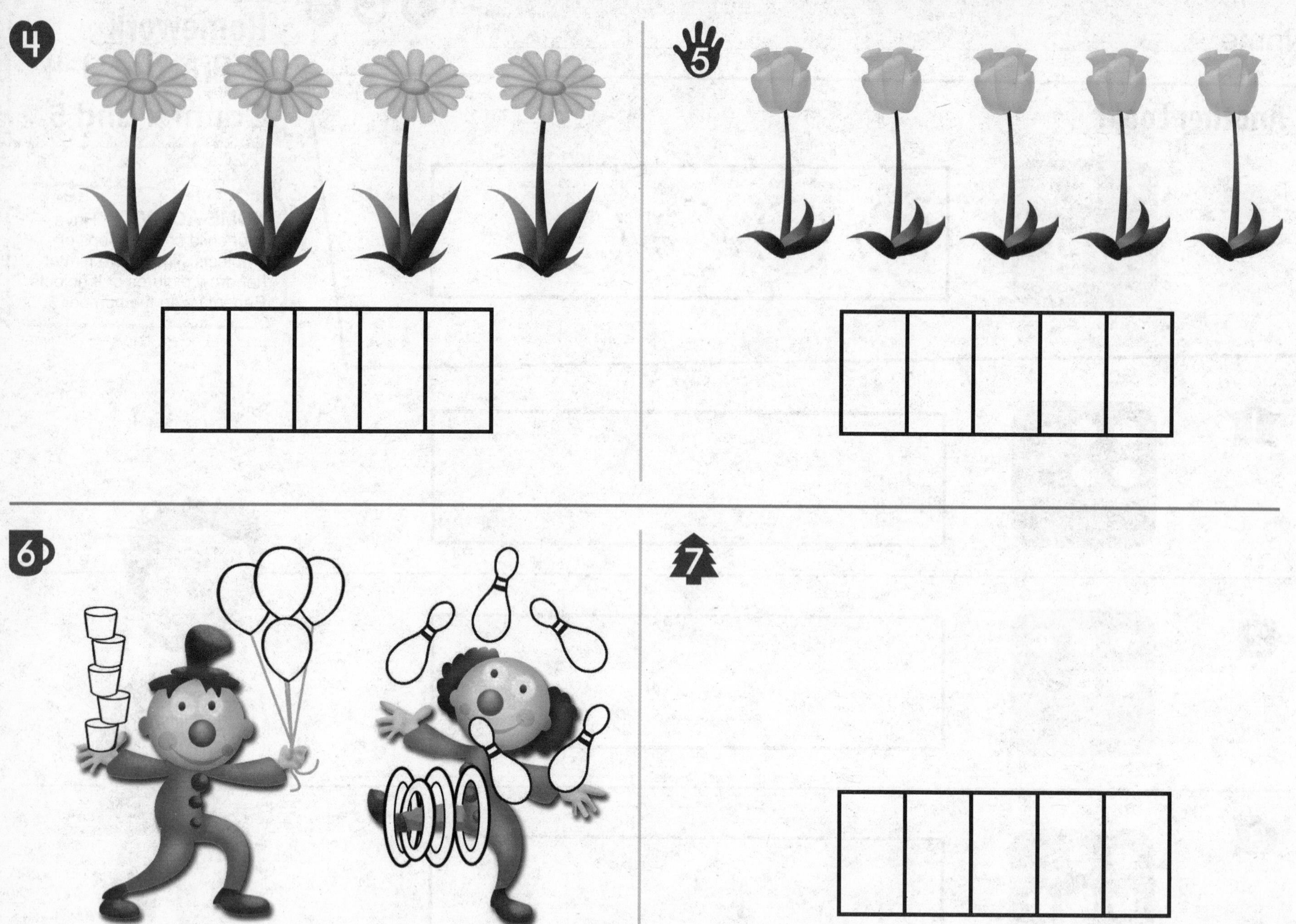

Directions 4 and 5 Have students color a box as they count each flower to show how many. 6 **Higher Order Thinking** Have students color red each group of 4 objects the clowns have and color yellow each group of 5 objects the clowns have. 7 **Higher Order Thinking** Have students draw 4 or 5 flowers, and then color a box as they draw each flower to show how many.

Solve & Share

Name ______________________________

Lesson 1-5

Recognize 4 and 5 in Different Arrangements

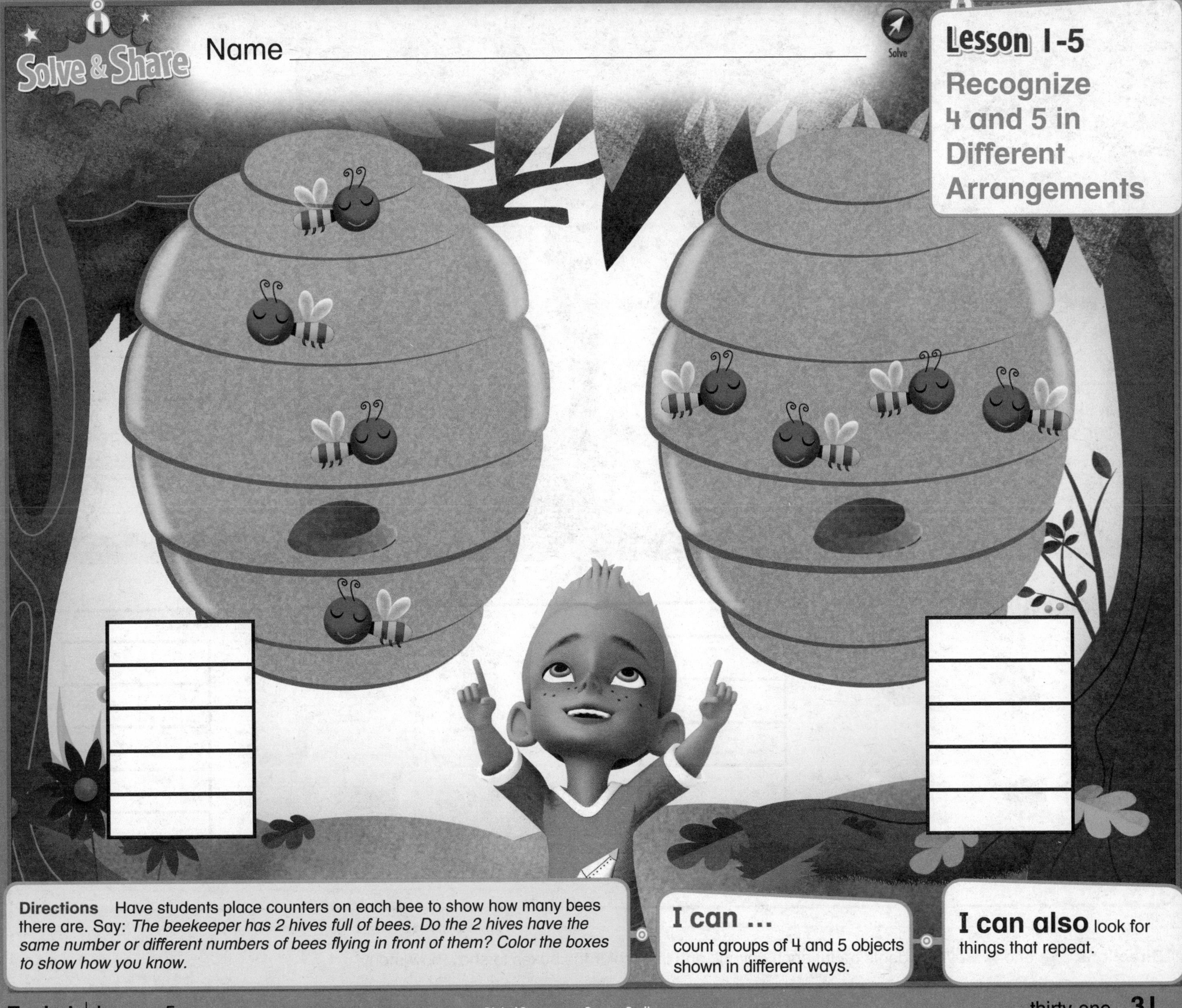

Directions Have students place counters on each bee to show how many bees there are. Say: *The beekeeper has 2 hives full of bees. Do the 2 hives have the same number or different numbers of bees flying in front of them? Color the boxes to show how you know.*

I can … count groups of 4 and 5 objects shown in different ways.

I can also look for things that repeat.

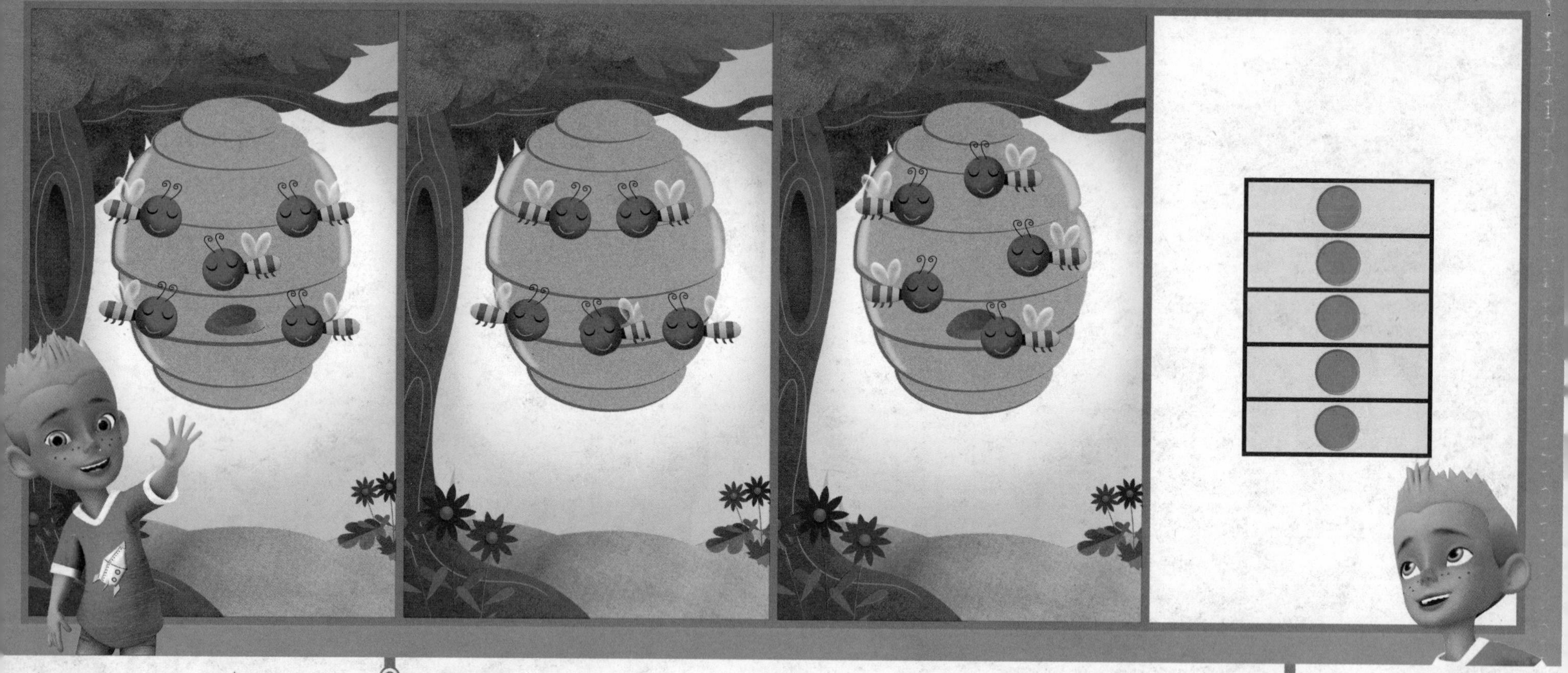

Guided Practice

1

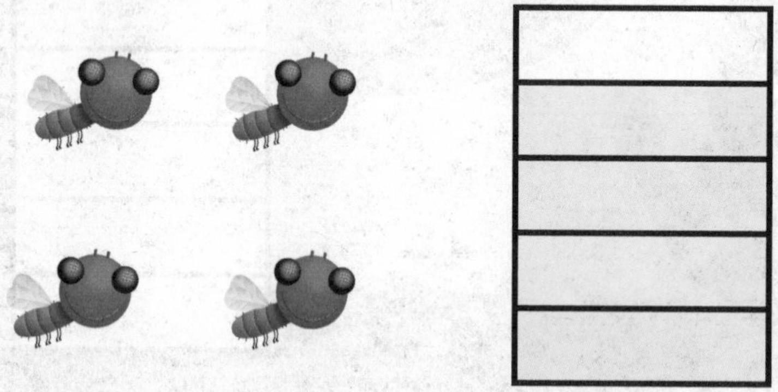

2

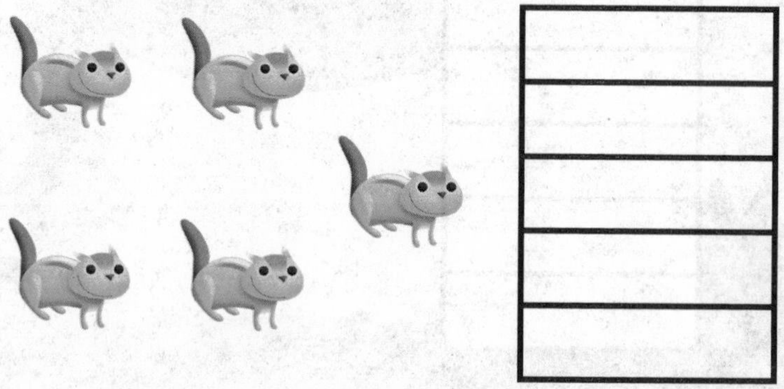

Directions 1 and 2 Have students count each animal, and then color the boxes to show how many.

Name ___

3

4

5

6

7

8

Directions 3–8 Have students count the birds, and then color the boxes to show how many.

Independent Practice

Tools Assessment

9

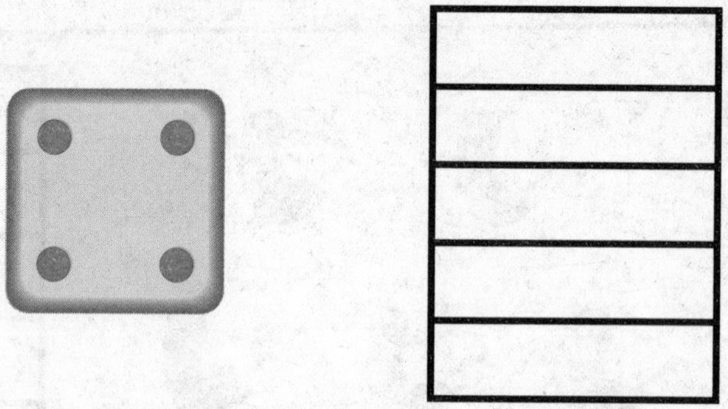

10

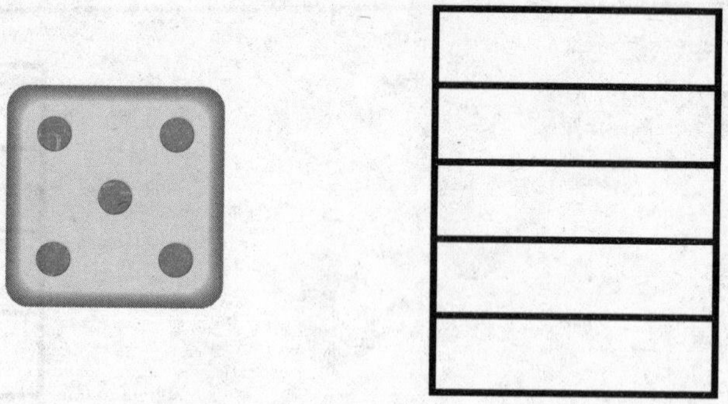

11

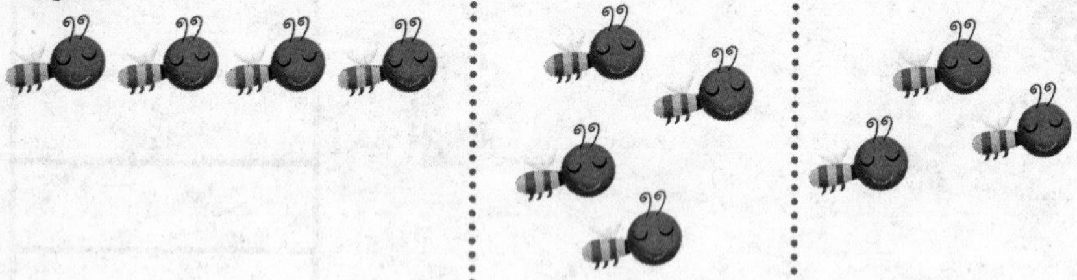

12

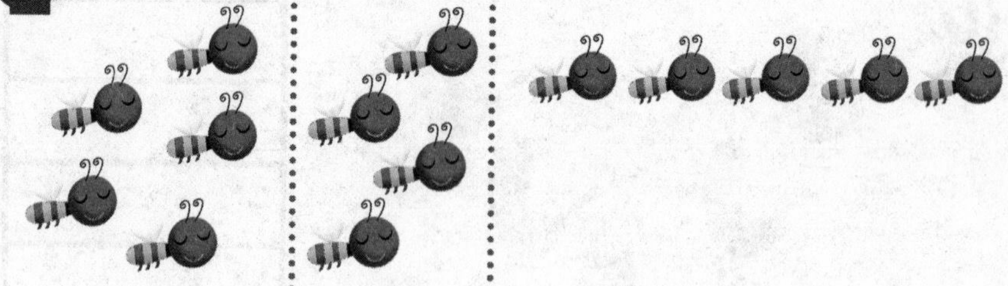

13

Directions Have students: 9 and 10 count the dots, and then color the boxes to show how many; 11 count the groups, and then draw a circle around the groups that show 4; 12 count the groups, and then draw a circle around the groups that show 5. 13 **Higher Order Thinking** Have students draw 5 counters in the first space, and then draw 5 counters in two different ways in the other two spaces.

Name ______________________________

Help

Tools
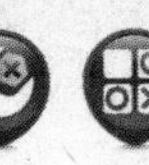
Games

Homework & Practice 1-5

Recognize 4 and 5 in Different Arrangements

HOME ACTIVITY Have your child recognize and count 4 and 5 objects in different arrangements.

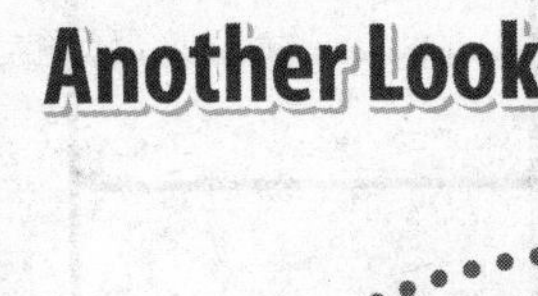

Another Look!

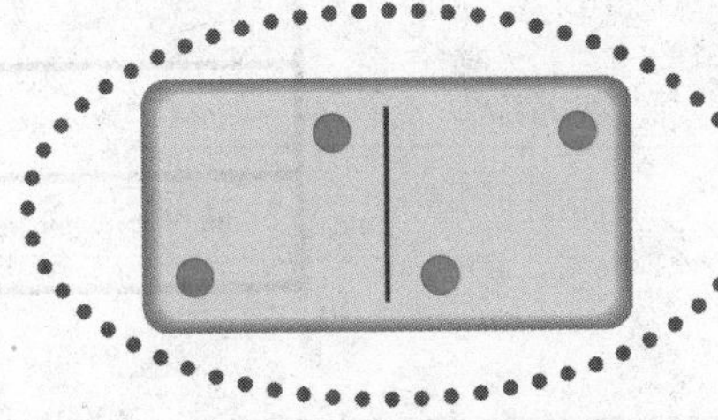

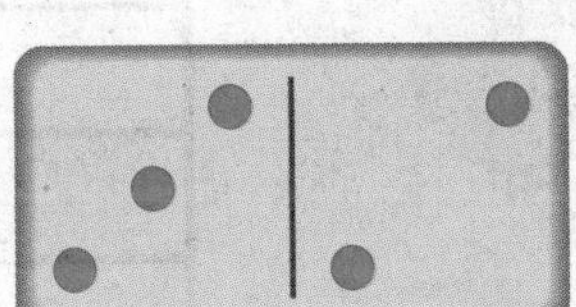
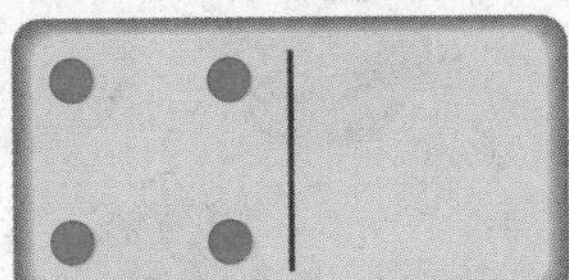
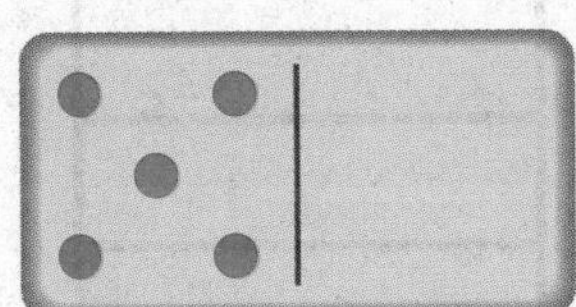

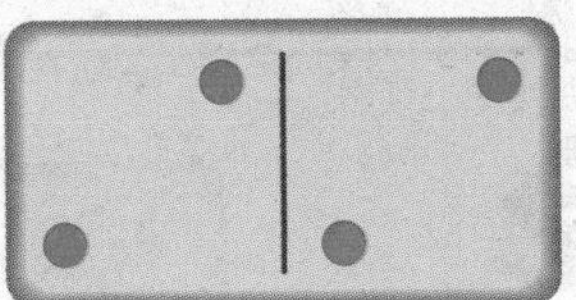
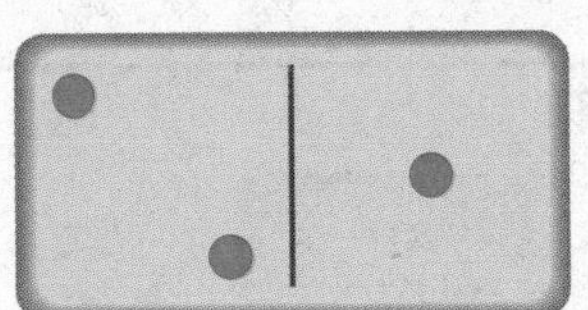

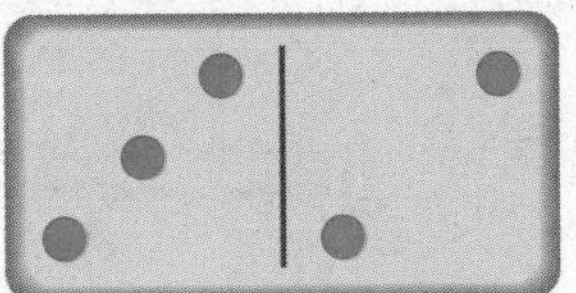
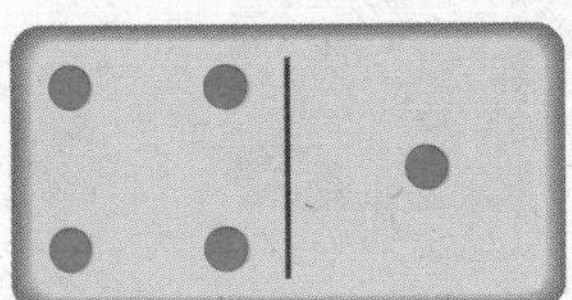

Directions Say: *Count the dots on each dot tile, and then draw a circle around the dot tiles with 4 dots.* Then have students: 1 draw a circle around the dot tiles with 5 dots; 2 draw a circle around the dot tiles with 4 dots; 3 draw a circle around the dot tiles with 5 dots.

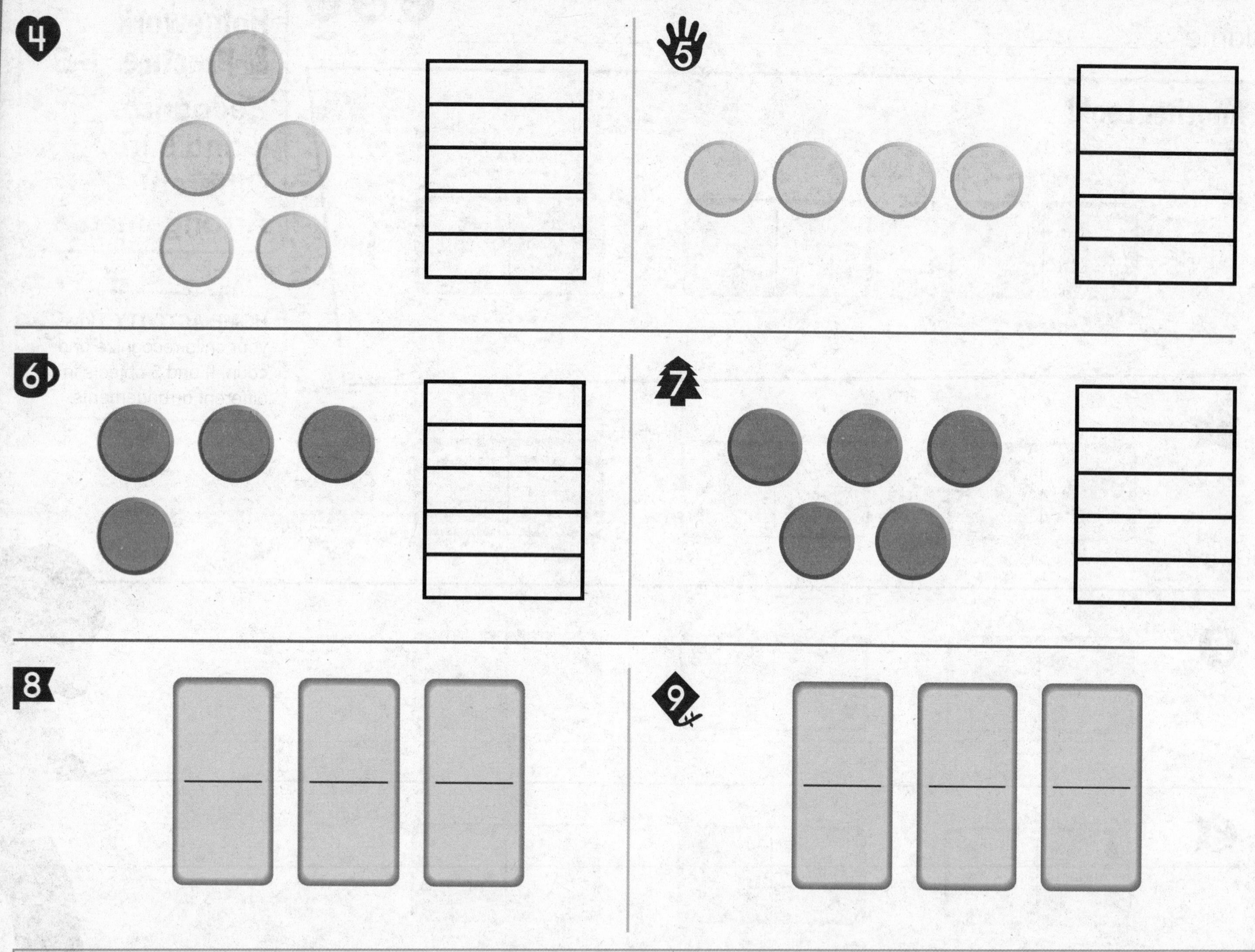

Directions 4–7 Have students count the counters, and then color the boxes to show how many. 8 **Higher Order Thinking** Have students draw 4 dots on each dot tile to show three different dot tiles. 9 **Higher Order Thinking** Have students draw 5 dots on each dot tile to show three different dot tiles.

Name ______________________________

Lesson 1-6

Read and Write 4 and 5

Directions Have students place 5 counters on the lily pad on the left side of the workmat. Say: *Alex sees 5 frogs on the lily pad. He glues pictures of 5 frogs on one lily pad. How can he show how many frogs in another way? Draw the other way on the empty lily pad.*

I can ...
read and write the numbers 4 and 5.

I can also reason about math.

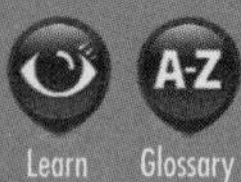

4

4

four

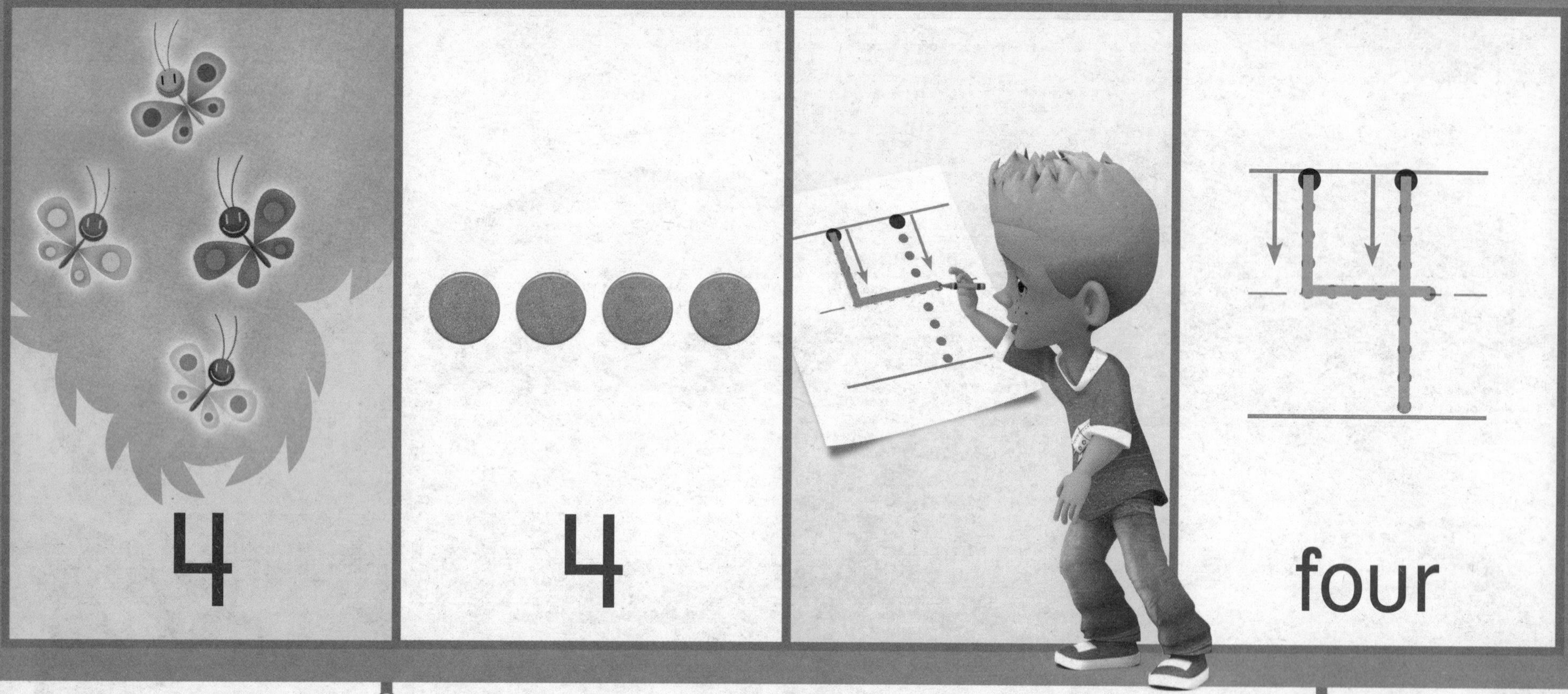

Guided Practice

1

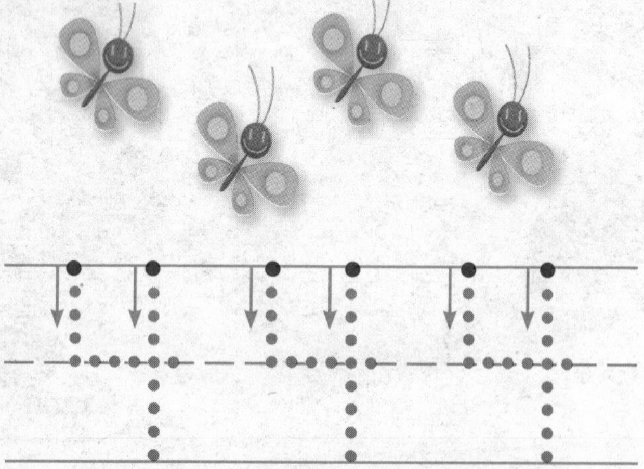

2

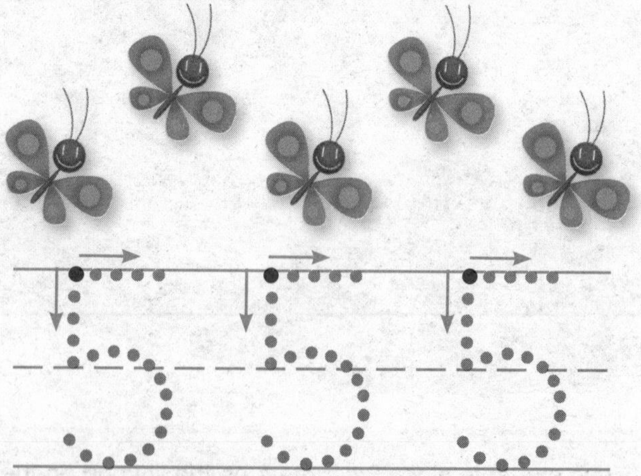

Directions 1 and 2 Have students count the butterflies, and then practice writing the number that tells how many.

Name ______________________________

3

4

5

6

Directions 3–6 Have students count the frogs, and then practice writing the number that tells how many.

Independent Practice

Tools Assessment

7

8

9

Directions 7 and 8 Have students count the dragonflies, and then practice writing the number that tells how many. 9 **Higher Order Thinking** Have students count the blue birds and the yellow birds, color a box for each bird, and then write the numbers to tell how many.

Name ______________________

Homework & Practice 1-6

Read and Write 4 and 5

HOME ACTIVITY Draw groups of 4 and 5 circles on 2 index cards. Have your child write the correct number on the back of each card. Then use the cards to practice counting and reading the numbers 4 and 5.

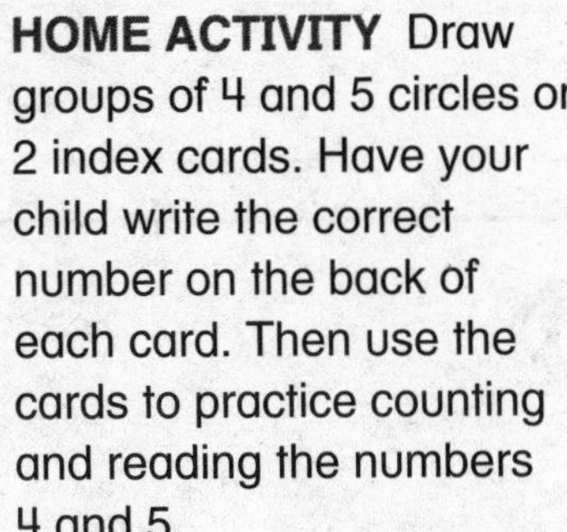

Another Look!

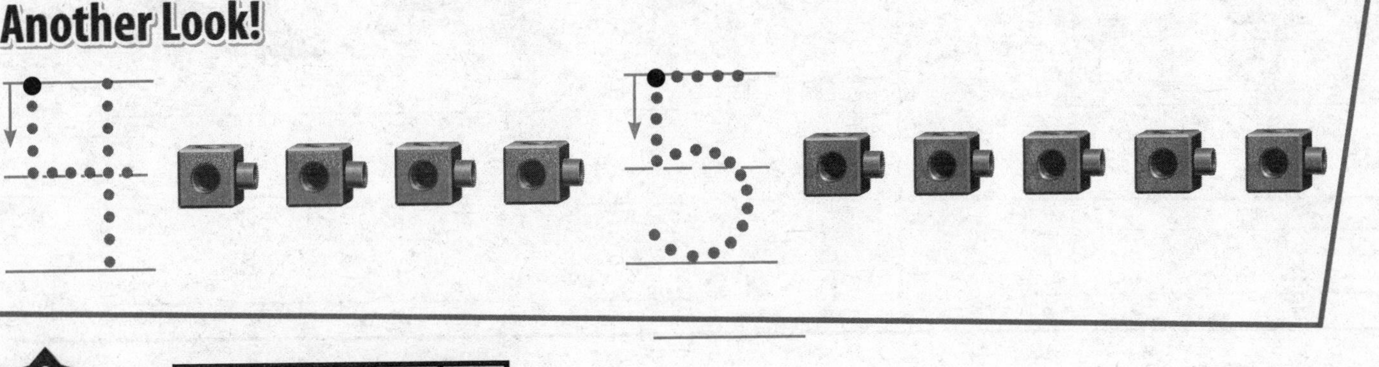

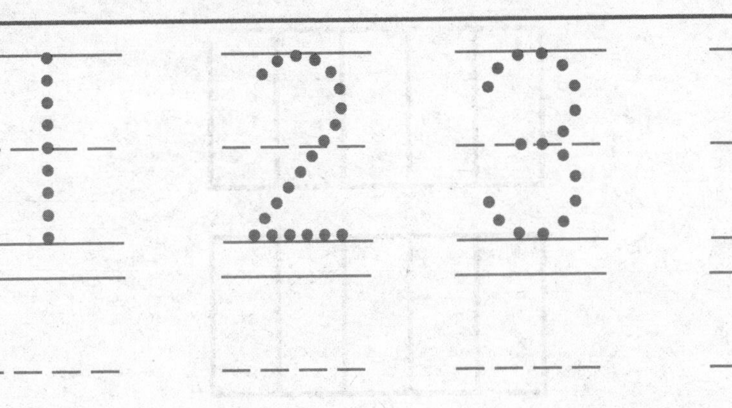

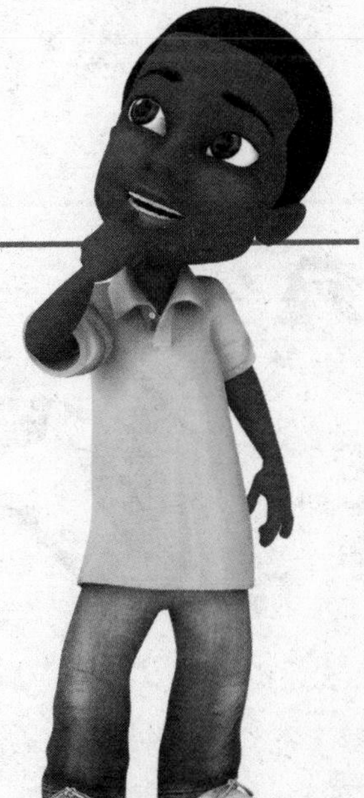

Directions Say: *Count the cubes, and then write the numbers to tell how many.* Have students: 1 and 2 count the colored boxes, and then write the number to tell how many; 3 write each number from 1 to 5, and then write each number again.

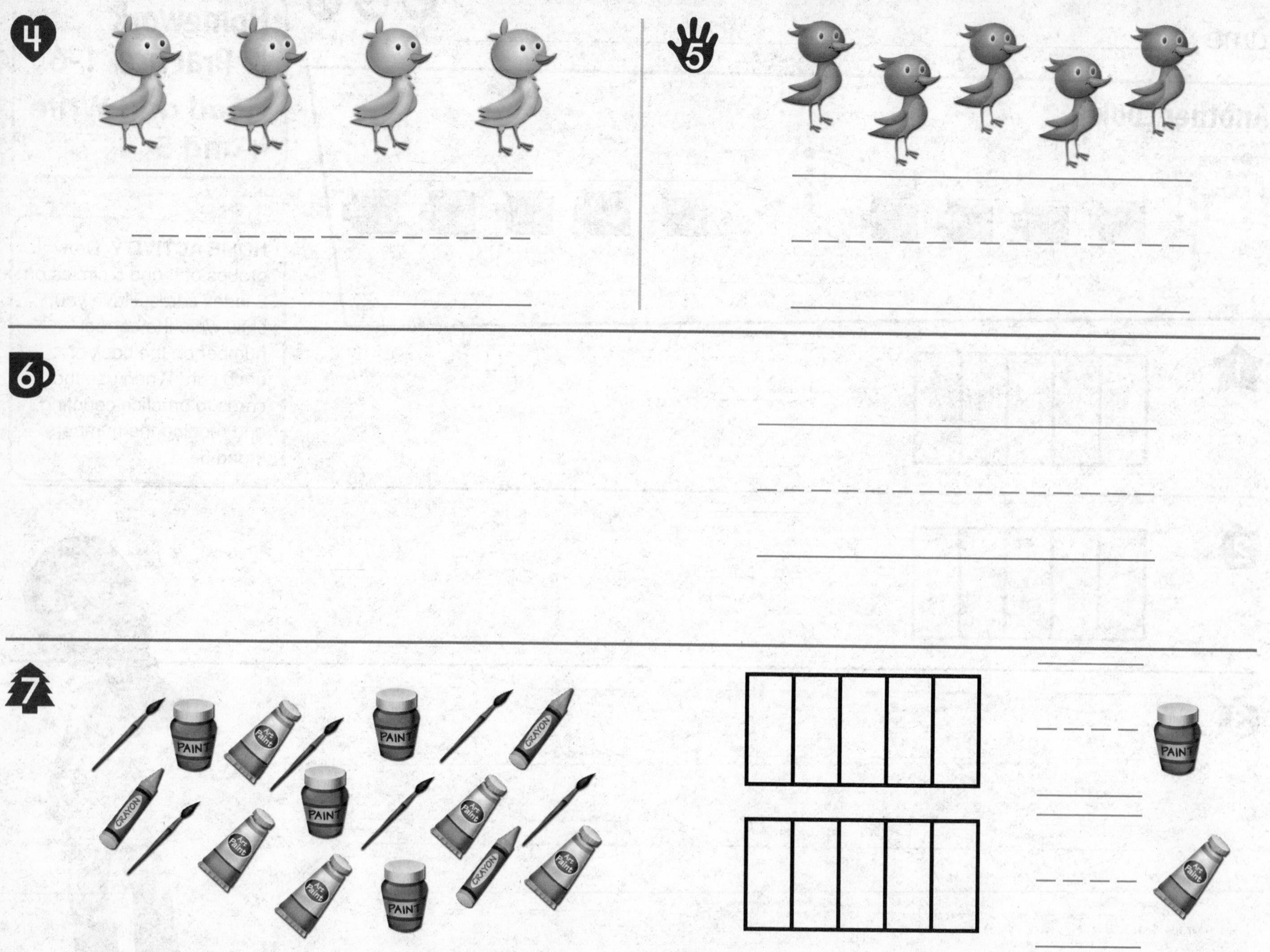

Directions 4 and 5 Have students count the number of birds, and then practice writing the number that tells how many. 6 **Higher Order Thinking** Have students draw 4 or 5 objects, and then practice writing the number that tells how many. 7 **Higher Order Thinking** Have students count the bottles of paint and the tubes of paint, color a box for each and then write the numbers to tell how many.

Name ______________________

Lesson 1-7
Identify the Number 0

Directions Have students place 0 counters in the basket on the workmat. Say: *Alex is in a vegetable garden. He does not see any potatoes in the basket. The basket is empty. How can Alex color the boxes to show that there are no potatoes in the basket?*

I can ...
use zero to tell when there are no objects.

I can also make math arguments.

1

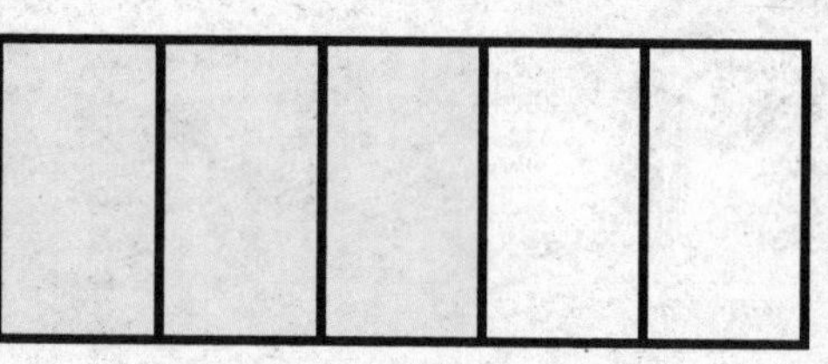

2

Directions 1 and 2 Have students color a box as they count each apple to show how many.

Name ___

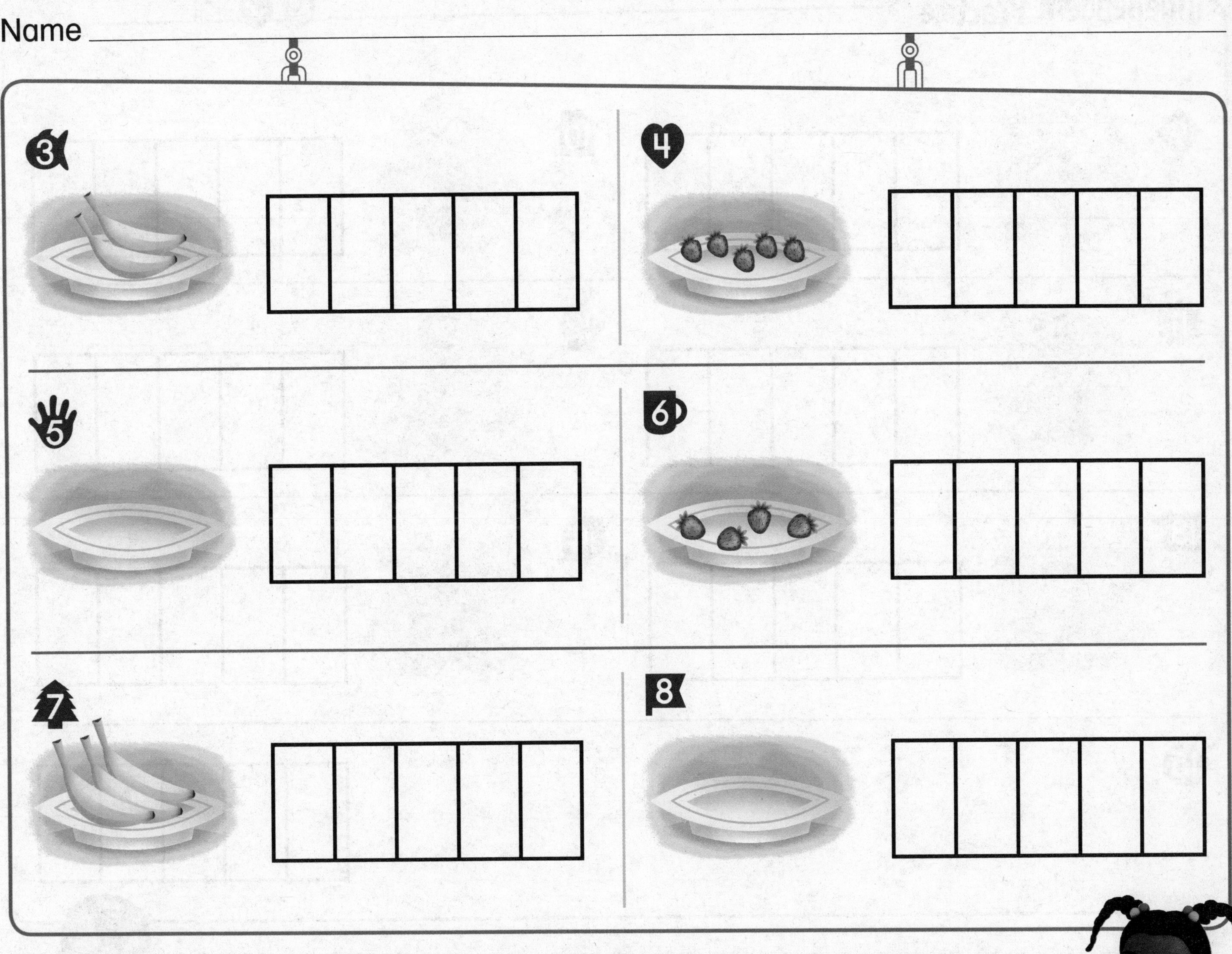

Directions 3–8 Have students color a box as they count each piece of fruit to show how many.

Independent Practice

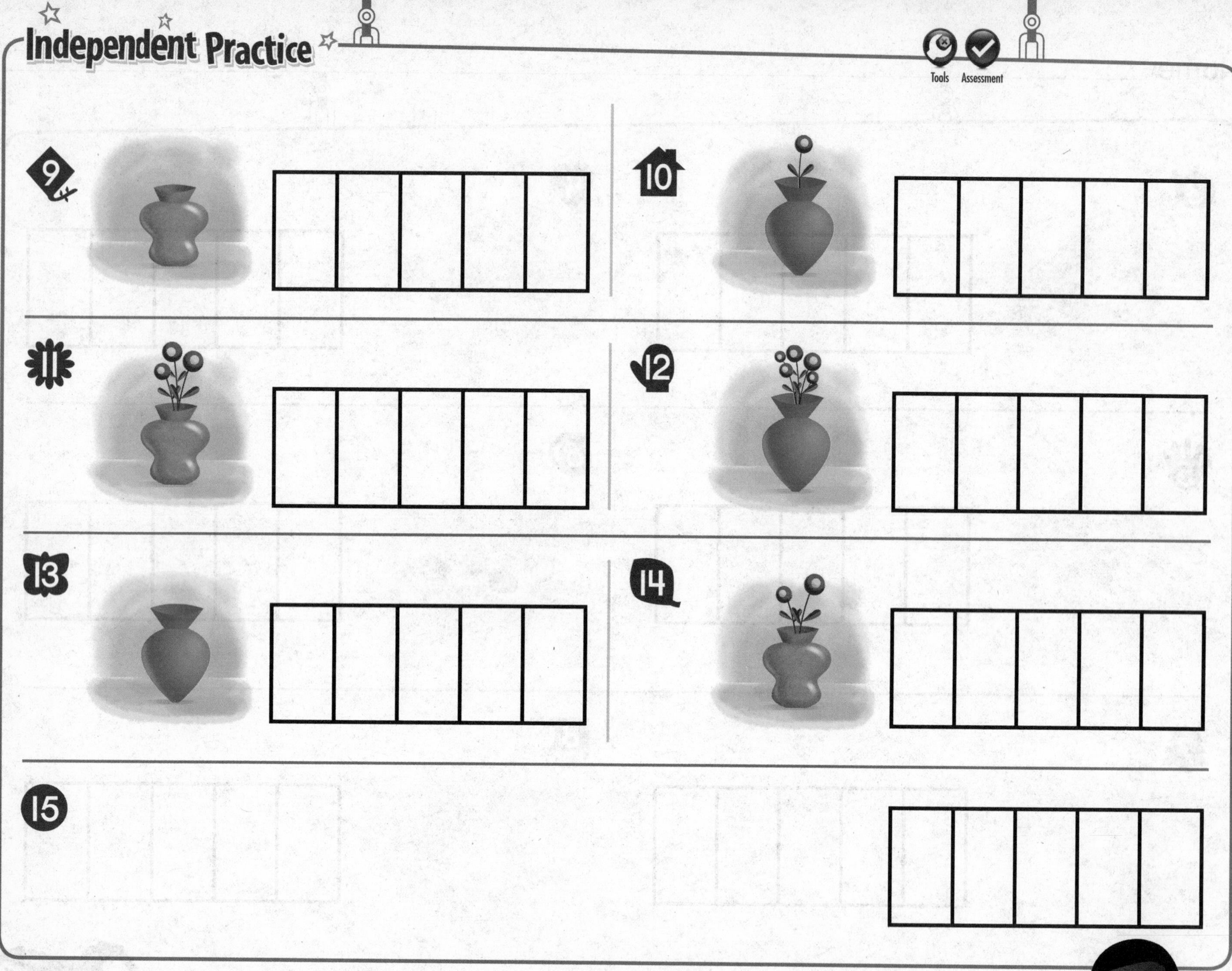

Directions 9–14 Have students color a box as they count each flower in the vase to show how many. 15 **Higher Order Thinking** Have students pick a number between 0 and 5, draw that many flowers, and then color the boxes to show how many.

Name ______________________________

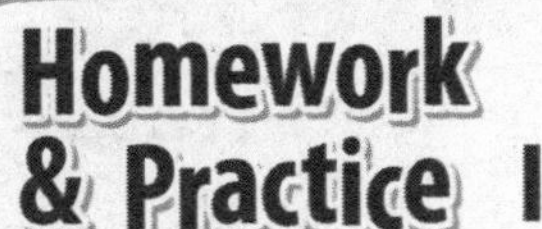

Homework & Practice 1-7

Identify the Number 0

HOME ACTIVITY Alternate putting objects on a plate and leaving it empty. Have your child identify when there are 0 objects on the plate.

Another Look!

1

2

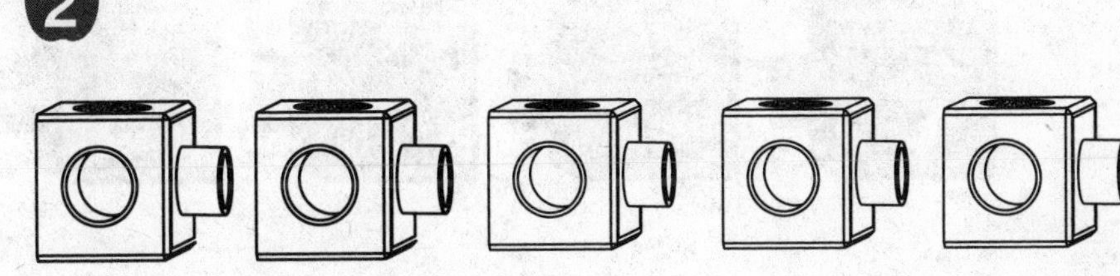

3

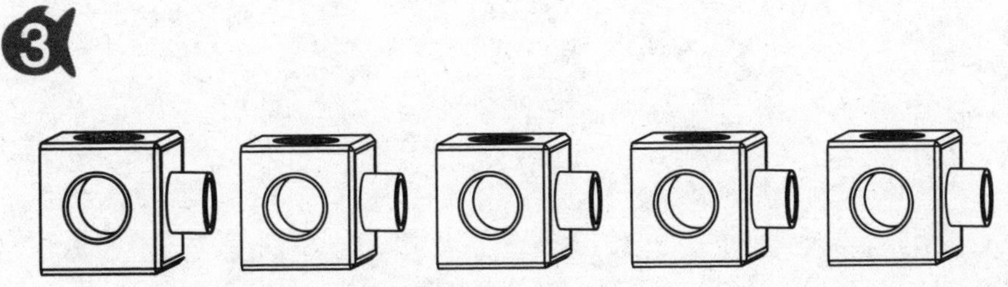

4

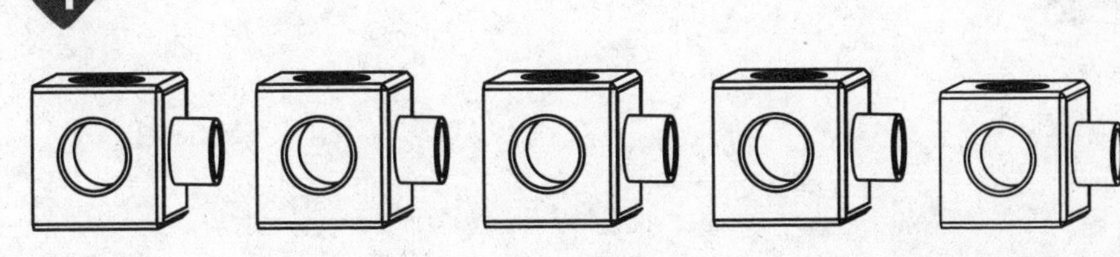

Directions Say: *How many toys are in the box? Use cubes or other objects to show 0, and then color 0 cubes.* Give students 5 cubes or 5 other objects. Have students: 1 choose 0 cubes or objects, and then color a cube as they count each cube to show how many; 2 choose 2 cubes or objects, and then color a cube as they count each cube to show how many; 3 choose 1 cube or object, and then color a cube as they count each cube to show how many; 4 choose 4 cubes or objects, and then color a cube as they count each cube to show how many.

7

Directions 5 Have students color a cube as they count each pear in the bowl to show how many. 6 **Higher Order Thinking** Have students draw an apple as they count each cube that shows how many. 7 **Higher Order Thinking** Have students draw a plate with some oranges on it, and then draw another plate with 0 oranges on it.

Solve & Share

Name ___

Solve

Lesson 1-8
Read and Write 0

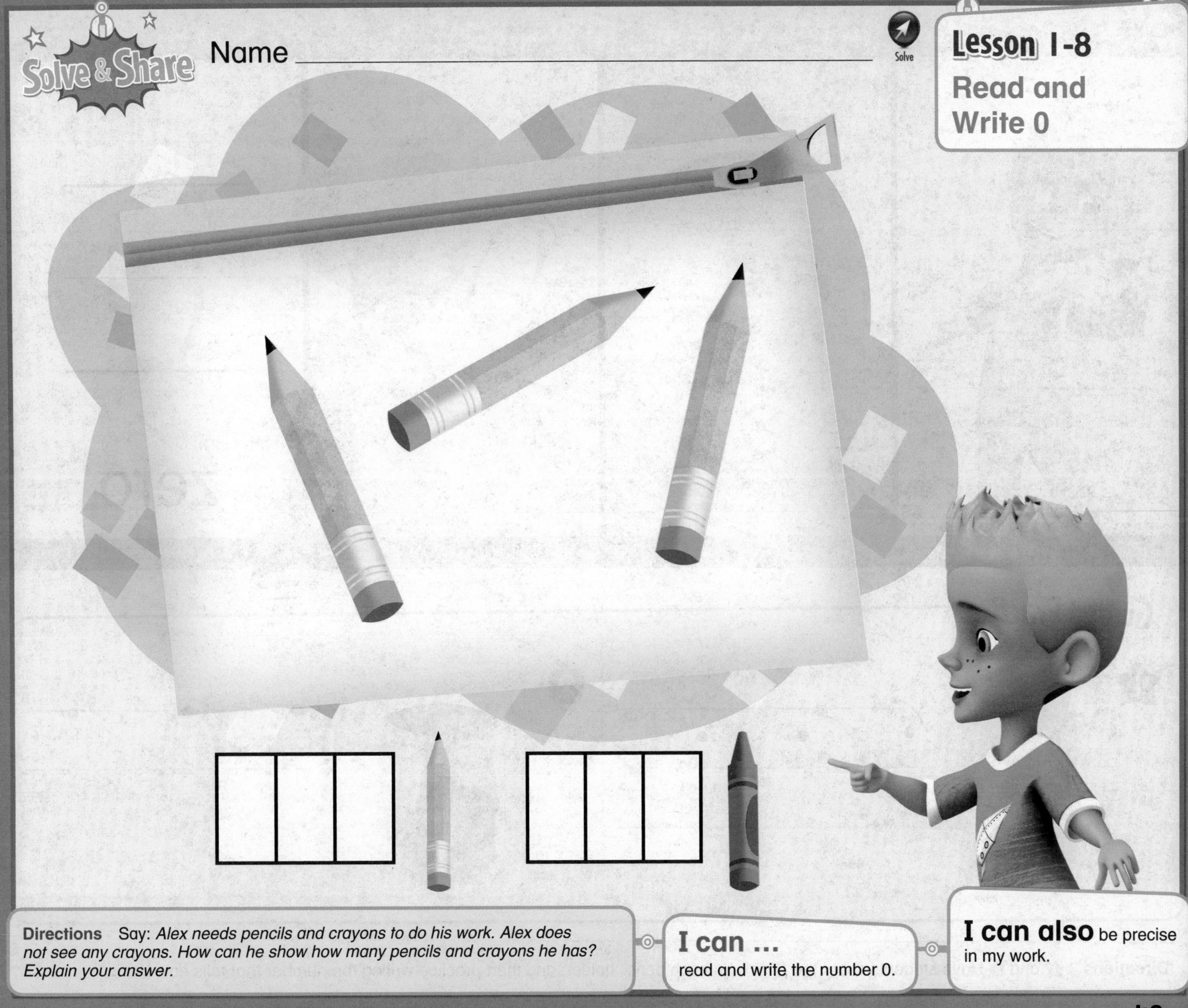

Directions Say: *Alex needs pencils and crayons to do his work. Alex does not see any crayons. How can he show how many pencils and crayons he has? Explain your answer.*

I can ...
read and write the number 0.

I can also be precise in my work.

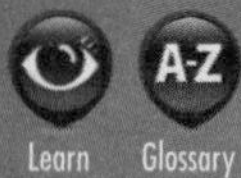

zero

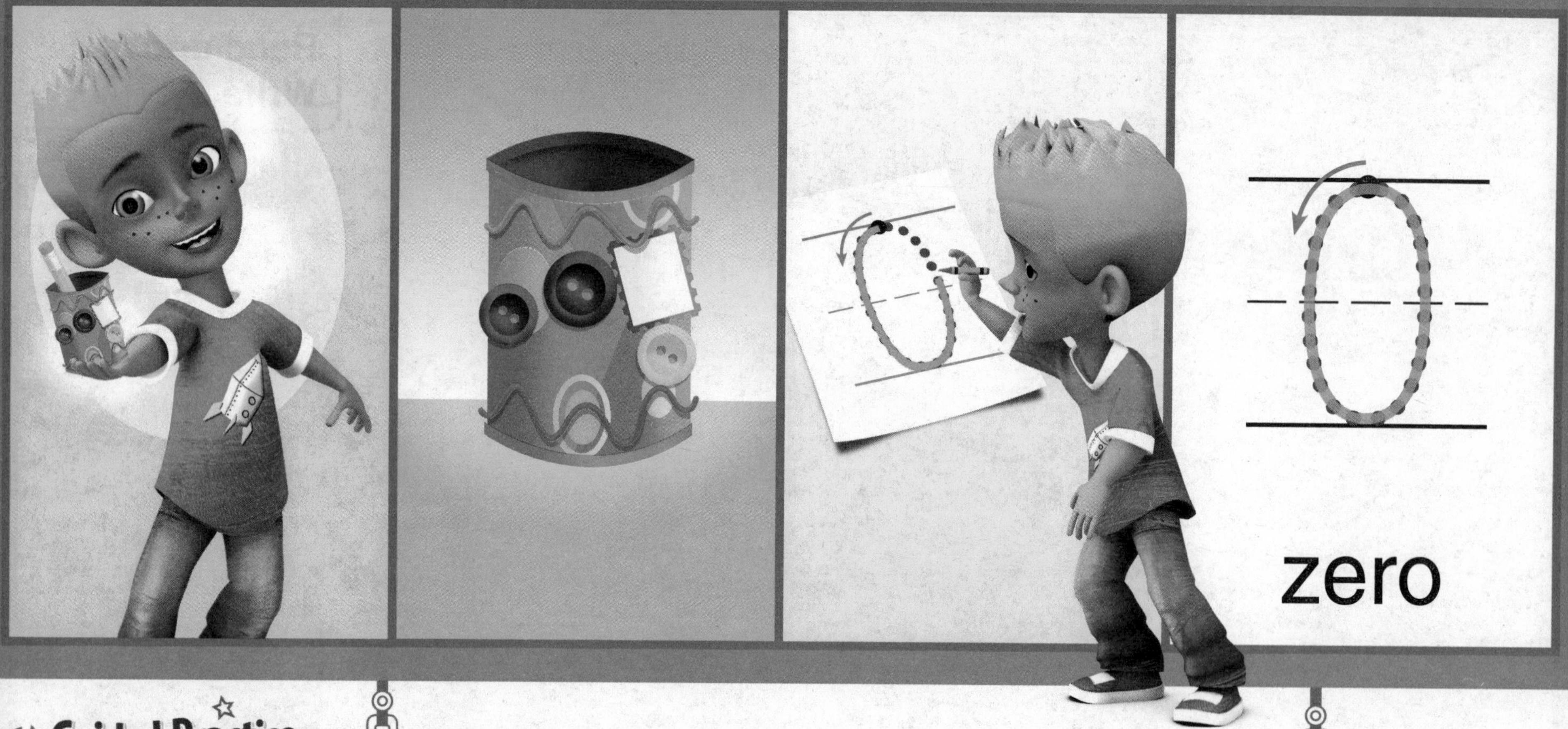

Guided Practice

1

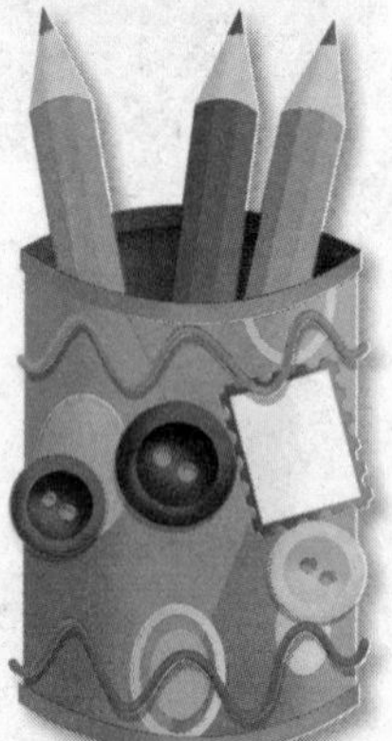

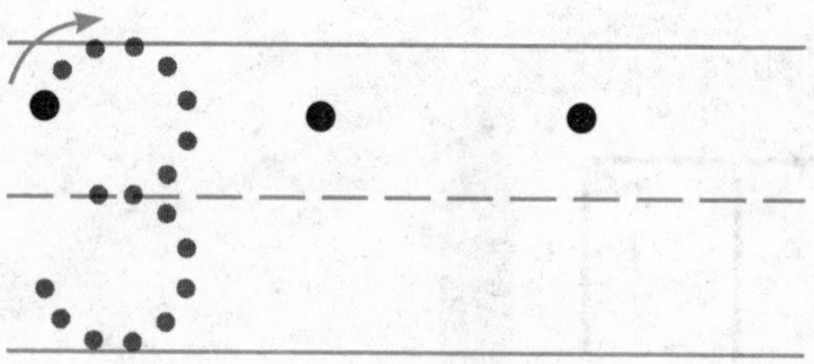

2

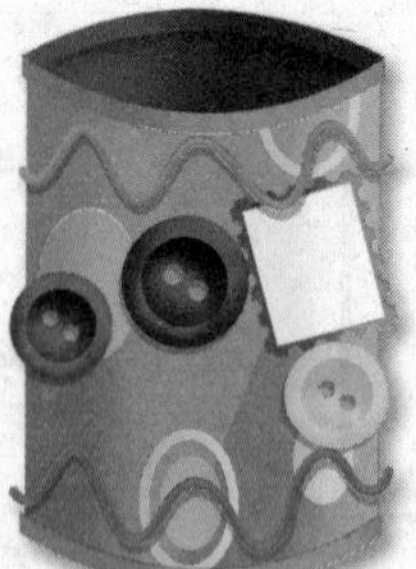

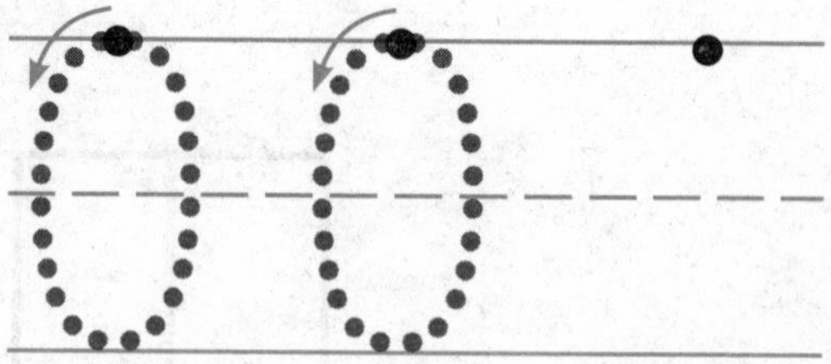

Directions 1 and 2 Have students count the pencils in each pencil holder, and then practice writing the number that tells how many.

Name

3

4

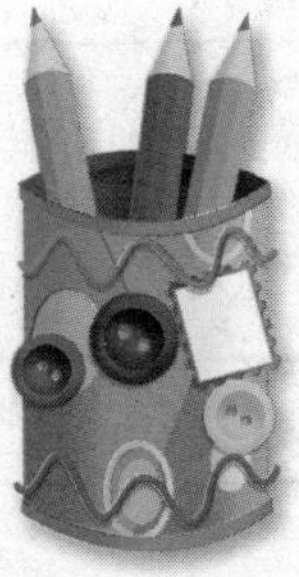

5

6

7

8

Directions 3–8 Have students count the pencils in each pencil holder, and then practice writing the number that tells how many.

Independent Practice

Tools Assessment

9

10

11

12

13

14

Directions Have students: 9–12 count the balls in each box, and then practice writing the number that tells how many; 13 practice writing the numbers 0 to 5. 14 **Higher Order Thinking** Have students draw zero counters and write the number to tell how many, and then draw 1 to 5 counters and write the number to tell how many.

Name ______________________

Help Tools Games

Homework & Practice 1-8

Read and Write 0

HOME ACTIVITY Have your child show how to read and write the number 0. Have your child use a bowl to model the number 0.

Another Look!

0 0 0 0

1

2

3

4

5

6

Directions Say: *Practice writing the number 0.* Have students: 1 and 2 count the colored boxes, and then practice writing the number that tells how many; 3 and 4 count the trucks in the box, and then write the number to tell how many; 5 and 6 count the counters in the hand, and then write the number to tell how many.

Directions 7–9 Have students count the books, and then write the number to tell how many. 10 **Higher Order Thinking** Have students draw 0 to 5 objects, and then practice writing the number that tells how many. 11 **Higher Order Thinking** Have students draw a circle around each animal that has 0 horns, and then mark an X on each animal that has 0 stripes.

Solve & Share

Name ____________________

Solve

Lesson 1-9
Ways to Make 5

Directions Say: *5 daisies are planted in a flowerpot. Some are yellow. Some are red. Use counters to show one way to make 5 daisies. Color the daisies yellow and red to show your work. Has the total number of counters changed? Why or why not?*

I can ... show ways to make 5.

I can also look for patterns.

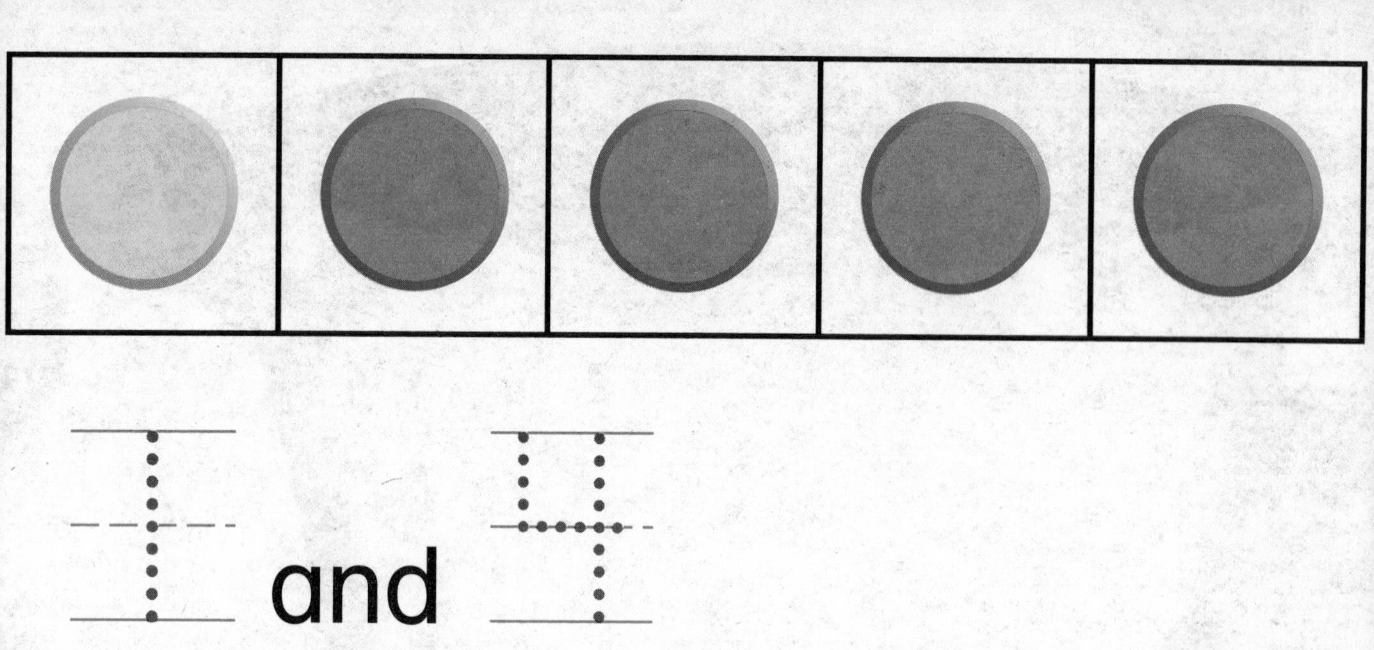

Guided Practice

Directions 1 Have students use counters to find a way to make 5, color the daisies to show the way, and then write the numbers to tell how many yellow and how many red daisies.

Name

2

and

3

and

Directions 2 and 3 Have students use counters to find two more ways to make 5, color the flowers yellow and red to show the ways, and then write the numbers to tell how many yellow and how many red flowers.

Independent Practice

Tools Assessment

4

and

5

and

Directions 4 Have students color the flowers yellow and red to show two different ways to make 5, and then write the numbers to tell how many yellow and how many red flowers. 5 **Higher Order Thinking** Have students draw a way to make 5 with flowers, and then write the numbers to tell the way to make 5. If needed, have them use counters.

Name ______________________

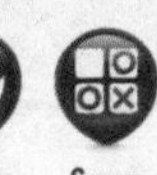

Homework & Practice 1-9

Ways to Make 5

HOME ACTIVITY Have your child show different ways to make 4 in two parts using 4 cards or pictures. Have your child show one part of the 4 cards or pictures facedown and another part faceup. Repeat using the number 5.

Another Look!

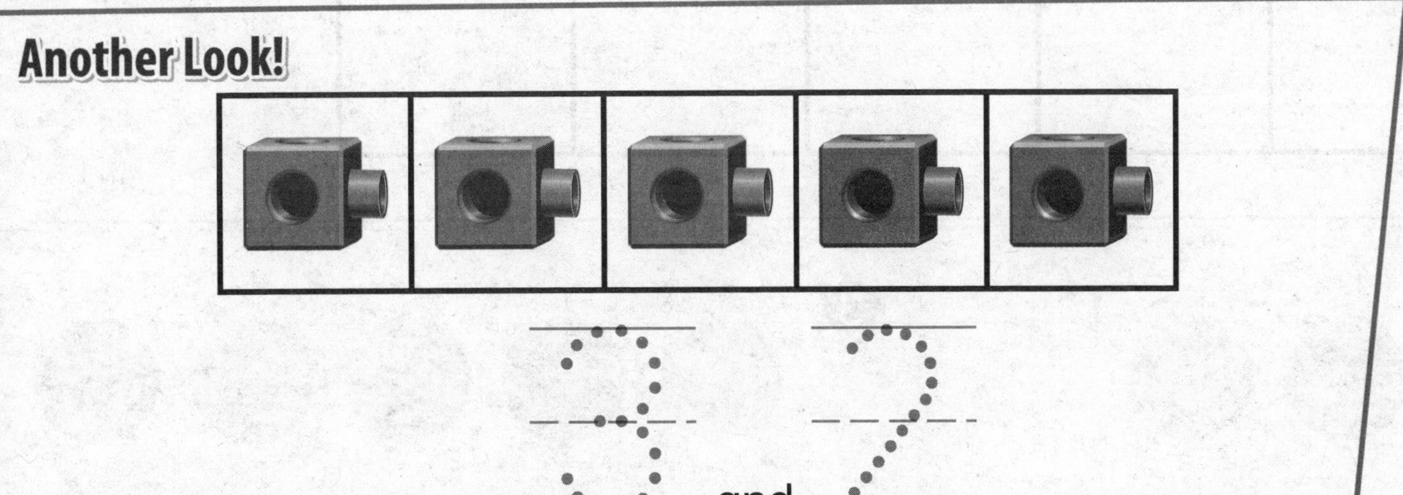

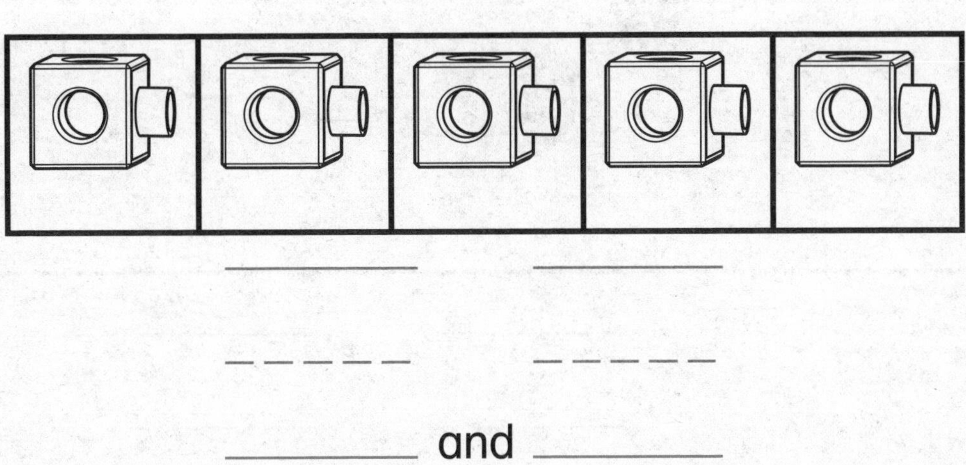

______ and ______

Directions Say: *Use red and blue cubes or pieces of paper to model a way to make 5, color the cubes to show the way, and then write the numbers to tell how many red and blue cubes.* **1** Have students color the cubes red and blue to show a different way to make 5, and then write the numbers to tell how many.

2

3

4

5

6

______ ______

______ and ______

Directions 2–5 Have students use the five-frame above, and then draw yellow counters to complete the ways to make 5. 6 **Higher Order Thinking** Have students draw a way to make 5 with flowers, and then write the numbers to tell how many.

Name ______________________

Lesson 1-10
Count Numbers to 5

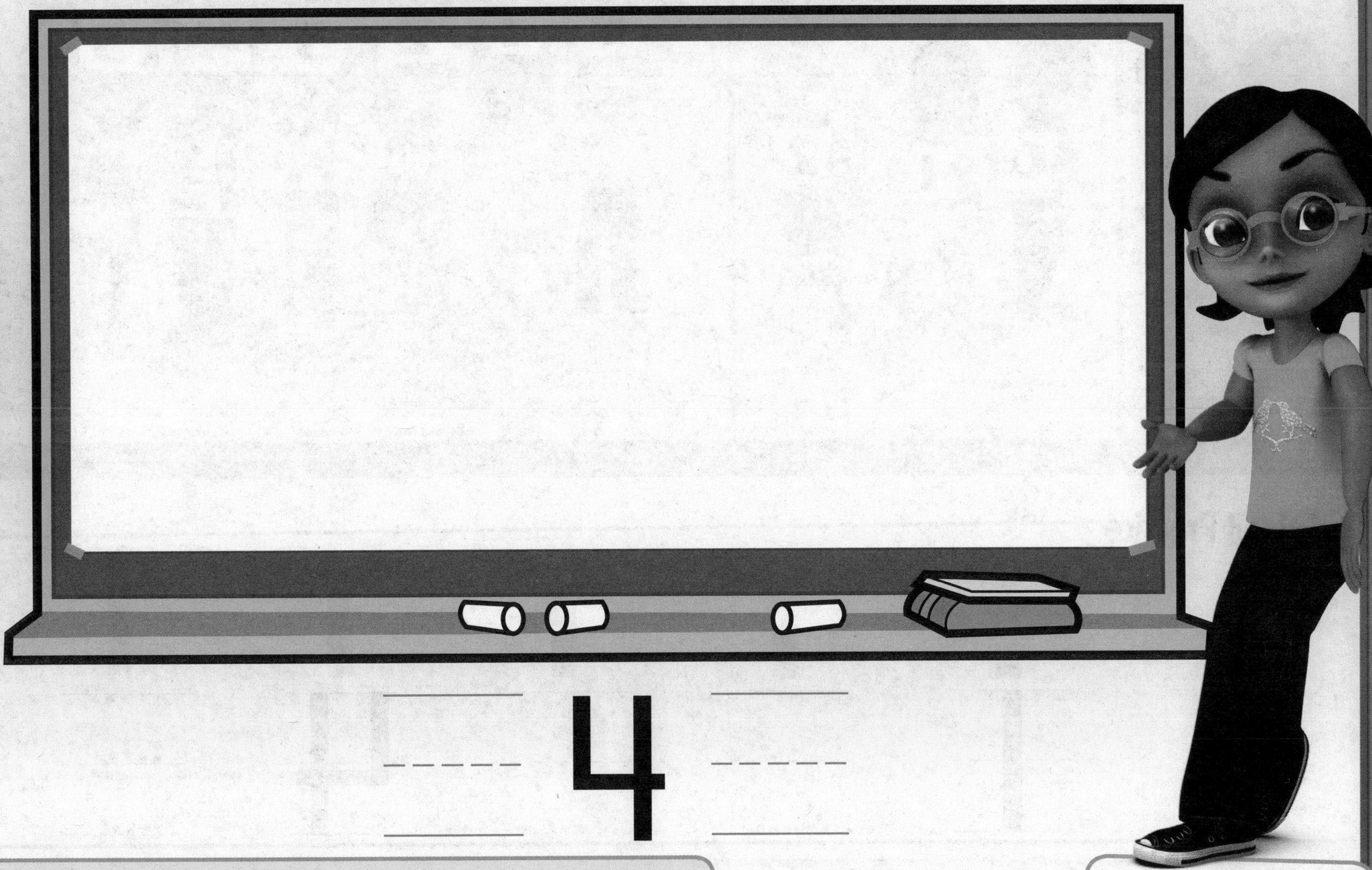

____ 4 ____

Directions Say: *Marta is thinking of two numbers—one is the number that comes just before 4 when counting, and the other is the number that comes just after 4 when counting. Write the two numbers Marta is thinking of. Show how you know you are correct.*

I can ... count up to the number 5.

I can also use math tools correctly.

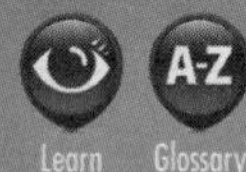

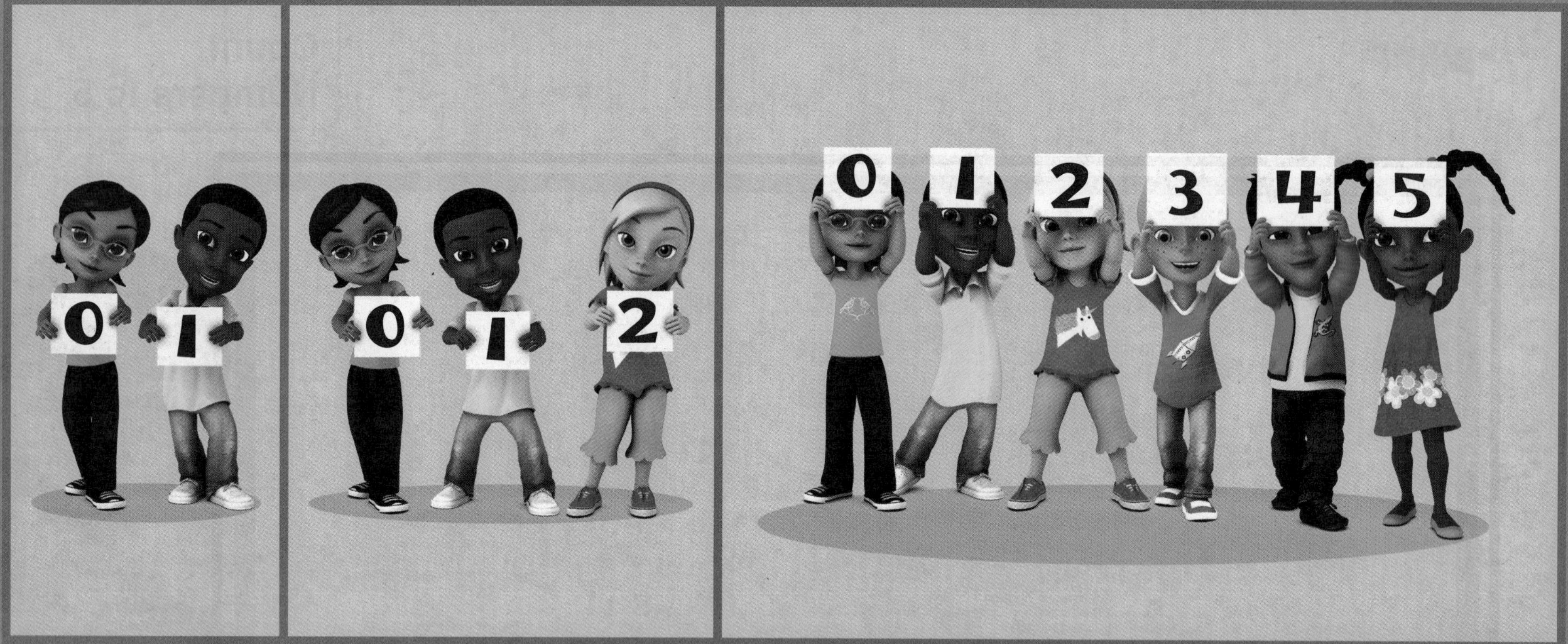

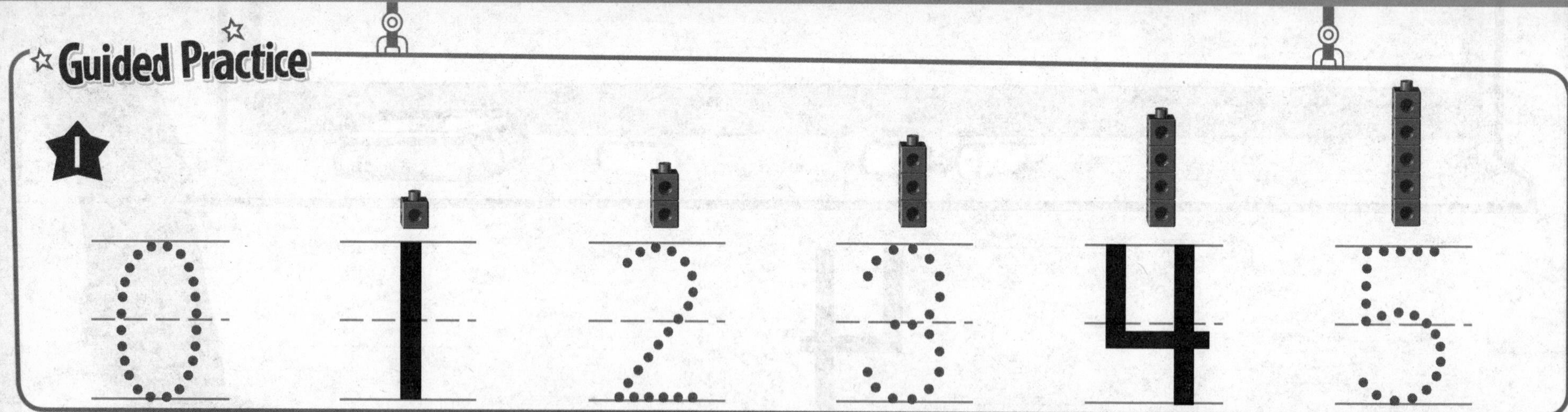

Directions 1 Have students write the number that comes just before 1 when counting, and the number that comes just after 1 when counting. Then have them write the number that comes just before 4 when counting, and the number that comes just after 4 when counting. Have them count the numbers in order from 0 to 5.

Name ___

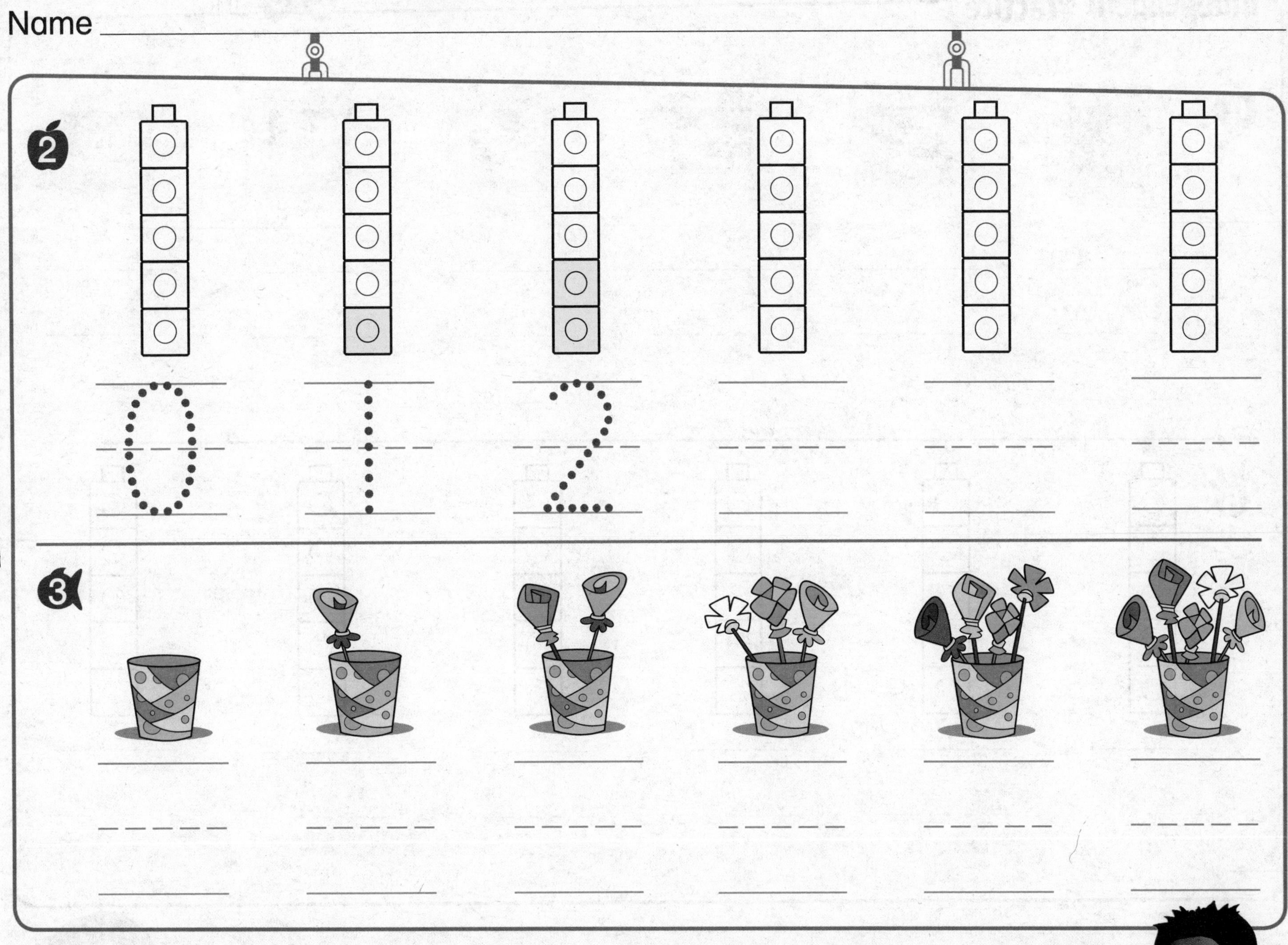

Directions Have students: 2 color the cubes to show each number, write the numbers in order, and then draw a circle around the number that comes just after 1 when counting; 3 count the flowers in each vase, write the numbers, and then count the numbers in order from 0 to 5.

Independent Practice

Tools Assessment

4

5

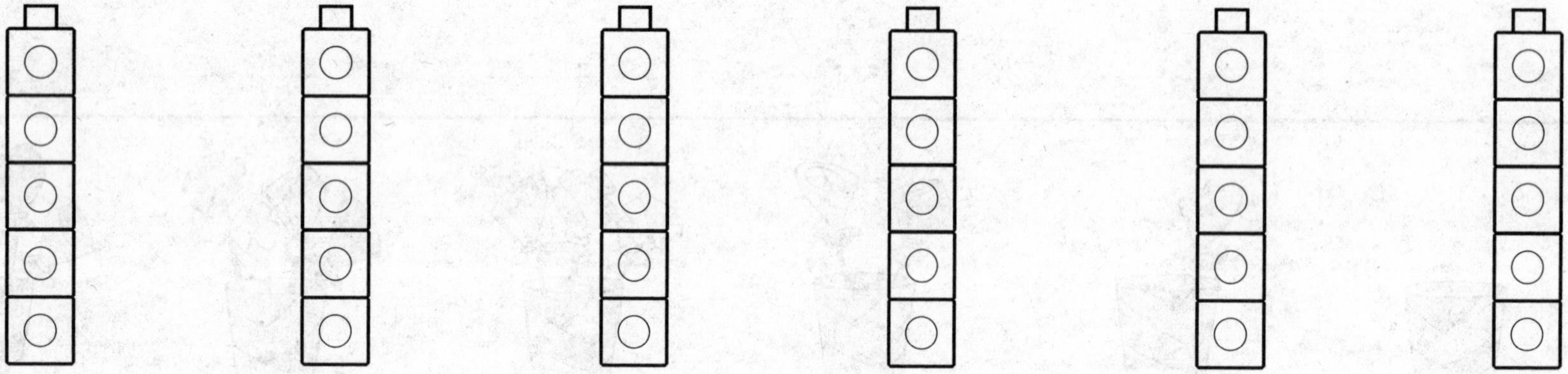

Directions 4 Have students count the toys in each box, write the numbers, and then draw a circle around the number that comes just after 4 when counting. 5 **Higher Order Thinking** Have students color 5 cubes, and then write the number. Have them color to show the number that comes just before it when counting in the next tower, and then write the number. Repeat for the remaining towers.

Name ______________________________

Homework & Practice 1-10

Count Numbers to 5

HOME ACTIVITY Ask your child to count the numbers from 0 to 5 in order, and then count backward from 5 to 0.

Another Look!

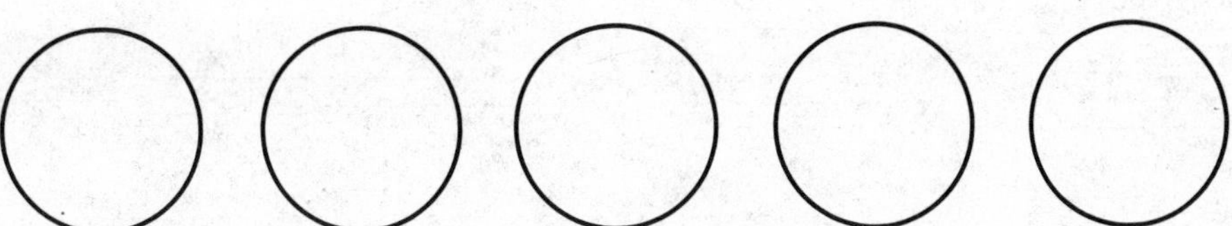

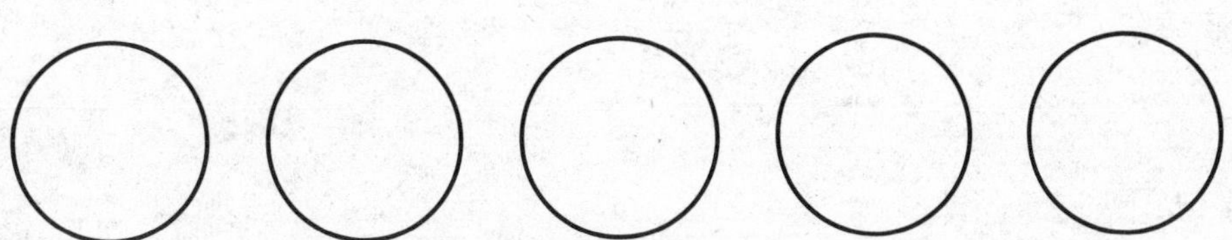

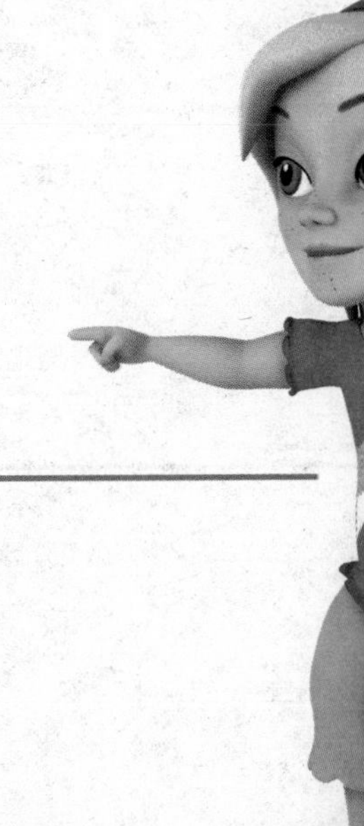

Directions Say: *The first row has zero counters colored. Write the number to tell how many. The next row shows 1 more counter colored. Write the number to tell how many.* 1 and 2 Have students color counters to add 1 more counter to each row than the row before, and then write the number to tell how many.

3

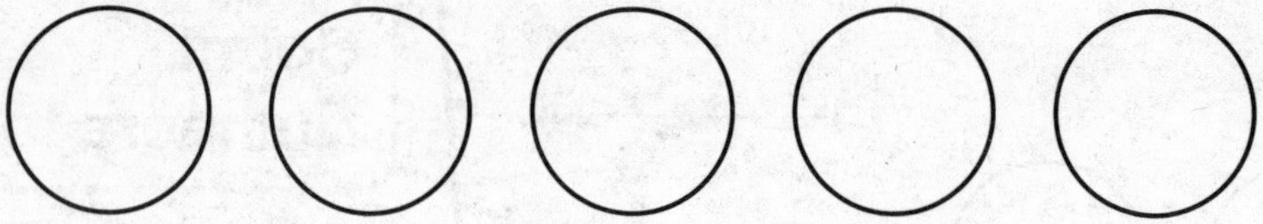

4

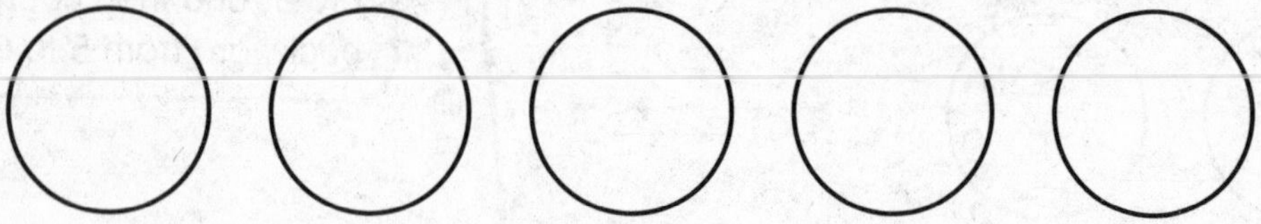

5

6

Directions 3 and 4 Have students color counters to add 1 more counter to each row than the counters in the item before, and then write the number to tell how many. 5 **Number Sense** Have students write the numbers in order from 0 to 5, draw a circle around the number that comes just before 1 when counting, and then mark an X on the number that comes just after 1 when counting. 6 **Higher Order Thinking** Have students count backward from 5 to 0, and then write the numbers.

Name ____________________

Problem Solving

Lesson 1-11

Construct Arguments

Think.

______

______

______

Directions Say: *Alex needs to count the group of shapes. How can you count these shapes? Use objects or words to help. Write the number to tell how many shapes. Tell why your number is correct.*

I can ... use math to explain what I know about counting.

I can also count to 5.

How can I explain?

1 2 3

Numbers

3

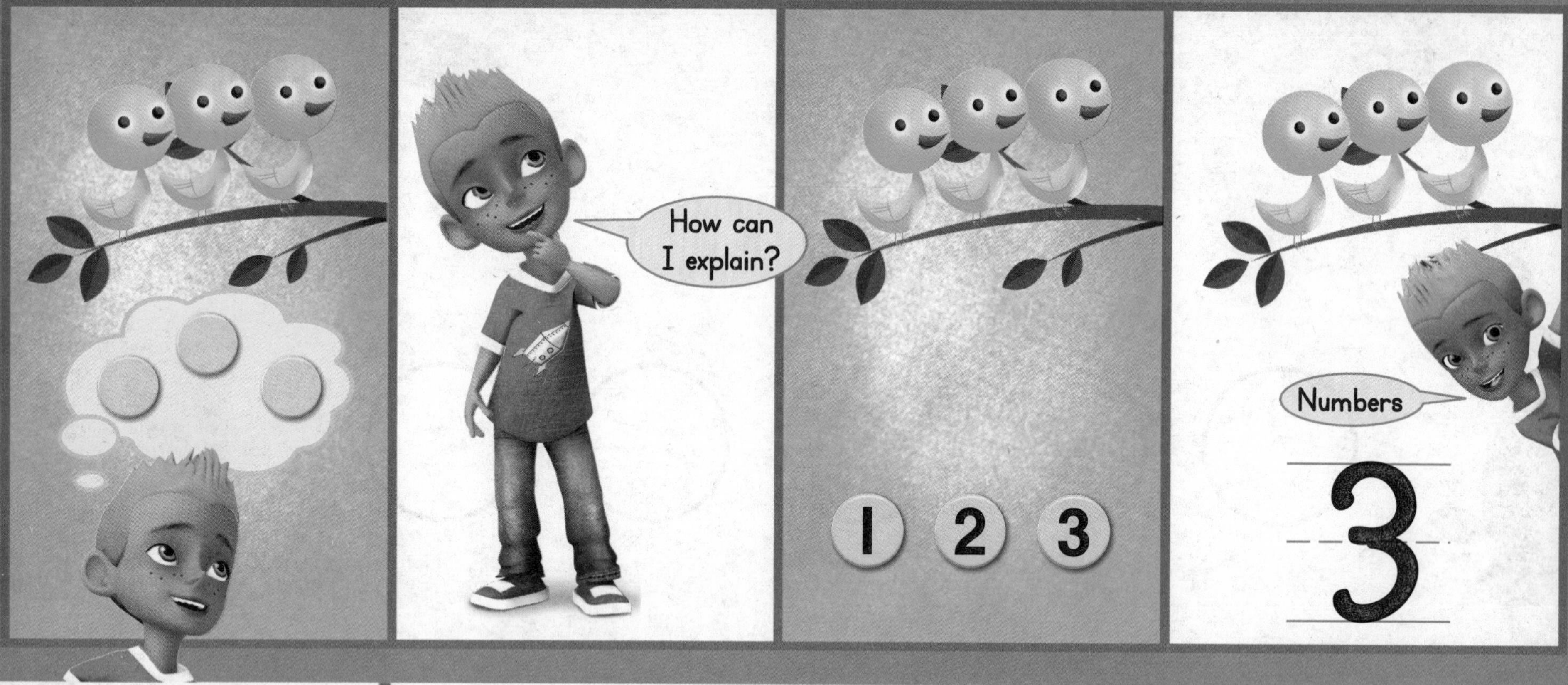

Guided Practice

Directions 1 and 2 Have students make a math argument about how many birds are in each row, and then write the number. Have them use objects, words, or a method of their choice to explain their arguments and tell why they are correct.

Tools Assessment

Name ______

Independent Practice

3

4

5

6

Directions 3–5 Have students make a math argument about how many leaves are in each row, and then write the number. Have them use objects, words, or a method of their choice to explain their arguments and tell why they are correct. 6 **Math and Science** Say: *Chlorophyll makes leaves green. There is less sunlight in the winter, so trees save their chlorophyll. This turns leaves brown, orange, red, and yellow.* Have students make a math argument about how many orange leaves are in the row, and then write the number. Have them use objects, words, or a method of their choice to explain their arguments and tell why they are correct.

Problem Solving

 Performance Assessment

Directions Read the problem to students. Then have them use multiple problem-solving methods to solve the problem. Say: *Brooke sees some rabbits. How many rabbits does she see?* **Reasoning** *How can you find the number of rabbits Brooke sees?* **Use Tools** *What tool can you use to help solve the problem?* **Explain** *How can you use math to explain why your work is correct?*

Name ________________

   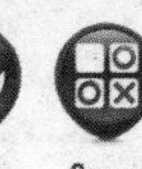
Help Tools Games

Homework & Practice 1-11

Construct Arguments

HOME ACTIVITY Place a row of up to 5 cups in front of your child. Have your child count the number of cups, write the number, and explain why his or her number is correct. Repeat with different numbers of cups up to 5.

Another Look!

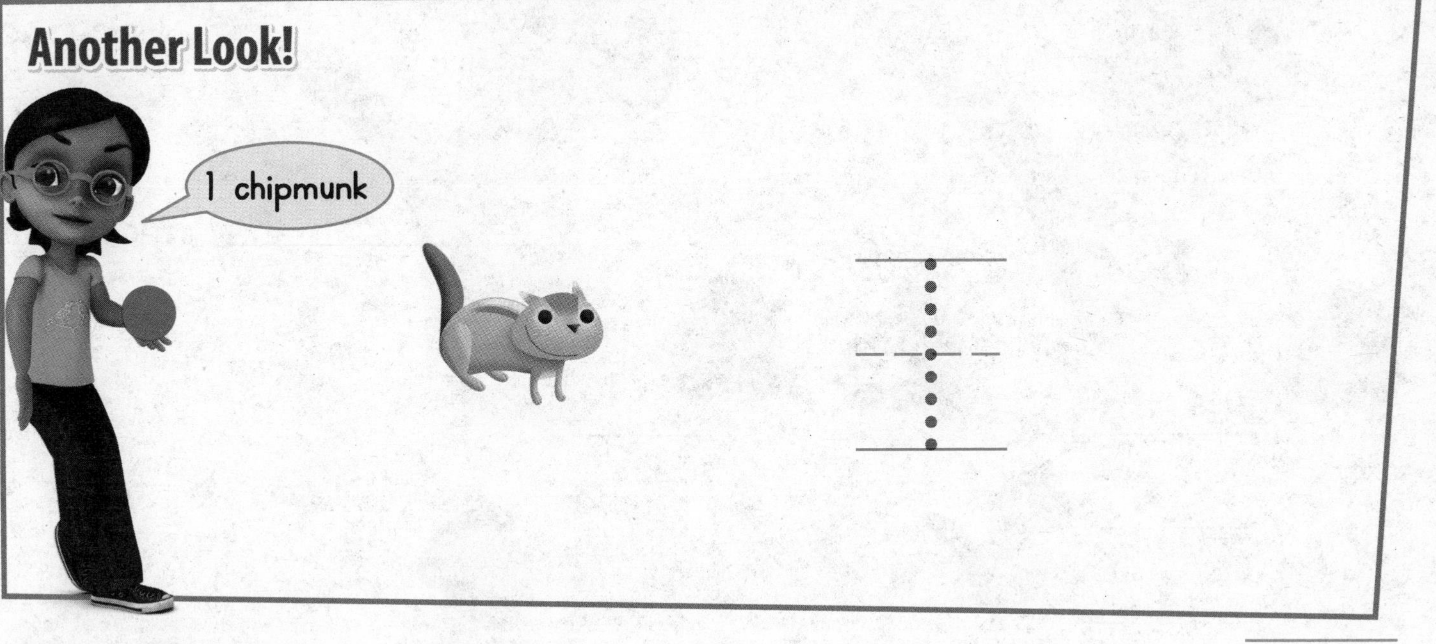

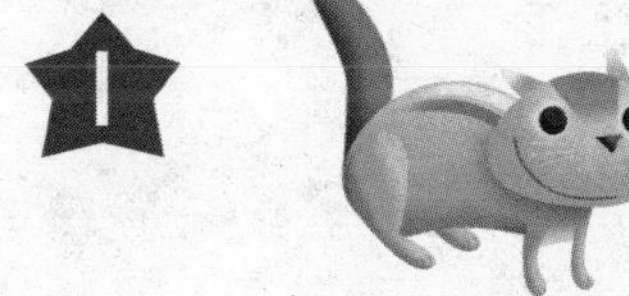 

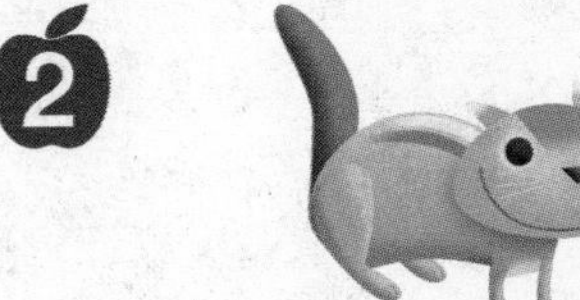   

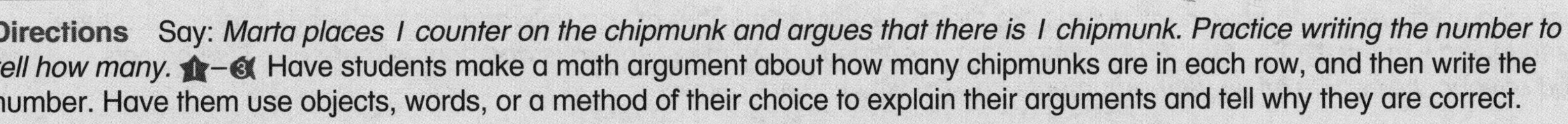

Directions Say: *Marta places 1 counter on the chipmunk and argues that there is 1 chipmunk. Practice writing the number to tell how many.* 1–3 Have students make a math argument about how many chipmunks are in each row, and then write the number. Have them use objects, words, or a method of their choice to explain their arguments and tell why they are correct.

Directions Read the problem to students. Then have them use multiple problem-solving methods to solve the problem. Say: *Some squirrels go out to gather acorns. How many squirrels and how many acorns are there?* **Make Sense** *What are you asked to find?* **Be Precise** *How many squirrels and how many acorns are there? Count the number of squirrels and the number of acorns, and then write the numbers to tell how many.* **Explain** *Make a math argument about how many squirrels and acorns there are. Use objects, words, or a method of your choice to explain your arguments and tell why you are correct.*

Name ______________________________

Glossary

TOPIC 1

Vocabulary Review

1

A 2

2

3

2 4

4

Directions **Understand Vocabulary** Have students: 1 draw a circle around the **number**; 2 write the number that means **none**; 3 draw a circle around the number **four**; 4 mark an X on a **part**, and then draw a circle around the **whole**.

I 3

7

8

Directions **Understand Vocabulary** Have students: 5 draw a circle around the number **one**; 6 write the number **three**; 7 **count** the number of cubes, and then write the number to tell how many; 8 write the numbers 0 to 5 in **order,** and then draw counters to show that many of each number.

Name

TOPIC 1

Set A

Reteaching

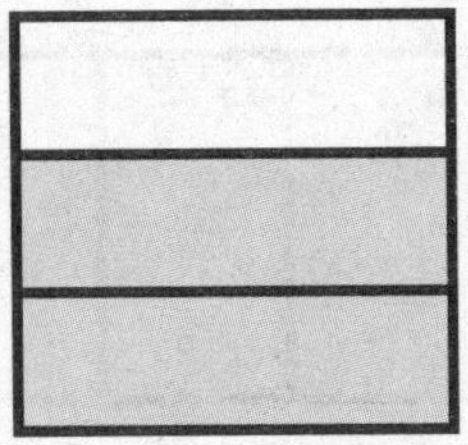

1

2

Set B

1

2

3

4

Directions Have students: 1 and 2 color a box as they count each ball to show how many; 3 and 4 count the flowers in the vase, and then practice writing the number that tells how many.

Set C

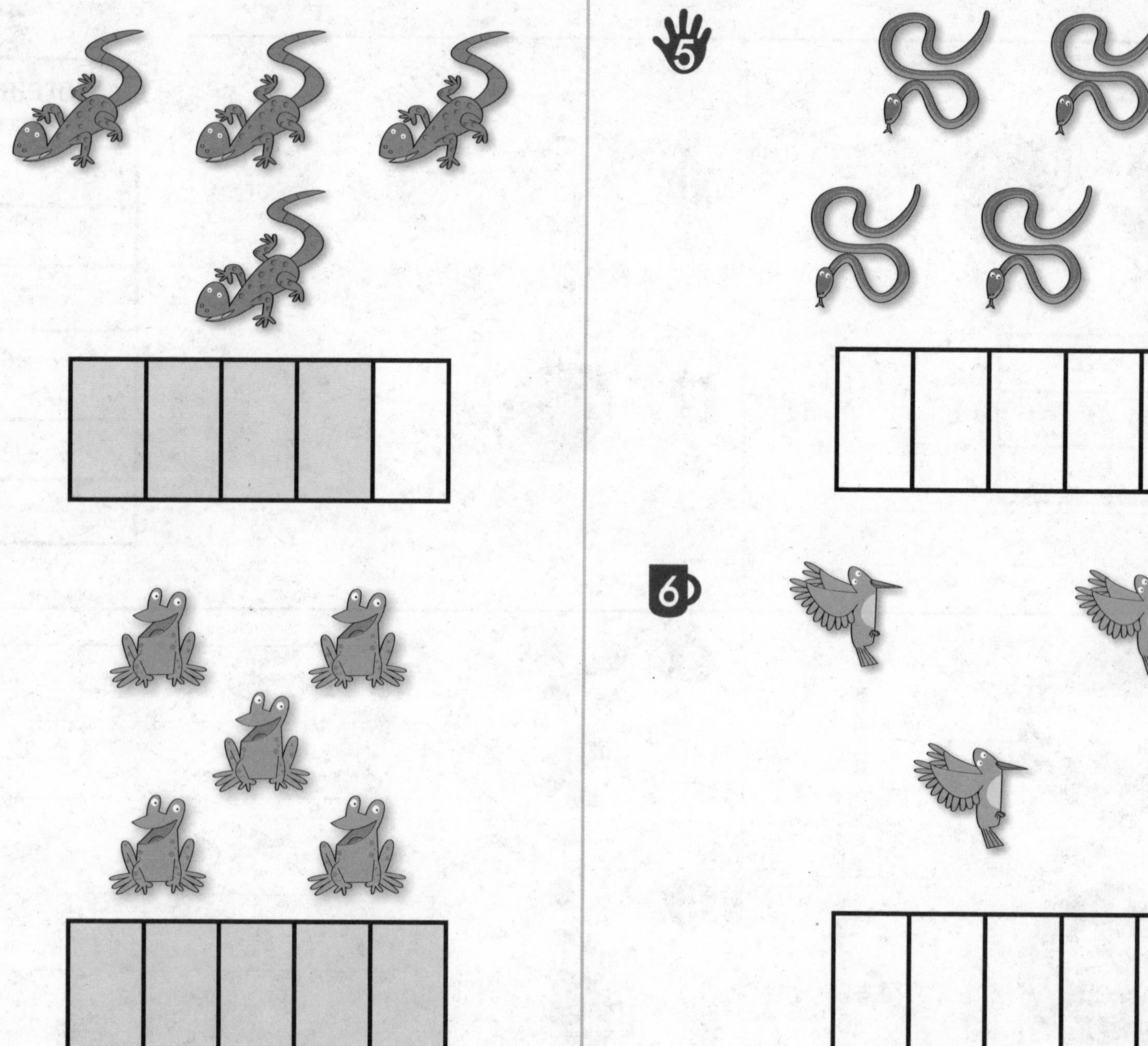

Directions 5 and 6 Have students color a box as they count each animal to show how many.

Name

Set D

7

3 and 2

and

Set E

0

8

9

Directions Have students: 7 use gray and brown crayons to color the animals to show a different way to make 5, and then write the numbers to tell how many gray and how many brown dogs; 8 and 9 count the flowers in the vase, and then practice writing the number that tells how many.

Set F

4

3

Directions 10 and 11 Have students count the octopuses, and then practice writing the number that tells how many.

Name ______________________________

Ⓐ 

Ⓑ 

Ⓒ 

Ⓓ 

☐ 

☐ 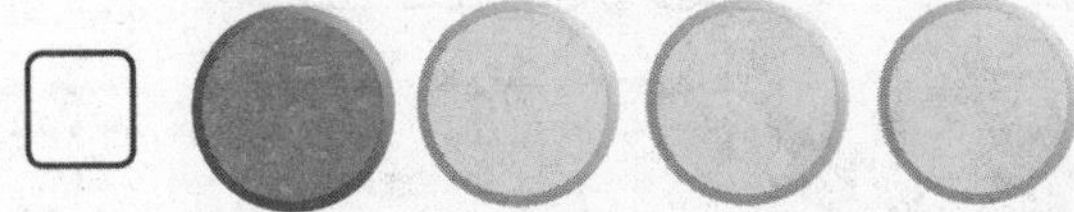

☐ 

☐ 

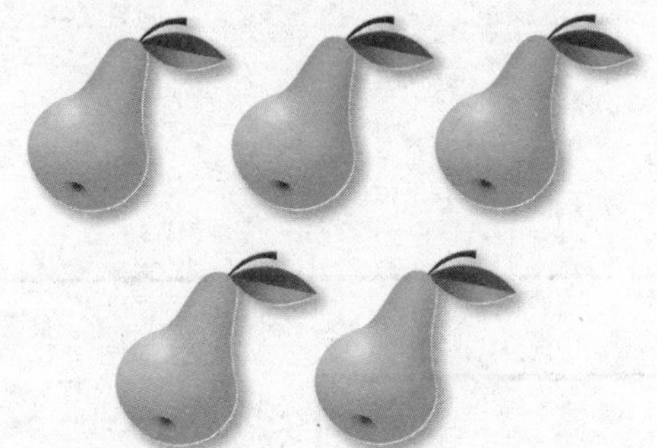

2	3	4	5
Ⓐ	Ⓑ	Ⓒ	Ⓓ

4

Ⓐ Ⓑ Ⓒ Ⓓ

Directions Have students mark the best answer. 1 Which shows 3 flowers? 2 Mark all the ways that do NOT show a way to make 5. 3 How many pears are there? 4 Which box has 0 toys in it?

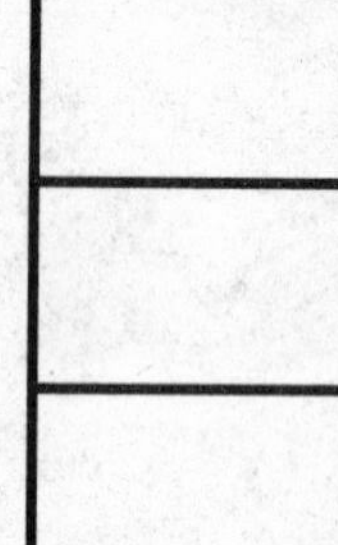

Directions Have students: 5 make a math argument about how many leaves are in each row, and then write the number; 6 count the butterflies, and then color the boxes to show how many; 7 count the number of dots and then draw counters in the box to show the same number of dots.

Name

8

9

and

Directions Have students: 8 count the snowflakes, and then write the number to tell how many; 9 color the leaves red and yellow to show a way to make 5, and then write the numbers to tell how many yellow and how many red leaves.

10

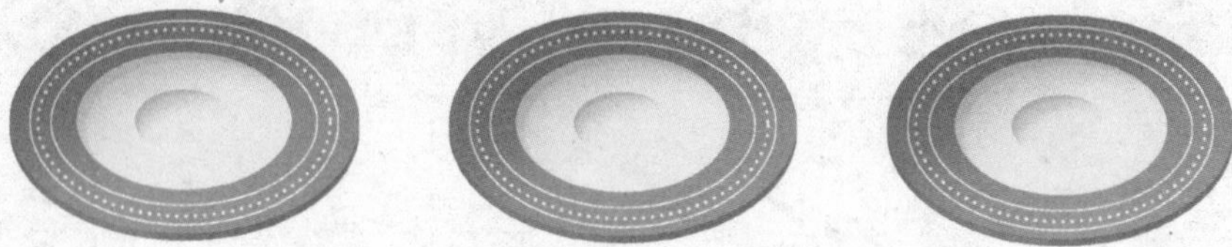

Directions Have students: 10 count the plates, and then write the number to tell how many; 11 count the number of apples on the plate, and then color the apples to show how many; 12 draw 5 marbles, and then write the number to tell how many.

Name ______________________________

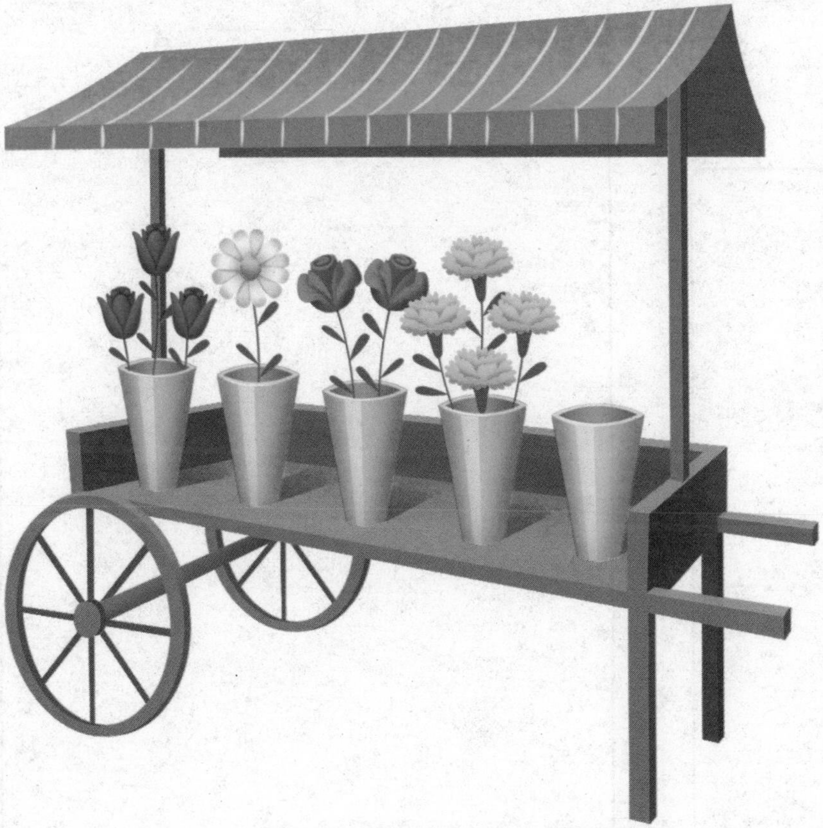

1

______

______

______

______

______

______

______

______

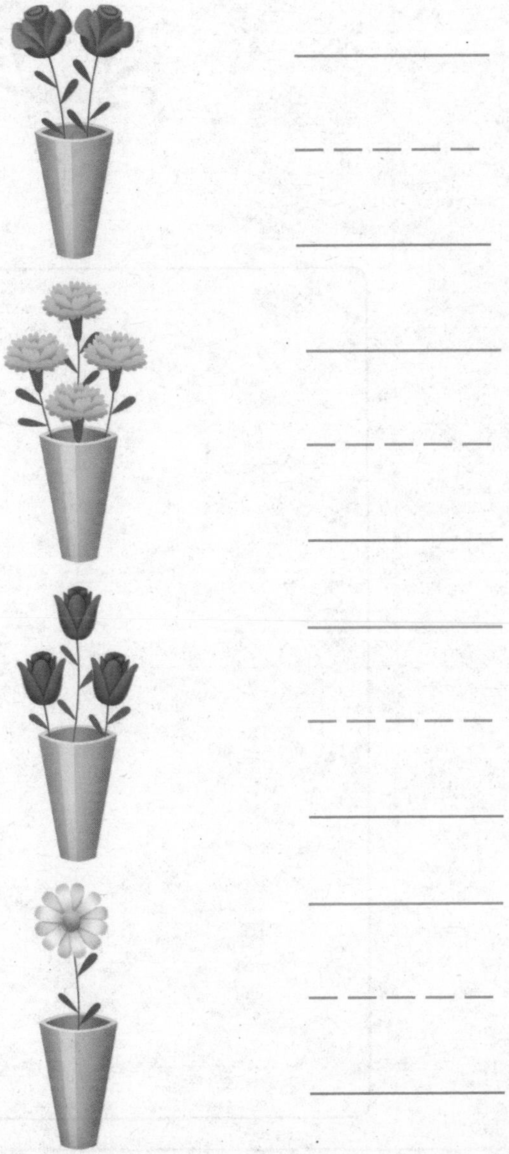

Directions **Flower Cart** Say: *Michael's family sells flowers from a flower cart.* 1 Have students count how many of each kind of flower, and then write the number to tell how many.

2

3

4

Directions 2 Say: *How can Michael show the number of flowers in the green vase?* Have students show two different ways. 3 Have students look at the 4 flowers, and then draw another way to show 4. 4 Say: *Michael wants to give his mother 5 flowers from the cart. What kinds of flowers can he give her?* Have students show one way that Michael can make an arrangement of 5 flowers, and then explain their answer.

TOPIC 2

Compare Numbers 0 to 5

Essential Question: How can numbers from 0 to 5 be compared and ordered?

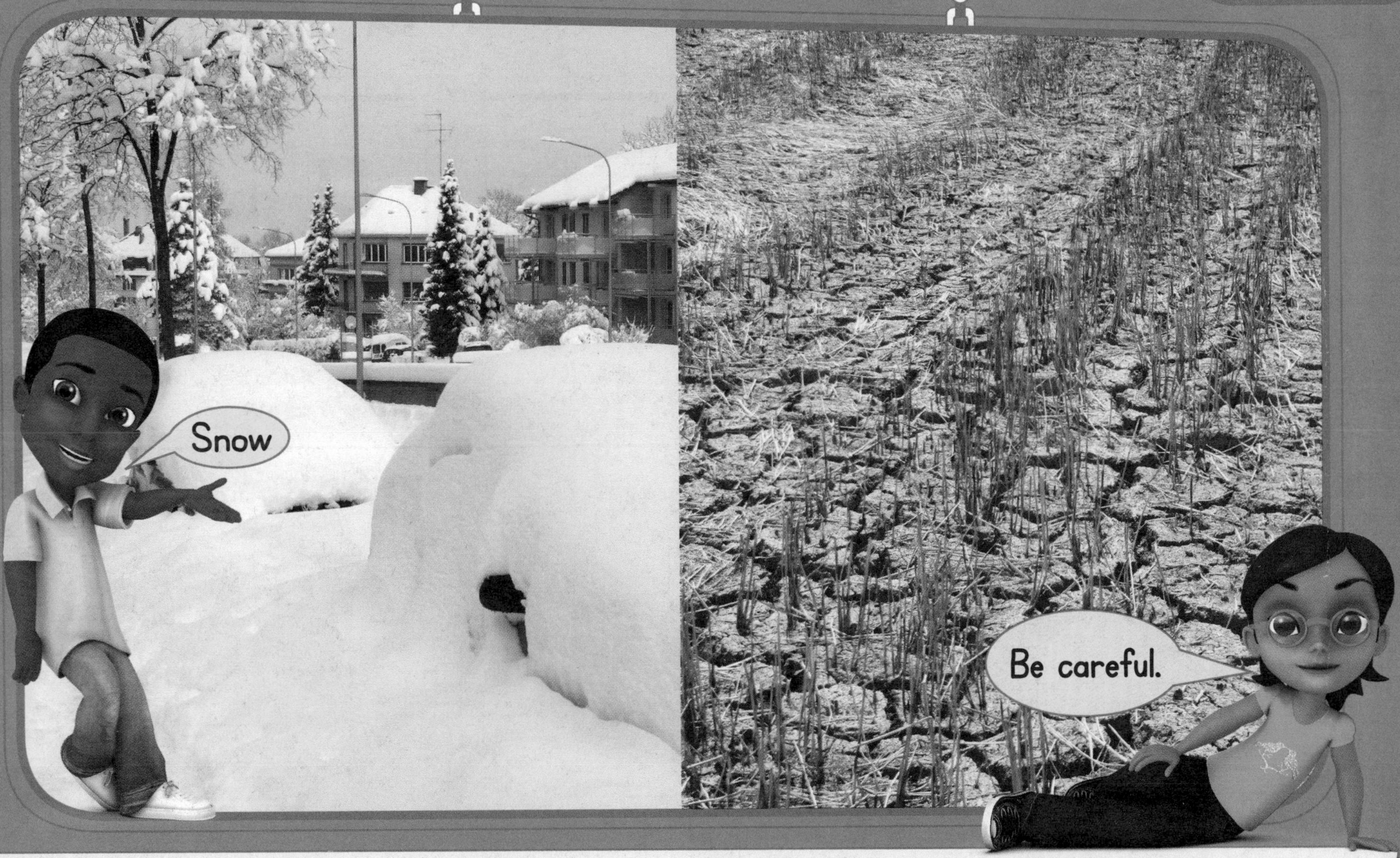

Math and Science Project: Severe Weather

Directions Read the character speech bubbles to students. **Find Out!** Have students name different types of severe weather that occur around the world. Say: *Not all places have the same types of severe weather. Talk to your friends and relatives about severe weather that has happened in the world in the past month. Ask them if they have ever seen that type of severe weather.* **Journal: Make a Poster** Have students make a poster. Ask them to draw up to 5 items people might need to be safe in a snowstorm. Have them draw up to 5 items people might need to be safe during a drought. Ask them to write the number of objects in each group, compare them, and then draw a circle around the number that is greater than the other number.

Name ___________________________

Review What You Know

1

0 2

2

3 1

3

4 5

4

5

6

Directions Have students: **1** draw a circle around the number zero; **2** draw a circle around the number one; **3** draw a circle around the number four; **4**–**6** count the toys and write the number to tell how many.

My Word Cards

Directions Have students cut out the vocabulary cards. Read the front of the card, and then ask them to explain what the word or phrase means.

equal	same number as	compare
group	greater than	less than

My Word Cards

Directions Review the definitions and have students study the cards. Extend learning by having students draw pictures for each word on a separate piece of paper.

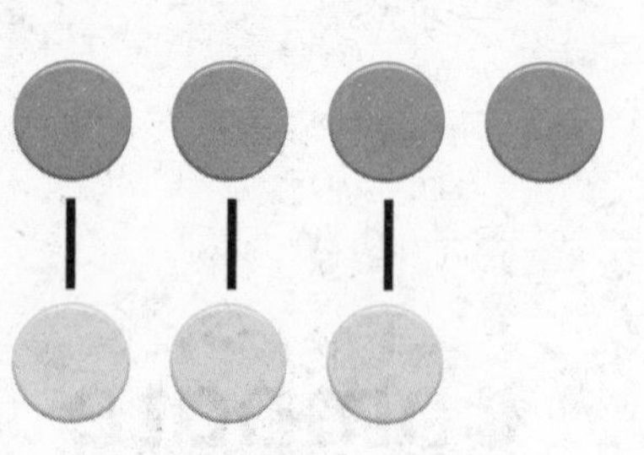

Point to the picture.
Say: *When we **compare** these groups, we see that they each have a different amount of counters.*

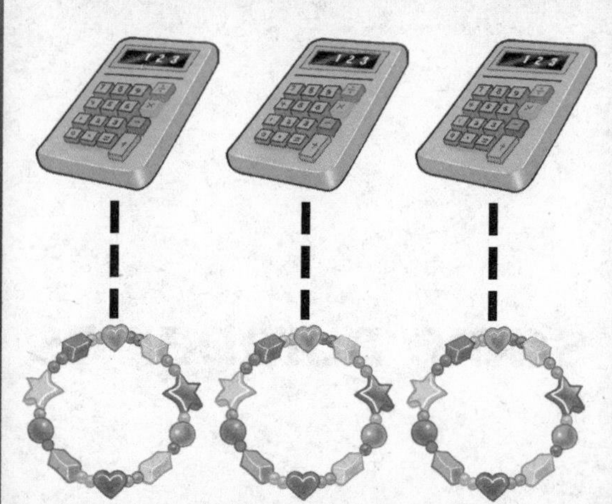

Point to the picture.
Say: *The top group has the **same number as** the bottom group.*

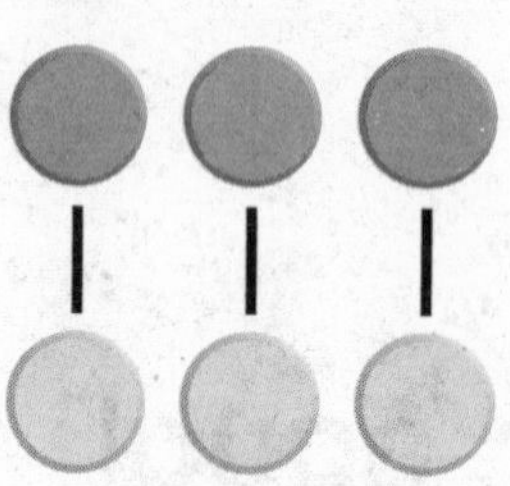

Point to the picture.
Say: *Both groups have 3 counters. They are **equal**.*

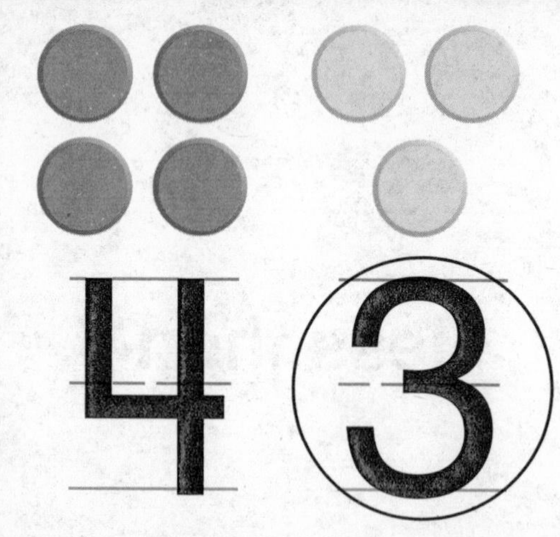

Point to the 3.
Say: *3 is **less than** 4.*

Point to the 4.
Say: *4 is **greater than** 3.*

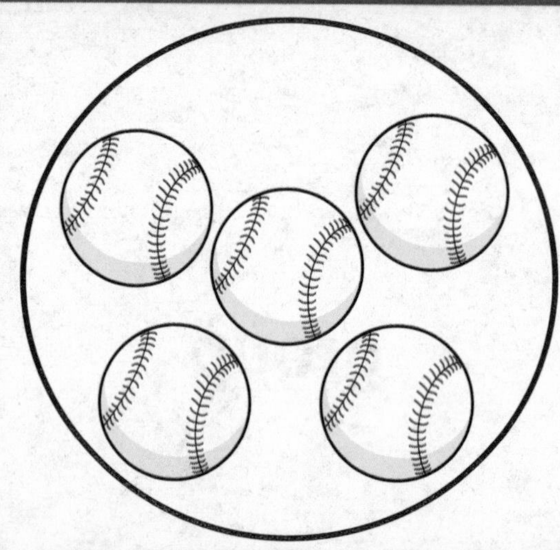

Point to the baseballs.
Say: *This is a **group** of baseballs.*

A-Z Glossary

My Word Cards

Directions Have students cut out the vocabulary cards. Read the front of the card, and then ask them to explain what the word or phrase means.

model

My Word Cards

Directions Review the definitions and have students study the cards. Extend learning by having students draw pictures for each word on a separate piece of paper.

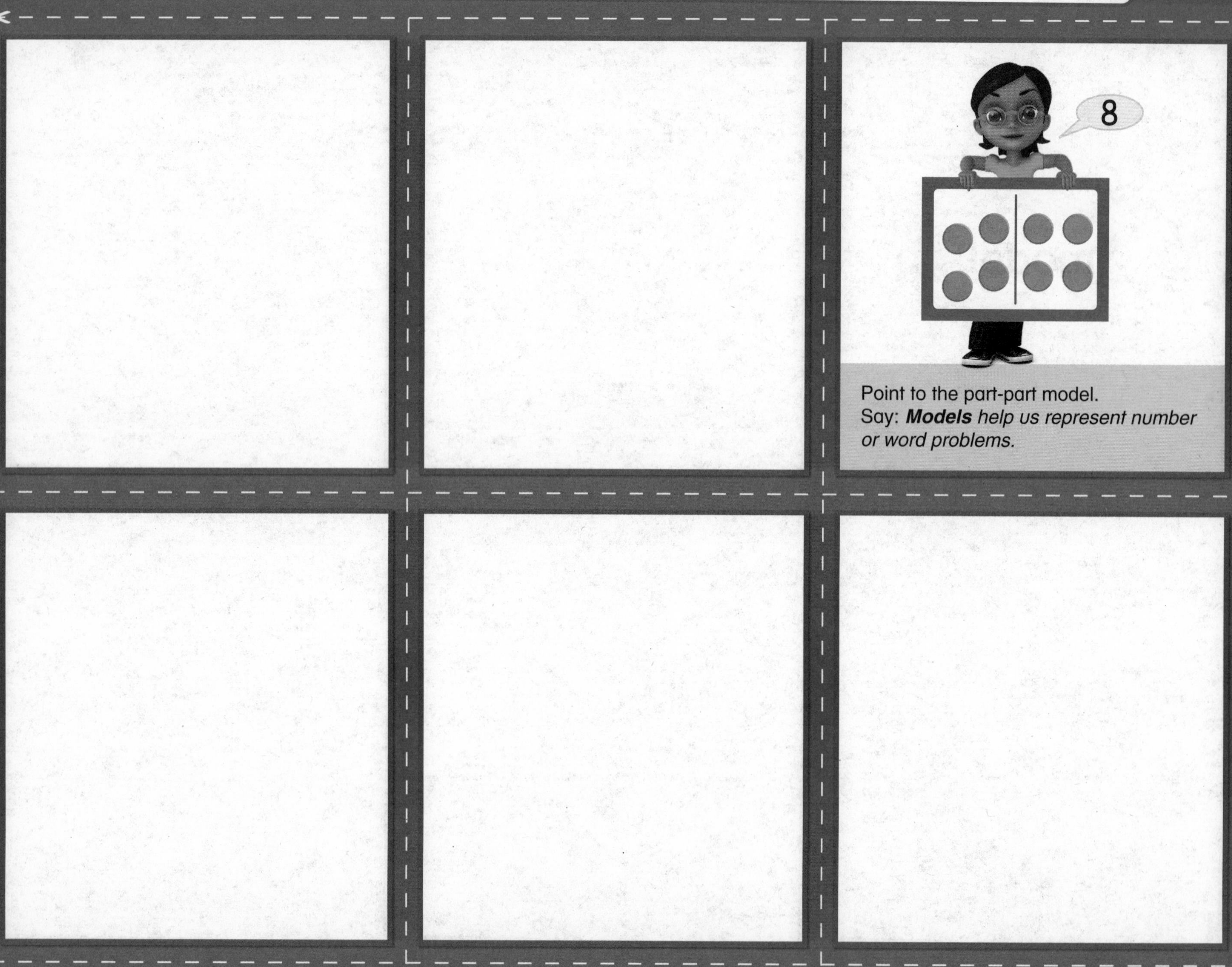

Point to the part-part model.
Say: ***Models*** *help us represent number or word problems.*

Name ____________________

Solve

Lesson 2-1
Equal Groups

Directions Say: *Marta has some toy cars. Are there the same number of red cars as there are yellow cars on the rug? How do you know? Use counters to show your work.*

I can ...
compare groups to see whether they are equal by matching.

I can also reason about math.

Guided Practice

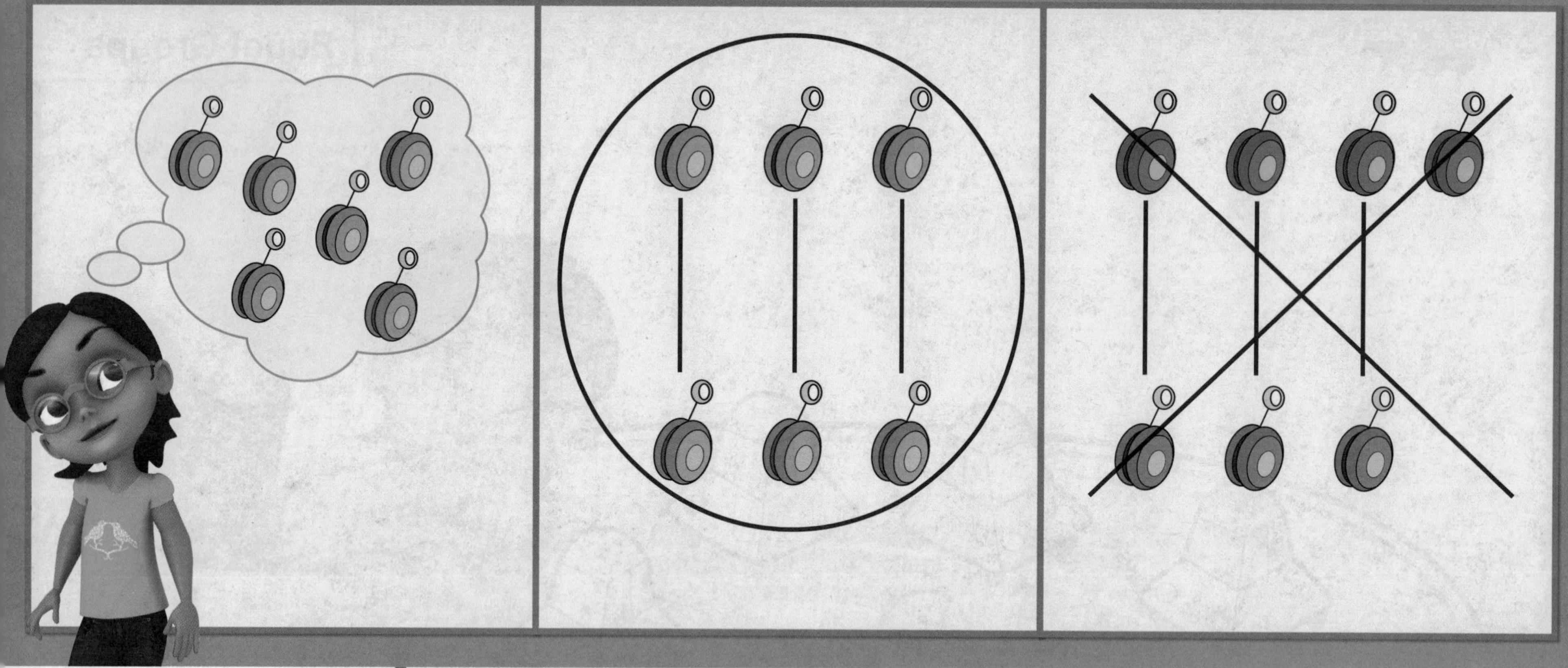

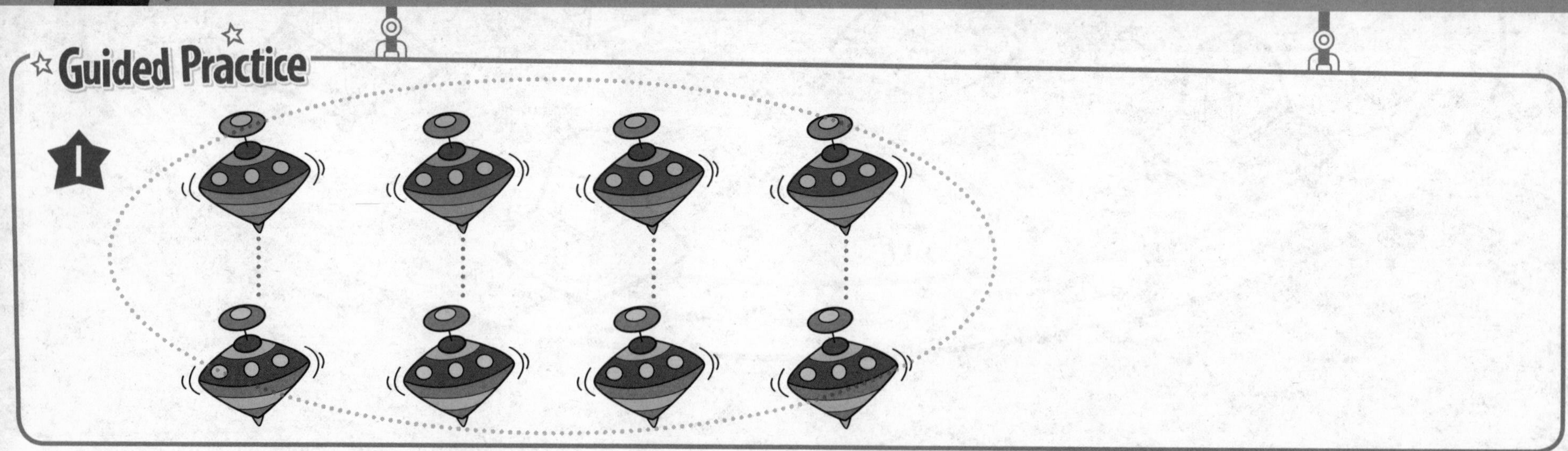

Directions 1 Have students draw lines between the toys in the top group to the toys in the bottom group. Then have them draw a circle around the groups if they are equal in number, or mark an X on the groups if they are NOT equal in number.

Name ______________________________

Directions 2–5 Have students draw lines from the blocks in one group to the blocks in the other group. Then have them draw a circle around the groups if they are equal in number, or mark an X on the groups if they are NOT equal in number.

Independent Practice

Tools Assessment

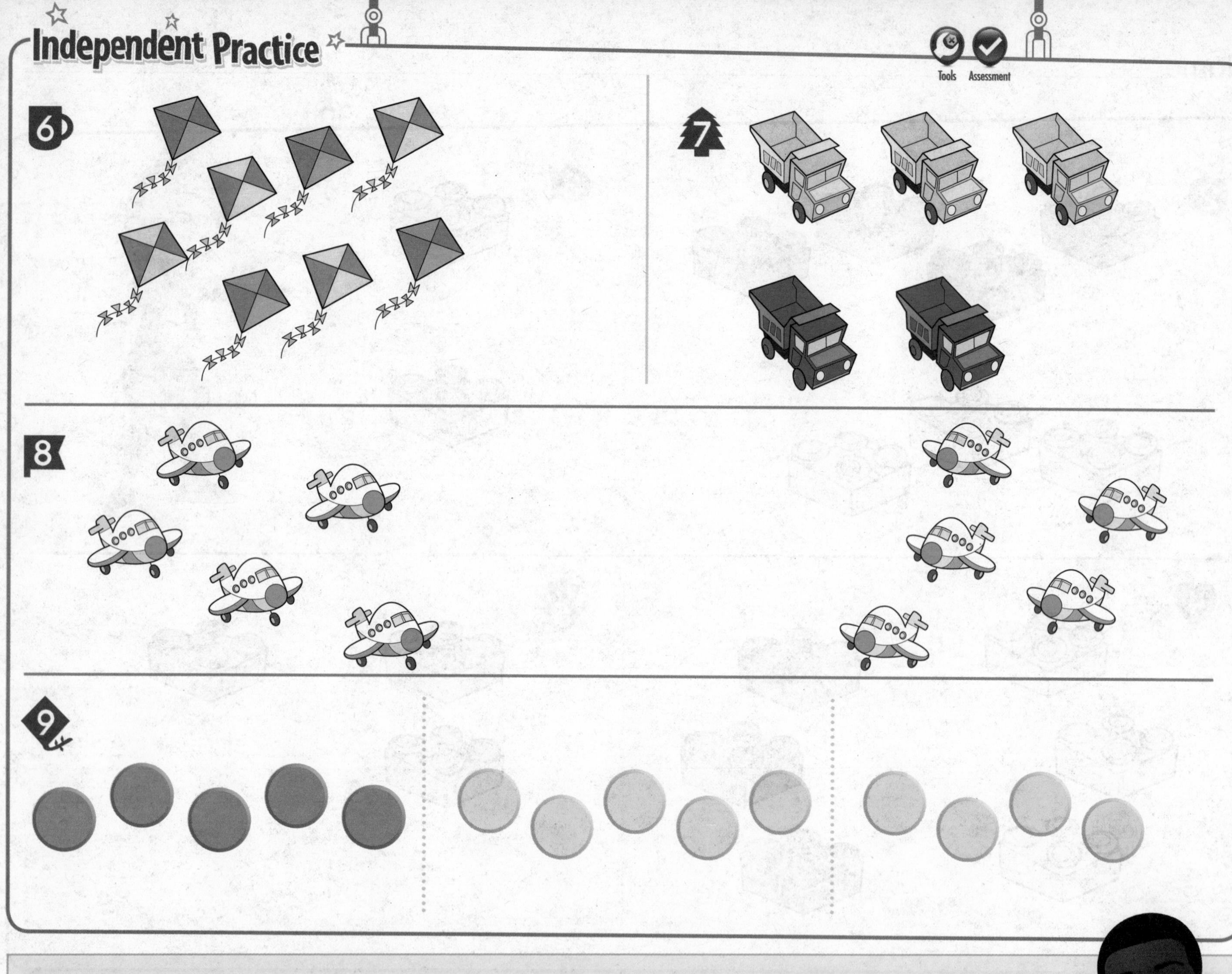

Directions 6–8 Have students draw lines from the toys in one group to the toys in the other group. Then have them draw a circle around the groups if they are equal in number, or mark an X on the groups if they are NOT equal in number. 9 **Higher Order Thinking** Have students draw a circle around the group of yellow counters that is NOT equal in number to the group of red counters.

Name ______________________________

Help Tools Games

Homework & Practice 2-1

Equal Groups

HOME ACTIVITY Give your child 5 objects. Place up to 5 objects on the table. Ask your child to make a group of objects that is equal in number to the group you made. Repeat with different numbers of objects. (Object suggestions: forks/spoons; pencils/pens)

Another Look!

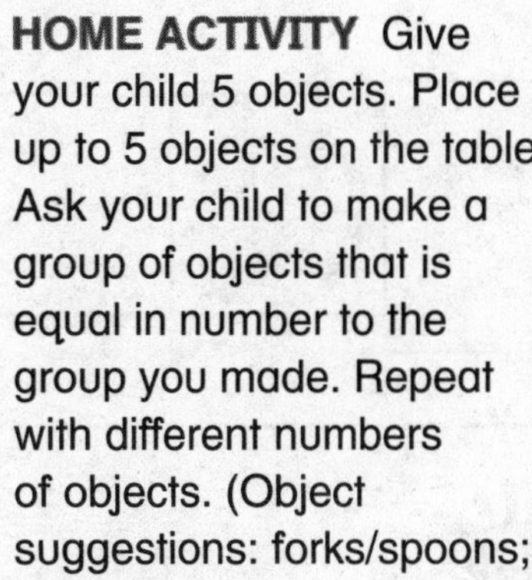

1

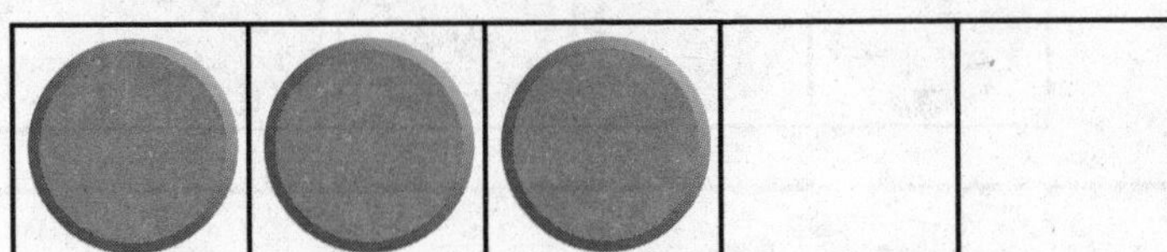

2

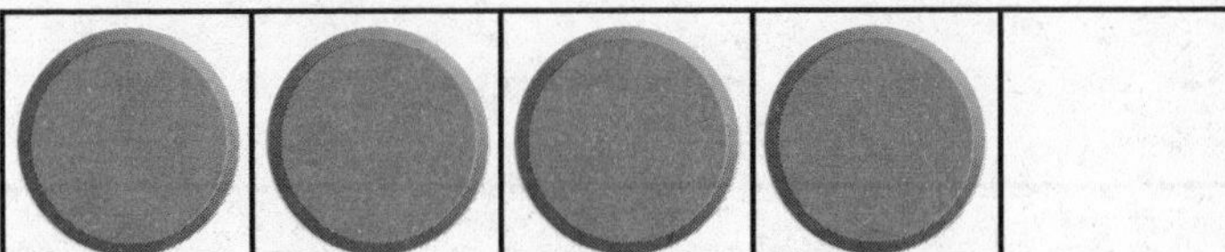

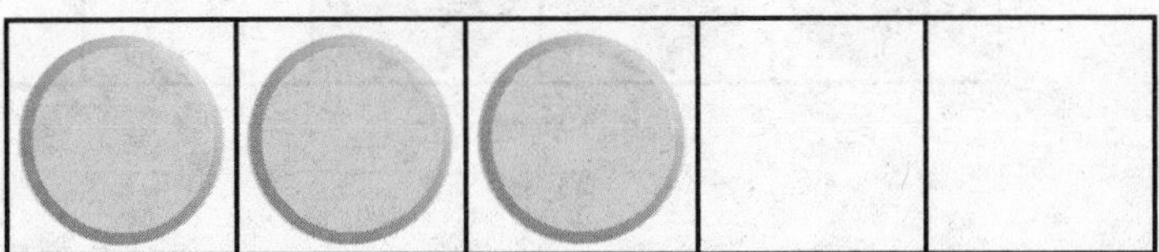

Directions Say: *How can you show that the group of yellow counters is equal in number to the group of red counters? Draw lines to match the counters from one group to the other group.* 1 and 2 Have students draw lines to match the counters from one group to the other group. Then have them draw a circle around the groups if they are equal in number, or mark an X on the groups if they are NOT equal in number.

3

4

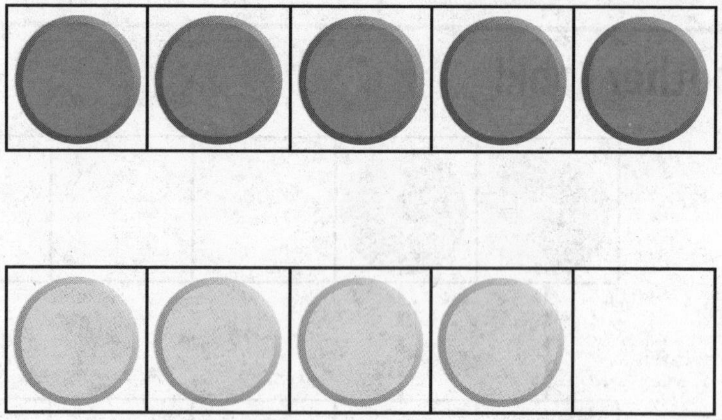

5

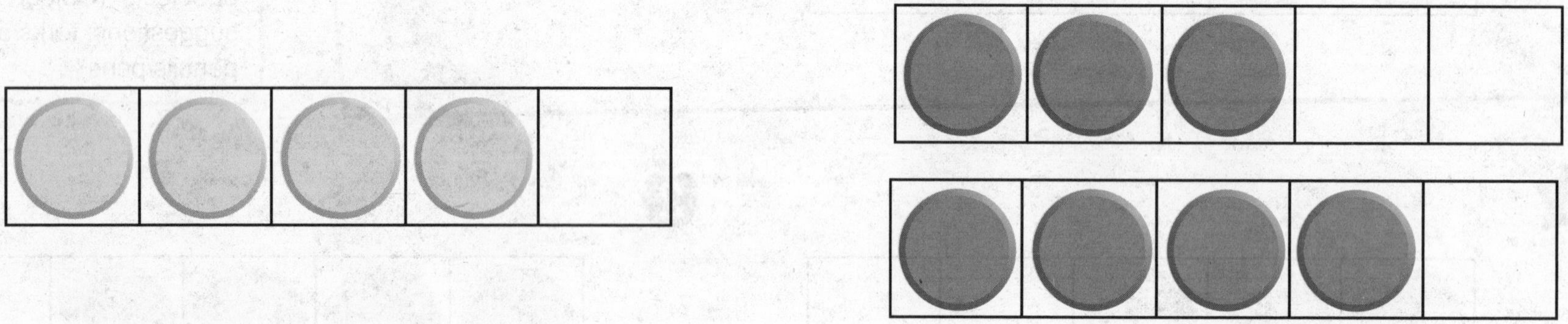

6

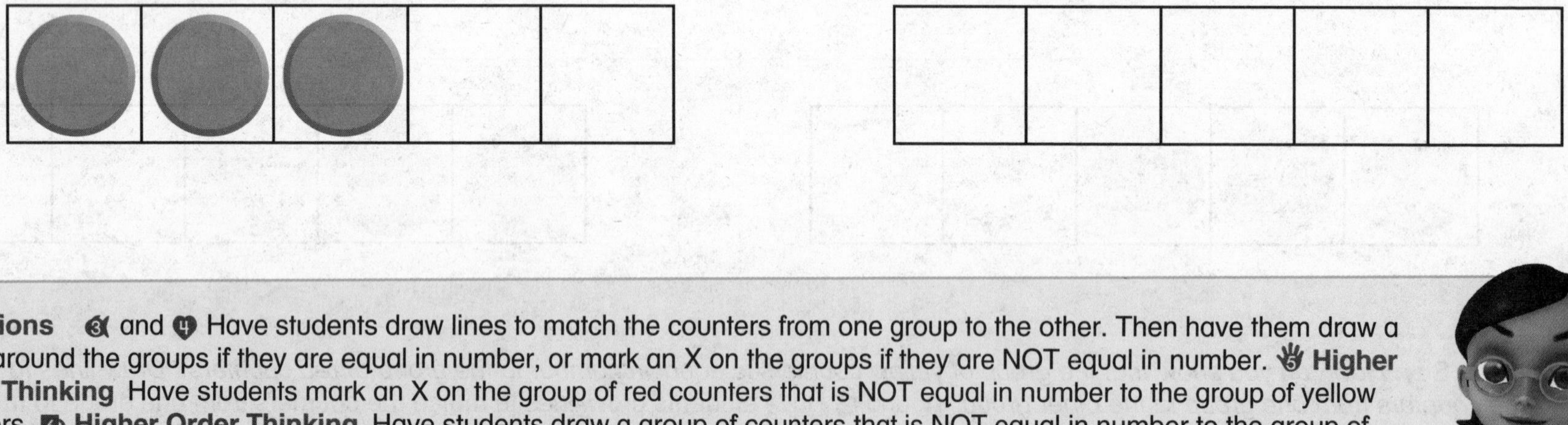

Directions 3 and 4 Have students draw lines to match the counters from one group to the other. Then have them draw a circle around the groups if they are equal in number, or mark an X on the groups if they are NOT equal in number. 5 **Higher Order Thinking** Have students mark an X on the group of red counters that is NOT equal in number to the group of yellow counters. 6 **Higher Order Thinking** Have students draw a group of counters that is NOT equal in number to the group of red counters shown.

Name ______________________________

Lesson 2-2
Greater Than

Directions Say: *Marta's class goes to the park. Mr. Leeman brings 4 soccer balls and 3 basketballs. Which group of balls has more? How do you know? Use counters to show your work.*

I can ...
tell whether one group is greater in number than another group.

I can also reason about math.

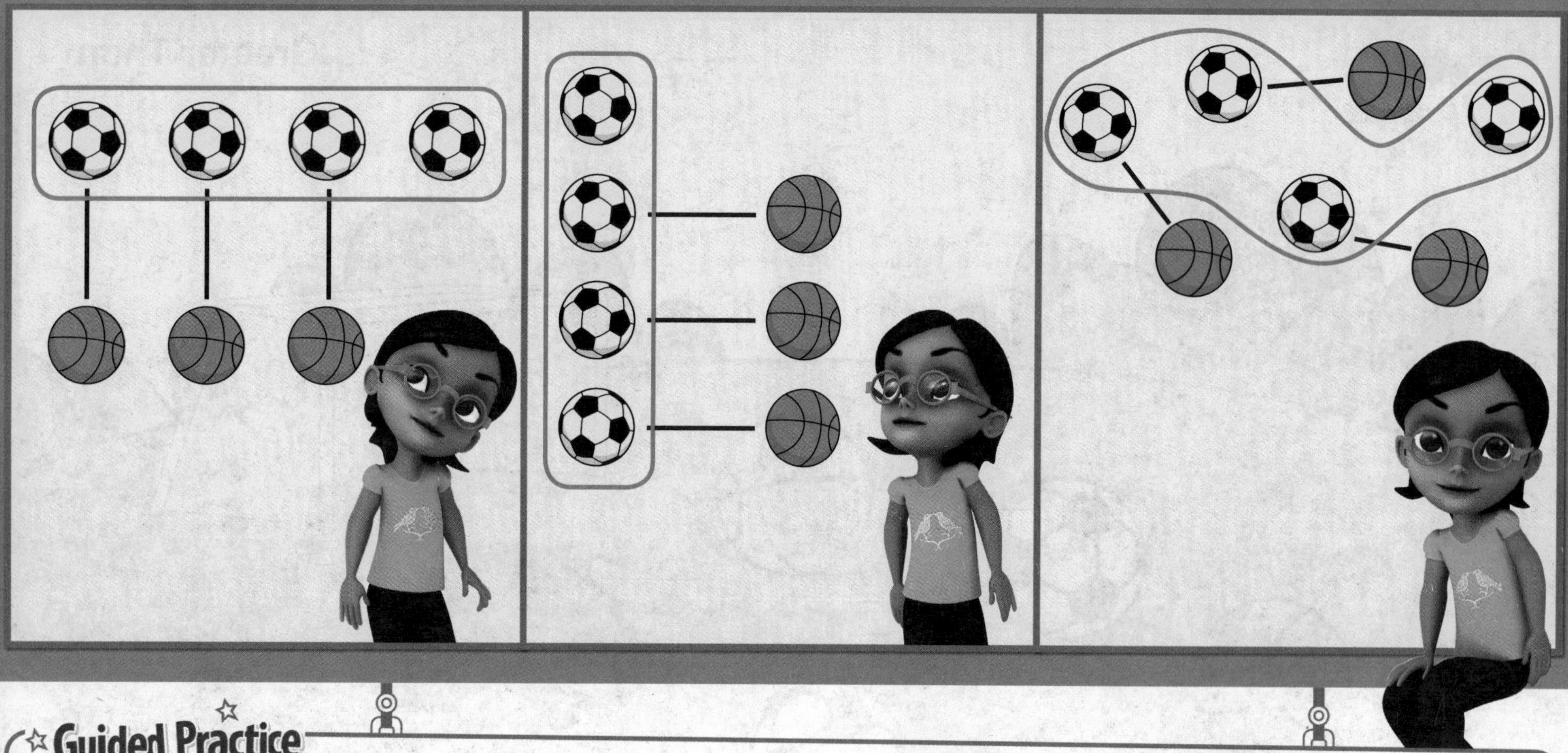

Guided Practice

1

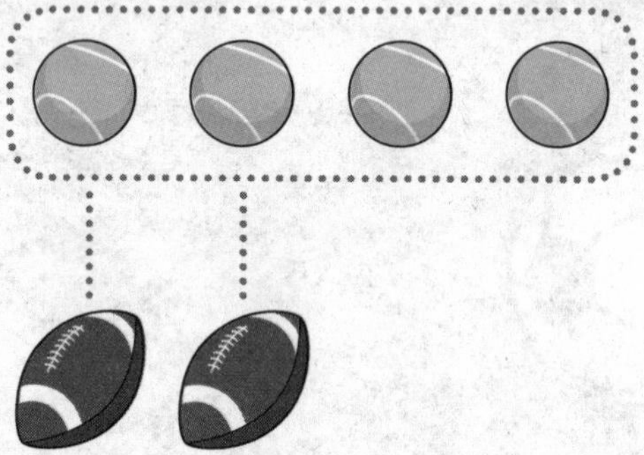

2

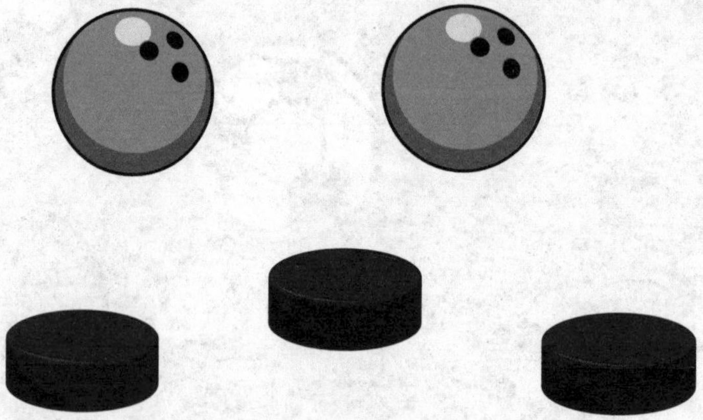

Directions 1 and 2 Have students draw lines to match objects from one group to the other group. Have them draw a circle around the group that is greater in number than the other group, and then explain why they are correct.

Name ______________________________

3

4

5

Directions 3–5 Have students draw lines to match objects from one group to the other group. Have them draw a circle around the group that is greater in number than the other group, and then explain why they are correct.

Independent Practice

Tools Assessment

6

7

8

9

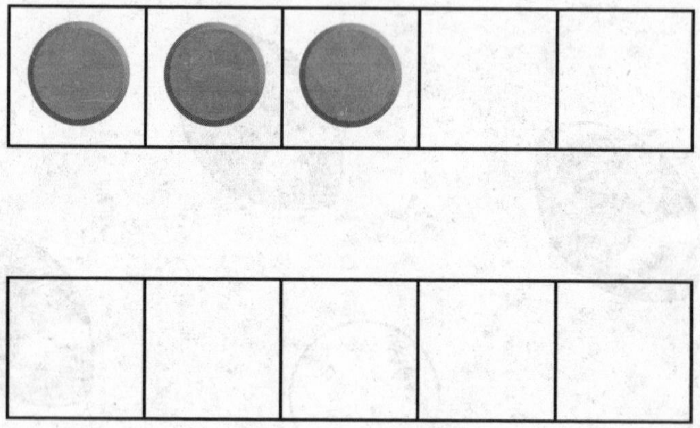

Directions 6–8 Have students draw lines to match objects from one group to the other group. Have them draw a circle around the group that is greater in number than the other group, and then explain why they are correct. 9 **Higher Order Thinking** Have students draw a group of counters in the bottom five-frame that is greater in number than the group of counters in the top five-frame. Have them explain their drawings.

Name ______________________________

Homework & Practice 2-2

Greater Than

HOME ACTIVITY Give your child 5 objects. Place up to 4 objects on the table. Ask your child to make a group that is greater in number than the group you made. Repeat with different numbers of objects.

Another Look!

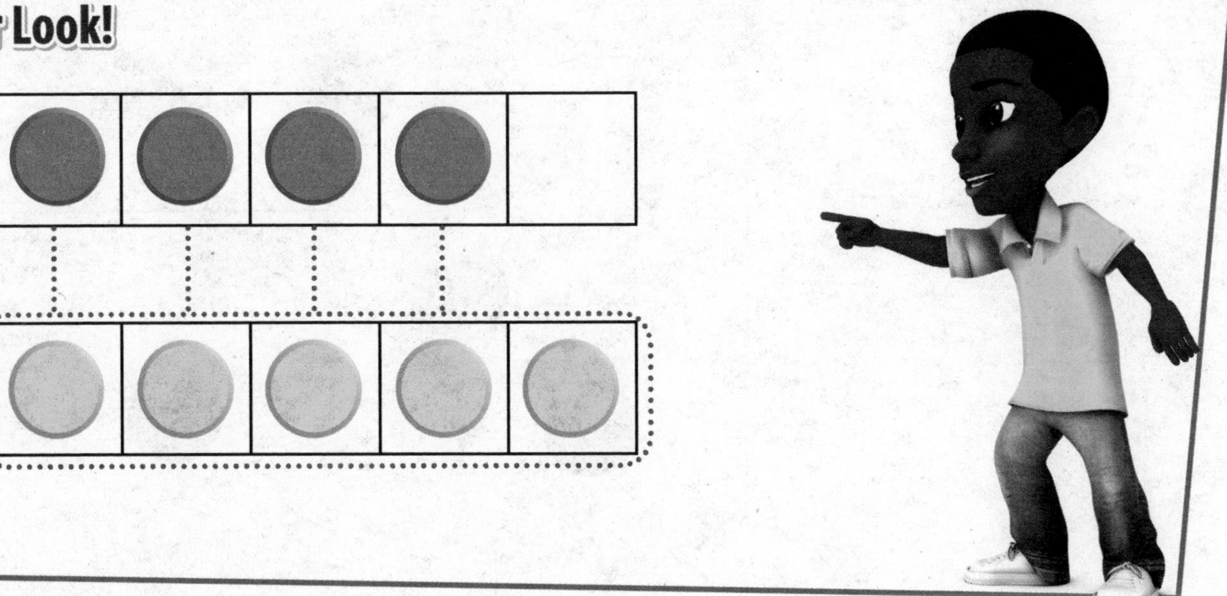

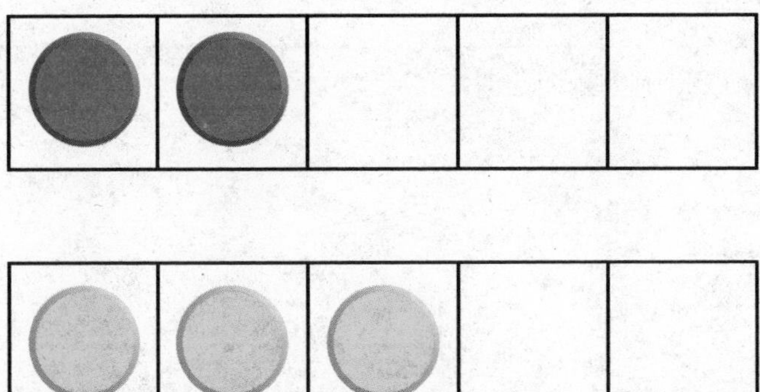

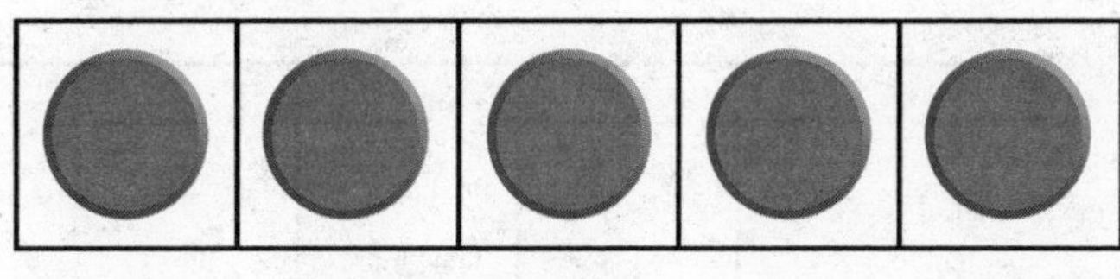

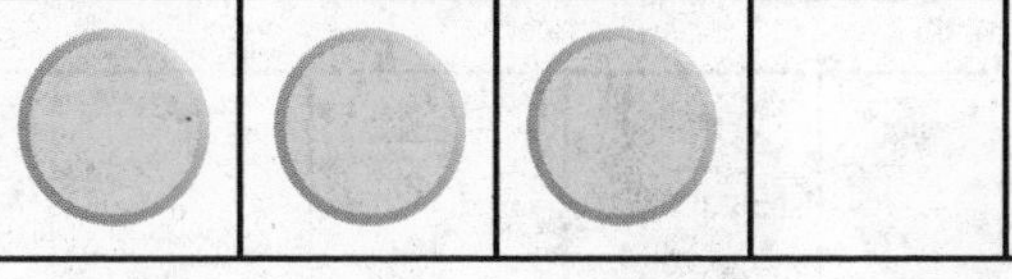

Directions Say: *How do you know which group of counters, the red or the yellow, is greater in number than the other? Draw a line from each red counter to a yellow counter. Draw a circle around the group that has counters left over.* 1 and 2 Have students draw lines to match the red and yellow groups of counters. Have them draw a circle around the group that is greater in number than the other group, and then explain why they are correct.

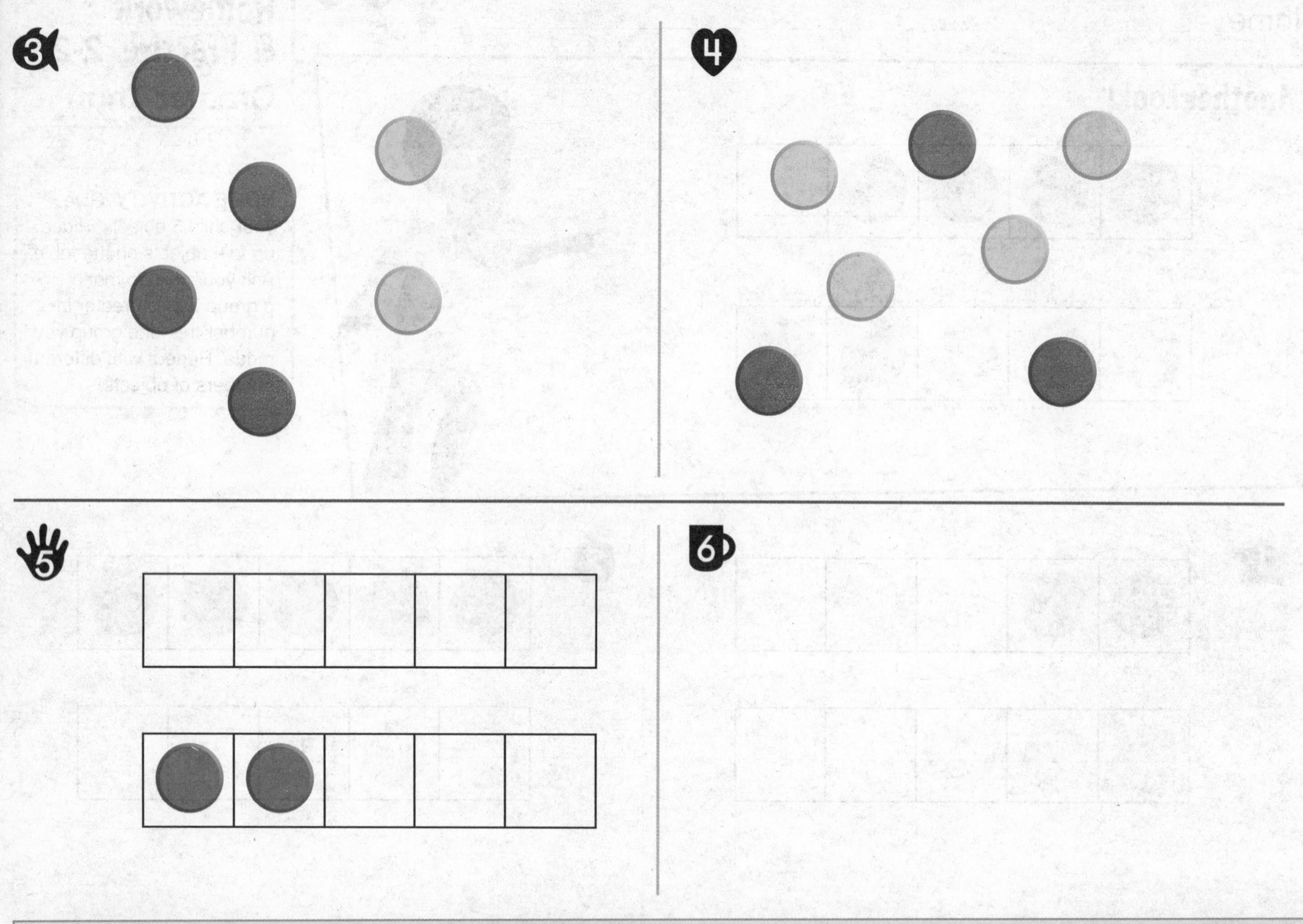

Directions 3 and 4 Have students draw lines to match the red and yellow groups of counters. Have them draw a circle around the group that is greater in number than the other group, and then explain why they are correct. 5 **Vocabulary** Have students draw a number of counters in the top five-frame that is greater than the number of counters in the bottom five-frame, and then explain how they know. 6 **Higher Order Thinking** Have students draw two different groups of counters or objects. Have them show and explain which group is greater in number than the other group.

Name ______________________________

Lesson 2-3
Less Than

Directions Say: *Marta puts 5 stuffed animals on a shelf. She puts 3 teddy bears on a different shelf. Which group has fewer stuffed toys? How do you know? Use counters to show your work.*

I can ...
tell whether one group is less in number than another group.

I can also reason about math.

Guided Practice

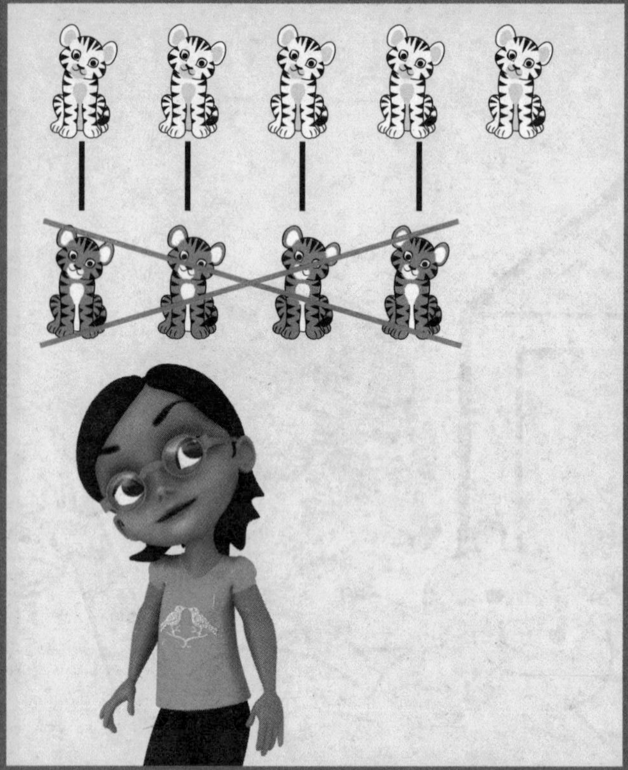

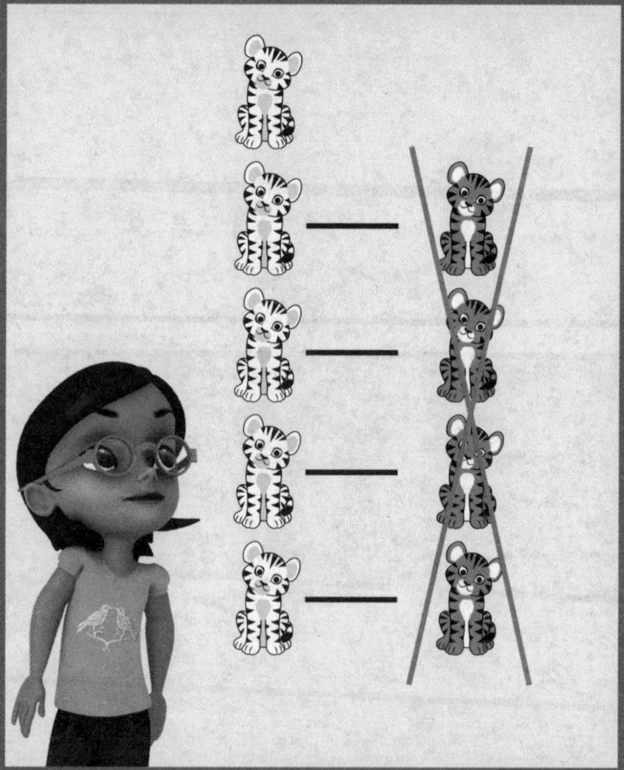

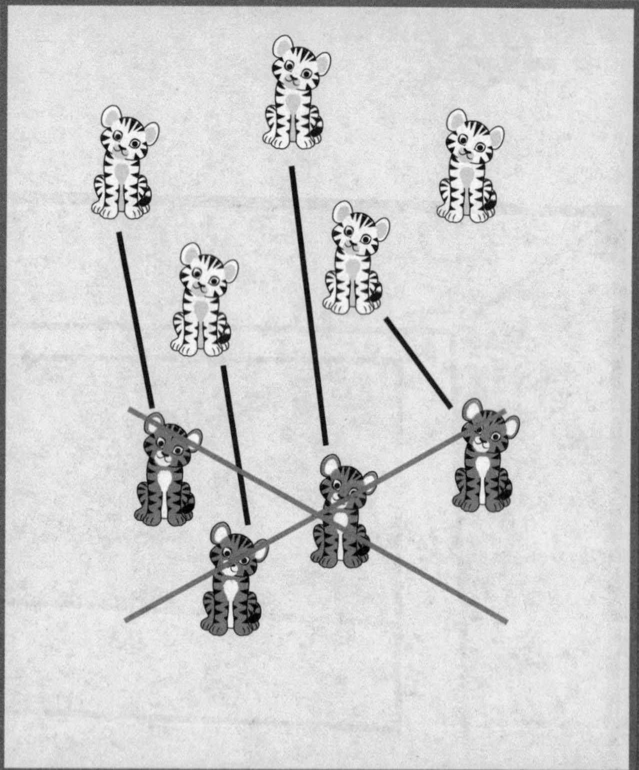

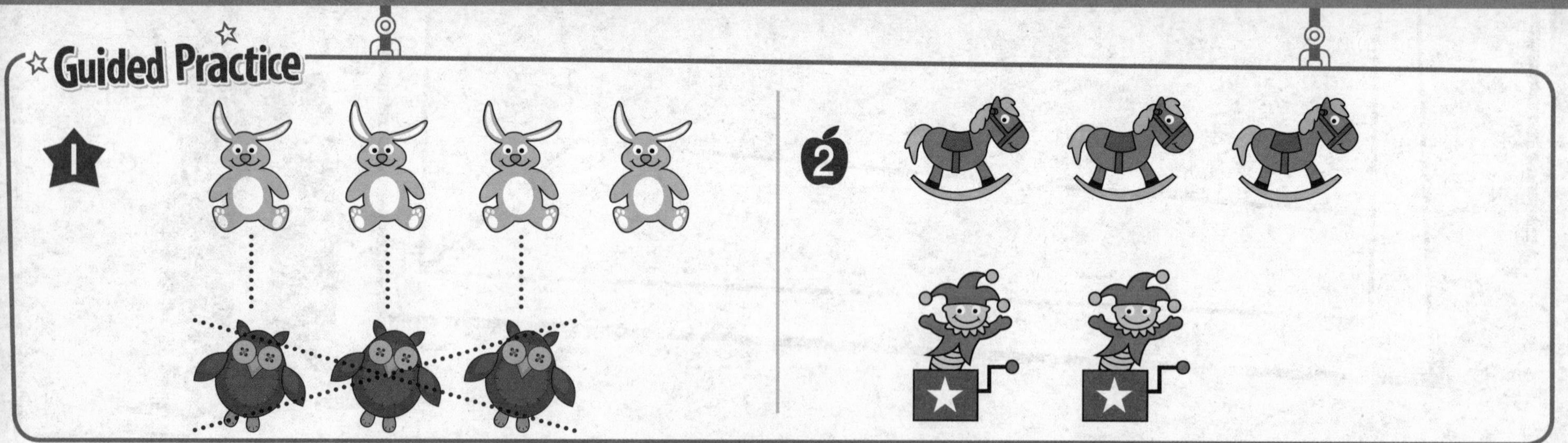

Directions 1 and 2 Have students draw lines to match the toys from one group to the other group. Have them mark an X on the group that is less in number than the other group, and then explain why they are correct.

Name ____________________

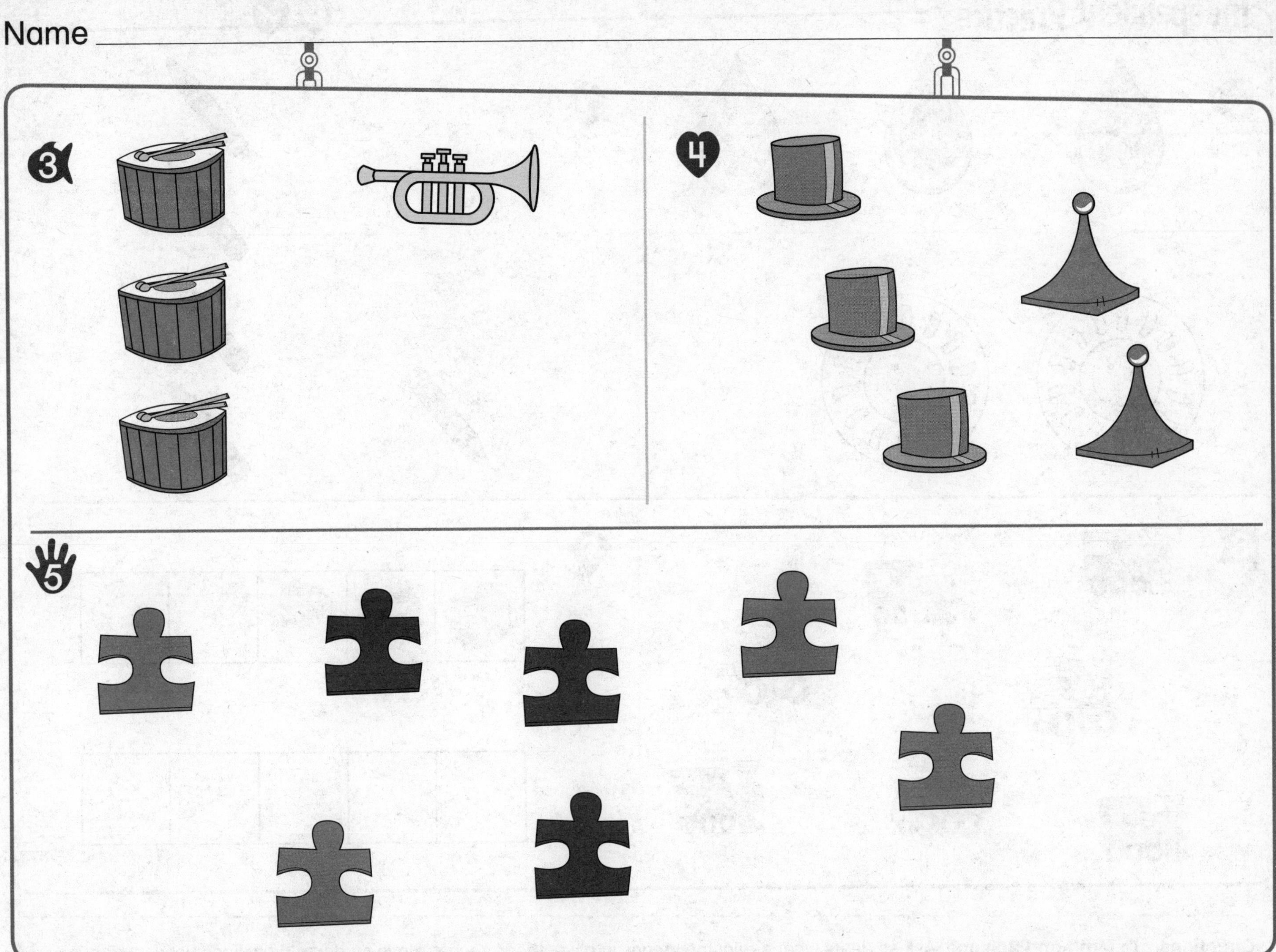

Directions 3–5 Have students draw lines to match the toys from one group to the other group. Have them mark an X on the group that is less in number than the other group, and then explain why they are correct.

Independent Practice

Directions 6 **Math and Science** Ask students what a raindrop means in a weather forecast. Have students draw lines between groups to match the raindrop stickers to the sun stickers. Have them mark an X on the group that is less in number than the other group, and then explain why they are correct. 7 and 8 Have students draw lines to match the objects from one group to the other group. Have them mark an X on the group that is less in number than the other group, and then explain why they are correct. 9 **Higher Order Thinking** Have students draw a group of yellow counters that is less in number than the group of red counters.

Name ______________________________

Help Tools Games

Homework & Practice 2-3

Less Than

HOME ACTIVITY Give your child 5 objects. Place at least 2 objects on the table. Ask your child to make a group that is less in number than the group you made. Repeat with different numbers of objects.

Another Look!

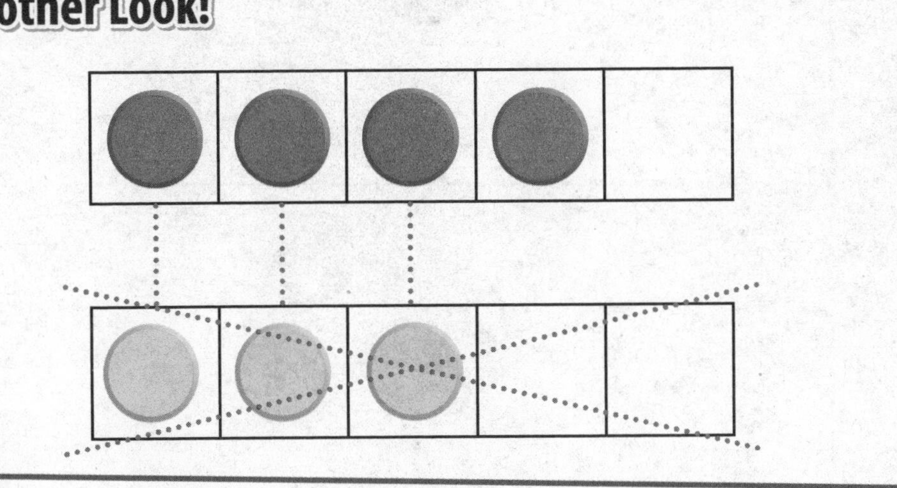

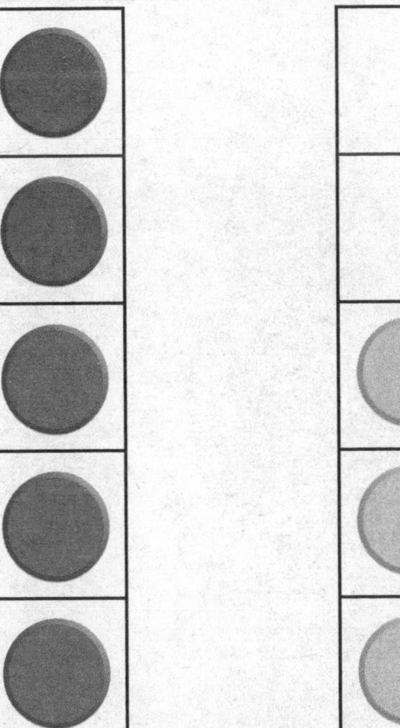

2

Directions Say: *How do you know which group of counters, the red or the yellow, is less in number than the other? Draw a line from each red counter to a yellow counter. Mark an X on the group that is less in number.* 1 and 2 Have students draw lines to match counters from one group to the other group. Have them mark an X on the group that is less in number than the other group, and then explain why they are correct.

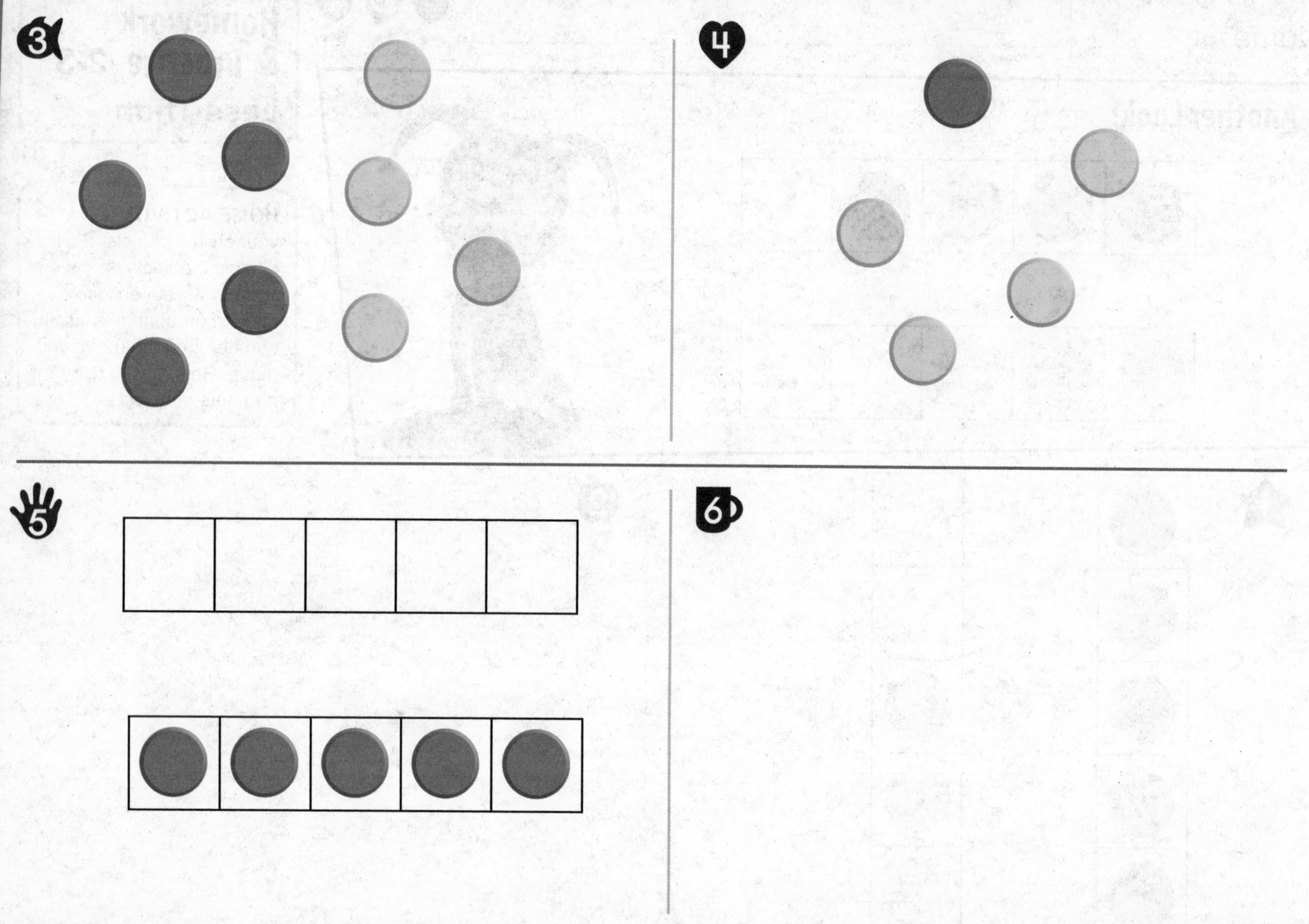

Directions 3 and 4 Have students draw lines to match counters from one group to the other group. Have them mark an X on the group that is less in number than the other group, and then explain why they are correct. 5 **Higher Order Thinking** Have students draw a group of counters that is less in number than the group of red counters shown. Then have them mark an X to show the group that is less in number than the other group. 6 **Higher Order Thinking** Have students draw two different groups of counters or objects. Have them show and explain which group is less in number than the other group.

Name ______________________

Lesson 2-4
Compare Groups to 5 by Counting

Directions Say: *Marta puts a group of elephant stickers on one page of her sticker book. She puts a group of lion stickers on another page. Compare the groups. Write the numbers to tell how many. Then draw a circle around the number of the group of stickers that is greater than the other group.*

I can ... compare groups by counting.

I can also be precise in my work.

3

4

Greater than

2

5

Less than

1 2 3 4 5

1 2 3 4 5

Directions 1 Have students count the monkey and banana stickers, and then write the numbers to tell how many. Then have them draw a circle around the number that is greater than the other number and mark an X on the number that is less than the other number.

Name ______________________________

2

3

4

5

Directions 2–5 Have students count the stickers, write the numbers to tell how many, and then draw a circle around the number that is greater than the other number and mark an X on the number that is less than the other number, or draw a circle around both numbers if they are equal.

Independent Practice

Tools Assessment

6

7

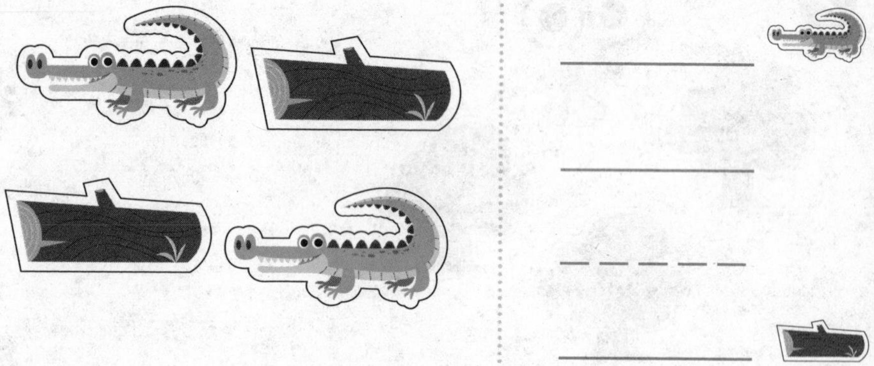

8

9

Directions 6–8 Have students count the stickers, write the numbers to tell how many, and then draw a circle around the number that is greater than the other number and mark an X on the number that is less than the other number, or draw a circle around both numbers if they are equal. 9 **Higher Order Thinking** Have students count the fish stickers, draw a group of fish stickers that is less in number than the group shown, and then write the numbers to tell how many.

Name ______________________

Homework & Practice 2-4

Compare Groups to 5 by Counting

Another Look!

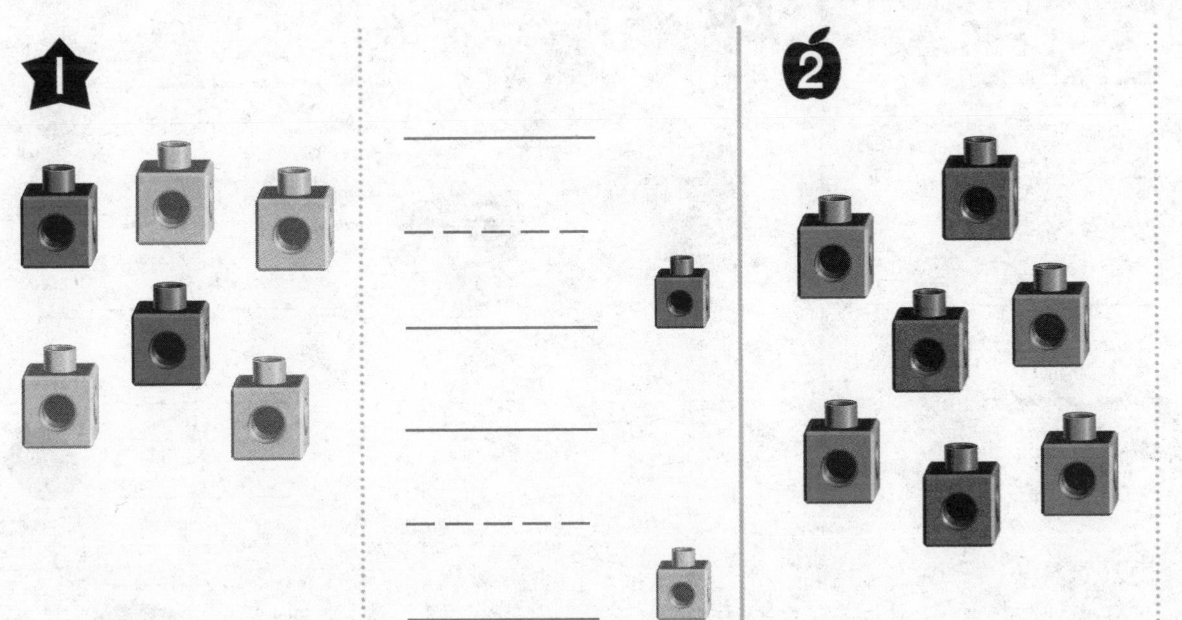

1

2

HOME ACTIVITY Gather 10 objects, such as buttons or straws. Show 4 objects randomly on a table. Ask your child to make a group of 2 objects. Have him or her write numbers to tell how many are in each group, and then explain which group is greater in number and which group is less in number.

Directions Say: *You can count the blue and green cubes to find out which group is greater in number. Count the cubes, and then write the numbers to tell how many. Draw a circle around the number that is greater than the other number and mark an X on the number that is less than the other number.* 1 and 2 Have students count the cubes, write the numbers to tell how many, and then draw a circle around the number that is greater than the other number and mark an X on the number that is less than the other number.

3

4

5

6

Directions 3 and 4 Have students count the cubes, write the numbers to tell how many, and then draw a circle around the number that is greater than the other number and mark an X on the number that is less than the other number. 5 **Higher Order Thinking** Have students count the bird stickers, draw a group of worms that is less in number than the group of birds shown, and then write the numbers to tell how many. 6 **Higher Order Thinking** Have students count the squirrel stickers, draw a group of nuts equal in number to the group of squirrels shown, and then write the numbers to tell how many.

Name ______________________

Solve

Lesson 2-5

Compare Numbers to 5

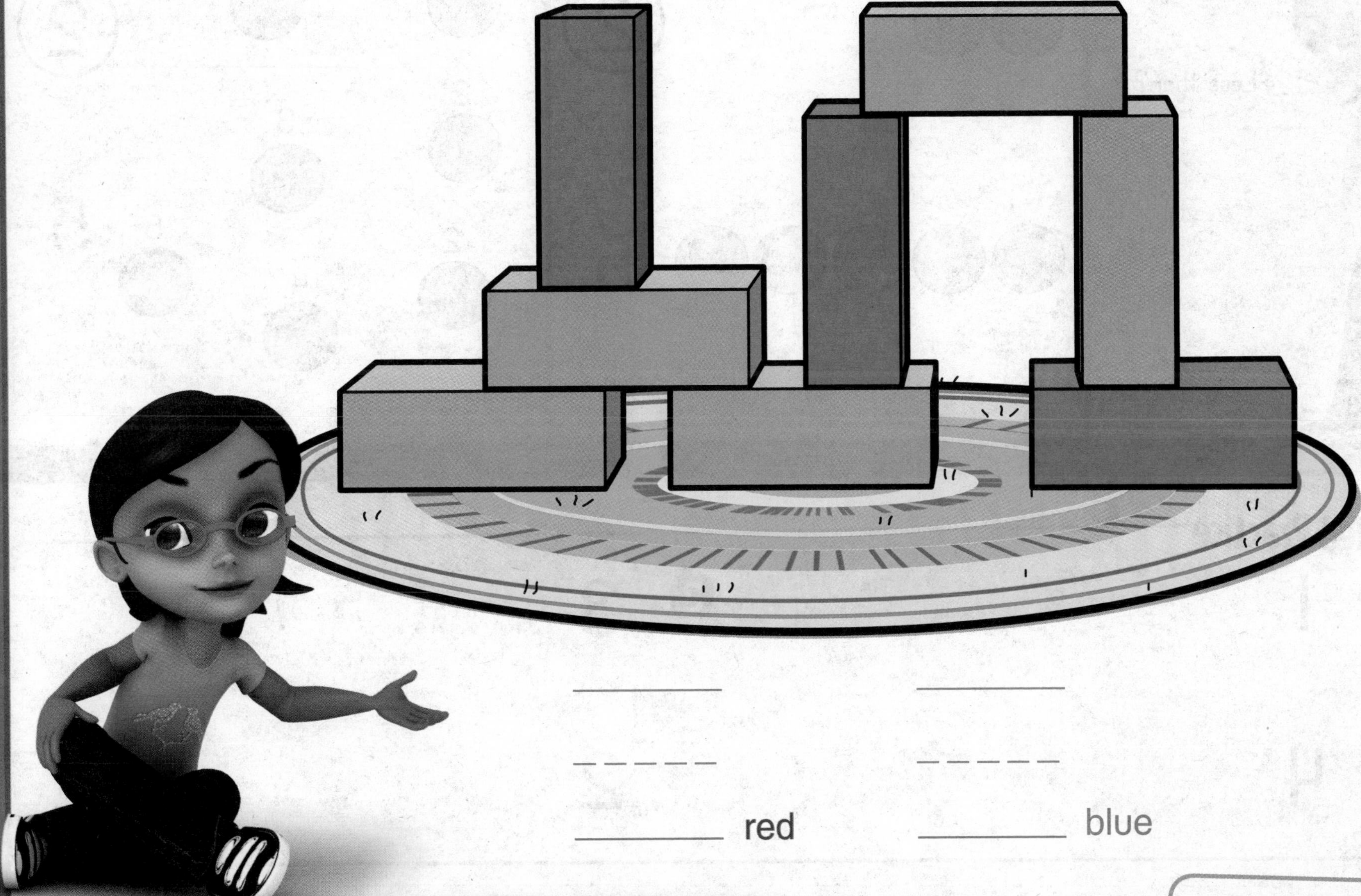

______ red ______ blue

Directions Say: *Marta builds a tower with red and blue blocks. Count how many red blocks and how many blue blocks she uses. Write the numbers to tell how many. Then draw a circle around the number that is less than the other number.*

I can ... compare numbers.

I can also reason about math.

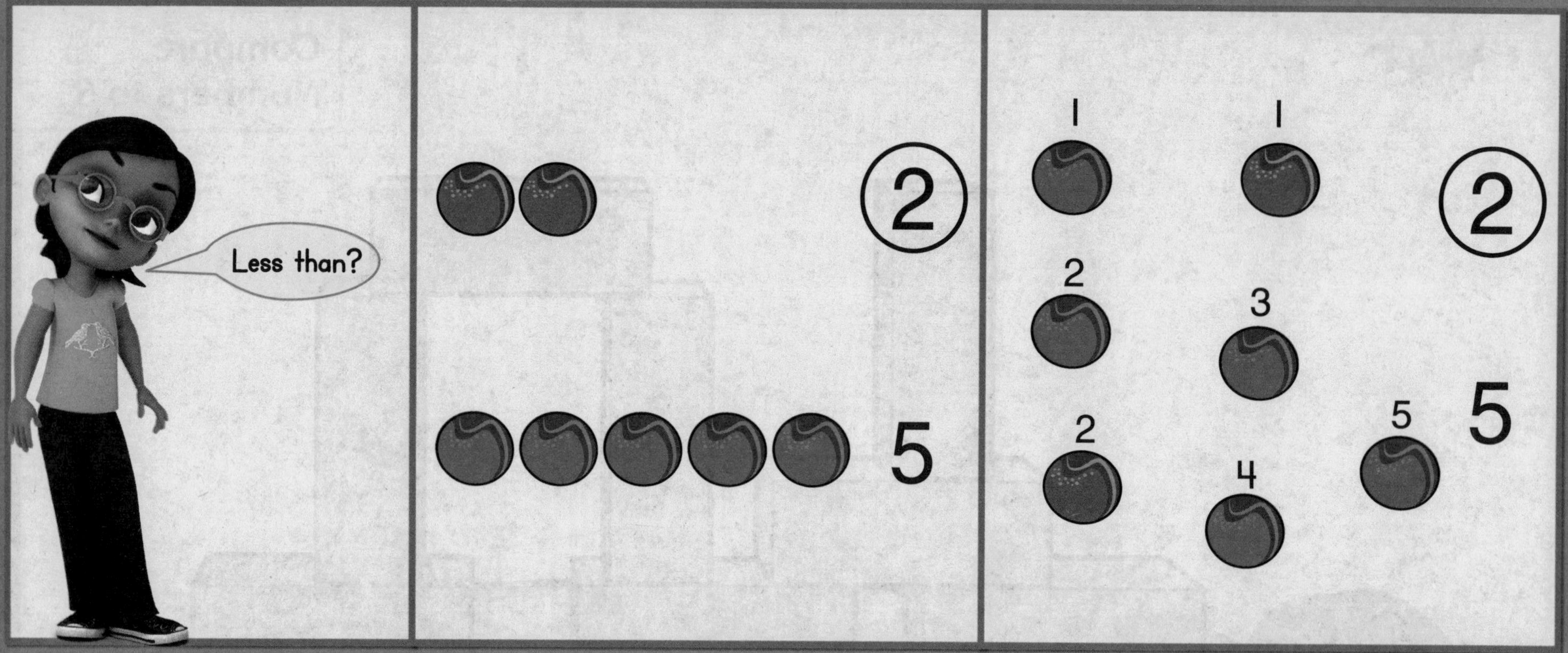

Less than?

2

5

1 1

2 3

2 4 5

2

5

Guided Practice

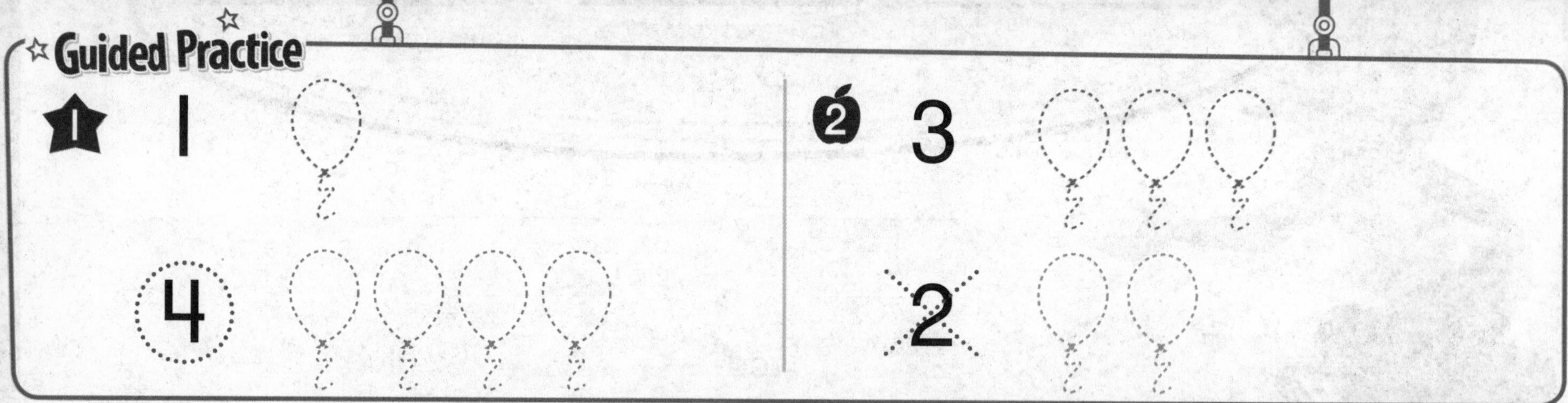

Directions Have students compare the numbers. Then have them: ★1 draw a circle around the number that is greater than the other number, or draw a circle around both numbers if they are equal. Have students draw pictures to show how they know; 2 mark an X on the number that is less than the other number, or draw a circle around both numbers if they are equal. Have students draw pictures to show how they know.

Name ______________________________

3 5

3

4 2

2

5 0

1

6 4

3

Directions Have students compare the numbers. Then have them: 3 and 4 draw a circle around the number that is greater than the other number, or draw a circle around both numbers if they are equal. Have students draw pictures to show how they know; 5 and 6 mark an X on the number that is less than the other number, or draw a circle around both numbers if they are equal. Have students draw pictures to show how they know.

Independent Practice

Tools Assessment

Directions Have students compare the numbers. Then have them: 7 mark an X on the number that is less than the other number, or draw a circle around both numbers if they are equal. Have students draw pictures to show how they know; 8 draw a circle around the number that is greater than the other number, or draw a circle around both numbers if they are equal. Have students draw pictures to show how they know. 9 **Higher Order Thinking** Have students look at the number card, and then write the number that is equal to that number. Then have them draw pictures to show how many. 10 **Higher Order Thinking** Have students look at the number card, and then write a number that is less than that number. Then have them draw pictures to show how many.

Name ______________________________

Homework & Practice 2-5

Compare Numbers to 5

HOME ACTIVITY Write two numbers between 0 and 5. Ask your child to compare the numbers. Have him or her point to the number that is greater than the other number. If needed, have your child use household objects, such as buttons or straws, to help show how many.

Another Look!

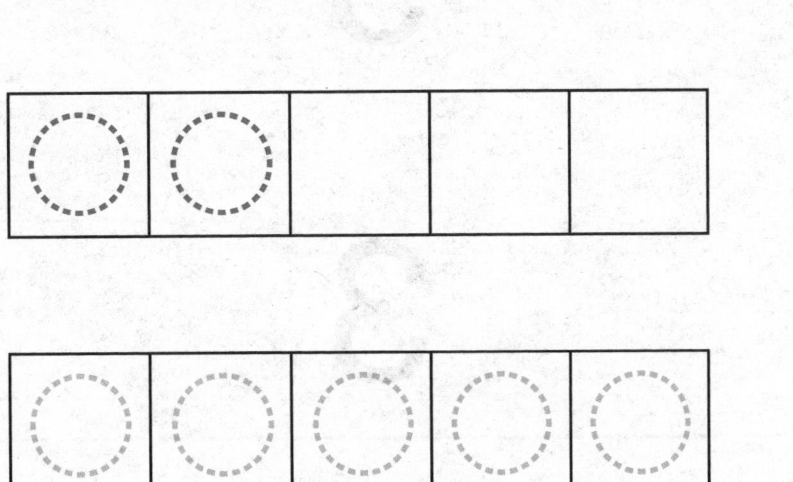

1

2

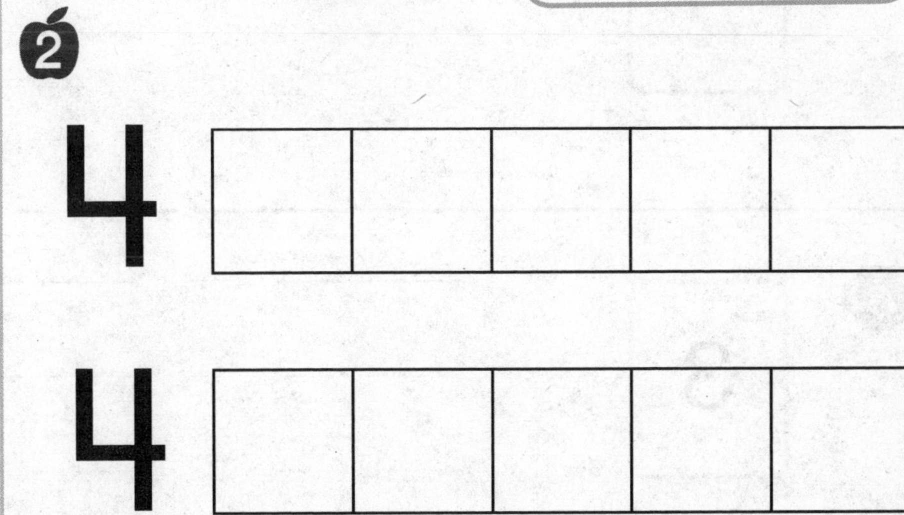

Directions Say: *A drawing can help to compare numbers. Draw 2 red counters and 5 yellow counters. Draw a circle around the number that is greater than the other number, or draw a circle around both numbers if they are equal.* Have students compare the numbers. Then have them: 1 mark an X on the number that is less than the other number, or draw a circle around both numbers if they are equal. Have students draw counters to show how they know; 2 draw a circle around the number that is greater than the other number, or draw a circle around both numbers if they are equal. Have students draw counters to show how they know.

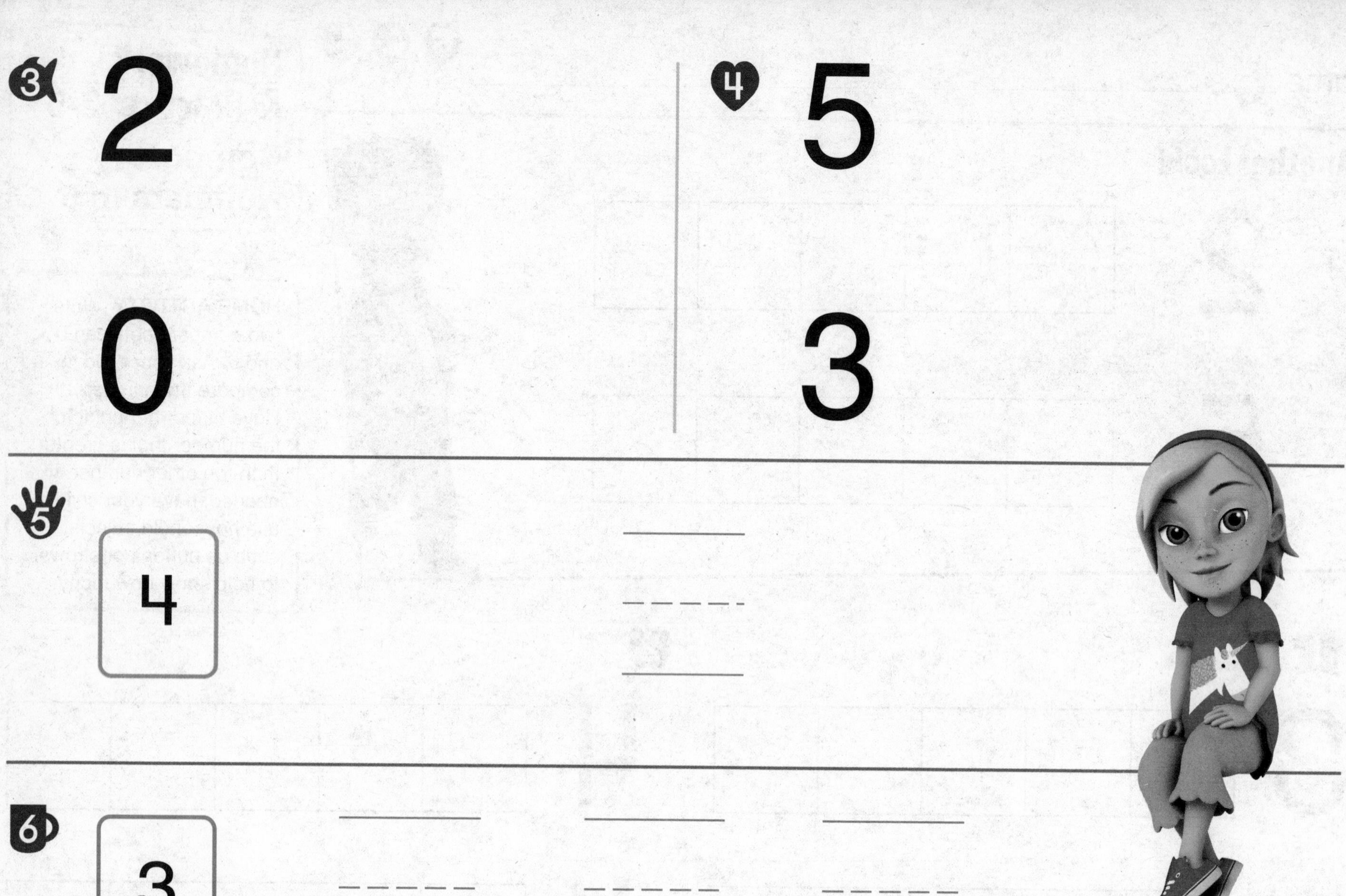

Directions Have students compare the numbers. Then have them: 3 draw a circle around the number that is greater than the other number, or draw a circle around both numbers if they are equal. Have students draw pictures to show how they know; 4 mark an X on the number that is less than the other number, or draw a circle around both numbers if they are equal. Have students draw pictures to show how they know. 5 **Number Sense** Have students look at the number card, and then write a number that is greater than that number. Then have them draw pictures to show how many. 6 **Higher Order Thinking** Have students look at the number card, and then write all the numbers that are less than that number.

Name ___________________________

Problem Solving

Lesson 2-6
Model with Math

Think.

Directions Say: *Work with your partner and take turns. Take 1 cube at a time from the bag and place it on your mat. Keep taking cubes until all the cubes are gone. Do you have a greater number of red cubes or blue cubes? How can you show your answer? Explain and show your work.*

I can ...
use objects, drawings, and numbers to compare numbers.

I can also write numbers to 5.

How can I show it?

Cubes

Drawings

Numbers

2

3

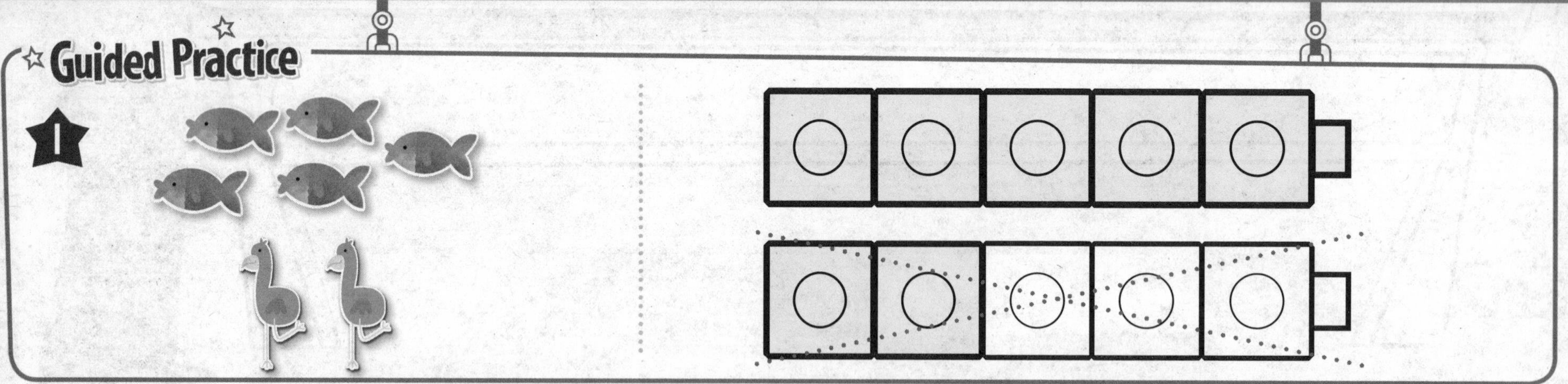

Directions 1 Say: *Marta has 5 fish stickers and 2 flamingo stickers. Which group of stickers is less in number than the other group? How can you use cubes to show how to find the answer?* Have students create cube trains for each group, color the number of cubes to show the number of stickers, and then mark an X on the cube train that shows less stickers in number than the other cube train. Have them explain their cube trains.

Name ______________________

Independent Practice

2

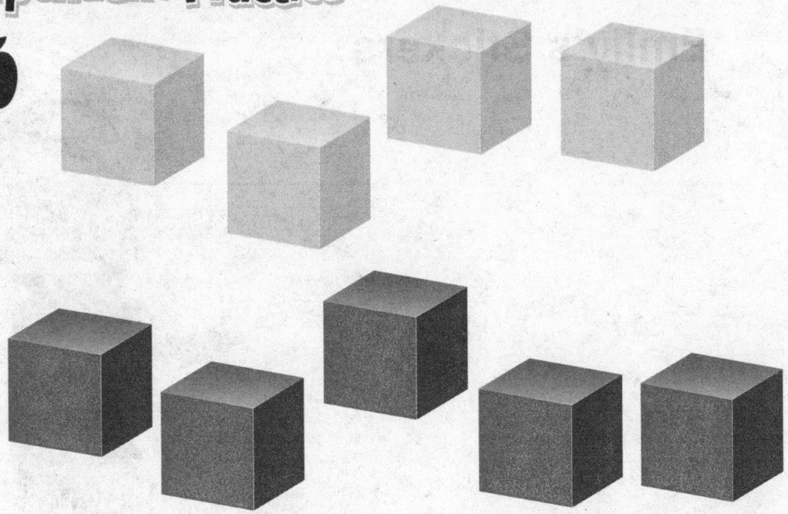

3

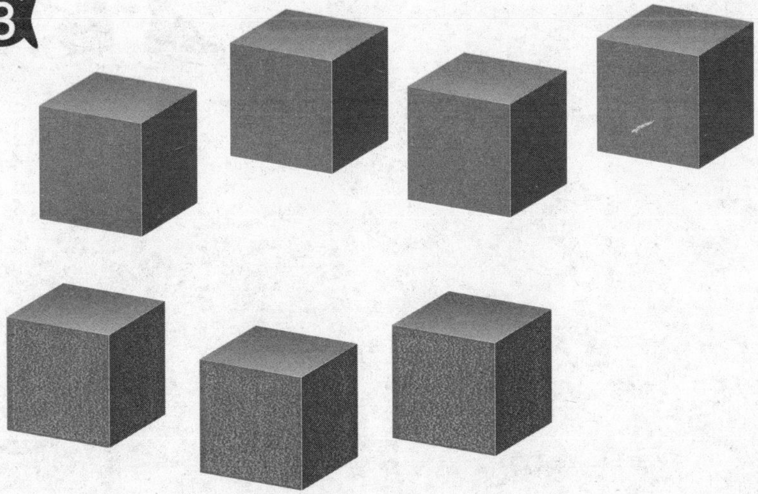

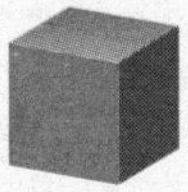

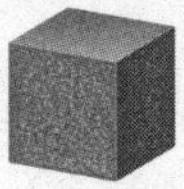

Directions 2 Say: *Carlos has 4 yellow blocks and 5 blue blocks. Which group of blocks is greater in number than the other group? How can you use a drawing to show your answer?* Have students create a drawing to show and explain their answer. 3 Say: *Carlos has 4 red blocks and 3 blue blocks. Which group of blocks is less in number than the other group? How can you use numbers to show your answer?* Have students use numbers to show and explain their answer.

Problem Solving

Performance Assessment

4 5 6

Marta's Stickers	Emily's Stickers

Directions Read the problem aloud. Then have students use multiple problem-solving methods to solve the problem. Say: *Marta has 2 stickers. Emily has a greater number of stickers than Marta. How many stickers could Emily have?* 4 **Make Sense** *What do you know about the problem? Can Emily have 1 sticker? Tell a partner why or why not.* 5 **Model** *Use cubes, draw a picture, or use numbers to show how many stickers Marta has and Emily could have.* 6 **Explain** *Tell a partner why your work for Emily's stickers is correct.*

Name ____________________

Homework & Practice 2-6
Model with Math

Another Look!

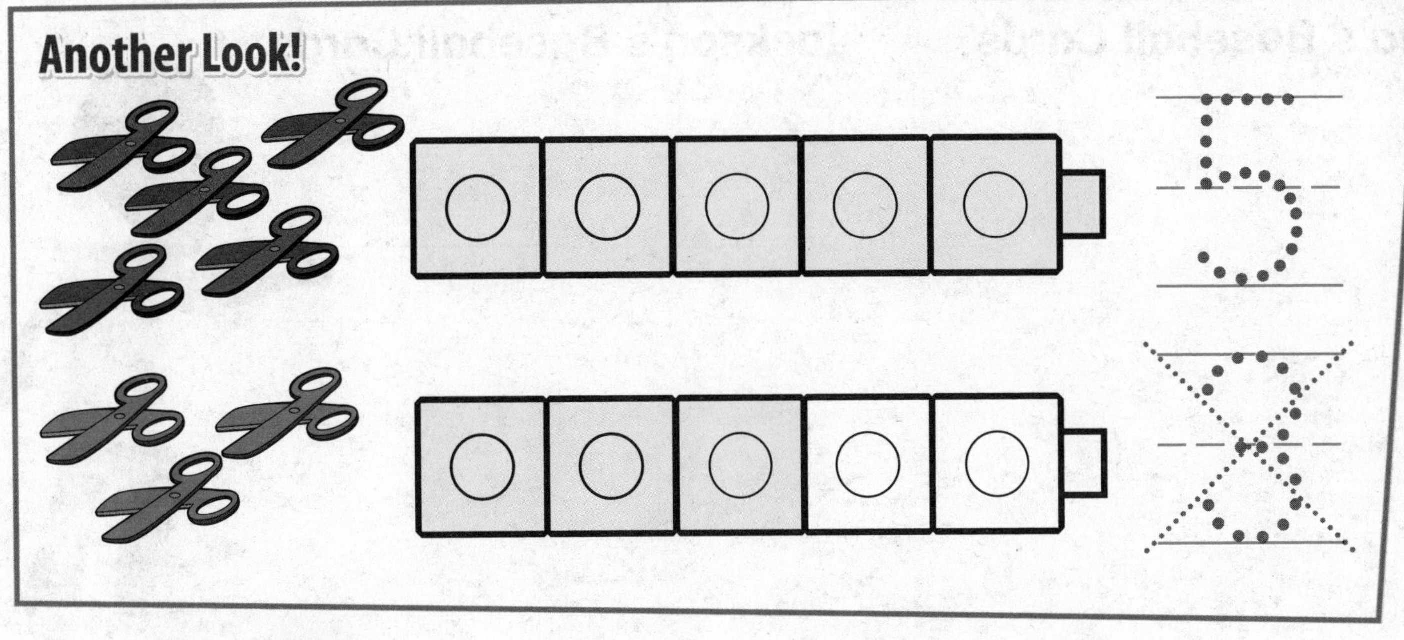

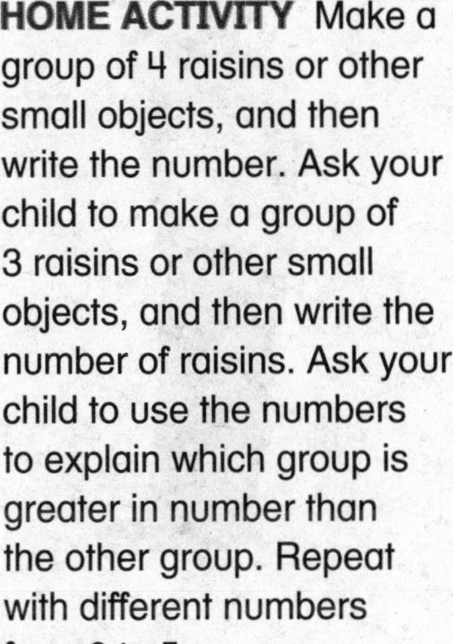

HOME ACTIVITY Make a group of 4 raisins or other small objects, and then write the number. Ask your child to make a group of 3 raisins or other small objects, and then write the number of raisins. Ask your child to use the numbers to explain which group is greater in number than the other group. Repeat with different numbers from 0 to 5.

1

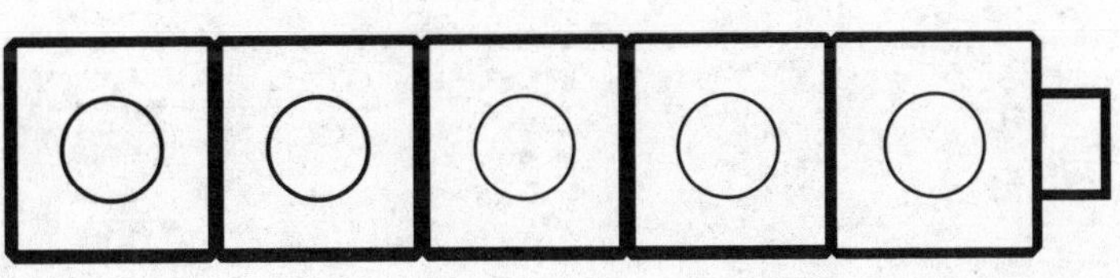

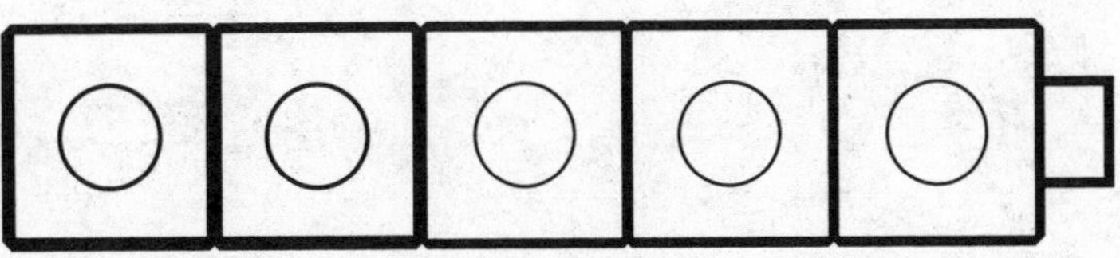

Directions Have students listen to the story. Say: *Mr. Davis has 5 blue scissors and 3 red scissors for his class. Which group of scissors has less than the other group? How can you use cubes, a drawing, or numbers to find out? Create cube or object trains for each group, color the number of cubes, and then write the numbers to tell how many. Mark an X on the number that is less than the other number.* Have students repeat the steps for this story: 1 *Candice has 4 purple blocks and 2 yellow blocks. Which group of blocks is less in number than the other group?*

Marta's Baseball Cards

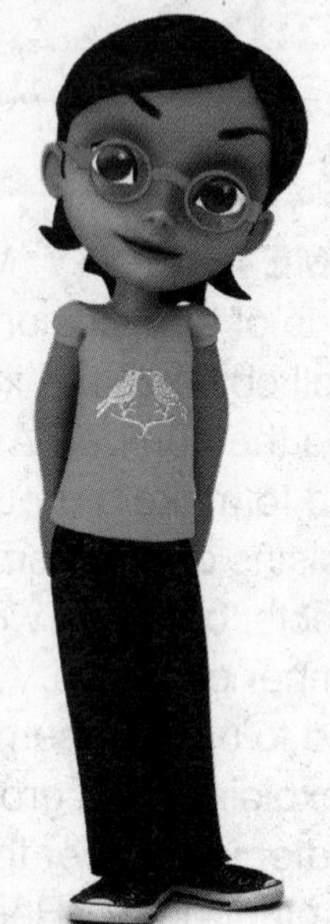

Jackson's Baseball Cards

Directions Read the problem aloud. Then have students use multiple problem-solving methods to solve the problem. Say: *Marta has 5 baseball cards. Jackson has less in number than Marta does. How many baseball cards could Jackson have?* **2 Make Sense** *What do you know about the problem? What is the number of baseball cards Jackson CANNOT have? Tell a partner and explain why.* **3 Model** *Use cubes, draw a picture, or use numbers to show how many baseball cards Marta has and Jackson could have.* **4 Explain** *Tell a partner why your work for Jackson's baseball cards is correct.*

Name ____________________

A-Z Glossary

1

2

1

3

4

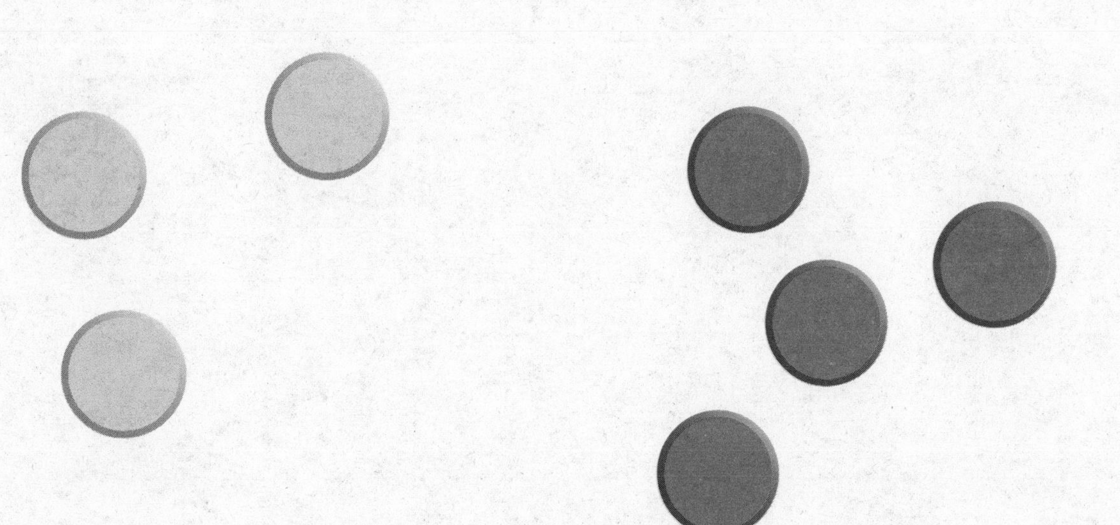

Directions **Understand Vocabulary** Have students: 1 draw 5 counters in a **group**; 2 write the number that is **less than** the number shown; 3 draw a group of counters that is **equal** in number to the group of counters shown; 4 **compare** red and yellow counters using matching to find which group is less in number than the other, and then mark an X on that group.

5

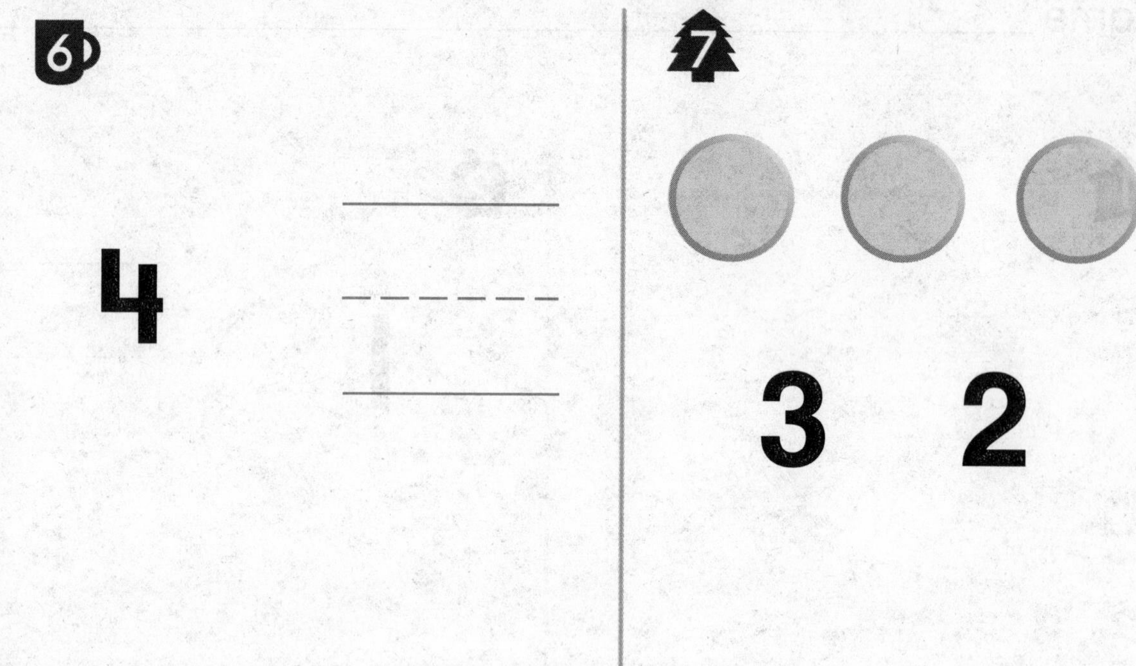

8

Directions **Understand Vocabulary** Have students: 5 draw counters to show a **model** of the given number; 6 write a number that is **greater than** the given number; 7 draw a circle around the number that is the **same number as** the number of counters shown; 8 draw two different ways to show a **group** of 7 counters.

Name ______________________

Reteaching

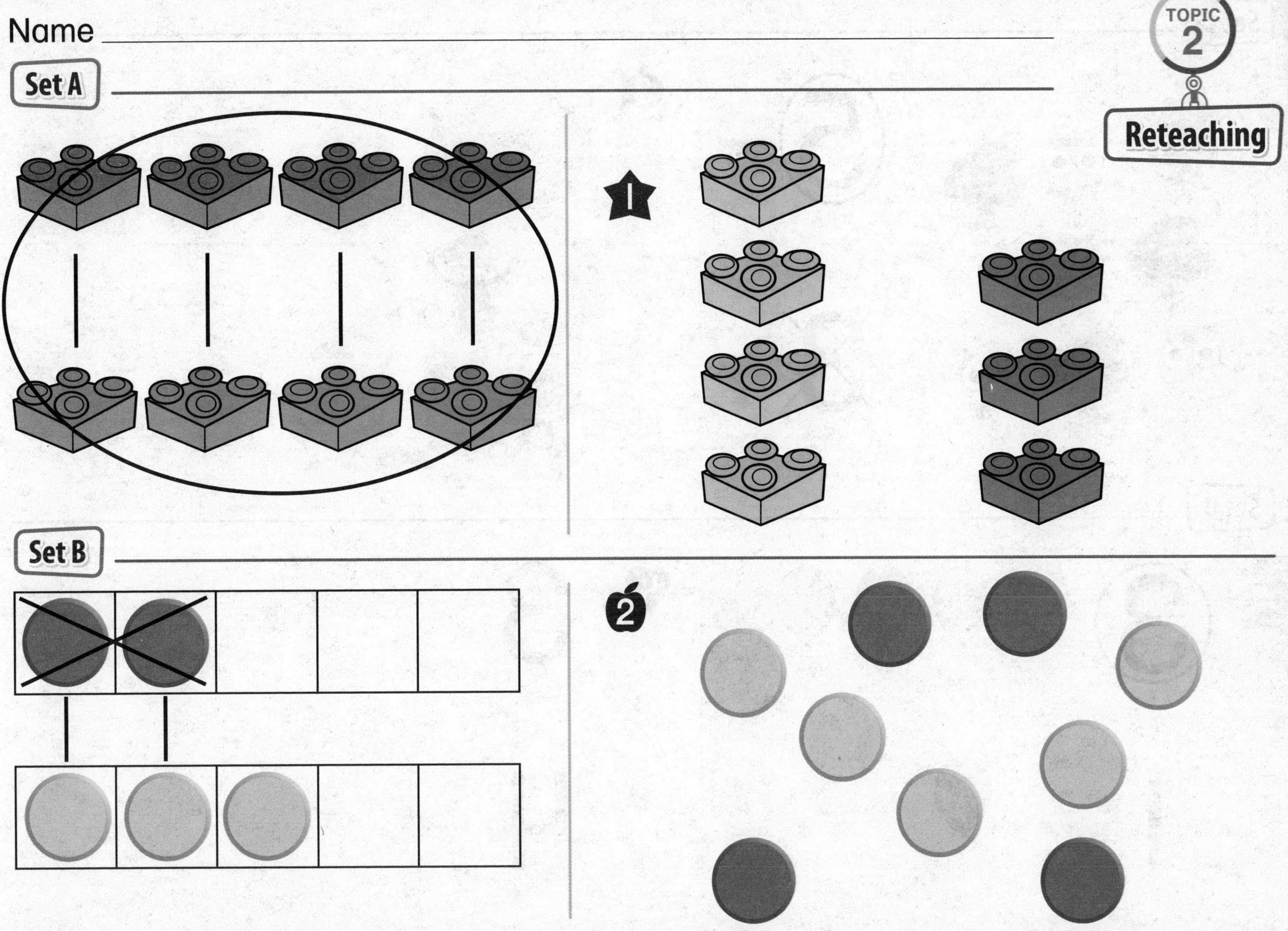

Directions Have students: 1 draw lines between the rows to match the blocks from one group to the other group. Then have them draw a circle around the groups if they are equal, or mark an X on the groups if they are NOT equal; 2 draw lines to match the groups of red and yellow counters. Have them draw a circle around the group that is greater in number than the other group, and then explain why they are correct.

Set C

Set D

3

1

4

Directions Have students: 3 count the stickers, and then draw a circle around the number that is greater than the other number and mark an X on the number that is less than the other number; 4 draw a circle around the number that is greater than the other number, or draw a circle around both numbers if they are equal. Have students draw pictures to show how they know.

Name ___

Ⓐ 

Ⓑ 

Ⓒ 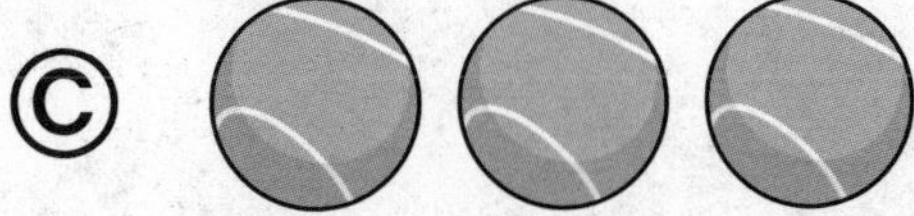

Ⓓ 

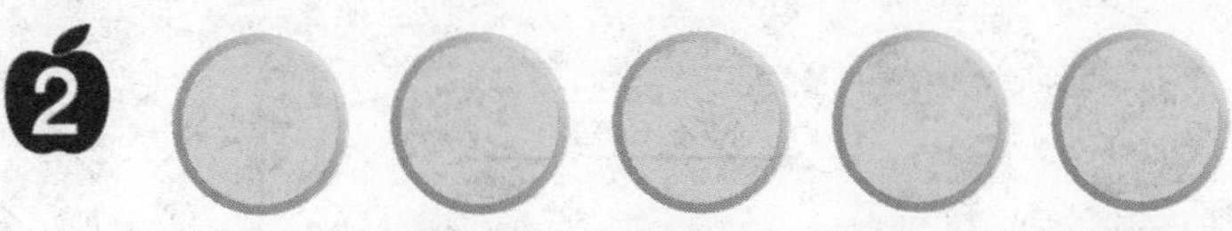

4

Directions ★ Which group of tennis balls is greater in number than the group of baseballs? ❷ Mark all the groups of red counters that are NOT equal in number to the group of yellow counters. ❸ Have students draw a circle around the number that is greater than the other number, or draw a circle around both numbers if they are equal. Then have students draw pictures to show how they know.

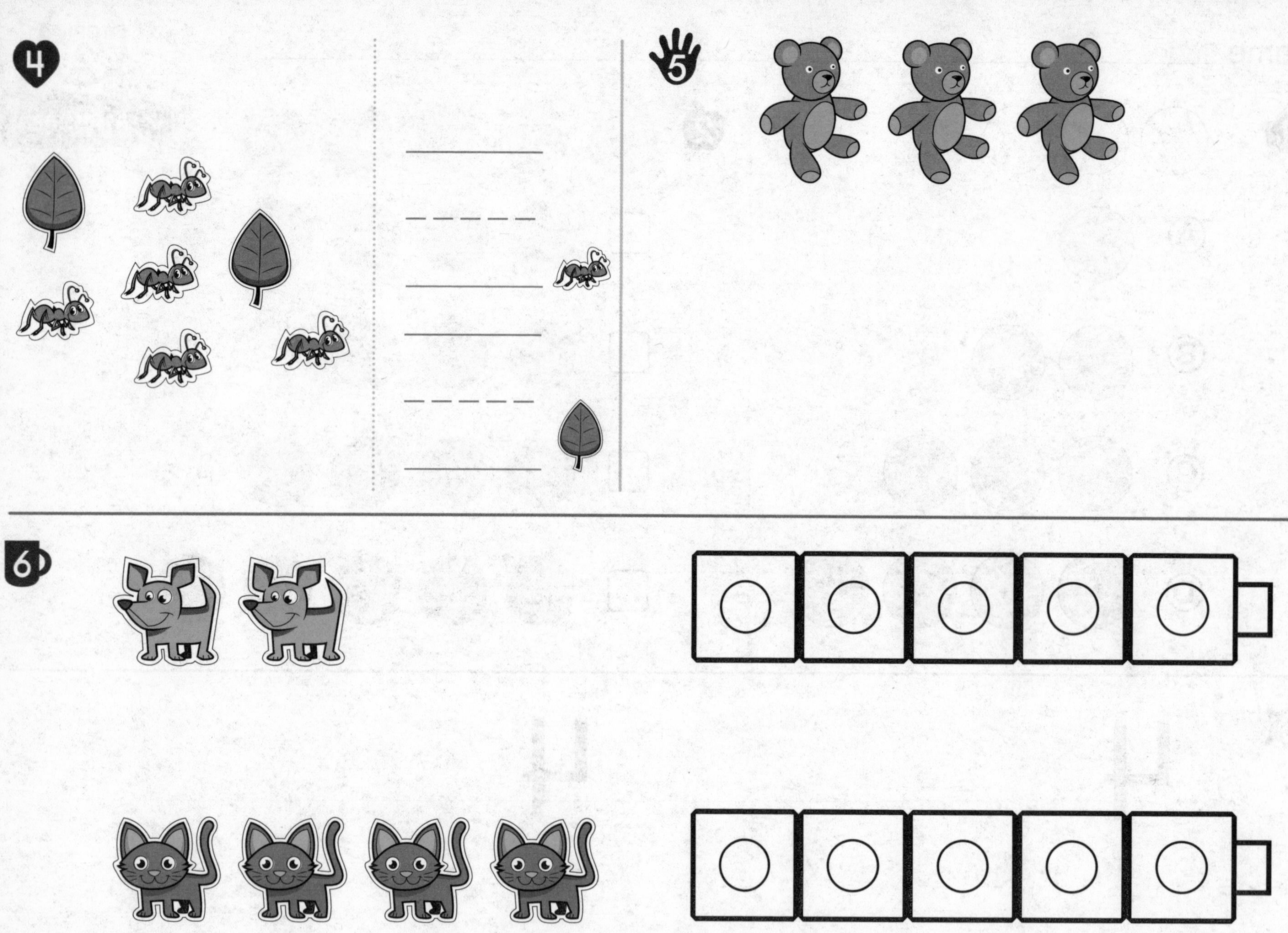

Directions Have students: ❹ count the stickers, write the numbers to tell how many, and then mark an X on the number that is less than the other number; ❺ draw a group of toys that is less in number than the group of stuffed bears shown. ❻ Say: *Ethan has 2 puppy stickers and 4 kitten stickers in his scrapbook. Color the cubes to show how many of each type of sticker, and then draw a circle around the cube train that is greater in number than the other cube train.*

Name ______________________________

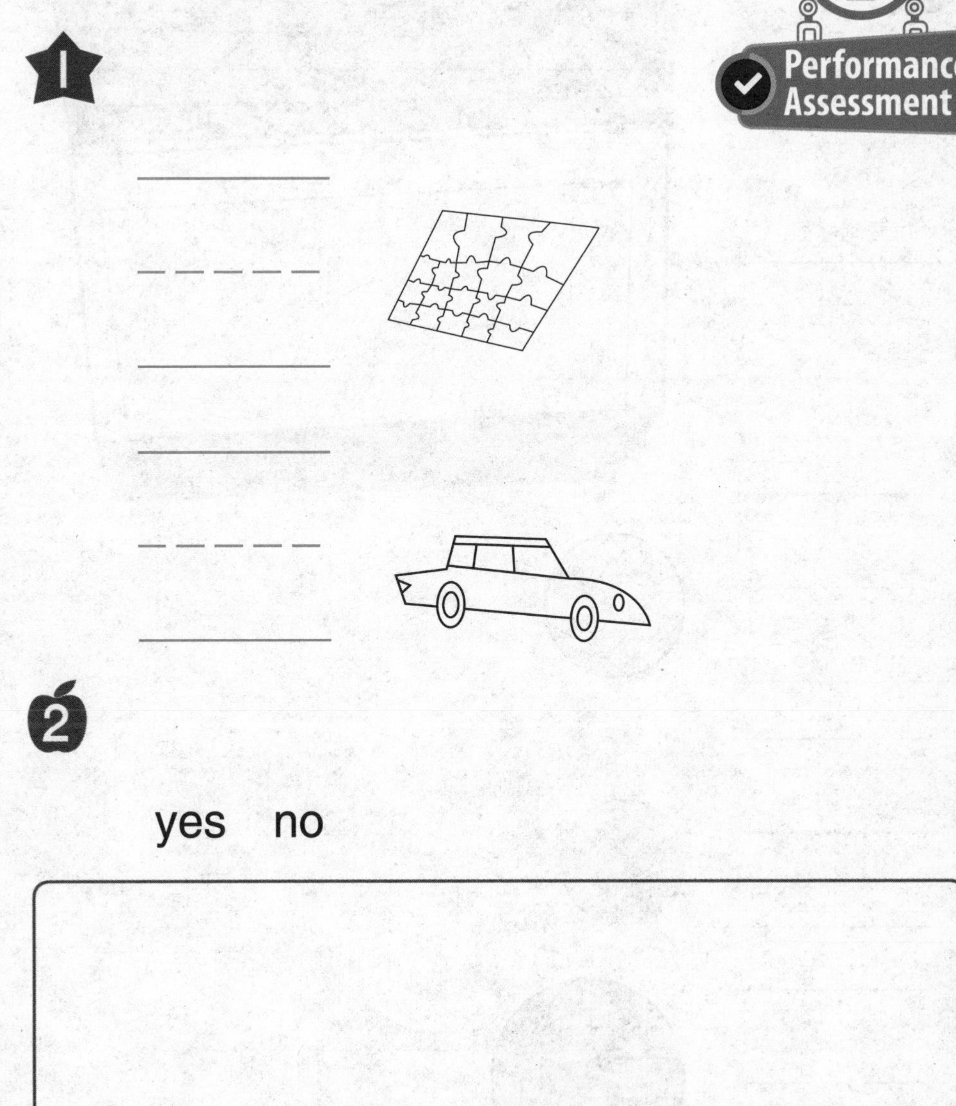

yes no

Directions **Toy Chest** Say: *David keeps his toys in a toy chest.* 1 Have students count the jigsaw puzzles and cars that David can see in the toy chest, and then write the numbers to tell how many. Then have them draw a circle around the number that is greater than the other number and mark an X on the number that is less than the other number. 2 Say: *David says that his group of toy cars is greater than his group of alphabet blocks. Do you agree with him?* Have students draw a circle around **yes** or **no**, and then have them draw a picture to explain their answer.

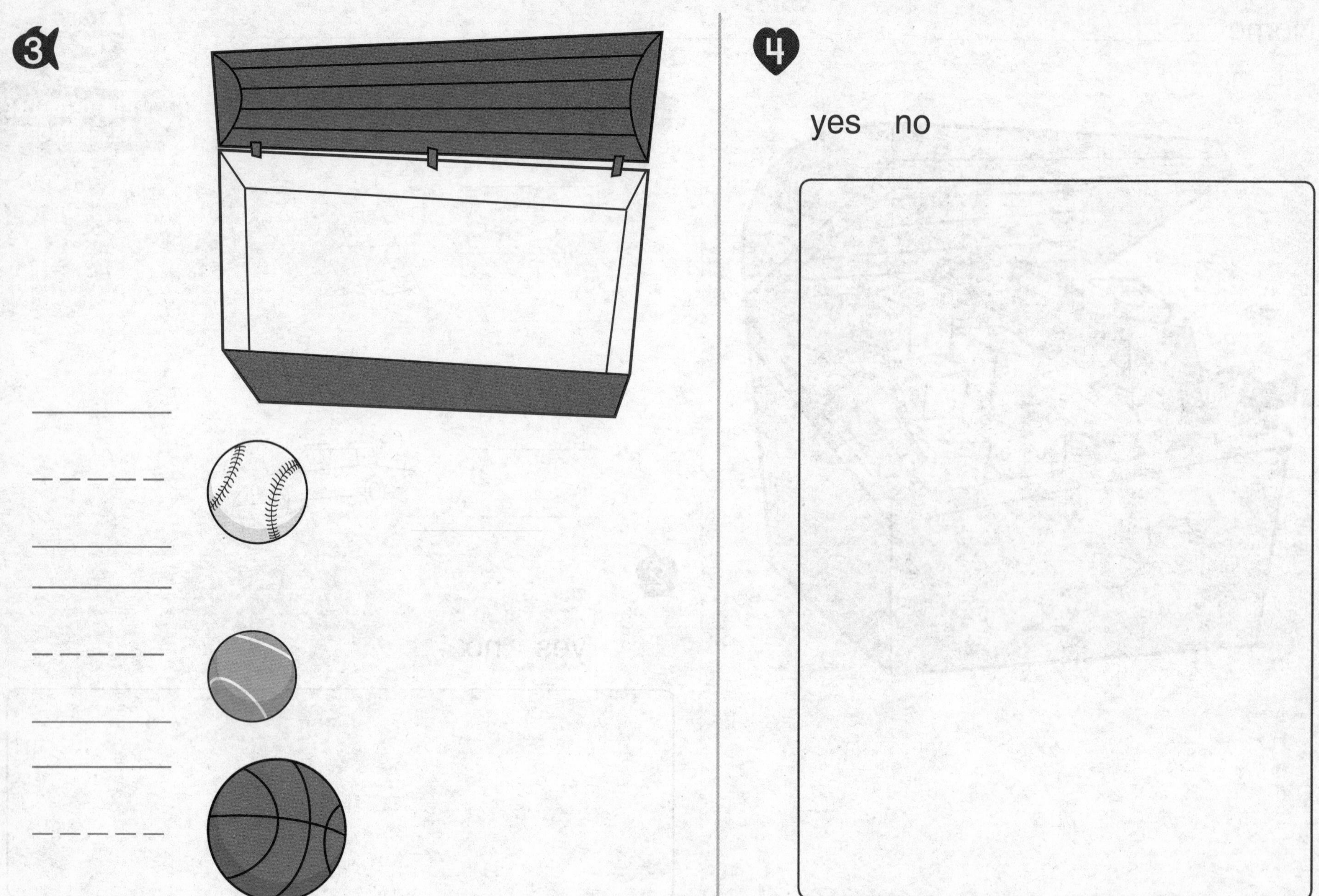

Directions 3 Say: *David's sister Sara likes sports. She keeps balls for different sports in her toy chest.* Then have students use the following clues to draw how many of each ball she could have in her toy chest, and then write the numbers to tell how many. *Sara has 3 baseballs. She has a group of tennis balls that is equal in number to the group of baseballs. Her group of basketballs is less in number than her group of tennis balls.* 4 Say: *David said that Sara could have zero basketballs in her toy chest. Do you agree with him? Draw a circle around **yes** or **no**.* Then have students draw a picture to explain their answer.

TOPIC 3

Numbers 6 to 10

Essential Question: How can numbers from 6 to 10 be counted, read, and written?

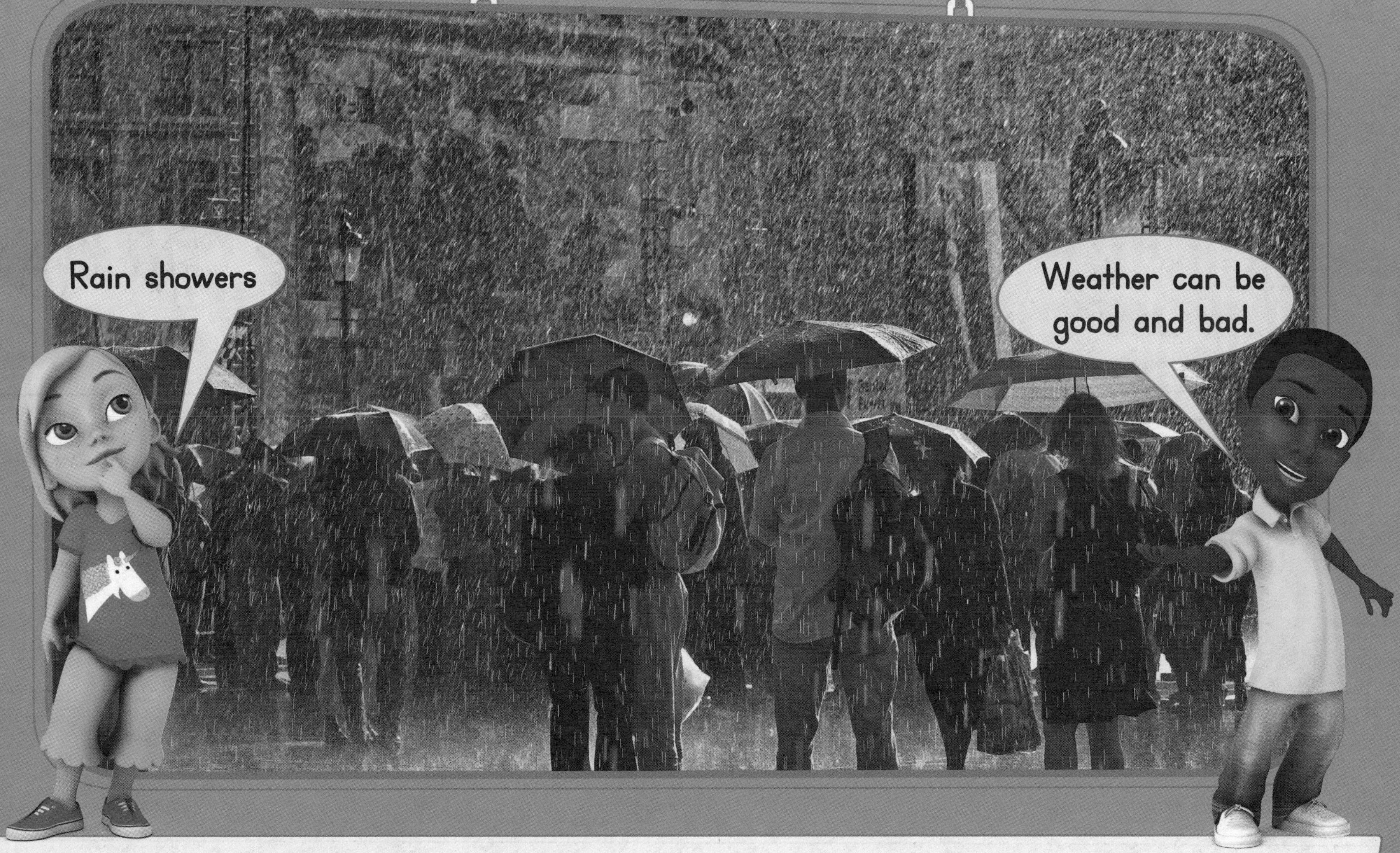

Math and Science Project: Types of Weather

Directions Read the character speech bubbles to students. **Find Out!** Have students discuss different types of weather they have experienced. Say: *Talk to friends and relatives about weather. Ask which types of weather they have seen.* **Journal: Make a Poster** Have students make a poster. Have them draw 10 pictures to represent good and bad weather they have experienced. Ask them to sort their pictures into two groups that show types of weather they enjoy and types they do not enjoy. Have students count how many are in each group and write the numbers.

Name ______________________________

Review What You Know

4

5

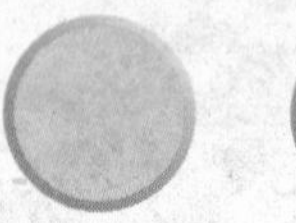

Directions Have students: 1 draw a circle around the group that is greater in number than the other group; 2 mark an X on the number that is less than the other number; 3 mark an X on the group that is less in number than the other group; 4 count the objects, write the number to tell how many of each, and then draw a circle around the number that is greater than the other number; 5 draw a group of counters that is equal in number to the group of counters shown.

A-Z Glossary

My Word Cards

Directions Have students cut out the vocabulary cards. Read the front of the card, and then ask them to explain what the word or phrase means.

six	**seven**	**eight**
nine	**ten**	

My Word Cards

Directions Review the definitions and have students study the cards. Extend learning by having students draw pictures for each word on a separate piece of paper.

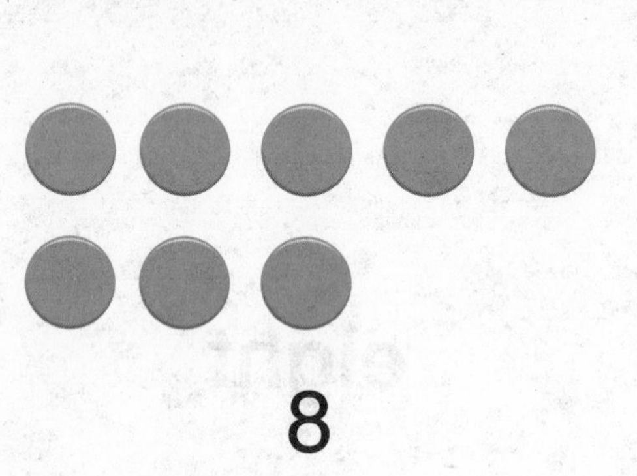

Point to the picture.
Say: *This is the number* ***eight***.

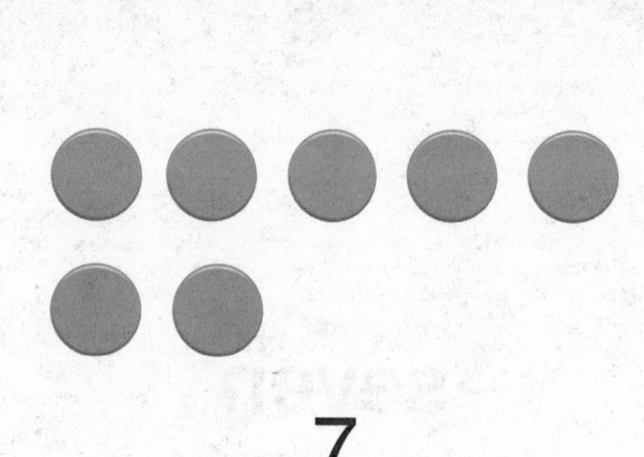

Point to the picture.
Say: *This is the number* ***seven***.

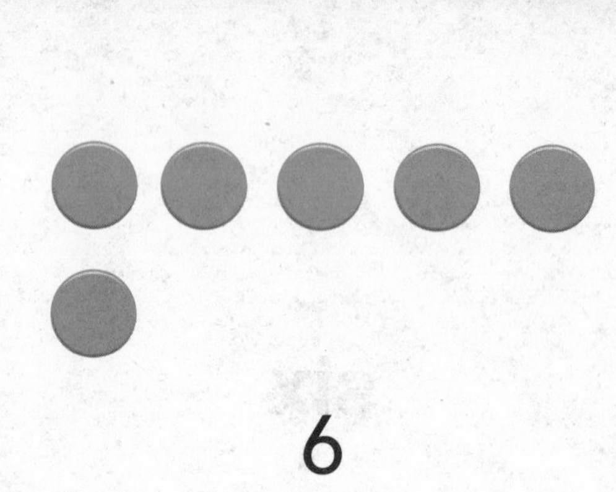

Point to the picture.
Say: *This is the number* ***six***.

Point to the picture.
Say: *This is the number* ***ten***.

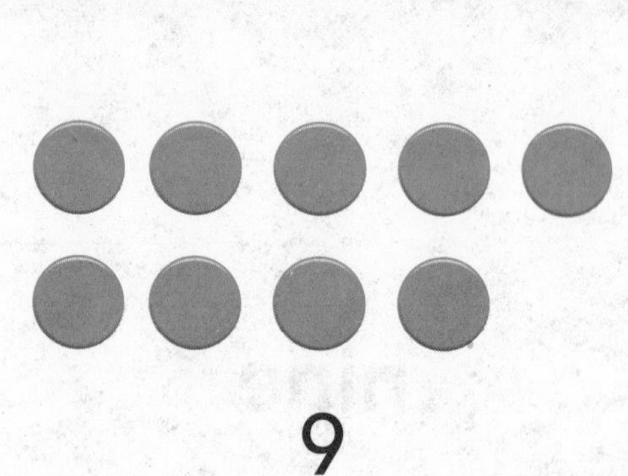

Point to the picture.
Say: *This is the number* ***nine***.

Name ____________________

Lesson 3-1
Count 6 and 7

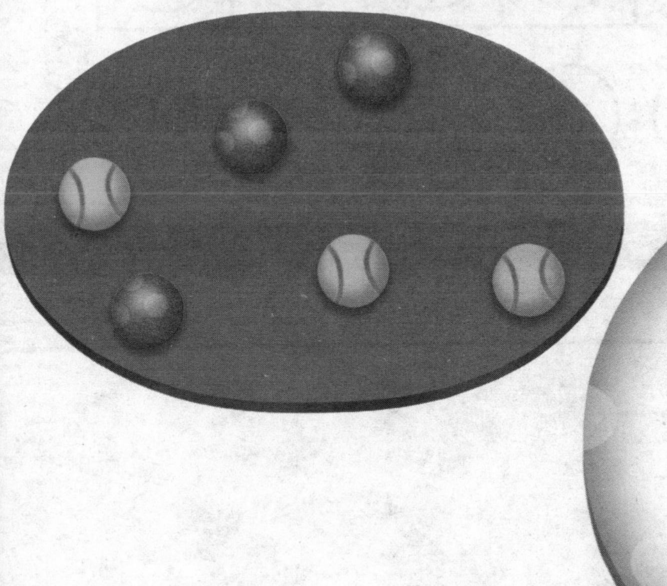

Directions Say: *Jackson's dog, Rex, has some balls on the red rug. Use counters and draw a picture on the empty dog bed to show how many balls Rex has. Tell how you know you are correct.*

I can ...
count the numbers 6 and 7.

I can also use math tools correctly.

Learn Glossary

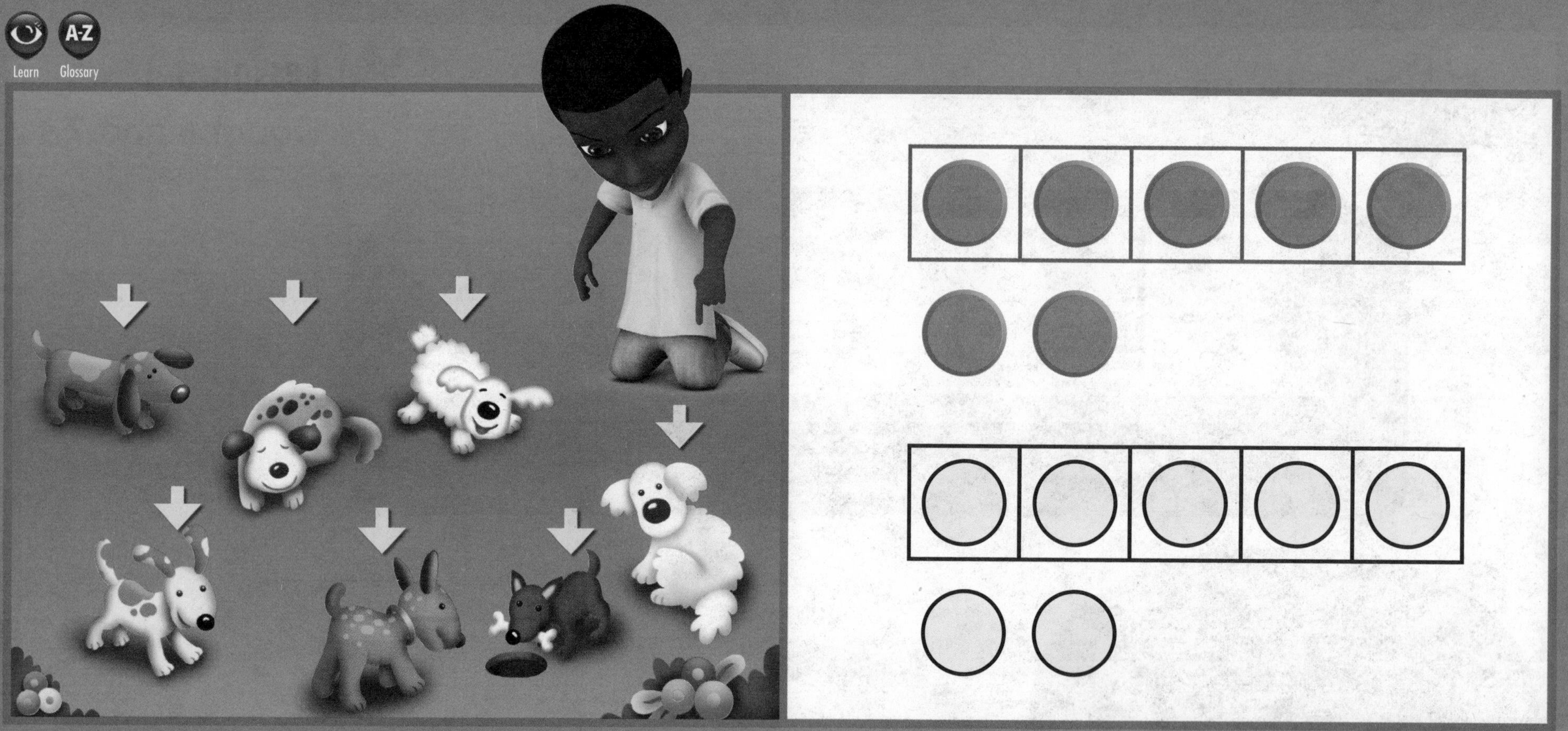

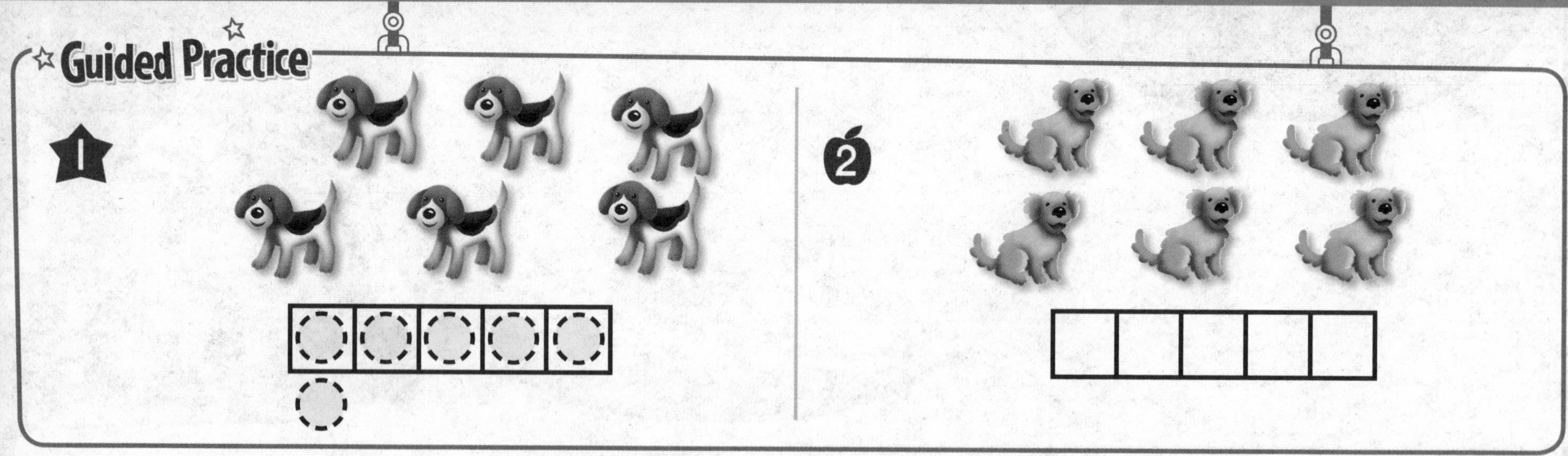

Directions 1 and 2 Have students draw a counter as they count each dog to show how many.

Name ______________________________

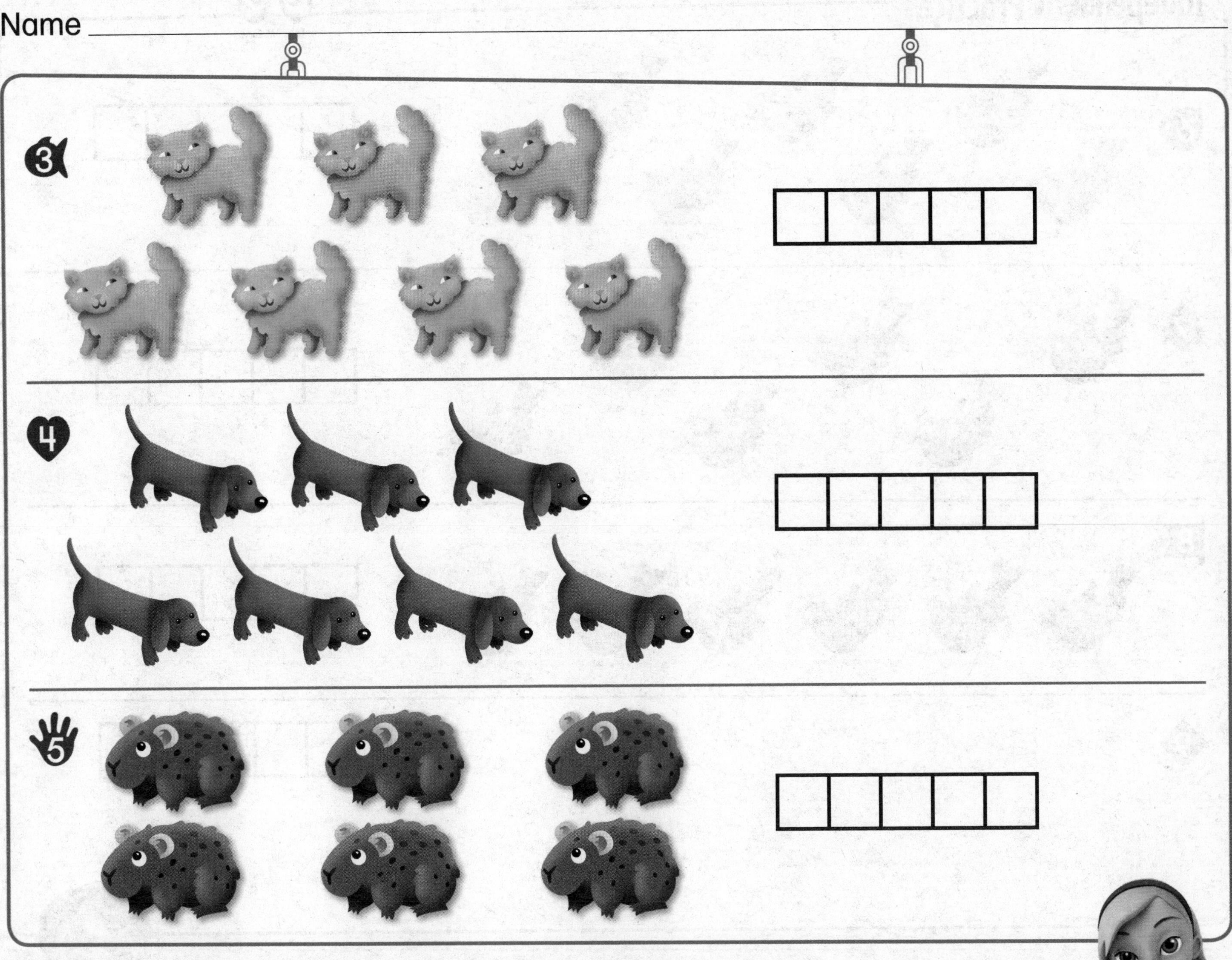

Directions 3–5 Have students draw a counter as they count each animal to show how many.

Independent Practice

Tools Assessment

6

7

8

9

Directions 6–8 Have students draw a counter as they count each bird to show how many. 9 **Higher Order Thinking** Have students draw 6 or 7 eggs, and then draw a counter as they draw each egg to show how many.

Name ______________________

Help Tools Games

Homework & Practice 3-1

Count 6 and 7

HOME ACTIVITY Have your child count groups of 6 objects. Then have him or her draw pictures of 6 objects. Repeat using the number 7.

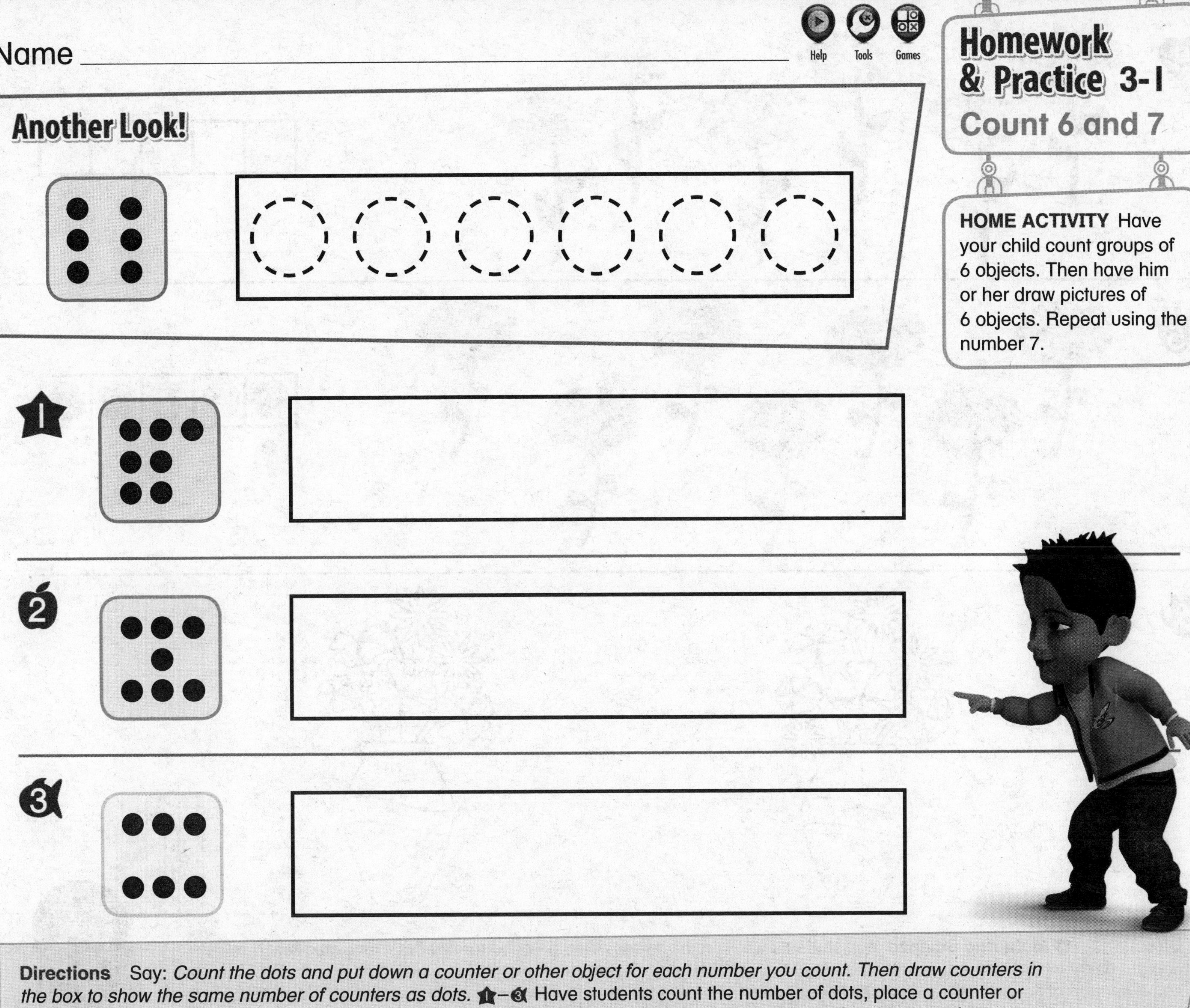

Directions Say: *Count the dots and put down a counter or other object for each number you count. Then draw counters in the box to show the same number of counters as dots.* 1–3 Have students count the number of dots, place a counter or other object for each dot they count, and then draw counters in the box to show the same number of counters as dots.

Directions **4 Math and Science** Ask students why a rain shower would be good for flowers. Have students draw a counter as they count each flower to show how many. **5 Higher Order Thinking** Have students draw a circle around the same number of flowers as counters. **6 Higher Order Thinking** Have students color red the vase with 6 flowers, and then color yellow the vase with 7 flowers.

Solve & Share

Name ______________________

Lesson 3-2

Read and Write 6 and 7

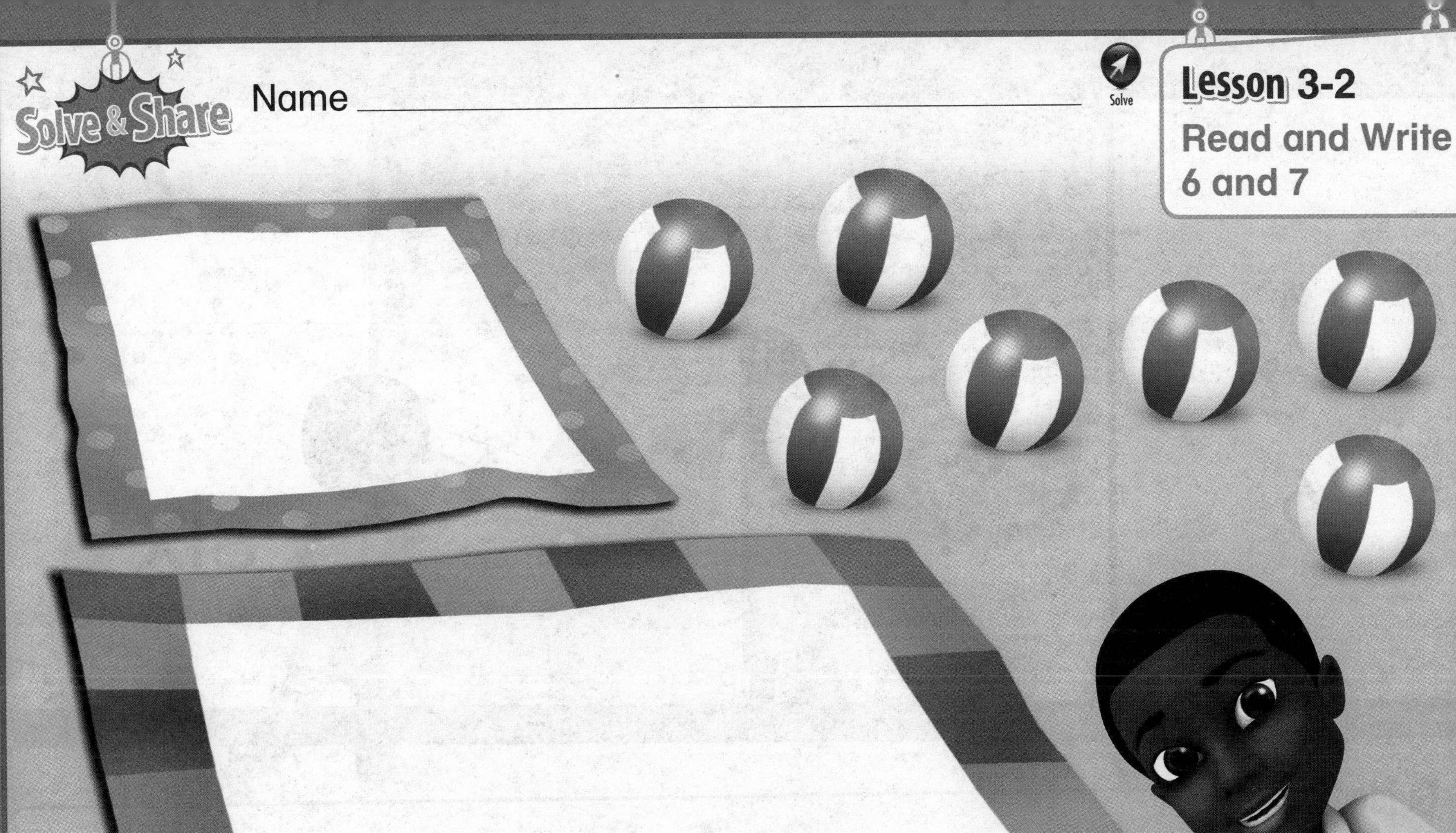

Directions Say: *Jackson sees 7 beach balls. How can he show how many beach balls in two different ways? Draw the ways on the blankets.*

I can ... read and write the numbers 6 and 7.

I can also make math arguments.

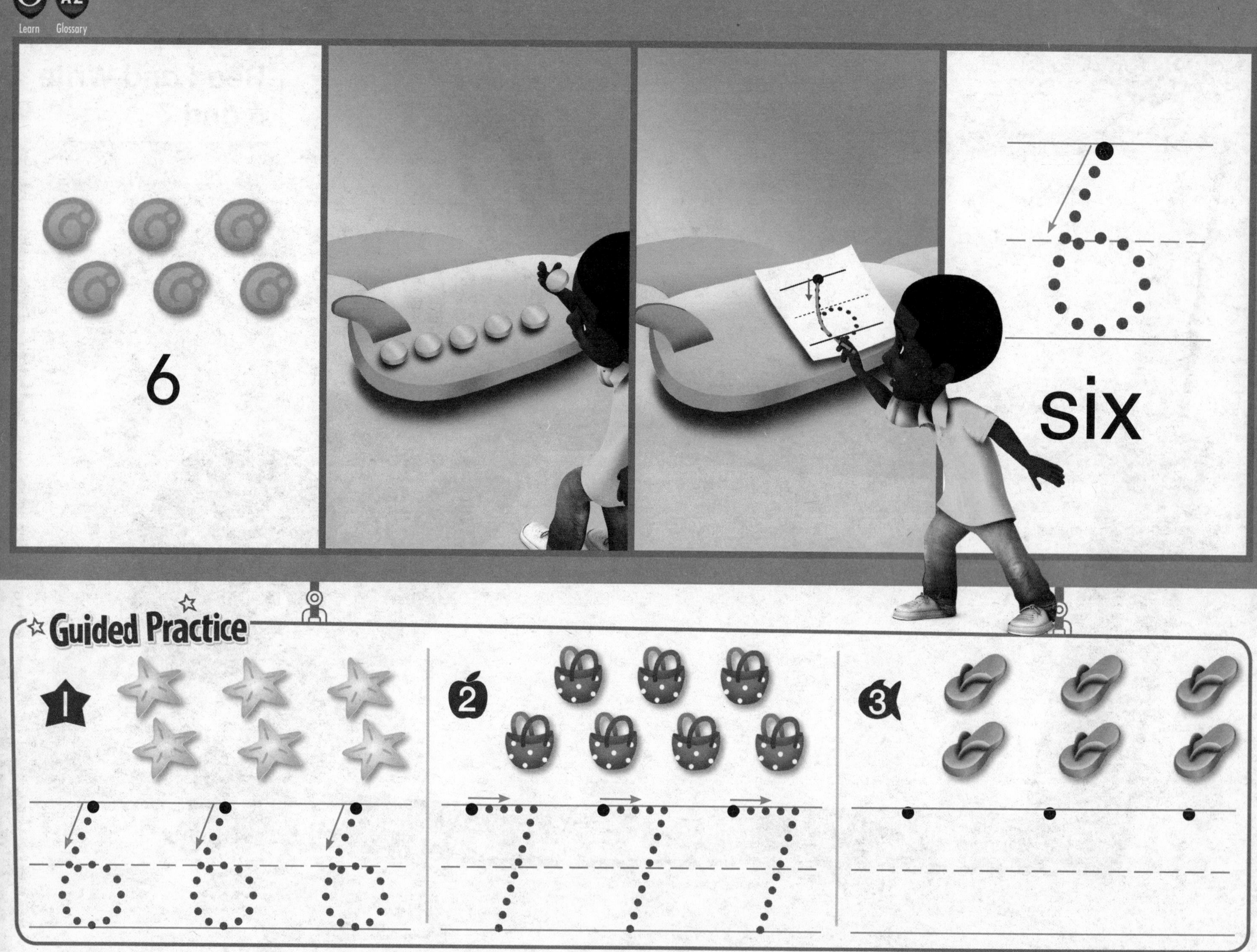

Directions 1–3 Have students count the objects, and then practice writing the number that tells how many.

Name

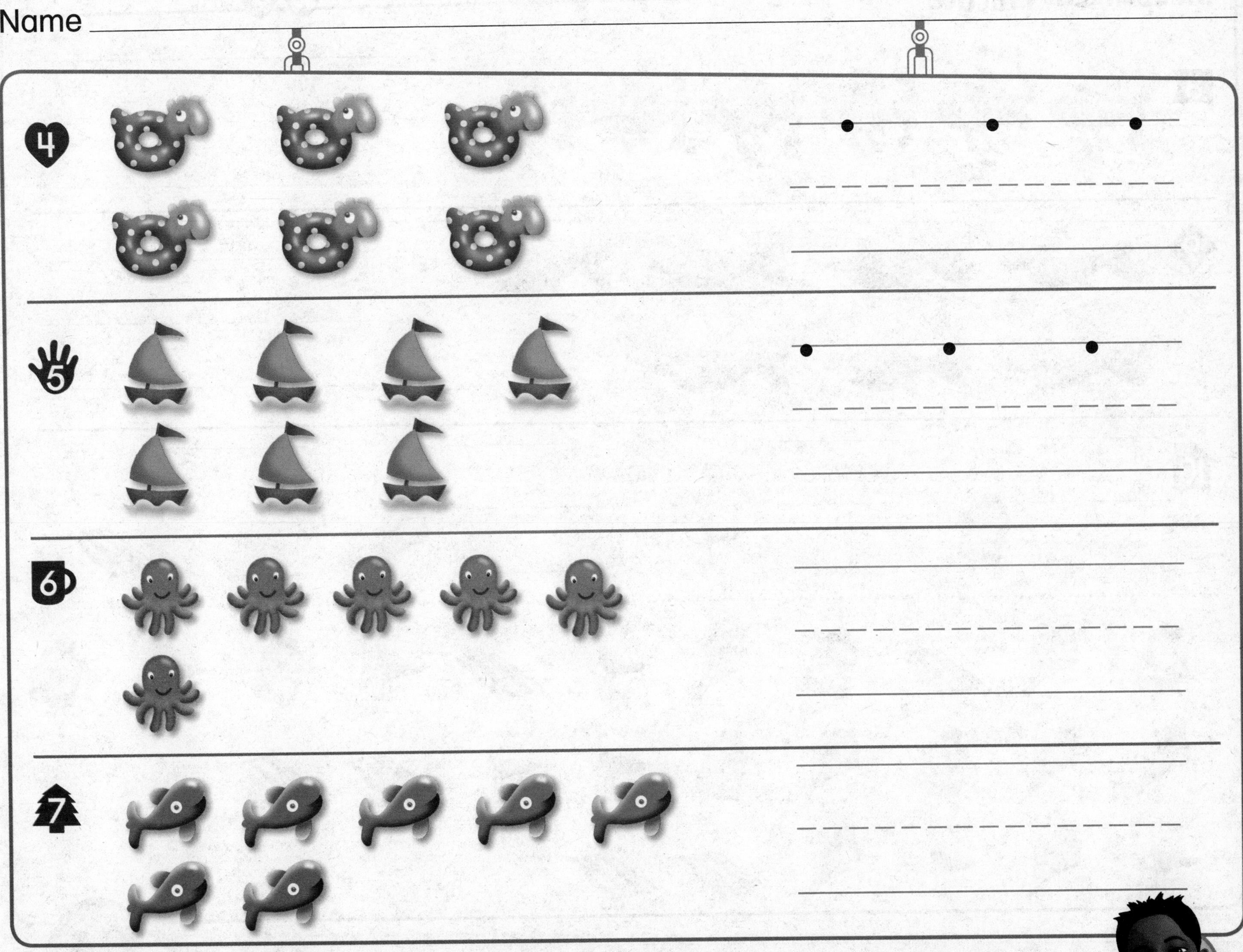

Directions 4–7 Have students count the objects, and then practice writing the number that tells how many.

Independent Practice

Tools Assessment

8

9

10

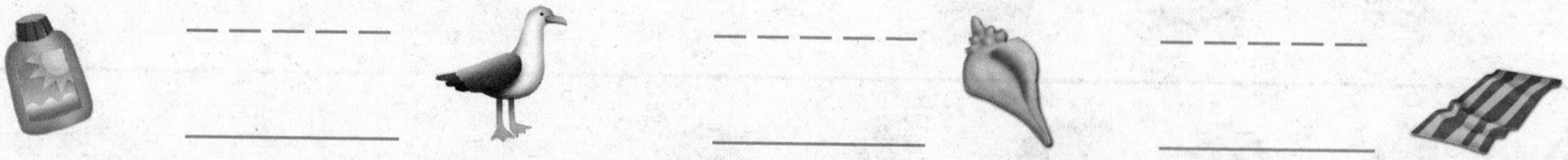

Directions 8 and 9 Have students count the fish, and then practice writing the number that tells how many. 10 **Higher Order Thinking** Have students count each group of objects, and then write the numbers to tell how many.

Name ______________________

Help Tools Games

Homework & Practice 3-2

Read and Write 6 and 7

HOME ACTIVITY Draw groups of 6 and 7 circles on 2 index cards. Have your child write the correct number on the back of each card. Then use the cards to practice counting and reading the numbers 6 and 7.

Another Look!

6 6 6

7 7 7

1

2

3

Directions Say: *Count the counters, and then practice writing the numbers that tell how many.* 1–3 Have students count the counters, and then practice writing the number that tells how many.

Directions 4 and 5 Have students count the objects, and then practice writing the number that tells how many. 6 **Higher Order Thinking** Have students draw more beach balls to show 7, and then practice writing the number 7. 7 **Higher Order Thinking** Have students draw 6 or 7 fish, and then practice writing the number that tells how many.

Name ____________________

Lesson 3-3
Count 8 and 9

Directions Say: *Jackson makes some sandwiches for lunch at the beach. Use counters and draw a picture on the blank sign to show how many sandwiches Jackson makes. Tell how you know you are correct.*

I can ...
count the numbers 8 and 9.

I can also model with math.

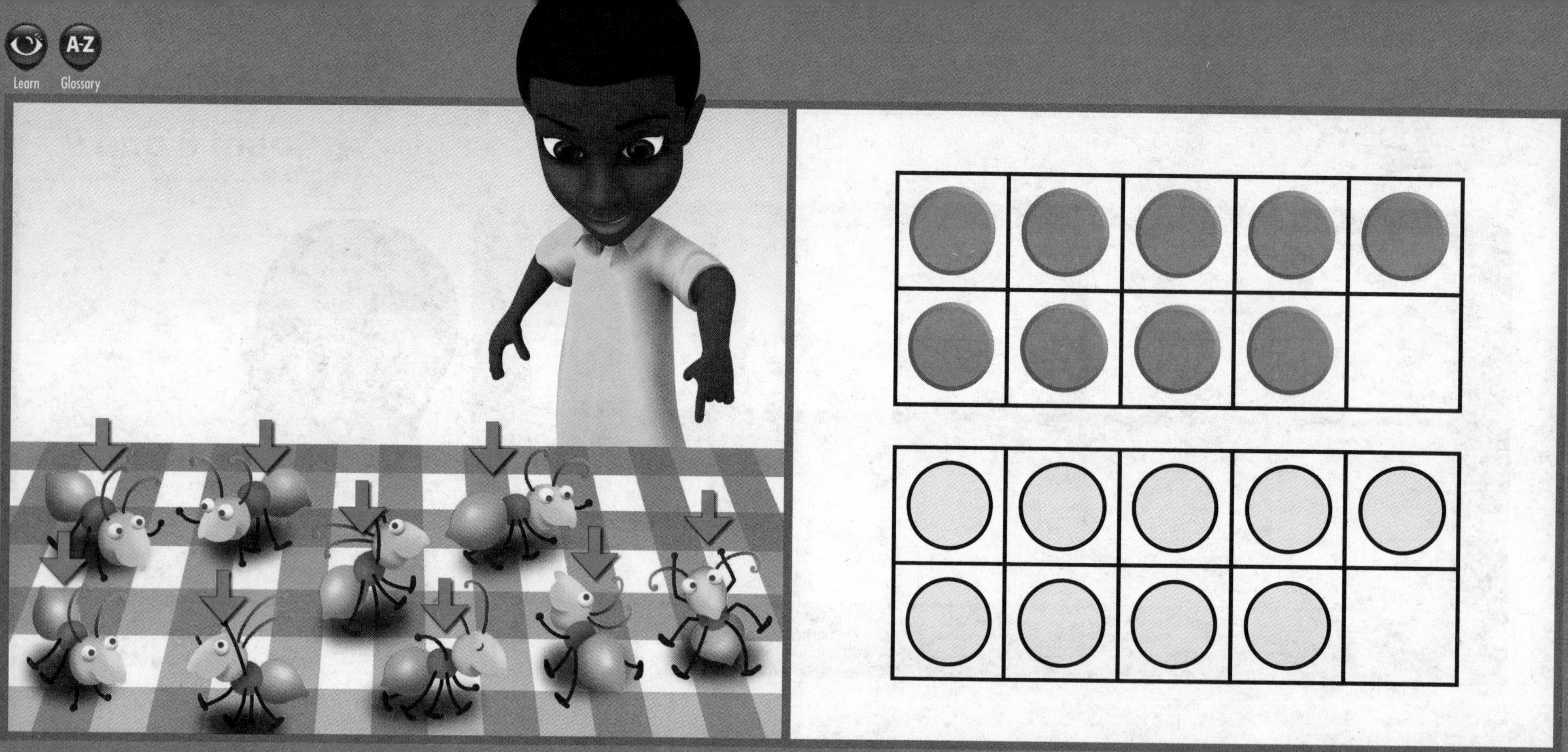

Learn Glossary

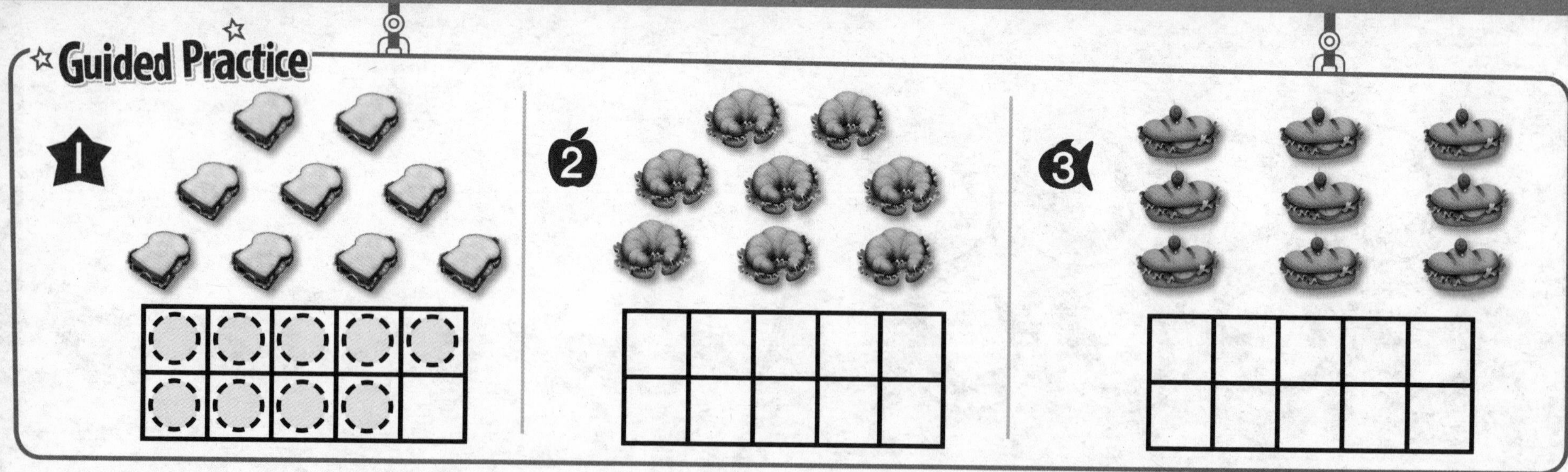

Directions 1–3 Have students count the sandwiches, and then draw counters to show how many.

Name

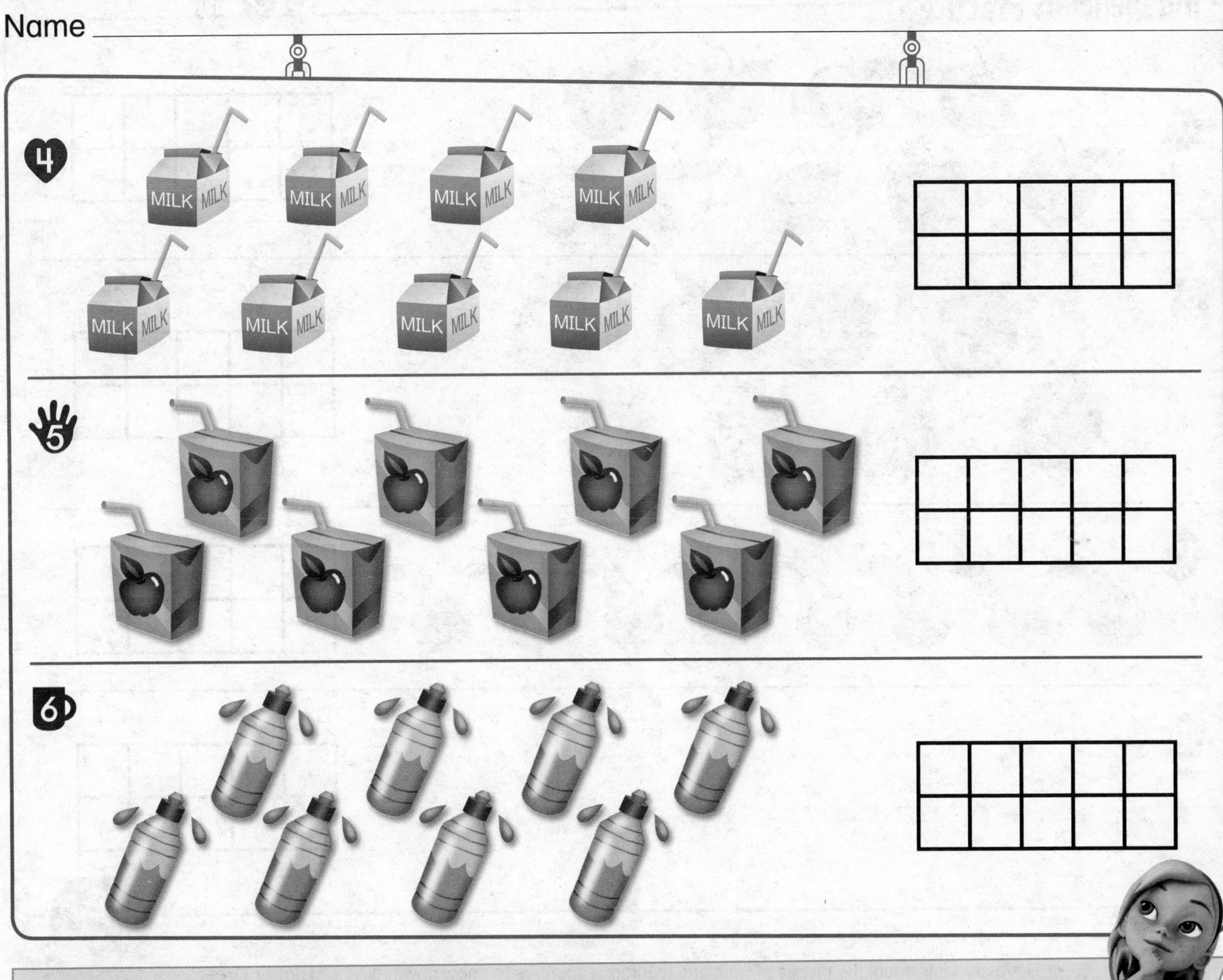

Directions 4–6 Have students count the drinks, and then draw counters to show how many.

Independent Practice

Tools Assessment

7

8

9

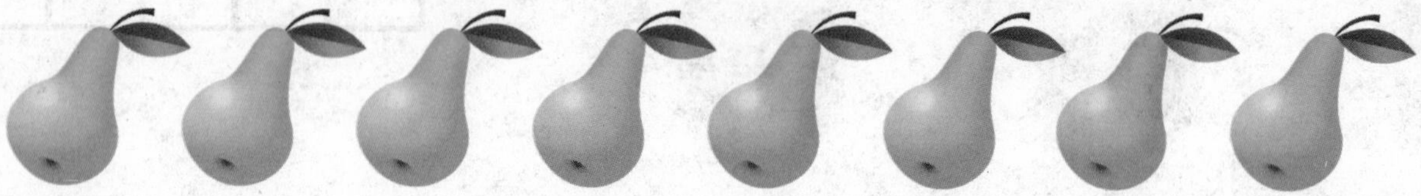

10

Directions 7–9 Have students count the pieces of fruit, and then draw counters to show how many. 10 **Higher Order Thinking** Have students draw 8 or 9 oranges, and then draw counters to show how many.

Name ______________________________

Help Tools Games

Homework & Practice 3-3

Count 8 and 9

HOME ACTIVITY Have your child count groups of 8 objects. Then ask him or her to draw pictures of 8 objects. Repeat using the number 9.

Another Look!

1

2

3

Directions Say: *Count the dots and use counters or other objects to show that number. Then draw counters in the box to show the same number of counters as dots.* 1–3 Have students count the number of dots, use counters or other objects to show that number, and then draw counters in the box to show the same number of counters as dots.

Directions 4 Have students count the sandwiches, and then draw counters to show how many. 5 **Higher Order Thinking** Have students draw a circle around the same number of sandwiches as counters. 6 **Higher Order Thinking** Have students color brown the dog with 8 spots, and then color black the dog with 9 spots.

Name ______________________________

Lesson 3-4
Read and Write 8 and 9

Directions Say: *Jackson sees 9 turtle eggs in the sand. How can he show how many turtle eggs in two different ways? Draw the ways on the turtle shells.*

I can ...
read and write the numbers 8 and 9.

I can also make math arguments.

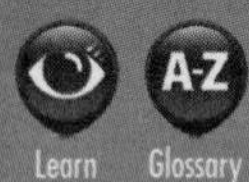

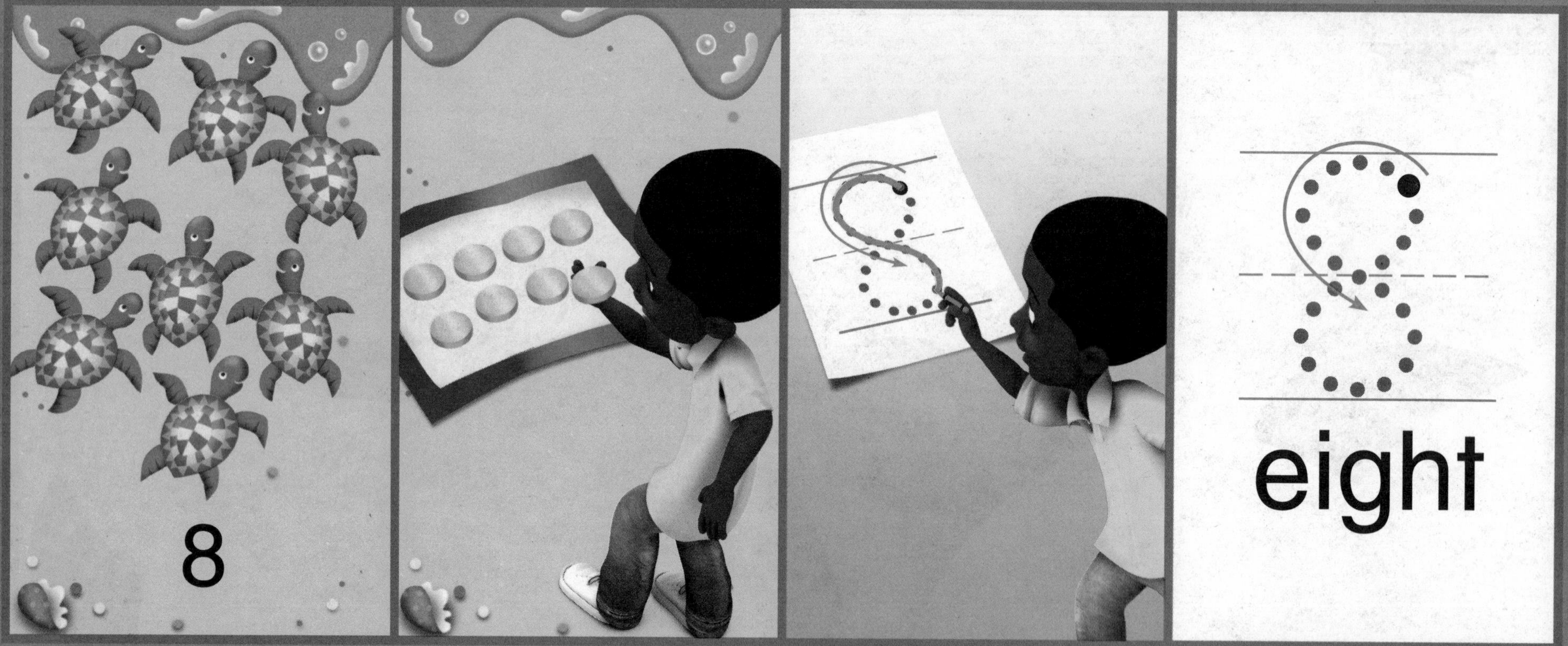

8

eight

Guided Practice

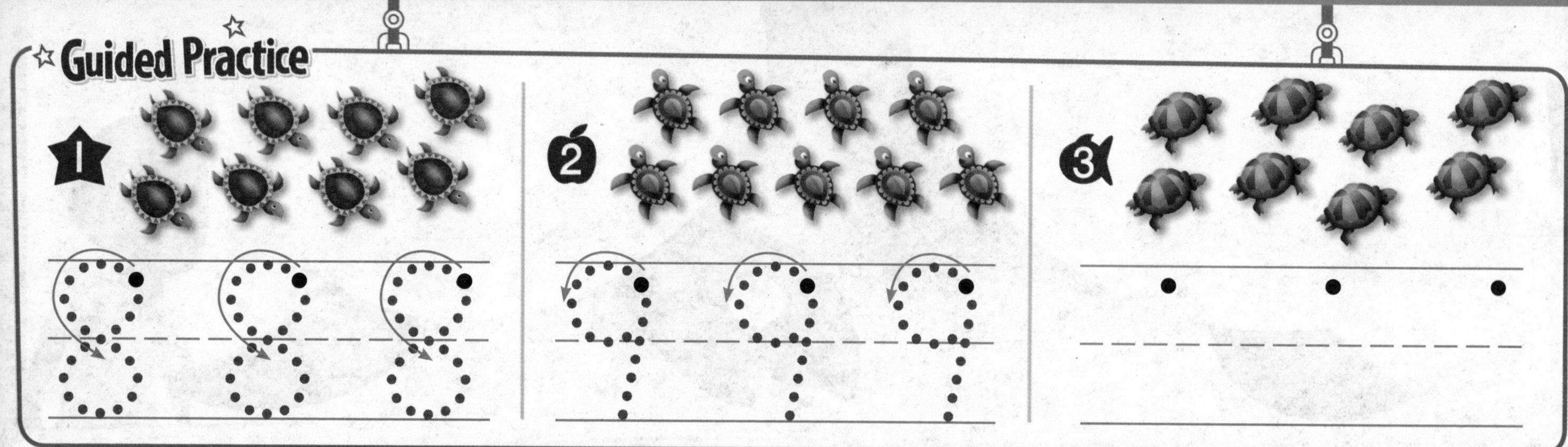

Directions 1–3 Have students count the turtles, and then practice writing the number that tells how many.

Name

Directions 4–7 Have students count the animals, and then practice writing the number that tells how many.

Independent Practice

Tools Assessment

Directions 8 and 9 Have students count the animals, and then practice writing the number that tells how many. 10 **Higher Order Thinking** Have students count each group of animals, and then write the numbers that tell how many.

Name ____________________

 Help  Tools  Games

Homework & Practice 3-4
Read and Write 8 and 9

Another Look!

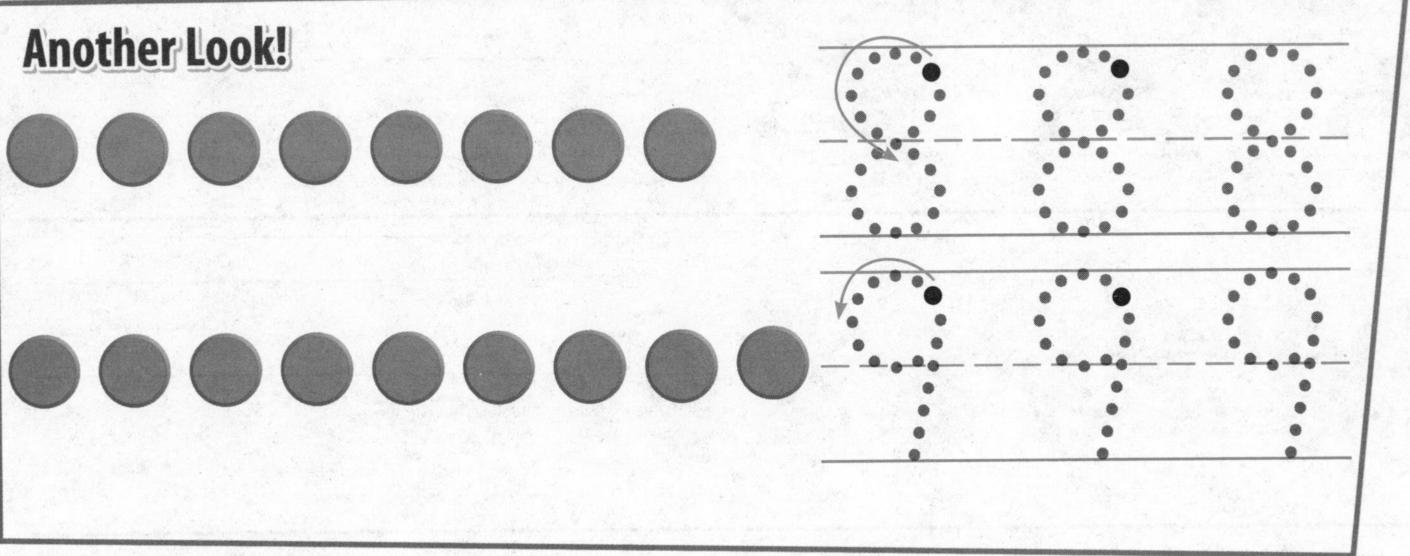

HOME ACTIVITY Draw groups of 8 and 9 circles on 2 index cards. Have your child write the correct number on the back of each card. Then use the cards to practice counting and reading the numbers 8 and 9.

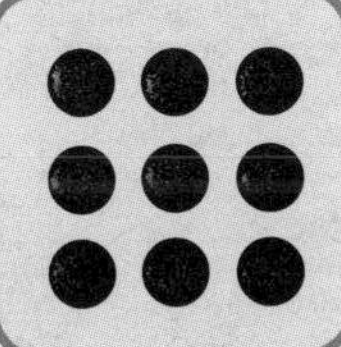

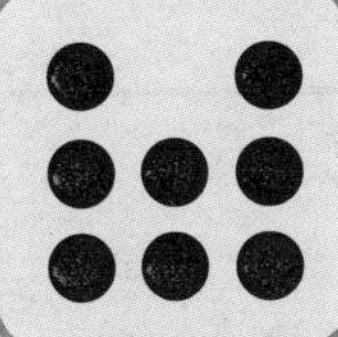

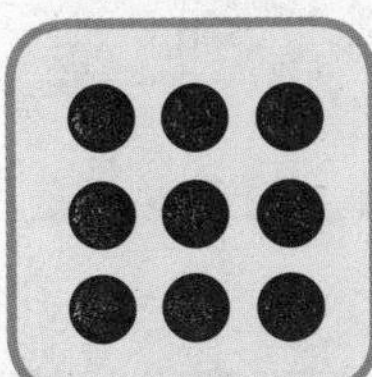

Directions Say: *Count the counters, and then practice writing the number that tells how many.* 1–3 Have students count the dots, and then practice writing the number that tells how many.

Directions 4 and 5 Have students count the animals, and then practice writing the number that tells how many. 6 **Higher Order Thinking** Have students draw more beach balls to show 9, and then practice writing the number 9. 7 **Higher Order Thinking** Have students draw 8 or 9 fish, and then practice writing the number that tells how many.

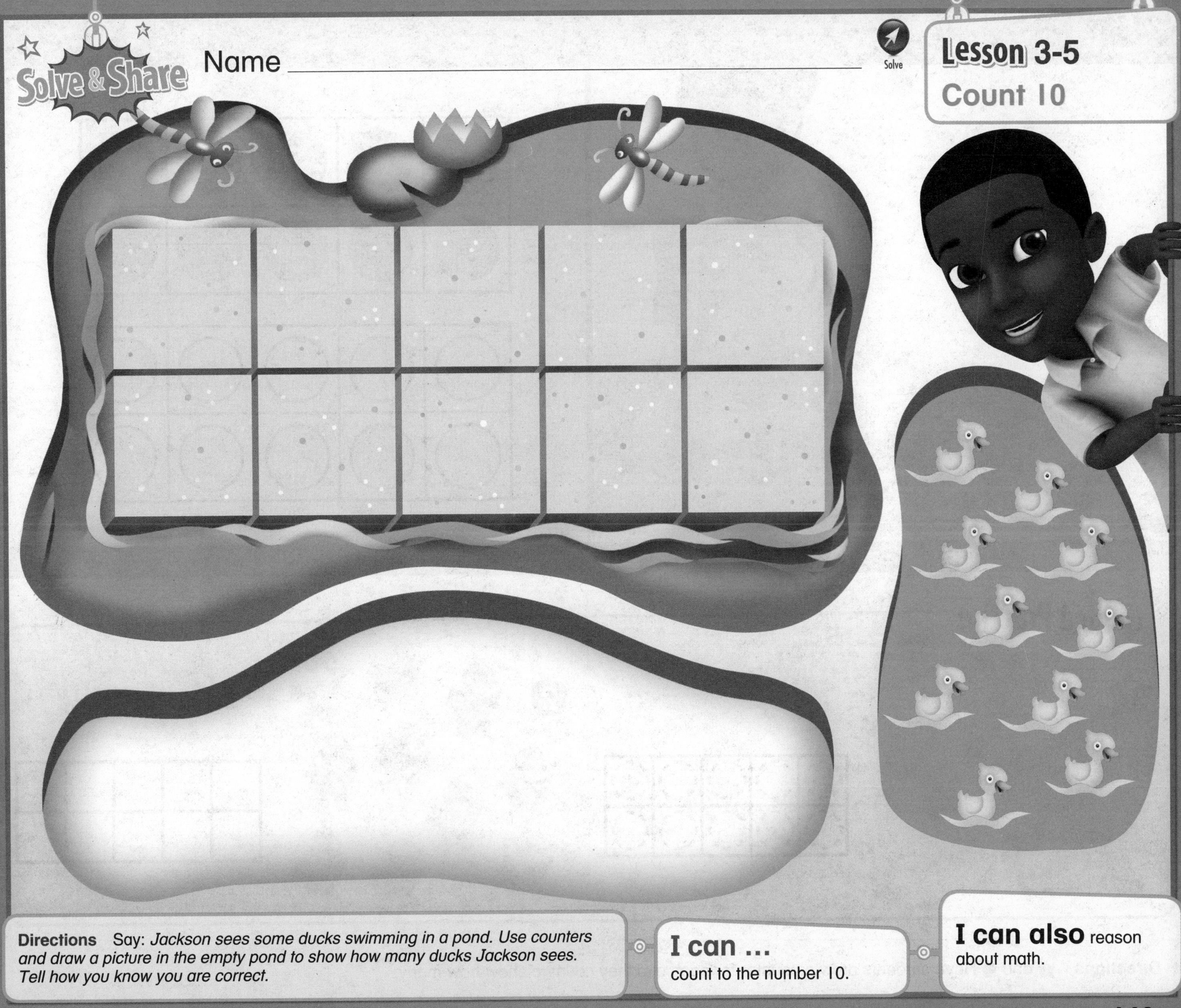

Directions Say: *Jackson sees some ducks swimming in a pond. Use counters and draw a picture in the empty pond to show how many ducks Jackson sees. Tell how you know you are correct.*

I can … count to the number 10.

I can also reason about math.

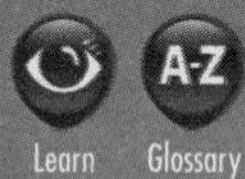

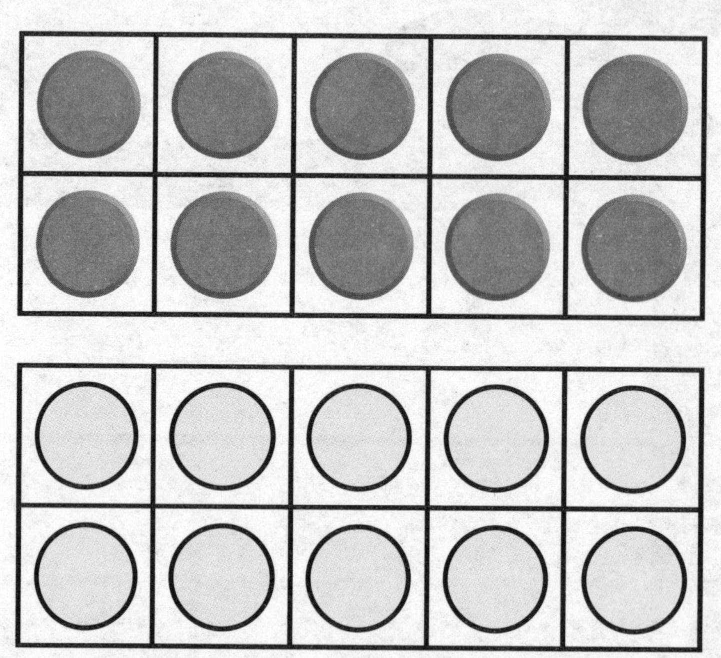

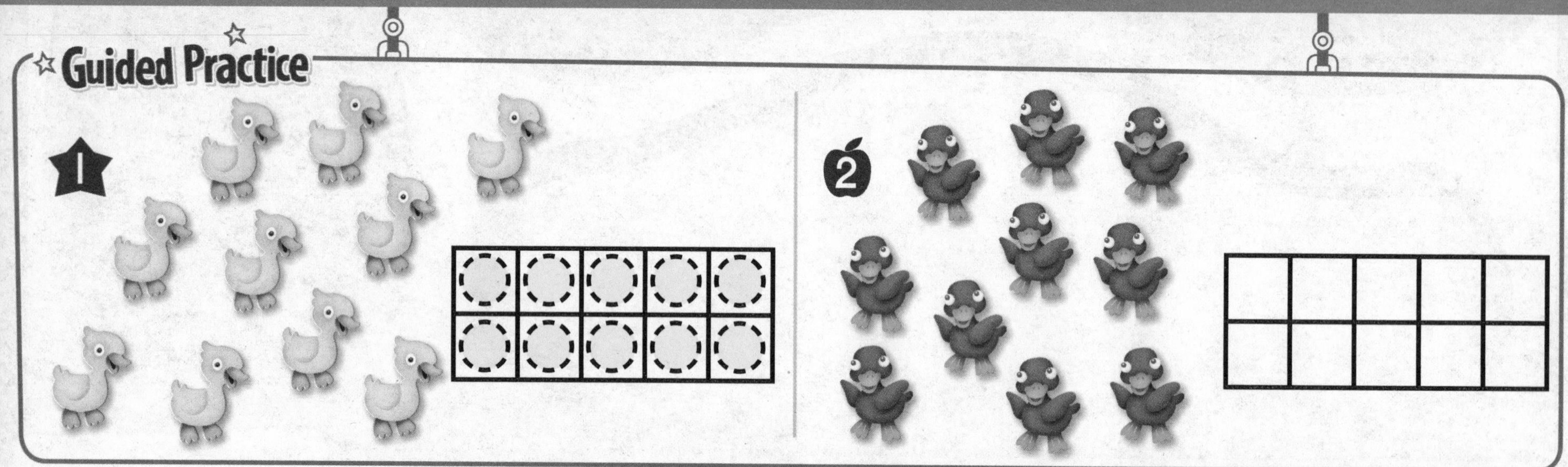

Directions 1 and 2 Have students draw a counter for each bird they count to show how many.

Name ______________________________

3

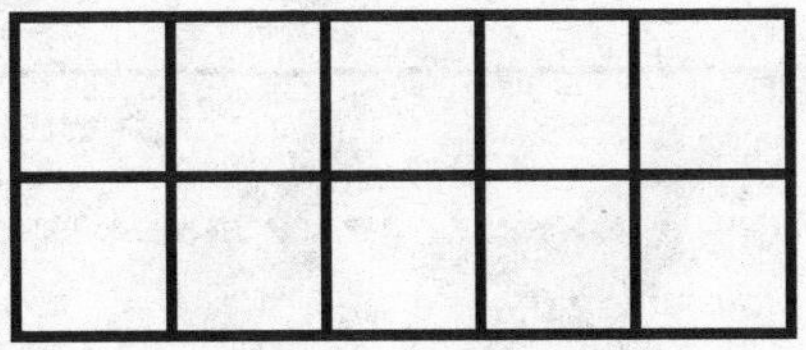

4

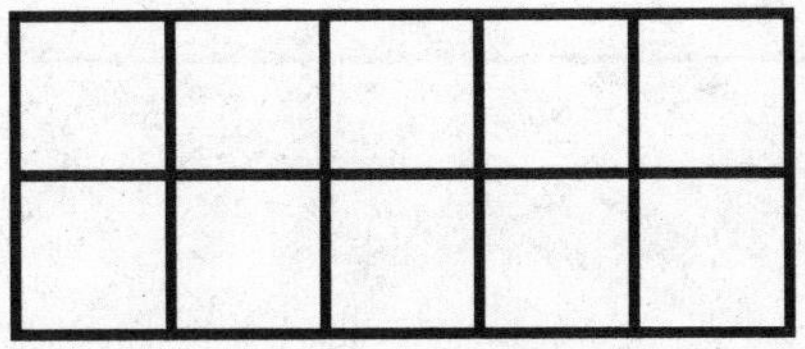

Directions 3 and 4 Have students draw a counter for each bird they count to show how many.

Independent Practice

Tools Assessment

5

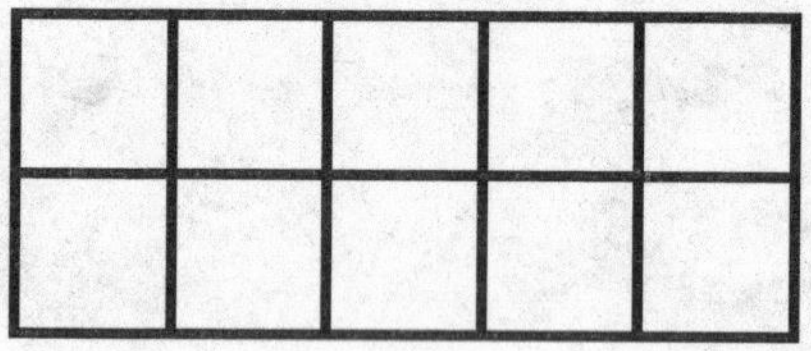

6

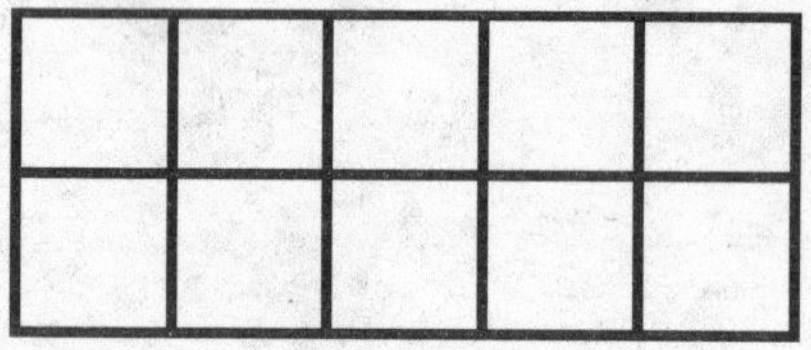

7

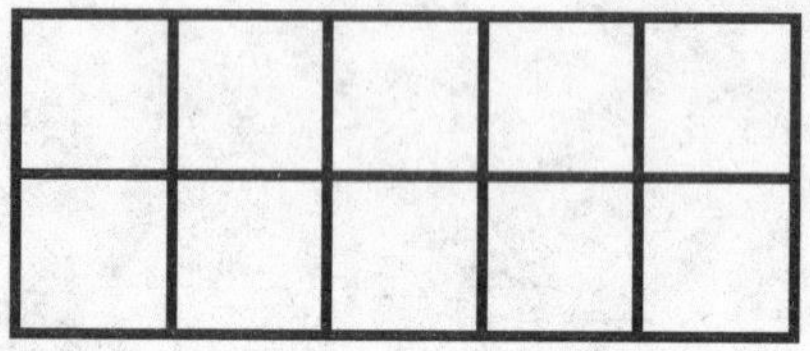

8

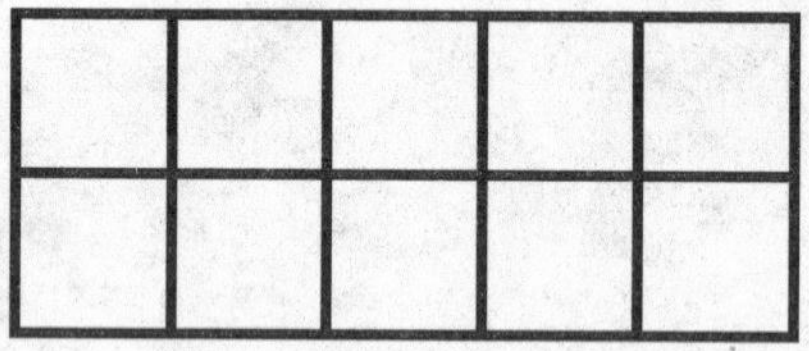

Directions 5–7 Have students draw counters as they count each bird to show how many. 8 **Higher Order Thinking** Have students draw 9 or 10 birds, and then draw a counter for each bird they draw to show how many.

Name ________________________________

 Help  Tools  Games

Homework & Practice 3-5

Count 10

HOME ACTIVITY Have your child count groups of 10 objects. Then have him or her draw pictures of 10 objects.

Another Look!

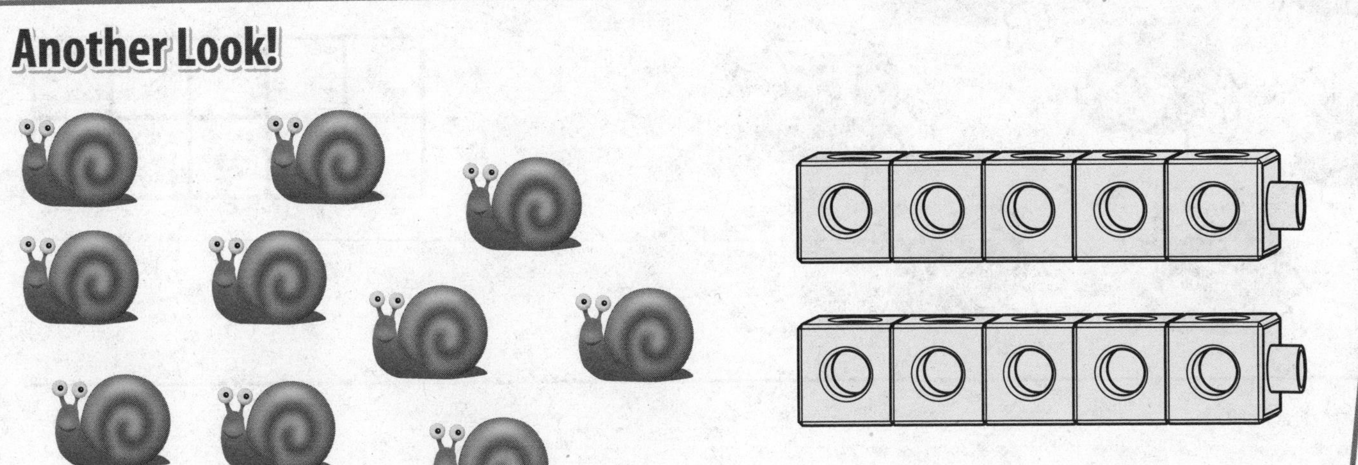

1

2

Directions Say: *Count the snails and use connecting cubes or other objects to show that number. Then color a connecting cube for each snail you counted to show the same number of cubes as snails.* 1 and 2 Have students count the insects, use connecting cubes or other objects to show that number, and then color a connecting cube for each insect they count to show the same number of cubes as insects.

3

4

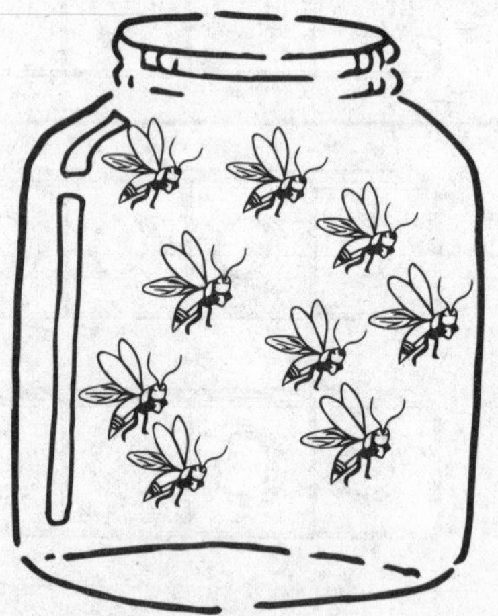

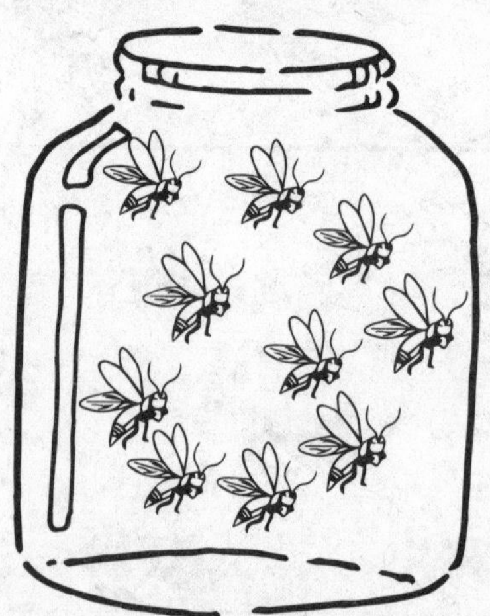

Directions 3 Have students count the ladybugs, and then draw counters to show how many. 4 **Higher Order Thinking** Have students draw more worms to show 10, and then draw counters to show how many. 5 **Higher Order Thinking** Have students look at the jars, color red the jar with 9 fireflies, and then color yellow the jar with 10 fireflies.

Name ________________________________

Lesson 3-6

Read and Write 10

Directions Say: *Jackson sees 10 fish in the water. How can he show how many fish he sees? Show or draw one way on the boat.*

I can ...
read and write the number 10.

I can also model with math.

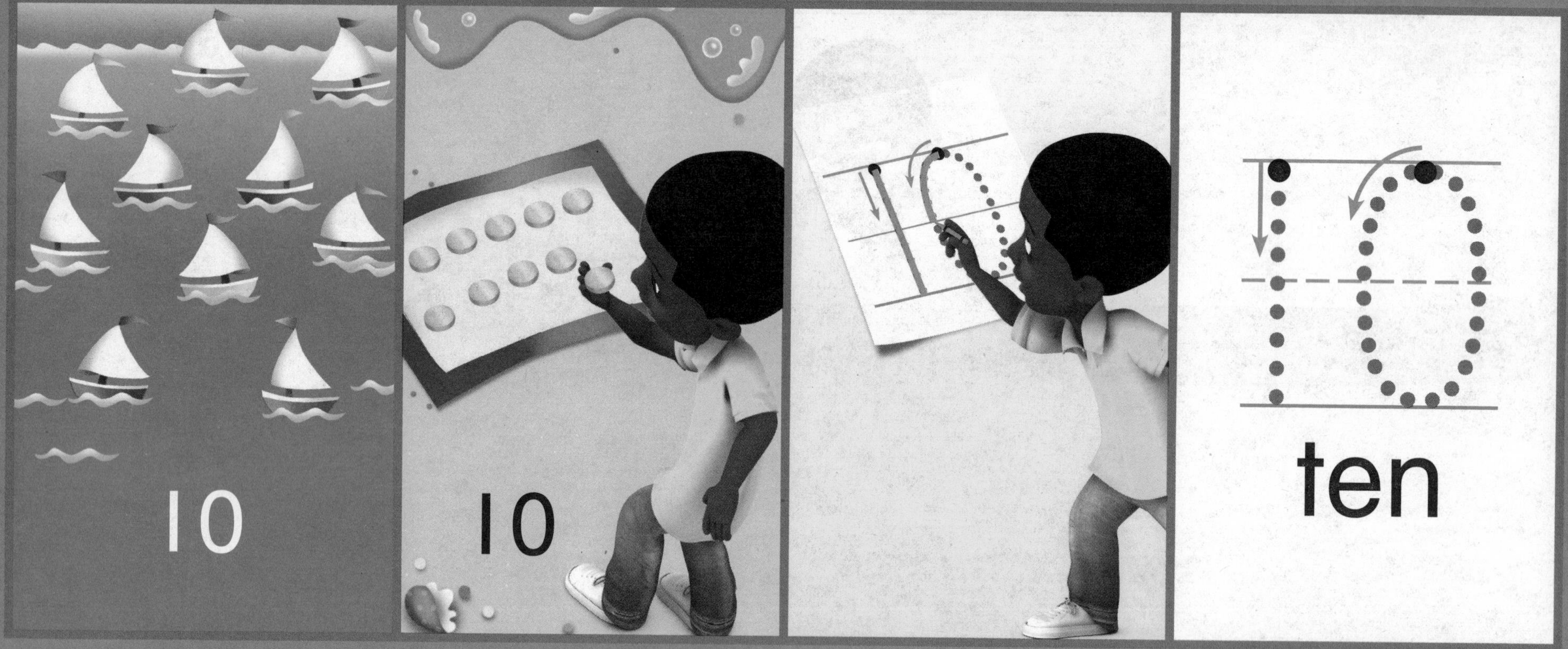

10

10

ten

Guided Practice

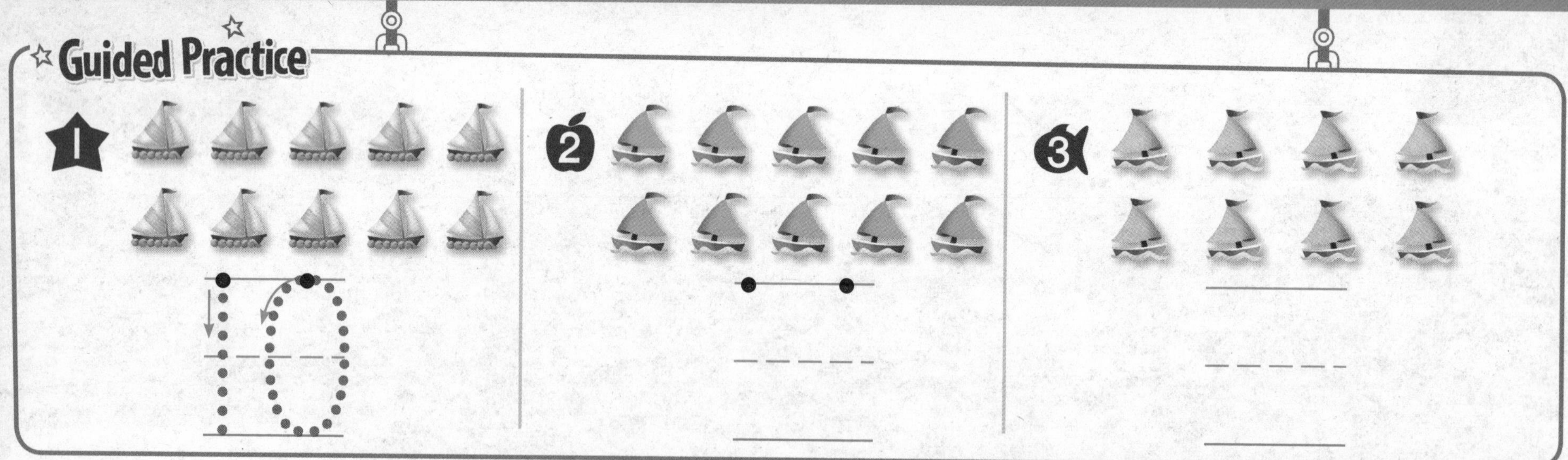

Directions ①–③ Have students count the boats, and then write the number to tell how many.

Name

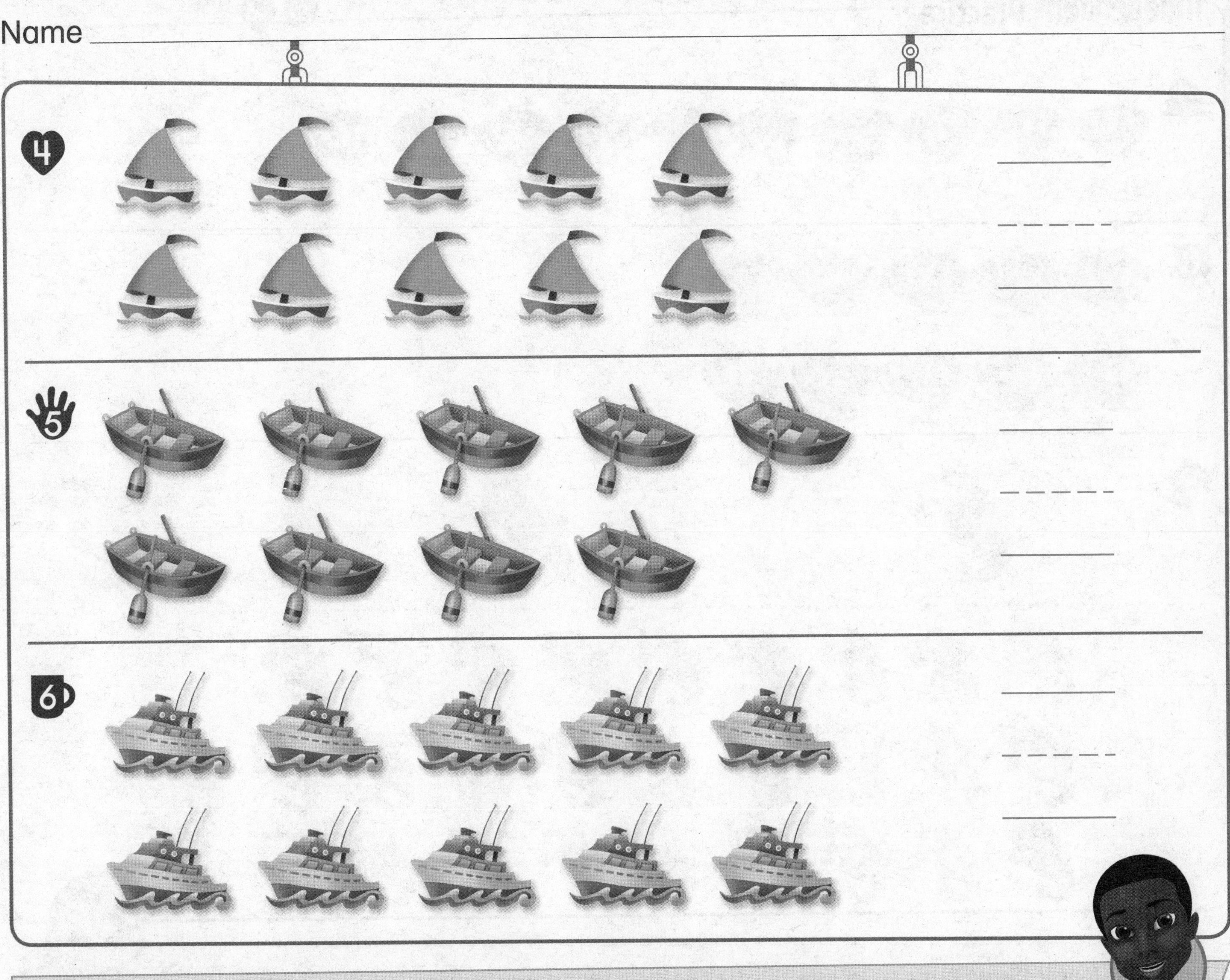

Directions 4–6 Have students count the boats, and then write the number to tell how many.

Independent Practice

Tools Assessment

7

8

9

Directions **Number Sense** 7 and 8 Have students count the shells, and then write the number to tell how many. 9 **Higher Order Thinking** Have students count each group of sea horses, and then write the numbers to tell how many.

Name ______________________________

Homework & Practice 3-6

Read and Write 10

Another Look!

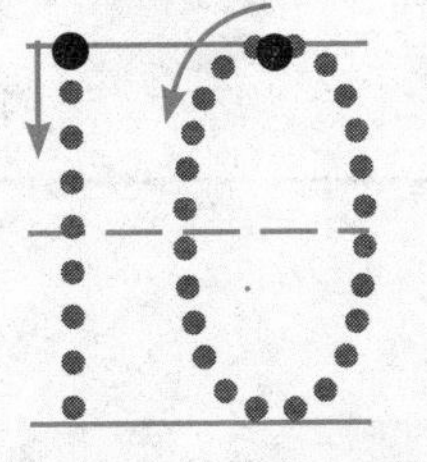

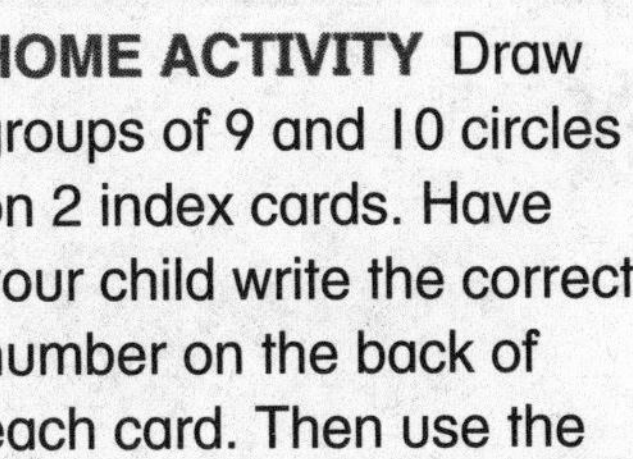

HOME ACTIVITY Draw groups of 9 and 10 circles on 2 index cards. Have your child write the correct number on the back of each card. Then use the cards to practice counting and reading the numbers 9 and 10.

Directions Say: *Count the sea stars, and then write the number to tell how many.* ★1 Have students count each group of sea stars, and then write the number to tell how many.

2

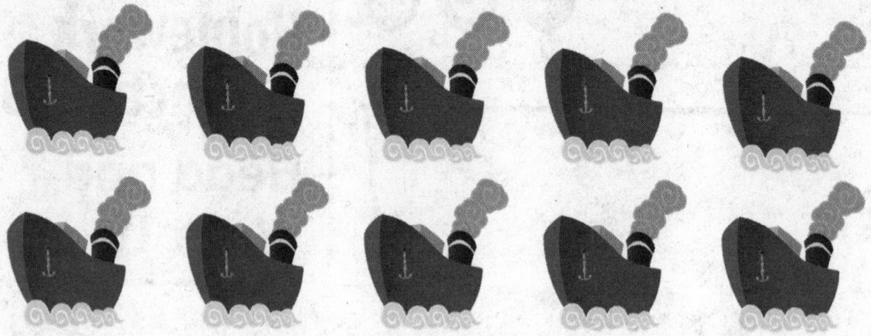

3

4

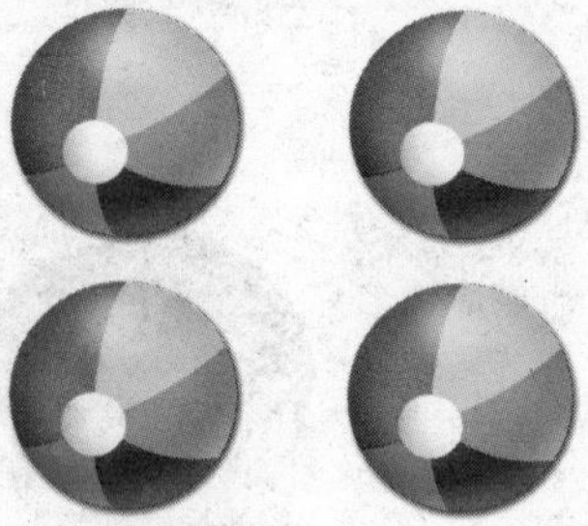

5

Directions Have students: 2 count the boats, and then practice writing the number that tells how many; 3 count the shells, and then write the number to tell how many. 4 **Higher Order Thinking** Have students draw more beach balls to show 10, and then practice writing the number 10. 5 **Higher Order Thinking** Have students draw 10 shells, and then write the number to tell how many.

Name ______________________________

Lesson 3-7

Ways to Make 10

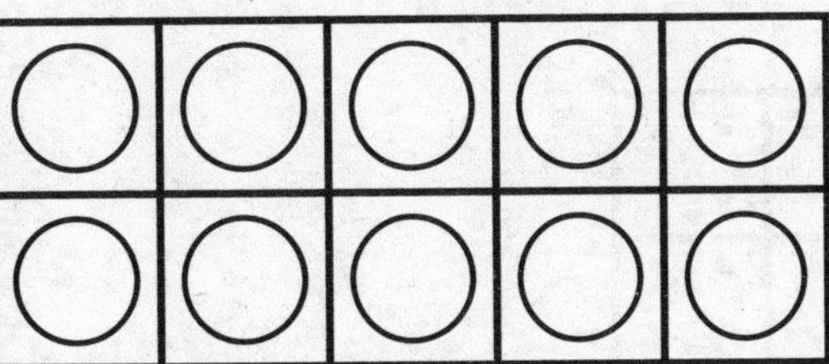

Directions Say: *Jackson puts 10 watering cans on a shelf in the garden store. How can you use counters to show the 10 watering cans in a different way? Color the counters red and yellow to show your work.*

I can ...
show how to make a group of 10.

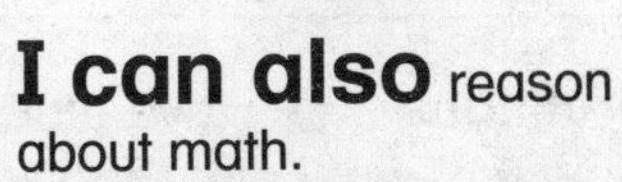

I can also reason about math.

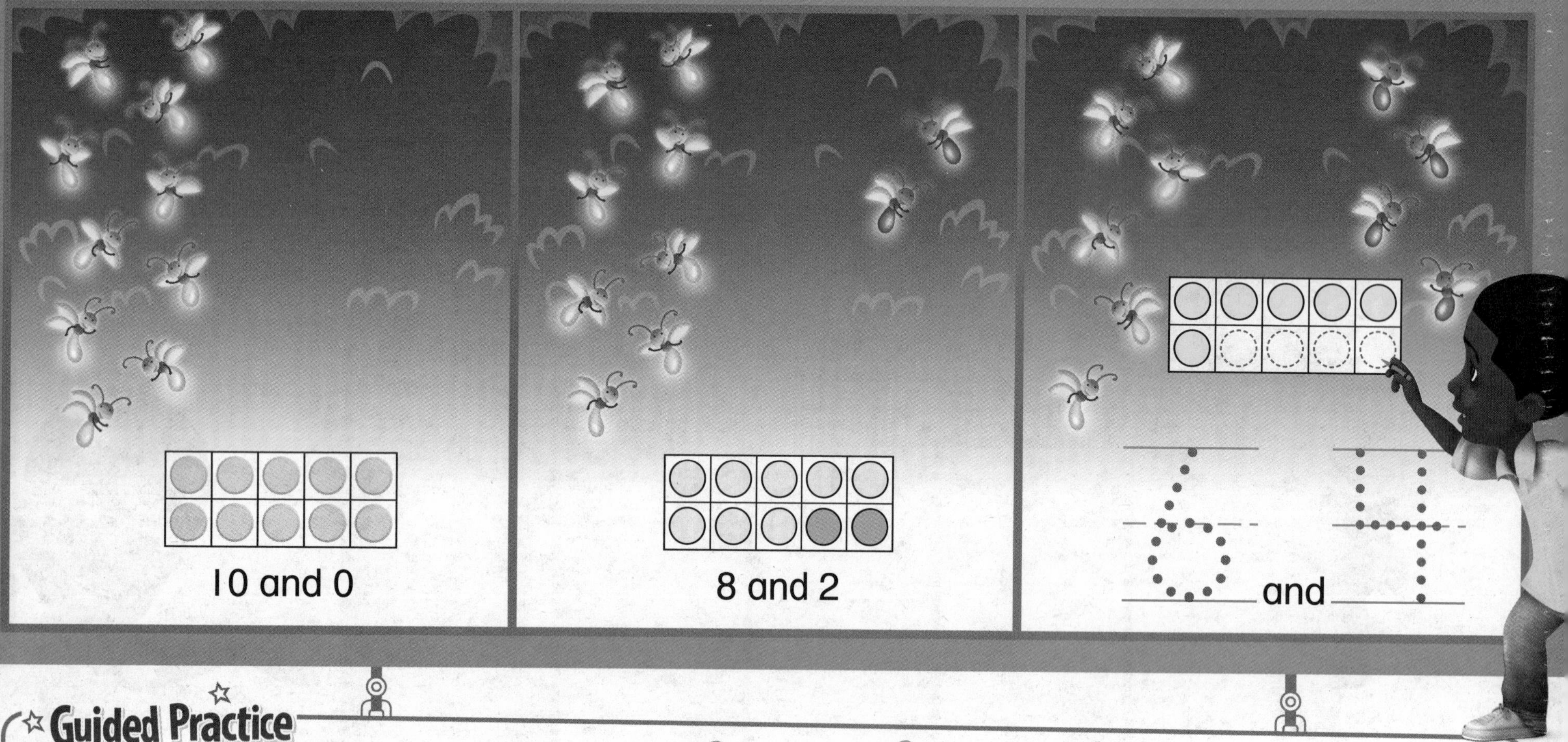

10 and 0

8 and 2

6 and 4

Guided Practice

1

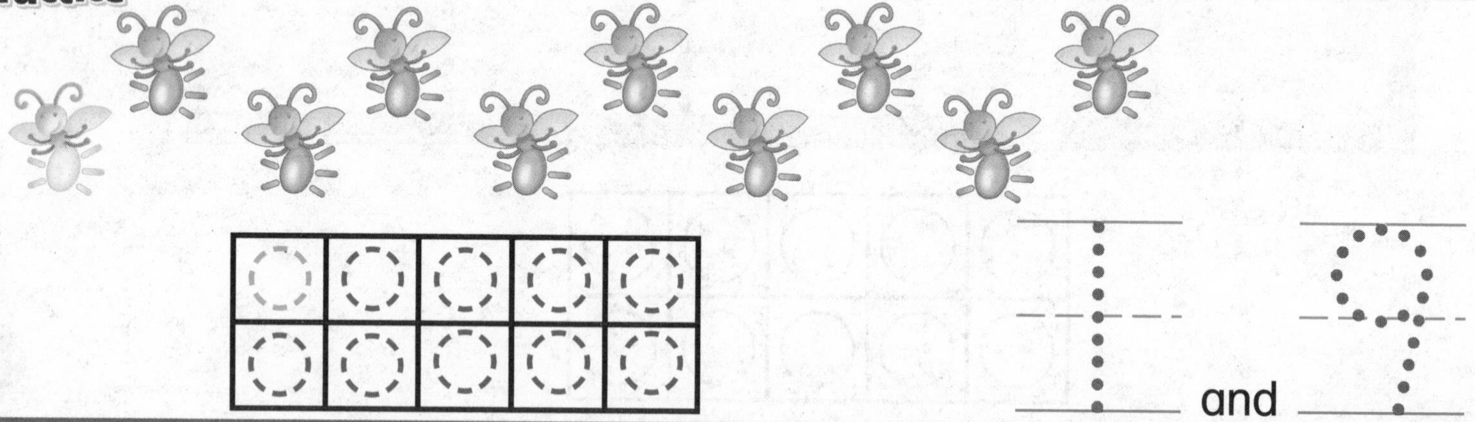

1 and 9

Directions 1 Have students draw and color counters red and yellow to show one way to make 10, color the fireflies red and yellow to show that way, and then write the numbers.

Name ______________________________

2

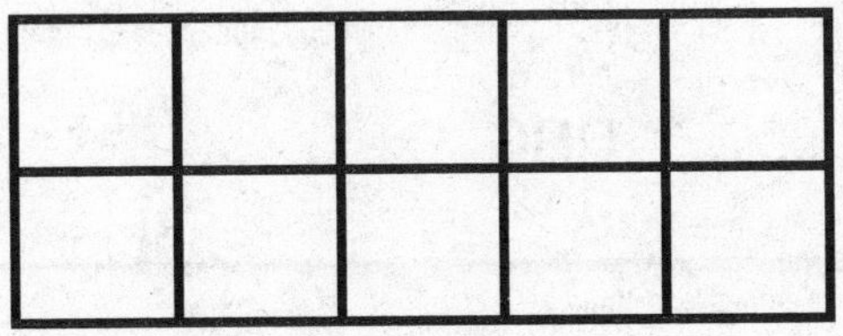

______ ______

______ ______

______ and ______

3

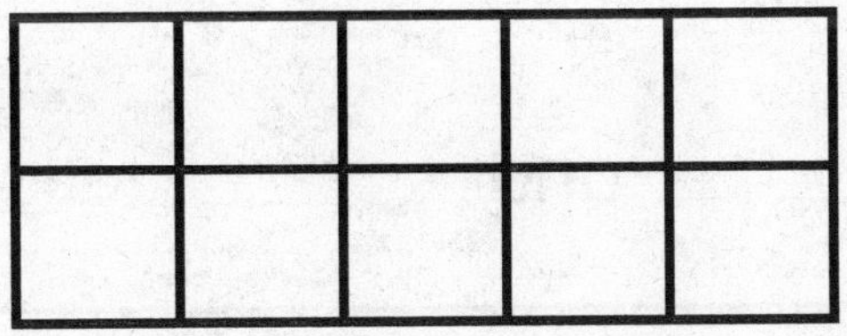

______ ______

______ ______

______ and ______

4

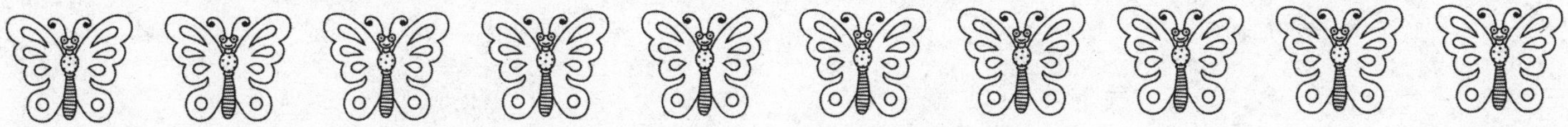

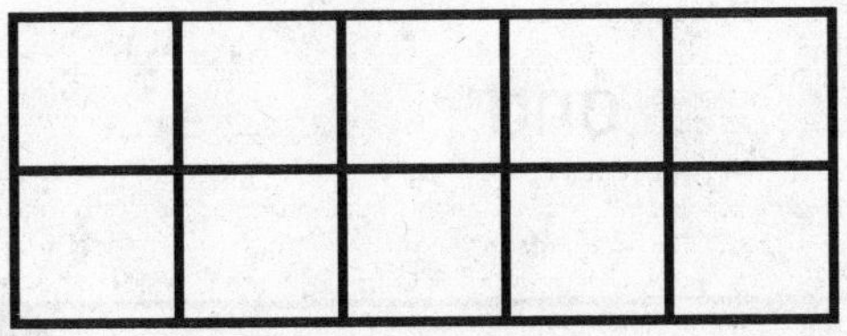

______ ______

______ ______

______ and ______

Directions 2–4 Have students draw and color counters red and yellow to show one way to make 10, color the insects red and yellow to show each way, and then write the numbers.

Independent Practice

Tools Assessment

5

______ ______

______ and ______

6

______ ______

______ and ______

7

______ ______

______ and ______

Directions 5 and 6 Have students draw and color counters red and yellow to show one way to make 10, color the insects red and yellow to show each way, and then write the numbers. 7 **Higher Order Thinking** Have students draw a way to make 10, and then write the numbers.

Name ______________________

Help Tools Games

Homework & Practice 3-7

Ways to Make 10

Another Look!

5 and 5

HOME ACTIVITY Have your child show the number 10 in different ways using 10 cards or pictures. Ask your child to tell the two parts that make the 10. Have your child show one part of the 10 pictures or cards facedown and the other part faceup.

1. ______ and ______

2. ______ and ______

Directions Say: *Use red and blue cubes or pieces of paper to model this way to make 10, and then write the numbers.* 1 and 2 **Vocabulary** Have students use red and blue cubes or pieces of paper to find two different ways to make **ten**, draw the cubes to show each way, and then write the numbers.

3

4 and

4

3 and

5

0 and

6

and

and

Directions Have students: 3 and 4 find the way to make 10, draw objects to show the way, and then write the numbers; 5 find the way to make 10, draw flowers to show the way, and then write the number. 6 **Higher Order Thinking** Have students draw red and yellow counters to show two different ways to make 10, and then write the numbers.

Name ___________________________

Problem Solving

Lesson 3-8

Look For and Use Structure

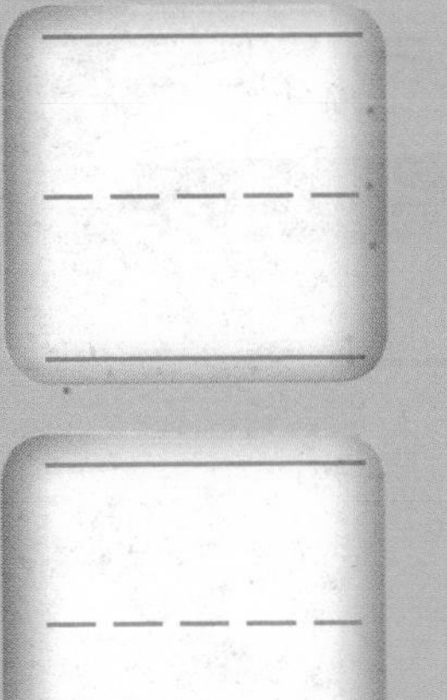

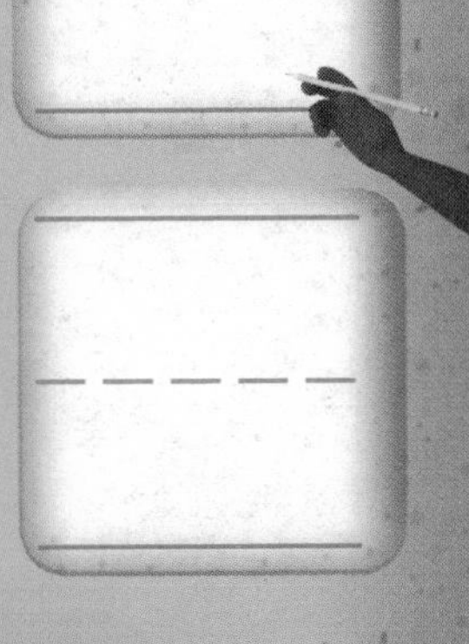

Directions Say: *Jackson decorates his sand castle with 3 shells. He has two different colors of shells. He wants to show all the ways to decorate his sand castle with 3 shells. How can he use a pattern to show all the ways to make 3?*

I can ...
use counting patterns to solve a problem.

I can also count to 10.

Guided Practice

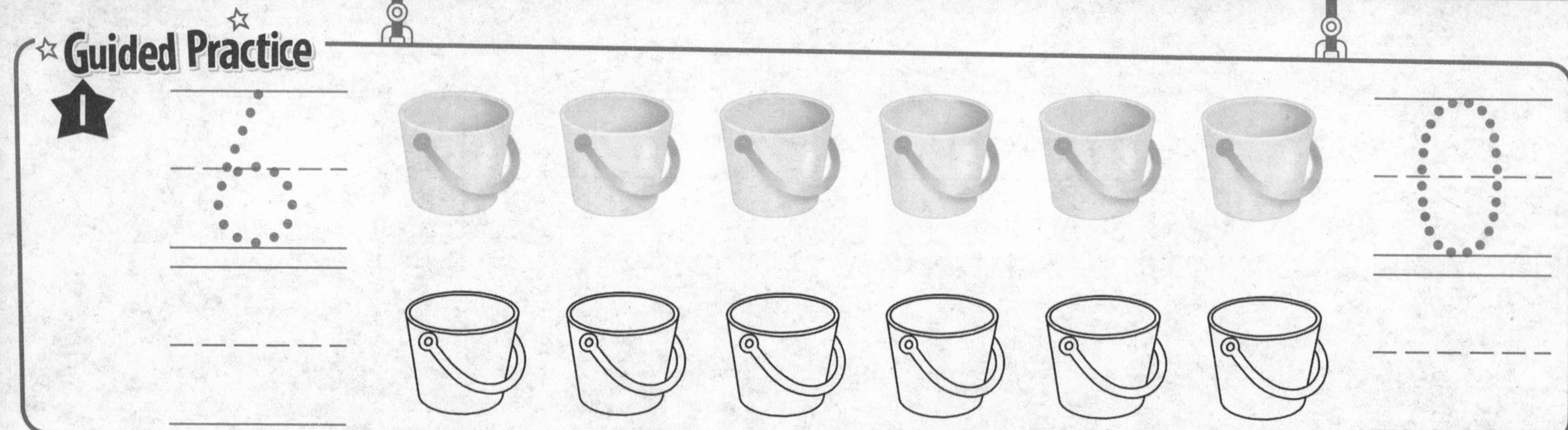

Directions Say: *How can you color the pails to show different ways to make 6?* **1** Have students use red and yellow crayons to make a pattern showing two ways to make 6, and then write the numbers. Have them describe the pattern.

Name

Independent Practice

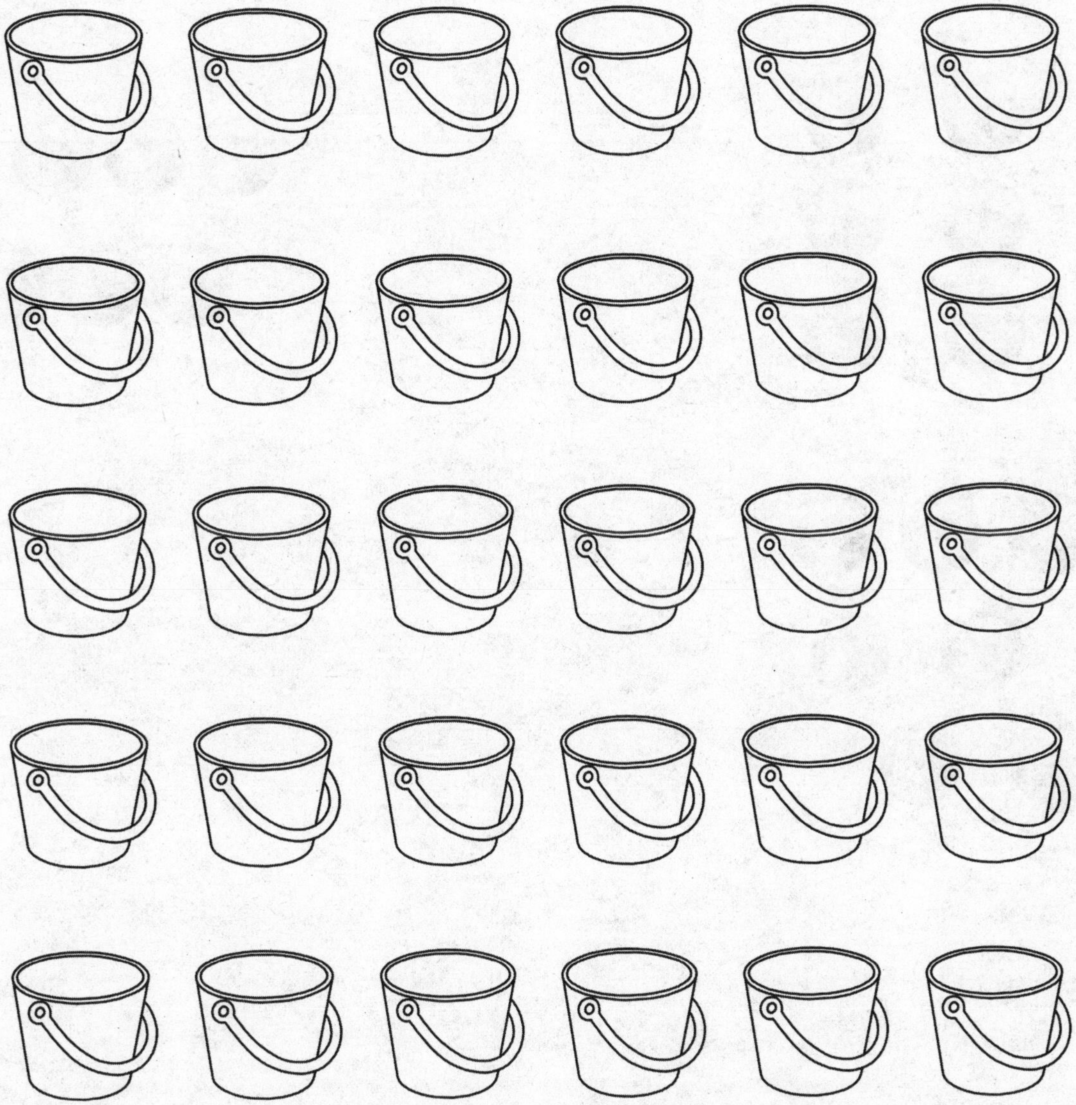

Directions Say: *How can you color the pails to show different ways to make 6?* ❷ Have students look at Items 1 and 2, and then use red and yellow crayons to complete the pattern showing five ways to make 6. Then have them write the numbers, and then describe the pattern.

Directions Read the problem to students. Then have them use multiple problem-solving methods to solve the problem. Say: *Mr. Sand runs a game at the beach. The prizes are red and blue beach balls. He displays them in a pattern. What is the next row in the pattern?* **Use Tools** *What tool can you use to help solve the problem?* **Generalize** *How can the ways that are shown help you find the next way to make 9?* **Look for Patterns** *What is the next way in the pattern to make 9? Write the numbers for that way.*

Name ______________________

Help

Tools
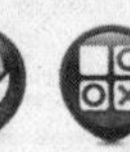
Games

Homework & Practice 3-8

Look For and Use Structure

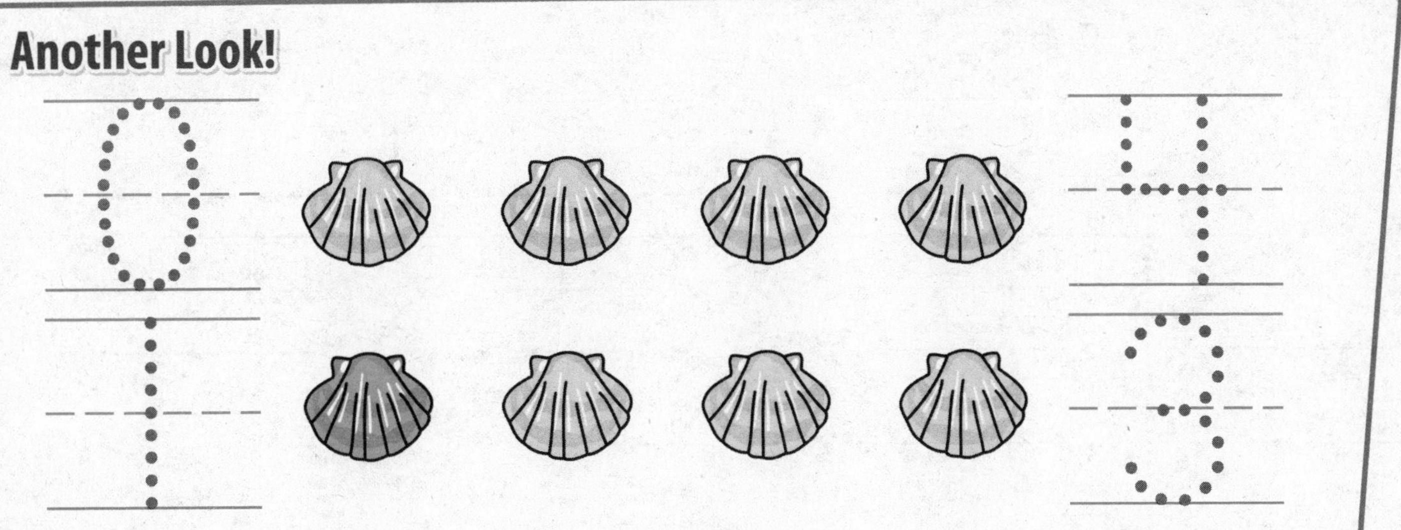

HOME ACTIVITY Place 10 crayons in a row across a table (pointing upward). Ask your child to show a way to make 10 by pointing 1 crayon down. Ask your child to write the numbers for the two groups (1 and 9). Then have your child use the crayons to show all the other ways to make 10 and then write the numbers.

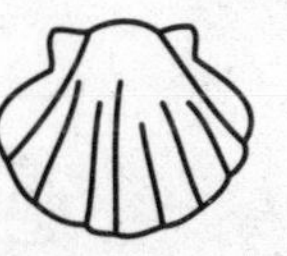  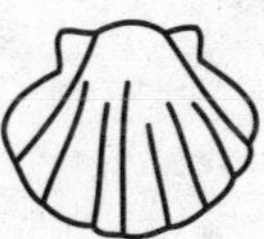 

 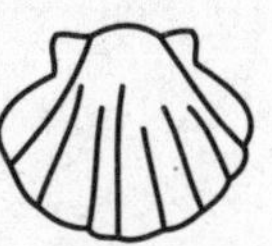 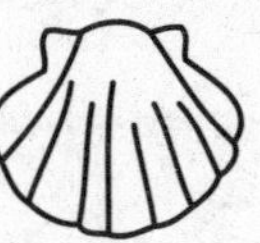 

  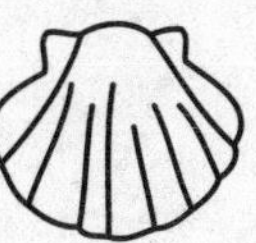 

Directions Say: *You can make a pattern to show all of the different ways to make 4. First, you can color to show 0 red shells and 4 yellow shells. Next, you can color to show 1 red shell and 3 yellow shells. Write the numbers.* ★1 Say: *Show three other ways to make 4.* Have students color the shells red and yellow to complete the pattern showing all the ways to make 4, and then write the numbers. Have them describe the pattern.

Performance Assessment

Directions Read the problem to students. Then have them use multiple problem-solving methods to solve the problem. Say: *Elijah has red and yellow napkins. He must set out napkins for 4 people. What are all the ways to make 4?* ❷ **Make Sense** *What is a good plan for solving the problem?* ❸ **Look for and Make Use of Structure** *What are all the ways to make 4? Write the ways on the lines at the top of the page.* ❹ **Reasoning** *How do you know that you have found all of the ways to make 4?*

Name ______________________

A-Z Glossary

1

2

8 9

3

5 _____ 7

4

Directions **Understand Vocabulary** Have students: 1 write the number **eight**; 2 draw a circle around the number **nine**; 3 write the missing number and then say it aloud; 4 write the parts that make 10.

5

10 9

6

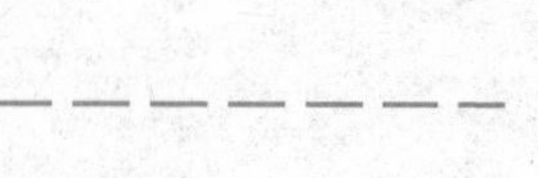

7

8

Directions **Understand Vocabulary** Have students: 5 draw a circle around the number **ten**; 6 write the number **seven**; 7 count the number of cubes, and then write the number to tell how many; 8 write numbers 1 to 10 in order.

Name ______

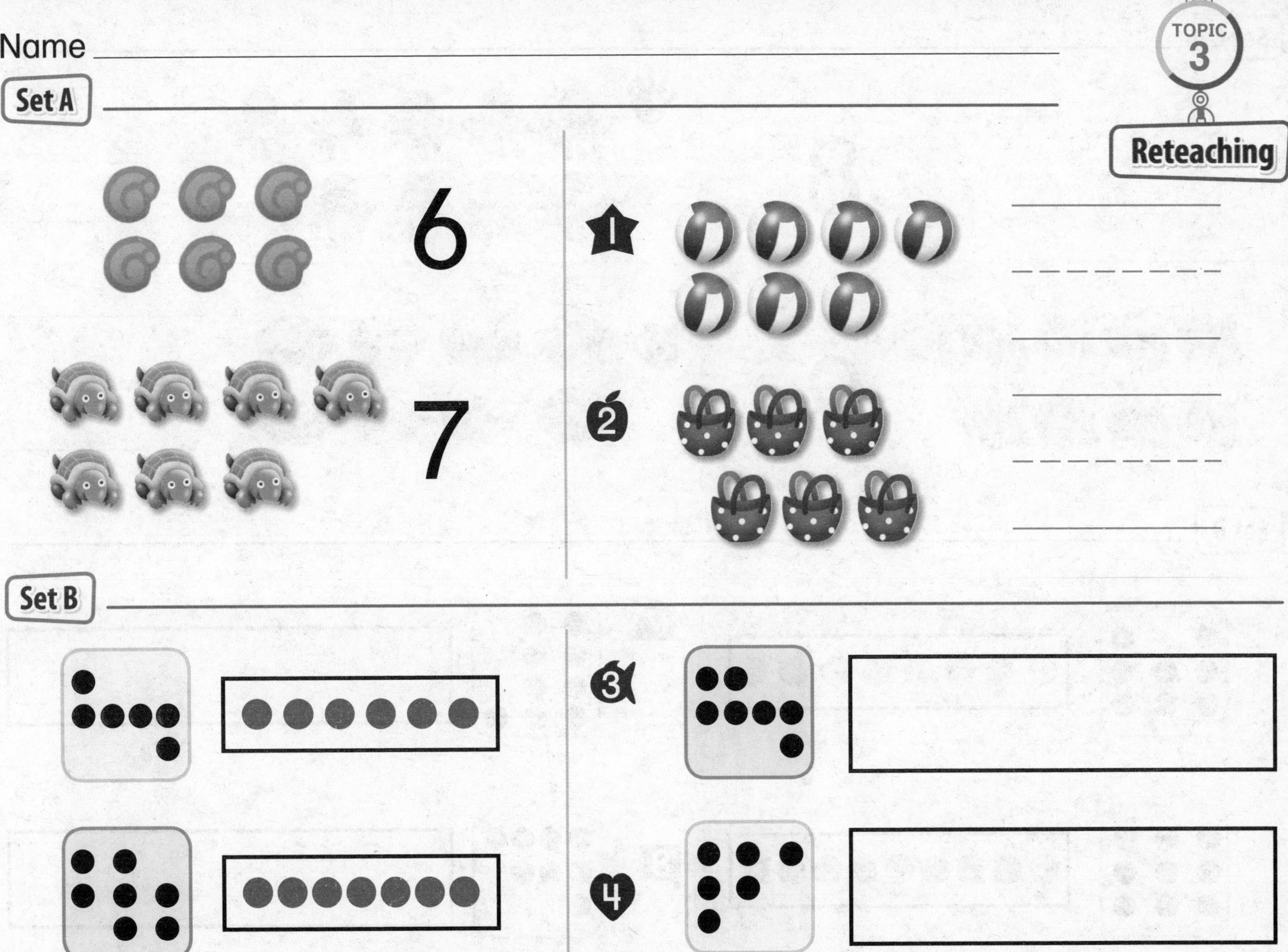

Directions Have students: 1 and 2 count the objects, and then write the numbers to tell how many; 3 and 4 count the number of dots, place a counter for each dot they count, and then draw counters in the box to show the same number of counters as dots in a different way.

Set C

8

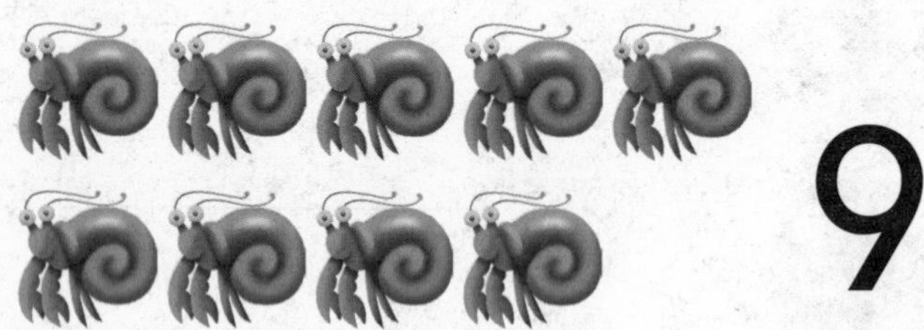

9

5

6

Set D

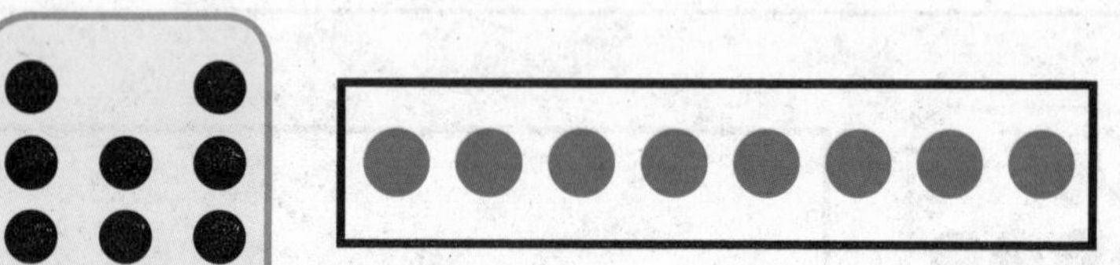

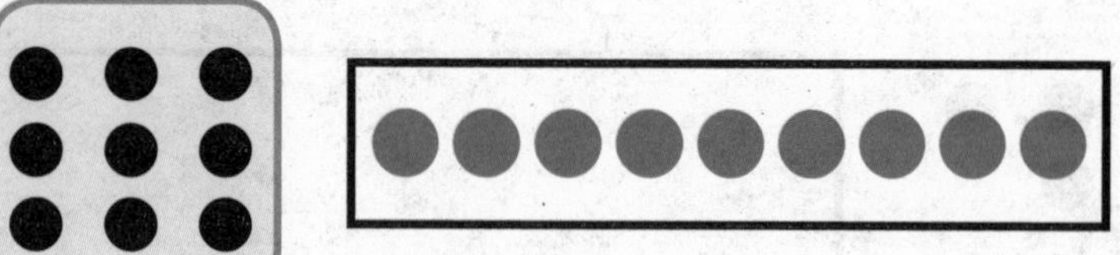

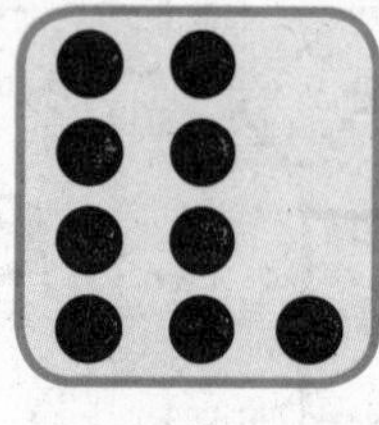

8

Directions Have students: 5 and 6 count the objects, and then write the number to tell how many; 7 and 8 count the number of dots, place a counter as they count each dot, and then draw counters in the box to show the same number of counters as dots in a different way.

Name ______________________________

Set E

9

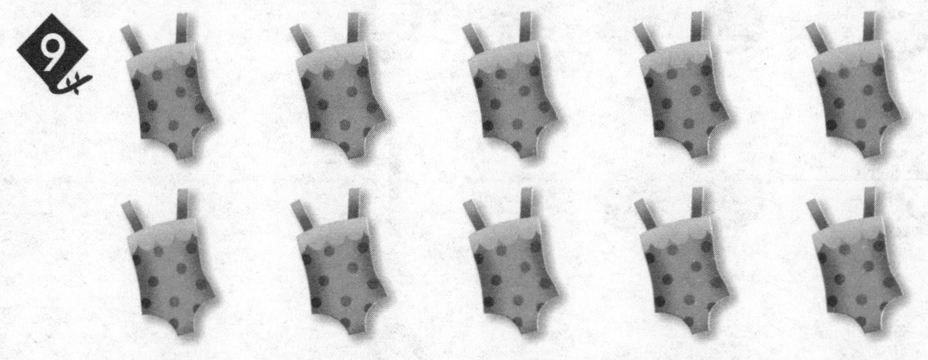

Set F

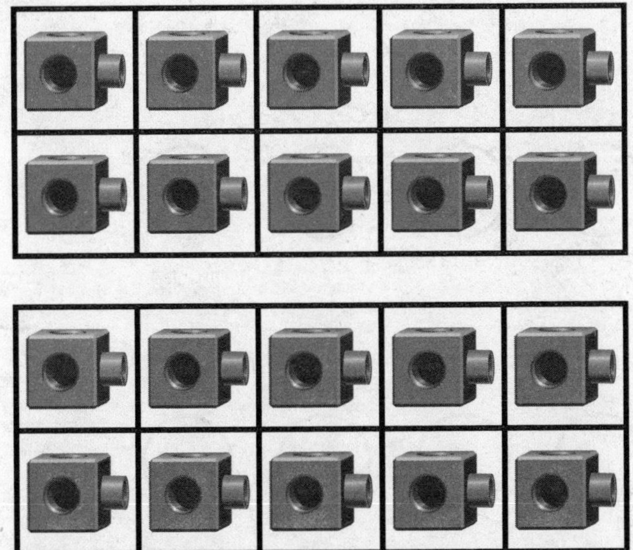

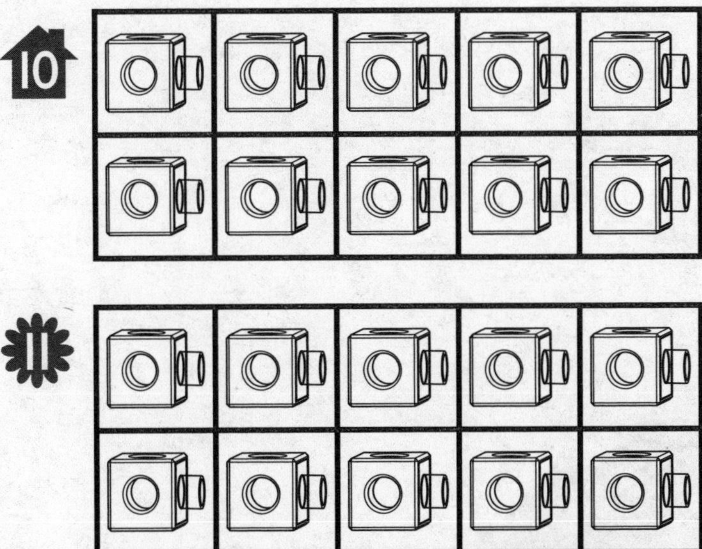

Directions Have students: count the objects, and then practice writing the number that tells how many; and color the connecting cubes red and blue to show two different ways to make 10.

Set G

3	● ● ●	0
2	● ● ○	1
1	● ○ ○	2
0	○ ○ ○	3

12 4 ○ ○ ○ ○ 0

○ ○ ○ ○

2 ○ ○ ○ ○

○ ○ ○ ○

○ ○ ○ ○

Directions 12 Have students use two different colored crayons to complete the pattern showing all of the ways to make 4, and then write the numbers.

Name ______________________________

4 Ⓐ 5 Ⓑ 6 Ⓒ 7 Ⓓ

2

7 Ⓐ 8 Ⓑ 9 Ⓒ 10 Ⓓ

3

Ⓐ 10 Ⓒ 8

Ⓑ 9 Ⓓ 7

4

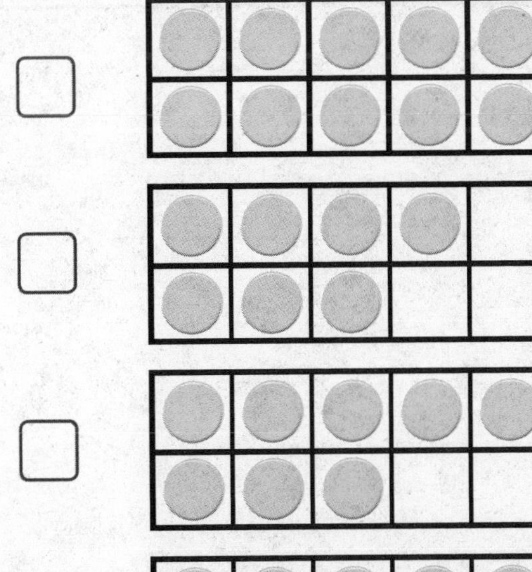

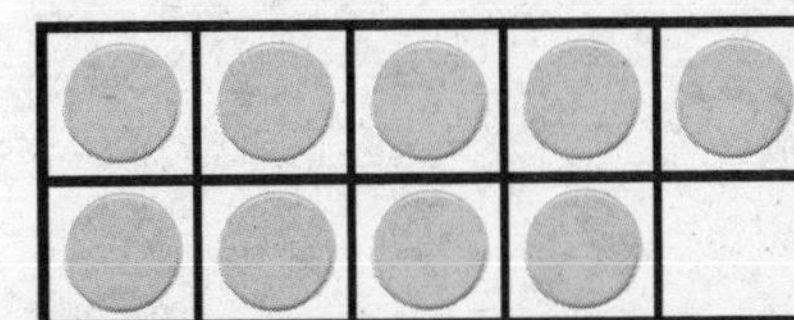

Directions Have students mark the best answer. 1 How many fish are there? 2 How many turtles are there? 3 Which number tells how many swimsuits? 4 Mark all the answers that do NOT show 9.

8

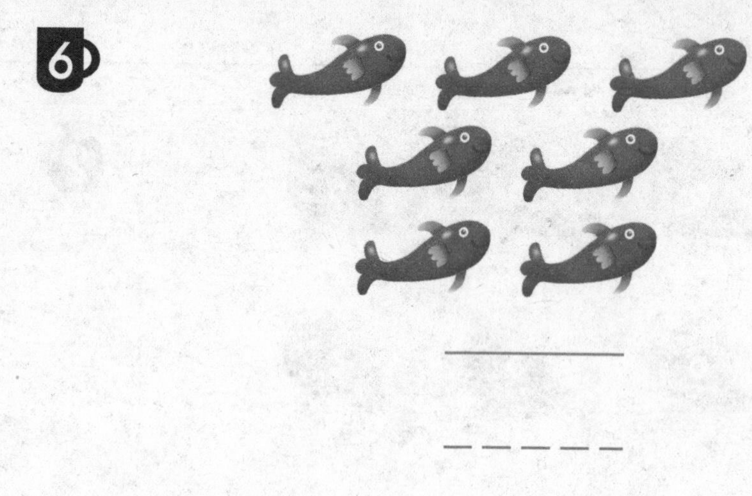

7

Directions Have students: 5 read the number, and then draw animals to show how many; 6 count the fish, and then write the number to tell how many; 7 draw ten shells, and then write the number to tell how many.

Name ______________________________

8

and

9

Directions Have students: **8** draw red and yellow counters to show one way to make 10, color the apples red and yellow to show that way, and then write the numbers; **9** draw more turtles to show 10, and then draw counters to show how many turtles in all.

Directions Have students use red and yellow crayons to complete the pattern showing six ways to make 5, and then write the numbers.

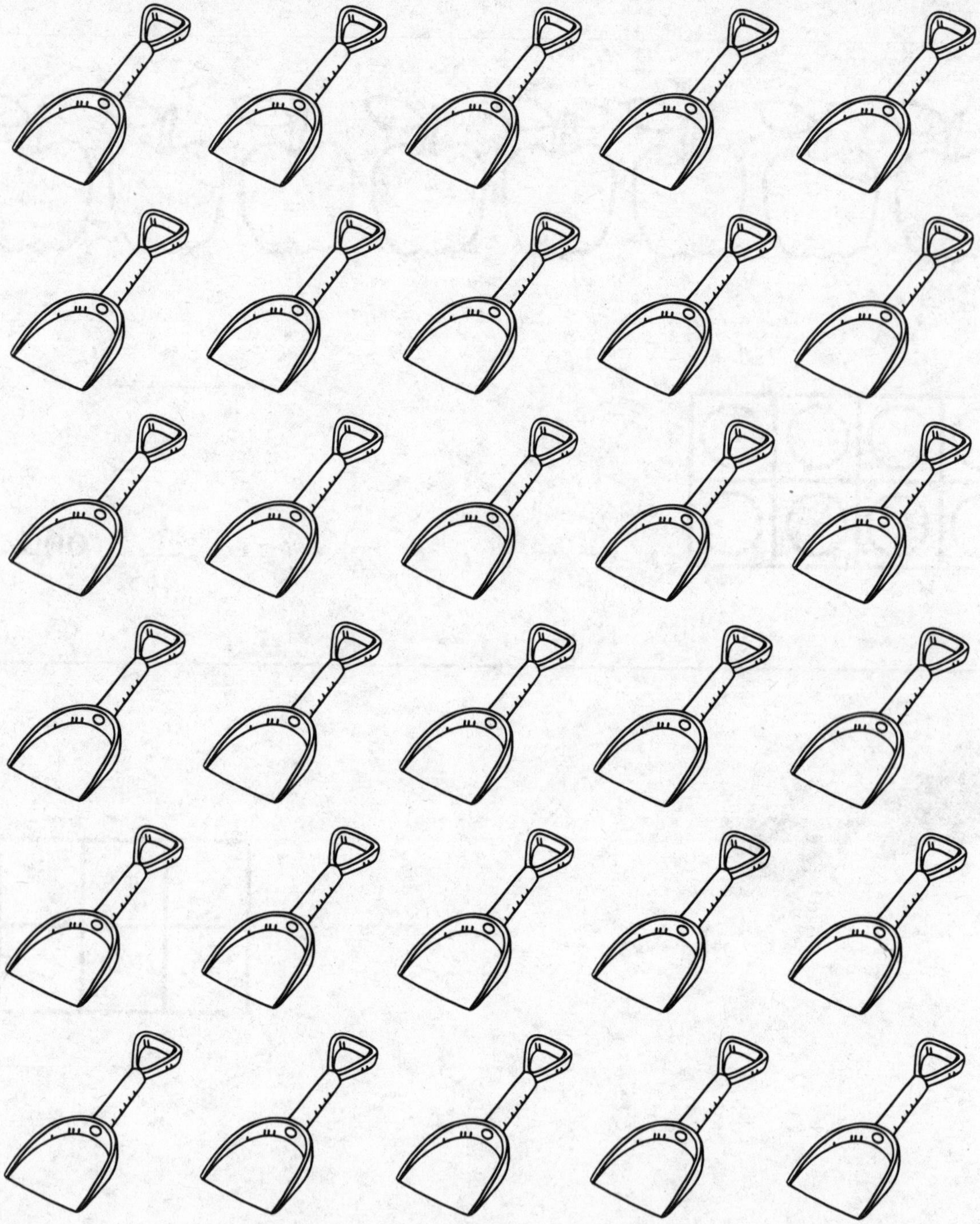

Name

Directions **The Beach** Say: *Lexi sees many interesting things at the beach.* Have students count how many there are of each object, and then write the number to tell how many. The fish that Lexi sees show one way to make 10. Color the fish red and yellow to show two different ways to make 10. Then write the numbers.

Directions Say: *The beach towels that Lexi sees show one way to make 7.* Have students color the beach towels blue and red to make a pattern that shows different ways to make 7, and then write the numbers.

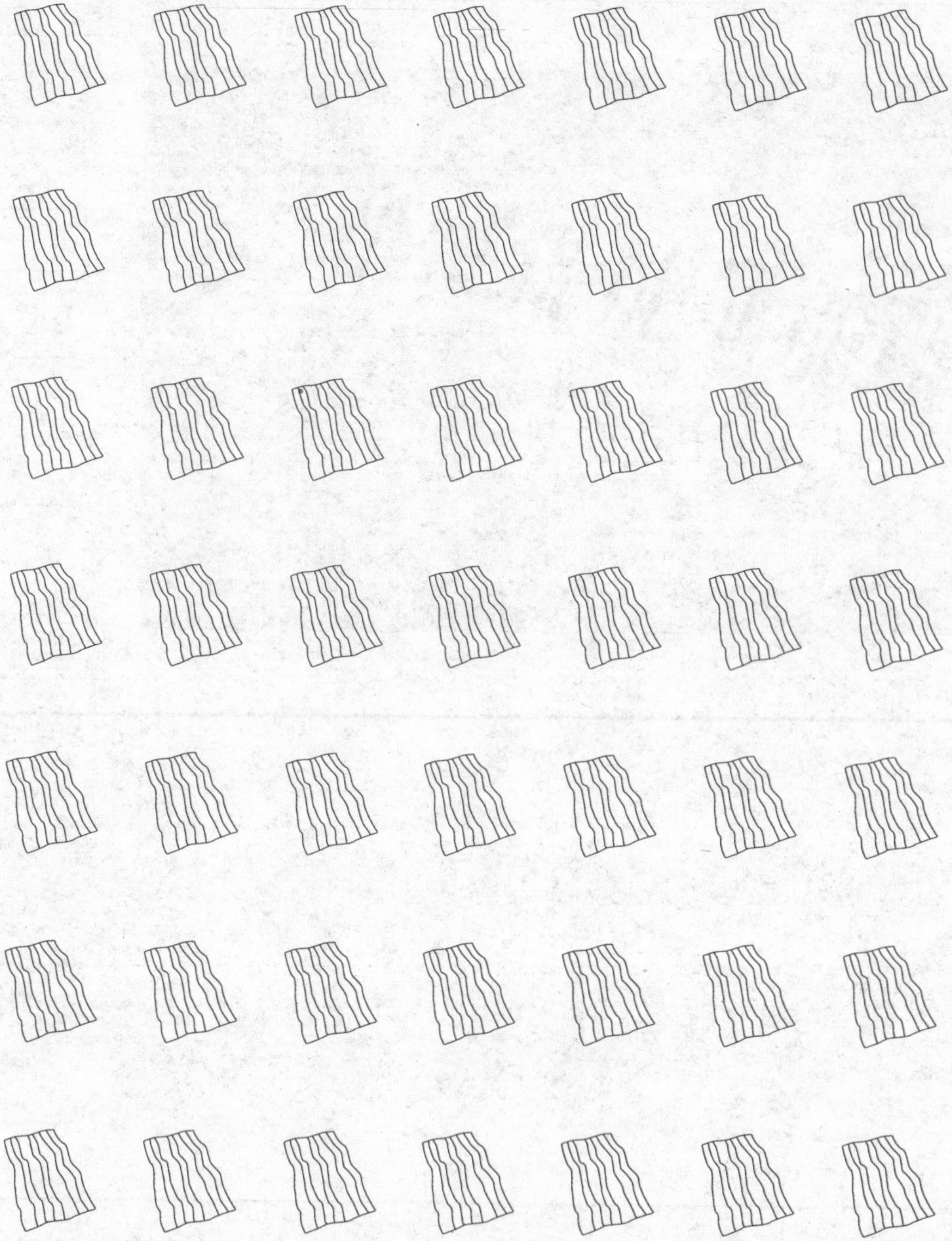

Compare Numbers 0 to 10

TOPIC 4

Essential Question: How can numbers from 0 to 10 be compared and ordered?

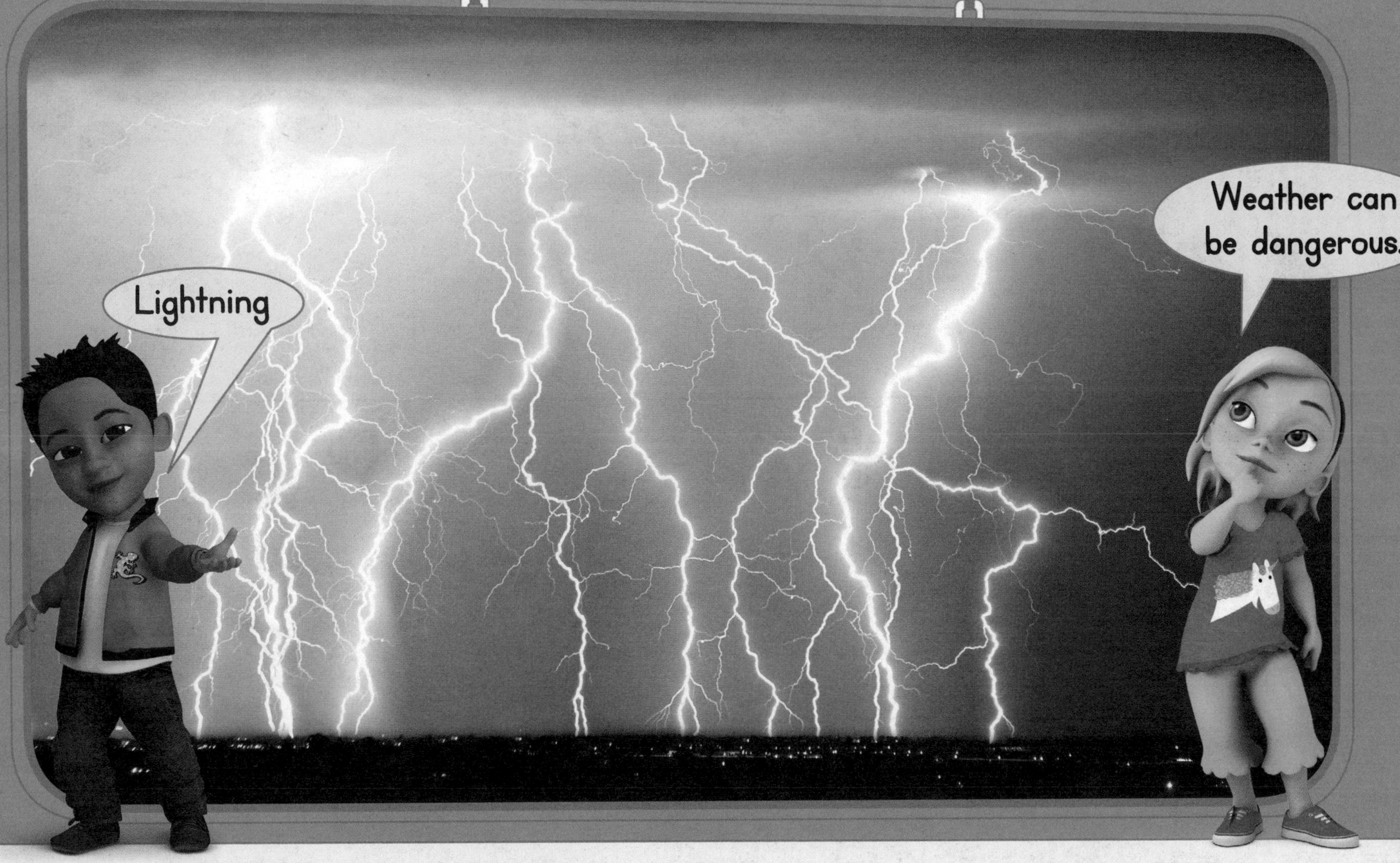

Math and Science Project: Weather Changes

Directions Read the character speech bubbles to students. **Find Out!** Have students find out about weather changes. Say: *The weather changes from day to day. Talk to friends and relatives about the weather. Ask them to help you record the number of sunny days and rainy days during the week.* **Journal: Make a Poster** Have students make a poster. Have them draw up to 10 lightning bolts above one house and up to 10 lightning bolts above another house. Ask them to write the number of lightning bolts above each house, and then draw a circle around the number that is greater than the other, or draw a circle around both numbers if they are the same.

Name ____________________

Review What You Know

2

3

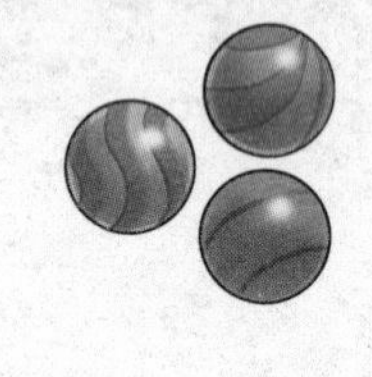

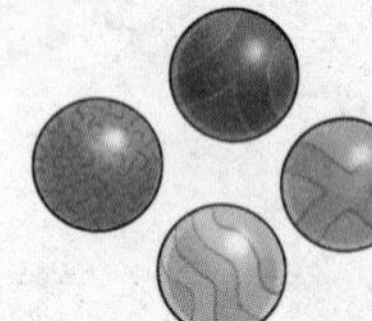

4

5

6

Directions Have students: 1 draw a circle around the group of birds that is less than the other group; 2 draw a circle around the group of dogs that is greater than the other group; 3 draw a circle around the two groups that have an equal number of marbles; 4–6 count the number of objects, and then write the number to tell how many.

Name ____________________

Lesson 4-1
Compare Groups to 10

Directions Say: *Emily visits a chicken farm. She sees a group of black chicks and a group of yellow chicks. Does Emily see more black or yellow chicks? How do you know?*

I can ...
compare groups of up to 10 objects.

I can also reason about math.

Guided Practice

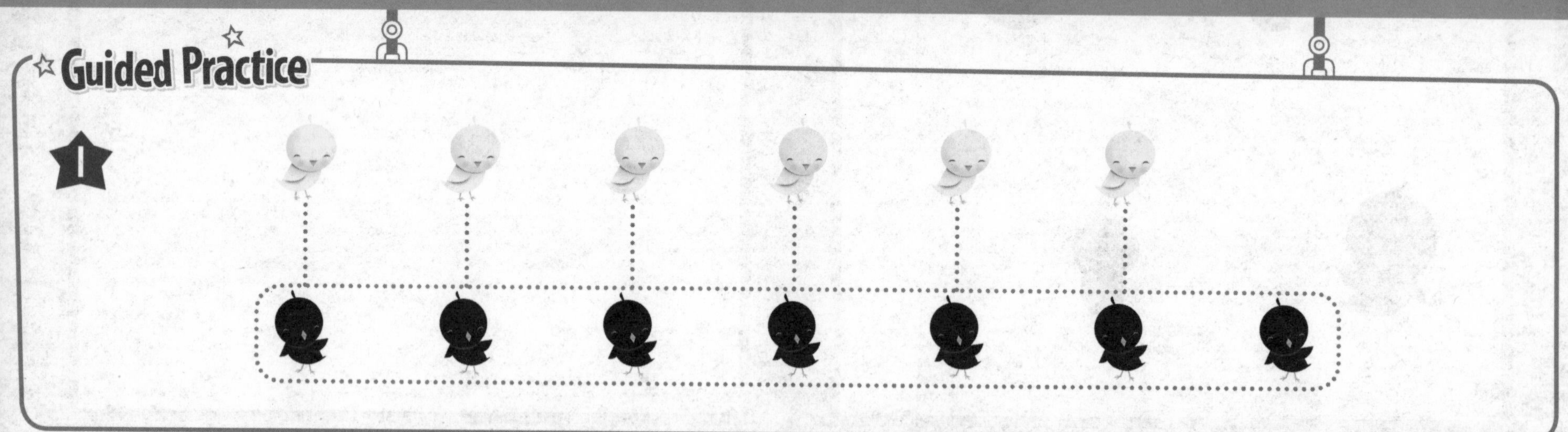

Directions Have students compare the groups, draw a line from each chick in the top group to a chick in the bottom group, and then draw a circle around the group that is greater in number than the other group.

Name ___

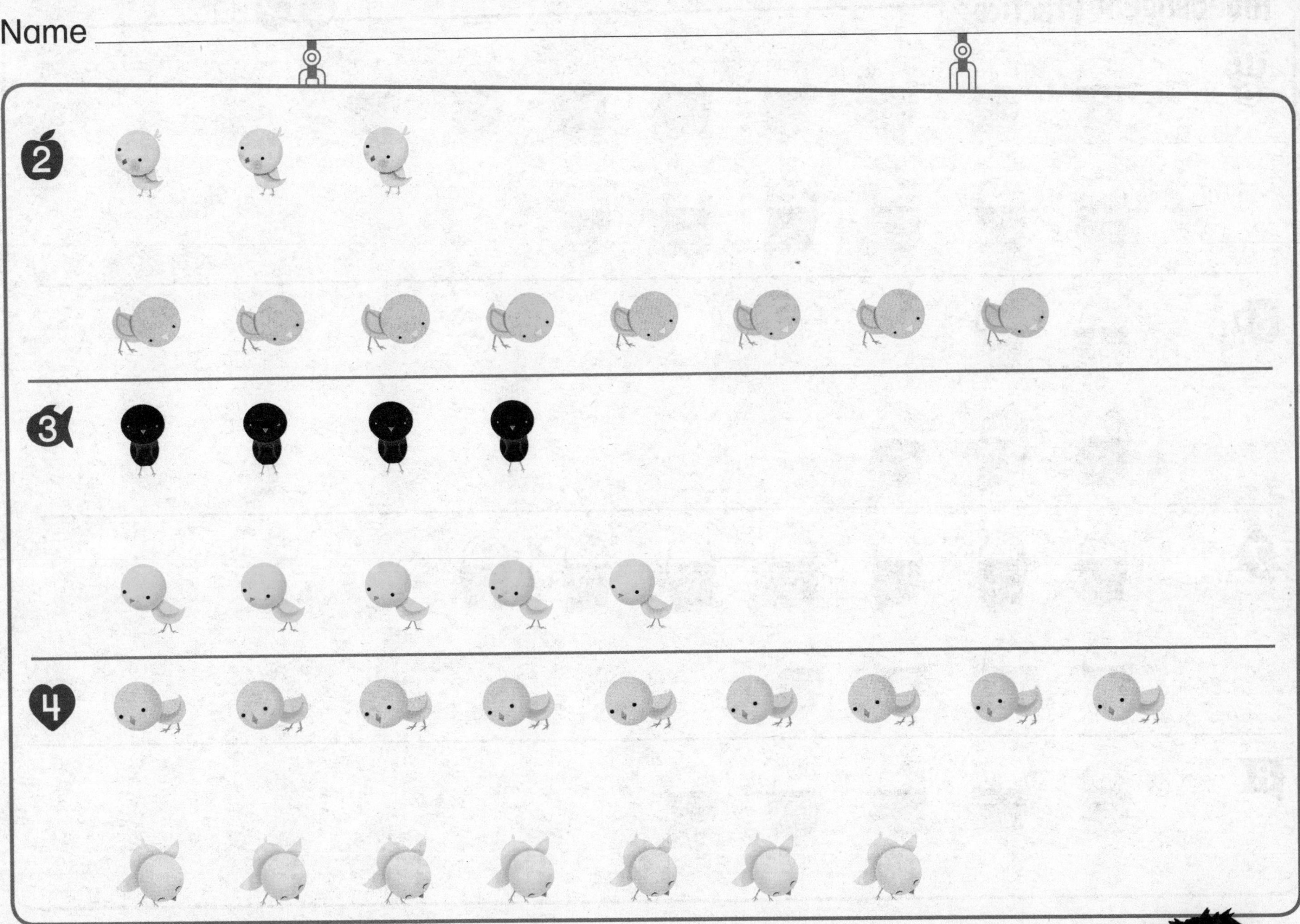

Directions ❷ **Math and Science** Say: *Chicks live in coops. Coops protect chicks in different types of weather.* Have students compare the groups, draw a line from each chick in the top group to a chick in the bottom group, and then draw a circle around the group that is greater in number than the other group. ❸ and ❹ Have students compare the groups, draw a line from each chick in the top group to a chick in the bottom group, and then draw a circle around the group that is less in number than the other group.

Independent Practice

Tools Assessment

5

6

7

8

Directions Have students: 5 compare the groups, draw a line from each bucket in the top group to a bucket in the bottom group, and then draw a circle around the group that is greater in number than the other group; 6 and 7 compare the groups, draw a line from each bucket in the top group to a bucket in the bottom group, and then draw a circle around the group that is less in number than the other group. 8 **Higher Order Thinking** Have students draw a group of buckets that is greater in number than the group shown.

Name ______________________________

Help Tools Games

Homework & Practice 4-1

Compare Groups to 10

Another Look!

HOME ACTIVITY Draw a group of up to 9 dots. Ask your child to draw a group that has more dots than the group of dots you drew. Then have your child draw a group that has fewer dots than the group of dots you drew.

1

2

3

Directions Say: *Compare the groups. Draw a circle around the group of counters that is greater in number than the other.* Have students: 1 compare the groups and draw a circle around the group of counters that is greater in number than the other group; 2 and 3 compare the groups and draw a circle around the group of counters that is less in number than the other group.

4

5

6

7

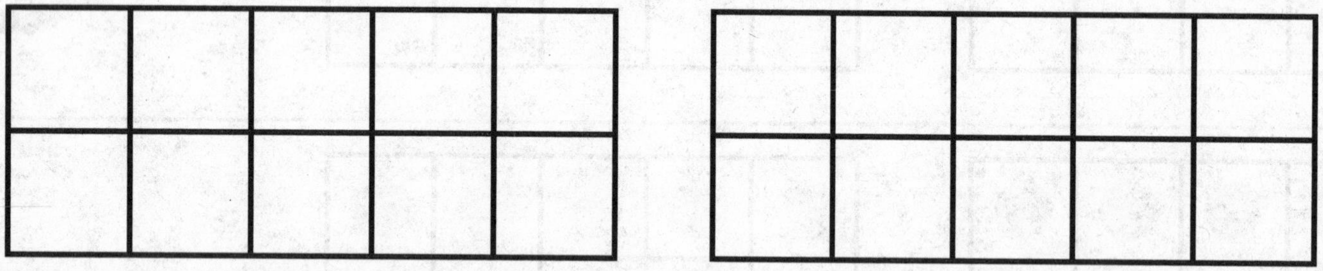

Directions Have students: 4 compare the groups and draw a circle around the group of chicks that is greater in number than the other group; 5 compare the groups and draw a circle around the group of chicks that is less in number than the other group. 6 **Higher Order Thinking** Have students draw a group of buckets that is less in number than the group shown. 7 **Higher Order Thinking** Have students draw a group of counters in the top part of the first ten-frame, and then draw a second group of counters in the other ten-frame that is greater in number than the first group of counters.

Solve & Share

Name ____________________

Lesson 4-2
Compare Numbers Using Numerals to 10

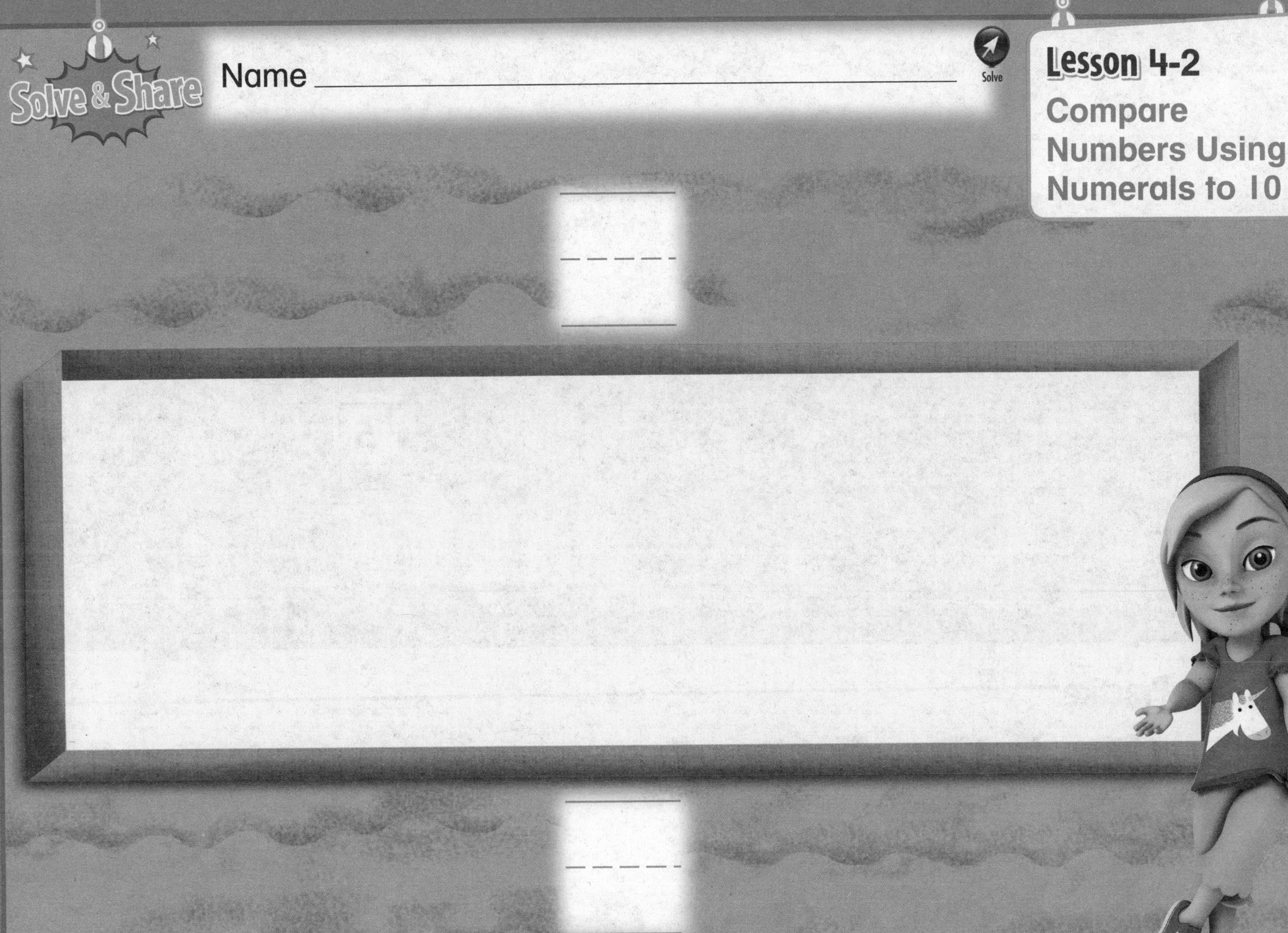

Directions Say: *Emily is planting seedlings, or little plants. She plants 5 red pepper seedlings and 7 yellow pepper seedlings. Use counters to show the groups of seedlings. Write the numbers, and then circle the number that tells which group has more.*

I can ...
compare groups of numbers using numerals to 10.

I can also make sense of problems.

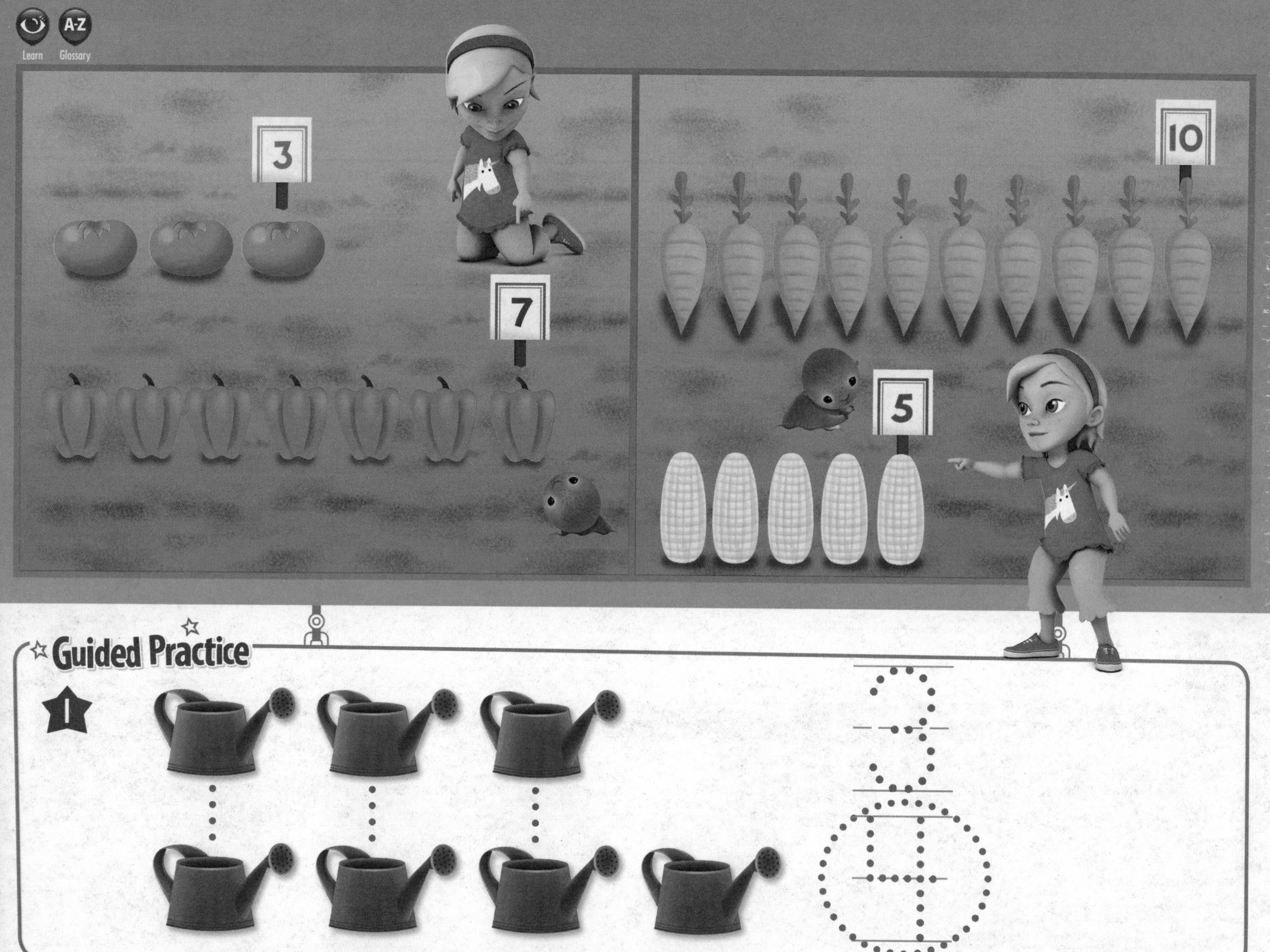

Guided Practice

Directions Have students count the watering cans in each group, write the number to tell how many, draw a line from each watering can in the top group to a watering can in the bottom group, and then draw a circle around the number that is greater than the other number.

Name

2

3

Directions 2 Have students count the vegetables in each group, write the number to tell how many, draw a line from each vegetable in the top group to a vegetable in the bottom group, and then mark an X on the number that is less than the other number. 3 **Number Sense** Have students count the vegetables in each group, draw more pea pods to make the groups equal, write the numbers to tell how many in each group, and then draw a line from each vegetable in the top group to a vegetable in the bottom group to compare.

Independent Practice

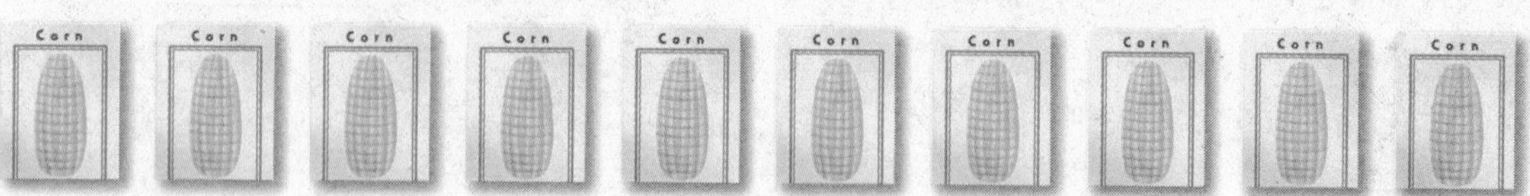

Directions 4 Have students count the seed packets in each group, write the number to tell how many, draw a line from each seed packet in the top group to a seed packet in the bottom group, and then mark an X on the number that is less than the other number. 5 **Higher Order Thinking** Have students count the flowers in the group, draw a group of flowers that is less than the group shown, and then write the numbers to tell how many.

Name ______________________

Help

Tools
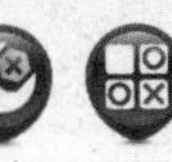
Games

Homework & Practice 4-2

Compare Numbers Using Numerals to 10

Another Look!

5

4

HOME ACTIVITY Show a group of up to 10 objects, such as buttons. Ask your child to show a group of objects that is greater in number than your group. Repeat with a group that is less in number than your group of objects.

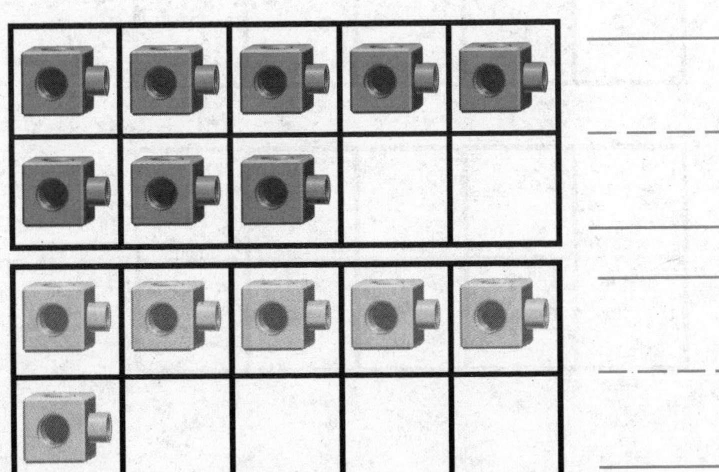

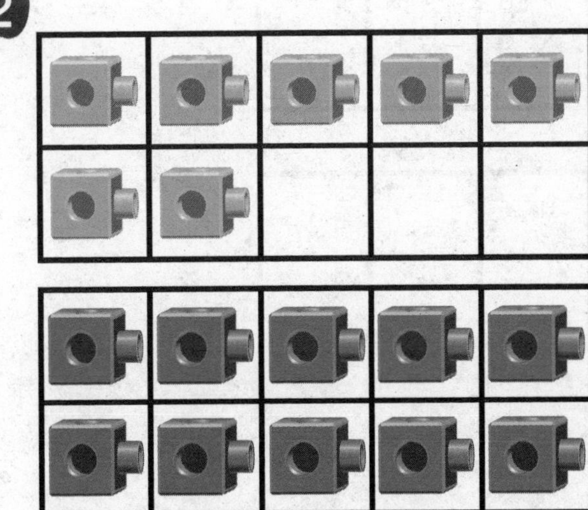

Directions Say: *Count the cubes in each group, write the number to tell how many, and then draw a circle around the number that is greater than the other number.* 1 and 2 Have students count the cubes in each group, write the number to tell how many, and then mark an X on the number that is less than the other number.

3

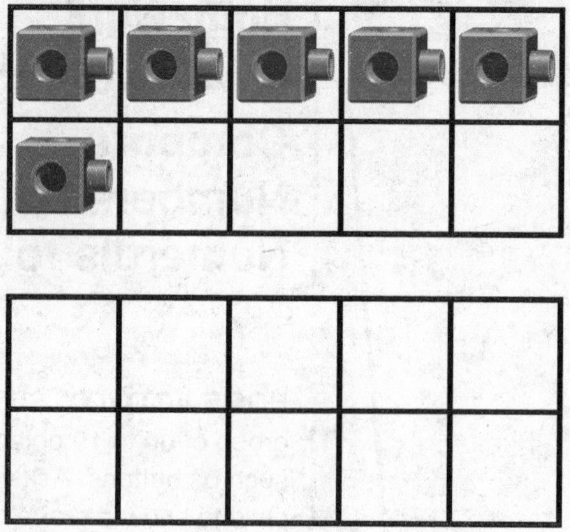

4

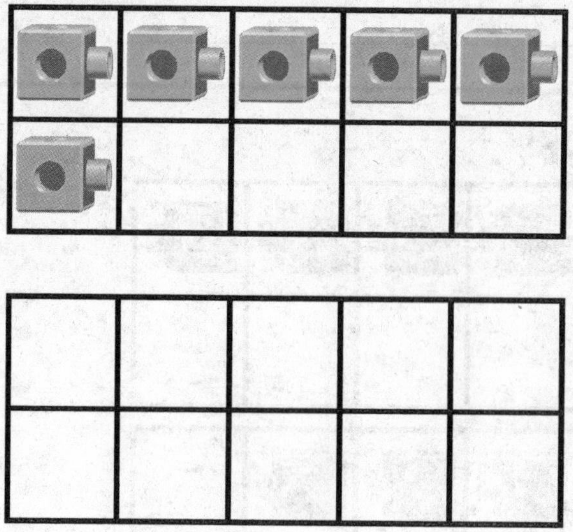

5

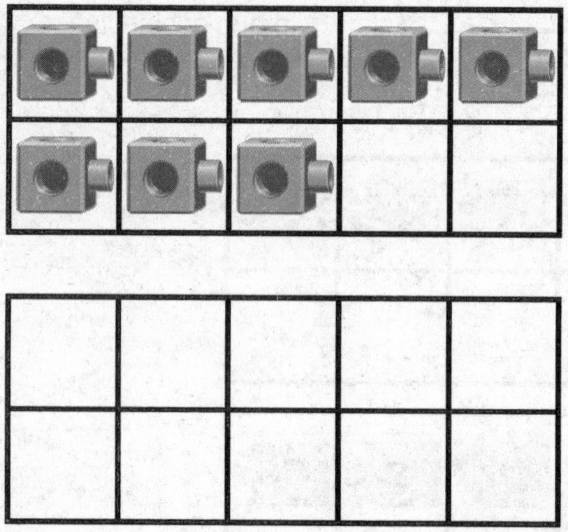

6

Directions Have students: 3 count the cubes, draw a group of cubes that is less in number than the number of cubes counted, and then write the number to tell how many; 4 and 5 count the cubes, draw a group of cubes that is greater in number than the number of cubes counted, and then write the numbers to tell how many. 6 **Higher Order Thinking** Have students draw a group of cubes in the top ten-frame, then in the bottom ten-frame draw a group of cubes that is equal in number to the first group they drew, and then write the numbers to tell how many.

Name ______________________

Lesson 4-3
Compare Groups to 10 by Counting

Directions Say: *The class aquarium has two kinds of fish, goldfish and tetras. Write numbers to tell how many of each kind. Draw a circle around the fish that has a number greater than the other. Show how you know you are right.*

I can ...
compare groups of numbers by counting.

I can also be precise in my work.

Guided Practice

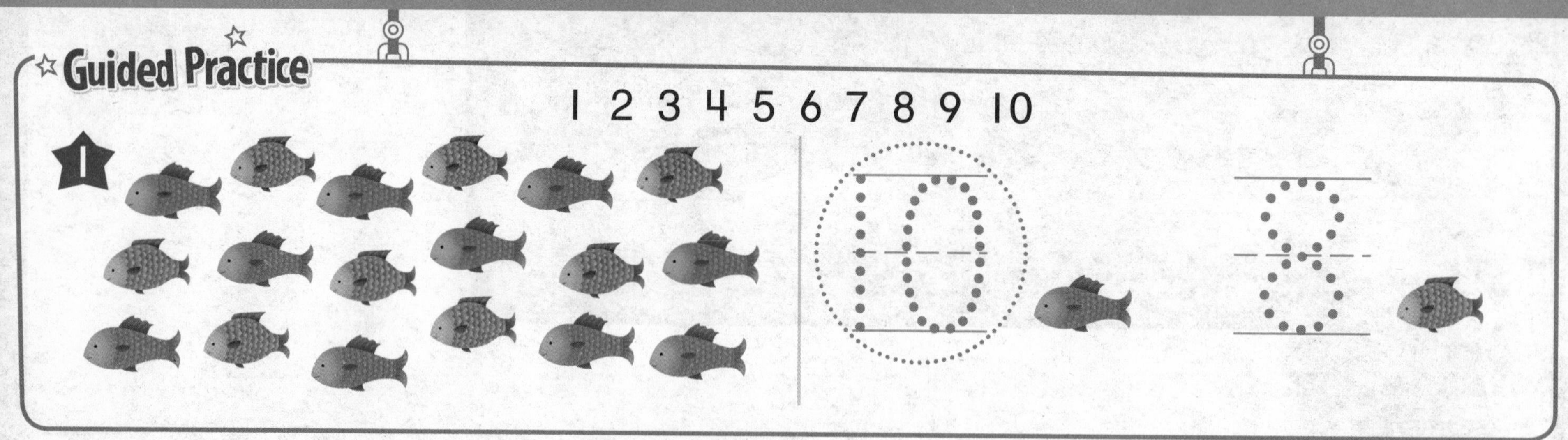

Directions 1 Have students count the number of each color fish, write the numbers to tell how many, and then draw a circle around the number that is greater than the other number. Use the number sequence to help find the answer.

Name ______________________________

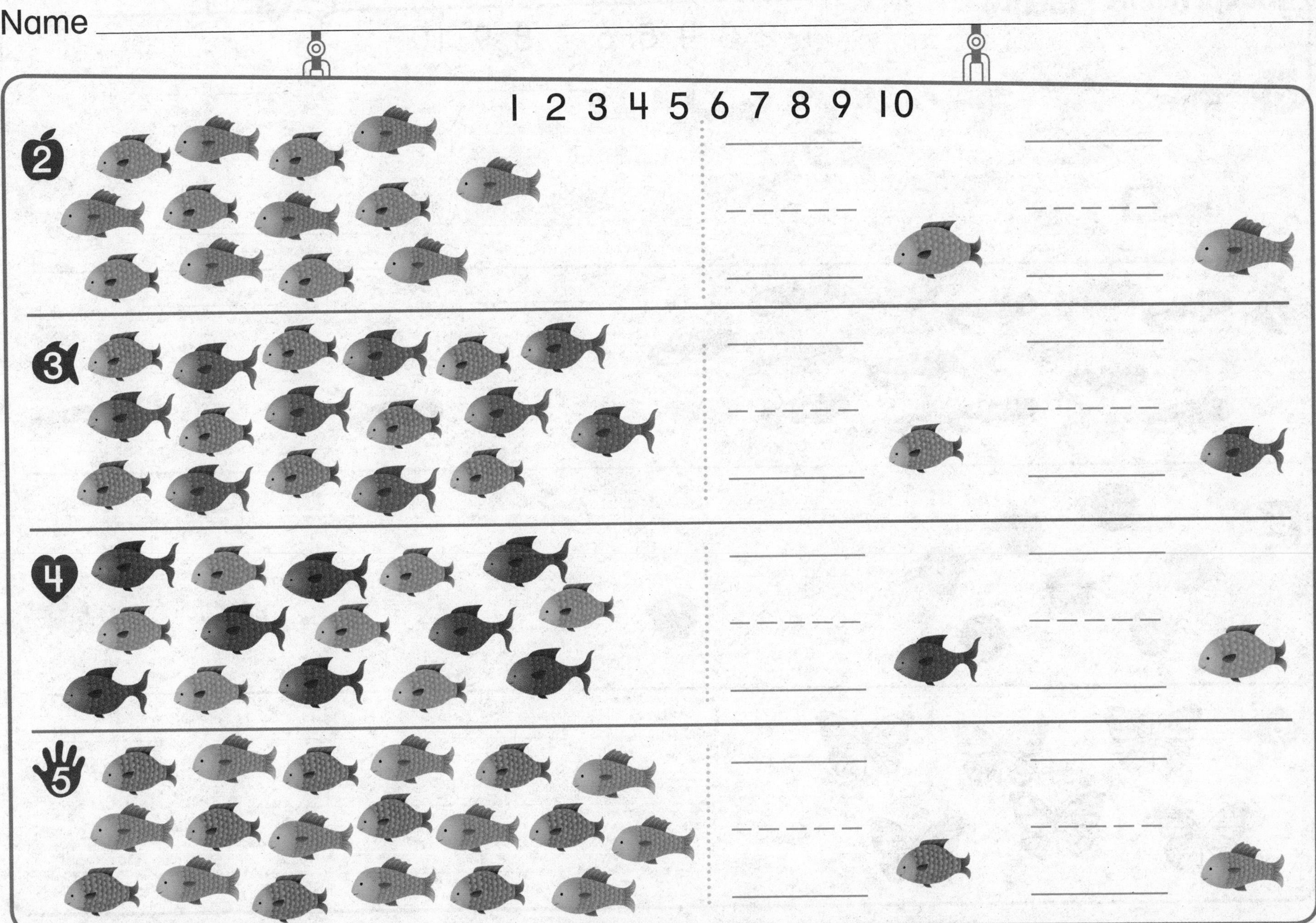

Directions **Math and Science** Say: *Fish keep warm in extreme cold by staying deep in the water.* Have students count the number of each color fish, write the numbers to tell how many, and then: 2 draw a circle around the number that is greater than the other number; 3 draw a circle around both numbers if they are equal, or mark an X on both numbers if they are NOT equal; 4 and 5 mark an X on the number that is less than the other number. Use the number sequence to help find the answer for each problem.

Directions Have students count the number of each critter, write the numbers to tell how many, and then: 6 draw a circle around both numbers if they are equal, or mark an X on both numbers if they are NOT equal; 7 mark an X on the number that is less than the other number; 8 draw a group of spiders that is two greater in number than the number of tarantulas shown, and then write the number to tell how many. 9 **Higher Order Thinking** Have students count the butterflies, and then write all the numbers up to 10 that are greater than the number of butterflies shown. Use the number sequence to help find the answer for each problem.

Name ____________________

Help Tools Games

Homework & Practice 4-3

Compare Groups to 10 by Counting

Another Look! 1 2 3 4 5 6 7 8 9 10

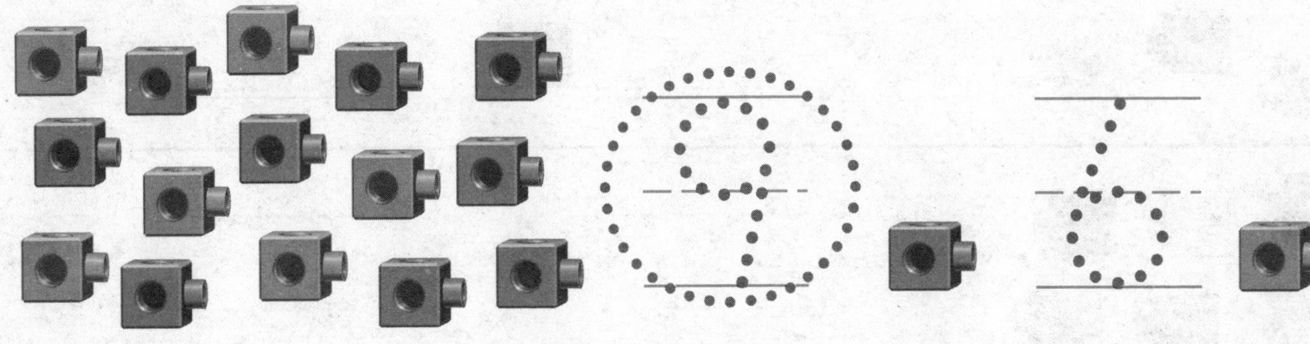

1 2 3 4 5 6 7 8 9 10

HOME ACTIVITY Shake up to 10 pennies and up to 10 nickels in your hand. Let them fall in a random group on the table. Have your child count the number of each coin, write the numbers, and then hold up the coin of the number that is greater. Repeat with different numbers of coins. Vary the activity by also asking them to hold up the coin of the number that is less, or hold up both if the numbers are equal.

Directions Say: *Count the red cubes. Then count the blue cubes. Write the numbers to tell how many of each color. Draw a circle around the number that is greater than the other number. Count the numbers 1 to 10 and use the number sequence to help find the answer.* 1 Have students count the number of each color cube, write the numbers to tell how many, and then draw a circle around the number that is greater than the other number. Use the number sequence to help find the answer.

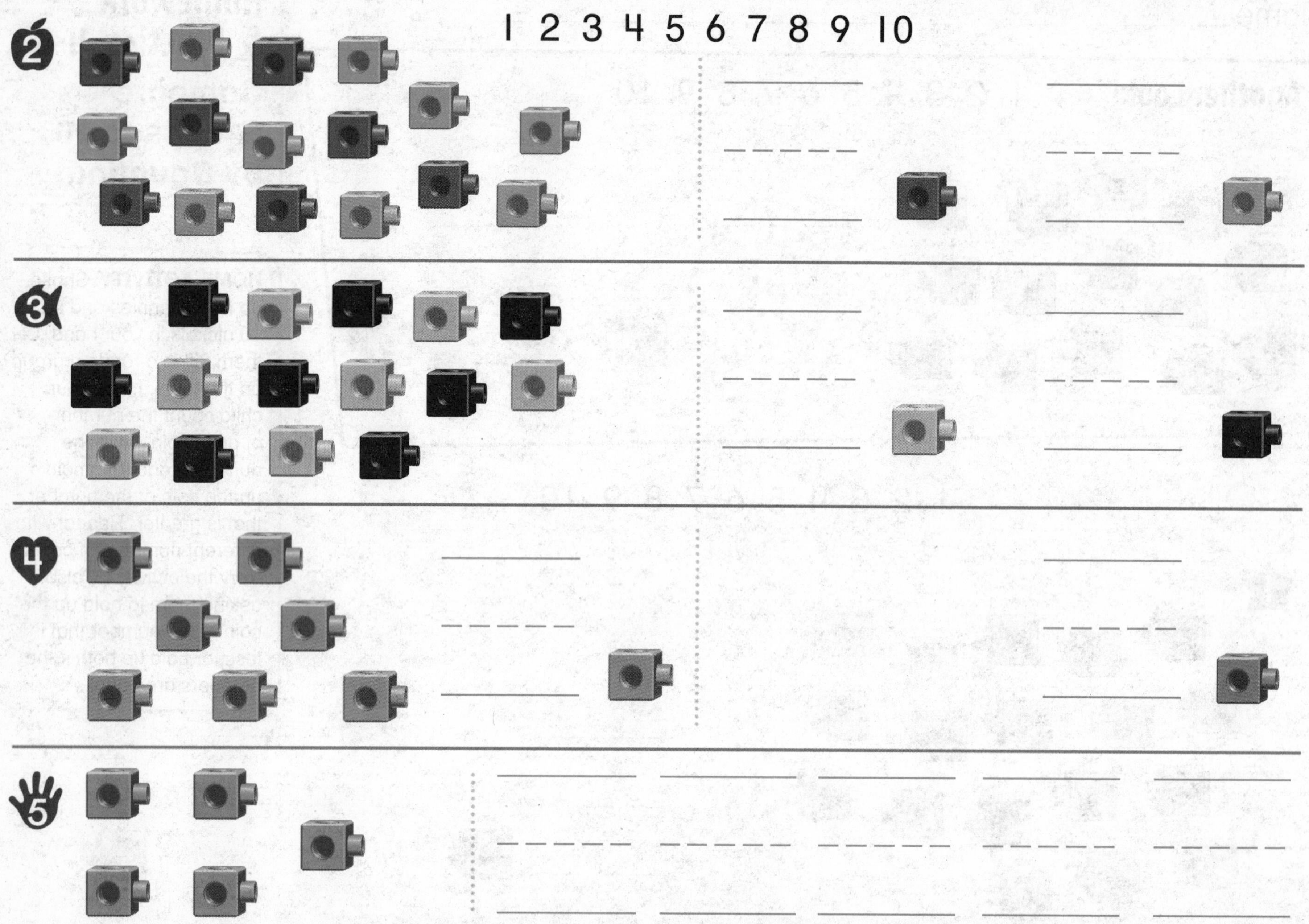

Directions Have students count the number of each color cube, write the numbers to tell how many, and then: 2 mark an X on the number that is less than the other number; 3 draw a circle around both numbers if they are equal, or mark an X on both numbers if they are NOT equal. 4 Have students draw a group of blue cubes that is equal to the number of cubes shown. 5 **Higher Order Thinking** Have students count the cubes, and then write all the numbers that are greater than the number of cubes shown up to 10. Use the number sequence to help find the answer for each problem.

Name ________________________________

Lesson 4-4
Compare Numbers to 10

1 2 3 4 5 6 7 8 9 10

Directions Say: *Emily's mother asked her to bring the towels in off the line. Her basket can hold less than 7 towels. How many towels might Emily bring in? You can give more than one answer. Show how you know your answers are right.*

I can ... compare two numbers.

I can also model with math.

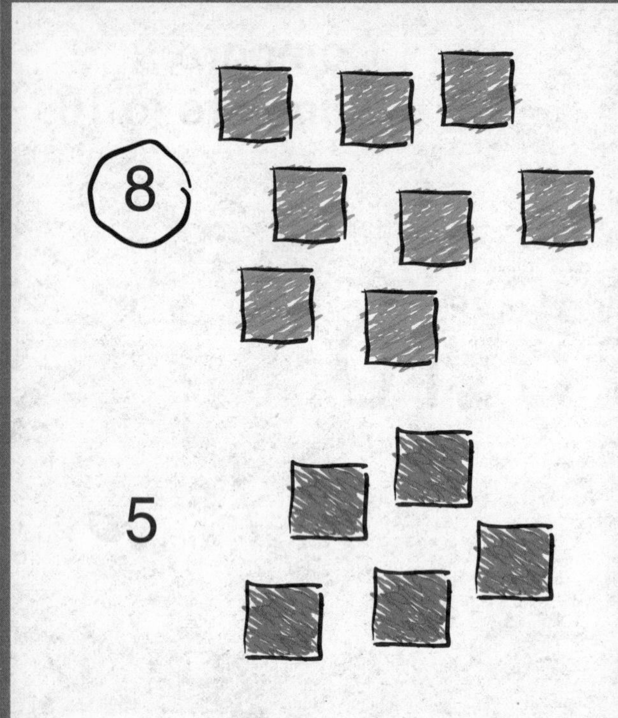

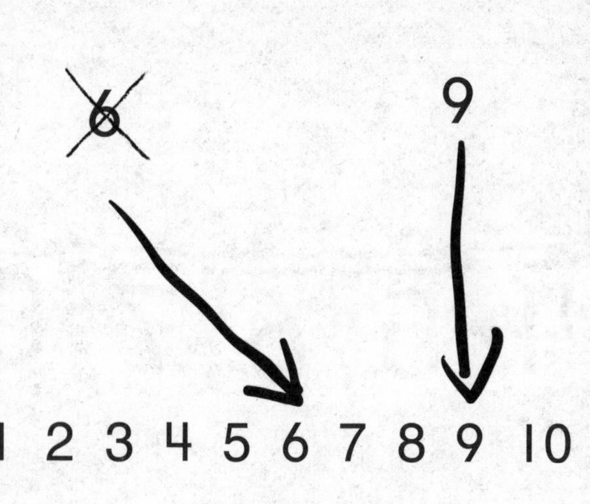

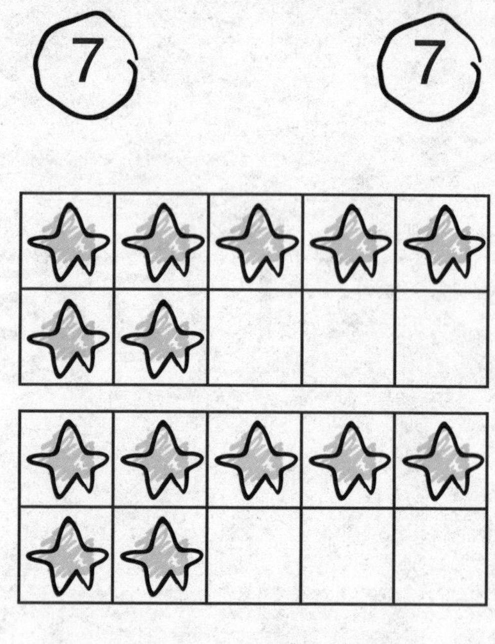

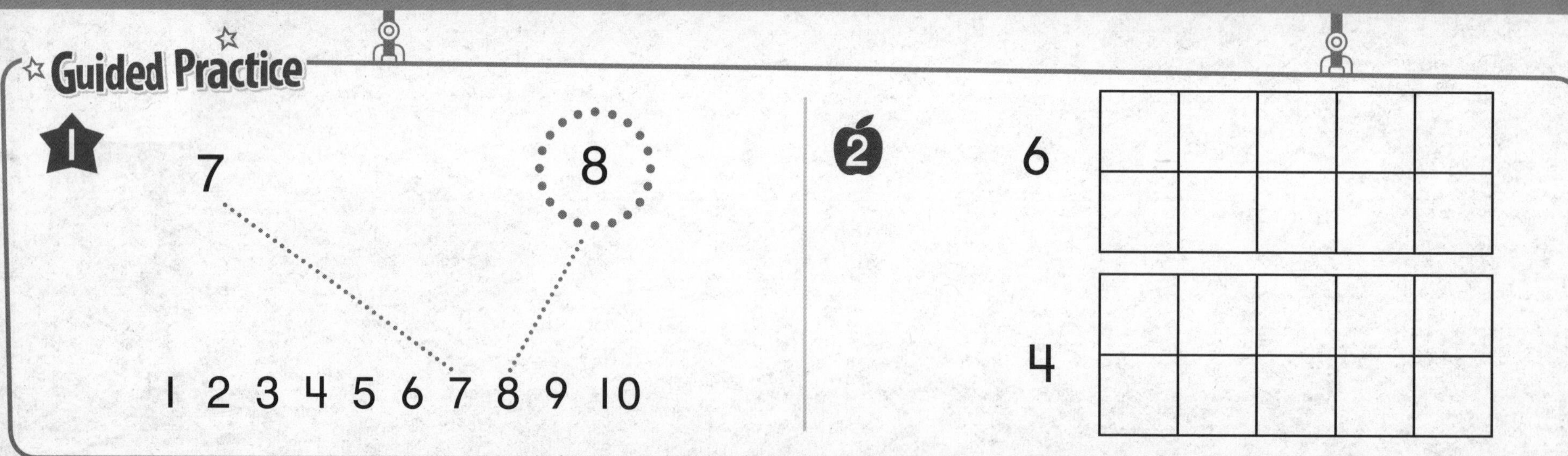

Directions Have students: 1 count the numbers 1 to 10 and use the number sequence to show how they know which number is greater than the other, and then draw a circle around the number that is greater; 2 draw counters in the ten-frames to show how they know which number is greater than the other, and then draw a circle around the number that is greater.

Name ______________________________

3

6

9

4

8

8

5

9 10

1 2 3 4 5 6 7 8 9 10

6

9

8

Directions Have students: 3 draw pictures to show how they know which number is greater than the other, and then draw a circle around the number that is greater; 4 draw counters in the ten-frames to show how they know if the numbers are equal, and then draw a circle around both numbers if they are equal, or mark an X on both numbers if they are NOT equal; 5 use the number sequence to show how they know which number is less than the other number, and then mark an X on the number that is less; 6 draw pictures to show how they know which number is less than the other number, and then mark an X on the number that is less.

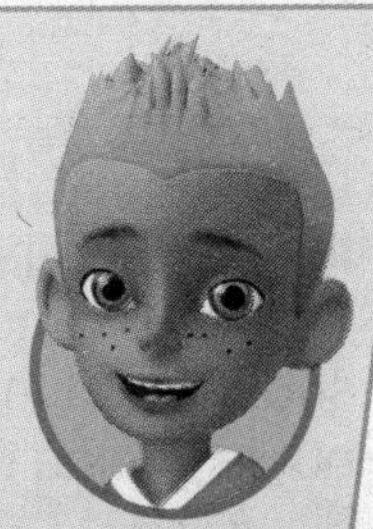

Independent Practice

Tools Assessment

7

6

8

8

9 7

1 2 3 4 5 6 7 8 9 10

9

8

10

5 9

Directions Have students: 7 draw pictures to show how they know which number is less than the other number, and then mark an X on the number that is less; 8 use the number sequence to show how they know which number is less than the other number, and then mark an X on the number that is less. 9 **Higher Order Thinking** Have students write the next two numbers that are greater than the number shown, and then tell how they know. 10 **Higher Order Thinking** Have students write a number that is greater than the number on the left, but less than the number on the right.

Name ______________________________

 Help  Tools  Games

Homework & Practice 4-4

Compare Numbers to 10

HOME ACTIVITY Give your child 10 pennies and 10 nickels. Write two numbers on a sheet of paper and ask your child to show the two numbers using the coins. Then have your child draw a circle around the number that is greater, mark an X on the number that is less, or draw a circle around both numbers if they are equal.

Another Look!

9

7

1

6

7

2

8

6

Directions Say: *Draw counters in the ten-frames to help find the answer. Then compare the numbers and draw a circle around the number that is greater than the other number.* Have students draw counters in the ten-frames to help find the answer, and then: 1 draw a circle around the number that is greater than the other number; 2 mark an X on the number that is less than the other number.

3

5

7

4

8

8

5

8

6

Directions Have students: 3 draw counters in the ten-frames, and then draw a circle around the number that is greater than the other number. Then have them show how they know; 4 use a number sequence, ten-frames, or draw pictures to show how they know the numbers are equal. 5 **Higher Order Thinking** Have students write a number that is less than the number shown, and then show how they know. 6 **Higher Order Thinking** *Talia went to the pet store to buy mealworms for her lizard. Her mom told her to buy more than 6, but less than 10. How many mealworms should Talia buy?* Have students write the number and show how they know their answer is correct.

Name ______________________

Lesson 4-5
Count Numbers to 10

8

Directions Say: *Emily thinks of two numbers, one that is 1 less than 8 and another that is 1 more than 8. Write the two numbers Emily is thinking of. Show how you know you are correct.*

I can ... count groups of numbers to 10.

I can also reason about math.

0 1 2 3 4 5 6 7 8 9 10

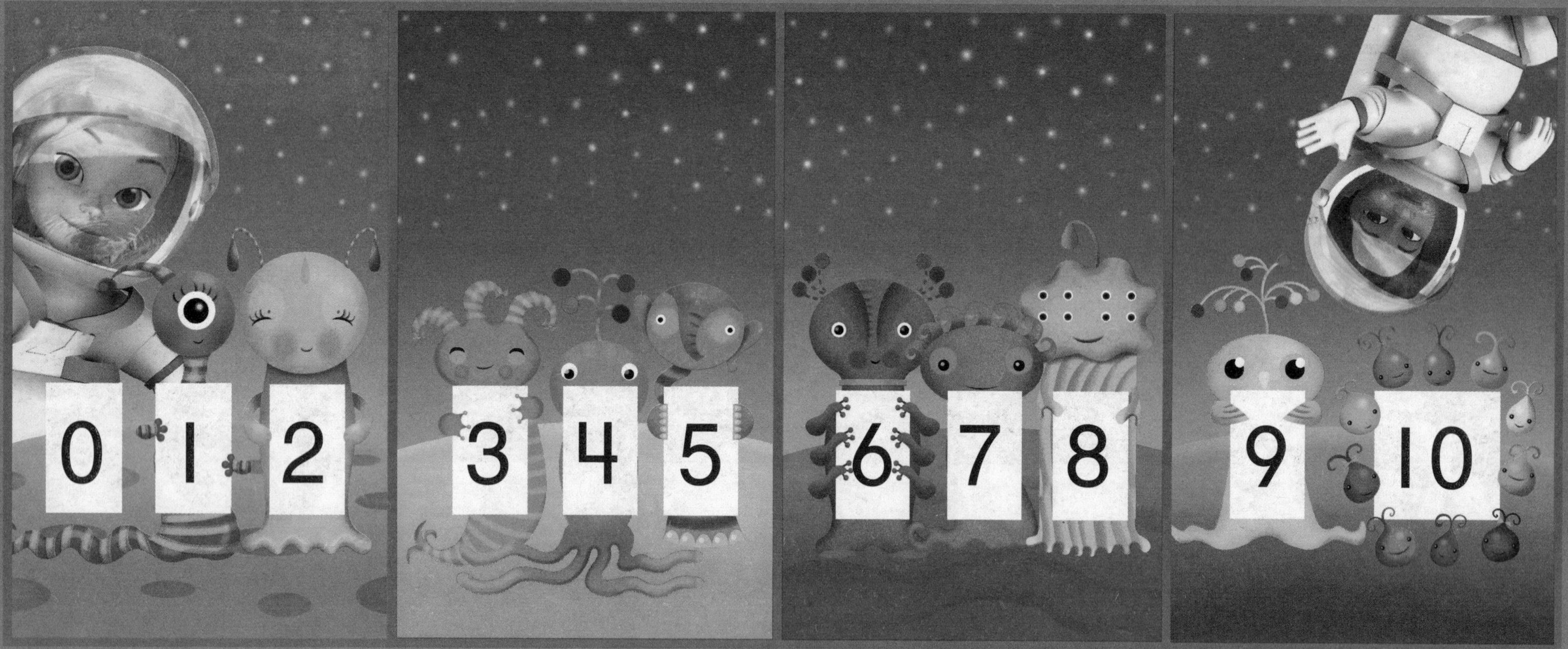

Directions ★ Have students count, and then write the number that is 1 greater than the number before.

Name ______

2

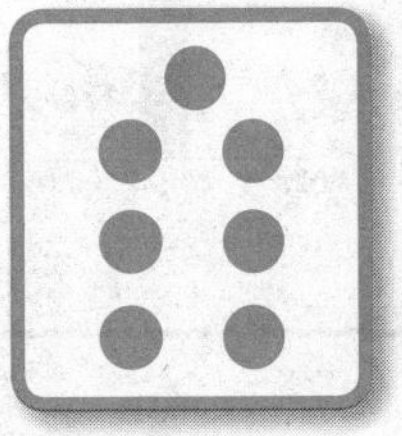

7

3

6 9

8 7

4

3 6

5 4

Directions 2 **Vocabulary** Have students count to find the number that is 1 **less than** and 1 **greater than** the given number, and then write the numbers. 3 and 4 Have students write the smallest number, and then count forward and write the number that is 1 greater than the number before.

Directions Have students: 5 and 6 count to find the number that is 1 less than and 1 greater than the given number, and then write the numbers; 7 compare the number cards, write the smallest number, and then count forward and write the number that is 1 greater than the number before. 8 **Higher Order Thinking** Have students find the missing number, and then count forward to write the number that is 1 greater than the number before.

Name ____________________

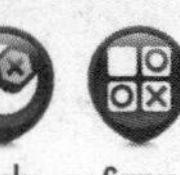

Help Tools Games

Homework & Practice 4-5

Count Numbers to 10

Another Look!

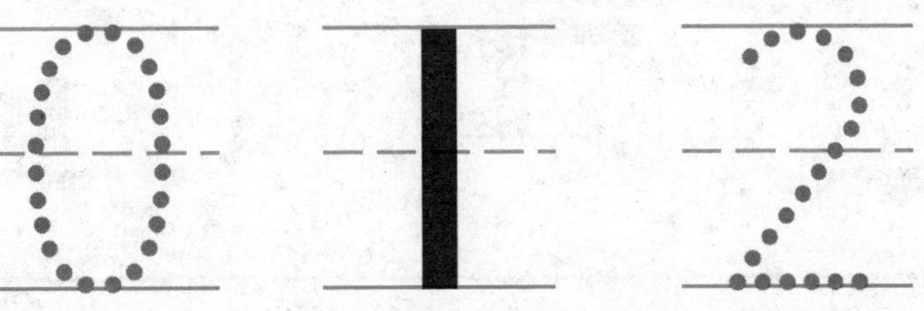

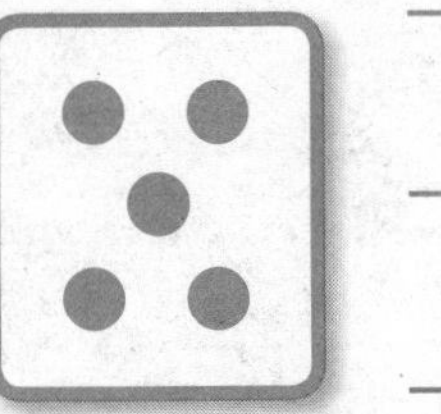

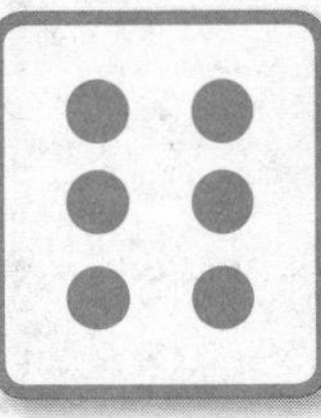

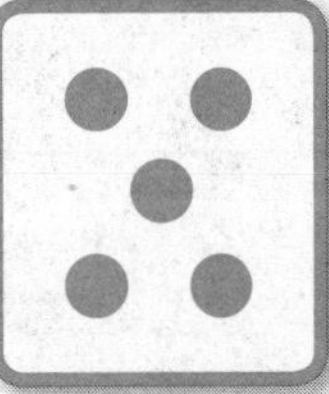

10 8 7 9

3 2 1 0

HOME ACTIVITY Write a number on a piece of paper and have your child write the number that is 1 greater. Then write another number and have your child write the number that is 1 less. Repeat with other numbers.

Directions Say: *Write the numbers that are 1 less than and 1 greater than 1. Count the numbers aloud.* Then have students: 1 and 2 count to find the number that is 1 less than and 1 greater than the given number, and then write the numbers; 3 and 4 compare the number cards, write the smallest number, and then count forward and write the number that is 1 greater than the number before.

Directions 5 and 6 Have students count to find the number that is 1 less than and 1 greater than the given number, and then write the numbers. 7 **Higher Order Thinking** Have students find the missing number and count to write the number that is 1 greater than the number before. 8 **Higher Order Thinking** Have students write the numbers from 5 to 10 so that each number is 1 greater than the number before.

Solve & Share

Name ______________________

Problem Solving

Lesson 4-6

Repeated Reasoning

Directions Say: *There are 7 fish in a bowl. Emily puts 1 more fish in the bowl. How many fish are in the bowl now? How can you solve this problem?*

I can ...
repeat something from one problem to help me solve another problem.

I can also compare numbers to 10.

Guided Practice

     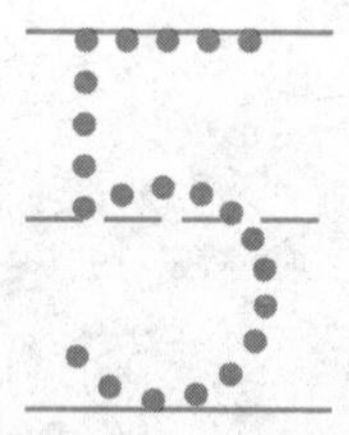

Directions 1 Say: *Carlos sees 4 frogs at the pond. Then he sees 1 more. How many frogs are there now?* Have students use reasoning to find the number that is 1 greater than the number of frogs shown. Draw counters to show the answer, and then write the number. Have students explain their reasoning.

Tools Assessment

Name ______

Independent Practice

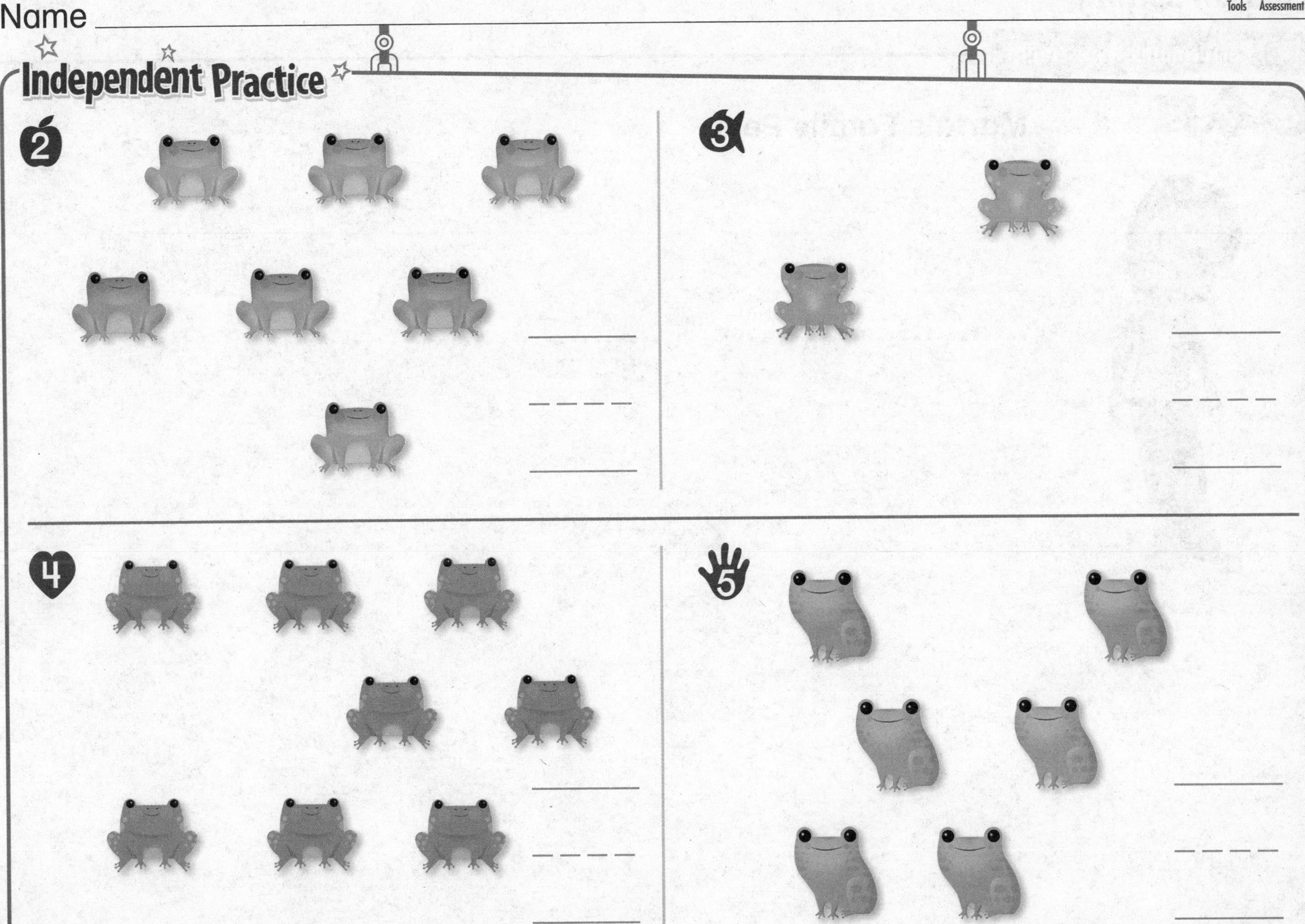

Directions Say: *Alex sees frogs at the pond. Then he sees 1 more. How many frogs are there now?* 2–5 Have students use reasoning to find the number that is 1 greater than the number of frogs shown. Draw counters to show the answer, and then write the number. Have students explain their reasoning.

Problem Solving

Performance Assessment

6 7 8

Marta's Family Pets

Directions Read the problem aloud. Then have students use multiple problem-solving methods to solve the problem. Say: *Marta's family has 5 pets. Then her family gets 1 more. How many pets do they have now?* **6 Generalize** *Does something repeat in the problem? How does that help?* **7 Use Tools** *What tool can you use to help solve the problem? Use the tool to find the number of pets in Marta's family now.* **8 Make Sense** *Should the answer be greater than or less than 5?*

Name ____________________

Help Tools Games

Homework & Practice 4-6

Repeated Reasoning

HOME ACTIVITY Give your child 10 crayons. Then place a row of 8 paper clips, or other small objects, on a table. Ask your child to make a row of crayons that is 1 greater in number than the number of paper clips and then tell how many. Repeat with other numbers.

Another Look!

7

1

2

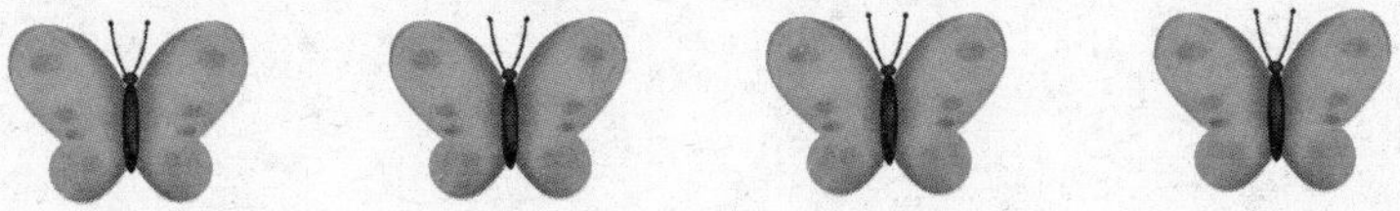

3

Directions Say: *You can show 1 more than the group of butterflies using counters. Use reasoning to find the number that is 1 greater than the number of butterflies shown. Draw counters to show your answer, and then write the number.* Have students explain their reasoning. Have students: 1 and 2 use reasoning to find the number that is 1 greater than the spiders or butterflies shown. Draw counters to show the answer, and then write the number; 3 use counters to find the number that is 2 greater than the number of spiders shown, draw the counters, and then write the number. Have students explain their reasoning.

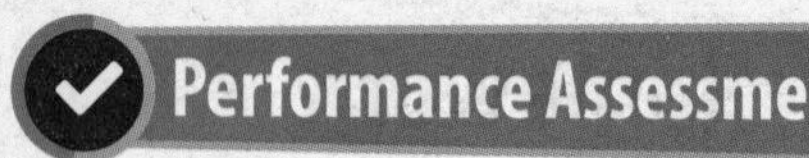

Comparing Goldfish

Directions Read the problem aloud. Then have students use multiple problem-solving methods to solve the problem. Say: *Alex has 7 goldfish. Marta has 1 more goldfish than Alex. Emily has 1 more goldfish than Marta. How many goldfish does Emily have?* **4 Generalize** *What part of the problem repeats? How does that help to solve the problem?* **5 Use Tools** *What tool can you use to help solve the problem? Use the tool to find the number of goldfish Emily has.* **6 Make Sense** *Which person should have a number of goldfish greater than the others? How do you know?*

Name ______________________

A-Z Glossary

6 9

2

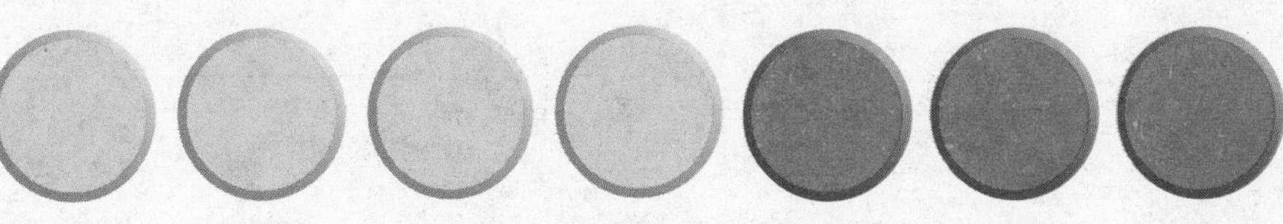

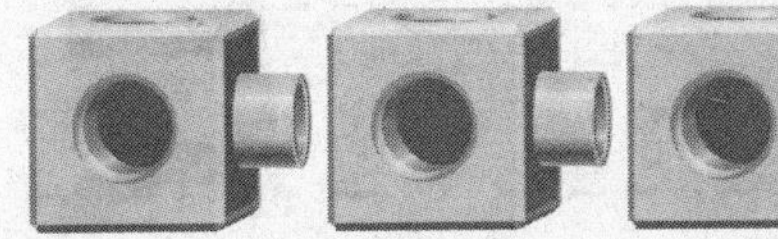

Directions **Understand Vocabulary** Have students: 1 draw a circle around the number that is **greater than** 7; 2 **count** the counters, and then write the number to tell how many; 3 write the number that means **none**; 4 count how many of each color cube there is, draw a circle around the group that has a number of cubes that is **less than** the other group, and then write the number to tell how many there are in that group.

3 8

7

8

5

9

Directions **Understand Vocabulary** Have students: 5 **compare** the numbers, draw a circle around the number that is greater, and then mark an X on the number that is less; 6 write a number that is greater than 3, but less than 5; 7 draw 5 counters in a **row** and then write the number to tell how many; 8 write the missing numbers in **order**.

Name

TOPIC 4

Reteaching

Set A

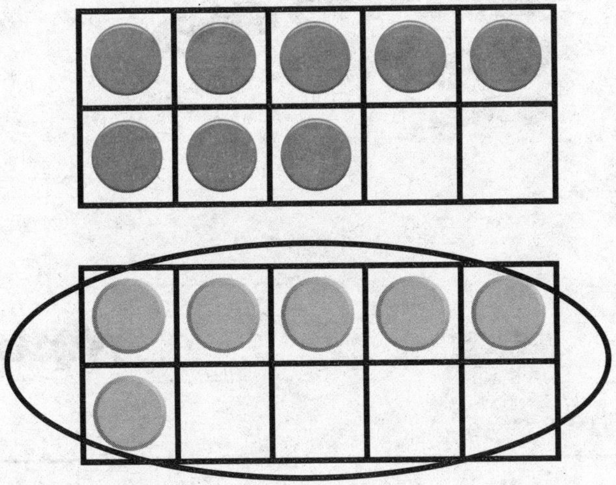

1

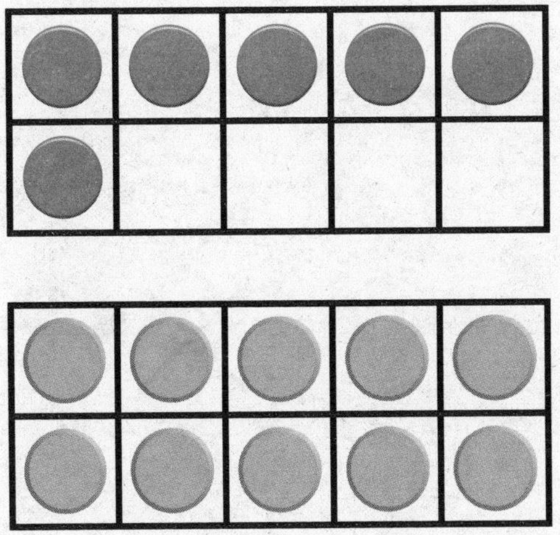

Set B

6

4

2

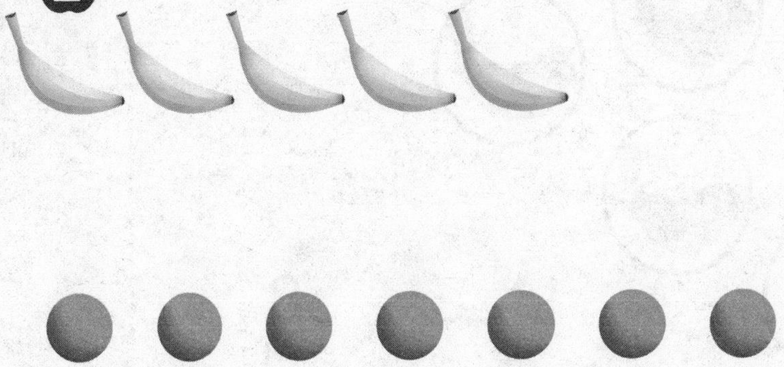

Directions Have students: 1 compare the groups, and draw a circle around the group that is less in number than the other group; 2 count the fruit in each group, write the numbers that tell how many, draw a line from each piece of fruit in the top group to a piece of fruit in the bottom group, and then draw a circle around the number that is greater than the other number.

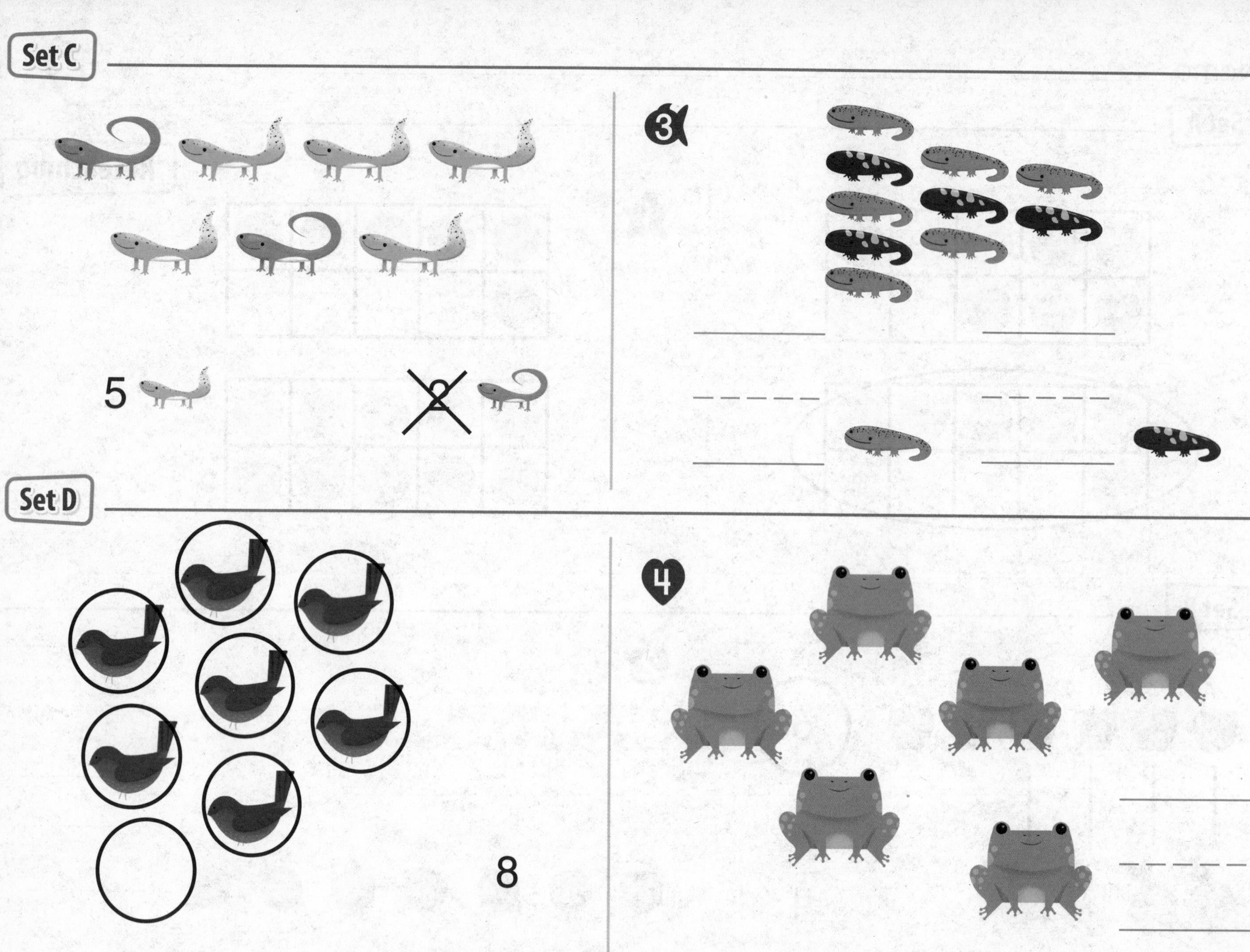

Directions Have students: 3 count the number of each critter, write the numbers, and then mark an X on the number that is less than the other number; 4 Say: *April sees frogs at the pond. Then she sees 1 more. How many frogs does she see now?* Have students use reasoning to find the number that is 1 greater than the number of frogs shown. Draw counters to show the answer, and then write the number.

Name ______________________________

TOPIC 4

Assessment

1

Ⓐ

Ⓑ

Ⓒ

Ⓓ

2

7

☐ 9

☐ 6

☐ 5

☐ 3

3

Directions Have students mark the best answer. 1 Which group of blue birds is greater in number than the group of yellow birds? 2 Mark all the numbers that are less than the number on the card. 3 Have students count the number of lemons and limes, write the number that tells how many of each, and then draw a circle around the number that is greater.

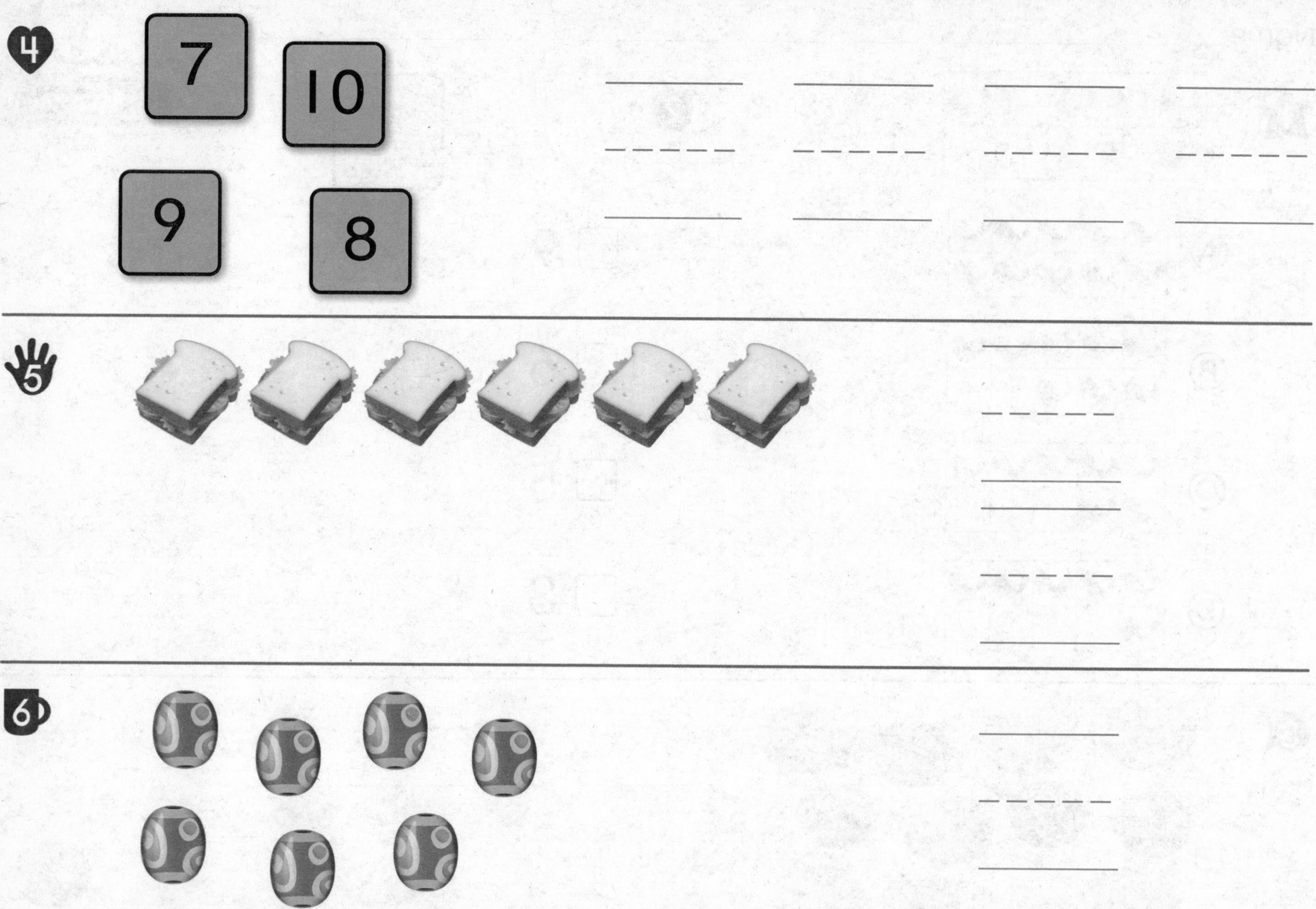

Directions Have students: 4 write the smallest number, and then count forward and write the number that is 1 greater than the number before; 5 count the sandwiches in the group, draw a group of juice boxes that is less in number than the group of sandwiches shown, and then write the numbers to tell how many. 6 Say: *Kayla has 7 beads to make a bracelet. Then she buys 1 more. How many beads does she have now?* Have students use reasoning to find the number that is 1 greater than the number of beads shown. Draw counters to show the answer, and then write the number to tell how many.

Name ______________________________

1 2 3 4 5 6 7 8 9 10

Directions **Forest Animals** Say: *The forest is home to woodland animals. One part of the forest has many different animal homes in it.* ★ Have students study the picture. Say: *How many skunks live in this part of the forest? How many raccoons live in this part of the forest? Count the number of each type of animal and write the numbers.* Then have students draw a circle around the number that is greater than the other number and mark an X on the number that is less than the other number. Have them use the number sequence to help find the answers.

2

3

5

5

4

Directions Have students look at the picture on the page before. 2 Say: *How many foxes live in this part of the forest? Count how many and write the number.* Then have students write all the numbers through 10 that are greater than the number of foxes. 3 Say: *5 chipmunks and 5 frogs move out of this part of the forest. Draw a circle around both numbers if they are equal, or mark an X on both numbers if they are NOT equal. Show how you know you are correct.* 4 Say: *How many birds live in this part of the forest? Count how many and write the number. 1 more bird flies into the forest. How many birds are in this part of the forest now?* Have students use tools to solve the problem and write the number. Then have them show how they found the answer.

TOPIC 5 Classify and Count Data

Essential Question: How can classifying data help answer questions?

Some cows are brown and some are black.

Cows can be different colors.

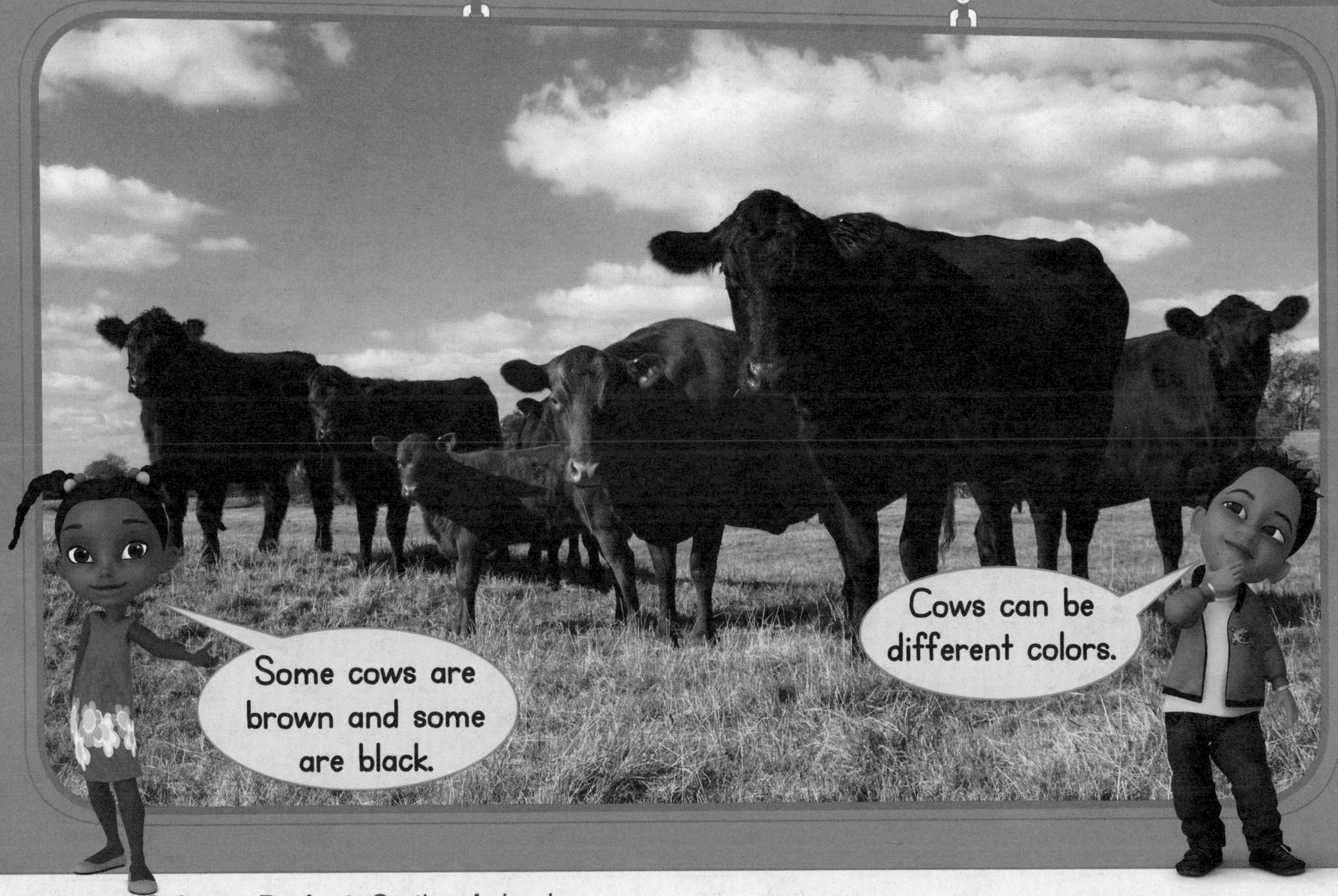

Math and Science Project: Sorting Animals

Directions Read the character speech bubbles to students. **Find Out!** Have students find out about animals that can be organized by color. Say: *Talk to friends and relatives about animals. Talk about how an animal can be one color, but another of the same animal can be a different color.* **Journal: Make a Poster** Have students make a poster. Have them choose one animal they learned about, and then draw a group of 6–10 animals. Ask them to color the animals using two different colors, and then write the numbers to tell how many of each color.

Name ______________________________

Review What You Know

1

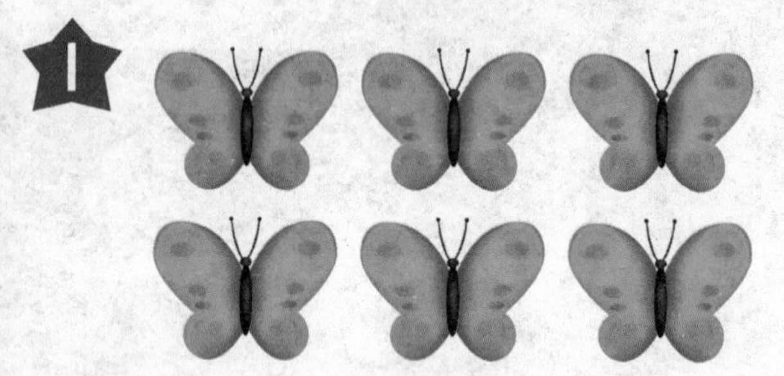

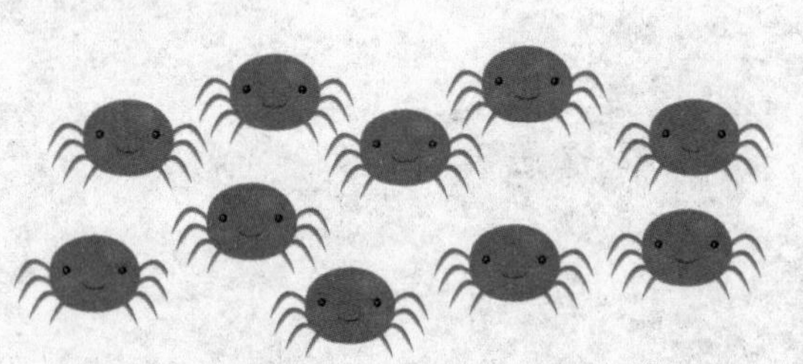

2

3

4

5

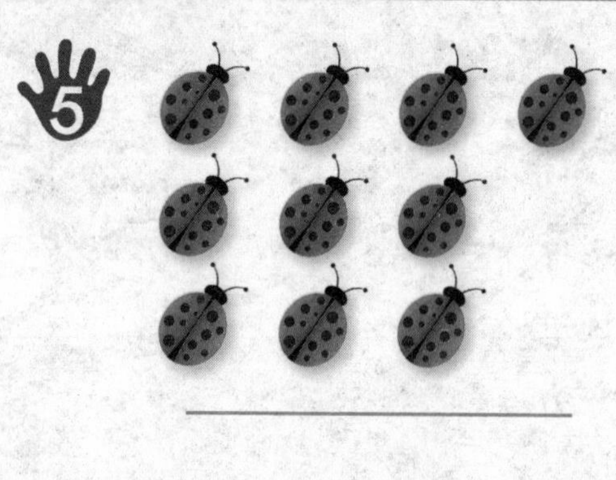

6

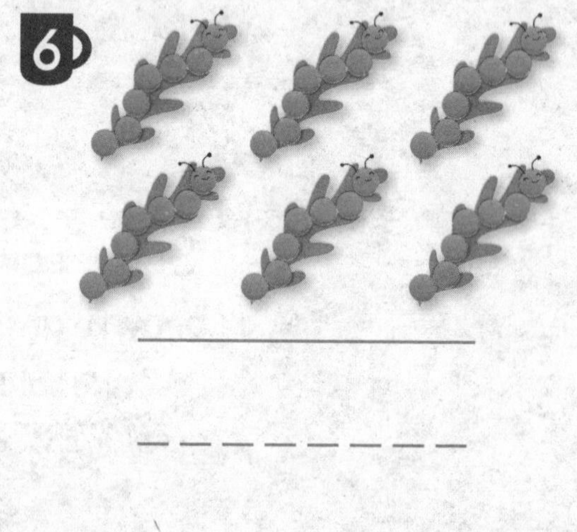

Directions Have students: 1 draw a circle around the group with 10 bugs; 2 draw a circle around the group that has a number of birds that is less than 5; 3 draw a circle around the group that has a number of birds that is greater than 5; 4–6 count the frogs or bugs in each group, and then write the number to tell how many.

A-Z Glossary

My Word Cards

Directions Have students cut out the vocabulary cards. Read the front of the card, and then ask them to explain what the word or phrase means.

category

classify

chart

tally mark

My Word Cards

Directions Review the definitions and have students study the cards. Extend learning by having students draw pictures for each word on a separate piece of paper.

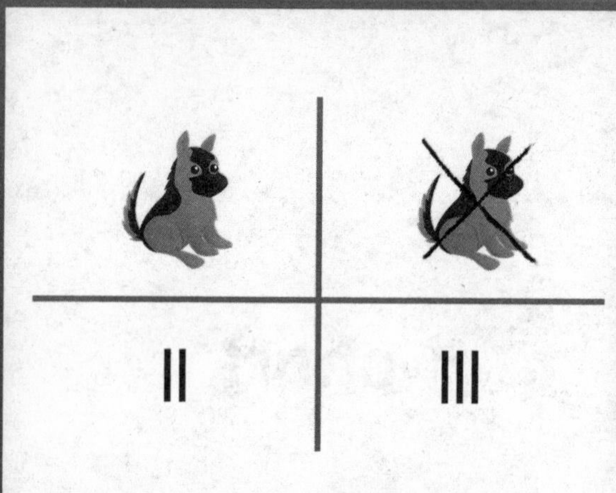

Point to the chart.
Say: *A **chart** is where information is organized.*

Point to the cats.
Say: *To **classify** objects is to sort them into categories. These are all cats.*

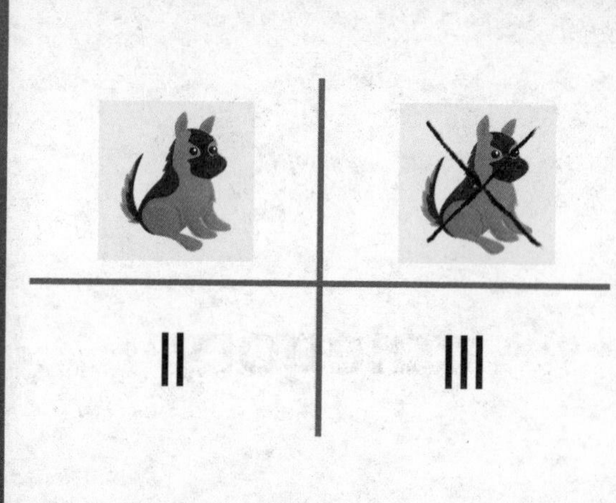

Point to the dog category.
Say: *A **category** groups things by similar attributes.*

Point to the tally marks.
Say: *A **tally mark** is a mark that helps record data. 1 mark represents 1 object.*

Name ______________________________

Lesson 5-1
Classify Objects into Categories

4 legs 

NOT 4 legs 

Pet Fair

Directions Say: *Carlos's kindergarten class is having a pet fair. The pets need to be put into two tents. One tent is for pets with 4 legs. The other tent is for pets that do NOT have 4 legs. Draw pictures of 5 pets. Where should you put them? How do you know you put them in the right tent?*

I can ...
classify objects into categories and tell why they are in each category.

I can also reason about math.

Guided Practice

Directions 1 Have students draw a circle around the animals that have feathers, and then mark an X on the animals that do NOT have feathers.

Name ______________________________

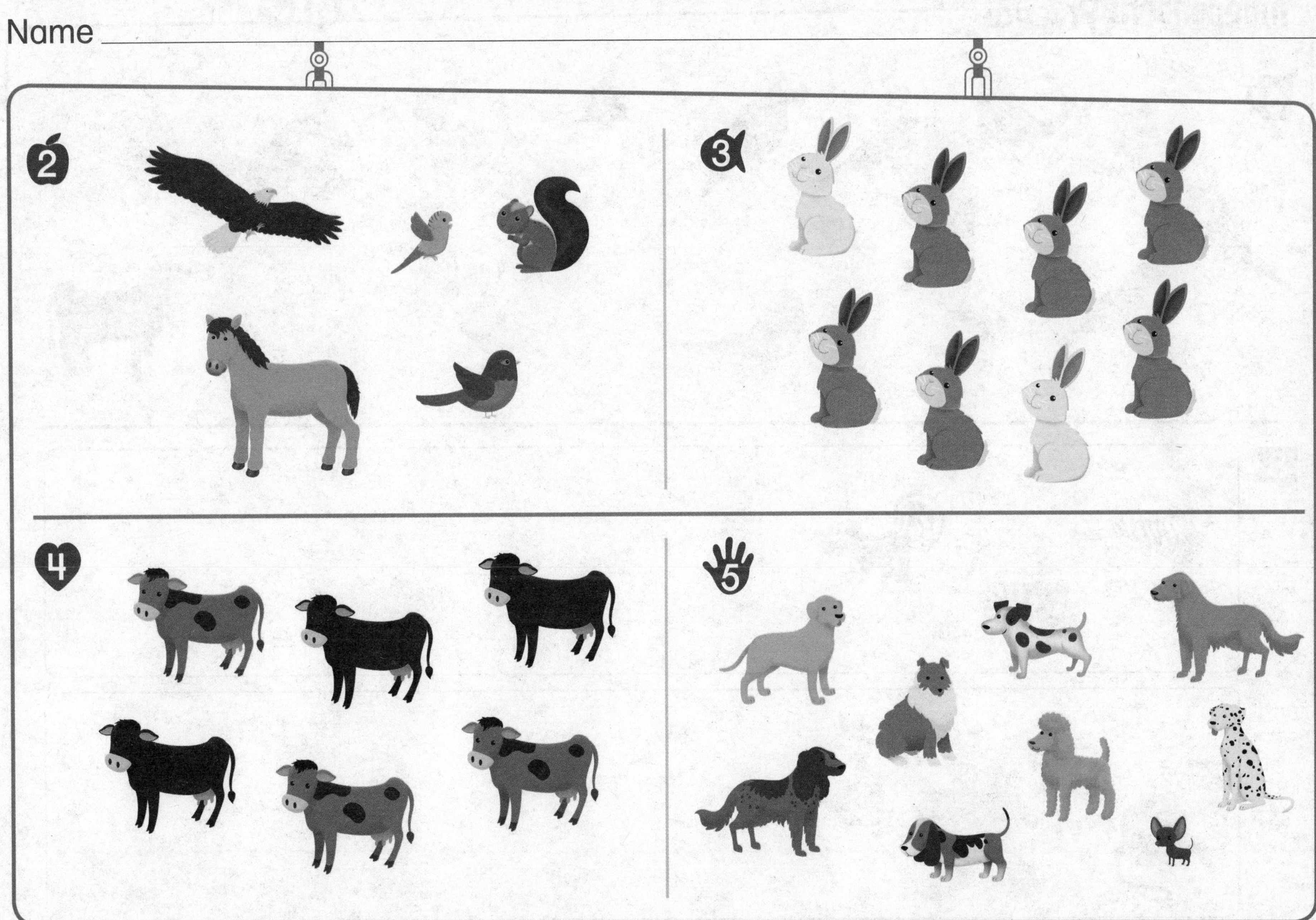

Directions 2 **Math and Science** Say: *What can most animals with wings do?* Have students draw a circle around the animals that have wings, and then mark an X on the animals that do NOT have wings. Have students: 3 draw a circle around the rabbits that are white, and then mark an X on the rabbits that are NOT white; 4 draw a circle around the cows that are brown, and then mark an X on the cows that are NOT brown; 5 draw a circle around the dogs that have spots, and then mark an X on the dogs that do NOT have spots.

Directions Have students: 6 draw a circle around the birds that are green, and then mark an X on the birds that are NOT green; 7 draw a circle around the animals that have tails, and then mark an X on the animals that do NOT have tails. 8 **Higher Order Thinking** Say: *The animals have been classified into two categories. How were the animals classified?* Have students draw a picture of an animal that belongs in each category.

Name ______________________________

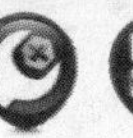

Homework & Practice 5-1

Classify Objects into Categories

HOME ACTIVITY Show your child two categories of objects that are different in at least one way. For example, show 6 coins that are silver and 4 coins that are not silver. Ask your child to classify the objects and explain how he or she classified them. Repeat the activity with other categories using up to 10 objects.

Another Look!

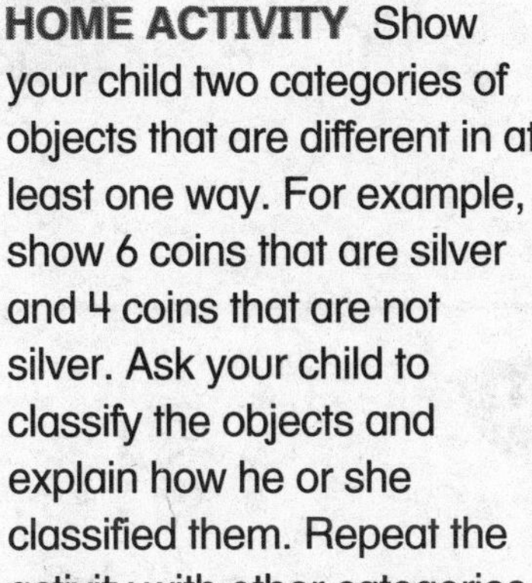

1

Directions Say: *You can classify objects into categories and tell how you classified them. Draw a circle around the animals that are adults, and then mark an X on the animals that are NOT adults.* 1 Have students draw a circle around the animals that have beaks, and then mark an X on the animals that do NOT have beaks.

2

3

4

Directions Have students: 2 draw a circle around the animals that are spotted, and then mark an X on the animals that are NOT spotted; 3 draw a circle around the fish that are yellow, and then mark an X on the fish that are NOT yellow. 4 **Higher Order Thinking** Say: *The mice are classified into two categories. One group has cheese and the other group does NOT have cheese. What is another way you could classify the mice?* Have students draw pictures to show how they could classify the mice in another way.

Solve & Share

Name ______________________

Lesson 5-2

Count the Number of Objects in Each Category

______

On the ground

______

NOT on the ground

Directions Say: *Carlos goes outside and sees some creatures. How many creatures does he see on the ground? How many does he see that are NOT on the ground? Tell how you know you counted all of the creatures.*

I can ...
count how many objects are in different categories.

I can also be precise in my work.

Count.

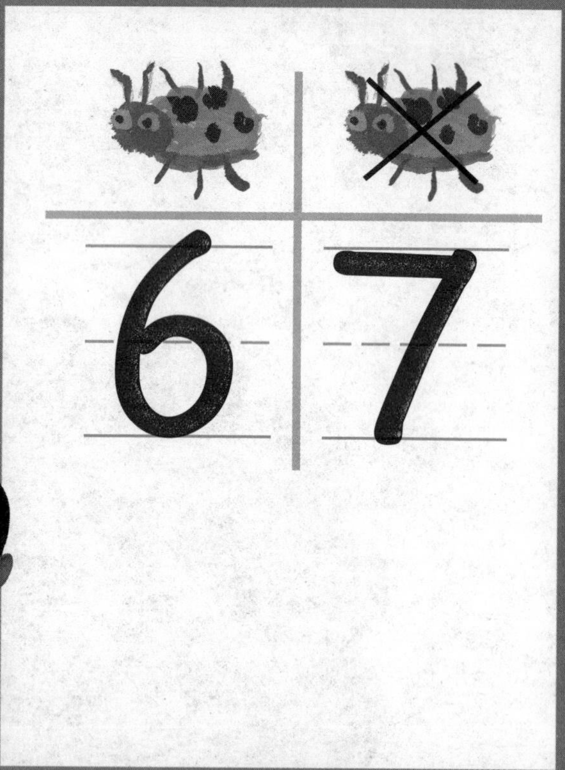

6 7

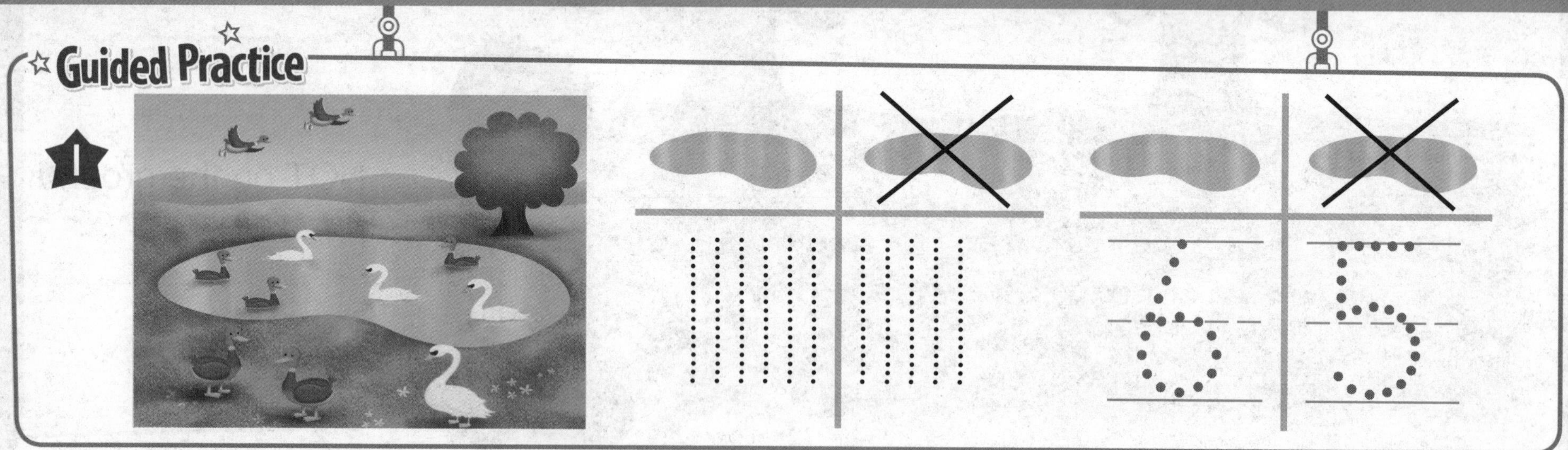

Directions 1 Have students draw lines in the chart as they count the animals that are in the pond and the animals that are NOT in the pond, and then write the numbers to tell how many in another chart.

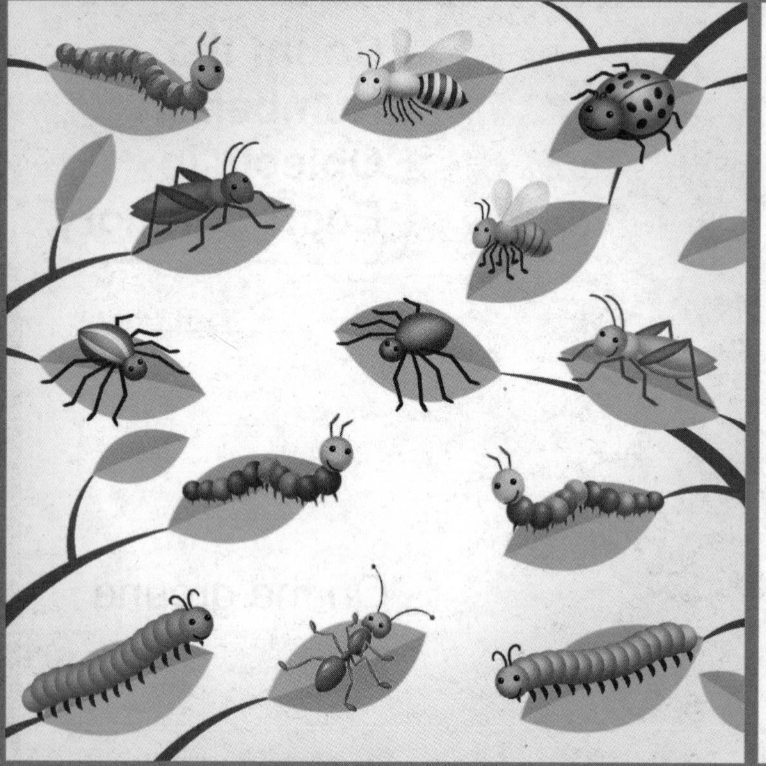

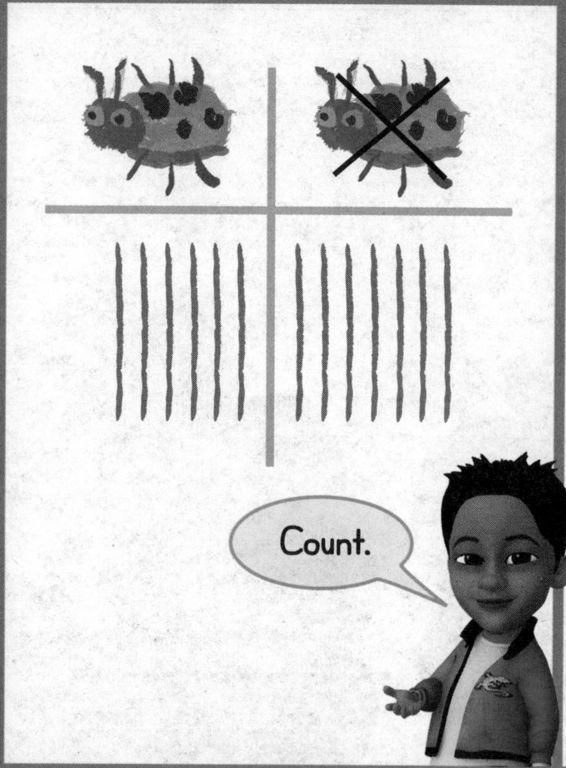

Name ____________________

2

3

Directions 2 **Vocabulary** Have students draw lines in the chart as they count the animals that have 8 legs and the animals that do NOT have 8 legs, and then write the numbers to tell how many are in each **category** in another chart. 3 Have students draw lines in the chart as they count the birds that are in the trees and the birds that are NOT in the trees, and then write the numbers to tell how many are in each category in another chart.

Independent Practice

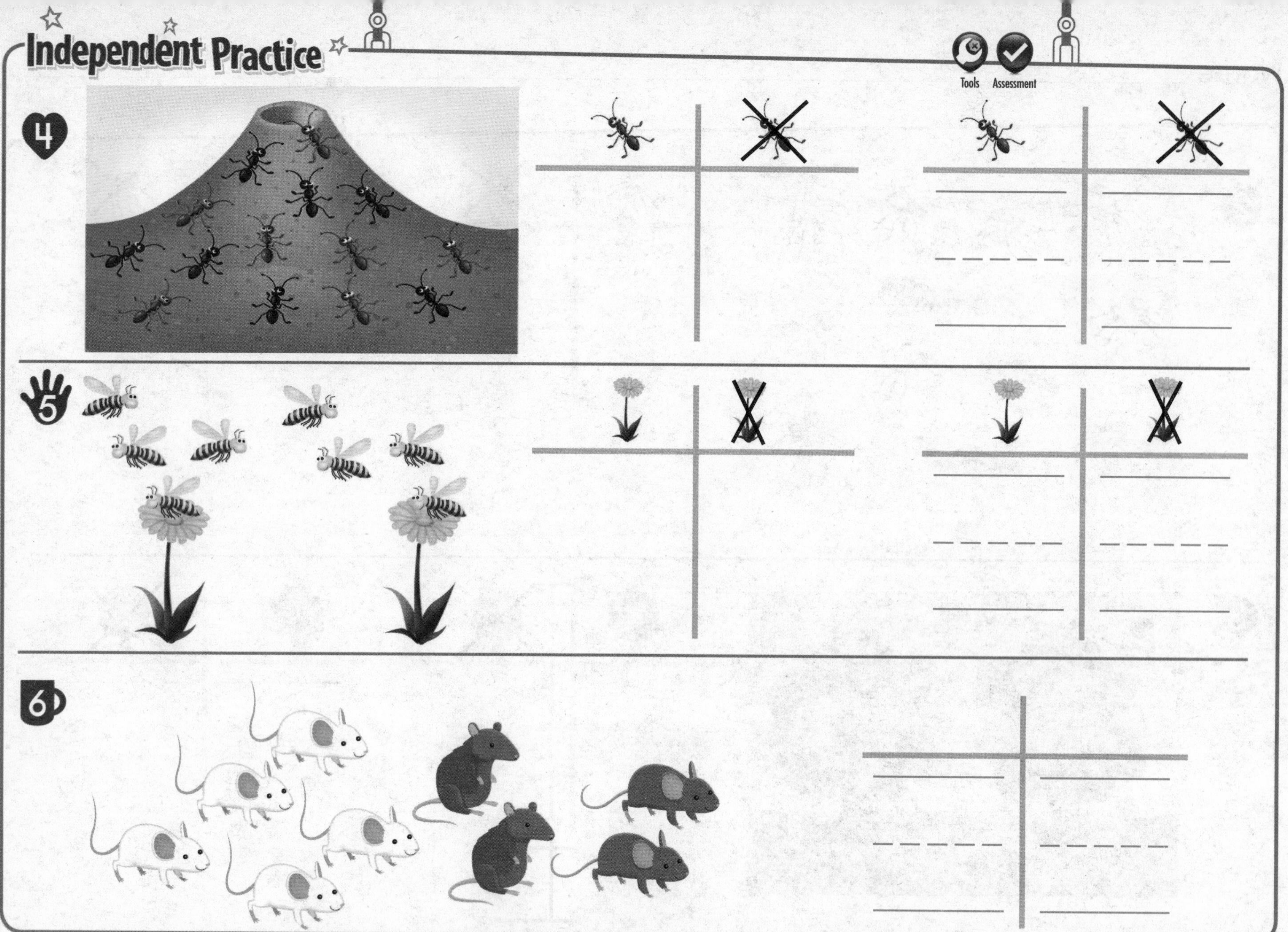

Directions Have students: 4 draw lines in the chart as they count the ants that are red and the ants that are NOT red, and then write the numbers to tell how many in another chart; 5 draw lines in the chart as they count the bees that are on flowers and the bees that are NOT on flowers, and then write the numbers to tell how many in another chart. 6 **Higher Order Thinking** Say: *These mice are sorted into two categories. How are they sorted?* Have students draw a picture in the chart to show the categories, and then write the numbers to tell how many mice are in each category.

Name ______________________

Homework & Practice 5-2

Count the Number of Objects in Each Category

Another Look!

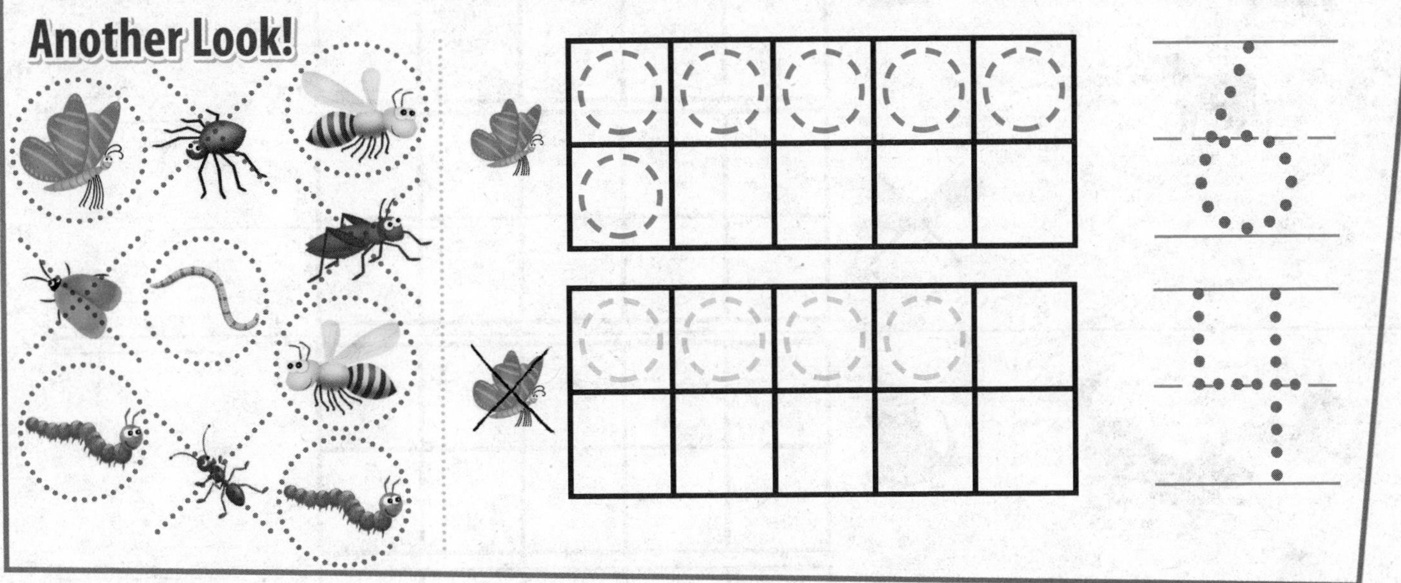

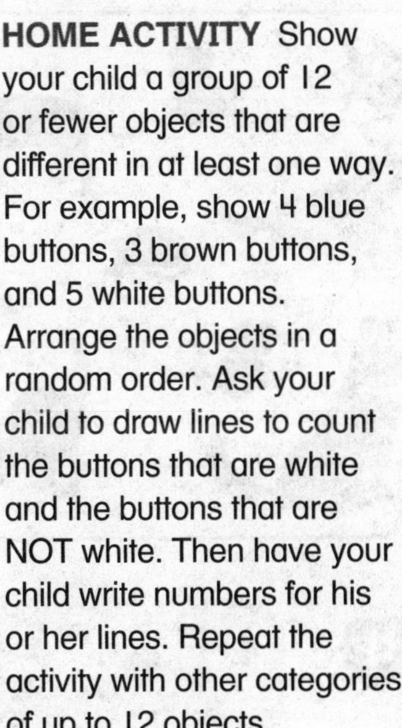

HOME ACTIVITY Show your child a group of 12 or fewer objects that are different in at least one way. For example, show 4 blue buttons, 3 brown buttons, and 5 white buttons. Arrange the objects in a random order. Ask your child to draw lines to count the buttons that are white and the buttons that are NOT white. Then have your child write numbers for his or her lines. Repeat the activity with other categories of up to 12 objects.

Directions Say: *You can use counters and a ten-frame to sort objects and count how many objects are in each category. Draw a circle around each animal that has stripes. Draw that many red counters in the top ten-frame, and then write the number to tell how many. Mark an X on each animal that does NOT have stripes. Draw that many yellow counters in the bottom ten-frame, and then write the number to tell how many.* ★1 Have students draw a circle around each animal that has 4 legs, draw that many red counters in the top ten-frame, and then write the number to tell how many. Have students mark an X on each animal that does NOT have 4 legs, draw that many yellow counters in the bottom ten-frame, and then write the number to tell how many.

Directions Have students draw a circle around animals in one category, draw that many red counters in the top ten-frame, and then write the number to tell how many. Then have them mark an X on animals in the other category, draw that many yellow counters in the bottom ten-frame, and then write the number to tell how many. 2 Categories: animals that have wings, animals that do NOT have wings 3 Categories: dogs that are puppies, dogs that are NOT puppies. 4 **Higher Order Thinking** Say: *Gretchen is going to put 1 more striped fish in the aquarium. Draw red counters in the top ten-frame to show how many striped fish will be in the aquarium. Write the number to tell how many.* Have students mark an X on the fish that are NOT striped, draw yellow counters in the bottom ten-frame, and then write the number to tell how many.

Name ______________________________

Lesson 5-3
Sort the Categories by Counting

Directions Say: *Carlos's kindergarten class has a new playground area. Sort the new playground into toys that have wheels and toys that do NOT have wheels. Draw a circle around the category that is greater than the other category. Tell how you know.*

I can ...
use counting to compare how many objects are in categories.

I can also be precise in my work.

Guided Practice

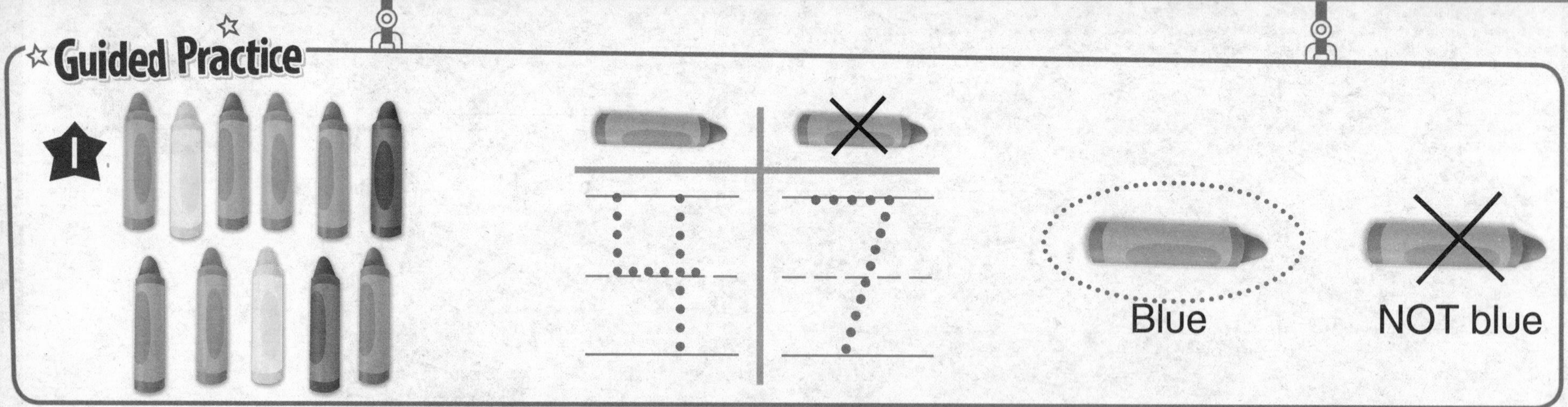

Directions 1 Have students sort the crayons into crayons that are blue and crayons that are NOT blue, count them, and then write numbers in the chart to tell how many. Have students draw a circle around the category that is less in number than the other category and tell how they know.

Name ______________________

2

3

Directions Have students: 2 sort the blocks into blocks that have letters and blocks that do NOT have letters, count them, and then write numbers in the chart to tell how many. Then have students draw a circle around the category that is greater in number than the other category and tell how they know; 3 sort the books into books that are open and books that are NOT open, count them, and then write numbers in the chart to tell how many. Then have students draw a circle around the category that is less in number than the other category and tell how they know.

Independent Practice

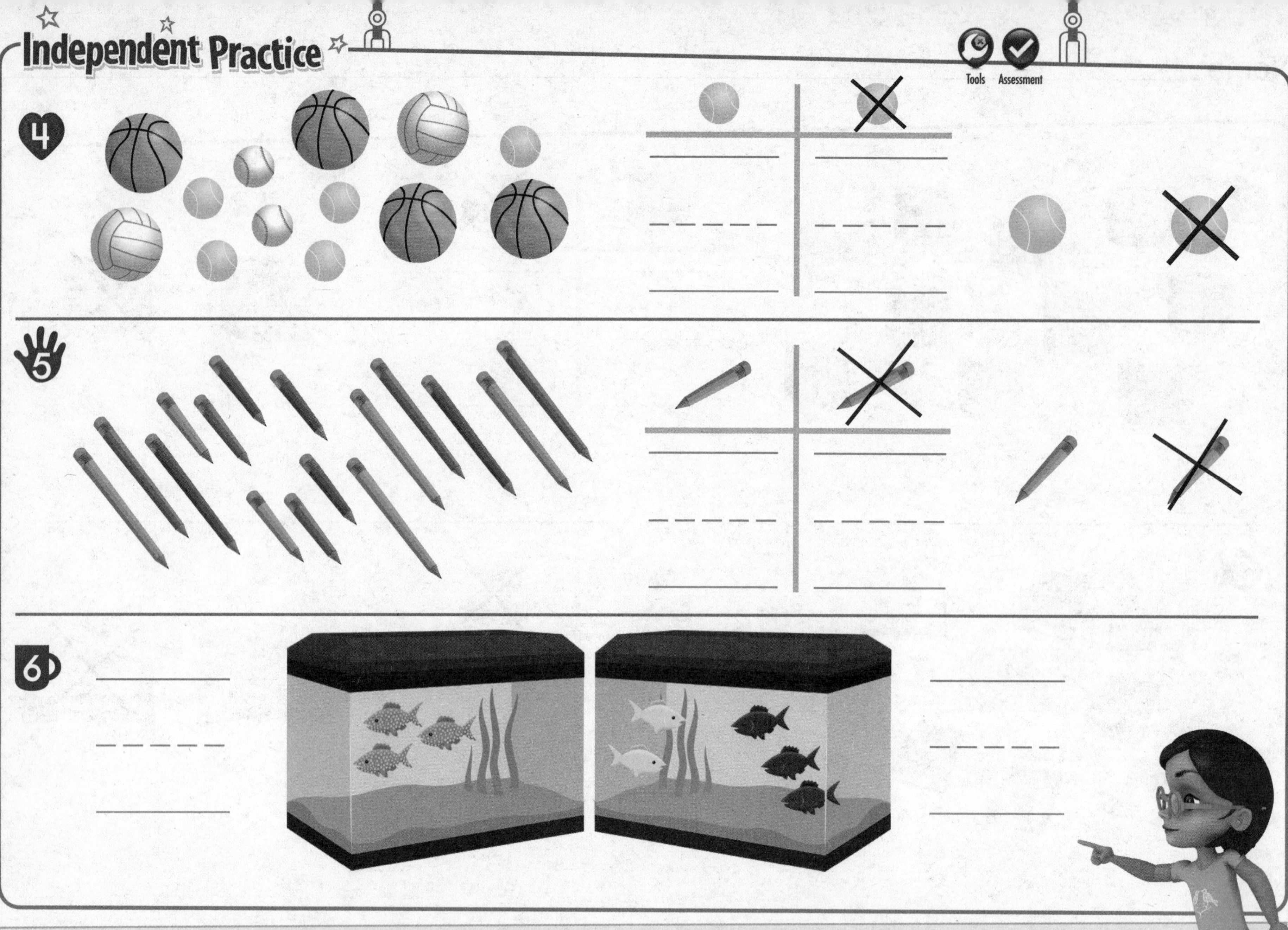

Directions Have students: 4 sort the balls into balls that are yellow and balls that are NOT yellow, count them, and then write numbers in the chart to tell how many. Then have students draw a circle around the category that is greater in number than the other category and tell how they know; 5 sort the pencils into pencils that are short and pencils that are NOT short, count them, and then write numbers in the chart to tell how many. Then have students draw a circle around the category that is greater in number than the other category and tell how they know. 6 **Higher Order Thinking** Say: *The fish are sorted into fish that have spots and fish that do NOT have spots.* Have students draw fish so the categories have an equal number of fish, and then write the number of fish in each category. Ask: *How do you know the categories have an equal number of fish?*

Name ______________________________

Homework & Practice 5-3

Sort the Categories by Counting

Another Look!

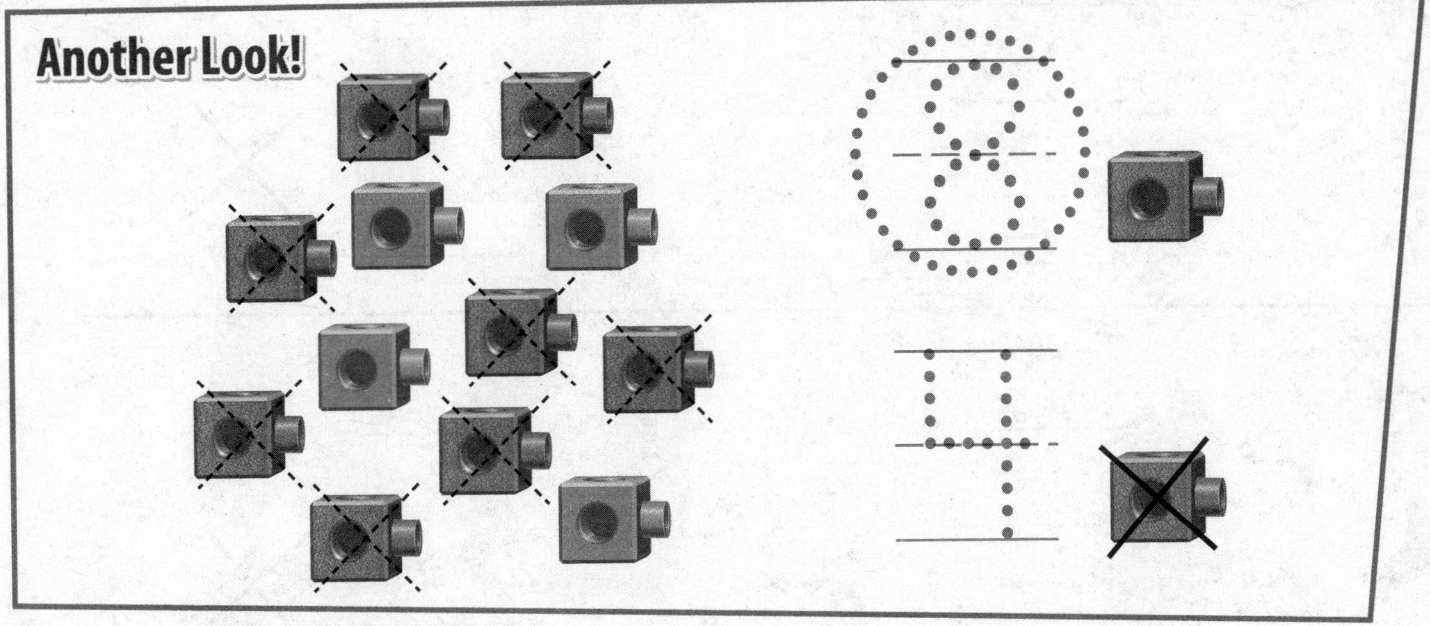

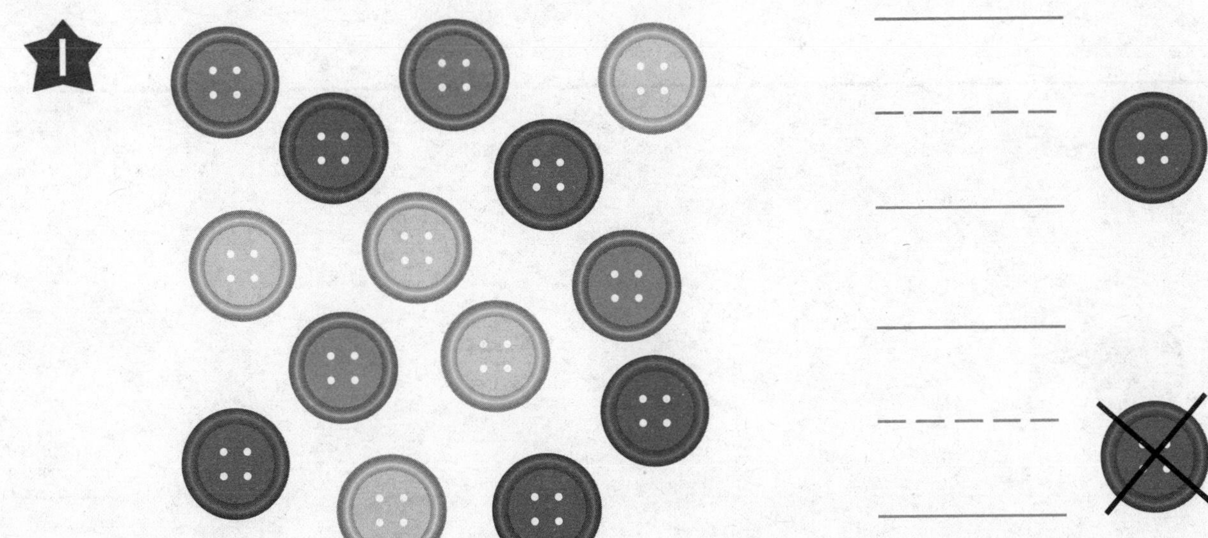

HOME ACTIVITY Show your child a group of 12 or fewer objects that are different in at least one way. For example, show 5 spoons and 6 forks. Arrange them in a random order. Ask your child to count the objects that are forks and the objects that are NOT forks, tell which category has a greater number of objects, and then explain how he or she knows. Repeat with another group of objects and have your child tell you which category has a number of objects that is less than the other category.

Directions Say: *Mark an X on the blue cubes, count the blue cubes, and then write how many. Count the cubes that are NOT blue, and then write how many. Draw a circle around the number that is greater than the other number. Tell how you know.* 1 Have students mark an X on each purple button, count them, and then write how many. Have students count the buttons that are NOT purple, write how many, and then draw a circle around the number that is less than the other number. Have them tell how they know.

Directions ❷ Have students mark an X on each large paper clip, count them, and then write how many. Have them count the paper clips that are NOT large, and then write how many. Then have students draw a circle around the number that is greater, and then tell how they know. ❸ **Number Sense** Have students mark an X on each sticker that is a sun, count them, and then write how many. Have students count the stickers that are NOT suns, and then write how many. Then have them draw a circle around the number that is greater, and then tell how they know. ❹ **Higher Order Thinking** Say: *These counters are sorted into red counters and counters that are NOT red.* Have students draw yellow counters so that the number of yellow counters is greater in number than the counters that are NOT yellow, and then tell how they know.

Name ______________________

Problem Solving

Lesson 5-4
Critique Reasoning

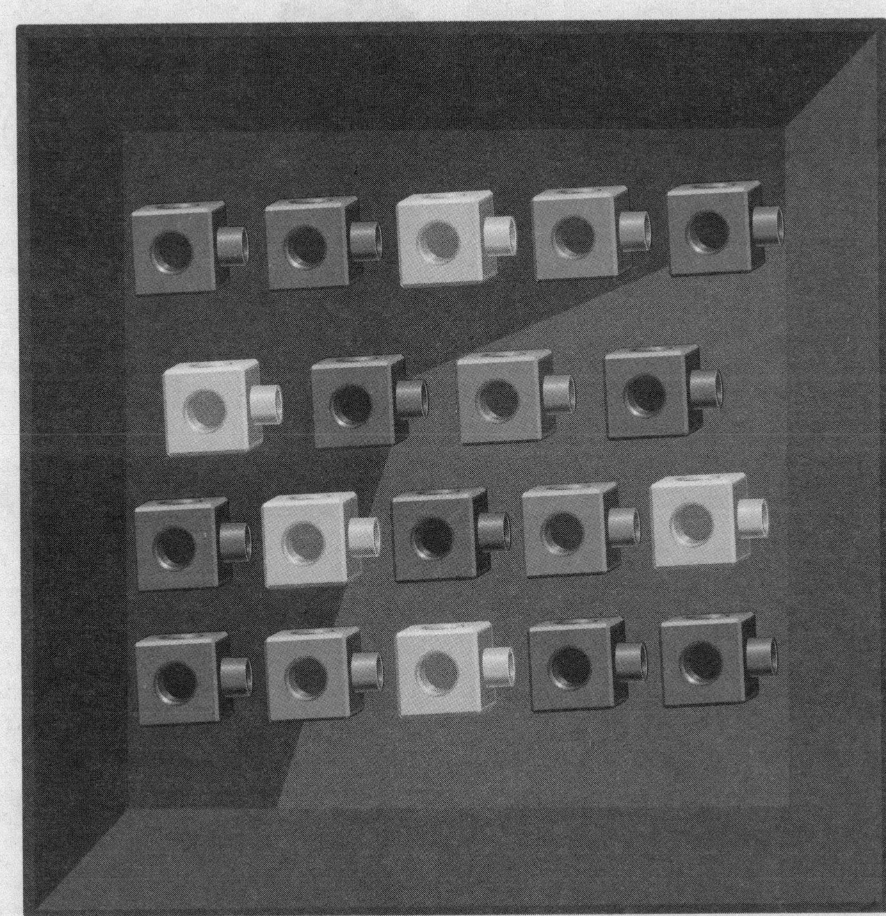

Directions Say: *Carlos says that the number of blue cubes is equal to the number of cubes that are NOT blue. Does his answer make sense? Use numbers, pictures, or words to explain your answer.*

I can ...
tell whether the way objects have been sorted, counted, and compared makes sense. I can explain how I know.

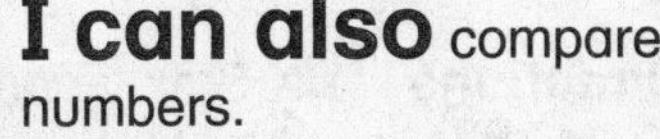

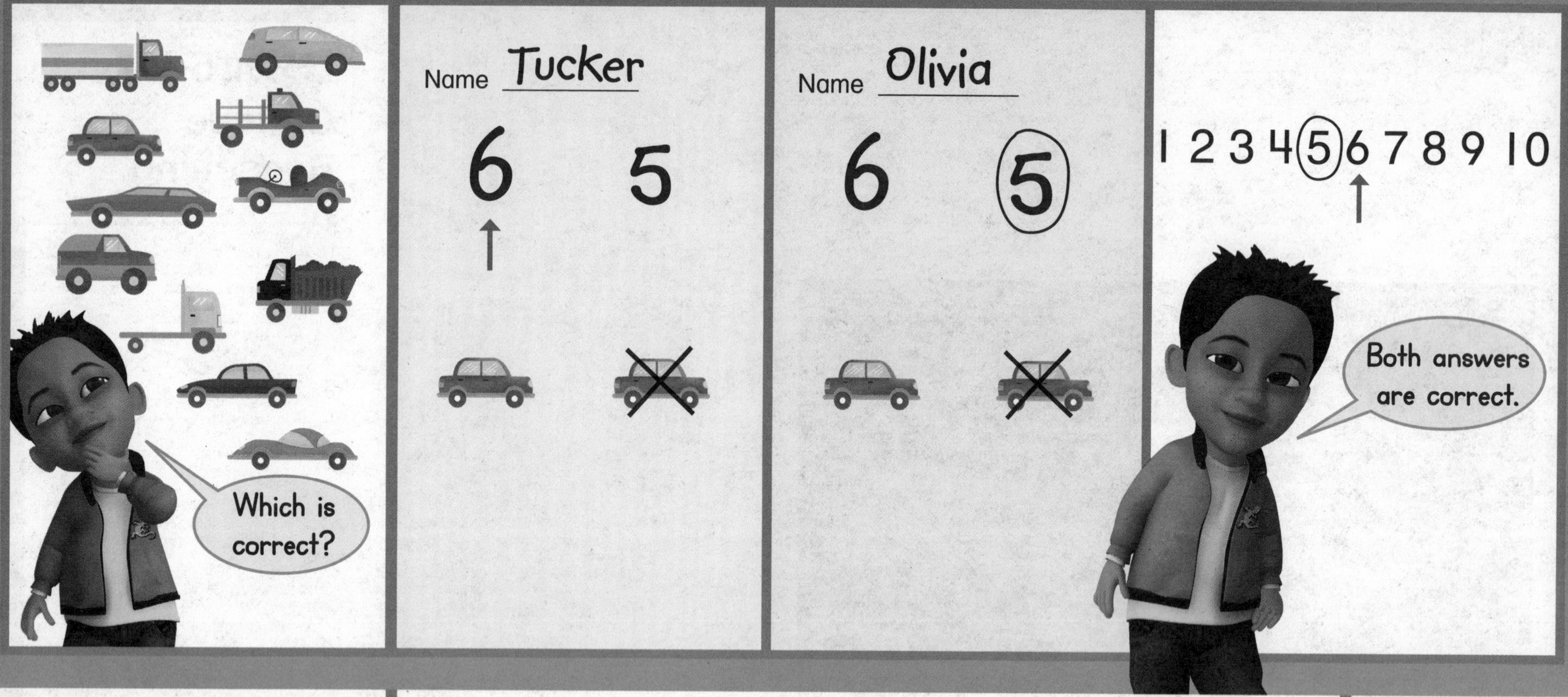

Which is correct?

Name Tucker

6 5

Name Olivia

6 5

1 2 3 4 5 6 7 8 9 10

Both answers are correct.

Guided Practice

Directions 1 Say: *Gabbi says that the category of airplanes is greater in number than the category that is NOT airplanes. Does her answer make sense?* Have students draw a circle around *yes* or *no*, and then use the sorting and counting of each category to explain their reasoning.

Tools Assessment

Name

Independent Practice

2

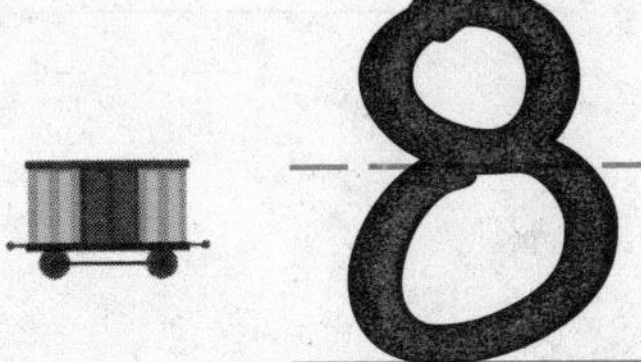

yes no

3

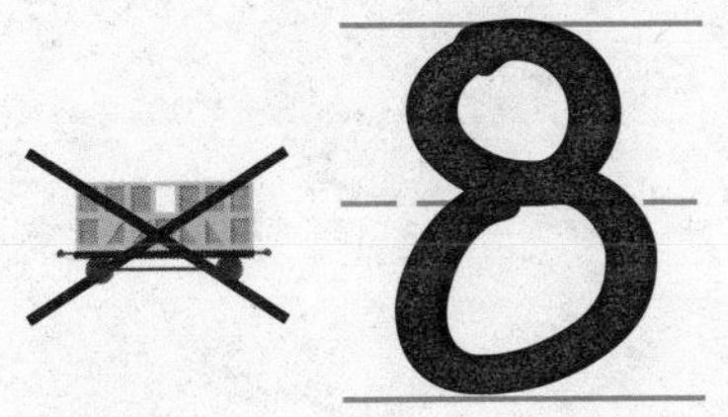

yes no

4

yes no

Directions Have students listen to each problem, draw a circle around *yes* or *no*, and then use the sorting and counting of each category to explain their reasoning. 2 *Damon says that he counted 8 yellow train cars and 6 train cars that are NOT yellow. Does his answer make sense?* 3 *Malinda says that the category of yellow train cars is less than the category of train cars that are NOT yellow. Does her answer make sense?* 4 *Aaron says that the category of red train cars is greater than the category of train cars that are NOT red. Does his answer make sense?*

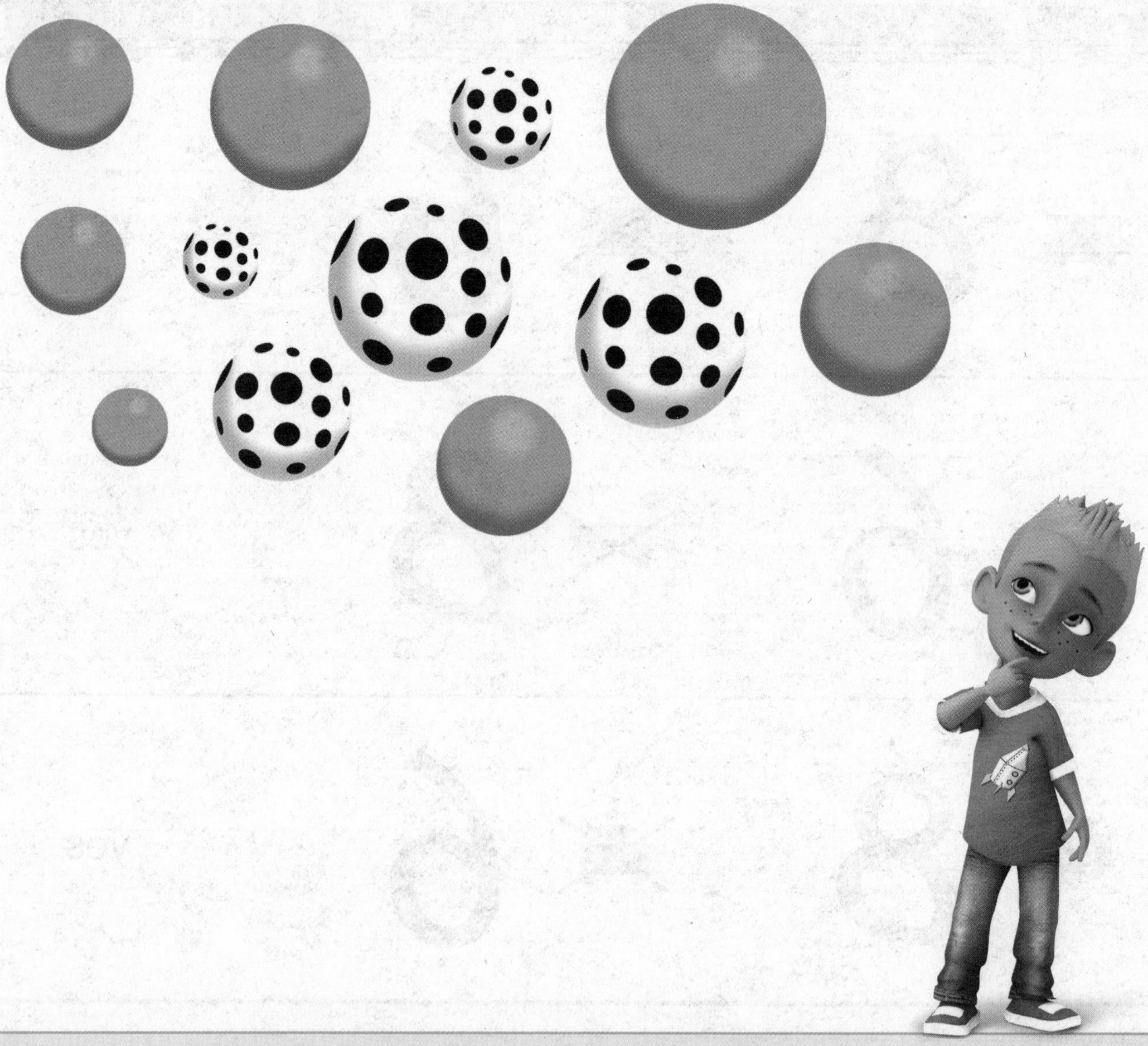

Directions Read the problem aloud. Then have students use multiple problem-solving methods to solve the problem. Say: *Alex says that if there was 1 fewer orange ball, then the category of orange balls would be equal in number to the category of balls that are NOT orange. Does his answer make sense?* **Reasoning** *Think about it. How many orange balls would there be if there was 1 fewer orange ball? Use numbers, tools, or draw a picture to show how many orange balls there would be.* **Be Precise** *Is the number of orange balls equal to the number of balls that are NOT orange?* **Critique Reasoning** *Use the sorting and counting of each category to explain your reasoning.*

Name ____________________

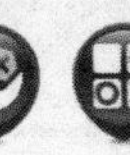

Help Tools Games

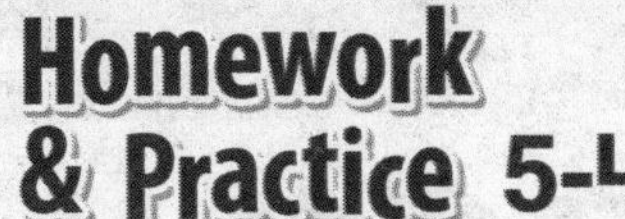

Homework & Practice 5-4

Critique Reasoning

Another Look!

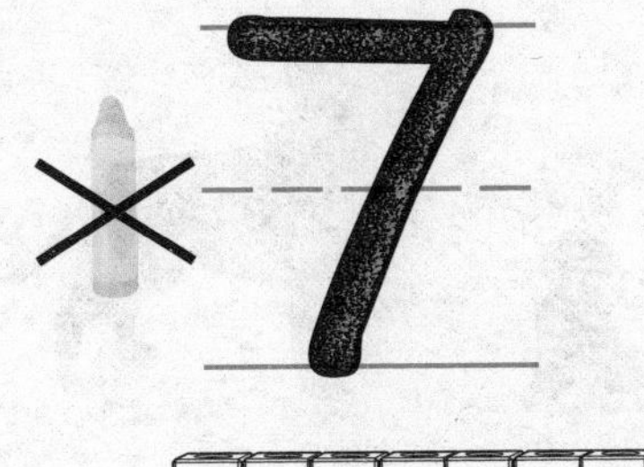

6 7

yes no

HOME ACTIVITY Show your child a group of up to 19 objects that are different in at least one way; for example, 9 plates and 8 cups. Arrange the objects in a random order and make a statement comparing the objects. For example, say: *The category of plates is greater than the category of cups.* Ask your child whether your statement makes sense and to explain how he or she knows. Repeat the activity with other groups of objects and statements that either make sense or do NOT make sense.

1

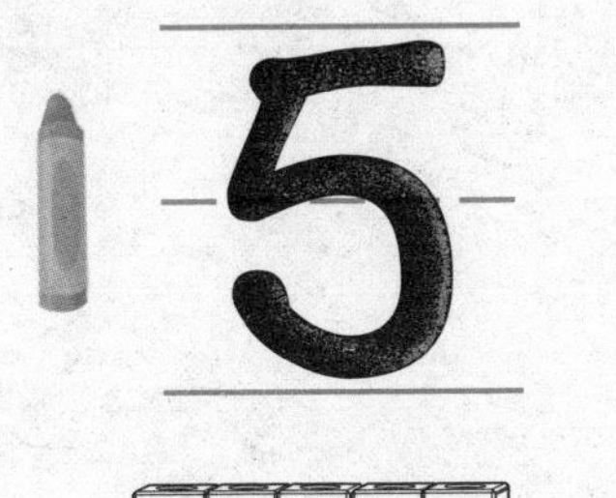

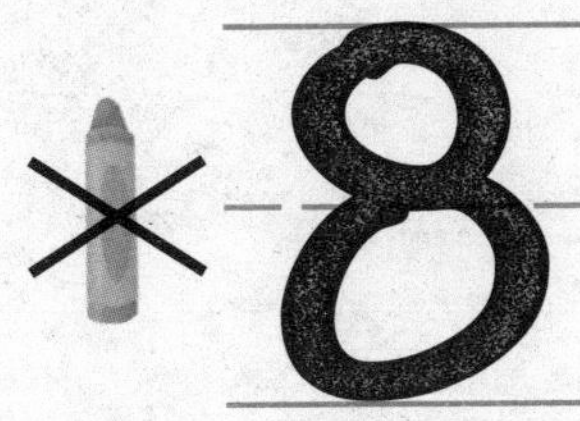

5 8

yes no

Directions Say: *Tanya used cubes to show how many crayons are yellow and how many crayons are NOT yellow. She says that the category of yellow crayons is less in number than the category of crayons that are NOT yellow. Does her answer make sense? Draw a circle around* yes *or* no. *Then use the sorting and counting of each category to explain their reasoning.* 1 Say: *Jared says that the category of green crayons is greater than the category that is NOT green. Does his answer make sense?* Then have students draw a circle around *yes* or *no*, and then use the sorting and counting of each category to explain their reasoning.

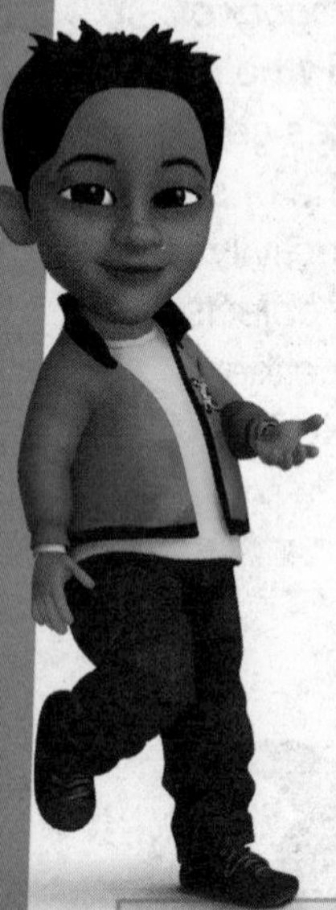

Directions Read the problem aloud. Then have students use multiple problem-solving methods to solve the problem. Say: *Carlos says that if there were 3 more brown dogs, then the category of brown dogs would be greater in number than the category of dogs that are NOT brown. He uses cubes to show the categories of dogs. Does his answer make sense?* **2 Model** *How can you show whether or not his answer makes sense? Use tools or draw a picture to show how many brown dogs there would be if 3 more brown dogs join the category.* **3 Be Precise** *Is the number of brown dogs now greater than the number of dogs that are NOT brown?* **4 Critique Reasoning** *Use the sorting and counting of each category to explain your reasoning.*

Name ______________________________

1

2

Directions **Understand Vocabulary** Have students: 1 draw an animal that fits each **category**, and then tell how the groups are organized; 2 sort books into books that are open and books that are NOT open. Have them draw **tally marks** in the chart as they count, and then write the number in another chart.

4

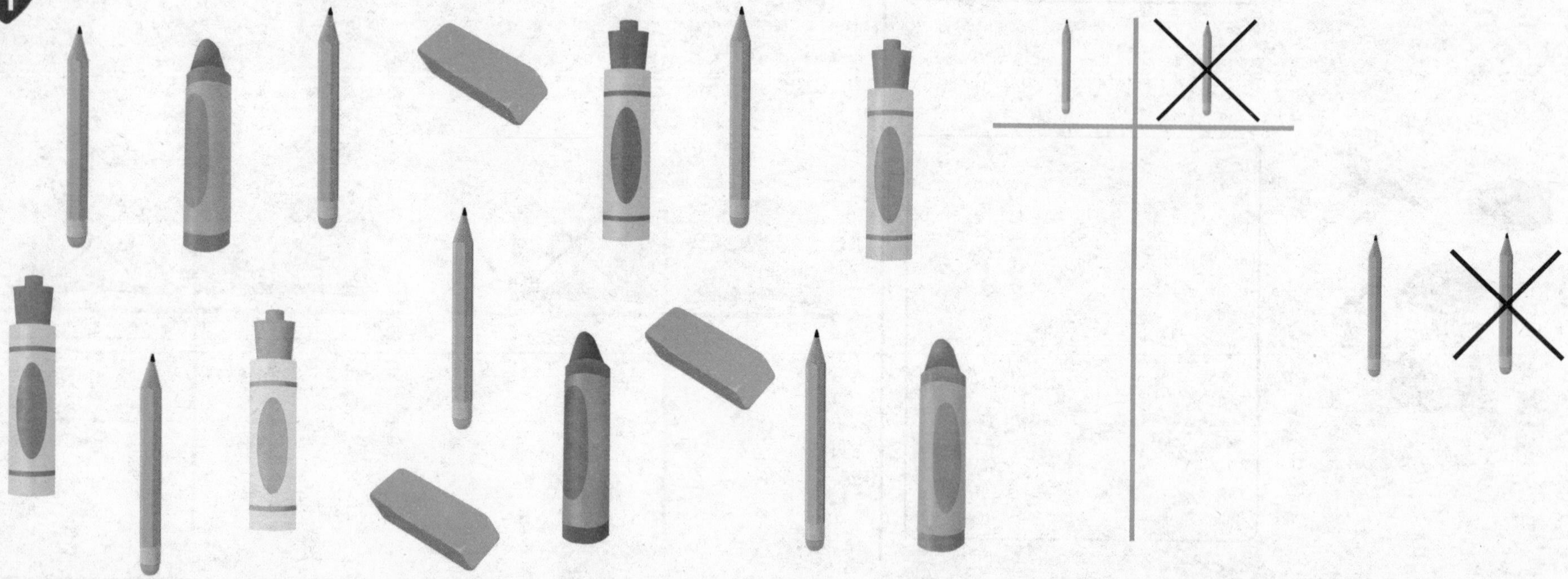

Directions **Understand Vocabulary** Have students: 3 **classify** the dogs by drawing circles and marking Xs, and then explain how they organized them; 4 draw lines in the **chart** to show how many in each group, and then draw a circle around the group that is greater in number than the other group.

Name ______________________

TOPIC 5

Reteaching

Set A

Directions Have students: 1 draw a circle around the animals that walk on 2 legs, and then mark an X on the animals that do NOT walk on 2 legs; 2 draw lines in the chart as they count the toys that are on the rug and the toys that are NOT on the rug. Then have them write the numbers to tell how many are in each group in another chart.

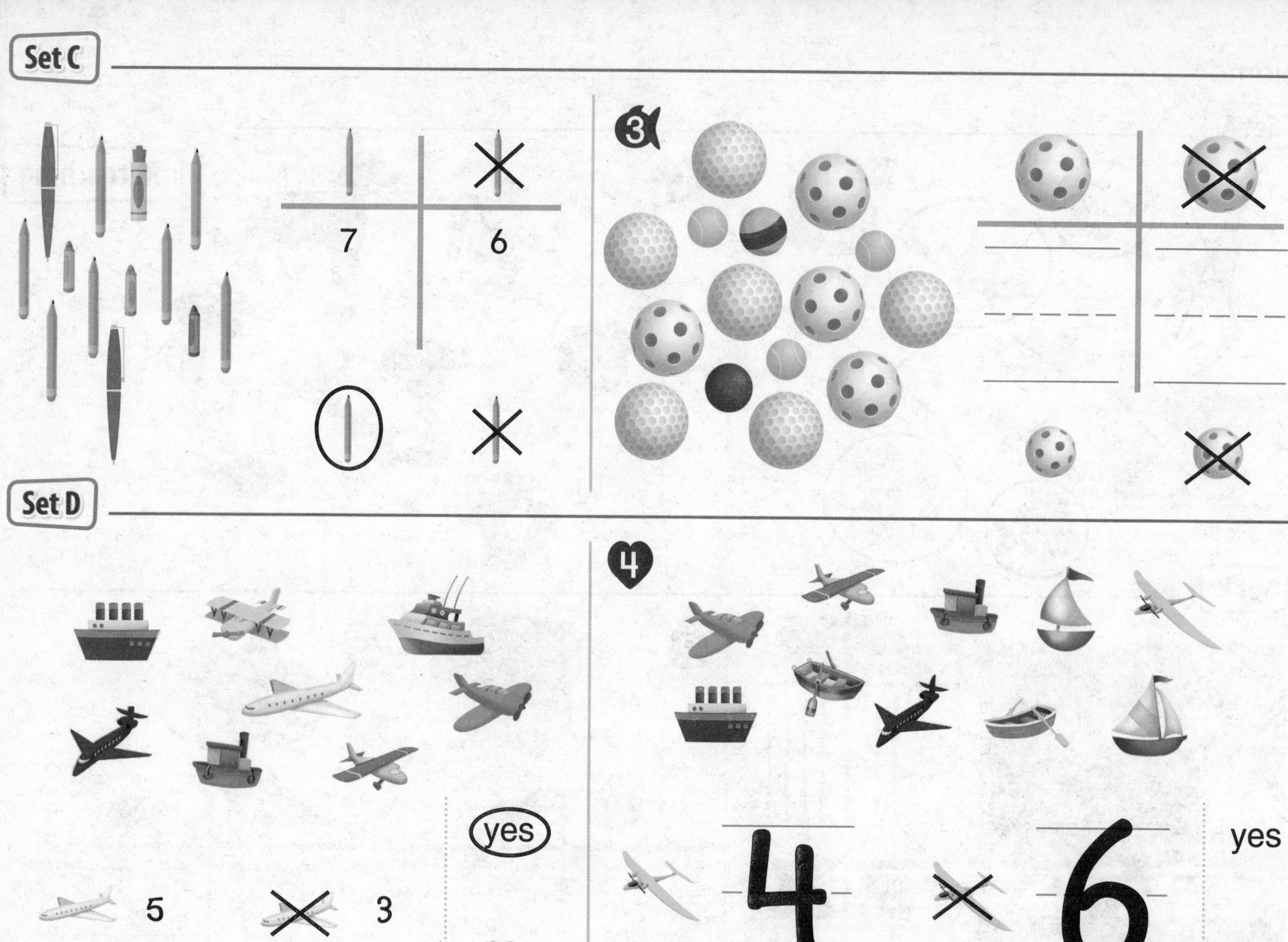

Directions 3 Have students sort the balls into balls that are white and balls that are NOT white, and then write numbers in the chart to tell how many. Then have students draw a circle around the group that is greater in number than the other group and tell how they know. 4 Say: *Malik says that the group of airplanes is greater than the group that is NOT airplanes. Does his answer make sense?* Have students draw a circle around *yes* or *no*, and then use the sorting and counting of each category to explain their reasoning.

Name ___________________________________

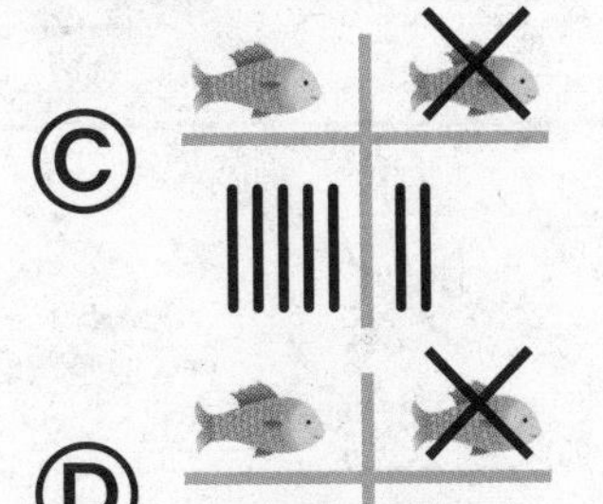

Ⓐ Ⓑ Ⓒ Ⓓ

Directions Have students mark the best answer. **1** Which chart shows how many fish are yellow and how many fish are NOT yellow? **2** Say: *The animals have been classified into two categories. Mark all the animals that belong in the category of animals inside the circle.* **3** Have students draw a circle around the animals that fly, and mark an X on the animals that do NOT fly.

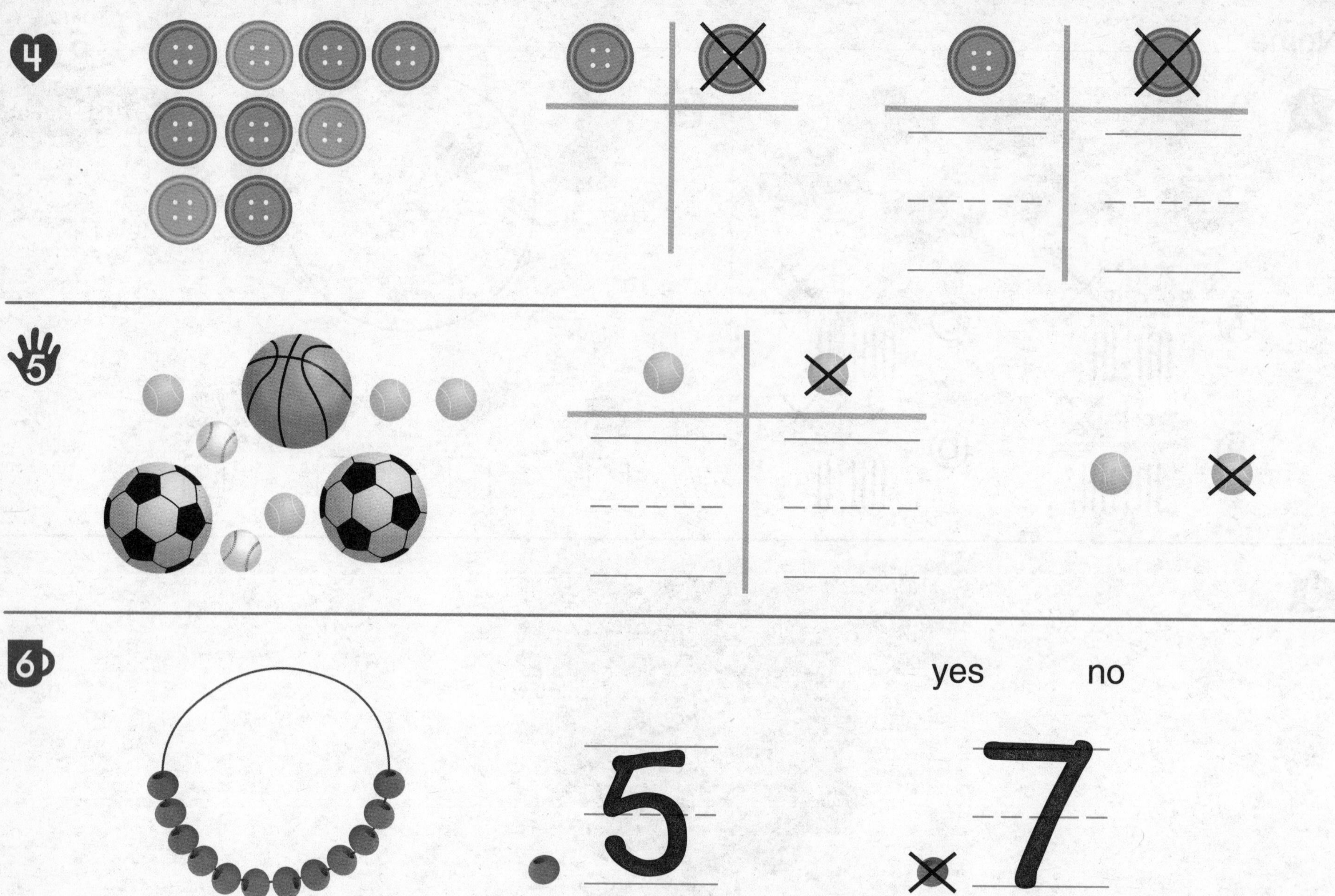

Directions Have students: 4 draw lines in the chart as they count the buttons that are green and the buttons that are NOT green, and then write the numbers to tell how many in another chart; 5 sort the balls into balls that are tennis balls and balls that are NOT tennis balls, count them, and then write numbers in the chart to tell how many. Then have students draw a circle around the category that is less in number than the other category; 6 listen to the problem, draw a circle around *yes* or *no*, and then use numbers, pictures, or words to explain how they know whether the answer makes sense. Say: *Dana says that the category of blue beads is greater in number than the category of beads that are NOT blue. Does her answer make sense?*

Name ______________________________

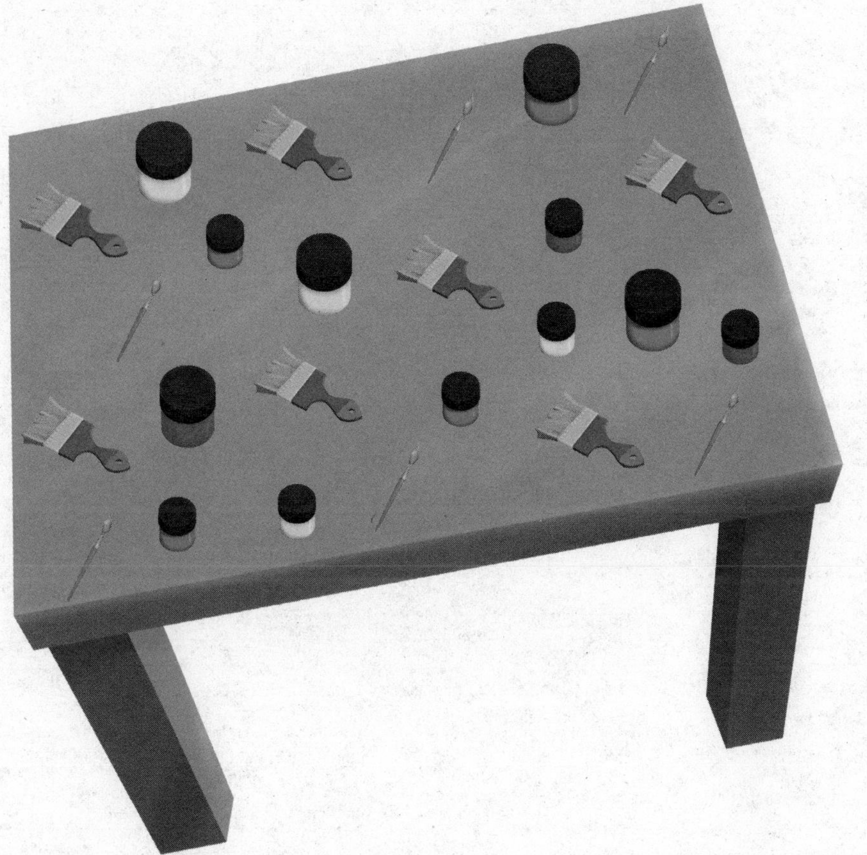

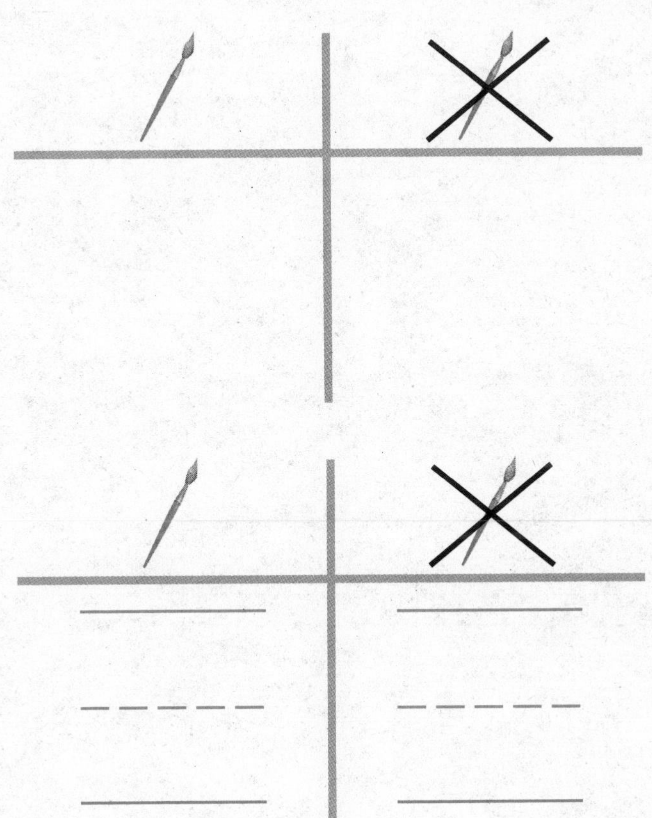

Directions **Works of Art** Say: *A kindergarten class uses paintbrushes and paint to draw pictures.* Have students: 1 draw a circle around the little paintbrushes, and then mark an X over the paintbrushes that are NOT little; 2 draw lines in the first chart as they count the paintbrushes that are little and the paintbrushes that are NOT little. Then have them write the number to tell how many are in each group in the second chart, and draw a circle around the number of the group that is less than the number of the other group.

yes no

Directions 3 Have students show one way to organize the jars of paint they see on the page before, and then explain how they sorted them. 4 Say: *Tina says that the number of small jars of paint is equal to the number of large jars of paint. Does her answer make sense?* Have students look at the paint on the page before, draw a circle around *yes* or *no*, and then use the sorting and counting of each category to explain their reasoning.

TOPIC 6

Understand Addition

Essential Question: What types of situations involve addition?

Babies

Cats can have kittens.

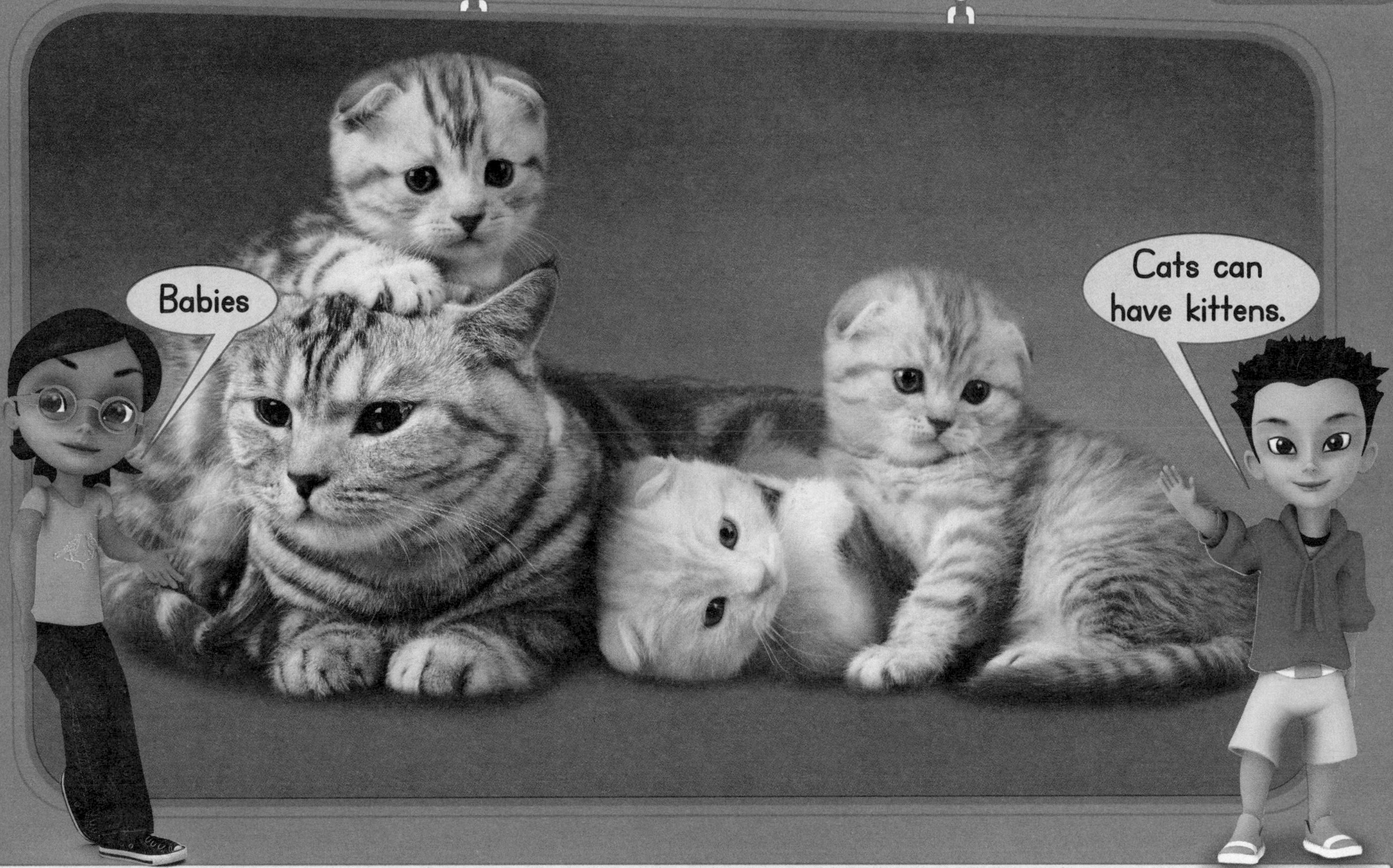

Math and Science Project: Baby Animals

Directions Read the character speech bubbles to students. **Find Out!** Have students explore the difference between animals and non-living things. Say: *Animals can have babies. Non-living things cannot have babies. Talk to friends and relatives about different animals and their babies.* **Journal: Make a Poster** Have students make a poster. Have them draw a cat with 5 kittens, circle the mother cat and the kittens to join them into one group, and then tell a joining story about how many cats there are in all.

Name ______________________________

Review What You Know

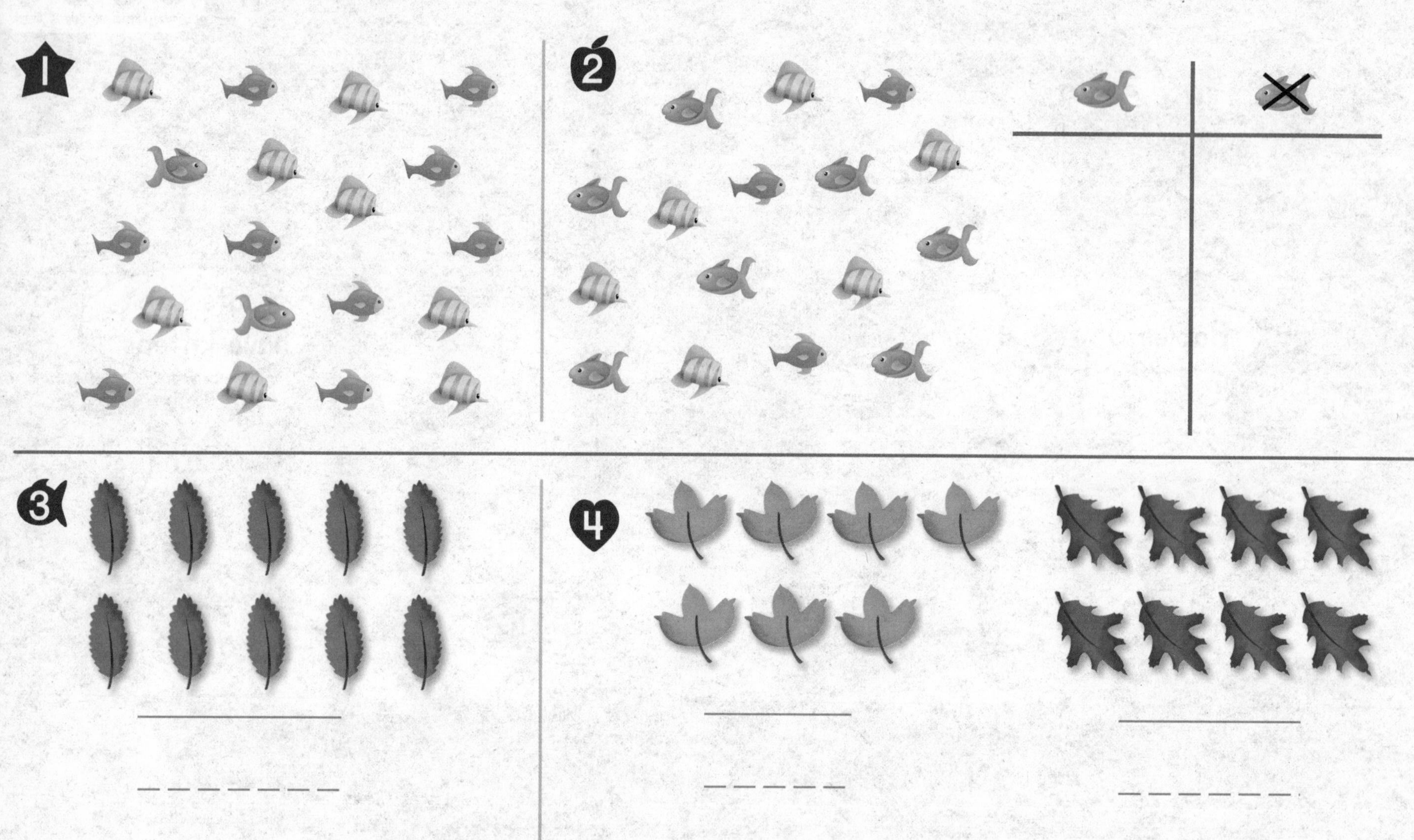

Directions Have students: 1 draw a circle around the fish that are purple, and then mark an X on the fish that are NOT purple; 2 draw lines in the chart as they count the fish that are blue and the fish that are NOT blue. Then have them draw a circle around the picture at the top of the chart of the group that is greater than the other; 3 count the leaves, and then write the number to tell how many; 4 count the leaves, write the numbers to tell how many, and then draw a circle around the number that is less than the other number.

My Word Cards

Directions Have students cut out the vocabulary cards. Read the front of the card, and then ask them to explain what the word or phrase means.

join	in all	addition sentence
add	plus sign (+)	equal sign (=)

My Word Cards

Directions Review the definitions and have students study the cards. Extend learning by having students draw pictures for each word on a separate piece of paper.

3 and 5 is 8.

Point to the addition sentence.
Say: *3 and 5 is 8 is an **addition sentence**. It tells how many there are in all.*

Point to the blue and red blocks.
Say: *There are 6 blocks **in all**.*

Point to each group of flowers.
Say: ***Join** the groups together to find how many flowers there are in all.*

$4 + 3 = 7$

Point to the equal sign.
Say: *This is the **equal sign**. It shows that the part on one side is the same amount as the part on the other side.*

$3 + 1 = 4$

Point to the plus sign.
Say: *This is the **plus sign**. It means add.*

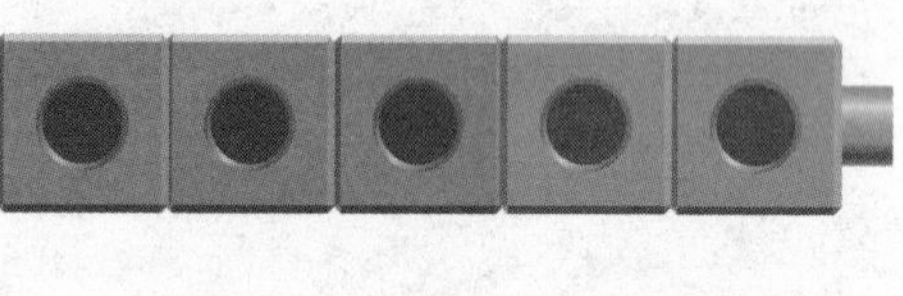

$3 + 2 = 5$

Point to the connecting cubes.
Say: *When you **add** 3 blue cubes to 2 green cubes, you have 5 cubes.*

A-Z Glossary

My Word Cards

Directions Have students cut out the vocabulary cards. Read the front of the card, and then ask them to explain what the word or phrase means.

sum	**equation**	

My Word Cards

Directions Review the definitions and have students study the cards. Extend learning by having students draw pictures for each word on a separate piece of paper.

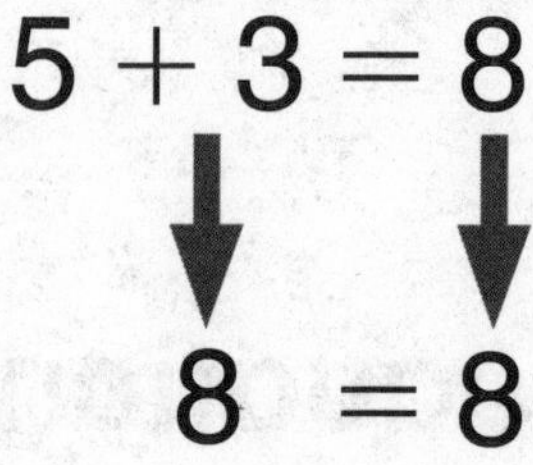

Point to one side of the equation at a time.
Say: *An* ***equation*** *uses an equal sign to show two sides are the same amount.*

$2 + 3 = 5$

Point to the 5.
Say: *The* ***sum*** *tells how many in all.*

Solve & Share

Name ______________________________

Lesson 6-1
Explore Addition

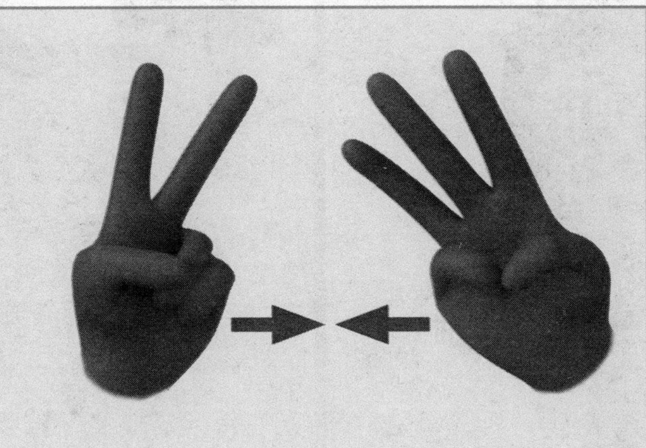

4 5 6

Directions Say: *Carlos holds up 2 flowers in one hand and 3 flowers in another hand. How many flowers does he have in all? Think about the problem in your head. Then act out the story with your fingers to explain. Draw a circle around your answer.*

I can ... show numbers in many ways.

I can also model with math.

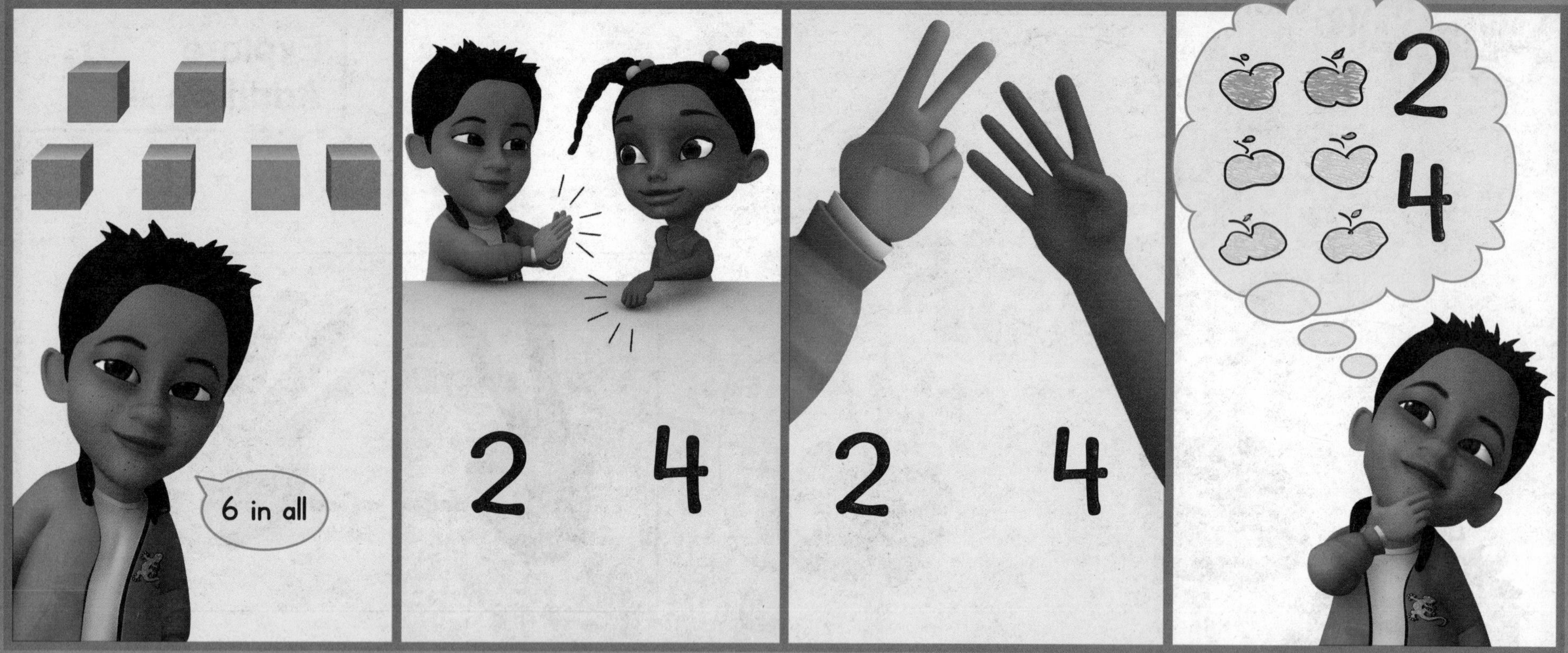

6 in all

2 4

2 4

2 4

Guided Practice

Directions 1 Have students listen to the story, and then do all of the following to show each part to find how many in all: clap and knock, hold up fingers, and give an explanation of a mental image. Ask them to show how many of each color crayon, and then write the number to tell how many in all. *Parker has 2 orange crayons. He has 3 purple crayons. How many crayons does he have in all?*

Name ______

2

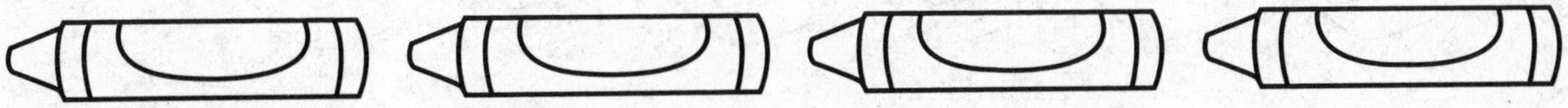

3 and 1 is ___ in all.

3

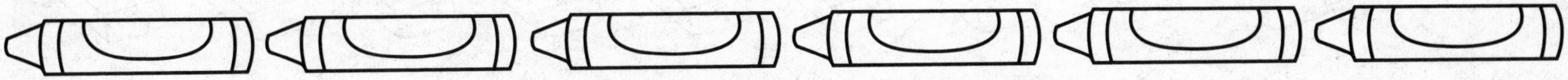

1 and 5 is ___ in all.

Directions Have students listen to the story, and then do all of the following to show each part to find how many in all: clap and knock, hold up fingers, and give an explanation of a mental image. Ask them to color the number of each part, and then write the number to tell how many in all. 2 *Cami has 3 green crayons. She has 1 blue crayon. How many crayons does she have in all?* 3 *Sammy has 1 brown crayon. He has 5 purple crayons. How many crayons does he have in all?*

Independent Practice

Directions 4 Have students listen to the story, and then do all of the following to show each part to find how many in all: clap and knock, hold up fingers, and give an explanation of a mental image. Ask them to color the number of each part, and then write the number to tell how many in all. *Junie has 5 erasers in one pocket. She has 2 erasers in her other pocket. How many erasers does she have in all?* 5 **Higher Order Thinking** Have students listen to the story, color the erasers to show the parts, and then write the numbers to tell how many of each. *Miguel has 9 erasers. He gives some to Aaron. He gives some to Bella. How many does he give to each friend?*

Name ______________________

Homework & Practice 6-1

Explore Addition

Another Look!

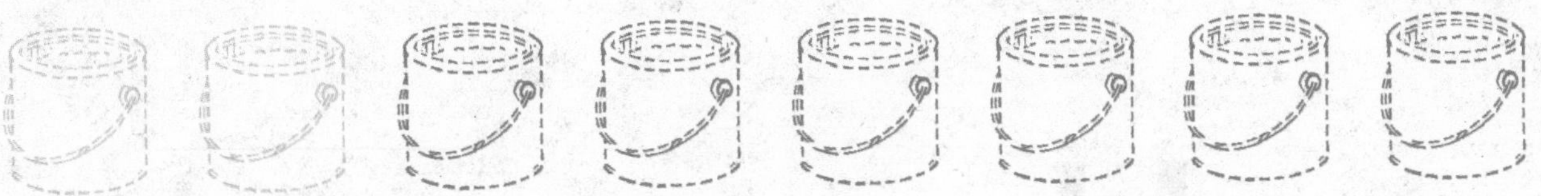

2 and 6 is 8 in all.

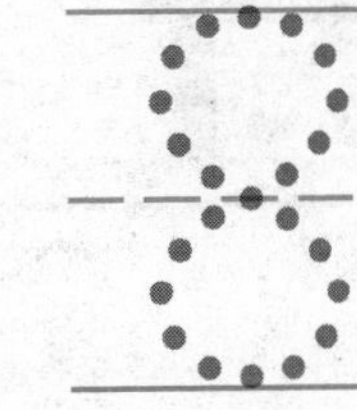

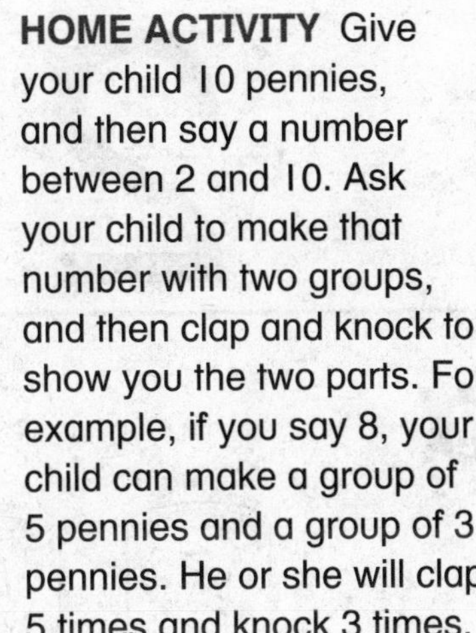

HOME ACTIVITY Give your child 10 pennies, and then say a number between 2 and 10. Ask your child to make that number with two groups, and then clap and knock to show you the two parts. For example, if you say 8, your child can make a group of 5 pennies and a group of 3 pennies. He or she will clap 5 times and knock 3 times.

1

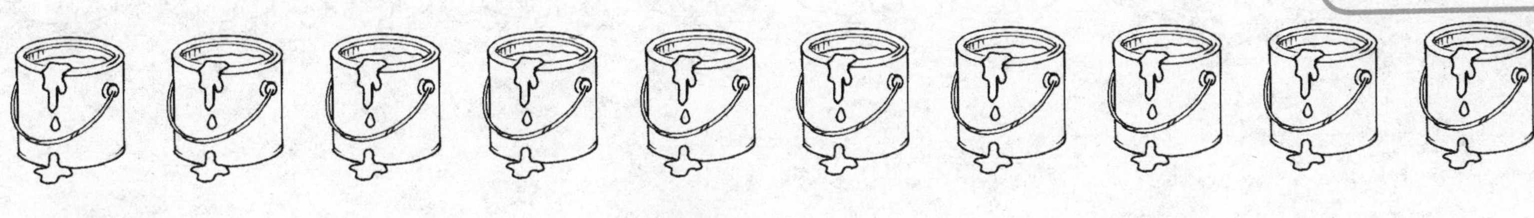

5 and 5 is ______ in all.

Directions Say: *There are 2 yellow paint buckets. There are 6 orange paint buckets. How many paint buckets are there in all?* Model how to clap and knock each part, how to show the parts with fingers, and how to think of the parts with a mental image to find the whole. Then have students color the number of each part, and then write the number to tell how many in all. **1** Have students listen to the story, and then do all of the following to show each part to find how many in all: clap and knock, hold up fingers, and give an explanation of a mental image. Ask them to color the number of each part, and then write the number to tell how many in all. *Mattias has 5 red paint buckets. He has 5 blue paint buckets. How many paint buckets does he have in all?*

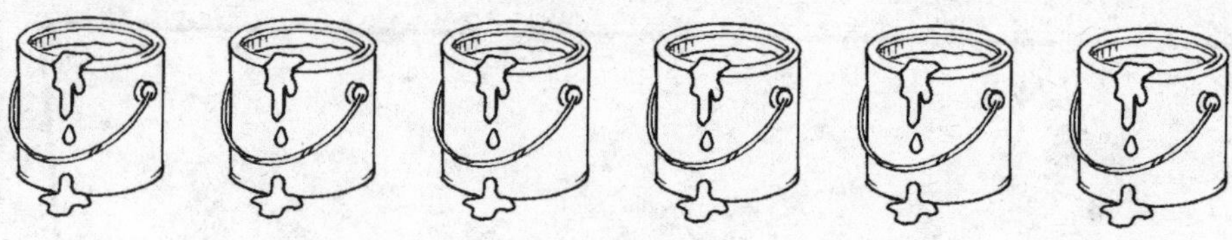

2 and 4 is ____ in all.

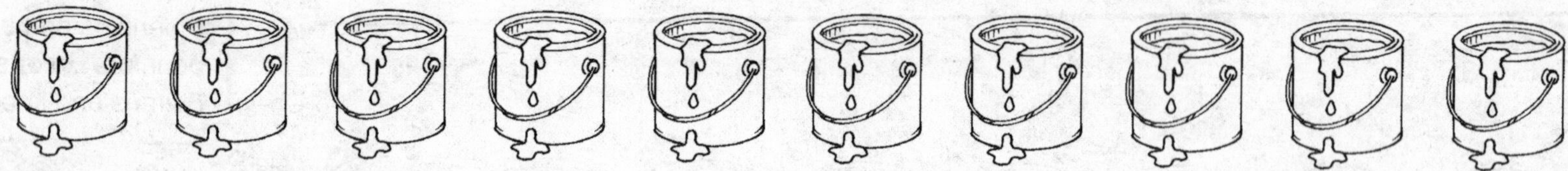

10 is ____ and ____ in all.

Directions ❷ Have students listen to the story, and then do all of the following to show each part to find how many in all: clap and knock, hold up fingers, and give an explanation of a mental image. Ask them to color the number of each part, and then write the number to tell how many in all. *Shruthi has 2 green paint buckets. She has 4 blue paint buckets. How many paint buckets does she have in all?* ❸ **Higher Order Thinking** Have students listen to the story, color the paint buckets to show the parts, and then write the numbers to tell how many of each. *Freddy has 10 paint buckets. He fills some with purple paint. He fills the others with red paint. How many does he fill with each color?*

Name ____________________

Lesson 6-2

Represent Addition as Adding To

______ and ______ is ______.

Directions Say: *Daniel sees 1 boat on the water. Then 4 more boats go out onto the water. How many boats are there in all? Show how you know.*

I can ... represent addition as adding to a number.

I can also use math tools correctly.

1 and 2 is 3.

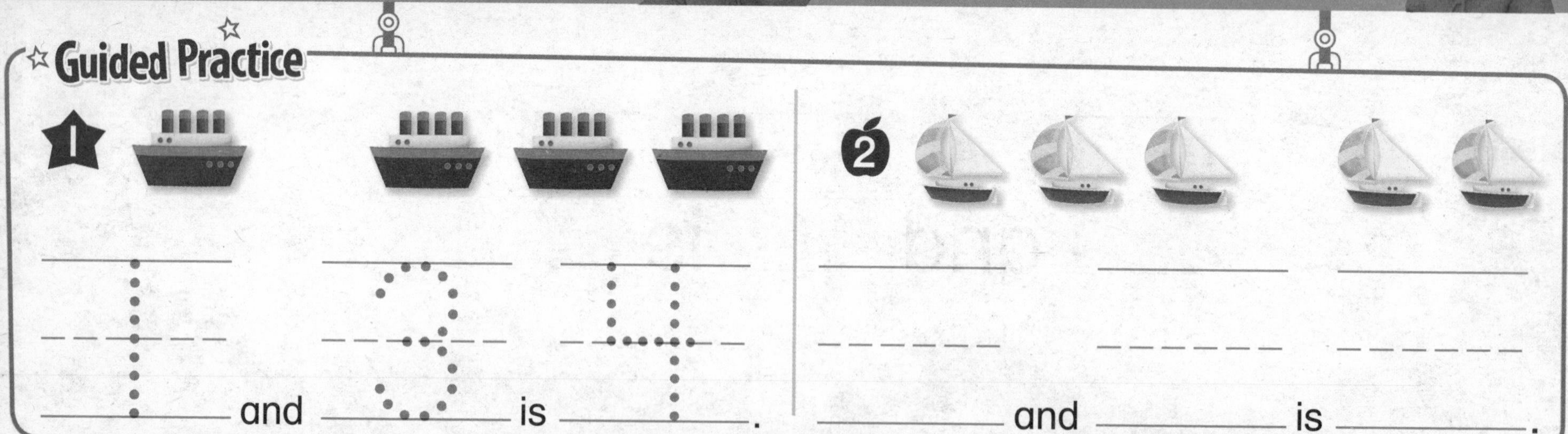

Directions 1 and 2 Have students use connecting cubes to model adding to the group when more boats come, and then write an addition sentence to tell how many in all.

Name ______________________________

3

______ ______ ______

______ and ______ is ______.

4

______ ______ ______

______ and ______ is ______.

5

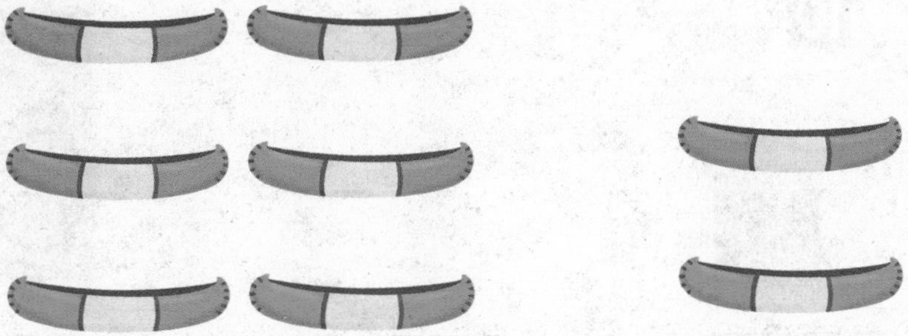

______ ______ ______

______ and ______ is ______.

6

______ ______ ______

______ and ______ is ______.

Directions 3–6 Have students use connecting cubes to model adding to the group when more boats come, and then write an addition sentence to tell how many in all.

Independent Practice

Tools Assessment

7

_____ _____ _____

_____ and _____ is _____.

8

_____ _____ _____

_____ and _____ is _____.

9

_____ _____ _____

_____ and _____ is _____.

10

_____ _____ 3

_____ and _____ is 3.

Directions 7–9 Have students use counters to model adding to the group when more fish or boats come, and then write an addition sentence to tell how many in all. 10 **Higher Order Thinking** Have students draw the number of green connecting cubes to add to the given connecting cube to make 3 connecting cubes in all, and then complete the addition sentence.

Name ______________________

Homework & Practice 6-2

Represent Addition as Adding To

HOME ACTIVITY Have your child model counting on with paper clips or pennies. For example, ask your child to make a group of 4 paper clips and a group of 3 paper clips. Have your child count the first group, and then from that number, count on the number of paper clips in all.

Another Look!

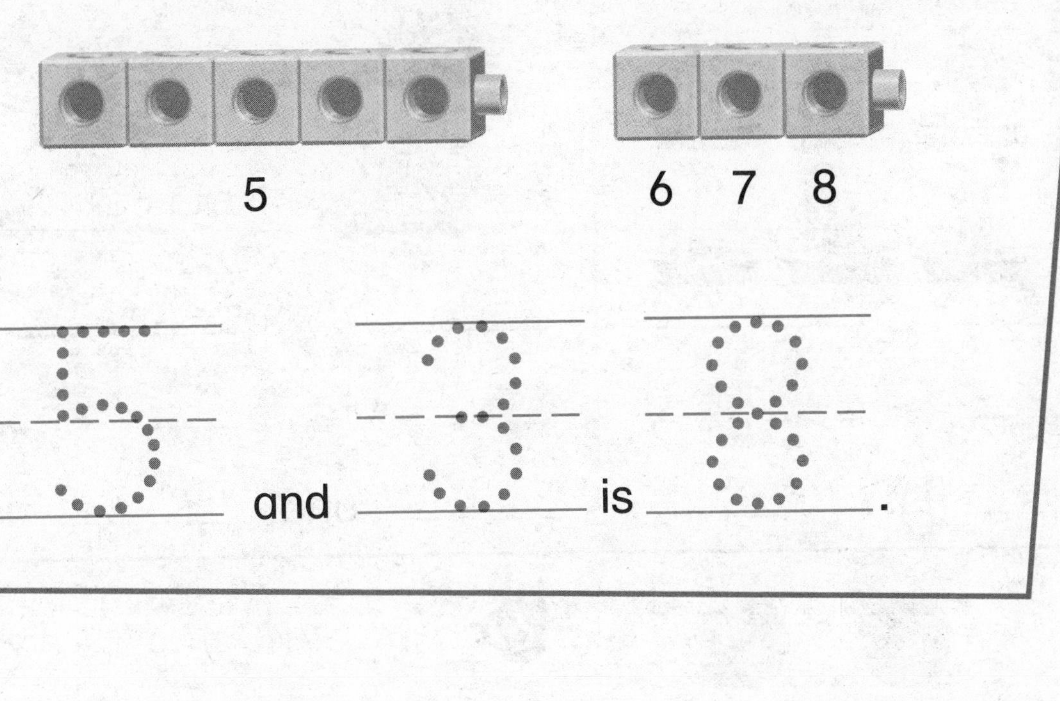

5 and 3 is 8.

1

______ and ______ is ______.

2

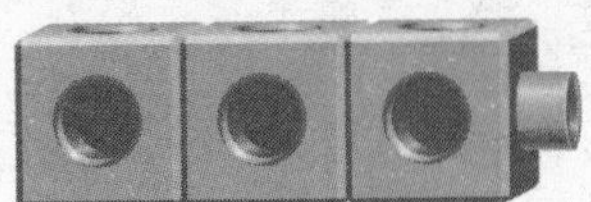

______ and ______ is ______.

Directions Say: *Marta has some cubes. Then she gets some more. You can write numbers to show how Marta counts on to add more to the group of cubes. Then write an addition sentence to tell how many in all.* 1 and 2 Say: *Daniel has some cubes. Then he gets some more.* Have students count on to add to the group of cubes, and then write an addition sentence to tell how many in all.

3

_____ and _____ is _____.

4

_____ and _____ is _____.

5

_____ and _____ is _____.

6

_____ and _____ is 6.

Directions 3 and 4 Have students write the numbers to tell how many to add to the group when more boats come, and then write how many there are in all. 5 **Higher Order Thinking** Have students listen to the story, draw the other group of counters, and then write an addition sentence to match the story. *There are some boats in the water. 6 more boats come. There are 9 boats in all.* 6 **Higher Order Thinking** Have students draw a group of up to 6 connecting cubes. Then have them draw the number of cubes they need to add to equal 6, and then complete the addition sentence.

Name ______________________

Lesson 6-3
Represent Addition as Putting Together

______ and ______ is ______.

Directions Say: *Daniel sees 3 tomatoes on a plant. He sees 5 tomatoes on another plant. How many tomatoes are there in all? Show how you know.*

I can ...
represent addition as putting two or more numbers together.

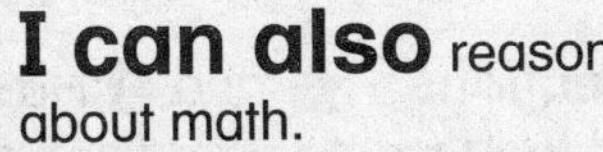

I can also reason about math.

2 and 4 is 6.

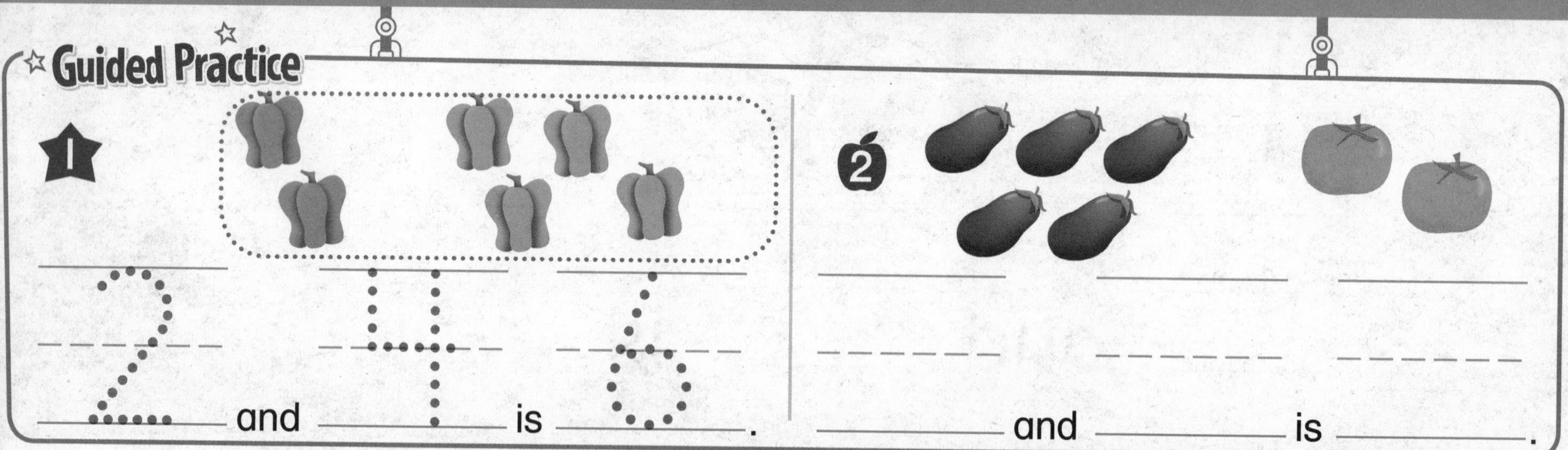

Directions 1 and 2 Have students use counters to model putting together the groups, draw a circle around the groups to put them together, and then write an addition sentence to tell how many in all.

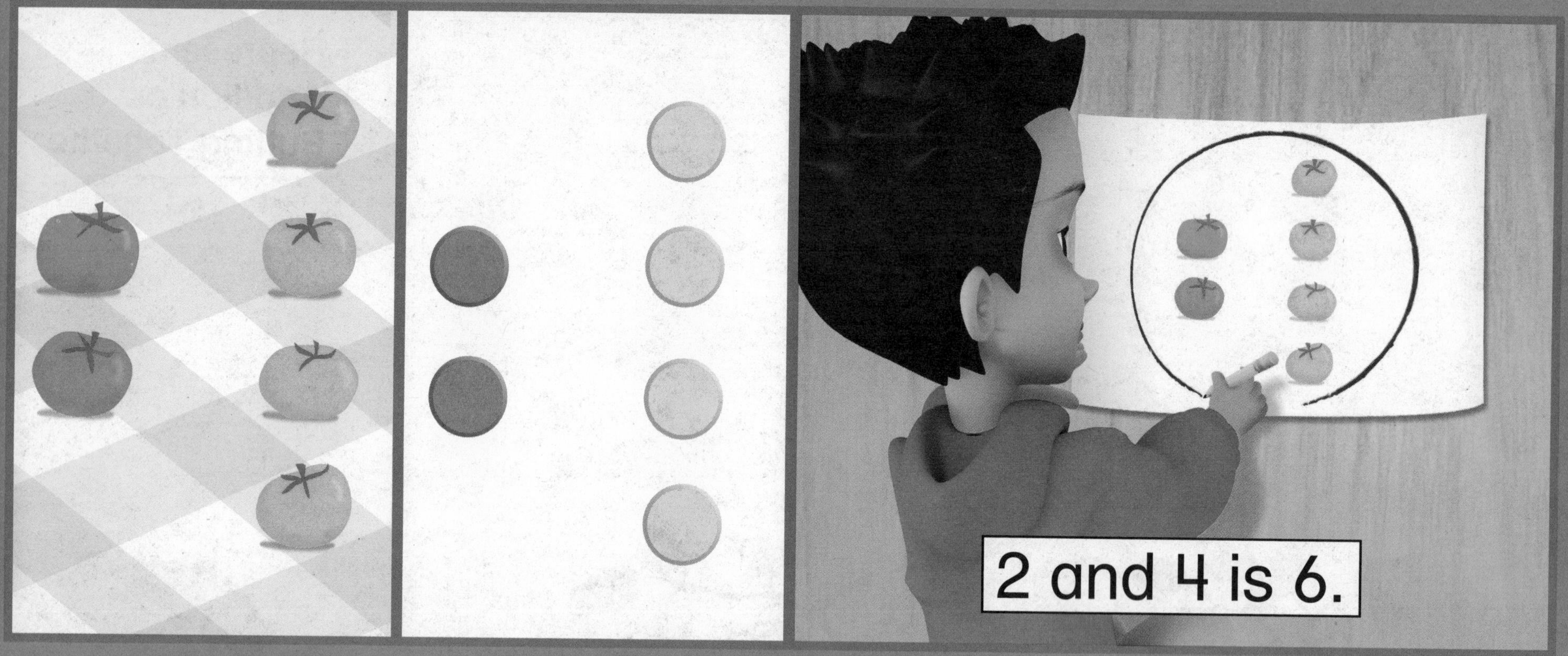

Name ______________________________

3

_______ _______ _______

_______ and _______ is _______.

4

_______ _______ _______

_______ and _______ is _______.

5

_______ _______ _______

_______ and _______ is _______.

6

_______ _______ _______

_______ and _______ is _______.

Directions 3 **Vocabulary** Have students draw a circle around the groups to put them together, write an **addition sentence** to tell how many in all, and then say the sentence aloud. 4–6 Have students use counters to model putting together the groups, draw a circle around the groups to put them together, and then write an addition sentence to tell how many in all.

Independent Practice

Tools Assessment

7

_____ and _____ is _____.

8

_____ and _____ is _____.

9

_____ and _____ is _____.

10

_____ and _____ is 8.

Directions 7 **Math and Science** Say: *What do plants need to grow?* Have students name the vegetables, draw a circle around the groups to put them together, and then write an addition sentence to tell how many in all. 8 and 9 Have students use counters as a model to put together the groups, draw a circle around the groups to put them together, and then write an addition sentence to tell how many in all. 10 **Higher Order Thinking** Have students draw the other group of counters, draw a circle around the groups to put them together, and then complete the addition sentence.

Name ____________________

Homework & Practice 6-3

Represent Addition as Putting Together

Another Look!

1 and 4 is 5.

HOME ACTIVITY Take turns choosing a problem on this page and making up a number story about it. One person tells the story, and the other person writes the complete addition sentence. For example, 1 and 4 is 5.

1

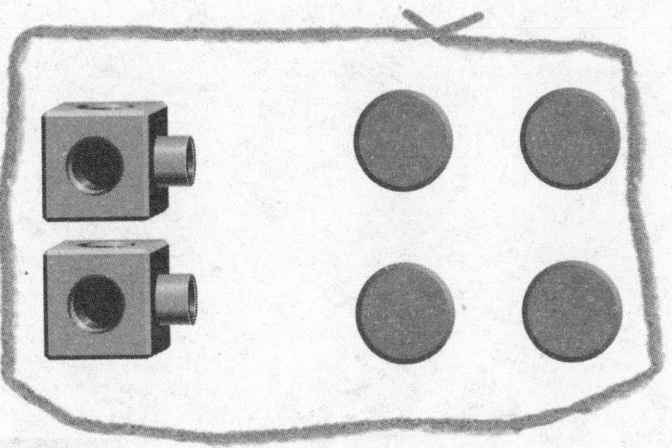

____ ____ ____

____ and ____ is ____.

2

____ ____ ____

____ and ____ is ____.

Directions Say: *How many cubes are there? How many counters are there? When you put the math tools together with yarn, you can count them all to find how many. Write how many of each math tool there is, and then write an addition sentence to tell how many in all.* **1** and **2** Have students write the numbers to tell how many of each math tool there is, and then write an addition sentence to tell how many in all.

3

_____ and _____ is _____.

4

_____ and _____ is _____.

5

_____ and _____ is 9.

6

_____ and _____ is 7.

Directions 3 and 4 Have students put together the math tools, draw a circle around the groups to put them together, and then write an addition sentence to tell how many in all. 5 **Higher Order Thinking** Have students draw the other group, draw a circle around the groups to put them together, and then complete the addition sentence. 6 **Higher Order Thinking** Have students draw counters to show two groups that equal 7 when put together, and then complete the addition sentence.

Name ______________________________

Lesson 6-4

Use the Plus Sign

Directions Say: *There are 4 crayons in a box. Daniel puts 3 red crayons in the box. How can you find how many crayons there are in all?*

I can ...
add numbers together.

I can also reason about math.

4 and 2

4 + 2

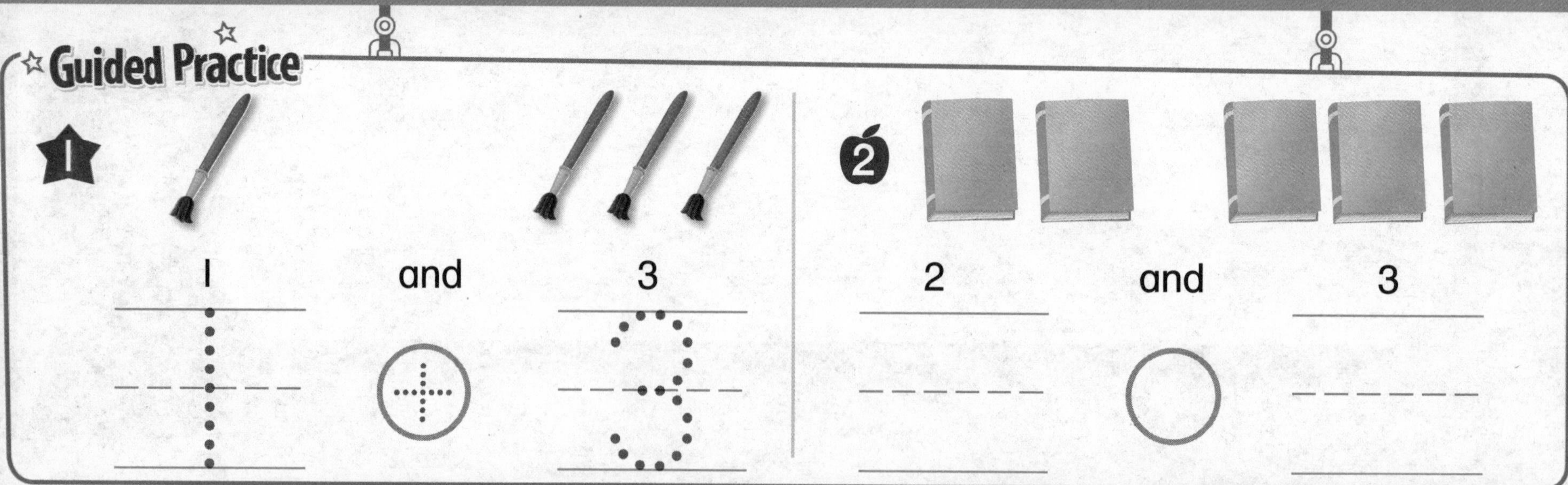

Directions 1 and 2 Have students count the school supplies in each group, and then write the numbers and the plus sign to show adding the groups.

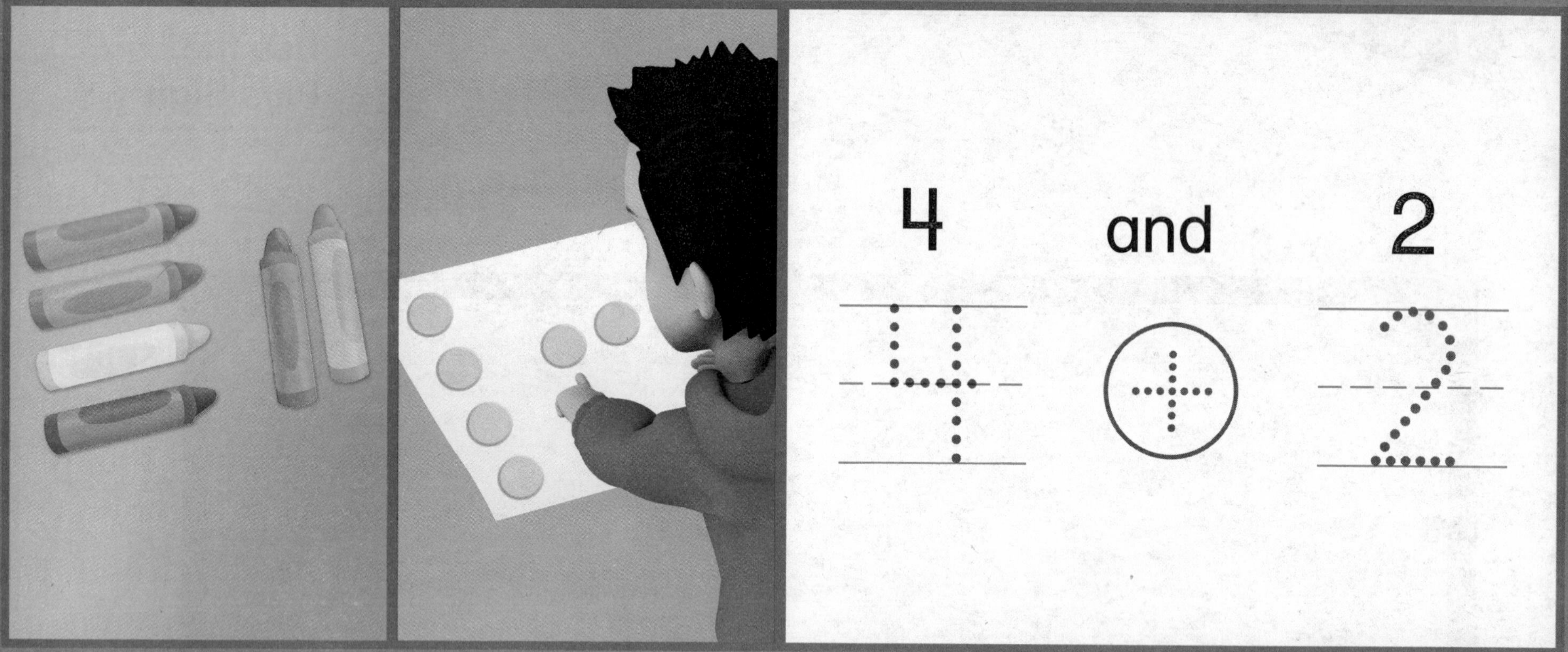

Name ______________________________

3

3 and 4

4

5 and 1

5

3 and 3

6

2 and 1

Directions 3–5 Have students count the school supplies in each group, and then write the numbers and the plus sign to show adding the groups. 6 **Number Sense** Have students count all the bookmarks, write the numbers and the plus sign to show adding, and then explain how counting forward relates to adding.

Independent Practice

Tools Assessment

7

5 and 1

8

2 and 5

9

1 and 2

10

Directions 7–9 Have students count the school supplies in each group, and then write the numbers and the plus sign to show adding the groups. 10 **Higher Order Thinking** Have students draw two groups of counters to show 5 in all, and then write the number of counters in each group and the plus sign to show adding the groups.

Name ______________________

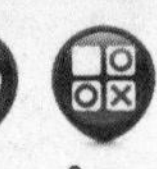

Help Tools Games

Homework & Practice 6-4

Use the Plus Sign

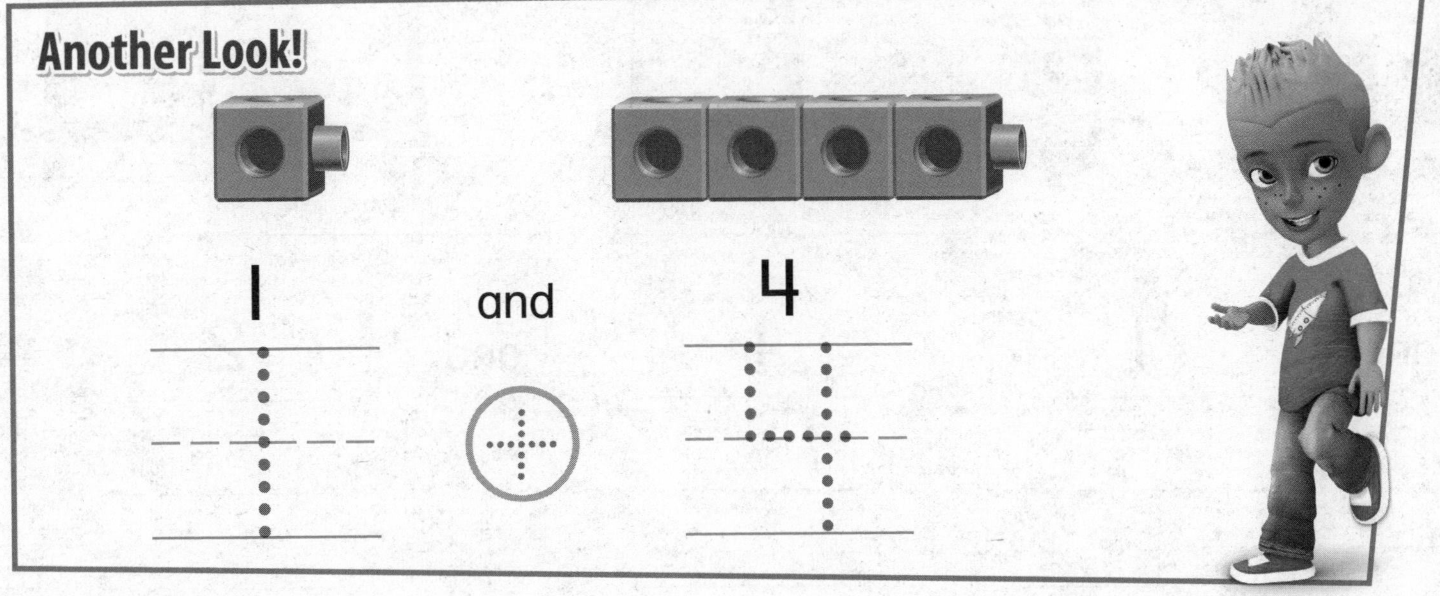

HOME ACTIVITY Show your child two groups of pennies and have your child write an addition expression with a plus sign to show adding the groups. For example, show a group of 2 pennies and a group of 5 pennies. Help your child write the addition expression 2 + 5.

4 and 2

2 and 3

Directions Say: *You can use connecting cubes or other objects to add 1 and 4. Write the numbers and the plus sign to show how to add the groups.* 1 and 2 Have students count the objects in each group, and then write the numbers and the plus sign to show adding the groups.

3

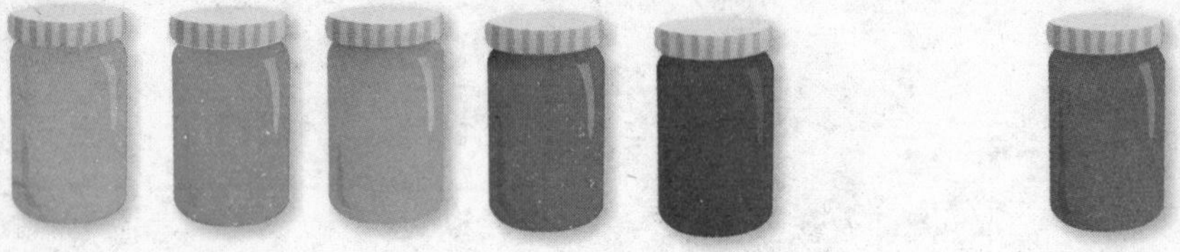

5 and 1

4

1 and 2

5

6

Directions 3 and 4 Have students count the art supplies in each group, and then write the numbers and the plus sign to show adding the groups. 5 **Higher Order Thinking** Have students count the connecting cubes in each group, and then write the numbers and the plus sign to show adding the groups. 6 **Higher Order Thinking** Have students draw two groups of apples that equal 6 apples in all when added together, and then write the number of apples in each group and the plus sign to show adding the groups.

Name ______________________________

Lesson 6-5

Represent and Explain Addition with Equations

Directions Say: *Daniel counts 4 drums in a parade. Then he sees 1 more drum. What numbers do you add to find how many drums he sees in all? How can you show the adding?*

I can ...
write an equation to show addition.

I can also reason about math.

Guided Practice

1

2 and 6 is 8.

2 + 6 = 8

2

4 and 1 is 5.

Directions 1 and 2 Have students add the groups to find the sum, and then write an equation to show the addition.

Name ______________________________

3 2 and 4 is 6.

4 4 and 4 is 8.

5 6 and 1 is 7.

6 3 and 4 is 7.

Directions 3–6 Have students add the groups to find the sum, and then write an equation to show the addition.

Independent Practice

Tools Assessment

7

8 and 2 is 10.

8

5 and 4 is 9.

9

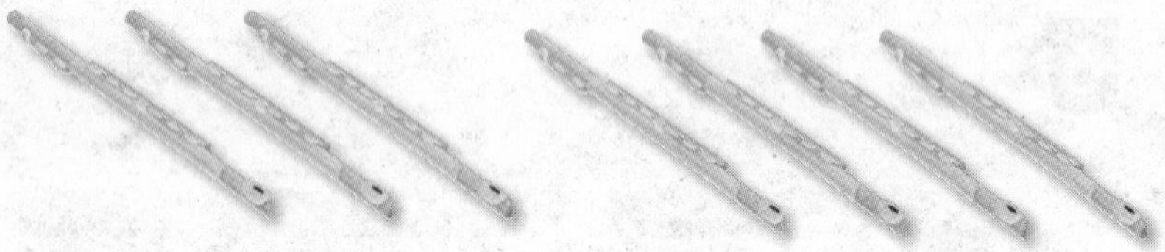

3 and 4 is 7.

10

7

Directions 7–9 Have students add the groups to find the sum, and then write an equation to show the addition. 10 **Higher Order Thinking** Have students listen to the story, draw the groups and add to find the sum, and then complete the equation. *There are some counters on the page. Emily puts 3 more on the page. There are now 7 counters in all.*

Name ________________

Help Tools Games

Homework & Practice 6-5

Represent and Explain Addition with Equations

Another Look!

4 and 5 is 9.

4 + 5 = 9

HOME ACTIVITY Make a set of number cards from 1 to 5. Shuffle them and place them facedown on a table. Take turns picking 2 number cards and finding the sum of the two numbers. Work with your child to write a number sentence using the plus and equal signs.

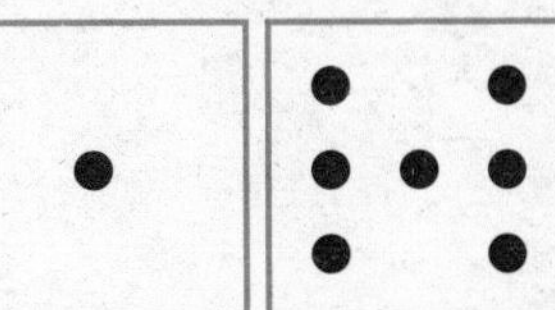

1 and 7 is 8.

2

2 and 2 is 4.

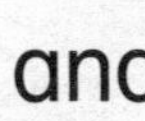

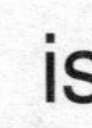

Directions Say: *What numbers do the dot cards show? Write the numbers, the plus sign, the equal sign, and the sum to show addition.* 1 and 2 Have students add the groups to find the sum, and then write an equation to show the addition.

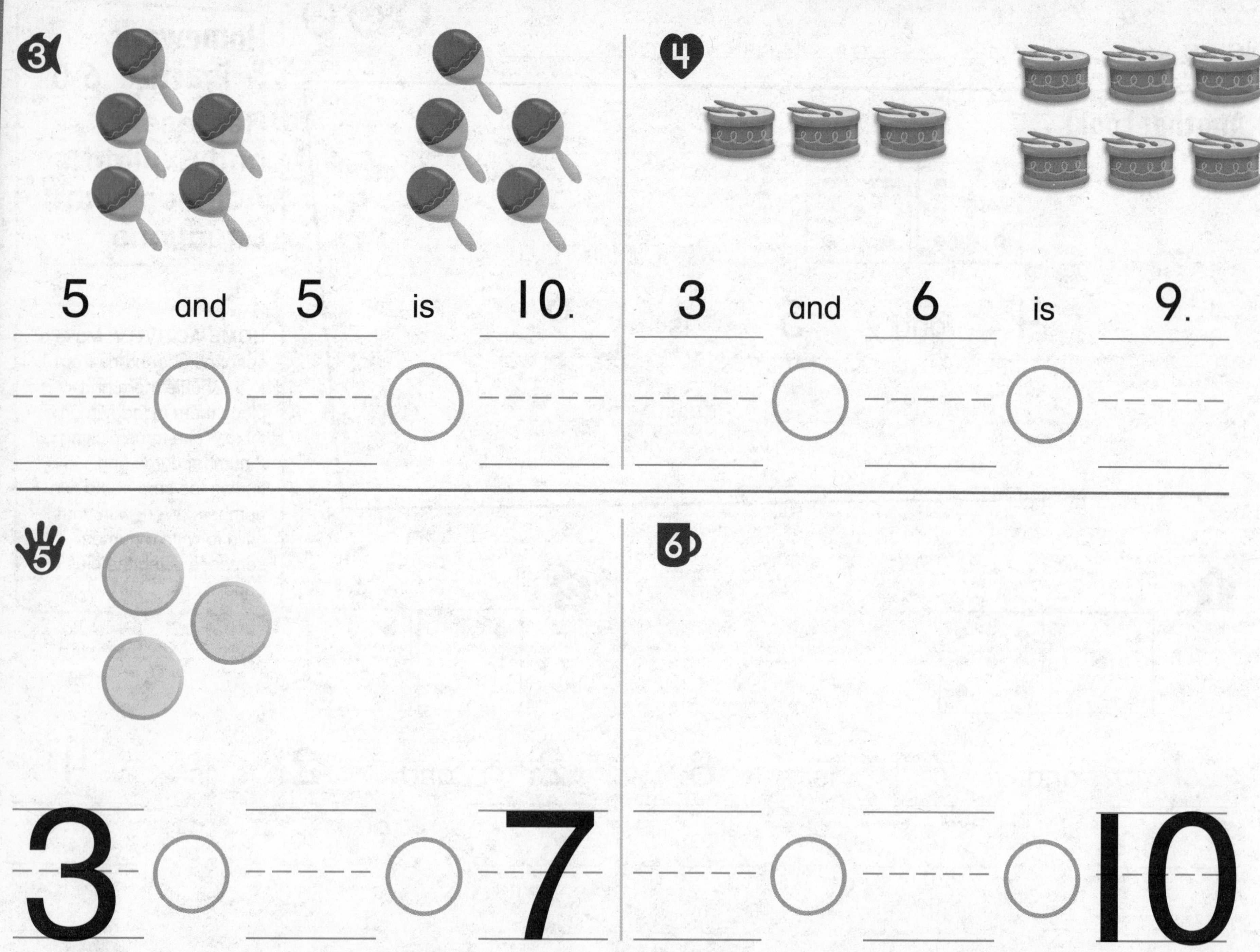

Directions 3 and 4 Have students add the groups to find the sum, and then write an equation to show the addition. 5 **Algebra** Have students draw the other group, add the groups to find the sum, and then complete the equation. 6 **Higher Order Thinking** Have students draw counters to show two groups that add up to 10, and then complete the equation.

Solve & Share

Name ______________________

Solve

Lesson 6-6

Continue to Represent and Explain Addition with Equations

_____ ○ _____ ○ _____

Directions Say: *Daniel sees 2 rabbits under a bush. He sees 5 other rabbits eating grass. How many rabbits are there in all? What equation can you write to solve the problem?*

I can ...
use the plus sign and equal sign in an equation.

I can also use math tools correctly.

$3 + 3 = 6$

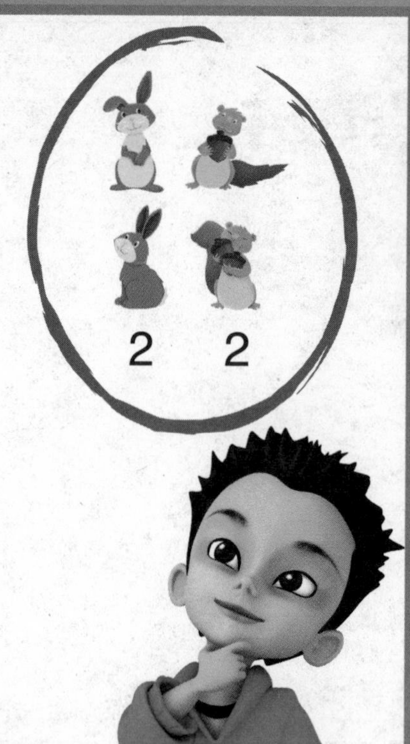

$2 + 2 = 4$

Guided Practice

Directions 1 Have students add one group of foxes to the other, and then write an equation to show the addition. 2 Have students put together the groups of animals, and then write an equation to show the addition.

Name ______________________________

3

______ ______ ______

______ ◯ ______ ◯ ______

______ ______ ______

4

______ ______ ______

______ ◯ ______ ◯ ______

______ ______ ______

5

______ ______ ______

______ ◯ ______ ◯ ______

______ ______ ______

6

______ ______ ______

______ ◯ ______ ◯ ______

______ ______ ______

Directions 3 and 4 Have students put together the groups of animals, and then write an equation to show the addition. 5 and 6 Have students add one group of animals to the other, and then write an equation to show the addition.

Independent Practice

Tools Assessment

7

8

9

10

Directions 7 and 8 Have students add one group of birds to the other, and then write an equation to show the addition. 9 Have students put together the groups of animals, and then write an equation to show the addition. 10 **Higher Order Thinking** Have students draw counters to show two groups that add up to 9, and then write an equation to show the addition.

Name ____________________

Help

Tools
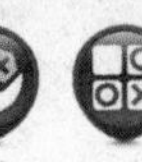
Games

Homework & Practice 6-6

Continue to Represent and Explain Addition with Equations

Another Look!

4 + 3 = 7

5 + 5 = 10

HOME ACTIVITY Make two groups of pennies and have your child write an equation that shows joining the groups together. For example, show a group of 5 pennies and a group of 4 pennies, and help your child write 5 + 4 = 9.

1

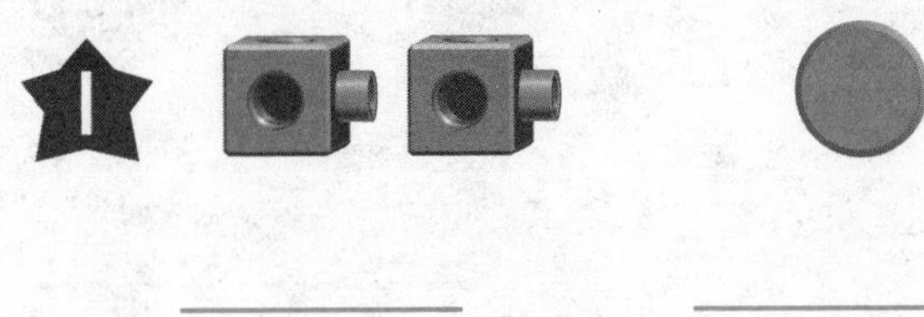

____ ◯ ____ ◯ ____

2

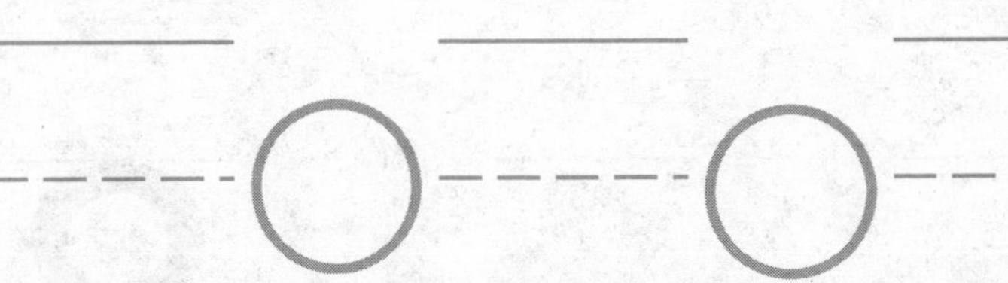

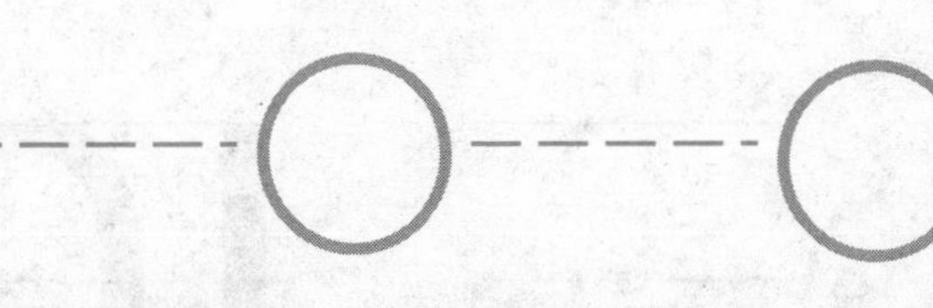

____ ◯ ____ ◯ ____

Directions Say: *Make a group of 4 connecting cubes or other objects, and a group of 3 counters or other objects. Now put the groups together to find out how many there are in all. Write the numbers, plus sign, equal sign, and sum to make the equation that shows the addition. Now make a group of 5 connecting cubes or other objects, and another group of 5 connecting cubes or other objects. Add one group to the other to find how many there are in all. Write an equation to show the addition.* 1 Have students put together the groups of math tools, and then write an equation to show the addition. 2 Have students add one group of math tools to the other, and then write an equation to show the addition.

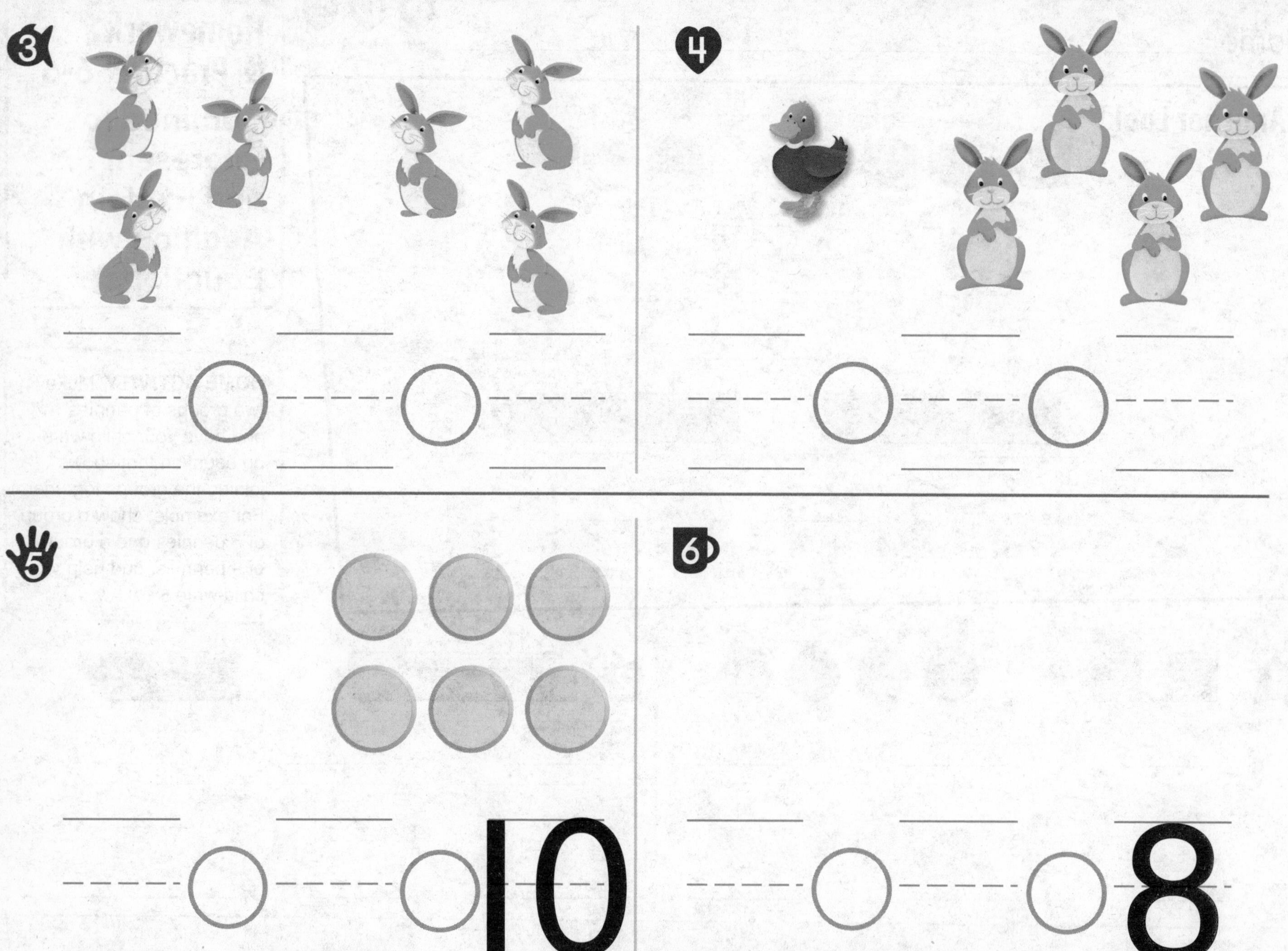

Directions 3 Have students add one group of rabbits to the other, and then write an equation to show the addition. 4 Have students put together the groups of animals, and then write an equation to show the addition. 5 **Higher Order Thinking** Have students draw the other group, add to or put the groups together, and then complete the equation to show addition. 6 **Higher Order Thinking** Have students draw counters to show two groups that add up to 8, and then complete the equation to show addition.

Directions Say: *4 squirrels are eating lunch at the squirrel feeder. 2 more join them. How many are eating at the feeder now? Show how you know in two ways, and then explain how you know.*

I can ...
solve addition problems.

I can also model with math.

Learn Glossary

9 in all

9 in all

$6 + 3 = 9$

Guided Practice

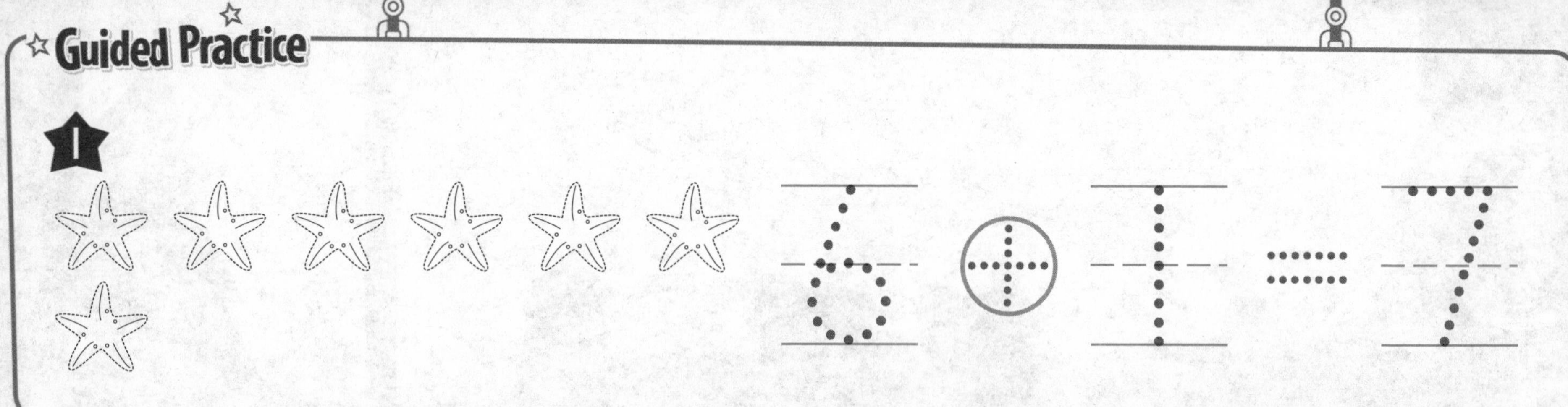

Directions Have students listen to the story, draw a picture to show what is happening, and then write the equation. Then have them explain their work. 1 *There are 6 sea stars on the beach. 1 more joins them. How many sea stars are there in all?*

Name ______________________________

2

3

4

5

Directions Have students listen to the story, use counters to show the addition, draw a picture, and then write an equation to tell how many in all. 2 *3 crabs sit on the beach. 7 more join them. How many crabs are sitting in all?* 3 *5 crabs look for food. 4 more join them. How many crabs are there in all?* 4 *There is 1 turtle on the beach. 5 more walk up. How many turtles are there in all?* 5 *2 turtles swim in the water. 6 more join them. How many turtles are swimming in all?*

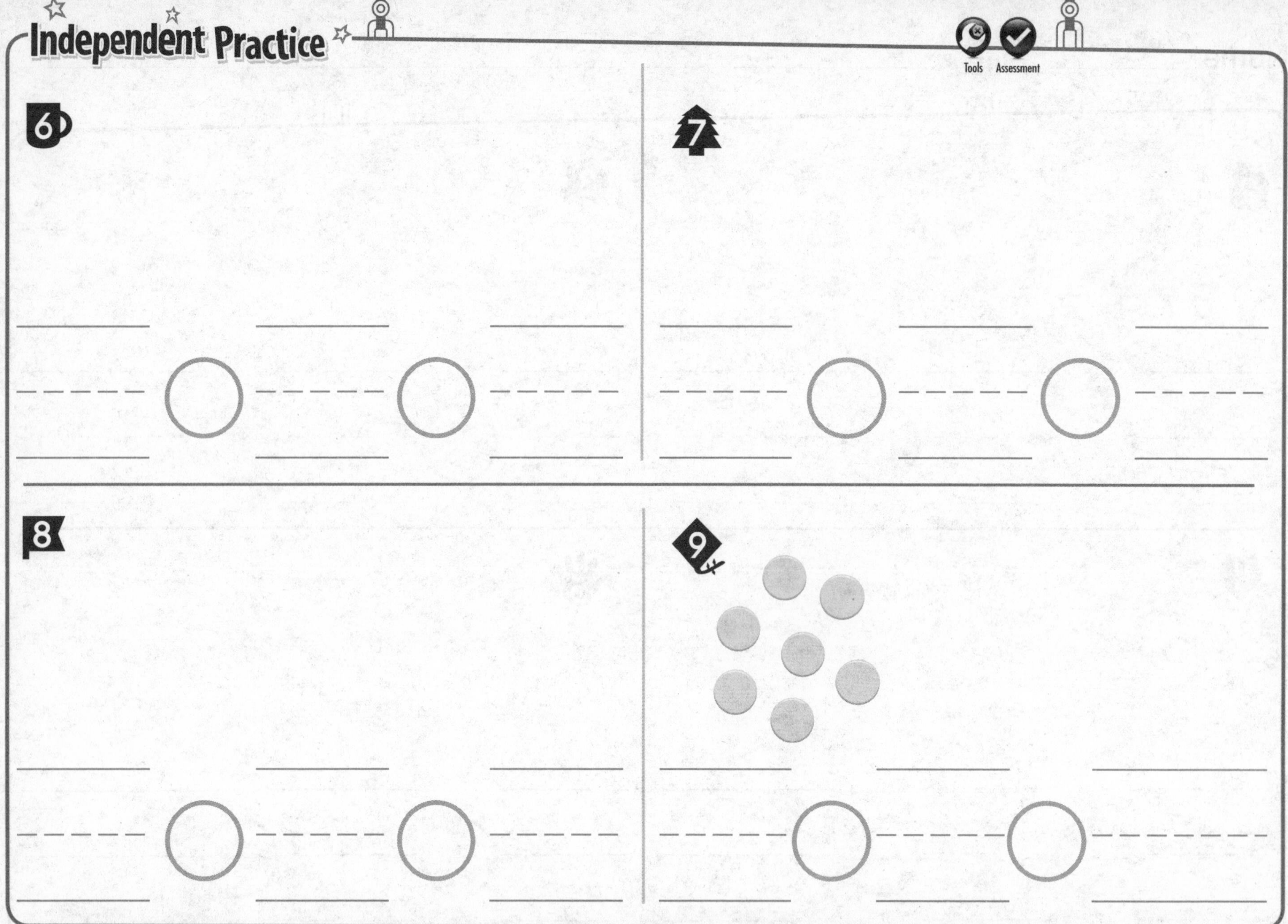

Directions Have students listen to the story, use counters to show the addition, draw a picture, and then write an equation to tell how many in all. **6** *4 girls play at the beach. 4 boys join them. How many children are there in all?* **7** *8 children rest on the sand. 1 girl joins them. How many children are there in all?* **8** *2 boys play in the water. 5 girls join them. How many children are there in all?* **9** **Higher Order Thinking** Have students listen to the story, draw counters to complete the picture, and write an equation. *7 children build a sand castle. Some more help them. There are 10 children building in all. How many more come to help them?*

Name ____________________

Homework & Practice 6-7

Solve Addition Word Problems: Add To

HOME ACTIVITY Give your child two numbers up to 10. Ask him or her to tell an addition story using the numbers. Repeat with different numbers.

Another Look!

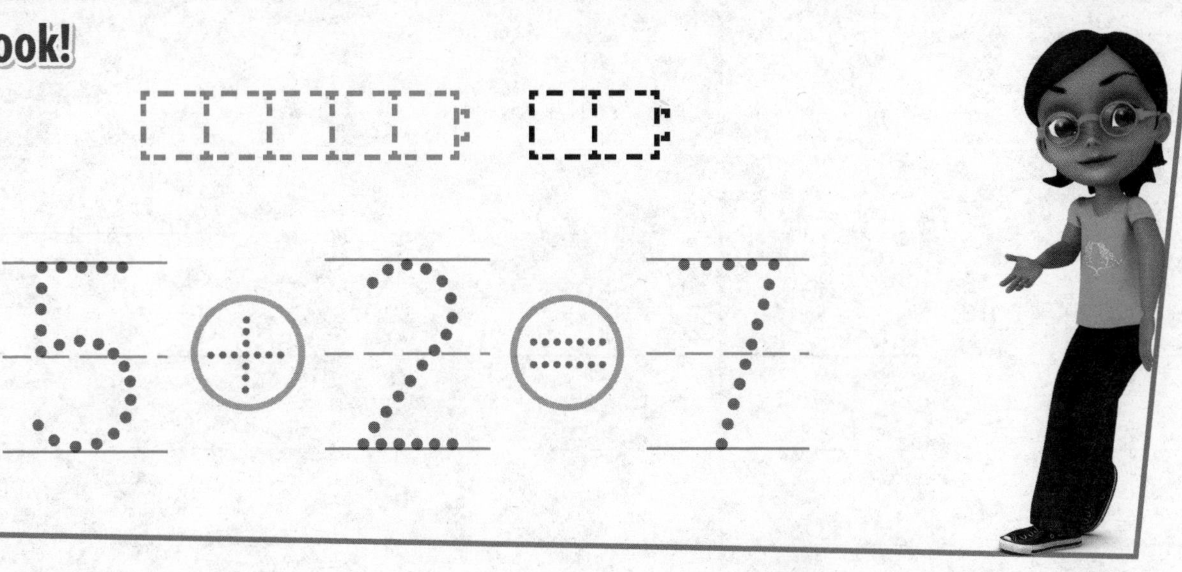

1

___ ◯ ___ ◯ ___

2

___ ◯ ___ ◯ ___

Directions Say: *How can you explain the equation* 5 + 2 = 7*?* Guide students to tell an addition story using the equation. Have students listen to the story, use connecting cubes to show the addition, draw a picture, and write an equation. 1 *4 fish swim in the water. 6 more join them. How many fish are there in all?* 2 *2 sea stars lie on a rock. 3 more join them. How many sea stars are there in all?*

3

4

5

8 + 2 = 10

6

Directions Have students listen to the story, use a model to show the addition, draw a picture, and write an equation. 3 *4 flowers grow in a pond. 3 more grow. How many flowers are there in all?* 4 *2 butterflies sit on a bush. 6 more join them. How many butterflies are there in all?* 5 **Higher Order Thinking** Have students tell an addition story that matches the equation, and then draw a picture to show what is happening. 6 **Higher Order Thinking** Have students tell an addition story that matches the picture, and then write an equation to match.

Lesson 6-8
Solve Addition Word Problems: Put Together

Directions Say: *Daniel's teacher is making name tags for her students. She makes 3 name tags for boys. She makes 2 more for girls. Now she has 5 name tags. How does Daniel's teacher know that she has made 5 name tags? Explain and then show how you know.*

I can ...
use equations to represent and explain addition.

I can also make math arguments.

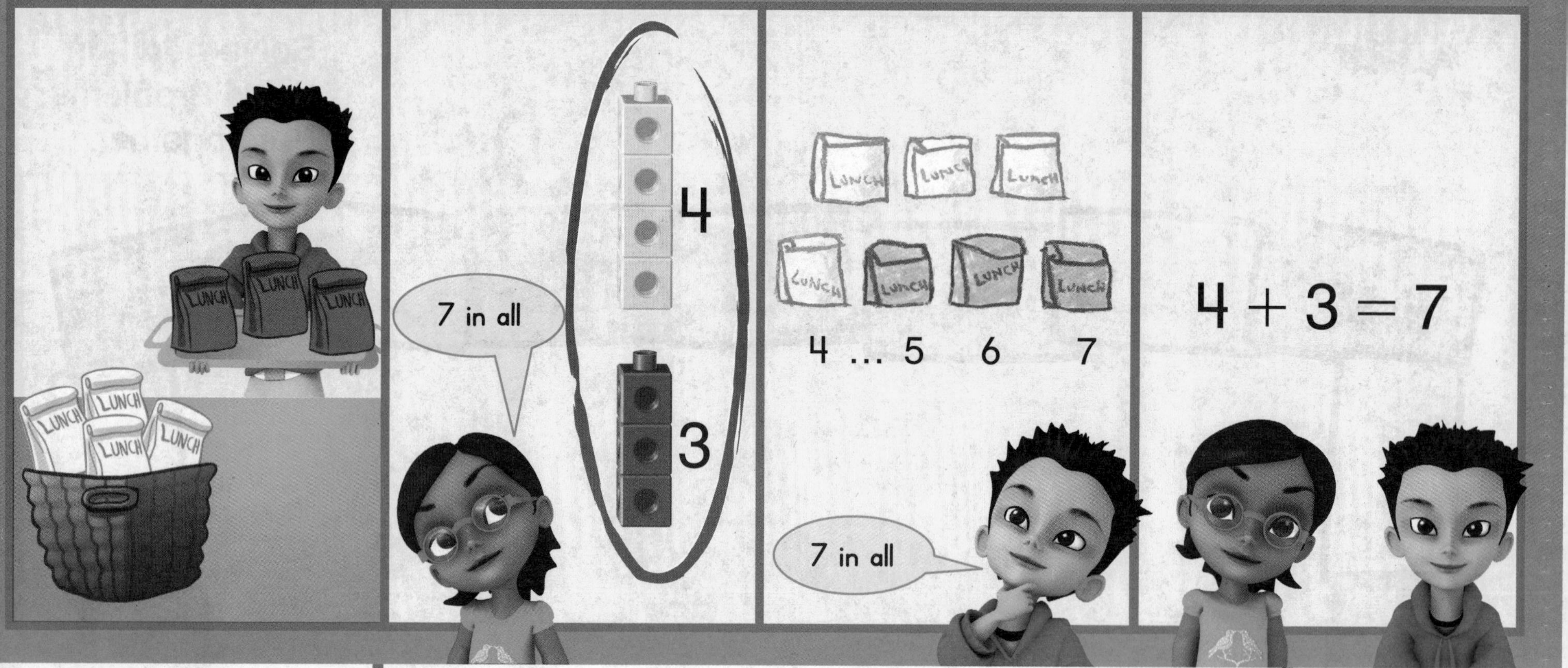

Guided Practice

1

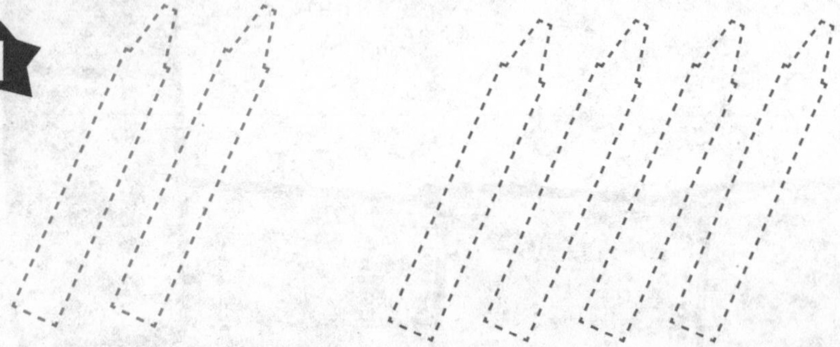

2 + 4 = 6

Directions Have students listen to the story, draw a picture to show what is happening, and then write an equation. Then have them explain their work. *Daniel puts 2 red crayons and 4 blue crayons on the table. Now there are 6 crayons in all. How can Daniel tell there are 6 crayons?*

Name ____________

2

3

4

5

Directions Have students listen to each story, draw a picture to show what is happening, and then write an equation. Then have them explain their work. 2 *Jorge puts 4 blue paint jars and 3 red paint jars in the art room. How many paint jars are there in all?* 3 *Maya has 3 green pencils and 2 orange pencils. How many pencils are there in all?* 4 *Rex has 1 sheet of blue paper and 8 sheets of yellow paper. How many sheets of paper does he have in all?* 5 *Reagan has 4 green blocks and 4 yellow blocks. How many blocks does she have in all?*

Independent Practice

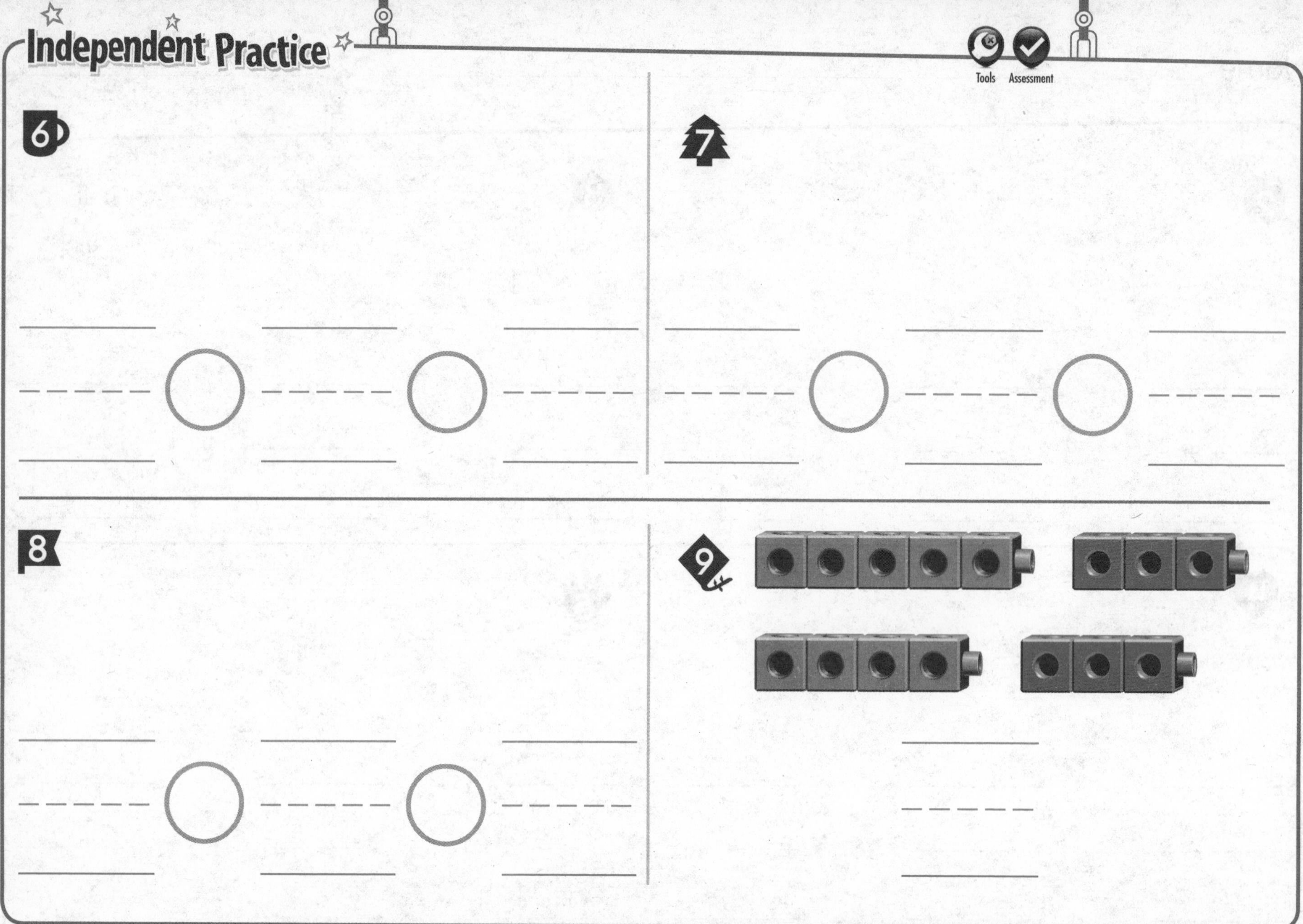

Directions Have students listen to each story, draw a picture to show what is happening, and then write an equation. 6 *Benny puts 5 bananas in a bowl and 4 bananas on a plate. How many bananas does he have in all?* 7 *Kris eats 2 grapes at lunch and 6 grapes for her snack. How many grapes does she eat in all?* 8 *There are 4 girls and 2 boys on a train ride. How many children ride the train in all?* 9 **Higher Order Thinking** Have students listen to the story, circle the connecting cubes that show the story and tell why the other cubes do not show the story, and then write the number to tell how many in all. Say: *Jimmy picks 5 raspberries. Then he picks 3 more. How many raspberries does he have in all?*

Name ____________________

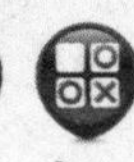

Homework & Practice 6-8

Solve Addition Word Problems: Put Together

Another Look!

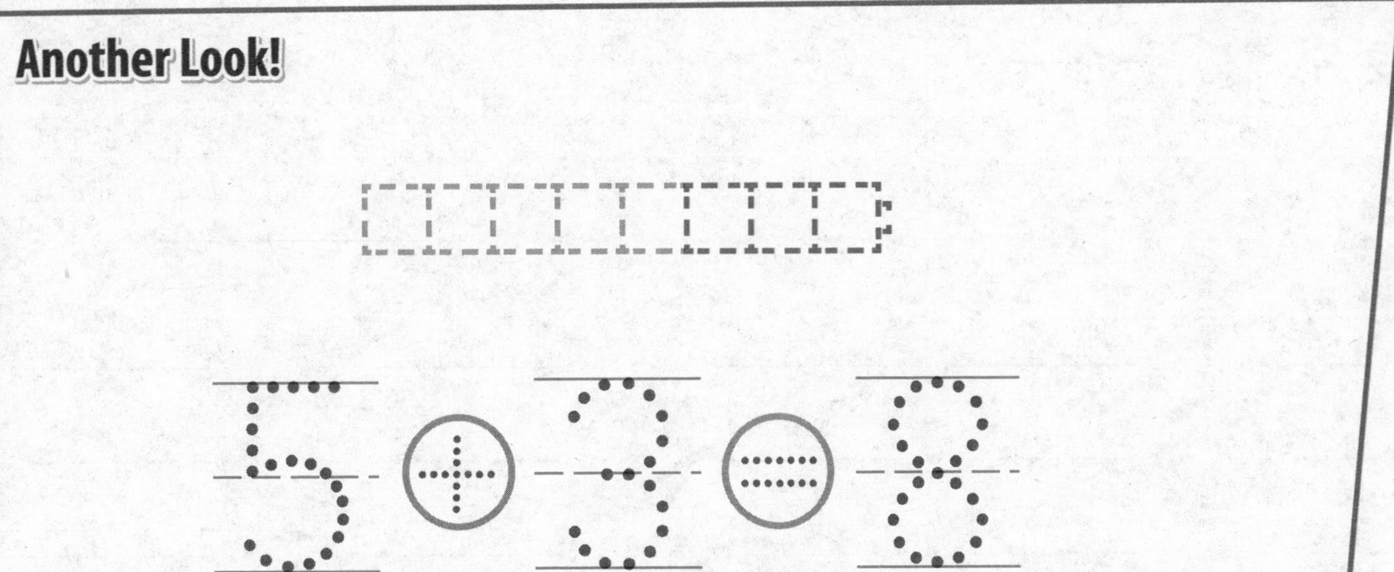

HOME ACTIVITY Give your child a group of 2 pennies and a group of 3 pennies and ask: *How can you tell there are 5 coins in all?* Encourage your child to show how he or she knows by lining up the coins and using words to describe how to add the groups together.

Directions Say: *How can you explain the equation* $5 + 3 = 8$? Guide students to connect cubes or put together other objects to model the addition. Encourage students to explain their thinking. Have students listen to each story, draw a picture to show what is happening, and then write an equation. **1** *There are 2 cherries on a plate and 3 cherries in a bowl. How many cherries are there in all?* **2** *There are 4 apples on the counter and 6 apples in a bag. How many apples are there in all?*

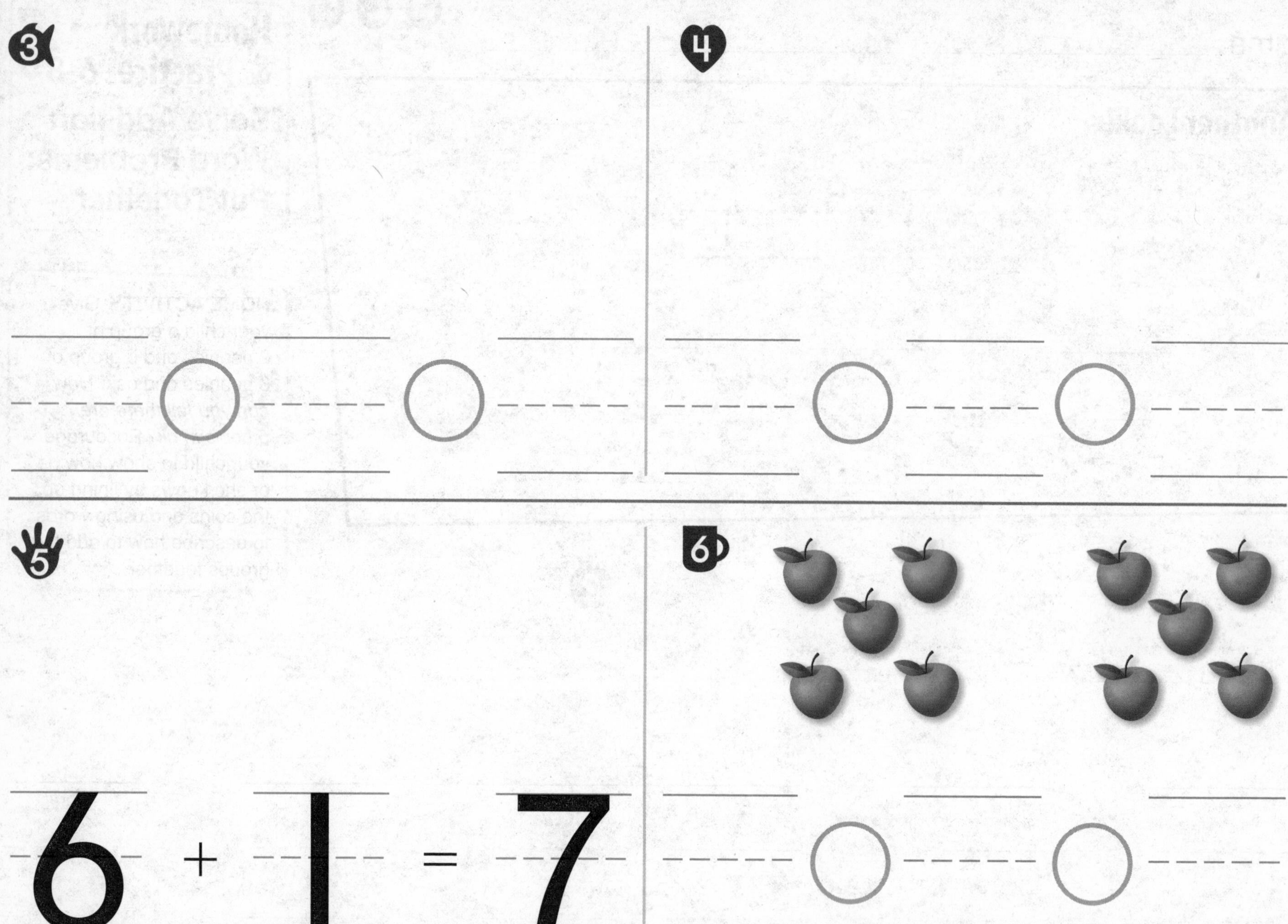

Directions Have students listen to each story, draw a picture to show what is happening, and then write an equation. 3 *There are 3 cardinals and 5 robins sitting on a tree branch. How many birds are there in all?* 4 *There are 4 rabbits and 4 squirrels looking for food by a tree. How many animals are there in all?* 5 **Higher Order Thinking** Have students tell an addition story that matches the equation, and then draw a picture to show what is happening. 6 **Higher Order Thinking** Have students tell an addition story about the groups of apples, and then write an equation to tell how many in all.

Name ______________________

Lesson 6-9

Use Patterns to Develop Fluency in Addition

____ + ____ = ____

____ + ____ = ____

____ + ____ = ____

Directions Say: *Use blue and red cubes to make stacks of 2 cubes. How many different ways can you make a stack of 2 cubes? Write equations to describe your stacks. Use a blue crayon to tell how many blue cubes and a red crayon to tell how many red cubes.*

I can ...
use patterns to add numbers together.

I can also look for patterns.

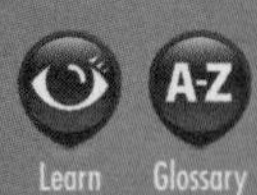

$5 + 0 = 5$
$4 + 1 = 5$
$3 + 2 = 5$
$2 + 3 = 5$
$1 + 4 = 5$
$0 + 5 = 5$

$5 + 0 = 5$ $1 + 4 = 5$
$0 + 5 = 5$ $4 + 1 = 5$

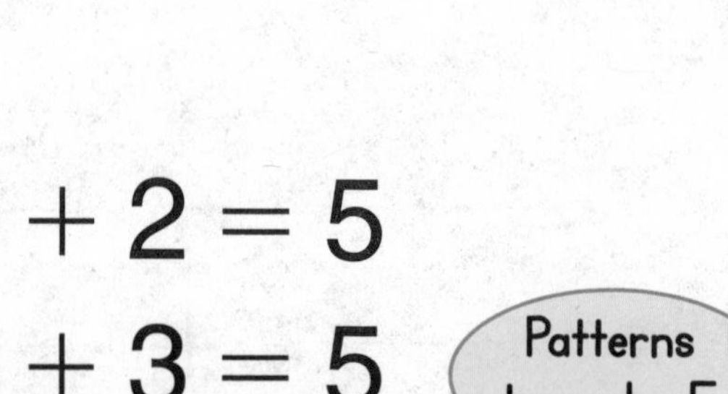
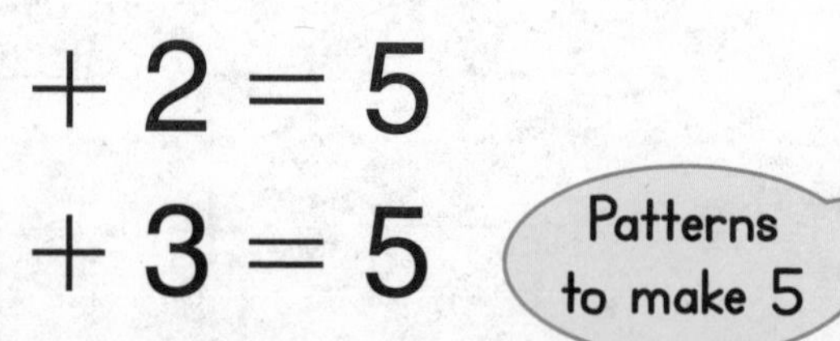

$3 + 2 = 5$
$2 + 3 = 5$

Patterns to make 5

Guided Practice

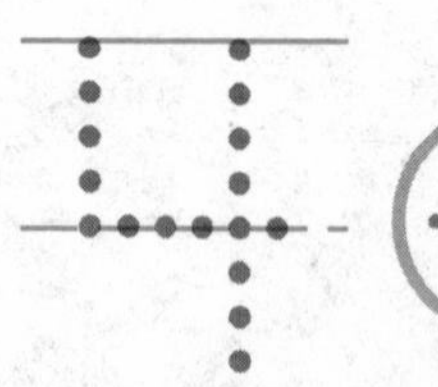  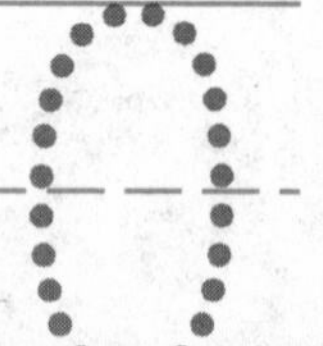 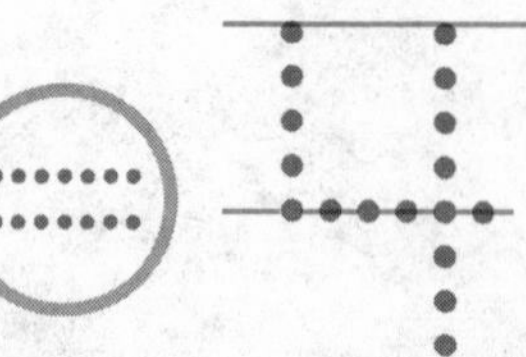

$4 + 0 = 4$

Directions ★ Have students color a way to make 4, and then write an equation to match the boxes.

Name

2

3

2

4

3

5

Directions 2–5 Have students color the boxes to complete the pattern started on the page before of ways to make 4, and then write an equation to match the boxes.

Independent Practice

6

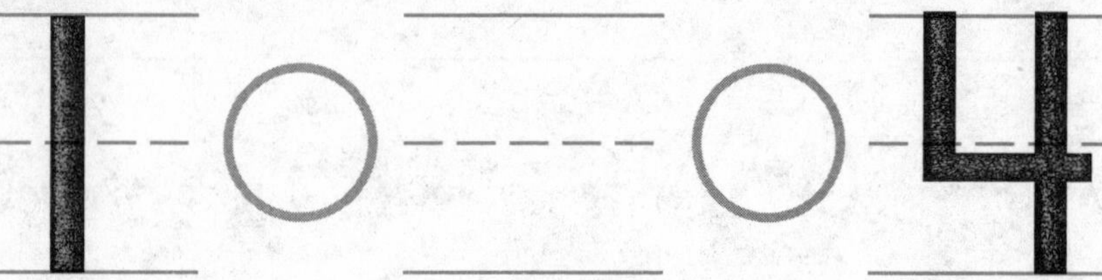

1 ◯ ____ ◯ 4

3 ◯ ____ ◯ 4

7

2 ◯ ____ ◯ 5

____ ◯ 2 ◯ 5

8

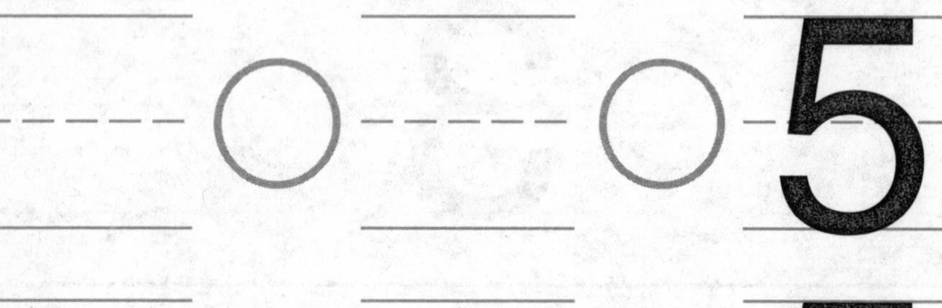

____ ◯ ____ ◯ 5

____ ◯ ____ ◯ 5

9

$100 + 200 = 300$

$200 + 100 = ?$

____

Directions 6 and 7 Have students complete the pair of equations to show a pattern. 8 **Higher Order Thinking** Have students write a pair of equations in a pattern that equal 5. 9 **Higher Order Thinking** Have students listen to the story: *If* $100 + 200 = 300$, *then what does* $200 + 100$ *equal?*

Name ________________________

Help Tools Games

Homework & Practice 6-9

Use Patterns to Develop Fluency in Addition

Another Look!

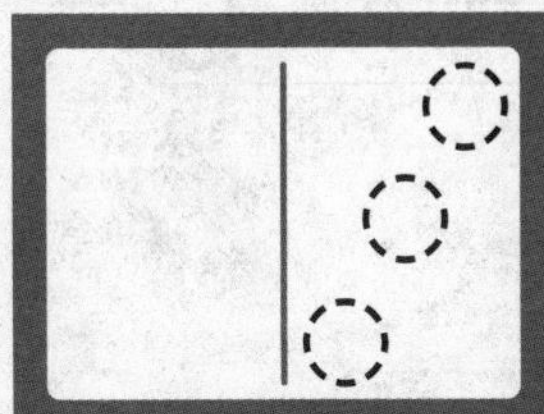
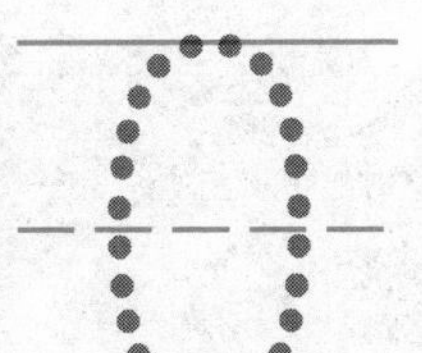
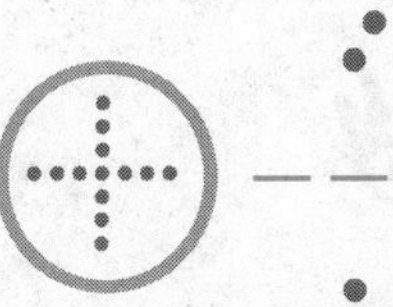
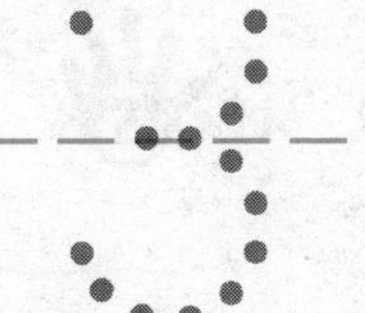
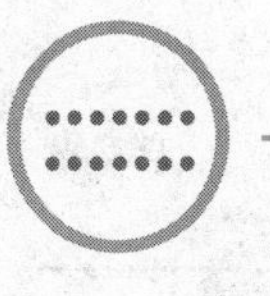
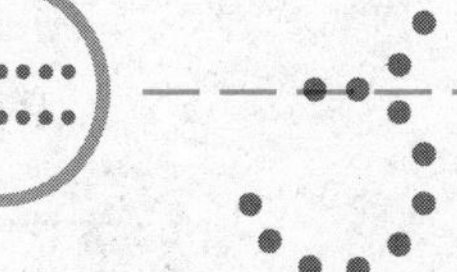

HOME ACTIVITY Give your child an equation with sums up to 5. Ask him or her to write the matching pair. For example, write $1 + 3 = 4$. Your child should write $3 + 1 = 4$.

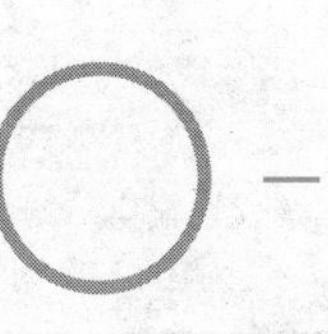

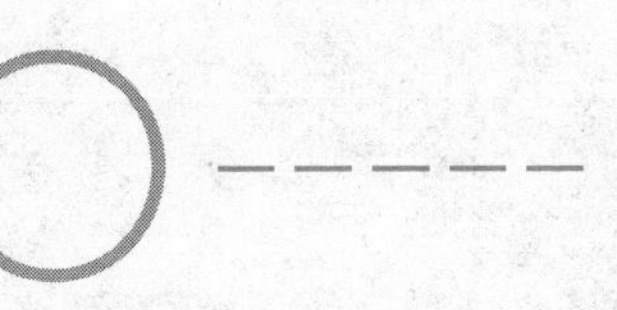

Directions Say: *Draw counters to show how to make 3. Write an equation to match the counters.* 1 and 2 Have students draw counters to complete the pattern of ways to make 3, and then write an equation to match the counters.

Directions Have students: 3 draw counters to complete the pattern, from page 339, of ways to make 3, and then write an equation to match the counters; 4 and 5 complete the pair of equations to show a pattern to make 5. 6 **Higher Order Thinking** Have students write a pair of matching equations that equal 5.

Name ______________________

Problem Solving

Lesson 6-10
Model with Math

______ + ______ = ______

Directions Say: *Daniel sees a group of 3 fluffy, white clouds in the sky. Marta sees 1 gray cloud. How many clouds do they see in all? Draw a picture to show what is happening, and then write the equation to tell how many clouds in all. Explain how you know.*

I can ...
model adding different numbers together by drawing, counting, or writing equations.

I can also find correct sums.

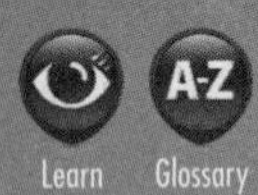

How can I show it?

3 + 3

Draw.

3 + 3 = 6

Count.

6 fish

Guided Practice

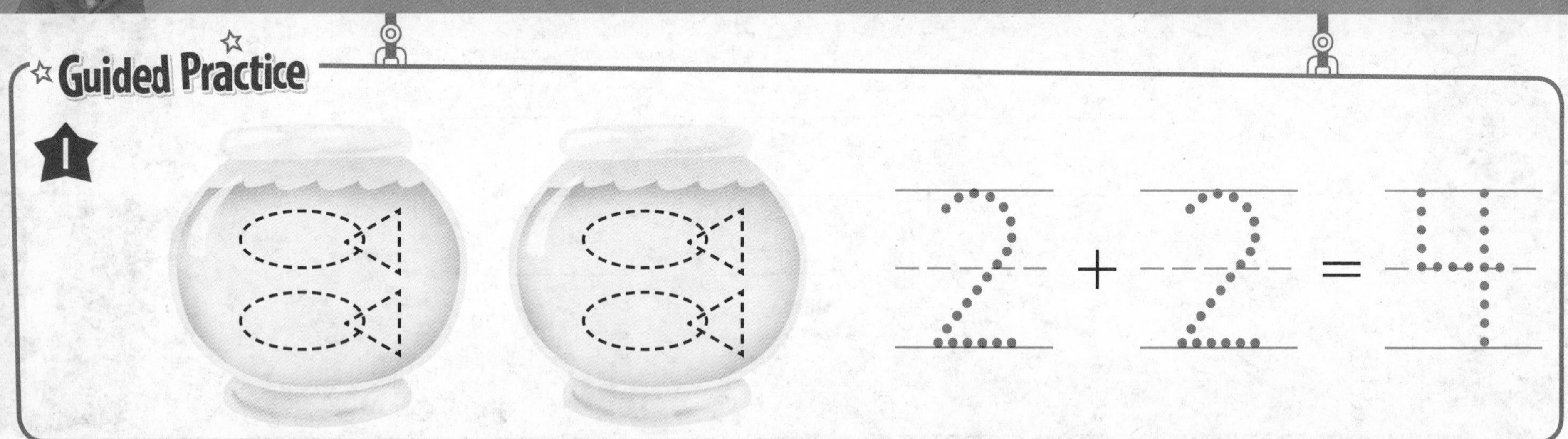

Directions Have students listen to the story, and then draw a picture to model what is happening. Then have them write an equation and explain their answer. *Daniel sees 2 fish in one bowl and 2 fish in another bowl. How many fish does he see in all?*

Name

Tools Assessment

Independent Practice

2

___ + ___ = ___

3

___ + ___ = ___

4

___ + ___ = ___

5

___ + ___ = ___

Directions Have students listen to each story, and then draw a picture to model what is happening. Then have them write an equation and explain their answer. 2 *Julie sees 5 stones in one pail and 3 stones in another pail. How many stones does she see in all?* 3 *A hen laid 2 eggs one day and 3 eggs the next day. How many eggs did she lay in all?* 4 *Maria threw a baseball 5 times in one inning and 2 times in the next inning. How many times did she throw the baseball in all?* 5 *Zak scored 2 goals during a soccer game, and then he scored 4 more goals during another soccer game. How many goals did he score in all?*

Problem Solving

Performance Assessment

6 7 8

2 + ___ = ___

2 + 1 = ___

___ + ___ = ___

Directions Read the problem aloud. Then have students use multiple problem-solving methods to solve the problem. Say: *There are 2 rabbits in a hole. The same number of rabbits come in to join them. How many rabbits are there in all?* **Reasoning** *What can you answer? How many rabbits join the group?* **Explain** *Emily says that the answer is 3 rabbits. Is she right or wrong? Explain how you know.* **Model** *Use cubes, draw pictures, or use numbers to show how many rabbits in all. Then write the equation.*

Name ______________________

Help

Tools

Games

Homework & Practice 6-10

Model with Math

HOME ACTIVITY Help your child make simple drawings to solve addition problems. For example, say: *I had 3 marbles, and then I got 2 more. How many do I have in all? How do you know?*

Another Look!

___ + ___ = ___

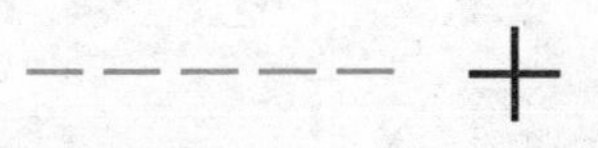

___ + ___ = ___

Directions Say: *Carlos finds 2 apples on a tree. Then he finds 3 more on the ground. How many apples does Carlos find in all? Draw the apples, count the apples to find out how many in all, and then write an equation.* Have students listen to each story, and then draw a picture to model what is happening. Then have them write an equation and explain their answer. **1** *There are 4 balls in the box. Paolo puts 1 more ball in the box. How many balls are there in all?* **2** *Layla has 3 oranges on a plate. Bryce has 3 oranges on a plate. How many oranges do Layla and Bryce have in all?*

Directions Read the problem aloud. Then have students use multiple problem-solving methods to solve the problem. *Daniel and Carlos each receive 3 flowers. They each put the flowers into vases. Daniel arranges his flowers in a different way than Carlos. Show how the students could have arranged the flowers.* **Reasoning** *What do you know? How many flowers does each student have?* **Model** *Use cubes, draw a picture, or use numbers to show two different ways that the students could have arranged their flowers. Then write the equation for each model.* **Explain** *How do you know that your models are correct? Explain your answer.*

Name ______________________

Vocabulary Review

2 ○ 7

4 + 3 ○ ____

Directions **Understand Vocabulary** Have students: 1 write the **plus sign** to show addition; 2 write the **equal sign,** and then complete the equation; 3 listen to the story, draw a picture to show what is happening, and then write an **equation** to match the story. *Max has 5 yellow cups and 5 orange cups. How many cups does he have in all?*

4

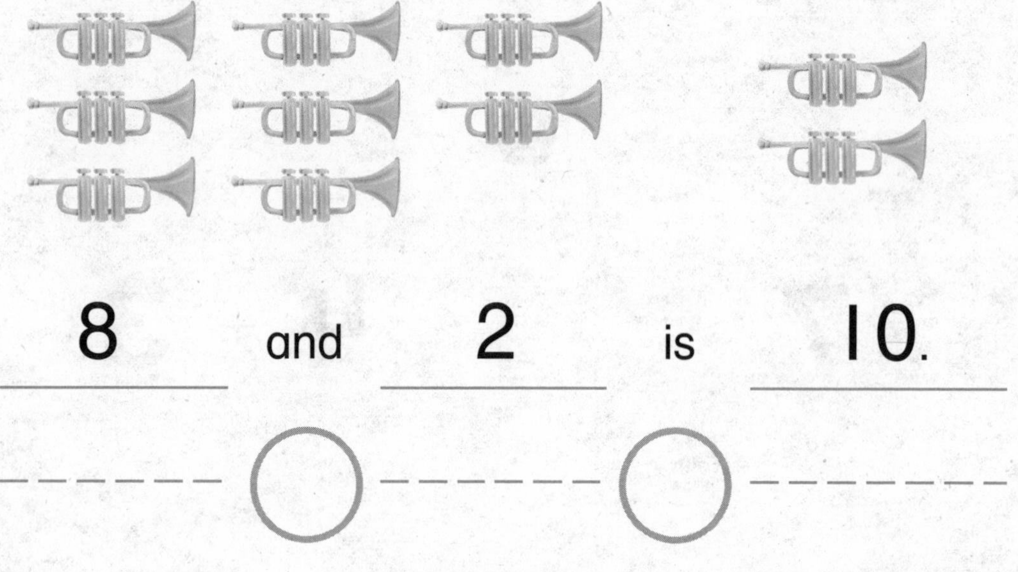

8 and 2 is 10.

Directions **Understand Vocabulary** Have students: 4 **add** the groups to find the sum, and then write an equation to show the addition; 5 listen to the story, draw a picture to show what is happening, and then write an equation. Have them draw a circle around the **sum**. *Bailey sees 3 apples in the tree. Then she sees 5 more. How many apples does she see in all?*

Name ___

Set A

Reteaching

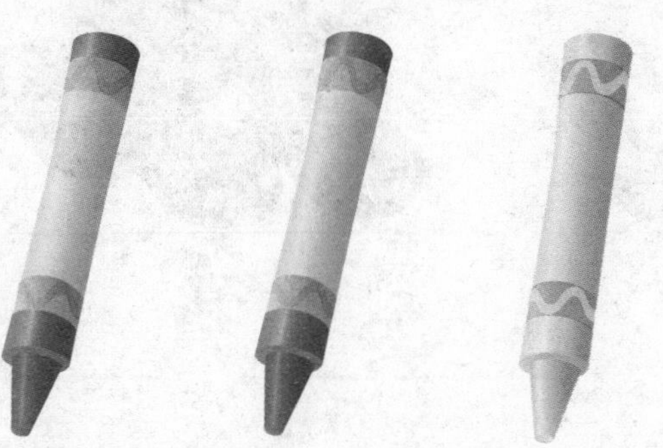

2 and 1 is 3 in all.

1 (crayons picture)

0 and 4 is ___ in all.

Set B

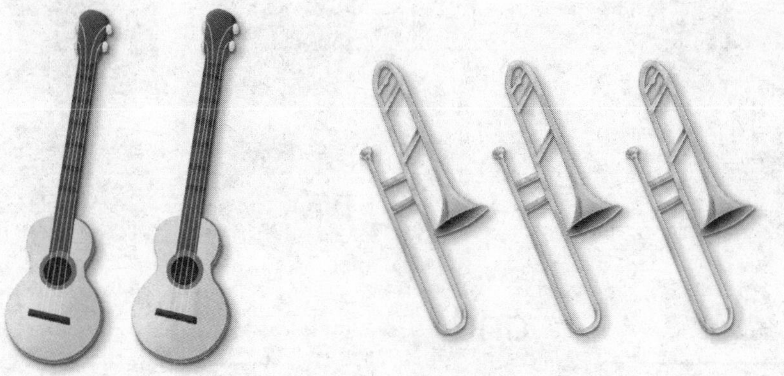

2 and 3 is 5.

2

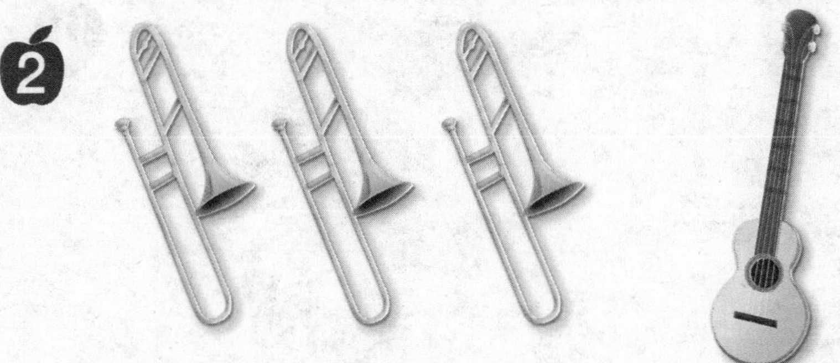

___ and ___ is ___.

Directions Have students: 1 listen to the story, color the number of each part, and then write the number to tell how many in all. *Margo has 0 red crayons. She has 4 blue crayons. How many crayons does she have in all?* 2 add to the first group of instruments, and then write an addition sentence to tell how many in all.

Set C

2 and 3 is 5.

3

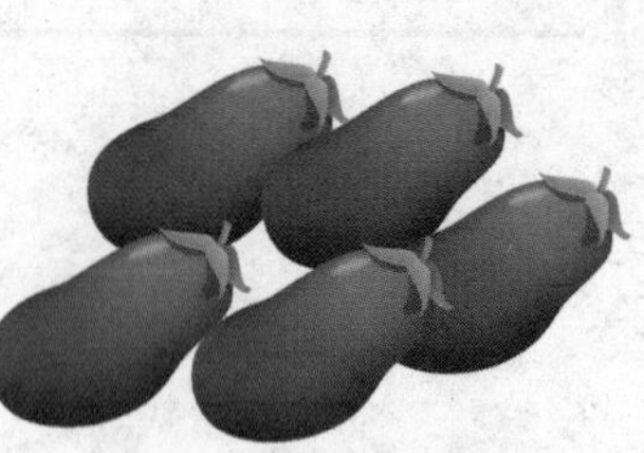

______ and ______ is ______.

Set D

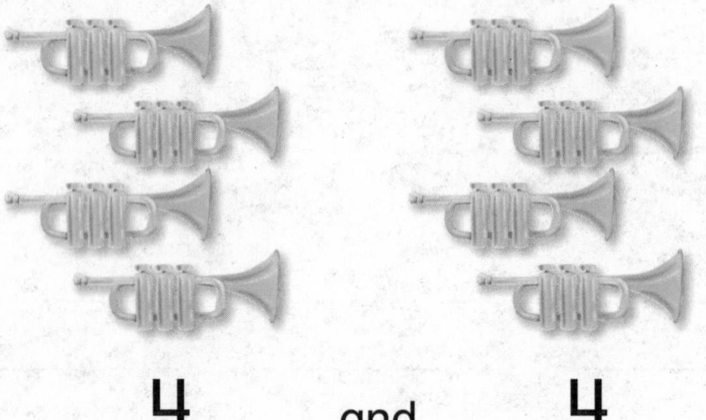

4 and 4

4  4

4

2 and 4

Directions Have students: 3 draw a circle around the groups to put them together, and then write an addition sentence to tell how many vegetables in all; 4 count the instruments in each group, and then write the numbers and the plus sign to add the groups.

Name ______________________

Set E

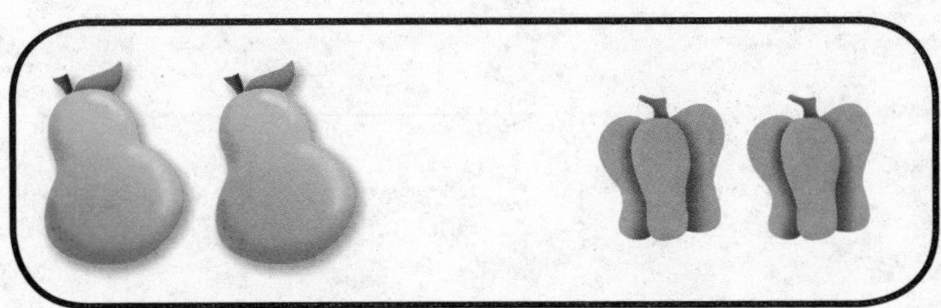

2 + 2 = 4

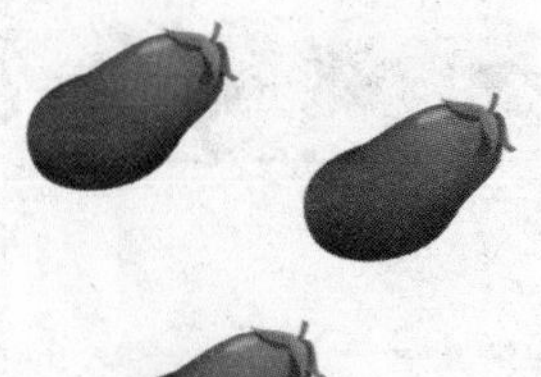

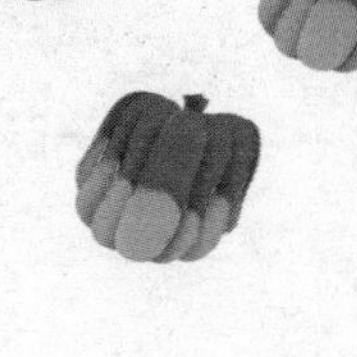

Set F

4 + 3 = 7

___ + ___ = ___

Directions Have students: 5 use counters to show how to put together the groups, draw a circle around the groups to put them together, and then write an equation to find the sum; 6 listen to the story, use counters to show the addition, draw a picture, and then write an equation to tell how many in all. *Mark has 3 flowers. He picks 2 more flowers. How many flowers does he have in all?*

Set G

$6 + 3 = 9$

7

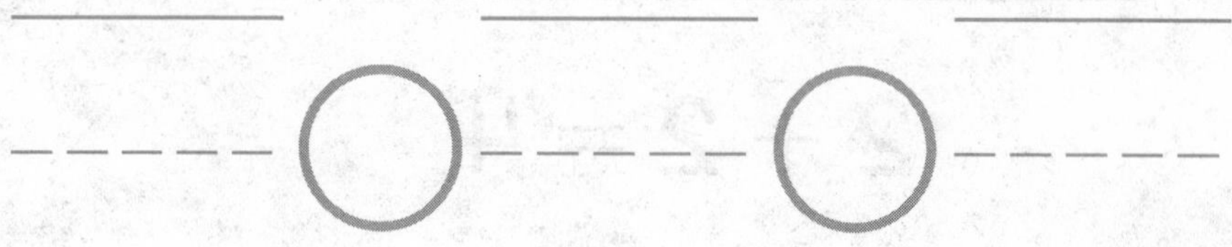

Set H

8 

$4 + 1 = 5$

Directions Have students: 7 listen to each story, draw a picture to show what is happening, and then write an equation. *Karina puts 4 red balls and 4 purple balls into the toy bin. How many balls are there in all?* 8 color a way to make 6, and then write an equation to match the boxes.

Name ______________________________

Assessment

Ⓐ I in all

Ⓑ 6 in all

Ⓒ 4 in all

Ⓓ 8 in all

2

Ⓐ I and 4 is 5.
I + 4 = 5

Ⓑ I and 5 is 6.
I + 5 = 6

Ⓒ I and 6 is 7.
I + 6 = 7

Ⓓ I and 3 is 4.
I + 3 = 4

Ⓐ 2 and 2 is 4.

Ⓑ 2 and 6 is 8.

Ⓒ 2 and 4 is 6.

Ⓓ 2 and 5 is 7.

4

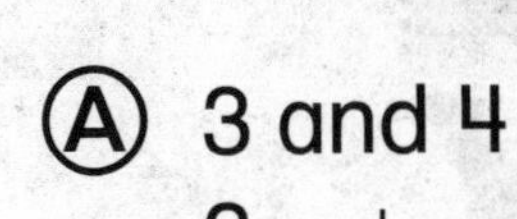

Ⓐ 3 and 4
3 + 4

Ⓑ 4 and 0
4 + 0

Ⓒ 3 and I
3 + I

Ⓓ 4 and I
4 + I

Directions Have students mark the best answer. 1 *Jen puts 2 teddy bears on her bed. Then she puts 2 more teddy bears on her bed. Which tells how many teddy bears she puts on her bed in all?* 2 *Hayden sees I scarecrow, and then he sees 3 more. Which number sentence tells how many scarecrows Hayden sees in all?* 3 *Which sentence tells about adding the groups of tambourines?* 4 *Which tells about the picture?*

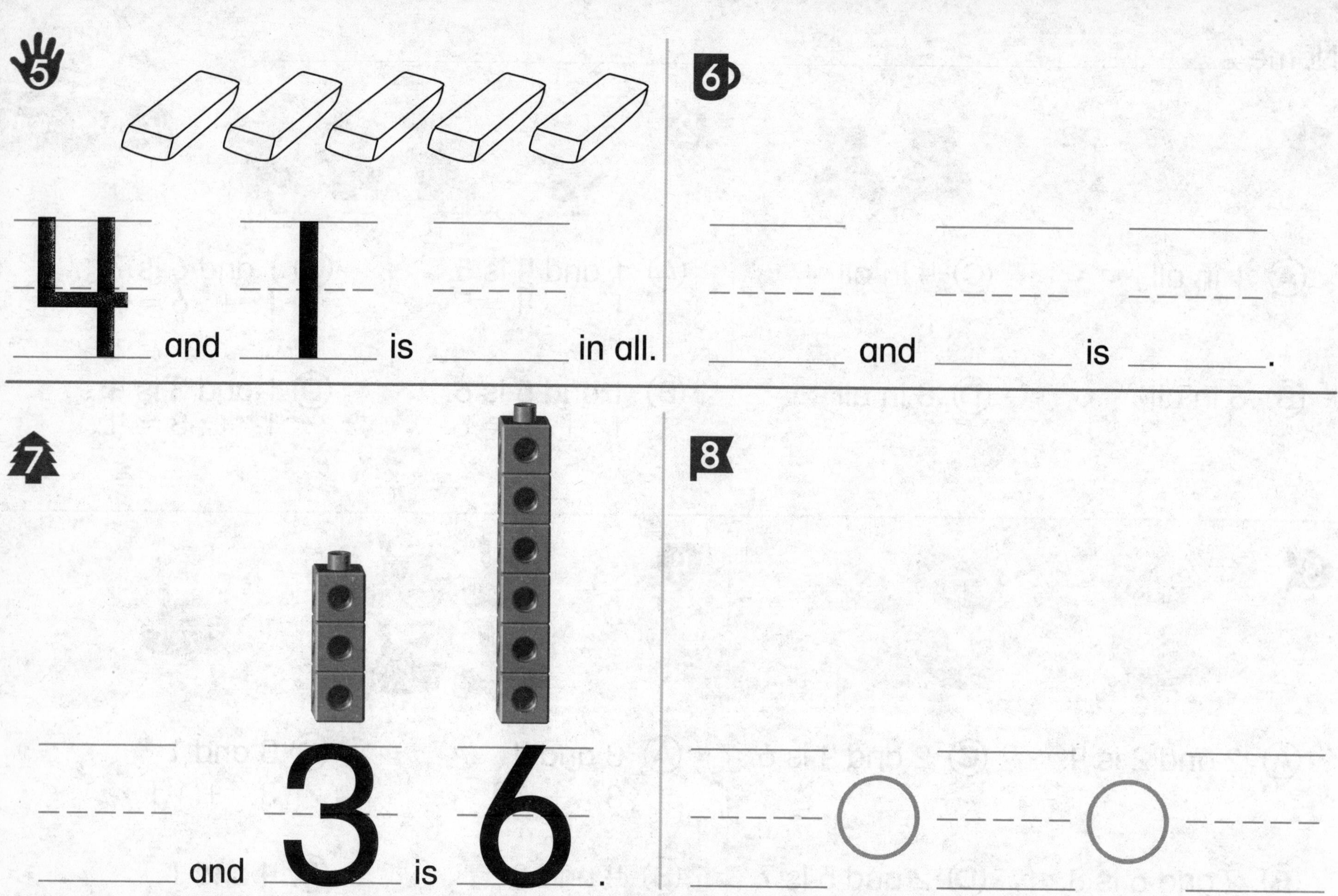

Directions 5 Have students listen to the story, and then do all of the following to show each part to find how many in all: clap and knock, hold up fingers, and give an explanation of a mental image. Ask them to color the number of each part, and then write the number to tell how many in all. *Ming buys 4 yellow erasers. She buys 1 purple eraser. How many erasers does she buy in all?* 6 Have students draw two groups of carrots to show 8 in all, and then write a number sentence to match the drawing. 7 Have students draw the number of cubes needed to make 6 cubes in all, and then complete the number sentence. 8 Have students listen to the story, use counters to model putting together the groups, draw the counters to show what is happening, and then write an equation for the story. *There are 6 brown bunnies in a garden and 3 white bunnies in the garden. How many bunnies are there in all?*

Name ______________________________

9

8

10

$5 + 2 = 7$

$4 + 4 = 8$

$1 + 7 = 8$

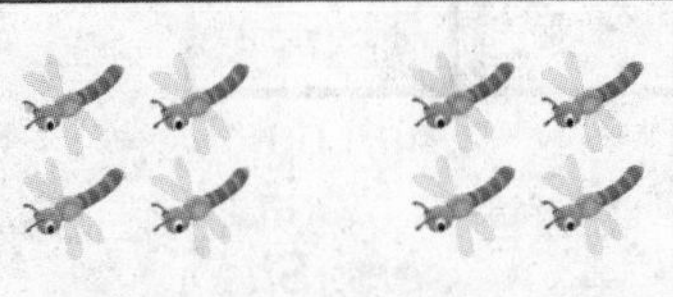

Directions Have students: 9 look at the number card, and then draw a circle to put together the groups that show how many in all; 10 match the pictures with the equation that shows the correct parts and how many in all.

11

Directions 11 Have students color the boxes to complete the pattern of ways to make 5, and then write an equation to match the boxes.

Name ______________________________

1

_____ and _____ is _____.

2

_____ + _____ = _____

Directions **Music Time** Say: *Students play many different instruments in music class.* 1 Say: *How many horns are there?* Have students count on to find the number of horns, and then write an addition sentence to tell how many in all. 2 Have students add one group of horns to the other group of horns, and then write an equation to find the sum.

3

\+ =

\+ =

\+ =

\+ =

4

\+ =

\+ =

5

\+ =

Directions 3 Say: *The music teacher puts 3 flutes on the shelves.* Have students color the boxes to complete a pattern to show the different ways she could put the flutes on the shelves. 4 Say: *The bells on the shelves show one way to make 4.* Have students write an equation to show the way, and then write the matching equation to make 4. 5 Say: *6 drums are on the shelf. Then Luisa puts more drums on the shelf. Now there are 8 drums on the shelf. How many drums did Luisa put on the shelf?* Have students draw counters to show what is happening, and then complete the equation.

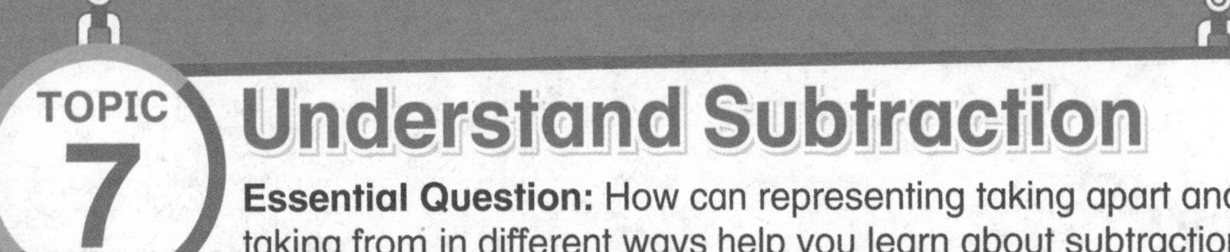

TOPIC 7 Understand Subtraction

Essential Question: How can representing taking apart and taking from in different ways help you learn about subtraction?

Food

Animals need food and water.

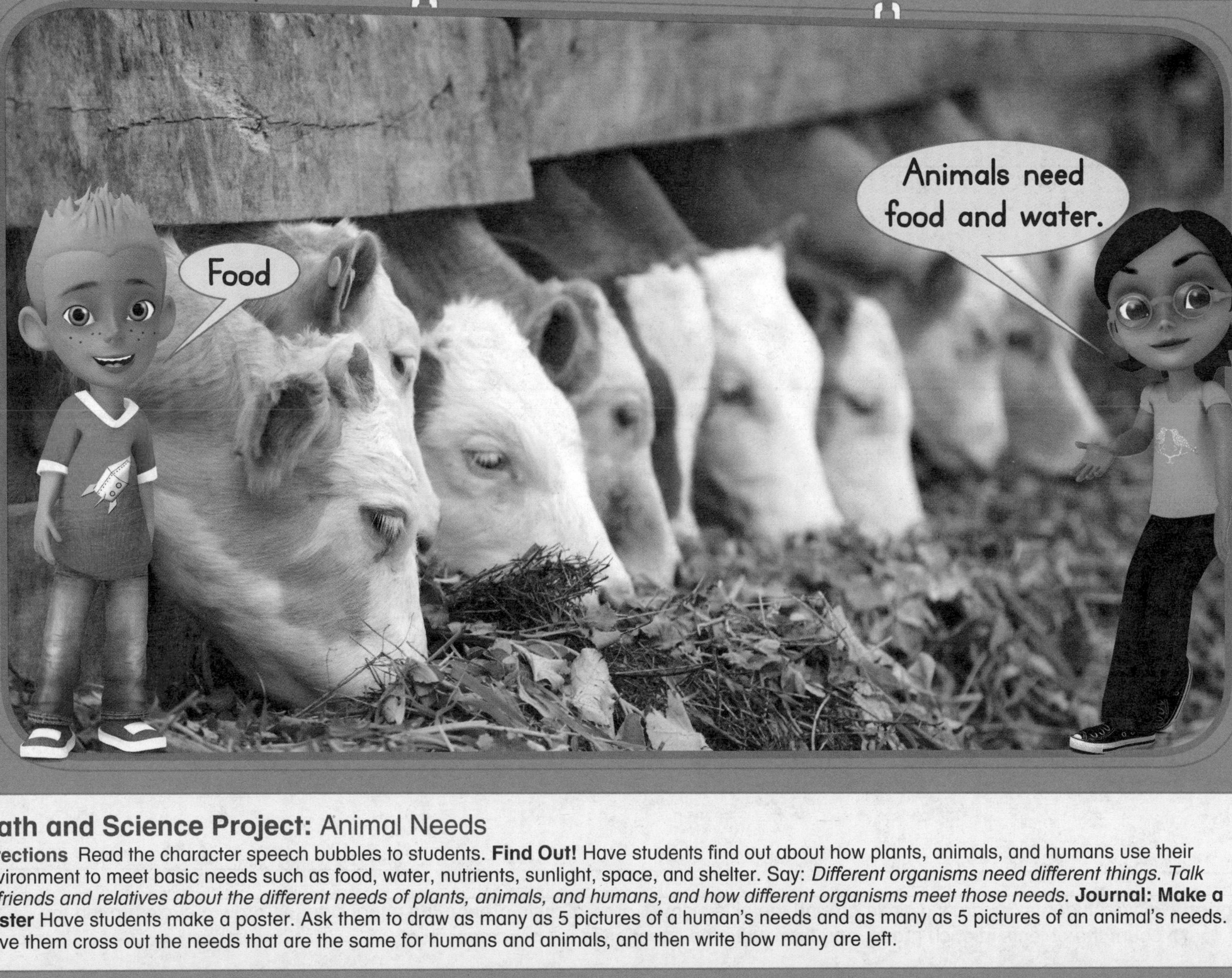

Math and Science Project: Animal Needs

Directions Read the character speech bubbles to students. **Find Out!** Have students find out about how plants, animals, and humans use their environment to meet basic needs such as food, water, nutrients, sunlight, space, and shelter. Say: *Different organisms need different things. Talk to friends and relatives about the different needs of plants, animals, and humans, and how different organisms meet those needs.* **Journal: Make a Poster** Have students make a poster. Ask them to draw as many as 5 pictures of a human's needs and as many as 5 pictures of an animal's needs. Have them cross out the needs that are the same for humans and animals, and then write how many are left.

Name ____________________

Review What You Know

$3 + 6 = 9$

2. $4 + 1 = 5$

3. $2 + 5 = 7$

4.

____ + ____ = ____

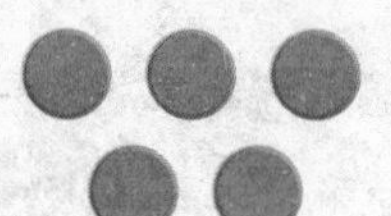 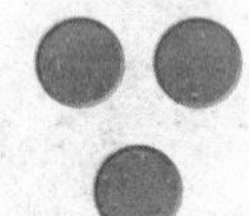

____ + ____ = ____

6.

____ + ____ = ____

Directions Have students: 1 draw a circle around the plus sign; 2 draw a circle around the equal sign; 3 draw a circle around the sum; 4–6 count the objects in each group, and then write the equation to tell how many in all.

A-Z Glossary

My Word Cards

Directions Have students cut out the vocabulary cards. Read the front of the card, and then ask them to explain what the word or phrase means.

left	separate	minus sign (–)
subtract	take away	difference

My Word Cards

Directions Review the definitions and have students study the cards. Extend learning by having students draw pictures for each word on a separate piece of paper.

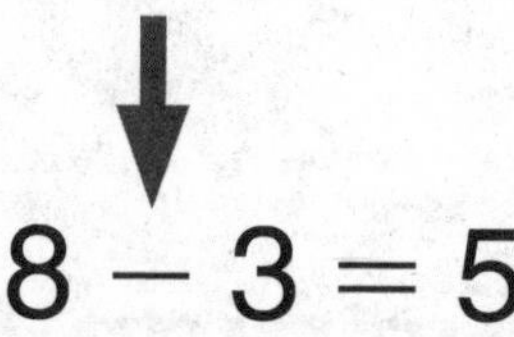

$8 - 3 = 5$

Point to the minus sign.
Say: *This is the* ***minus sign****. It means subtract.*

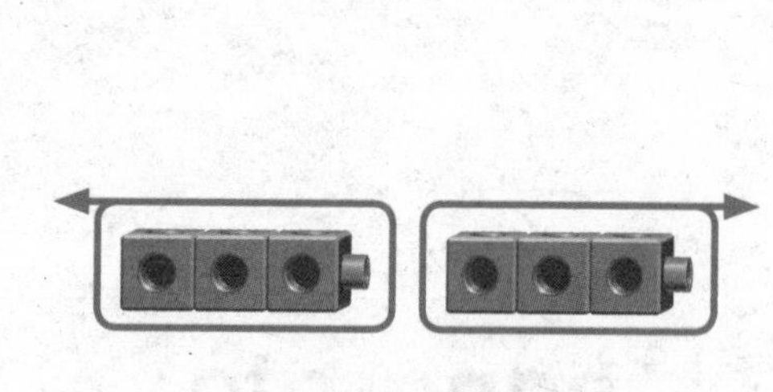

Point to the cube train.
Say: *When you* ***separate*** *groups, you pull or move them apart.*

Point to the jar of marbles.
Say: *There were 6 marbles in the jar. 1 marble was taken out. There are 5 marbles* ***left****.*

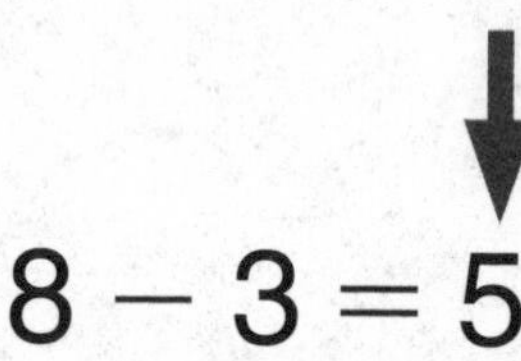

$8 - 3 = 5$

Point to the 5.
Say: *When you subtract, the answer is called the* ***difference****.*

Point to the 3 swans.
Say: *When you* ***take away****, you find out how many are left.*

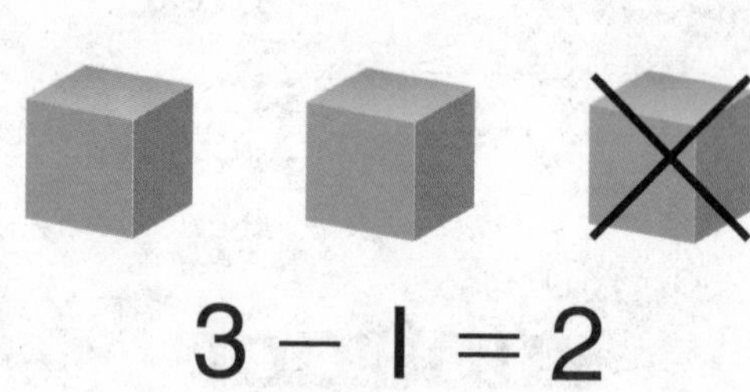

$3 - 1 = 2$

Point to the third box.
Say: ***Subtract*** *means "take away." 3 take away 1 is 2.*

My Word Cards

Directions Have students cut out the vocabulary cards. Read the front of the card, and then ask them to explain what the word or phrase means.

subtraction sentence

My Word Cards

Directions Review the definitions and have students study the cards. Extend learning by having students draw pictures for each word on a separate piece of paper.

4 take away 3 is 1.

Point to the subtraction sentence. Say: *4 take away 3 is 1 is a* ***subtraction sentence****. It tells how many are left.*

Directions Say: *Marta sees 5 goldfish in the pond. 1 swims away. How many fish are left? Think about the problem in your head. Then act out the story with your fingers to explain. Draw a circle around your answer.*

I can ... show numbers in many ways.

I can also model with math.

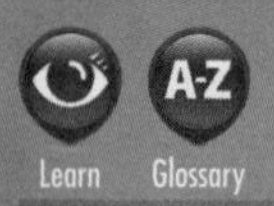

5 are left.

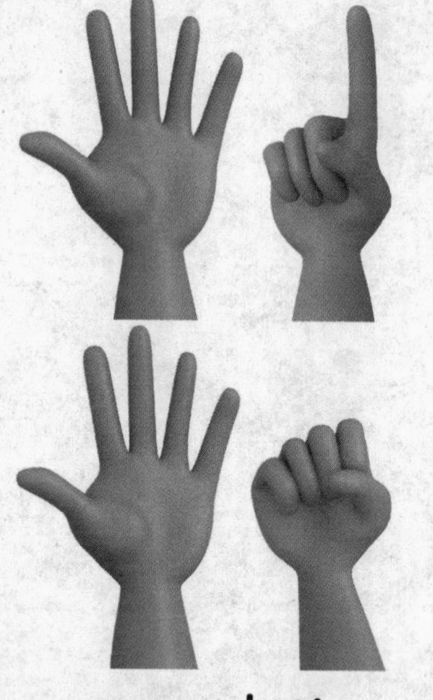

5 are left.

5 are left.

Guided Practice

Directions Have students listen to the story, and then do all of the following to find how many are left: give an explanation of a mental image, use objects to act it out, and hold up fingers. Have them mark Xs on how many birds fly away, and then write the number to tell how many are left. 1 *8 eagles sit on a branch. 2 fly away. How many eagles are left?* 2 *5 blue jays hop on the ground. 1 flies away. How many blue jays are left?*

Name ___

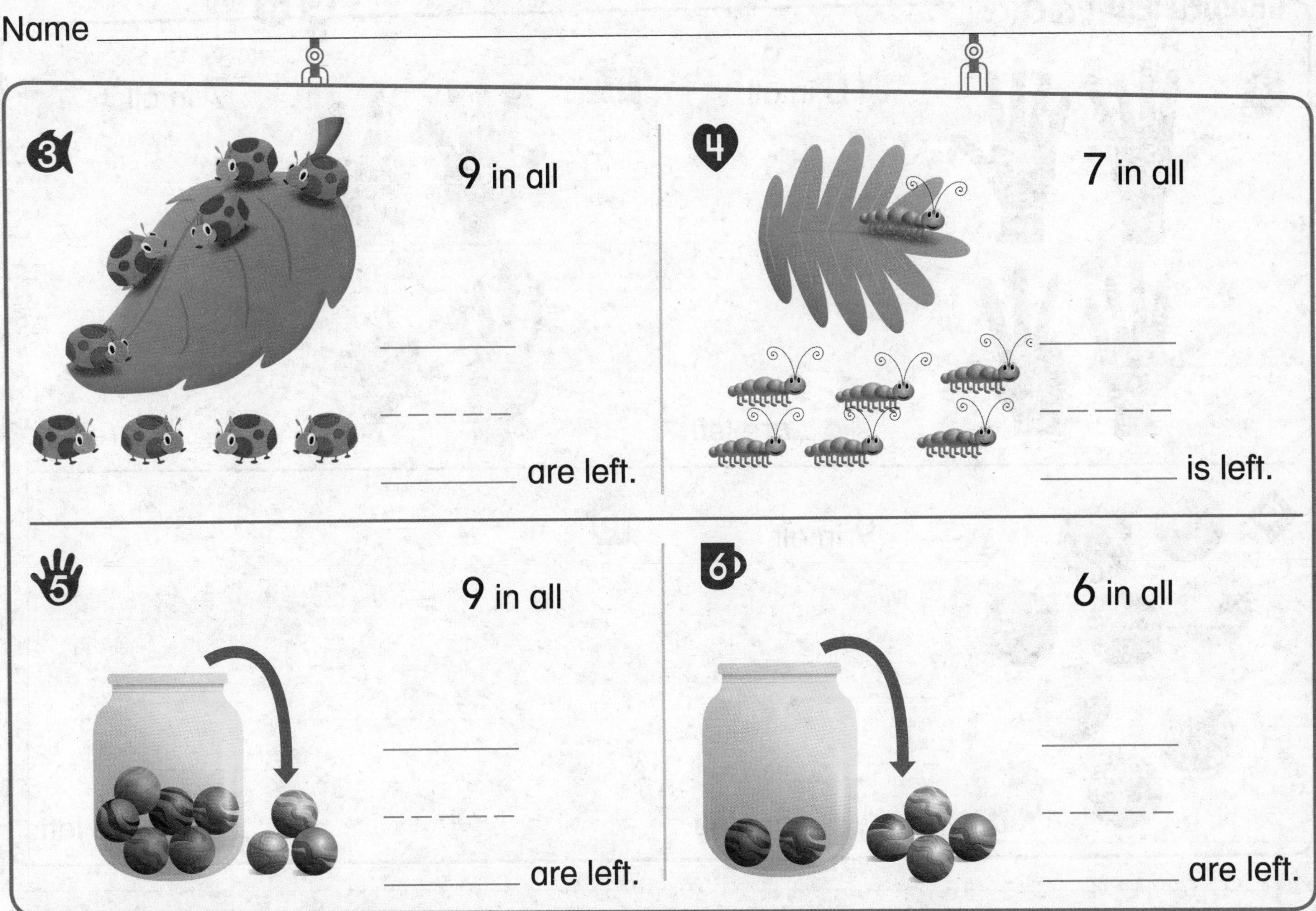

Directions Have students listen to the story, and then do all of the following to find how many are left: give an explanation of a mental image, use objects to act it out, and hold up fingers. Have them mark Xs on how many walk away or are taken out, and then write the number to tell how many are left. 3 *9 ladybugs are on a leaf. 4 walk away. How many ladybugs are left?* 4 *7 caterpillars are on a leaf. 6 walk away. How many caterpillars are left?* 5 *9 marbles are in a jar. 3 are taken out. How many marbles are left?* 6 *6 marbles are in a jar. 4 are taken out. How many marbles are left?*

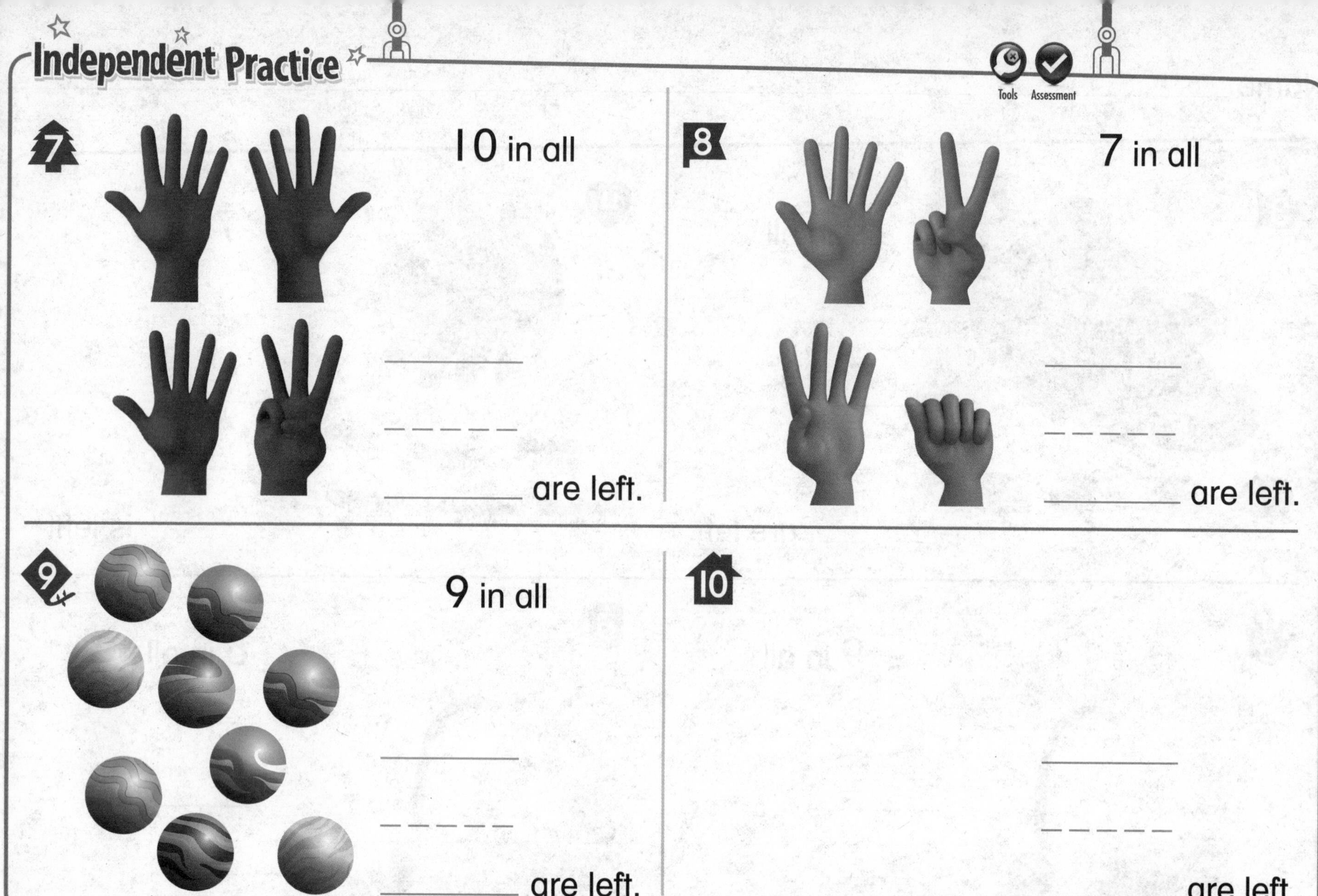

Directions Have students listen to the story, and then do all of the following to find how many are left: give an explanation of a mental image, use objects to act it out, and hold up fingers. Ask them to write the number to tell how many are left. 7 *10 fingers are in the air. 2 are put down. How many fingers are left?* 8 *7 fingers are in the air. 3 are put down. How many fingers are left?* 9 Have students listen to the story, and then do all of the following to find how many are left: give an explanation of a mental image, use objects to act it out, and then mark Xs on how many are taken away. Ask them to write the number to tell how many are left. *There are 9 marbles. 6 are taken away. How many marbles are left?* 10 **Higher Order Thinking** Have students draw 10 marbles. Have them mark Xs on some of them, and then write the number to tell how many marbles are left.

Name ______________________

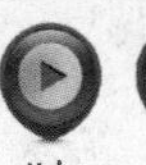

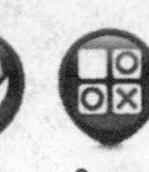

Help Tools Games

Homework & Practice 7-1

Explore Subtraction

HOME ACTIVITY Put up to 10 coins on a napkin and have your child count them. Then move some of the coins off of the napkin. Ask: *How many coins are left on the napkin?* Repeat the activity using a different number of coins.

Another Look!

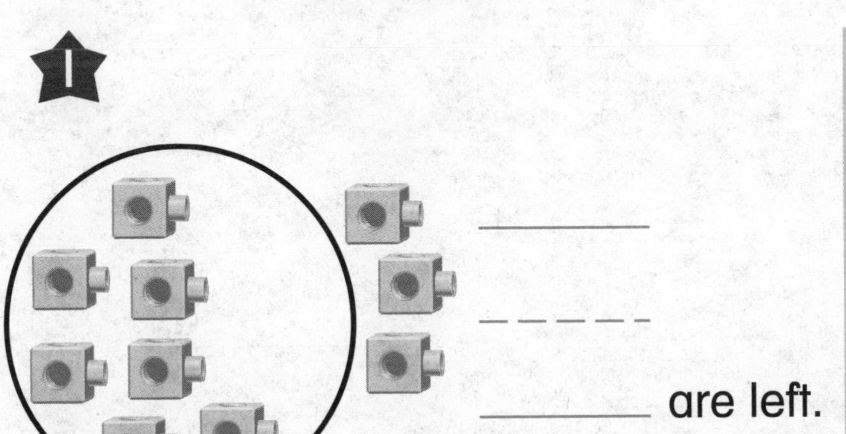

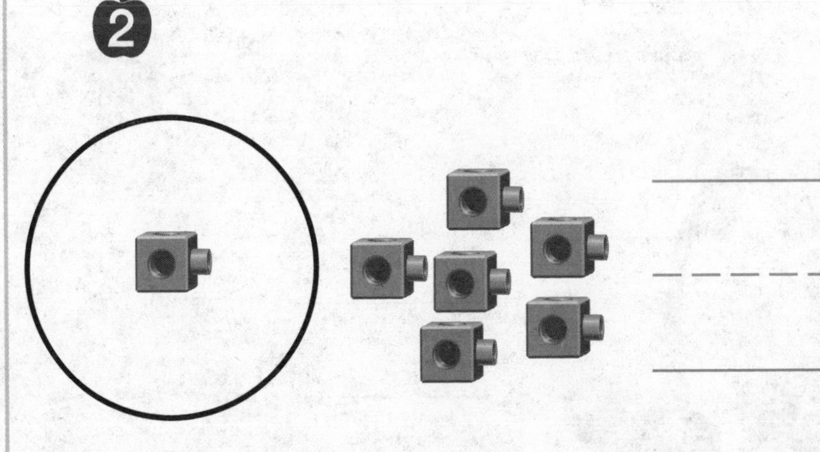

Directions Say: *Carlos puts 8 cubes inside a circle. He moves 4 of them outside the circle.* Model how to explain a mental image, how to act it out with objects, and how to hold up fingers to show how many cubes are left inside the circle. Have students listen to the story, and then do all of the following to find how many are left: give an explanation of a mental image, use objects to act it out, and hold up fingers. Have them write the number to tell how many are left. **1** *Carlos puts 10 cubes inside a circle. He moves 3 of them out. How many cubes are left?* **2** *Carlos puts 7 cubes inside a circle. He moves 6 of them out. How many cubes are left?*

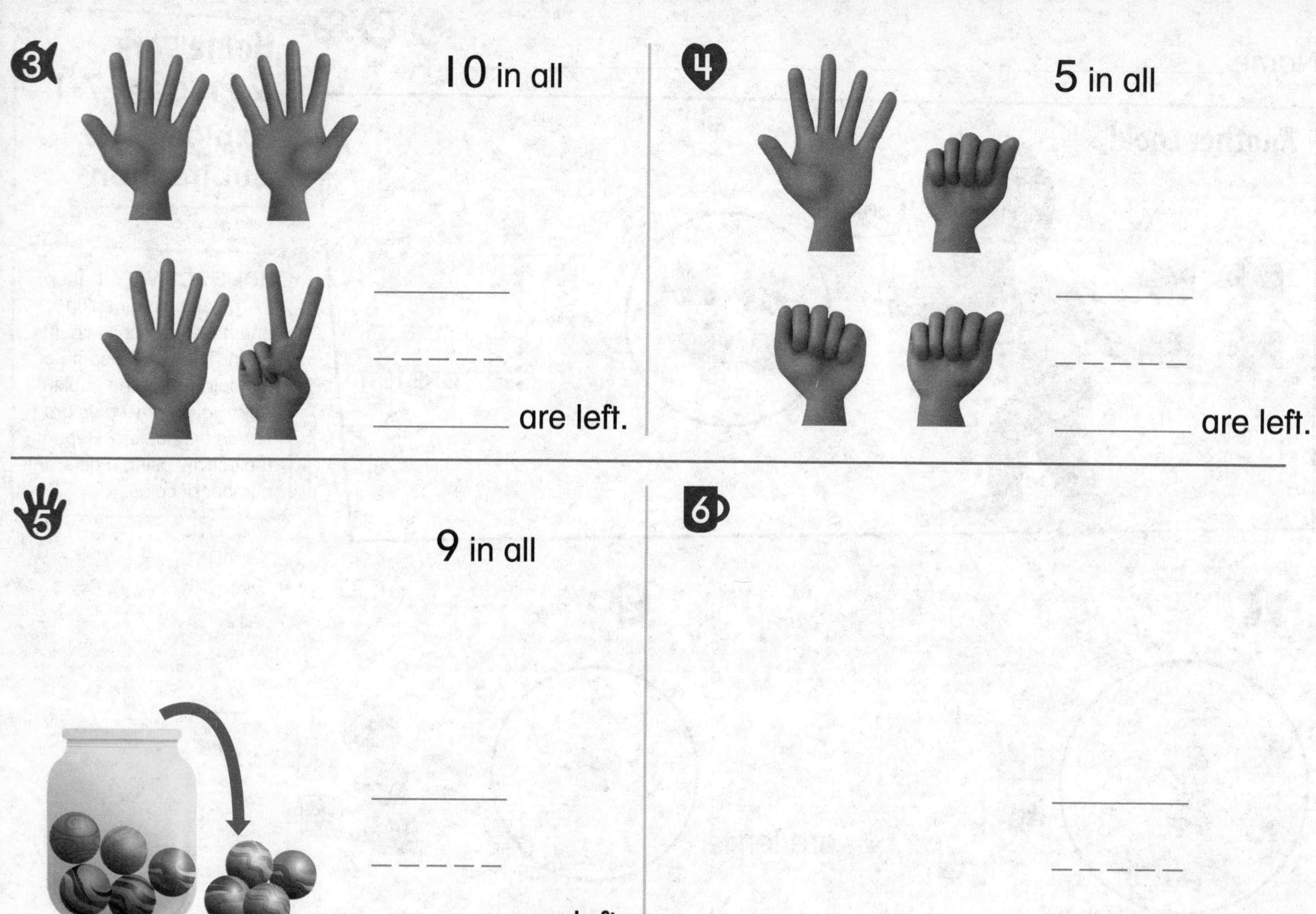

Directions Have students listen to the story, and then do all of the following to find how many are left: give an explanation of a mental image, use objects to act it out, and hold up fingers. Ask them to write the number to tell how many are left. **3** *10 fingers are in the air. 3 are put down. How many fingers are left?* **4** *5 fingers are in the air. 5 are put down. How many fingers are left?* **5** *9 marbles are in a jar. 4 are taken out. How many marbles are left?* **6** **Higher Order Thinking** Have students draw 8 marbles. Have them mark Xs on some of them, and then write the number to tell how many marbles are left.

Name ______________________________

Lesson 7-2
Represent Subtraction as Taking Apart

Directions Say: *Alex picks 7 apples. Some apples are red, and some are yellow. Alex wants to put the red apples in one basket and the yellow in the other. How many red apples and how many yellow apples can there be? Write the numbers to tell how many. Draw pictures to show your answer.*

I can ... take apart a number and tell the parts.

I can also reason about math.

Take apart 7.

Take apart 7.

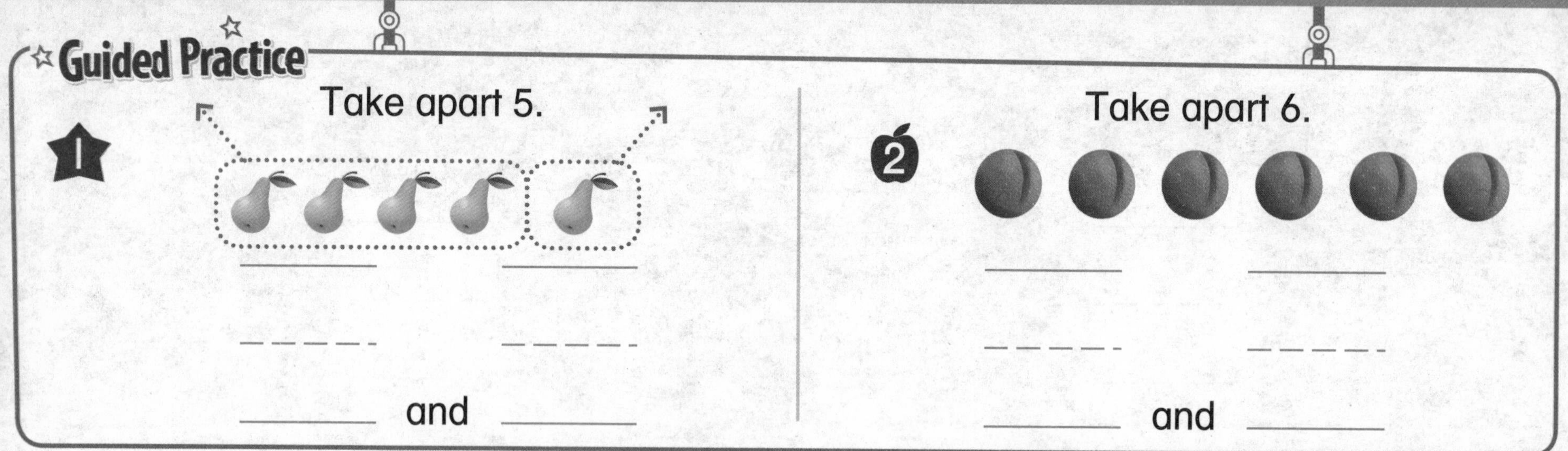

Directions Have students: 1 take apart the group of pears. Then have them draw a circle around the parts they made, and then write the numbers to tell the parts; 2 take apart the group of peaches. Then have them draw a circle around the parts they made, and then write the numbers to tell the parts.

Name ______

3 Take apart 4.

______ ______

and

4 Take apart 10.

______ ______

and

5 Take apart 3.

______ ______

and

6 Take apart 8.

______ ______

and

Directions 3–6 Have students take apart the group of fruit. Then have them draw a circle around the parts they made, and then write the numbers to tell the parts.

Independent Practice

Tools Assessment

7 Take apart 6.

______ ______

______ and ______

8 Take apart 2.

______ ______

______ and ______

9 Take apart 5.

______ ______

______ and ______

10 ______

Take apart ______.

______ ______

______ and ______

Directions 7 and 8 Have students take apart the group of fruit. Then have them draw a circle around the parts they made, and then write the numbers to tell the parts. 9 **Higher Order Thinking** Have students draw counters to show a group of 5. Then have them take apart the group of counters, draw a circle around the parts they made, and then write the numbers to tell the parts. 10 **Higher Order Thinking** Have students choose any number between 2 and 10, write that number on the top line, and then draw a group of counters to show that number. Have them take apart the group of counters, draw a circle around the parts they made, and then write the numbers to tell the parts.

Name ______________________

Homework & Practice 7-2

Represent Subtraction as Taking Apart

HOME ACTIVITY Give your child 8 coins. Have him or her use the coins to show a way to take apart 8 into two parts. Then have them write the parts.

Another Look! Take apart 9.

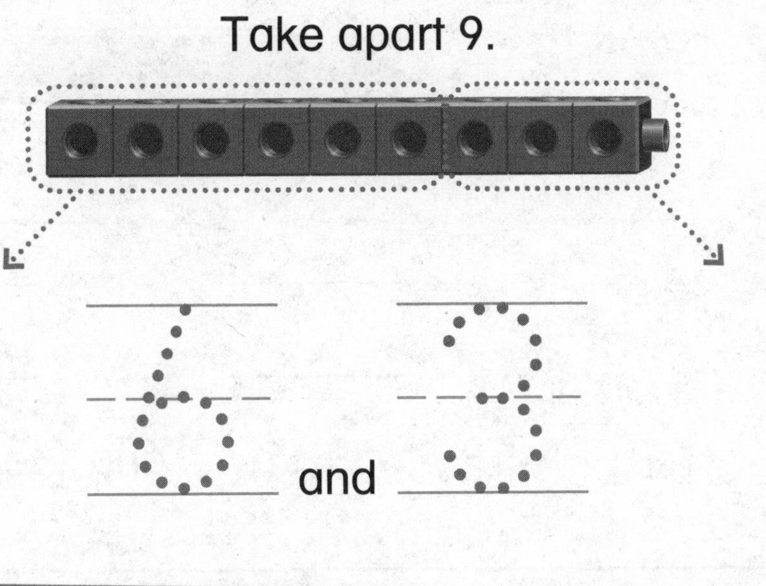

6 and 3

Take apart 6.

______ and ______

2 Take apart 7.

______ and ______

Directions Say: *Carlos takes apart his cube train. He makes a group of 6 and a group of 3. Draw circles around the cubes to show the parts he made, and then write the numbers to tell the parts.* 1 and 2 Have students take apart each cube train. Have them draw a circle around the parts they made, and then write the numbers to tell the parts.

3 Take apart 8.

Take apart 8.

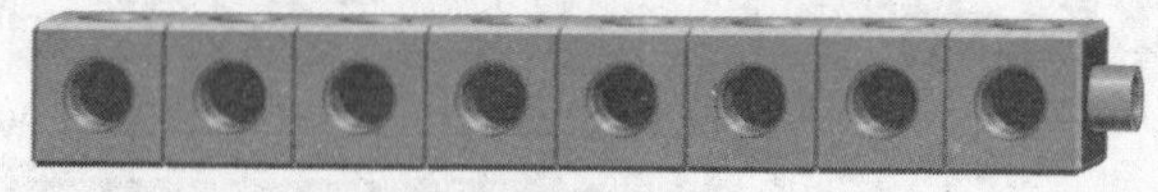

____ ____

____ and ____

____ ____

____ and ____

____ ____

____ and ____

____ ____

____ and ____

Directions 3 Have students take apart the cube train on the left. Have them draw a circle around the parts they made, and then write the numbers to tell the parts. Have them show a different way to take apart the cube train on the right, draw a circle around the parts they made, and then write the numbers to tell the parts. 4 **Higher Order Thinking** Have students draw two cube trains with the same amount of cubes. Have them take apart the cube trains in two different ways, draw a circle around the parts they made, and then write the numbers to tell the parts.

Name ______________________

Lesson 7-3
Represent Subtraction as Taking From

_____ take away _____ is _____.

Directions Say: *Marta is watching bugs. She sees 4 ladybugs. Then 2 crawl away. How can you complete the sentence to tell how many ladybugs are left?*

I can ...
represent subtraction as taking away from a whole.

I can also make sense of problems.

Guided Practice

1

6 take away 3 is 3.

2

___ take away ___ is ___.

Directions Have students listen to each story, and then complete the sentence to tell how many bugs are left. 1 *Marta sees 6 bumblebees. 3 leave. How many bumblebees are left?* 2 *Marta sees 7 ladybugs. 2 leave. How many ladybugs are left?*

Name ______________________________

3

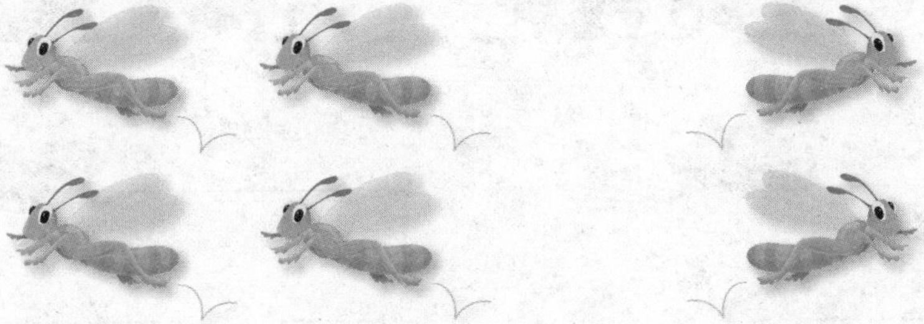

______ ______ ______

______ take away ______ is ______.

4

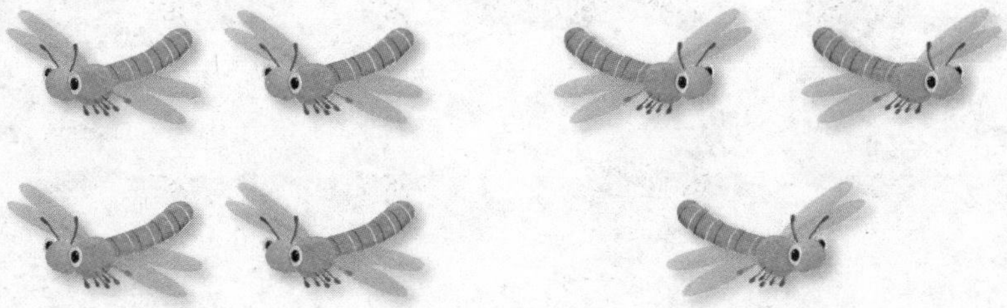

______ ______ ______

______ take away ______ is ______.

5

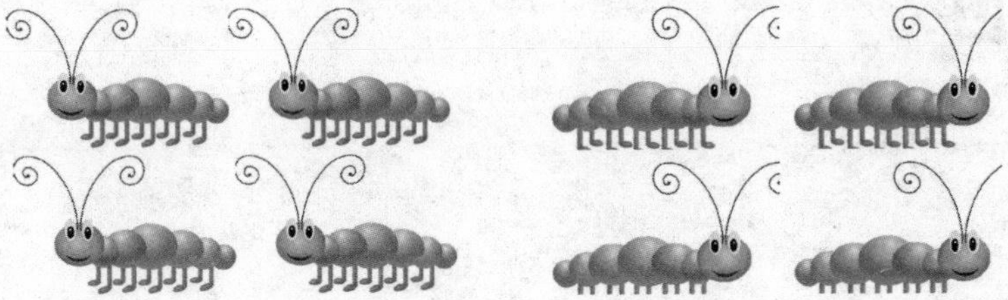

______ ______ ______

______ take away ______ is ______.

6

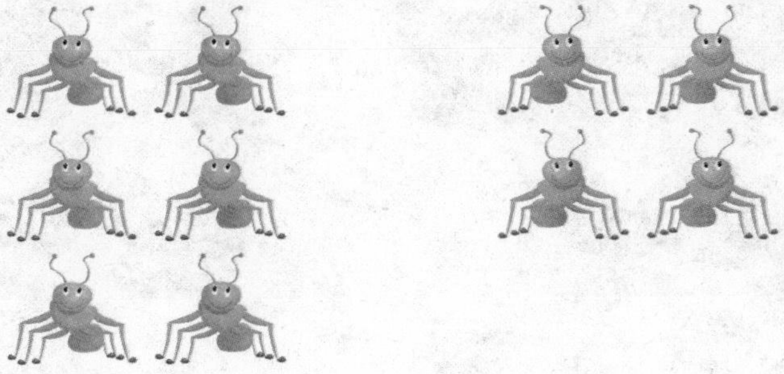

______ ______ ______

______ take away ______ is ______.

Directions Have students listen to each story, and then complete the sentence to tell how many bugs are left. 3 *Emily sees 6 grasshoppers on the table. 2 hop away. How many grasshoppers are left?* 4 *Emily sees 7 dragonflies. 3 fly away. How many dragonflies are left?* 5 *Emily sees 8 caterpillars resting on a branch. 4 crawl away. How many caterpillars are left?* 6 **Math and Science** Say: *Ants can move material much bigger than themselves. Emily sees 10 ants on a picnic blanket. 4 walk away. How many ants are left?*

Independent Practice

Tools Assessment

7

_____ _____ _____

_____ take away _____ is _____.

8

_____ _____ _____

_____ take away _____ is _____.

9

_____ _____ _____

_____ take away _____ is _____.

10

_____ _____ _____

_____ take away _____ is _____.

Directions Have students listen to each story, and then complete the sentence to tell how many are left. 7 *Jerome sees 8 snails on the sidewalk. 3 slink away. How many snails are left?* 8 *Jerome sees 6 grasshoppers in the grass. 3 hop away. How many grasshoppers are left?* 9 *Jerome sees 9 butterflies in the garden. 4 flutter away. How many butterflies are left?* 10 **Higher Order Thinking** Have students listen to the story, draw a picture to show the story, and then complete the sentence to tell how many are left. *Jerome sees 7 inchworms on a tree. 4 crawl away. How many inchworms are left?*

Name ______________________

Homework & Practice 7-3

Represent Subtraction as Taking From

Another Look!

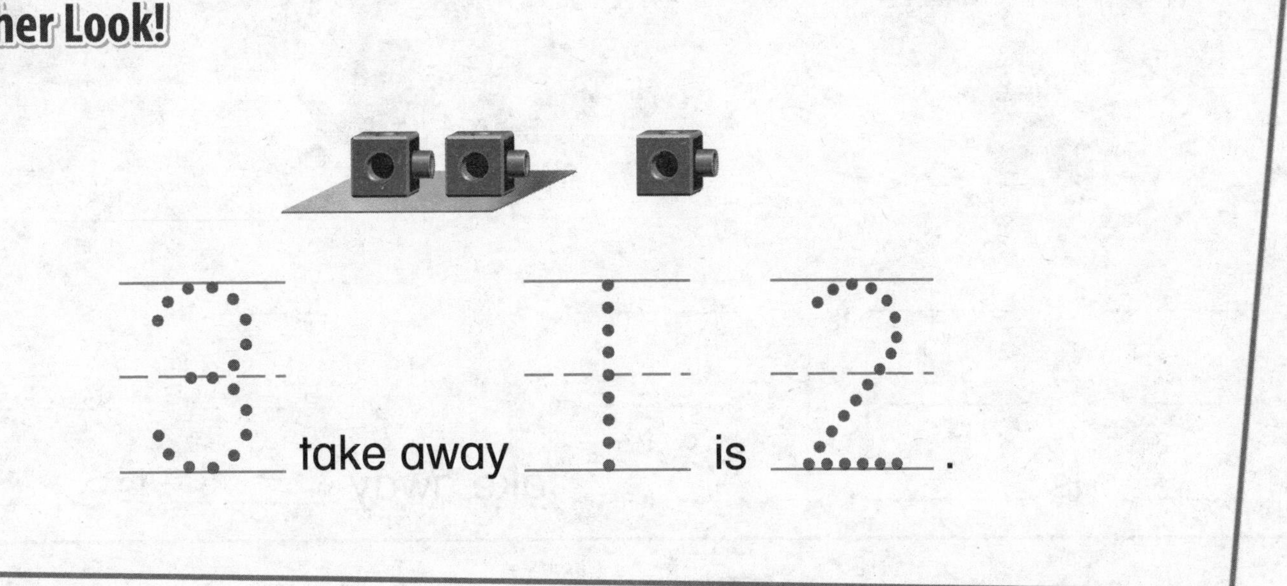

3 take away 1 is 2.

HOME ACTIVITY Place 7 toys or other small objects in front of your child. Ask him or her to tell you how many toys there are in all, and then move 3 of the toys to the side and tell how many toys are left. Have your child say a sentence that tells how many are left.

1

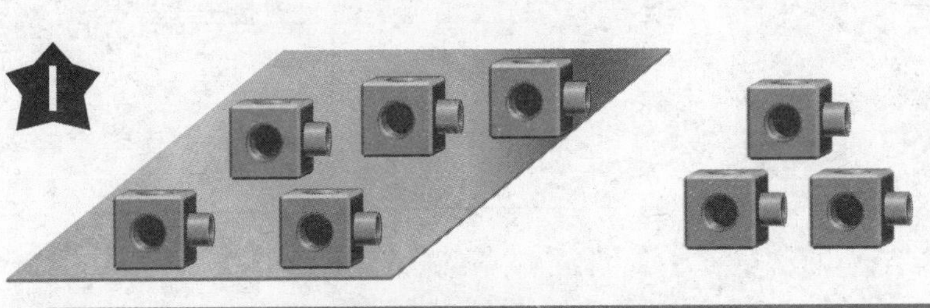

_____ take away _____ is _____.

2

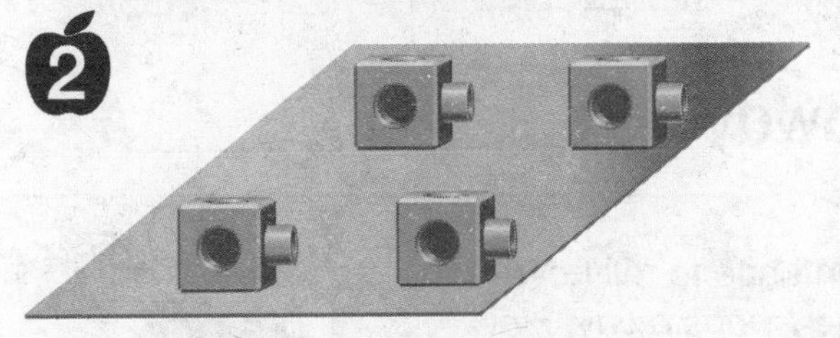

_____ take away _____ is _____.

Directions Say: *There are 3 cubes on a mat. Then Alex moves 1 away. How many cubes are left on the mat? Complete the sentence to tell how many are left.* Have students listen to each story, and then complete the sentence to tell how many are left. 1 *Alex puts 8 cubes on a mat. Then he moves 3 away. How many cubes are left on the mat?* 2 *Alex puts 5 cubes on a mat. Then he moves 1 away. How many cubes are left on the mat?*

3

_____ _____ _____

_____ take away _____ is _____.

4

_____ _____ _____

_____ take away _____ is _____.

5

_____ _____ _____

_____ take away _____ is _____.

6

_____ _____ _____

_____ take away _____ is _____.

Directions Have students listen to each story, count how many are left, and then complete the sentence to tell how many are left. 3 *Carlos sees 6 ducks. 3 fly away. How many ducks are left?* 4 *Carlos sees 6 frogs. 1 hops away. How many frogs are left?* 5 **Higher Order Thinking** Have students listen to the story, draw a picture to show what is happening, and then complete the sentence to tell how many are left. *Carlos sees 6 ants. 4 crawl away. How many ants are left?* 6 **Higher Order Thinking** Have students listen to the story, draw a picture to show what is happening, and then complete the sentence to tell how many are left. *Some oranges are on Carlos's plate. He eats 2 oranges. 4 are left. How many oranges were on the plate before Carlos ate some?*

Lesson 7-4
Use the Minus Sign

Directions Say: *There are 5 parrots in a tree. 2 fly away. Use counters or draw pictures to show how many parrots are left. Explain how you know you are correct.*

I can ...
separate numbers.

I can also reason about math.

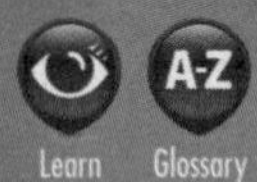

5 take away 2

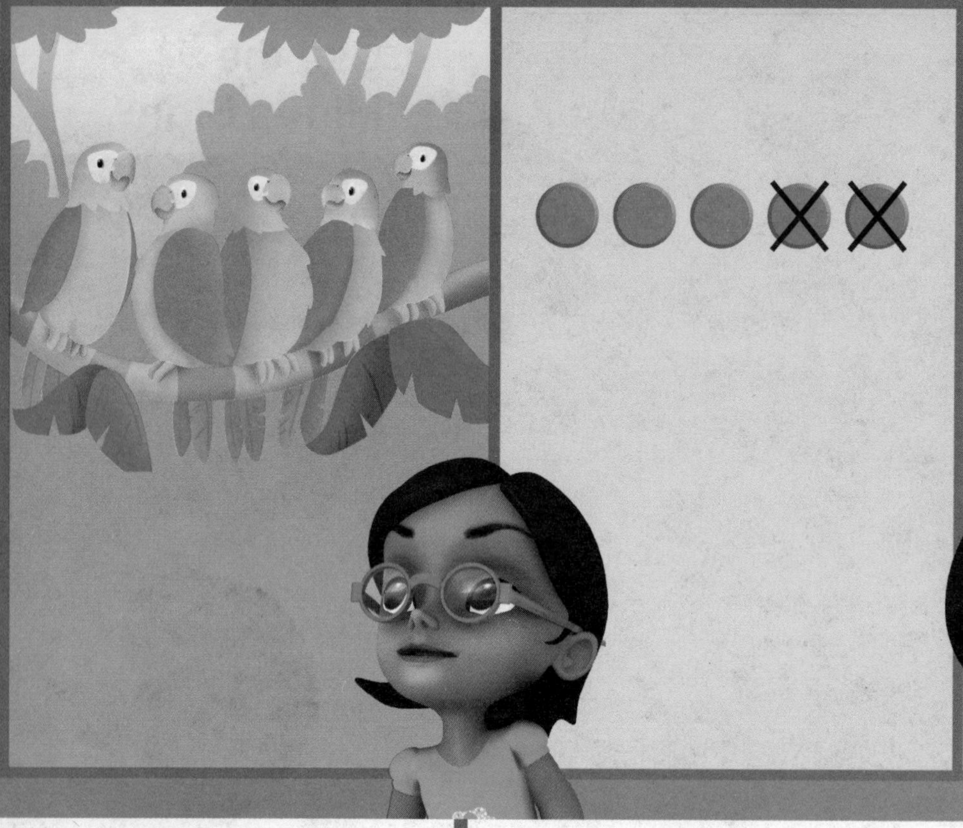

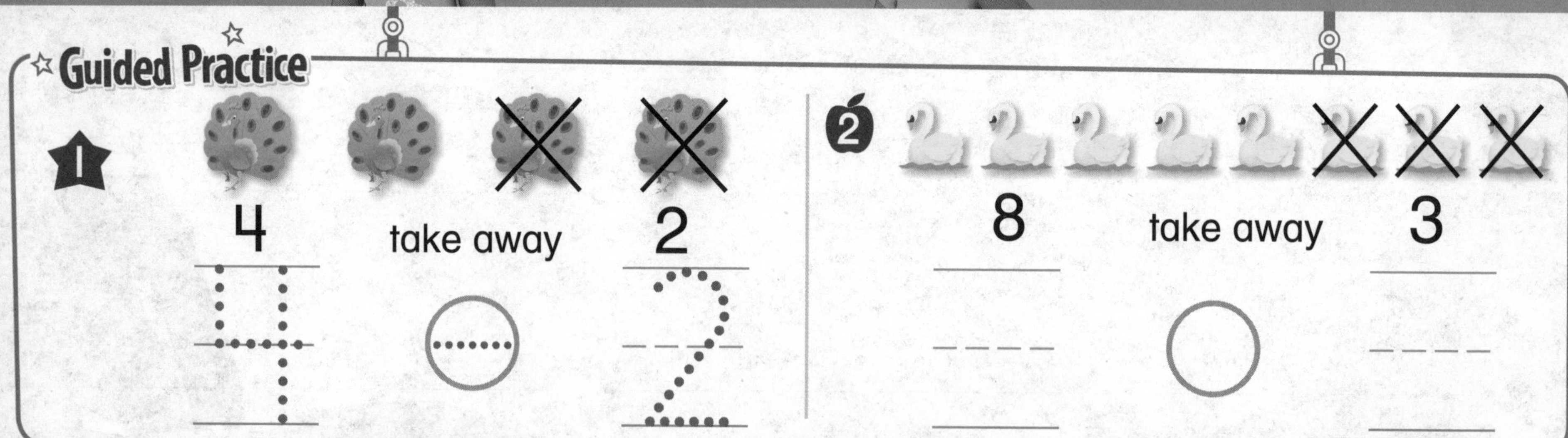

Directions 1 and 2 Have students count the birds and write the number to tell how many, and then write the minus sign and the number subtracted.

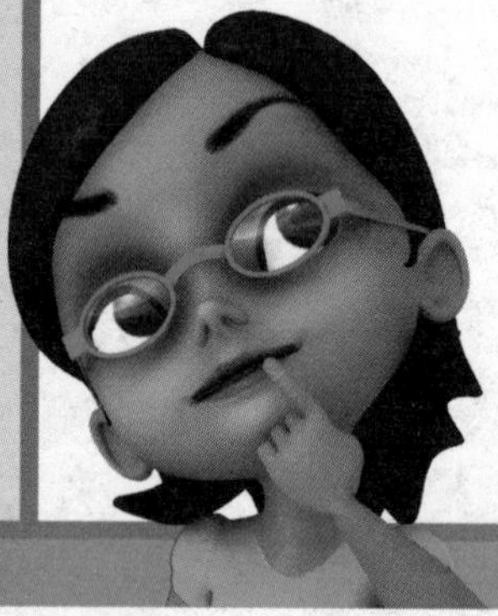

Name ________________________________

3

6 take away 2

4

7 take away 3

5

8 take away 3

6

9 take away 4

Directions 3–6 Have students count the birds and write the number to tell how many, and then write the minus sign and the number subtracted.

Independent Practice

5 take away 1

____ – ____

8 take away 5

____ ◯ ____

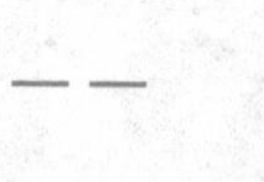

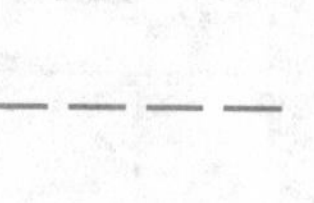

6 take away 2

____ ◯ ____

9 take away 6

____ ◯ ____

Directions 7 **Vocabulary** Have students listen to the story, and then show how a **minus sign** is represented by marking an X on the owl that flies away. Have them write a number to tell how many and the number subtracted. *There are 5 owls. 1 flies away.* 8 and 9 Have students count the birds and write the number to tell how many, and then write the minus sign and the number subtracted. 10 **Higher Order Thinking** Have students listen to the story, draw counters and mark Xs to show the subtraction, and then write the numbers and the minus sign to solve. *There are 9 birds. Some fly away. 3 birds are left.*

Name ____________________

Help

Tools
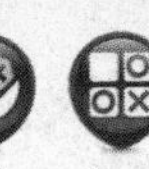
Games

Homework & Practice 7-4

Use the Minus Sign

Another Look!

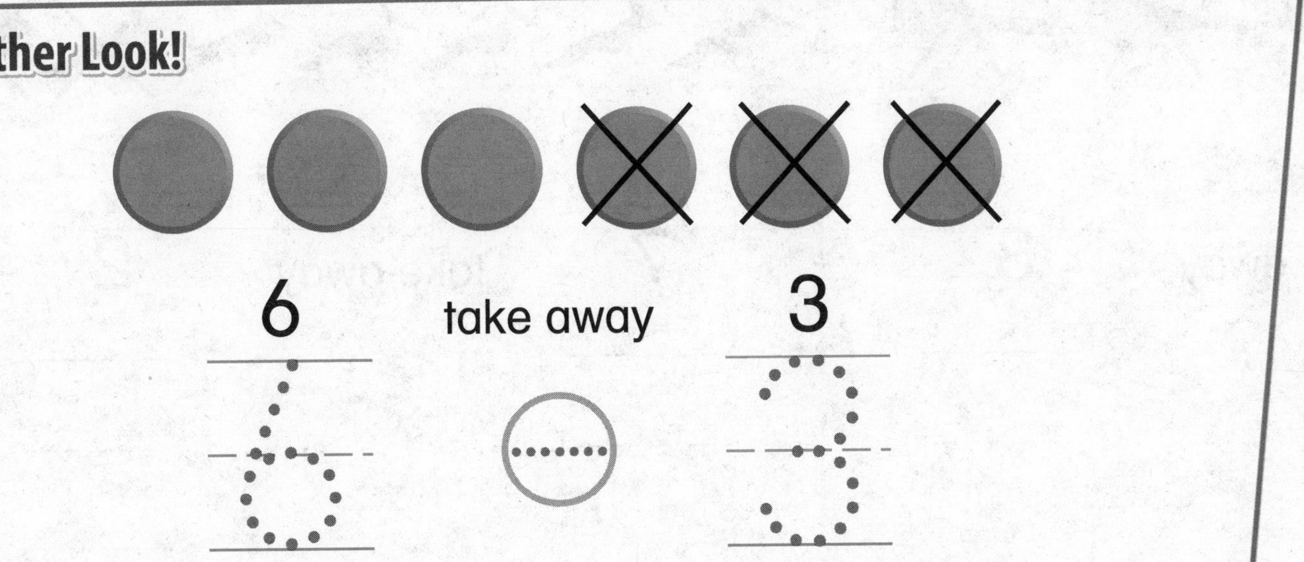

HOME ACTIVITY Have your child point to a minus sign on the page and explain what the minus sign means. Then encourage him or her to tell some number stories that involve subtracting.

1

2

Directions Say: *Write the number to tell how many counters in all, and then write the minus sign. How many counters are subtracted? Write the number to tell how many are subtracted.* 1 and 2 Have students count the counters and write the number to tell how many, write the minus sign, and then count the counters that are taken away and write the number.

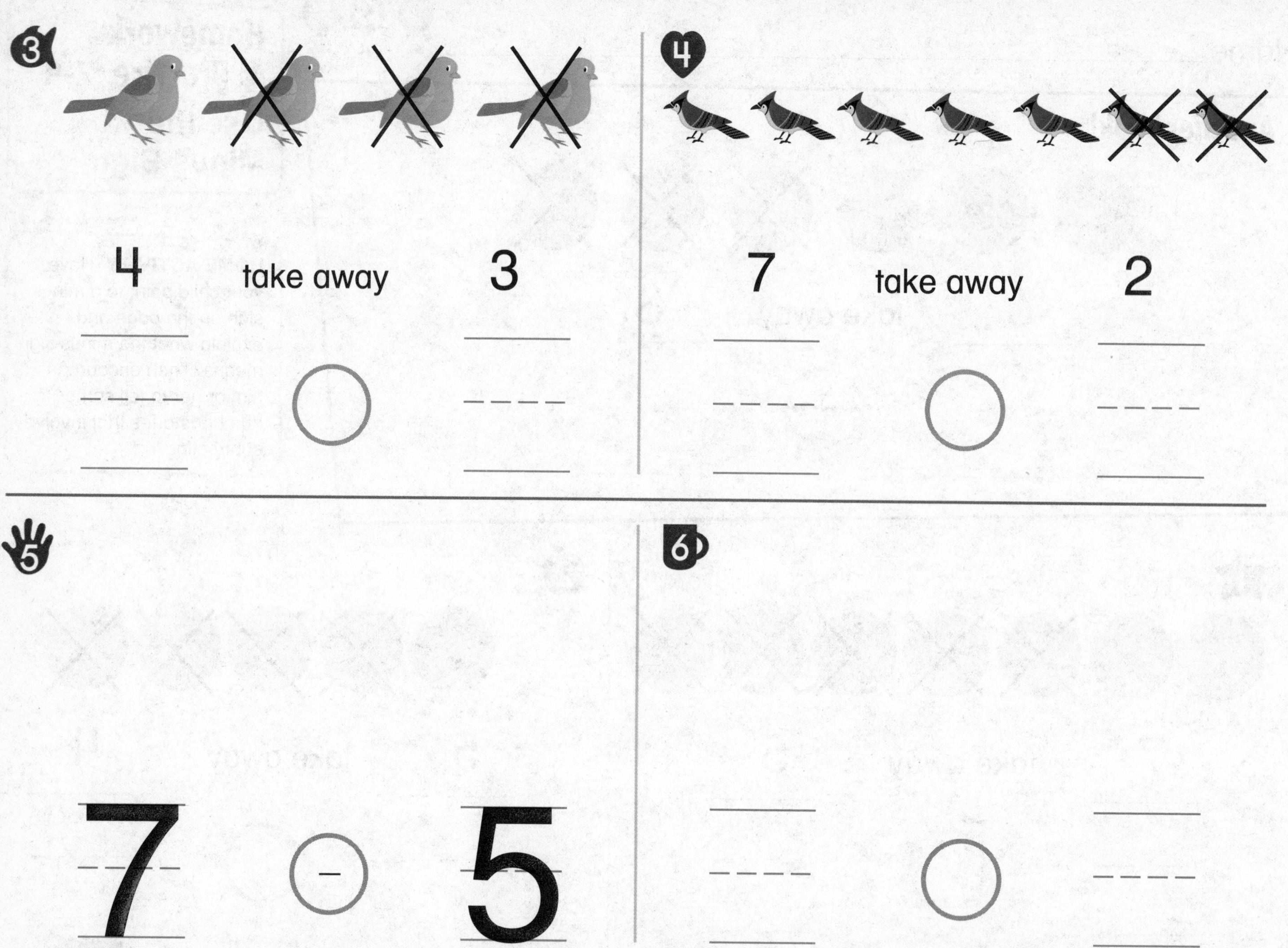

Directions 3 and 4 Have students count the birds and write the number to tell how many, and then write the minus sign and the number subtracted. 5 **Higher Order Thinking** Have students draw a picture to match the number sentence. 6 **Higher Order Thinking** Have students listen to the story, draw counters and mark Xs to show what is happening, and then write the numbers and the minus sign. *There are 6 parrots in a cage. A zookeeper takes some away for a show. 2 parrots are left in the cage.*

Name ______________________________

Lesson 7-5

Represent and Explain Subtraction with Equations

Directions Say: *There are 6 fire hats. Firefighters take 3 away. What numbers do you subtract to find how many hats are left? How can you show the subtraction?*

I can ...
separate more numbers.

I can also reason about math.

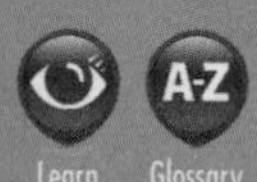

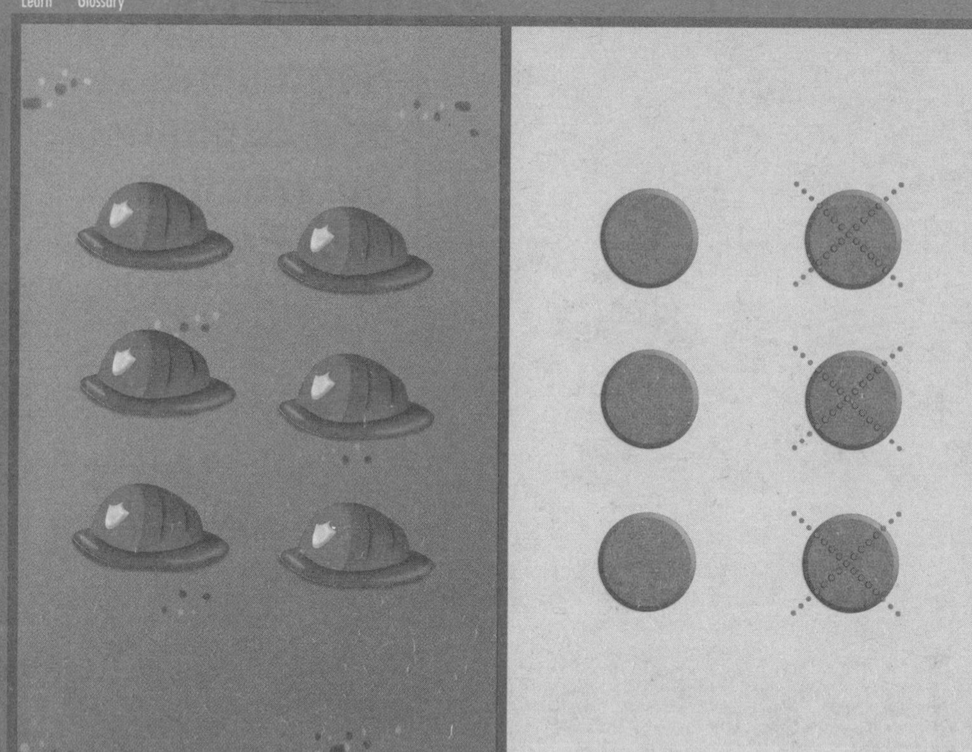

Guided Practice

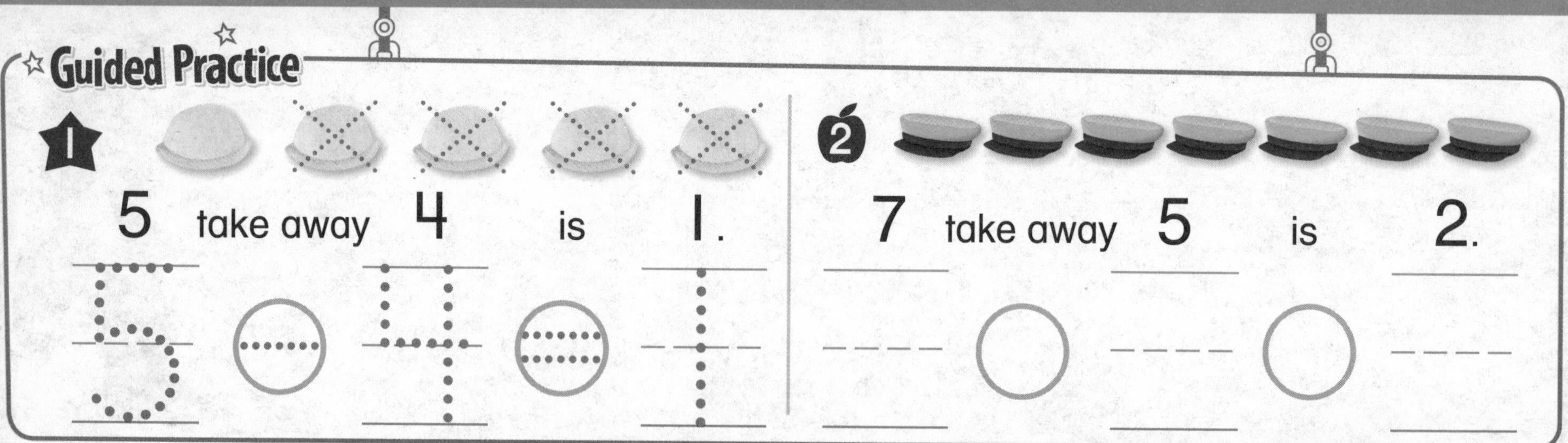

Directions 1 and 2 Have students use counters to model the problem, mark Xs to subtract, and then write a subtraction equation to find the difference.

Name

3 

8 take away 2 is 6.

4 

6 take away 5 is 1.

5 

9 take away 5 is 4.

6 

7 take away 2 is 5.

Directions 3–6 Have students use counters to model the problem, mark Xs to subtract, and then write an equation to find the difference.

Independent Practice

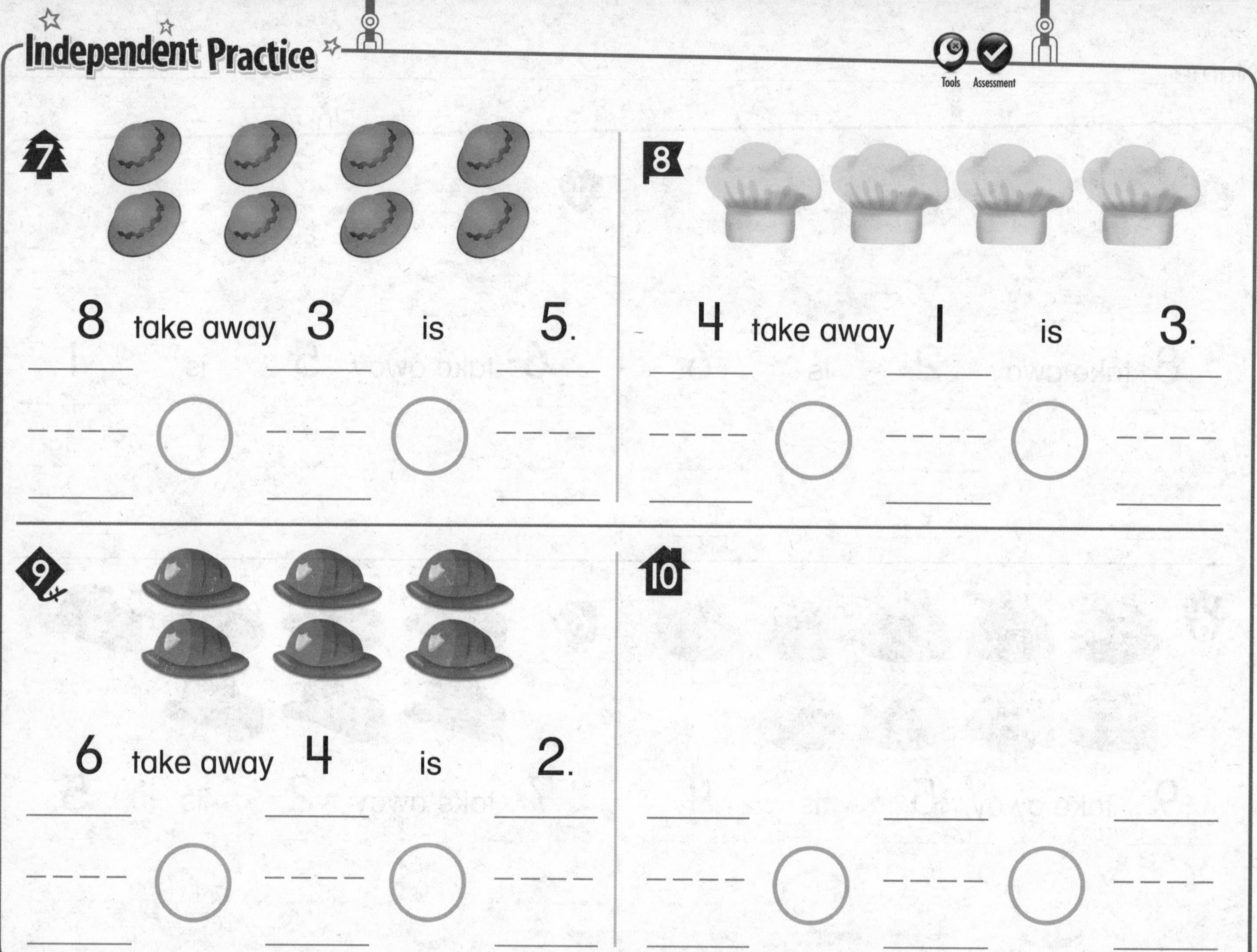

Directions 7–9 Have students use counters to model the problem, mark Xs to subtract, and then write an equation to find the difference. 10 **Higher Order Thinking** Have students listen to the story, draw counters and mark Xs to show the problem, and then write an equation to find the difference. *There are 7 baseball caps. Some are worn to a game. There are 4 left. How many caps were worn to the game?*

Name ________________

   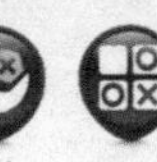

Homework & Practice 7-5

Represent and Explain Subtraction with Equations

Another Look!

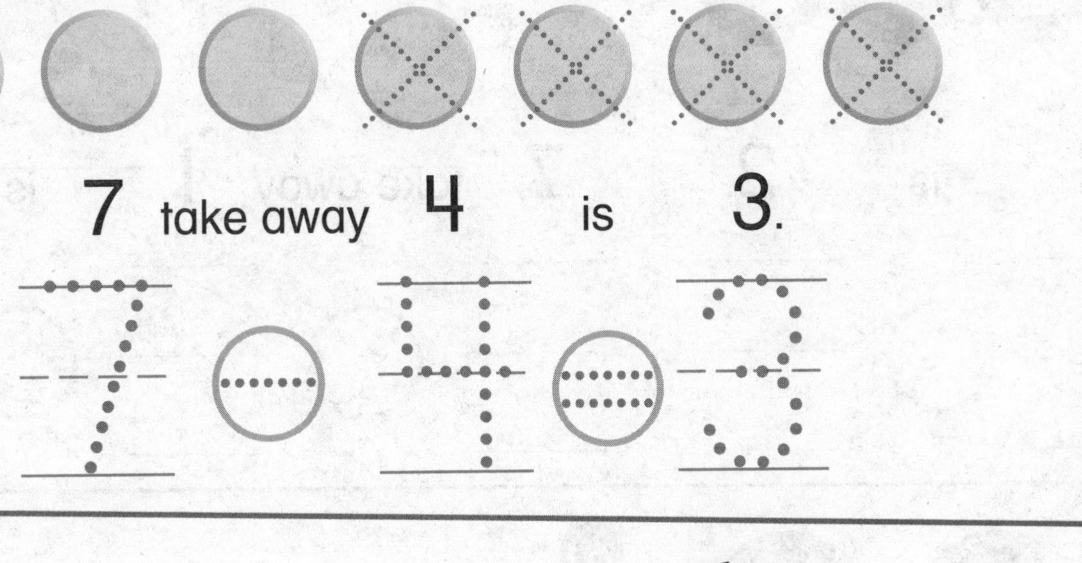

HOME ACTIVITY Have your child point to the difference in a number sentence on this page and explain the number. Then give your child 4 toys and help him or her tell a subtracting story. Ask him or her to find the difference. Repeat with other numbers and objects.

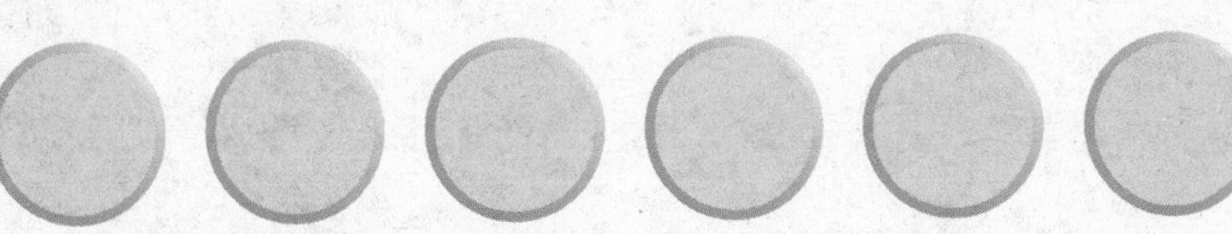

6 take away 4 is 2.

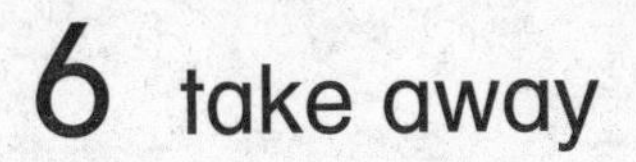

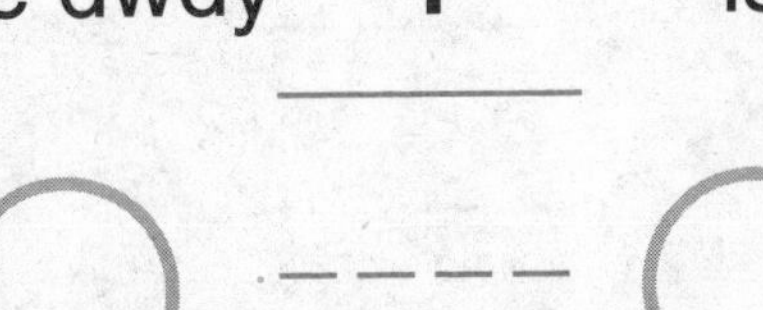

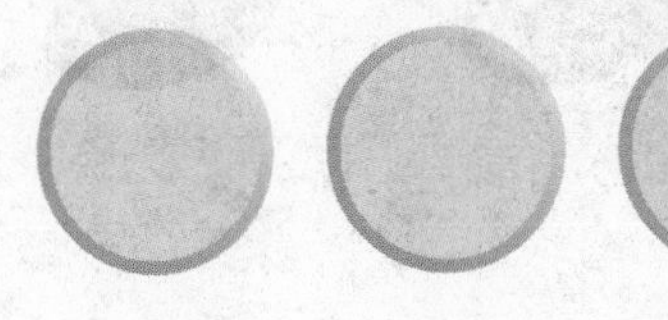

4 take away 3 is 1.

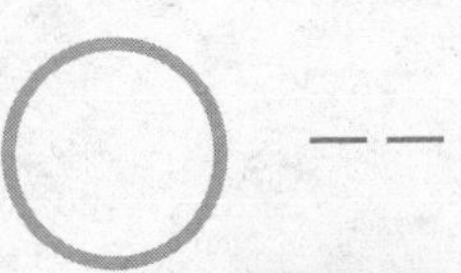

Directions Say: *What numbers are being subtracted? Mark Xs on the counters to show how many to take away, and then write the numbers, the minus sign, the equal sign, and the difference to write the equation.* 1 and 2 Have students mark Xs to show how many counters to take away, and then write an equation to find the difference.

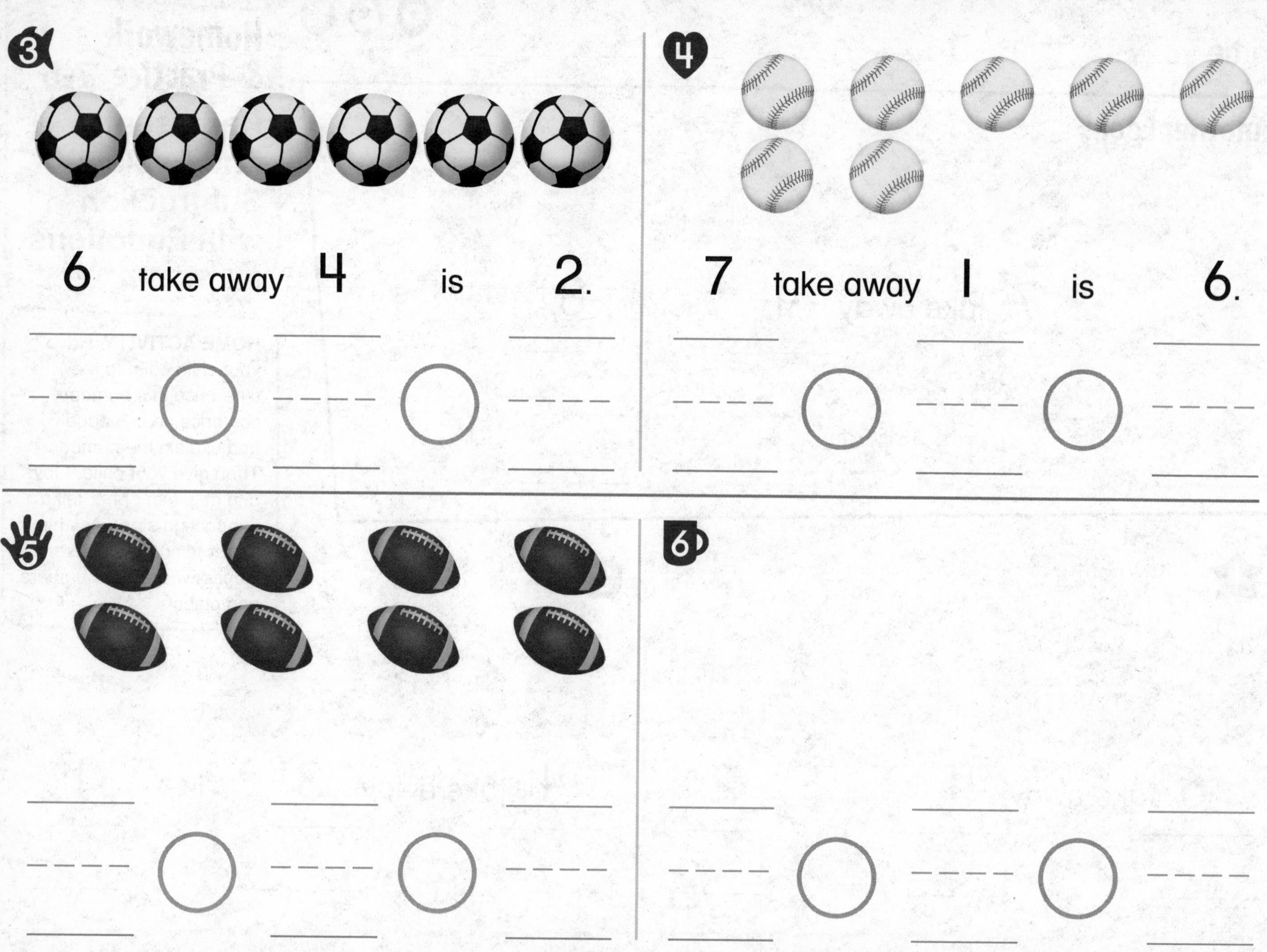

Directions 3 and 4 Have students mark Xs to subtract, and then write an equation to find the difference. 5 **Higher Order Thinking** Have students write how many balls there are in all, choose a number to subtract, mark Xs to show how many to take away, and then write the equation to find the difference. 6 **Higher Order Thinking** Have students listen to the story, draw counters and mark Xs to show the problem, and then write an equation to find the difference. *Some baseballs are in a bag. 3 are taken out. There are 6 baseballs left.*

Solve & Share

Name ______________________

Solve

Lesson 7-6

Continue to Represent and Explain Subtraction with Equations

______ ◯ ______ ◯ ______

Directions Say: *Marta has 10 puppets on the puppet stage. 4 leave the stage. How many puppets does Marta have left on stage? What number sentence can you write to solve the problem? Use counters or draw pictures to show your work.*

I can ... use the minus sign in an equation.

I can also reason about math.

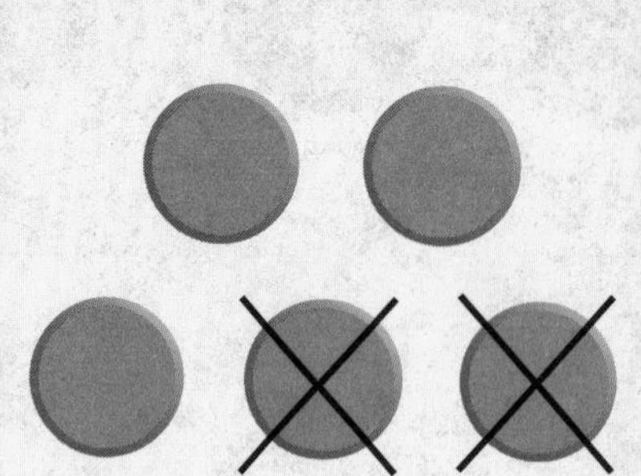

Guided Practice

Directions 1 and 2 Have students use counters to model the problem, and then write an equation to tell how many are left.

Name

3

4

5

6

Directions 3–6 Have students use counters to model the problem, and then write an equation to tell how many are left.

Independent Practice

Tools Assessment

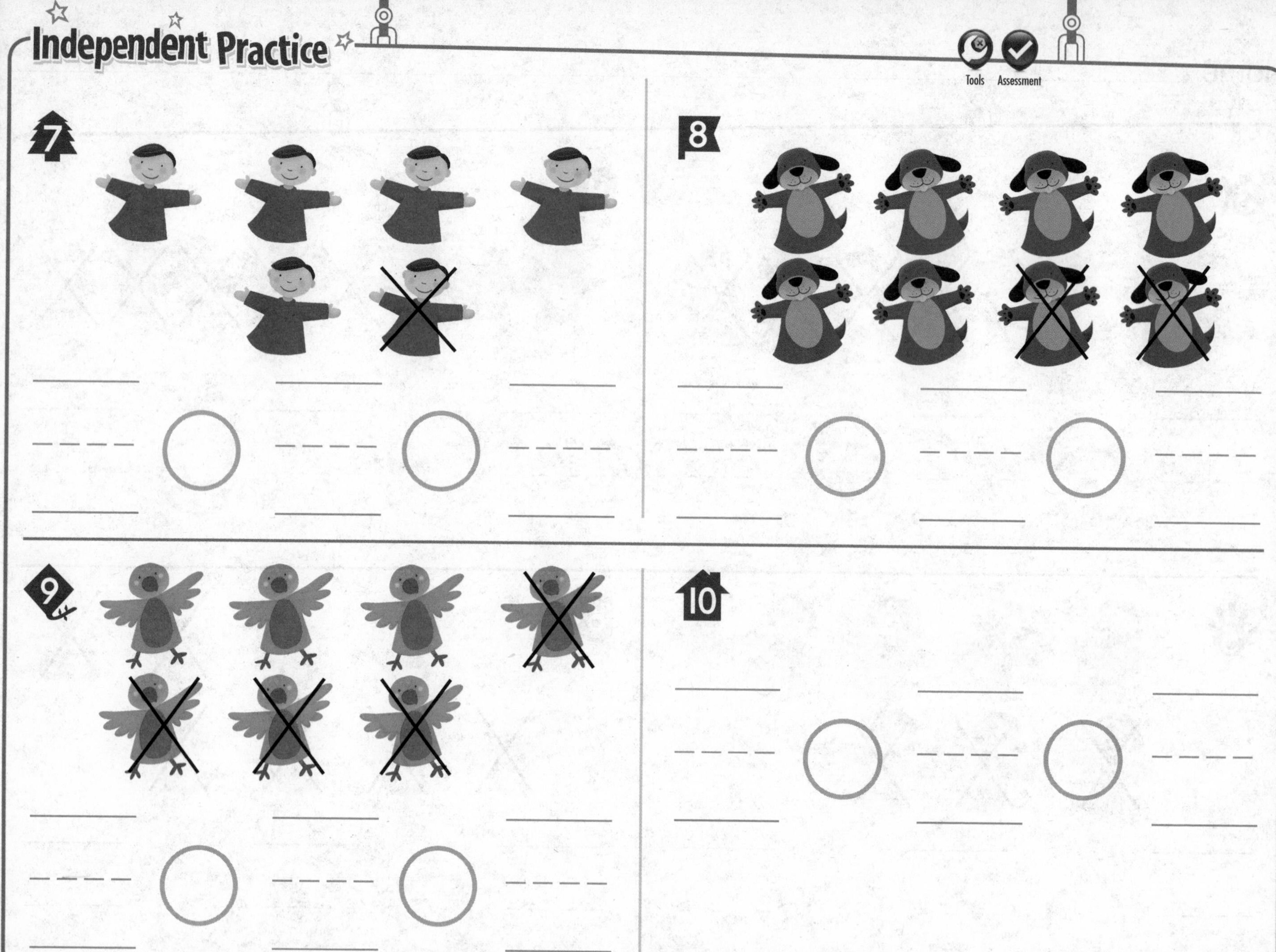

Directions 7–9 Have students use counters to model the problem, and then write an equation to tell how many are left. 10 **Higher Order Thinking** Have students listen to the story, and then write an equation to tell how many are left. *Marta has 8 puppets for the puppet show. She takes away some puppets to be fixed. Marta has 5 left for the show. How many puppets did she take away?*

Name ______________________

Homework & Practice 7-6

Continue to Represent and Explain Subtraction with Equations

HOME ACTIVITY Give your child 6 small objects and ask him or her to give you 3 of the objects. Ask your child to tell what he or she did and to write an equation (6 − 3 = 3). Repeat the activity, using other subtraction situations.

Another Look!

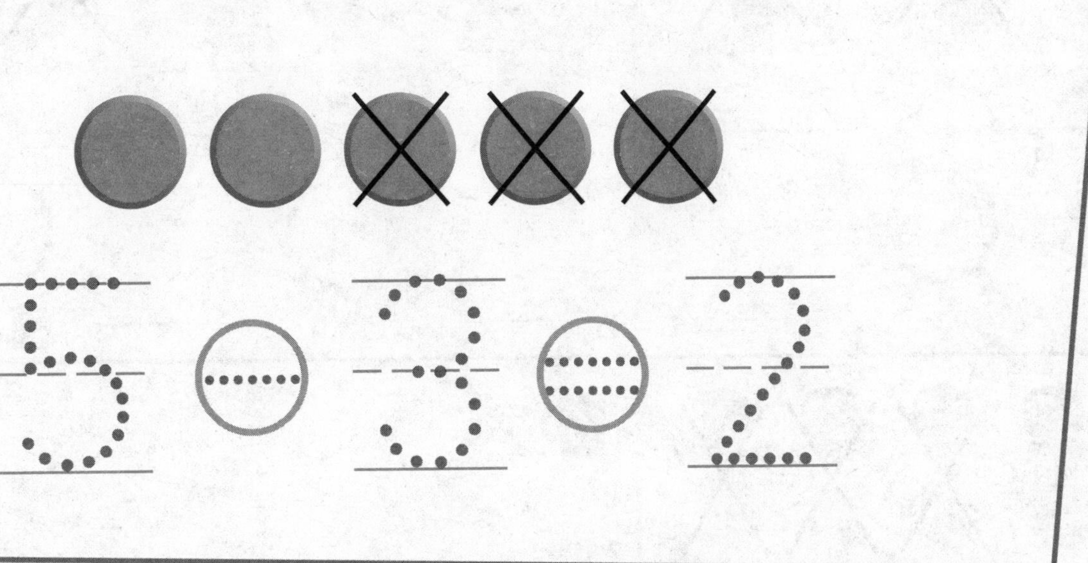

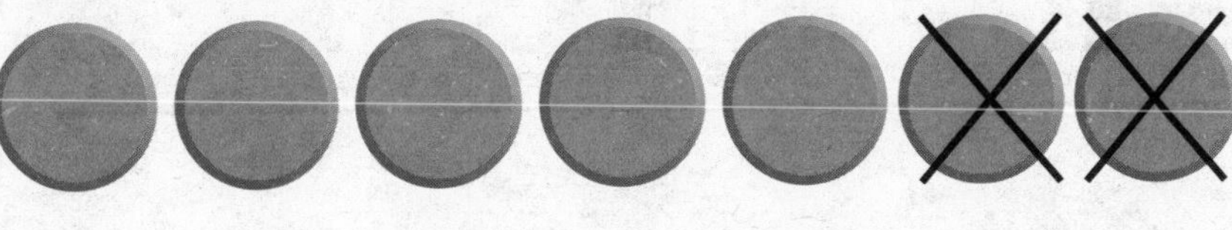

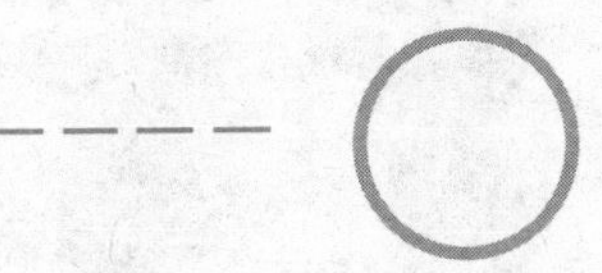

Directions Say: *How many counters are there in all? How many counters are being subtracted? How many are left? Write the numbers, the minus sign, the equal sign, and the difference to complete the equation.* 1 and 2 Have students subtract the group of counters that are marked with Xs, and then write an equation to tell how many are left.

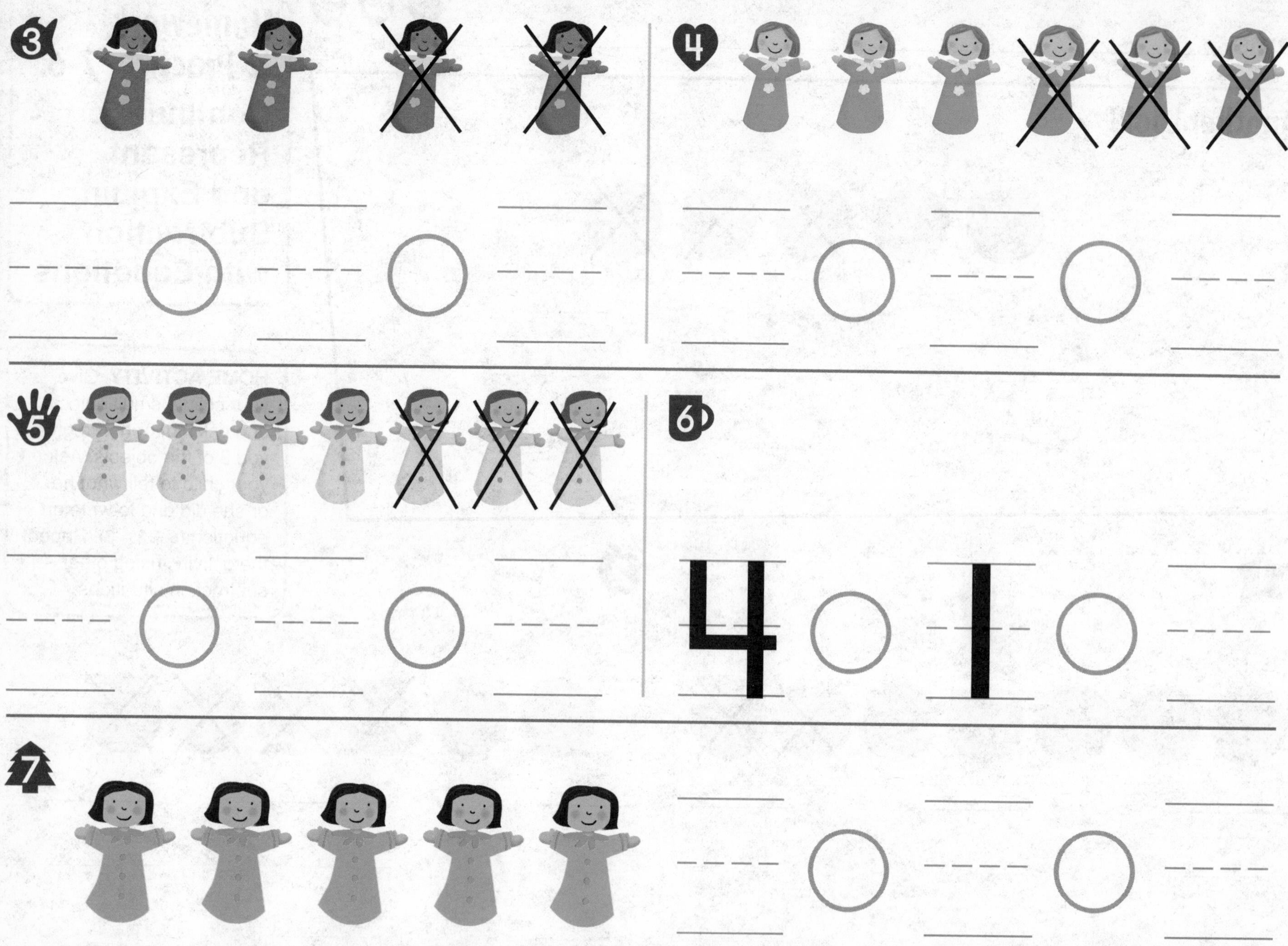

Directions 3–5 Have students write an equation to tell how many are left. 6 **Higher Order Thinking** Have students draw a picture to show the subtraction, and then complete the equation to find the difference. 7 **Higher Order Thinking** Have students listen to the story, mark Xs to show what is happening, and then write an equation to tell how many are left. *Marta has some puppets. She gives 2 puppets to her brother. She has 3 left. How many puppets did she have before?*

Name ________________________________

Lesson 7-7
Solve Subtraction Word Problems: Take From

Directions Say: *Marta's dog, Spot, loves to eat doggie biscuits. Marta put 6 biscuits in a bag. One day, Spot ate 4 biscuits. Now there are only 2 left. How does Marta know there are 2 biscuits left? Use counters, pictures, or numbers to explain and show your work.*

I can ... find the difference of two numbers.

I can also make math arguments.

2

3

1
2
3
4
5

2 are left.

2 are left.

$5 - 3 = 2$

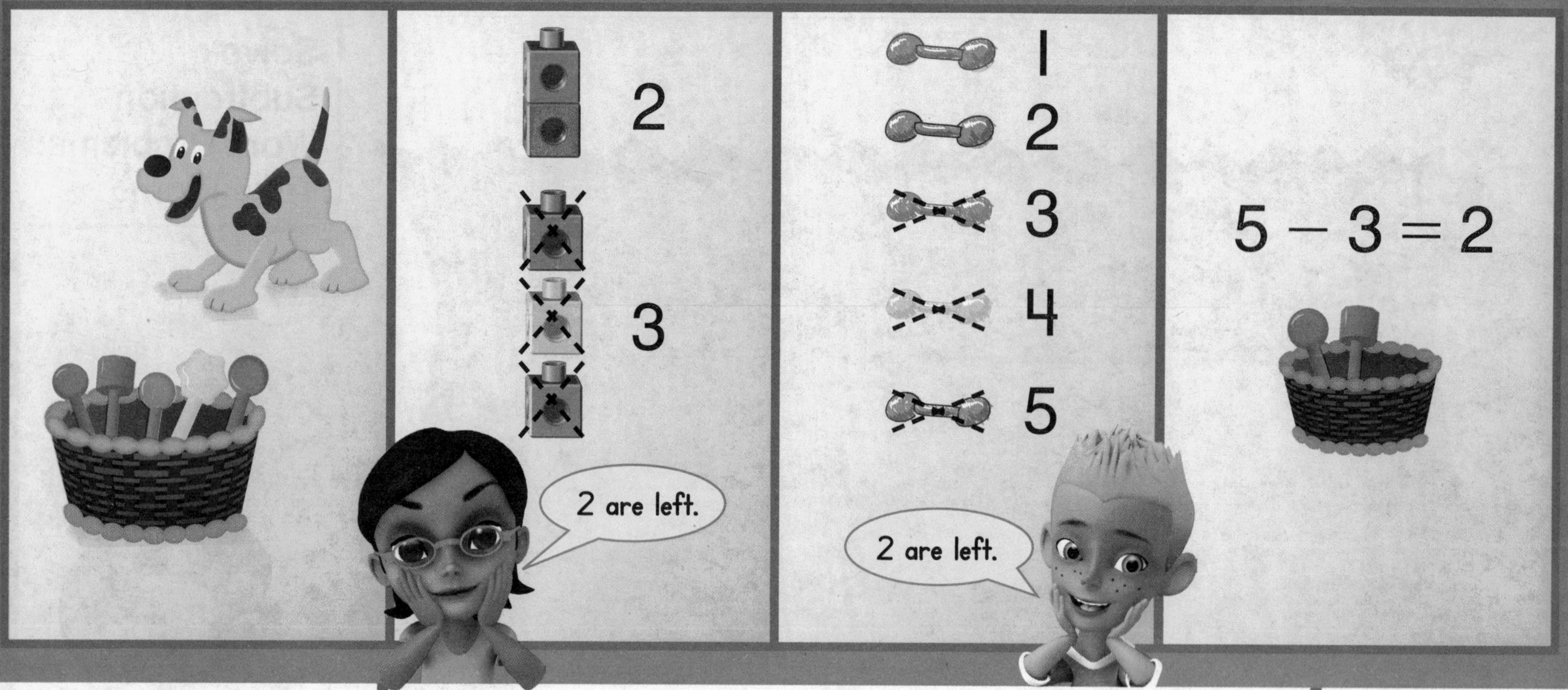

Guided Practice

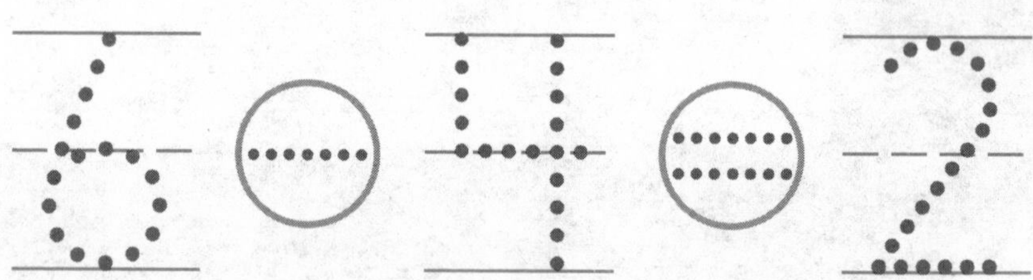

Directions Have students listen to the story, draw a picture to show what is happening, and then write a subtraction equation. Then have them explain their work aloud. Say: *Marta has 6 kittens. She gives them a big bowl of water to drink. But there is only room for 4 kittens to drink at the same time. How does Marta know that 2 kittens have to wait?*

Name ____________________

2

3

4

5

Directions Have students listen to each story, draw a picture to show what is happening, and then write an equation. Then have them explain their work aloud. 2 *Emily sees 8 rabbits in a pet store. Someone buys 3 of them. How many rabbits are left?* 3 *Emily sees 7 birds in a cage. The pet store owner opens the cage door and 3 fly out. How many birds are left?* 4 *Emily sees 8 puppies in the store. 6 of them are sold. How many puppies are left?* 5 *Emily sees 5 hamsters sleeping. I leaves to eat. How many hamsters are left?*

Independent Practice

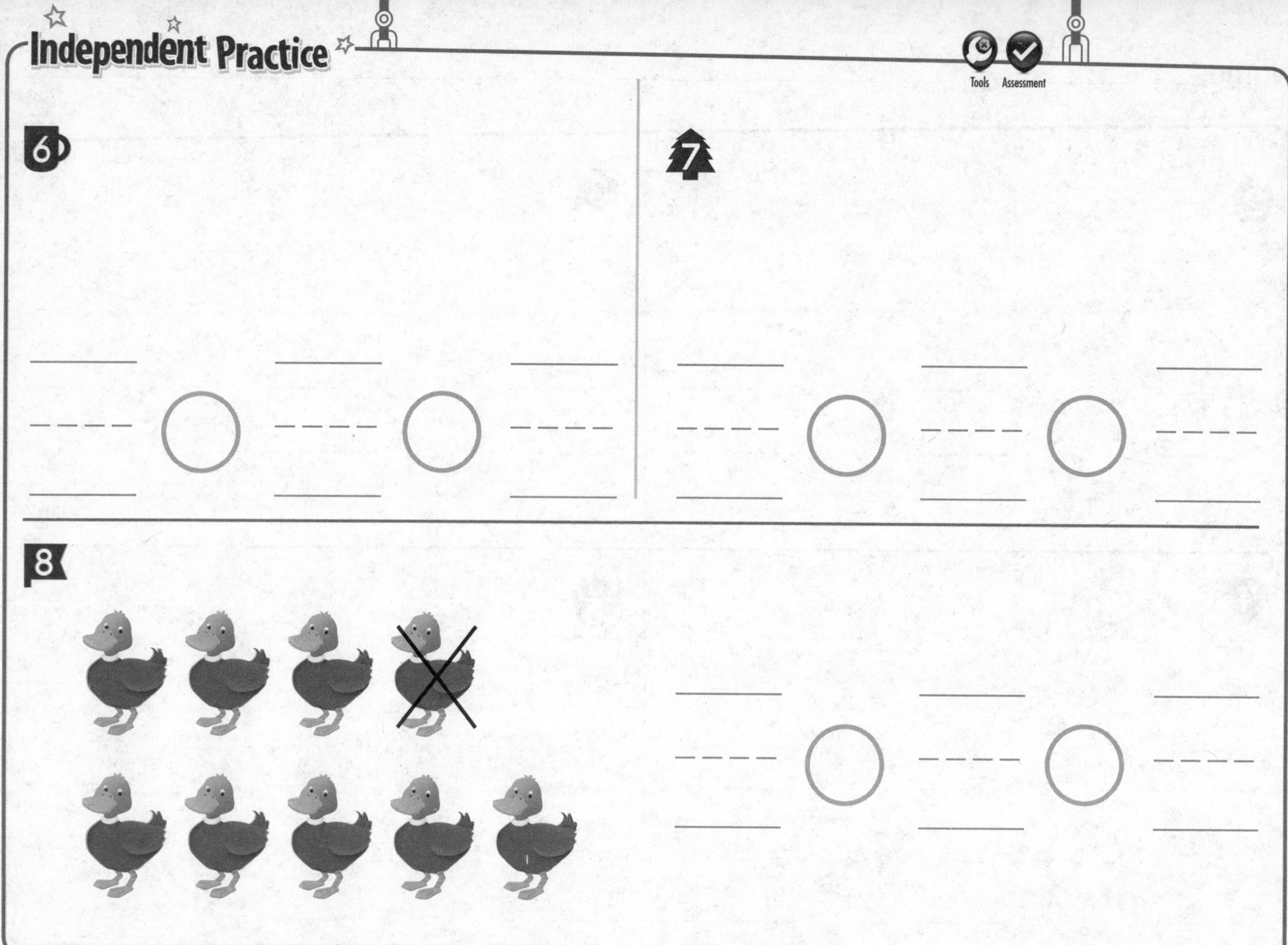

Directions Have students listen to each story, draw a picture to show what is happening, and then write an equation. 6 *There are 6 birds in a birdbath. 4 fly away. How many birds are left?* 7 *There are 5 acorns under a tree. A squirrel takes 3 of them. How many acorns are left?* 8 **Higher Order Thinking** Have students listen to the story, draw a circle around the picture that shows the story and tell why the other picture does NOT show the story, and then write an equation. *There are 4 ducks in a pond. 1 leaves. How many ducks are left?*

Name ______________________

 Help  Tools  Games

Homework & Practice 7-7

Solve Subtraction Word Problems: Take From

Another Look!

5 − 3 = 2

HOME ACTIVITY Give your child 7 small objects and ask him or her to give you 3 of the objects. Ask your child to tell you how many objects are left, and ask how he or she knows. Then ask your child to write an equation (7 − 3 = 4).

Directions Say: *There are 5 counters. 3 are taken away. How many counters are left? You can draw counters and mark Xs to show what is happening. Write an equation.* Have students listen to each story, draw pictures to show what is happening, and then write an equation. ★1 *There are 6 chipmunks. 4 run under a bush. How many chipmunks are left?* 2 *There are 5 raccoons. 2 climb up a tree. How many raccoons are left?*

3

4

5

$6 - 5 = 1$

6

Directions Have students listen to each story, draw a picture to show what is happening, and then write an equation. 3 *Marta has 9 dog biscuits. She gives her dog 5 of them. How many biscuits are left?* 4 *Marta buys 7 tennis balls. Her brother borrows 4 of them. How many balls are left?* 5 **Higher Order Thinking** Have students tell a number story that matches the equation, and then draw a picture to show what is happening. 6 **Higher Order Thinking** Have students tell a subtraction story about the cats, and then write an equation.

Name ______________________

Lesson 7-8
Use Patterns to Develop Fluency in Subtraction

0	1	2	3

$5 - \square = 2$

$5 - \square = 3$

$5 - \square = \_\_\_$

$5 - \square = \_\_\_$

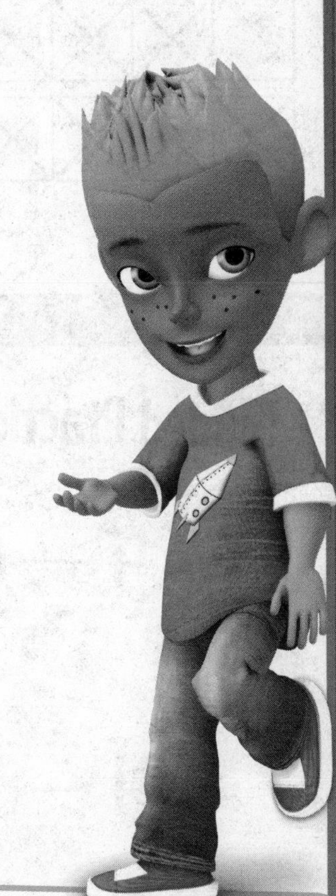

Directions Say: *Look at the first equation. Write the number from the number card that completes the equation on the orange space. Repeat for the next equation. Finish the pattern by placing the other number cards on the orange spaces, and then write the numbers to complete the equations. What patterns do you see?*

I can ... find patterns in subtraction equations.

I can also look for patterns.

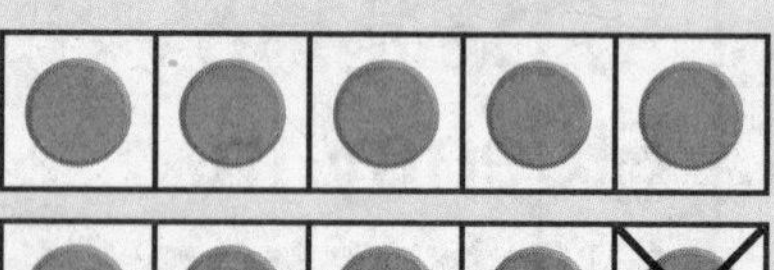

$$5 - 0 = 5$$
$$5 - 1 = 4$$
$$5 - 2 = 3$$
$$5 - 3 = 2$$
$$5 - 4 = 1$$
$$5 - 5 = 0$$

$$5 - 0 = 5 \qquad 5 - 1 = 4$$
$$5 - 5 = 0 \qquad 5 - 4 = 1$$

$$5 - 2 = 3$$
$$5 - 3 = 2$$

Guided Practice

$4 - 0 =$ _____

$4 - 1 =$ _____

$4 - 2 =$ _____

$4 - 3 =$ _____

Directions ⭑1 Have students complete each equation to find the pattern, and then explain the pattern they see.

Name ______________________________

2

3 − ______ = ______

3 − ______ = ______

3 − ______ = ______

3

1 − ______ = ______

1 − ______ = ______

Directions 2 and 3 Have students look for a pattern, explain the pattern they see, and then write equations for each row of insects.

Independent Practice

Tools Assessment

4

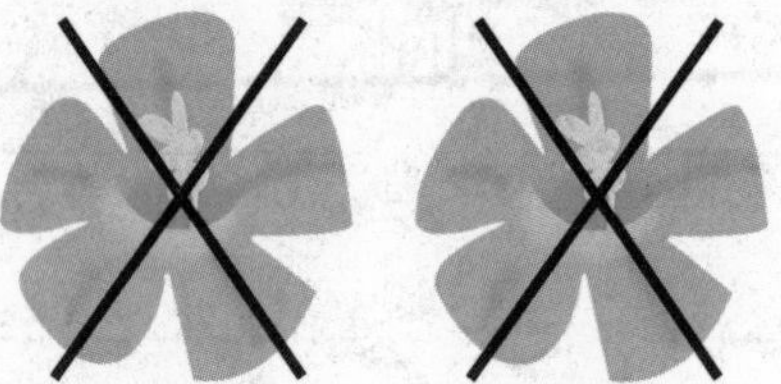

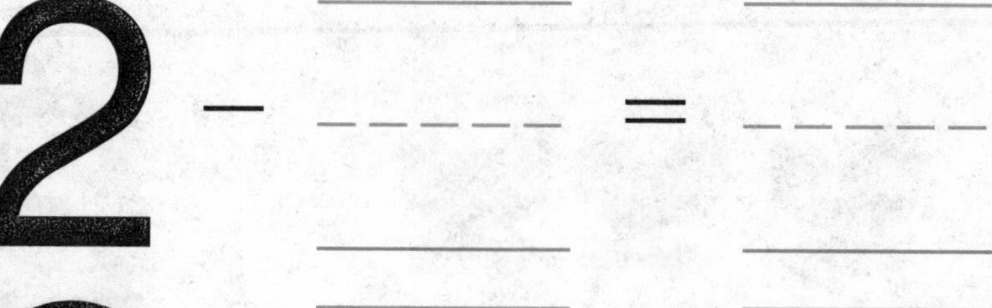

2 – ____ = ____

2 – ____ = ____

2 – ____ = ____

5 10 – 6 = 4

10 – 4 = ____

6 5 – 1 = 4

5 – ____ = 1

Directions 4 **Algebra** Have students mark Xs to complete the pattern, explain the pattern they see, and then write an equation for each row of flowers. 5 **Higher Order Thinking** Have students find the pattern, and then complete the equation. 6 **Higher Order Thinking** Have students find the pattern, and then write the missing number in the equation.

Name ______________________

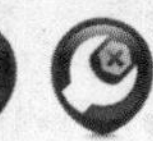

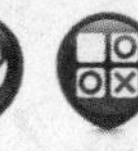

Help Tools Games

Homework & Practice 7-8

Use Patterns to Develop Fluency in Subtraction

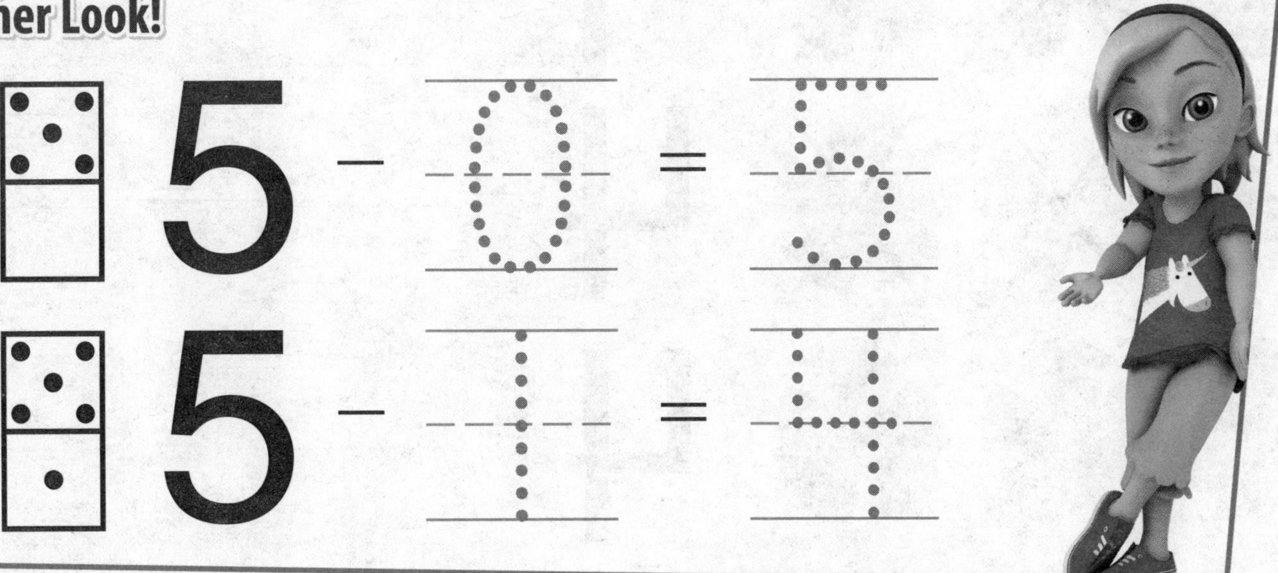

Another Look!

5 − 0 = 5

5 − 1 = 4

HOME ACTIVITY On a piece of paper, write: 3 − 3 = ?; 3 − 2 = ?; 3 − 1 = ?; 3 − 0 = ?. Have your child draw pictures for each problem, complete each equation, and then explain the pattern. (0, 1, 2, 3)

1

5 − ____ = ____

5 − ____ = ____

5 − ____ = ____

5 − ____ = ____

Directions Say: *Emily plays with dot tiles. She subtracts the side with fewer dots from the side with more dots. Write the numbers to tell how many dots are on each side, and then write how many are left after she subtracts.* 1 Have students use the dot tiles to complete the equations to find the pattern, and then explain the pattern they see.

$4 - \_\_\_ = \_\_\_$

$4 - \_\_\_ = \_\_\_$

$4 - \_\_\_ = \_\_\_$

3

$10 - 3 = 7$

$10 - 7 = \_\_\_$

4

$5 - 0 = 5$

$5 - \_\_\_ = 0$

Directions 2 Have students mark Xs to complete the pattern, and then write an equation for each row of flowers. 3 **Higher Order Thinking** Have students find the pattern, and then complete the equation. 4 **Higher Order Thinking** Have students find the pattern, and then write the missing number in the equation.

Name ______________________

Problem Solving

Lesson 7-9
Use Appropriate Tools

____ ◯ ____ = ____

Directions Say: *Alex has a food bar with 8 pieces of food for the flamingos at the lake. He takes apart 2 pieces of the bar to feed the flamingos. How many pieces does he have left on his bar? Use one of the tools you have to help solve the problem. Draw a picture of what you did, and then write the equation.*

I can ...
use tools to subtract numbers.

I can also subtract with numbers to 9.

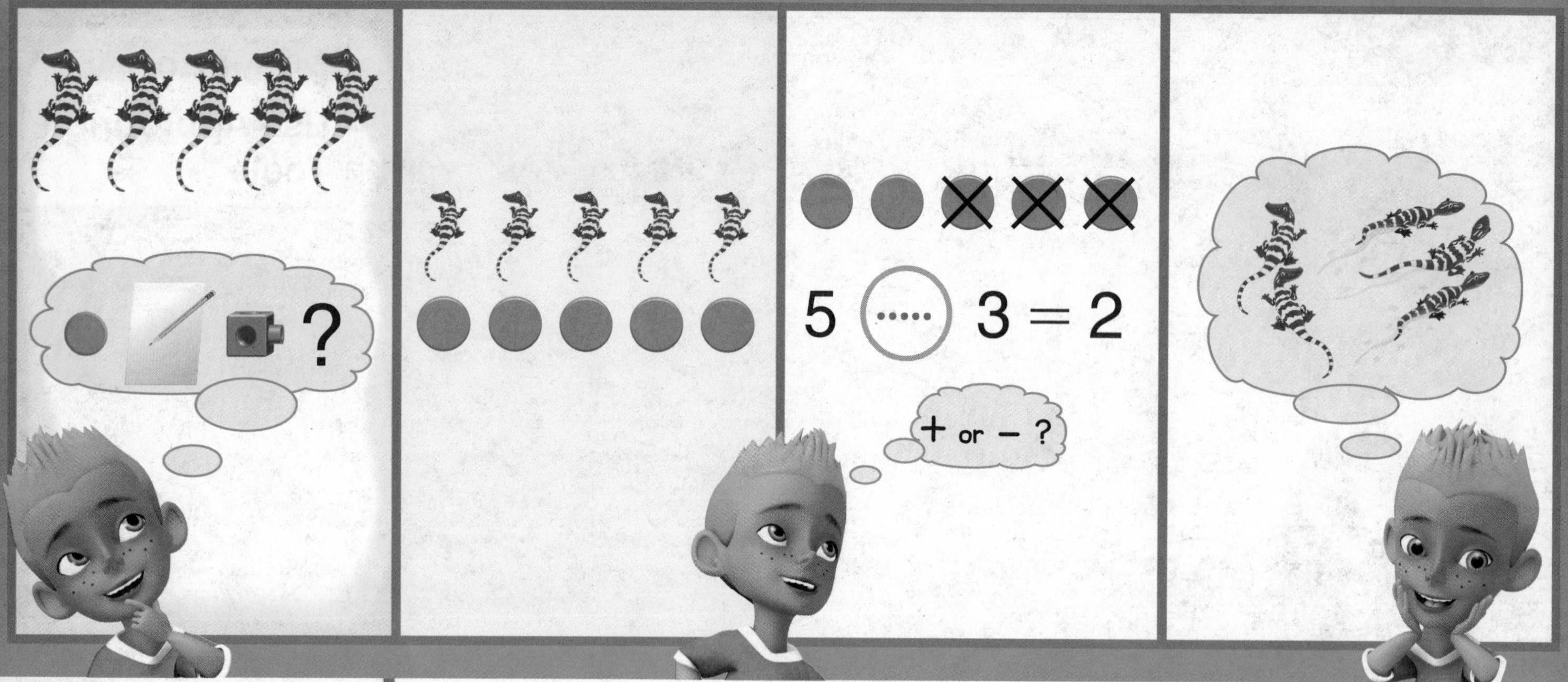

Guided Practice

1 1 + 8 = 9

2 ___ ..... ___ = ___

Directions Have students listen to each story, use a tool to help them solve the problem, and then write the equation. Then have them explain whether or not the tool they chose helped to solve the problem. **1** *There is 1 flamingo standing in the water. 8 more fly over to join it. How many flamingos are there in all?* **2** *Marta sees 7 seagulls. 4 fly away. How many seagulls are left?*

Name

Independent Practice

3

____ ◯ ____ = ____

4

____ ◯ ____ = ____

5

____ ◯ ____ = ____

6

____ ◯ ____ = ____

Directions Have students listen to each story, use a tool to help them solve the problem, and then write the equation. Then have them tell which tool they chose and whether or not it helped to solve the problem. 3 *There are 3 raccoons in a tree. 3 more climb the tree to join them. How many raccoons are there in all?* 4 *Marta sees 9 turtles swimming in a pond. 5 dive under the water. How many turtles are left?* 5 *There are 7 beavers in the water. 4 swim away. How many beavers are left?* 6 *Marta see 6 ducks in the lake. 2 more join them. How many ducks are there in all?*

Problem Solving

Performance Assessment

Stamps

USA 33

Directions Read the problem aloud. Then have students use multiple problem-solving methods to solve the problem. Say: *Carlos collects stamps. He has 9 stamps in all. He puts 1 stamp on the cover. He puts the rest inside the book. How many stamps does Carlos put inside his stamp book?* **Make Sense** *What are you trying to find out? Will you use addition or subtraction to solve the problem?* **Use Tools** *What tool can you use to help solve the problem? Tell a partner and explain why.* **Be Precise** *Did you write the equation correctly? Explain what the numbers and the symbols mean in the equation.*

Name ____________________

Homework & Practice 7-9
Use Appropriate Tools

HOME ACTIVITY Give your child 5 spoons and then 2 more spoons. Ask how many there are in all. Have him or her explain whether he or she added or subtracted. Then have your child use the spoons to model the equation.

Another Look!

5 − 2 = 3

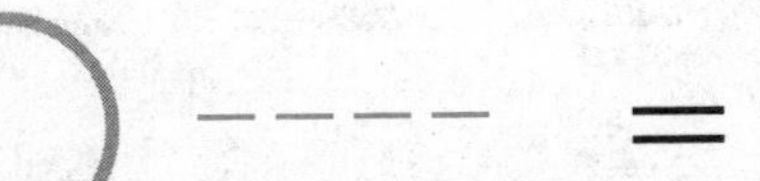

___ ◯ ___ = ___

2

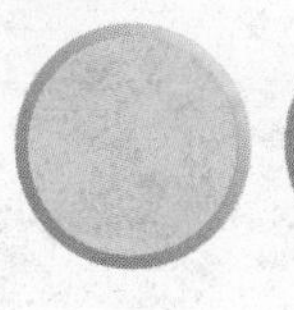
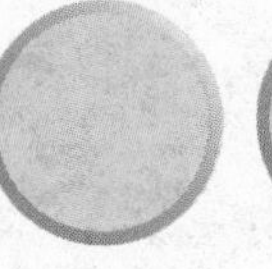

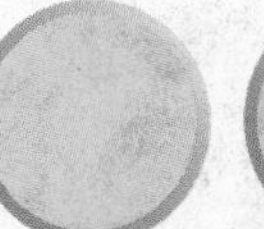

___ ◯ ___ = ___

Directions Say: *You can use counters to help you decide whether a story is an addition or subtraction problem. Listen to this story:* Emily built 5 sandcastles. Waves knocked down 2 of them. How many sandcastles are left? *Model this story with counters. Did you add or subtract? Mark Xs on the counters to show subtraction, and then write the equation.* Have students listen to each story, use counters or other objects to help them solve the problem, mark Xs on the counters to show subtraction or draw counters to show addition, and then write the equation. 1 *Emily sees 2 balls at the beach. Later that day, she sees 3 more. How many balls does Emily see in all?* 2 *Emily has 6 sand shovels. Her brothers lose 3 of them. How many sand shovels are left?*

Performance Assessment

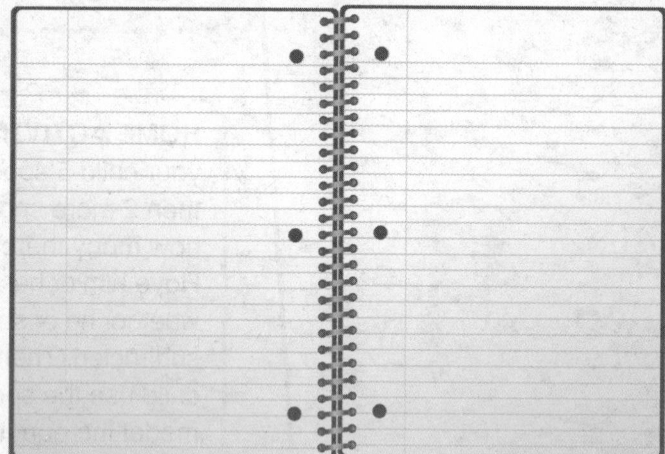

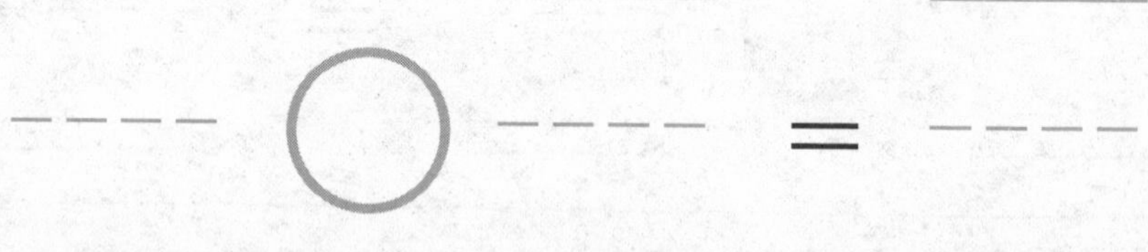

Directions Read the problem aloud. Then have students use multiple problem-solving methods to solve the problem. Say: *Emily has 7 stickers. She gives 2 to her brother. Then she sticks some stickers in her notebook. Emily has 3 stickers left. How many stickers did Emily put in her notebook?* **Make Sense** *What are you trying to find out? Will you use addition or subtraction to solve the problem?* **Use Tools** *What tool can you use to help solve the problem? Tell a partner and explain why.* **Be Precise** *Did you write the equation correctly? Explain what the numbers and the symbols mean in the equation.*

Name ______

Glossary

TOPIC 7

Vocabulary Review

7 ◯ 5

$9 - 6 = 3$

3

8 take away ______ is ______.

4

Directions **Understand Vocabulary** Have students: 1 write the **minus sign** to show subtraction; 2 draw a circle around the number that tells how many are **left**; 3 complete the **subtraction sentence**; 4 **separate** the tower into 2 parts, draw each part, and then write the numbers to tell the parts.

8 − 3 = 5

=

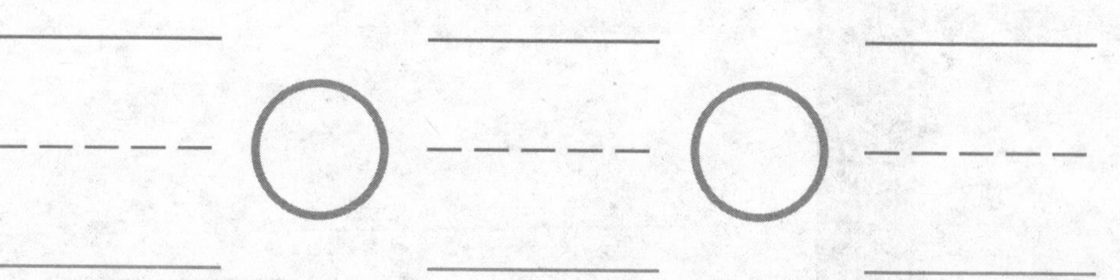

Directions **Understand Vocabulary** Have students: draw a circle around the **difference**; write an equation to show how to **subtract** 3 from 7 to find the difference; listen to the story, draw a picture to show how to **take away**, and then write an equation to match the story. *Lorin sees 6 apples on the table. She takes 3 away. How many apples are left?*

Name ______________________

TOPIC 7

Set A

Reteaching

2 are left.

1

______ are left.

Set B

Take apart 7.

2 and 5

2

Take apart 7.

______ and ______

Directions Have students: 1 count the bees, tell how many are NOT on the flower, and then write the number to tell how many are left on the flower; 2 take apart the group of apples. Have them draw a circle around the parts they made, and then write the numbers to tell the parts.

Set C

8 take away 4 is 4.

3 

____ take away ____ is ____.

Set D

6 take away 2 is 4.

$6 - 2 = 4$

4 take away 1 is 3.

____ ◯ ____ ◯ ____

Directions Have students: 3 listen to the story, and then complete the sentence to tell how many are left. *Javi sees 9 dragonflies. 4 fly away. How many dragonflies are left?* 4 use counters to model the problem, mark Xs to subtract, and then write an equation to find the difference.

Name

Set E

$7 - 5 = 2$

5

Set F

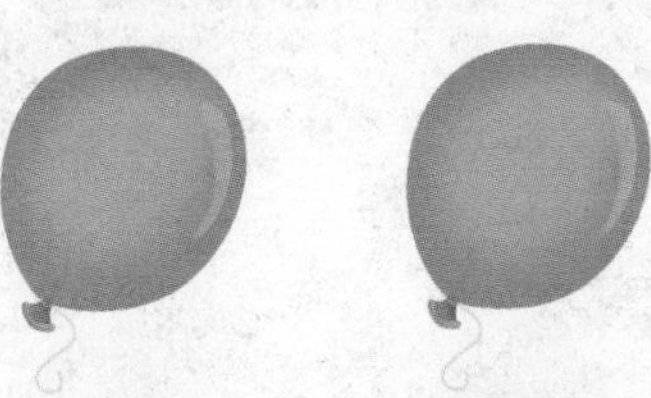

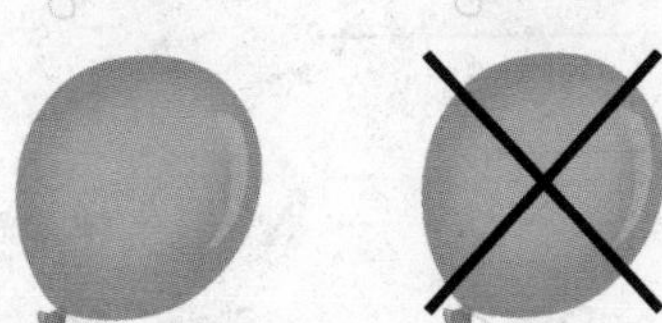

$4 - 1 = 3$

6

Directions Have students: 5 use counters to model the problem, and then write an equation to tell how many are left; 6 listen to the story, draw a picture to show what is happening, and then write an equation to match the story. *Lidia has 5 balloons. 2 balloons pop. How many balloons does she have left?*

Set G

$4 - 3 = 1$
$4 - 2 = 2$
$4 - 1 = 3$

7

$5 - \_\_\_ = \_\_\_$

$5 - \_\_\_ = \_\_\_$

$5 - \_\_\_ = \_\_\_$

Set H

$6 - 3 = 3$

8

___ ○ ___ ○ ___

Directions Have students: 7 complete each equation to find the pattern; 8 listen to the story, use counters to help solve the problem, and then write the equation. *Darla sees 3 frogs on the pond. 7 more join them. How many frogs are there in all?*

Name ______________________________

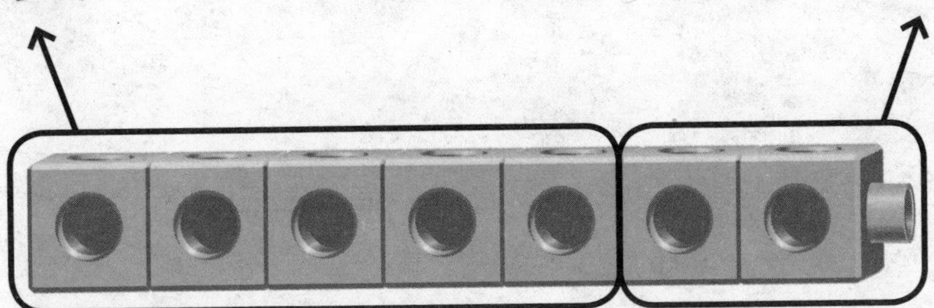

Ⓐ 6 and 2

Ⓑ 4 and 2

Ⓒ 5 and 2

Ⓓ 5 and 3

Ⓐ 3

Ⓑ 4

Ⓒ 5

Ⓓ 6

Ⓐ 4 take away 2 is 2.
$8 - 2 = 6$

Ⓑ 4 take away 3 is 1.
$4 - 3 = 1$

Ⓒ 3 take away 1 is 2.
$3 - 1 = 2$

Ⓓ 5 take away 3 is 2.
$5 - 3 = 2$

Ⓐ $5 - 3 = 2$

Ⓑ $5 - 2 = 3$

Ⓒ $7 - 3 = 4$

Ⓓ $7 - 2 = 5$

Directions Have students mark the best answer. 1 Which numbers tell the parts? 2 Which number tells how many are left? 3 Which sentence matches the picture? 4 Which equation matches the picture?

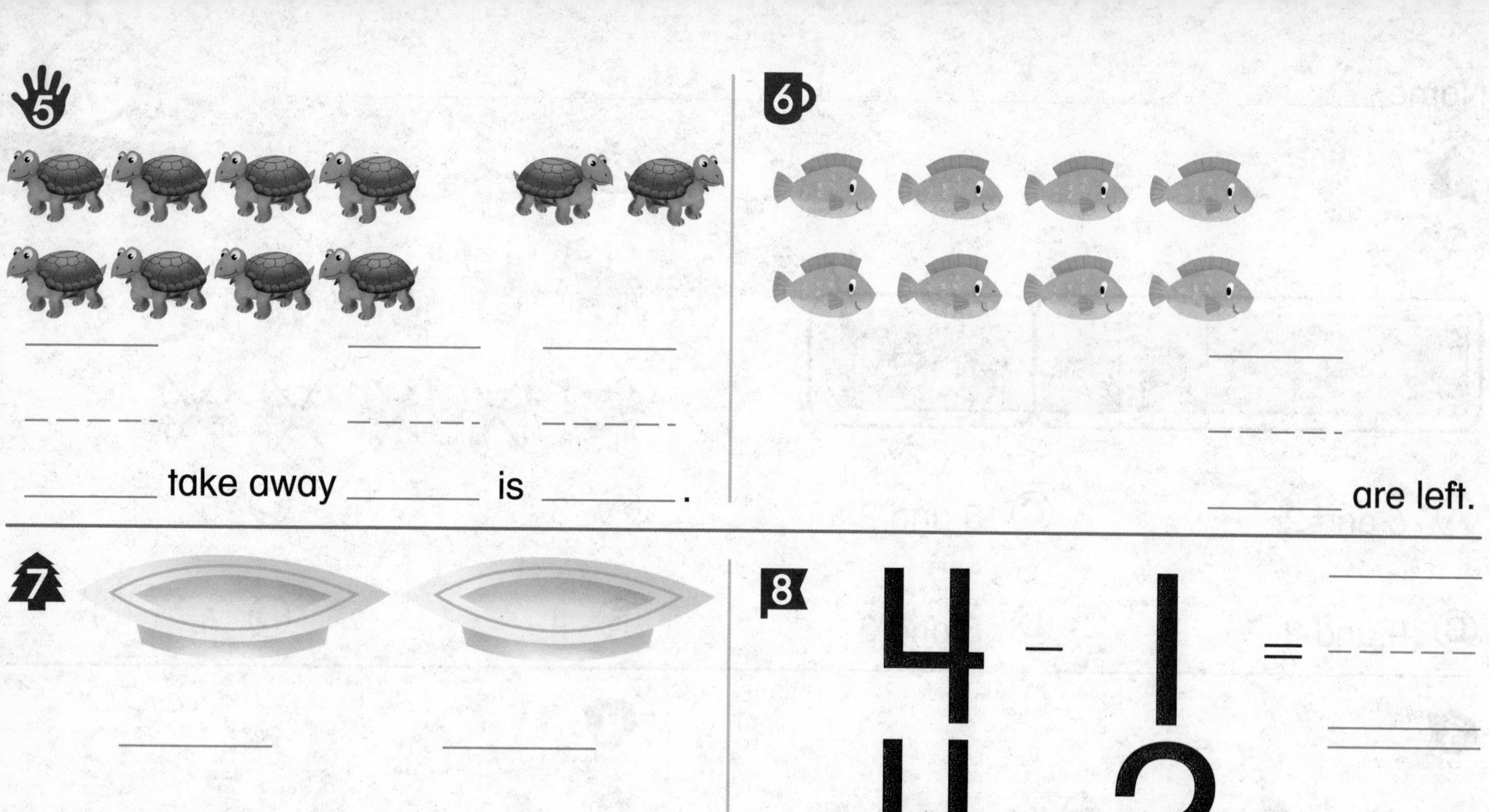

7

and

8

$4 - 1 =$

$4 - 2 =$

$- \quad =$

Directions 5 Have students listen to the story, and then complete the sentence to tell how many are left. *Kyle sees 10 turtles at the zoo. 2 turtles crawl away. How many turtles are left?* 6 Have students count the fish. Then have them mark Xs on some of the fish, and write the number to tell how many are left. 7 Say: *Ramona has 7 apples. She puts the apples on 2 plates. Draw apples to show how many Ramona could put on each plate. Then write the numbers to tell the parts.* 8 Have students complete each equation to find the pattern.

Name ___

9

___ ___ ___

10

Take apart 6.

___ and ___

11

___ ___ ___

Directions Have students: 9 listen to the story, draw a circle around the picture that shows the story, and then write an equation. *There were 7 lizards in the sand. 1 crawls away. How many are left?* 10 take apart the group of plums. Have them draw a circle around the parts they made, and then write the numbers to tell the parts; 11 listen to the story, draw a picture, use counters or other objects to help solve the problem, and then write the equation. *Kim collects 9 shells. She gives 6 away. How many shells does Kim have left?*

$5 - 1 = 4$

$5 - 0 = 5$

$5 - 3 = 2$

$5 - 4 = 1$

$5 - 2 = 3$

Directions 12 Have students match each equation with a row of flowers to find the pattern.

Name ________________________________

______ take away ______ is ______.

Directions **Puppet Show** Say: *Paco's class uses many puppets for their puppet show.* 1 Have students listen to the story, and then write a subtraction sentence to tell how many duck puppets are left. *Paco has 8 duck puppets at school. He takes 3 home. How many duck puppets are left at school?* 2 Write an equation to tell how many duck puppets Paco has left at school. 3 Say: *The picture shows that Paco put 1 cat puppet in a drawer. How many cat puppets are left?* Have students write an equation for the picture, and then write another equation to complete a pattern.

4

4 − ____ = ____

4 − ____ = ____

4 − ____ = ____

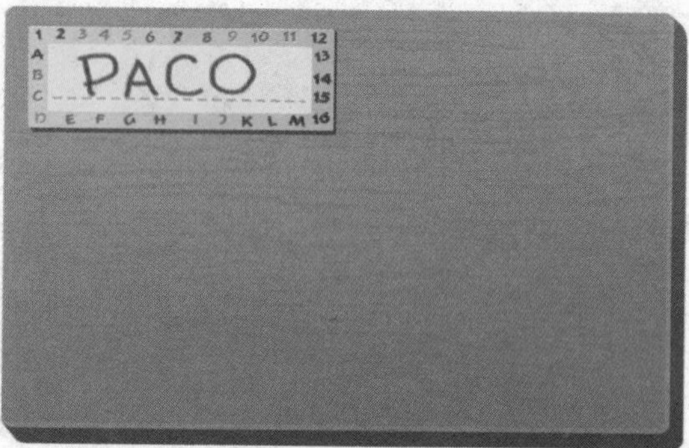

Directions 4 Say: *Paco's class puts on a play using 4 puppets. Each scene of the play has 1 more puppet leave the stage than the scene before.* Have students mark Xs to complete the pattern. Then have them write equations to show how many puppets leave each scene. 5 Have students listen to the story, use counters to help solve each part of the problem, and then write an equation. *Paco has 4 yellow bird puppets and 3 red bird puppets on his desk. How many bird puppets does Paco have in all? Then Paco moves 2 bird puppets to his friend Owen's desk. How many bird puppets are left on Paco's desk?*

TOPIC 8 More Addition and Subtraction

Essential Question: How can decomposing numbers in more than one way help you learn about addition and subtraction?

Digital Resources

Solve Learn Glossary Tools Assessment Help Games

Math and Science Project: Recycling

Directions Read the character speech bubbles to students. **Find Out!** Have students find out about the impact of littering and how recycling reduces human impact on the environment. Say: *Talk to friends and relatives about the items they recycle. Ask them how they are helping to protect the environment.* **Journal: Make a Poster** Then have students make a poster. Ask them to draw a playground littered with 4 paper, 3 plastic, and 2 metal recyclables. Have them draw a circle around the papers in green, the plastics in yellow, and the metals in orange. Finally, have students write an equation that adds the 4 paper and 3 plastic recyclables together.

Name ______________________________

Review What You Know

1

$7 - 5 = 2$

2

$8 - 6 = 2$

$3 + 2 = 5$

3

$+$ $-$

4

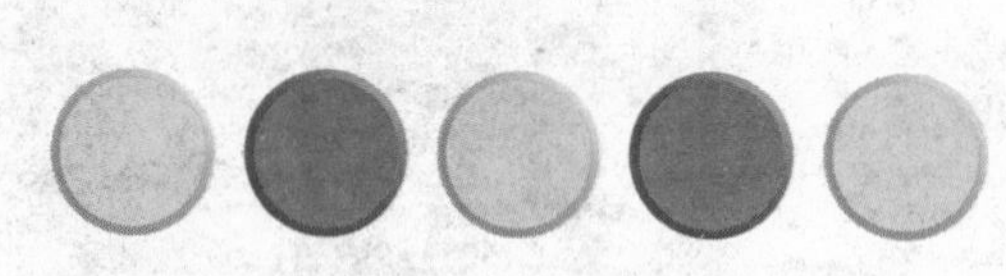

5

6

Directions Have students: 1 draw a circle around the difference; 2 draw a circle around the subtraction equation and mark an X on the addition equation; 3 draw a circle around the minus sign; 4 and 5 count the counters, and then write the number to tell how many; 6 count the counters, and then write the numbers to tell the parts.

My Word Cards

Directions Have students cut out the vocabulary cards. Read the front of the card, and then ask them to explain what the word or phrase means.

A-Z Glossary

break apart	operation	

My Word Cards

Directions Review the definitions and have students study the cards. Extend learning by having students draw pictures for each word on a separate piece of paper.

4 + 2 = 6

4 − 2 = 2

Point to the plus and minus signs. Say: *The* ***operation*** *tells us what to do with the numbers. Addition and subtraction are types of operations.*

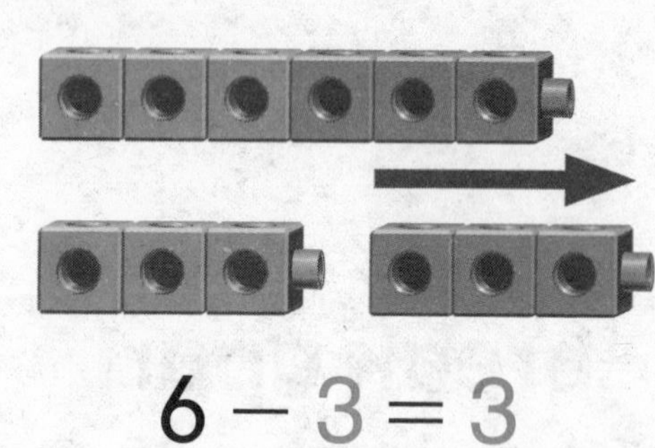

6 − 3 = 3

Point to the bottom row of blocks. Say: *We* ***break apart*** *numbers to show subtraction.*

Name ______________________

Lesson 8-1
Decompose and Represent Numbers to 5

Jada's Work

My Work

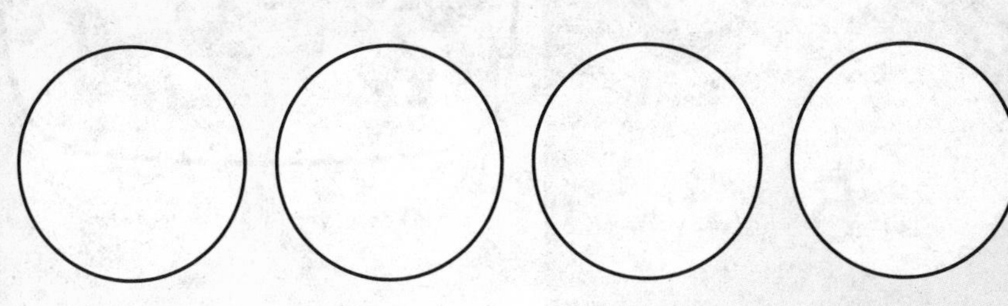

$4 = \_\_\_ + \_\_\_$

Directions Say: *Jada uses yellow and red counters to show that 4 = 2 + 2. Use red and yellow counters to show a different way to take apart 4. Color to show your counters, and then write an equation to match. Tell how your work is like Jada's work and then how it is different.*

I can ...
write equations to show the parts of numbers up to 5.

I can also use math tools correctly.

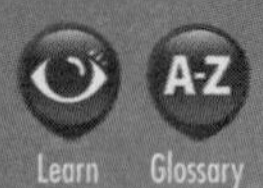

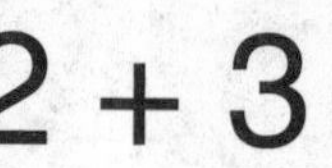

1

5 = 1 + 4

Directions 1 Have students use yellow and red counters to show how to break apart the 5 dogs, draw a circle around each group of dogs to show a number pair for 5, and then complete the equation to show the way to break apart 5.

Name ______

4 = ___ + ___

3

4 = ___ + ___

4

4 = ___ + ___

Directions 2 and 3 Have students use yellow and red counters to show how to break apart the 4 cats, draw a circle around two groups of cats to show a different number pair for 4, and then complete the equation to show the way to break apart 4. 4 **Math and Science** *How does pollution affect where animals live?* Have students use yellow and red counters to show how to break apart the 4 cats, draw a circle around two groups of cats to show a different number pair for 4, and then complete the equation to show the way to break apart 4.

Independent Practice

5 = ____ + ____

5 = ____ + ____

5 = ____ + ____

Directions 5 and 6 Have students use yellow and red counters to show how to break apart the 5 hamsters, draw a circle around two groups of hamsters to show a different number pair for 5, and then complete the equation to show the way to break apart 5. 7 **Higher Order Thinking** Have students draw 5 hamsters. Then have them draw a circle around two groups of hamsters to show a different number pair for 5, and then write an equation to show the way to break apart 5.

Name ______________________

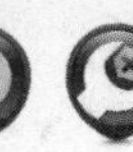

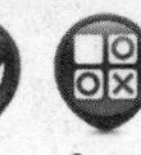

Homework & Practice 8-1

Decompose and Represent Numbers to 5

HOME ACTIVITY Give your child several household objects such as pennies or paper clips. Ask him or her to make a group of 4 or 5 objects. Then ask your child to break apart the objects to show pairs of 4 or 5, and then write an equation to show one way to break apart 4 or 5. Repeat this activity with a different number of objects.

Another Look!

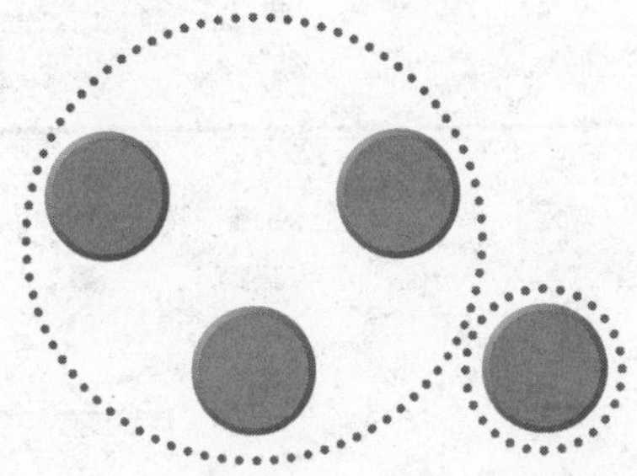

4 = 3 + 1

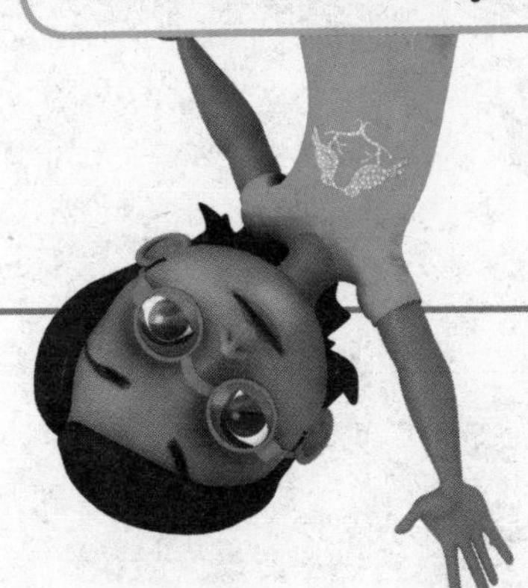

1

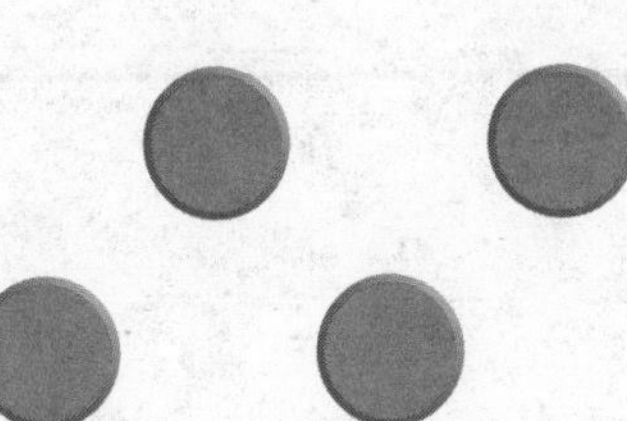

4 = ____ + ____

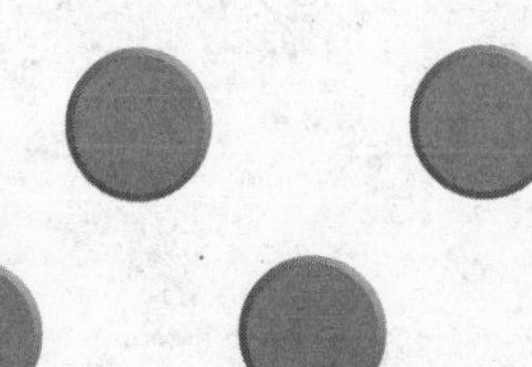

4 = ____ + ____

Directions Say: *You can break apart the dots to show number pairs for 4. Draw a circle around two groups of dots. You can also write an equation to show the way to break apart 4:* 4 = 3 + 1. **1** and **2** Have students draw a circle around two groups of dots to show a different number pair for 4, and then complete the equation to show the way to break apart 4.

3

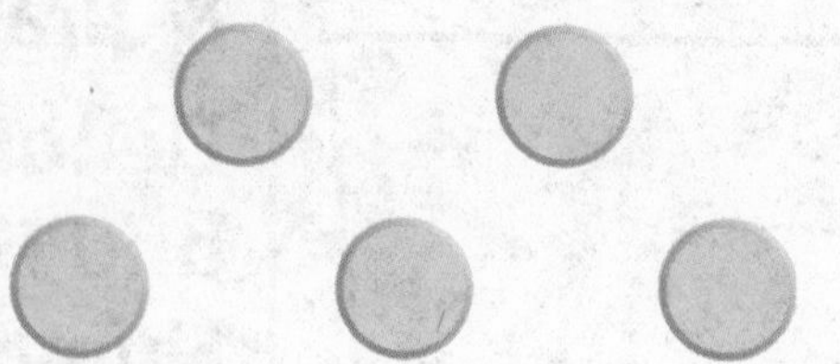

$5 = \_\_\_ + \_\_\_$

$5 = \_\_\_ + \_\_\_$

5

$\_\_\_ = \_\_\_ + \_\_\_$

Directions 3 Have students draw a circle around two groups of dots to show a different number pair for 5, and then complete the equation to show the way to break apart 5. 4 **Higher Order Thinking** Have students draw 5 dots. Then have them draw a circle around two groups of dots to show a different number pair for 5, and then complete the equation to show the way to break apart 5. 5 **Higher Order Thinking** Have students draw up to 5 dots. Then have them draw a circle around two groups of dots to show a different number pair for the number of dots they drew, and then write an equation to show the way to break apart the number they chose.

Name ________________________________

Lesson 8-2
Related Facts

$2 + 2 = 4$

$4 - 2 = 2$

Directions Say: *4 penguins play outside. 2 penguins go in the ice cave. How many penguins are left outside? Draw a circle around the equation that matches the story. Tell how you know.*

I can ...
solve related addition and subtraction equations.

I can also use math tools correctly.

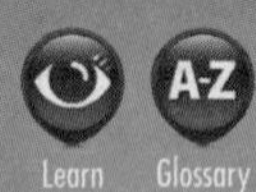

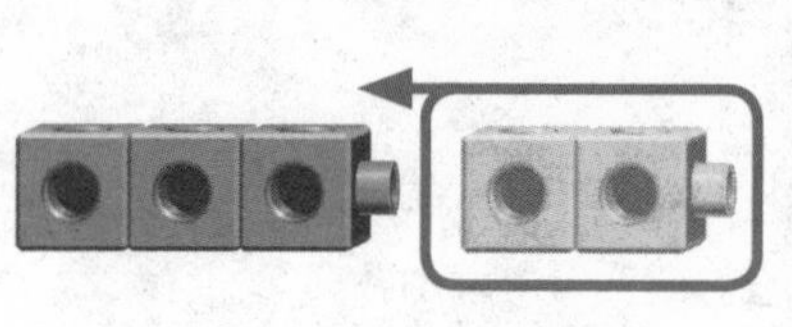

$$3 + 2 = 5$$

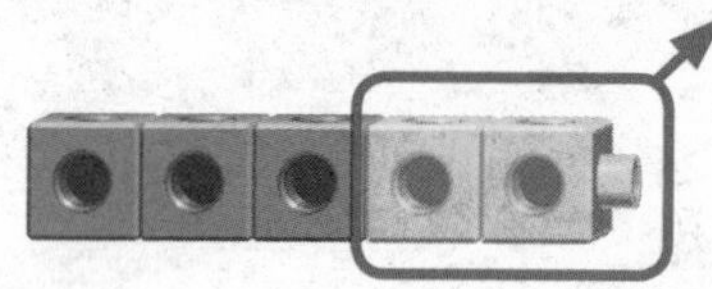

$$5 - 2 = 3$$

Guided Practice

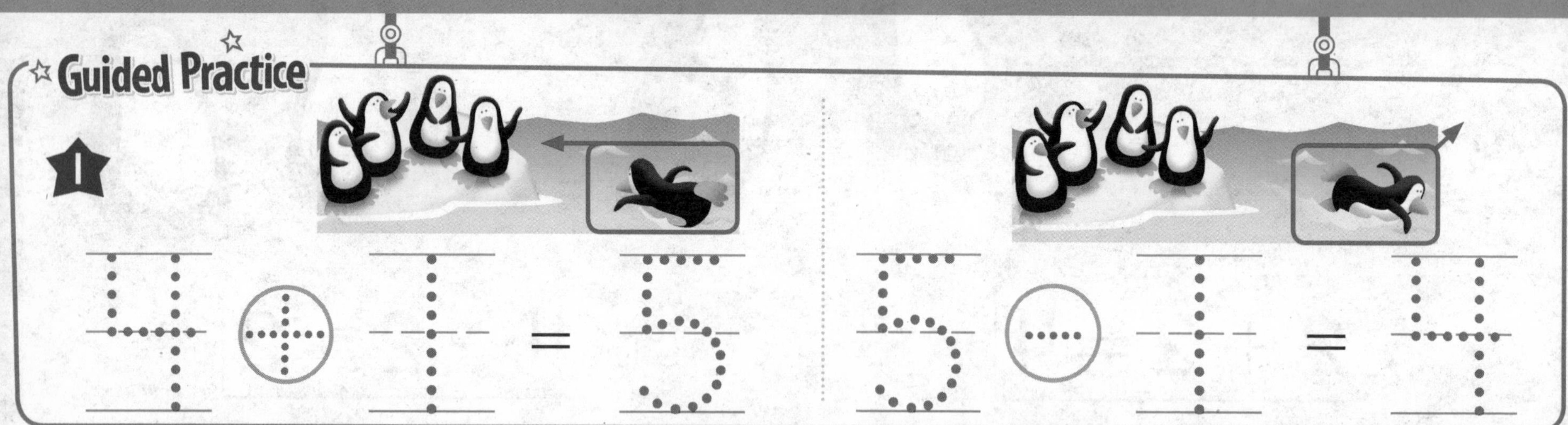

Directions Have students listen to each story and use connecting cubes to help act out each story to choose an operation. Then have students complete the equations to tell the related facts. *4 penguins are in a group. 1 joins them. How many penguins are there in all?* Then say: *5 penguins are in a group. 1 leaves. How many penguins are left?*

Name ______________________________

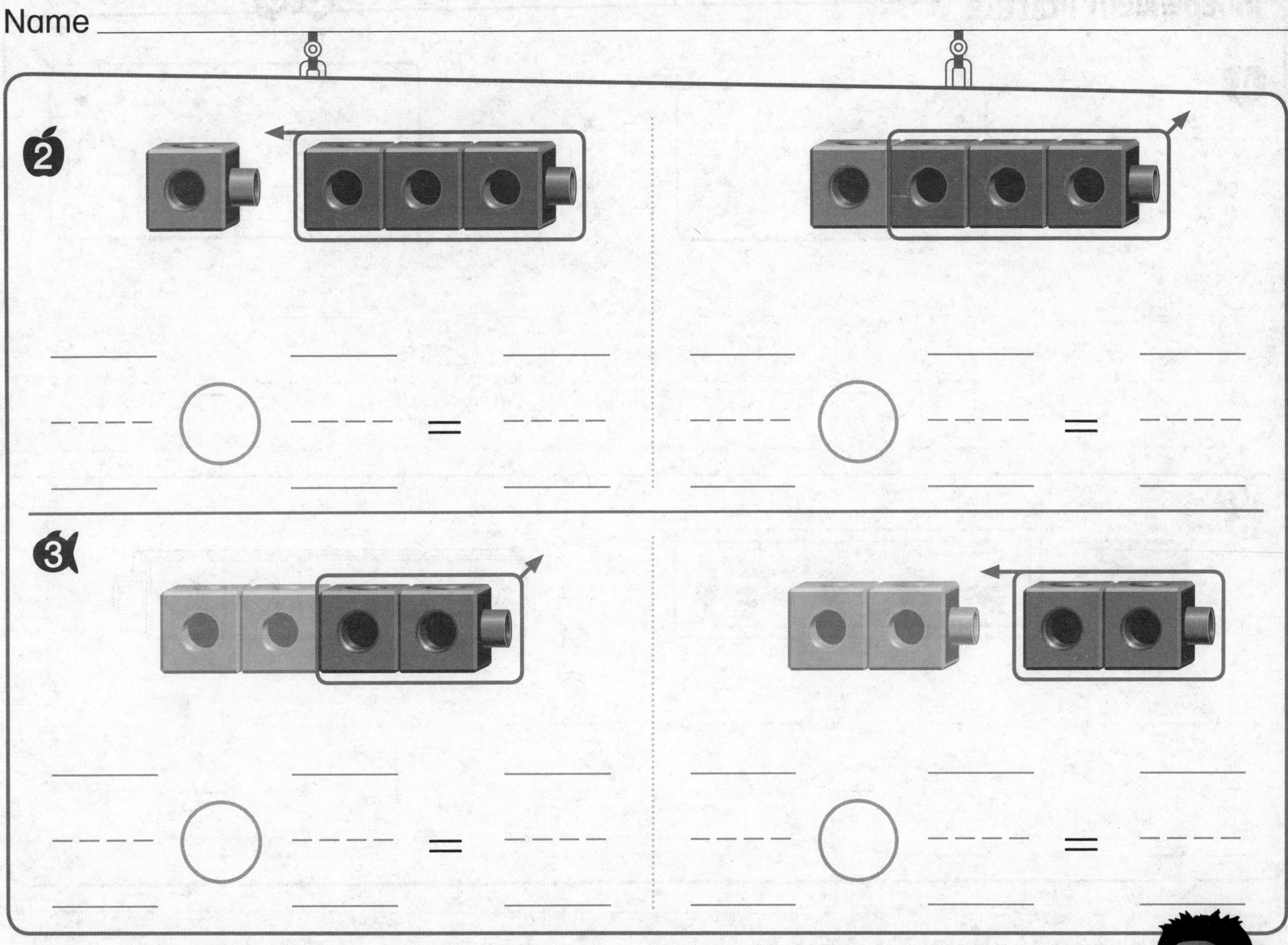

Directions 2 and 3 Have students use cubes for these facts with 4. Have them decide whether the cubes show addition or subtraction. Encourage students to make up their own stories to match the cubes. Then have them write equations to tell the related facts.

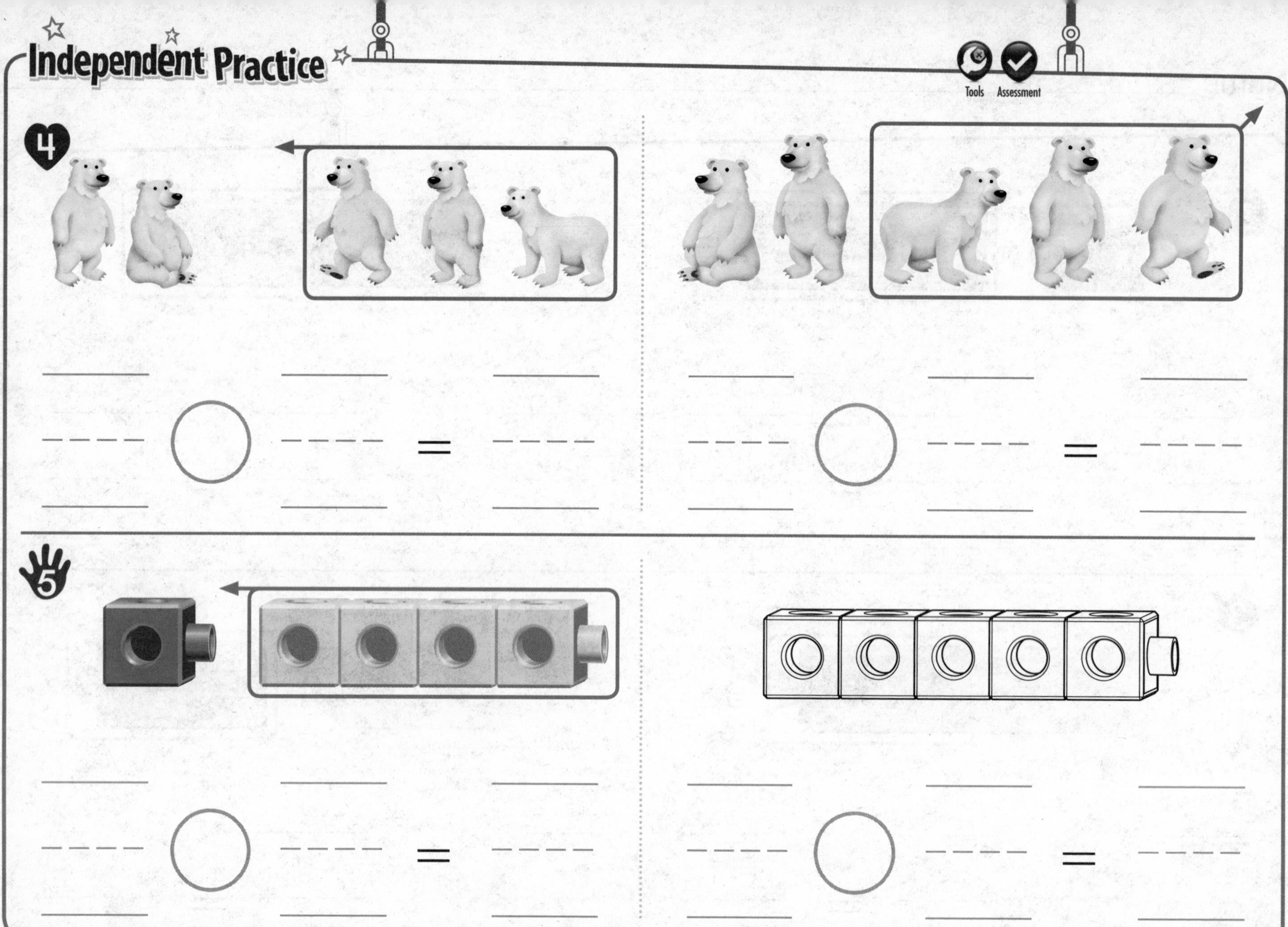

Directions 4 Have students listen to each story, use cubes to help act out each story to choose an operation, and then write the equations to tell the related facts. *2 bears are in a group. 3 join them. How many bears are there in all?* Then say: *5 bears are in a group. 3 leave. How many bears are there now?* 5 **Higher Order Thinking** Have students decide whether they want the cubes to show addition or subtraction, and then write an equation to match. Then have them color the cubes using the same numbers as the equation they just wrote, draw an arrow to tell the related fact, and then write the equation to match.

Name ______________________

Homework & Practice 8-2
Related Facts

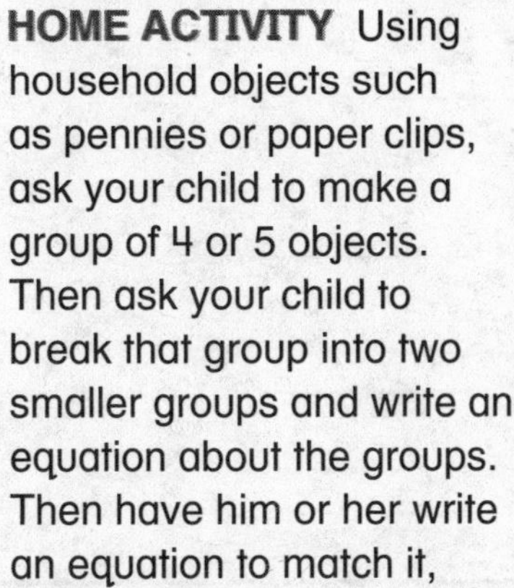

HOME ACTIVITY Using household objects such as pennies or paper clips, ask your child to make a group of 4 or 5 objects. Then ask your child to break that group into two smaller groups and write an equation about the groups. Then have him or her write an equation to match it, using a different operation.

Another Look!

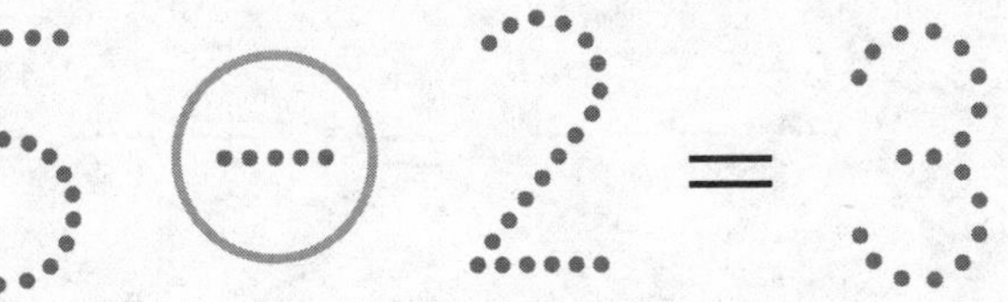

5 − 2 = 3　　3 + 2 = 5

1

____ ◯ ____ = ____　　____ ◯ ____ = ____

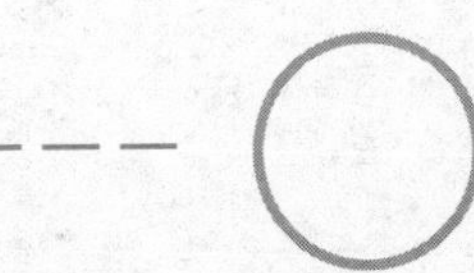

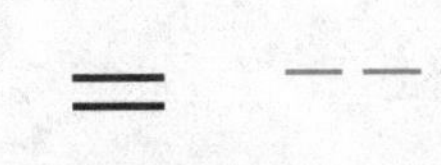

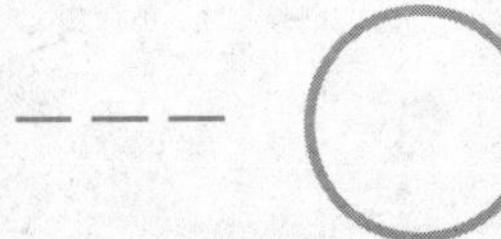

Directions Say: *Listen to each story and use counters or other objects to help act out each story to choose an operation. Then complete the equations to tell the related facts.* 5 seals are playing. 2 leave. How many seals are left? There are 3 seals playing and 2 join them. How many seals are there in all? **1** Have students listen to each story, use counters or other objects to help act out the story to choose an operation, and then write the equations to tell the related facts. *4 seals are in a group. 1 walks away. How many seals are left?* Then say: *3 seals are in a group. 1 joins them. How many seals are there in all?*

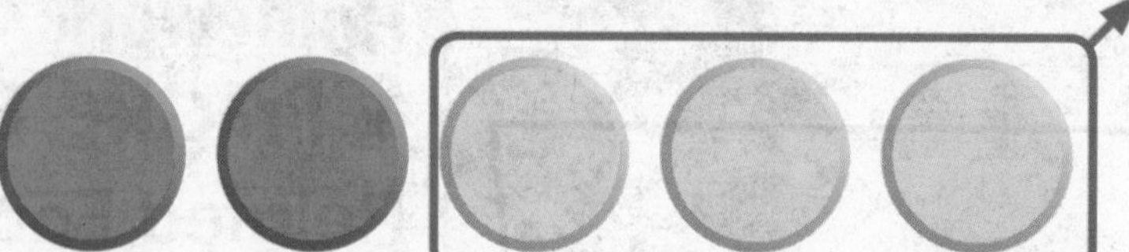

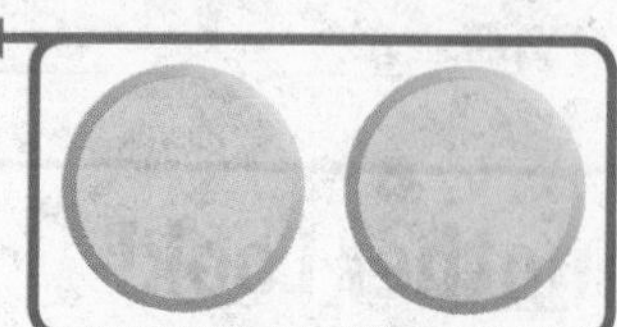

$4 + 1 = 5$

$5 - 1 = 4$

Directions ❷ Have students decide whether the counters show addition or subtraction, and then write equations to tell the related facts. ❸ **Higher Order Thinking** Have students draw and color counters to match the equation. ❹ **Higher Order Thinking** Have students draw and color counters to match the equation.

Name ________________________________

Problem Solving

Lesson 8-3

Reasoning

$4 - 2 = 2$

Think.

Directions Say: *Jada and Carlos are at the zoo. Each of them tells a story about an animal in a habitat. How could you tell a story to match the equation shown? Tell your story to a partner.*

I can ...
reason about numbers and operations.

I can also add and subtract within 5.

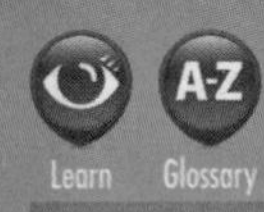

2 + 3 = ?

Guided Practice

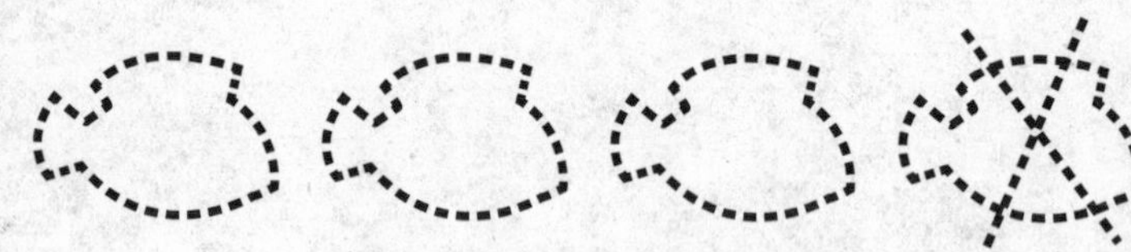

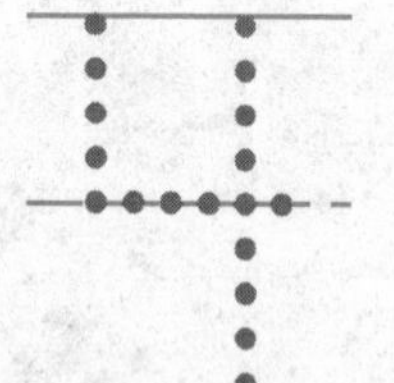

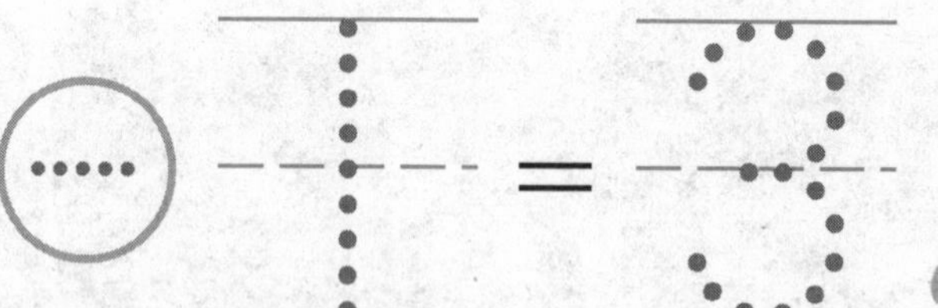

Directions Have students tell a story for 4 − 1. Then have them draw a picture to illustrate their story and write the equation.

Name ______________________

Tools Assessment

Independent Practice

___ ◯ ___ = ___

___ ◯ ___ = ___

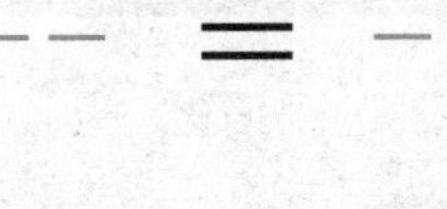

Directions Have students tell a story for: ❷ 1 + 3. Then have them draw a picture to illustrate their story and write the equation; ❸ 3 − 2. Then have them draw a picture to illustrate their story and write the equation.

Problem Solving

Performance Assessment

4 + ___ = 5

Directions Read the problem to students. Then have them use multiple problem-solving methods to solve the problem. Say: *Carlos's teacher wrote this equation on the chalkboard: 4 + ☐ = 5. Can you tell a story for that equation?* **Reasoning** *What story can you tell to help solve the problem and write the equation?* **Use Tools** *Does drawing a picture help to solve the problem? What does your picture show? What other tools can you use to solve the problem?* **Model** *Can a model help you solve the problem? Use the part-part model to check your answer.*

Name ______________________

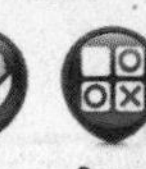

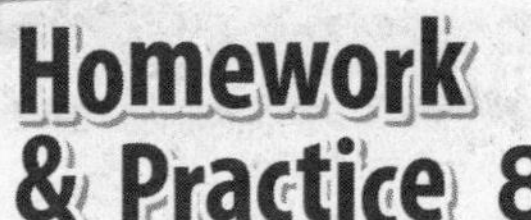

8-3

HOME ACTIVITY Tell your child simple addition and subtraction stories. Have your child solve them by drawing models, such as those in the lesson, or by using his or her own representations of the problems.

Another Look!

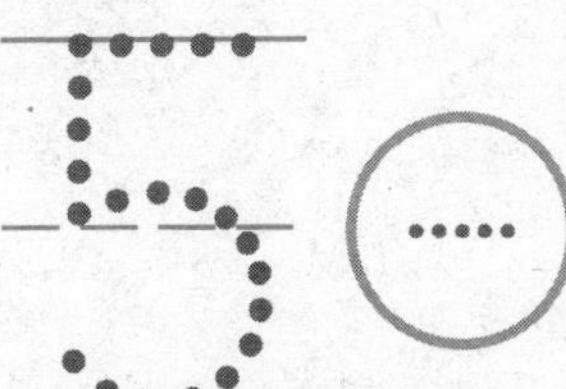
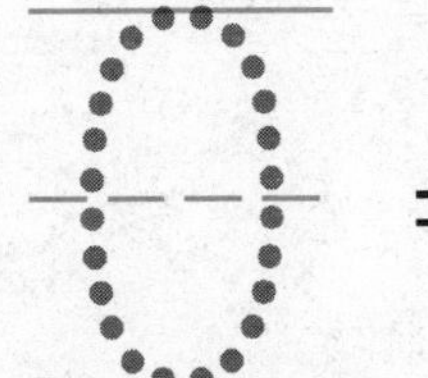
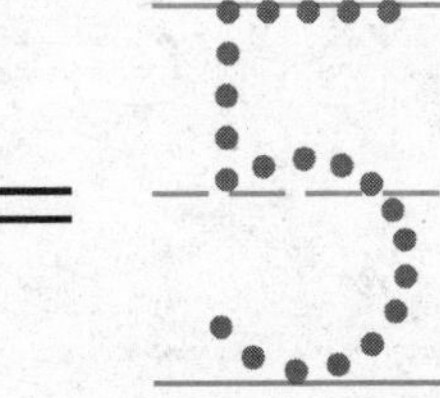

$5 - 0 = 5$

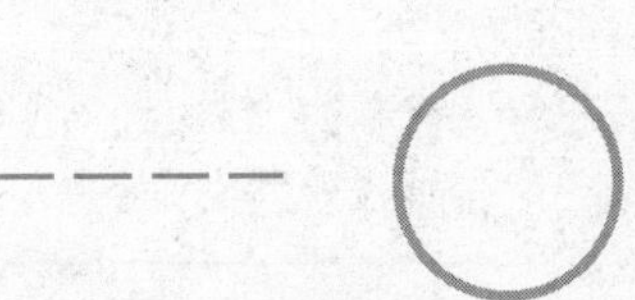

___ ◯ ___ = ___

Directions Say: *You can use a picture to tell a story for 5 − 0.* Have students use the picture to tell a story, and then write the equation. ★1 Have students tell a story for 3 − 1. Then have them draw a picture to illustrate their story and write the equation.

 Performance Assessment

2 3 4

3 + 2 = ____

Directions Read the problem to students. Then have them use multiple problem-solving methods to solve the problem. Say: *Marta's teacher challenges the class. She asks the class to tell two different stories for one equation:* 3 + 2 = ☐. *Can you tell two different stories for that equation?* **2 Reasoning** *What story can you tell first to help solve the problem and complete the equation?* **3 Generalize** *What can you use from your first story to help you tell the second story? What will repeat in the second equation?* **4 Use Tools** *Does drawing pictures help to solve the problem? What do your pictures show? What other tools can you use to solve the problem?*

Name ____________________

Lesson 8-4

Fluently Add and Subtract to 5

_____

- - - - -

$1 + 2 =$ _____

Directions Say: *Help Jada solve the equation. Solve any way you choose. Explain how you solved the problem.*

I can ...
write addition and subtraction equations within 5 and remember them.

I can also be precise in my work.

$3 + 2 = ?$

$3 + 2 = 5$

$3 - 1 = ?$

$3 - 1 = 2$

$3 - 1 = 2$

$4 + 1 = 5$

2

$5 - 1 =$ ___

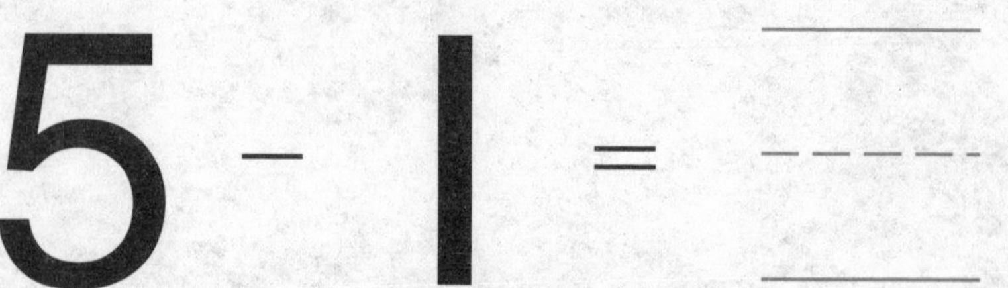

Directions 1 and 2 Have students solve the equation any way they choose, and then tell how they solved the problem.

Name ______________________

3

$2 + 1 =$ ______

4

$3 - 1 =$ ______

5

$2 - 2 =$ ______

6

$1 + 4 =$ ______

7

$4 + 0 =$ ______

8

$4 - 2 =$ ______

Directions 3–8 Have students solve the equation any way they choose, and then tell how they solved the problem.

Independent Practice

Tools Assessment

9

$4 - 1 =$ ____

10

$3 + 1 =$ ____

11

$3 - 2 =$ ____

12

$1 + 0 =$ ____

13

$5 - 2 =$ ____

14

$5 -$ ____ $= 5$

Directions 9–13 Have students solve the equation any way they choose, and then tell how they solved the problem. 14 **Higher Order Thinking** Have students solve for the missing number in the equation any way they choose, and then tell how they solved the problem.

Name ______________________

Help Tools Games

Homework & Practice 8-4

Fluently Add and Subtract to 5

Another Look!

1 + 1 = ?

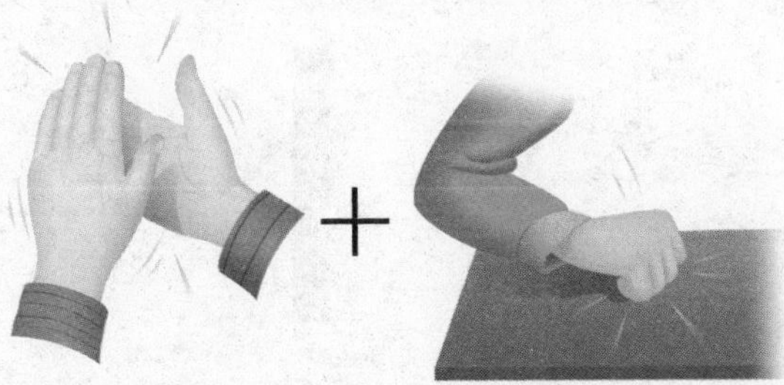

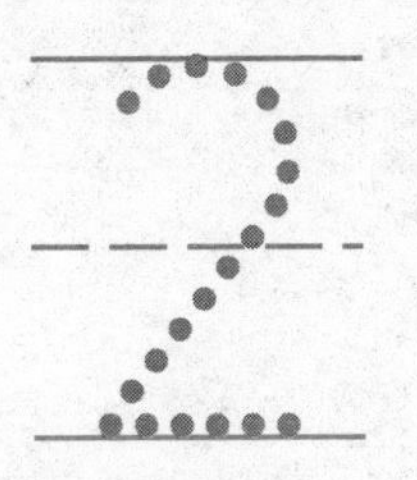

1 + 1 = 2

HOME ACTIVITY Show your child the equation 2 + 3 = ?. Have him or her solve the problem any way he or she chooses. Then have your child explain how to solve the problem. Repeat for the equation 3 − 3 = ?.

1. 2 + 2 = ____

2. 2 − 1 = ____

3. 0 + 3 = ____

4. 5 − 4 = ____

Directions Say: *There are many ways to solve an equation. Try clapping and knocking to solve 1 + 1. Write the number to tell how many in all.* 1–4 Have students solve the equation any way they choose, and then tell how they solved the problem.

5

$5 - 3 =$ ___

6

$1 + 3 =$ ___

7

$4 - 3 =$ ___

8

$5 + 0 =$ ___

9

$4 -$ ___ $= 2$

10

___ $+ 4 = 4$

Directions 5–8 Have students solve the equation any way they choose, and then tell how they solved the problem. 9 **Higher Order Thinking** Have students solve for the missing number in the equation any way they choose, and then tell how they solved the problem. 10 **Higher Order Thinking** Have students solve for the missing number in the equation any way they choose, and then tell how they solved the problem.

Name ________________________

Lesson 8-5
Decompose and Represent Numbers 6 and 7

6 = ____ + ____

Directions Say: *Alex uses yellow and red counters to show that 6 = 4 + 2. Use red and yellow counters to show a different way to break apart 6. Color to show your counters, and then write an equation to match. Tell how your work is like Alex's work and then how it is different.*

I can ... write equations to show the parts of 6 and 7.

I can also use math tools correctly.

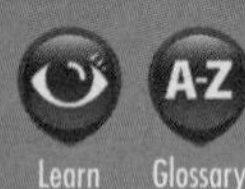

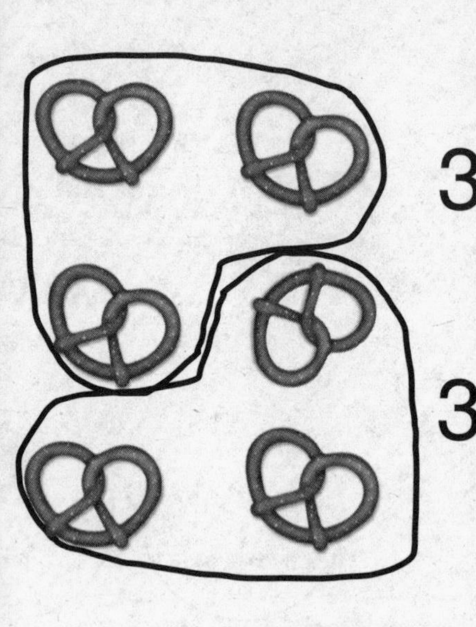

Guided Practice

Directions 1 Have students use yellow and red counters to show how to break apart the 6 pretzels, draw a circle around each group of pretzels to show a number pair for 6, and then complete the equation to tell the way to break apart 6.

Name ______________________________

2

7 = ____ + ____

3

7 = ____ + ____

4

7 = ____ + ____

Directions 2–4 Have students use yellow and red counters to show how to break apart the 7 crackers, draw a circle around two groups of crackers to show a different number pair for 7, and then complete the equation to tell the way to break apart 7.

Independent Practice

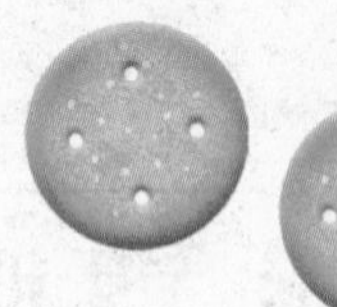 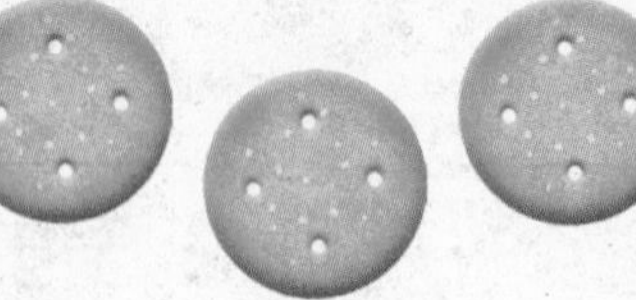 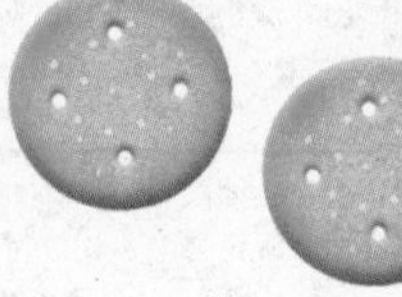 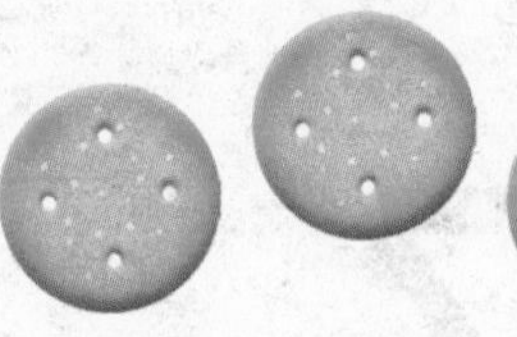 

6 = ___ + ___

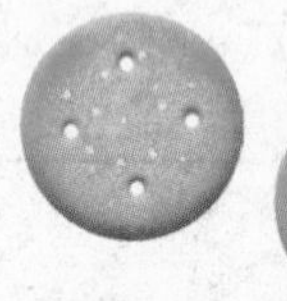 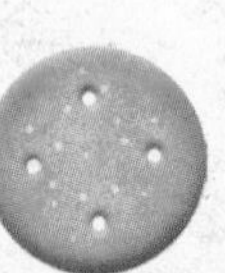 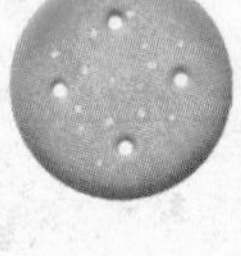 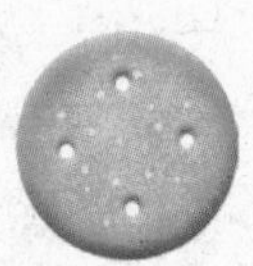  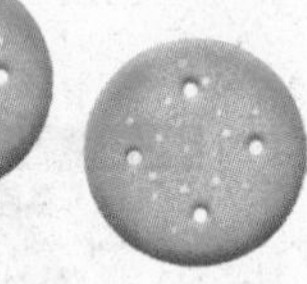

___ = ___ + ___

7

6 = ___ + ___

Directions 5 and 6 Have students use yellow and red counters to show how to break apart the 6 crackers, draw a circle around two groups of crackers to show a different number pair for 6, and then complete the equation to tell the way to break apart 6. 7 **Higher Order Thinking** Have students draw 6 crackers. Then have them draw a circle around two groups of crackers to show a different number pair for 6, and then write an equation to tell the way to break apart 6.

Name ______________________

Help Tools Games

Homework & Practice 8-5

Decompose and Represent Numbers 6 and 7

Another Look!

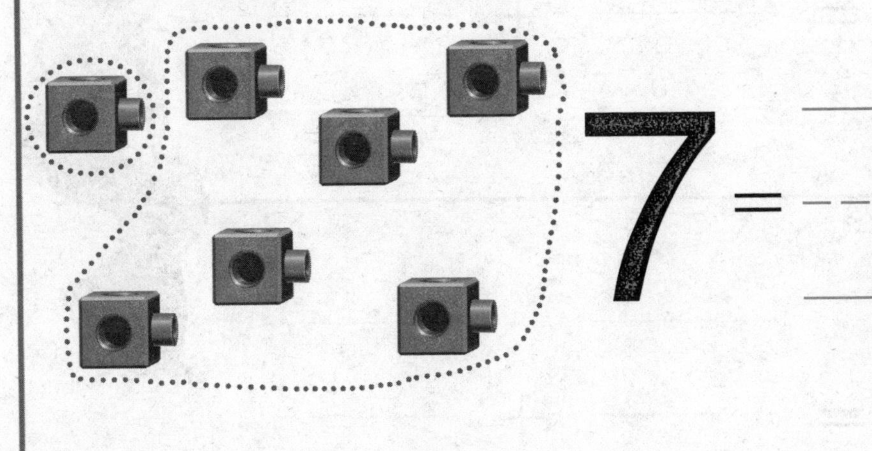

7 = 1 + 6

HOME ACTIVITY Give your child a group of objects, such as pennies, and have him or her make a group of 6 or 7. Have him or her break apart the group into two groups, and then write an equation about the objects.

1

7 = ____ + ____

2

7 = ____ + ____

Directions Say: *You can break apart the cubes to show number pairs for 7. Draw a circle around two groups of cubes. You can also write an equation to tell one way to break apart 7:* 7 = 1 + 6. 1 and 2 Have students draw a circle around two groups of cubes to show a different number pair for 7, and then complete the equation to tell the way to break apart 7.

3

6 = ___ + ___

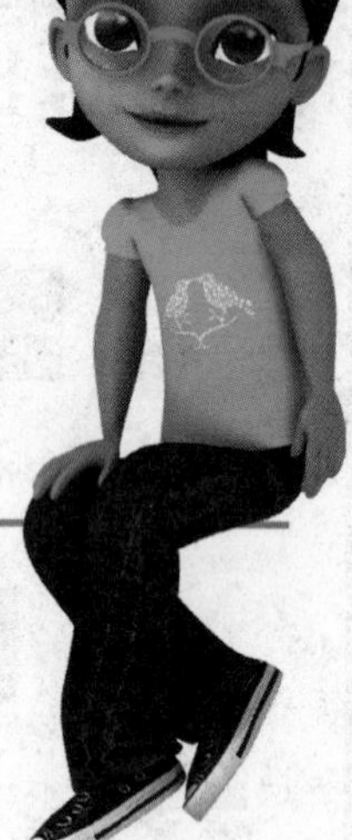

6 = ___ + ___

5

___ = ___ + ___

Directions 3 Have students draw a circle around two groups of cubes to show a different number pair for 6, and then complete the equation to tell the way to break apart 6. 4 **Higher Order Thinking** Have students draw 6 cubes. Then have them draw a circle around two groups of cubes to show a different number pair for 6, and then complete the equation to tell the way to break apart 6. 5 **Higher Order Thinking** Have students draw 6 or 7 cubes. Then have them draw a circle around two groups of cubes to show a different number pair for the number of cubes they drew, and then write an equation to tell the way to break apart the number they chose.

Name ______________________

Lesson 8-6

Decompose and Represent Numbers 8 and 9

My Work

8 = ___ + ___

Directions Say: *Toss 8 counters on the mat. Some land red-side up, and some land yellow-side up. Draw and color a picture of your counters, and then write an equation to match. Compare your work with a partner. How are your pictures and equations both alike and different?*

I can ...
write equations to show the parts of 8 and 9.

I can also model with math.

9

5

4

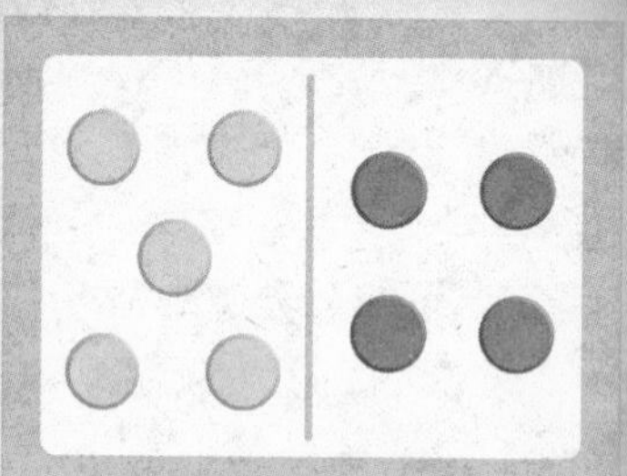

5 + 4

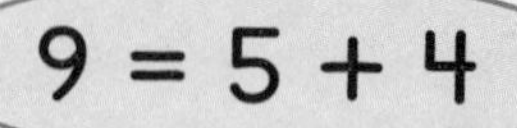

Guided Practice

9 = 8 + 1

Directions Have students use yellow and red counters to show how to break apart the 9 beets, draw a circle around two groups of beets to show a number pair for 9, and then complete the equation to tell the way to break apart 9.

Name ______________________________

2

$8 = \_\_\_ + \_\_\_$

3

$8 = \_\_\_ + \_\_\_$

4

$8 = \_\_\_ + \_\_\_$

Directions 2–4 Have students use yellow and red counters to show how to break apart the 8 peppers, draw a circle around two groups of peppers to show a different number pair for 8, and then complete the equation to tell the way to break apart 8.

Independent Practice

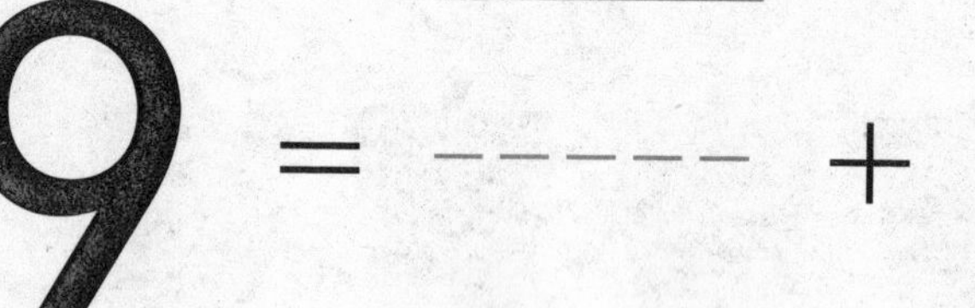

9 = ___ + ___

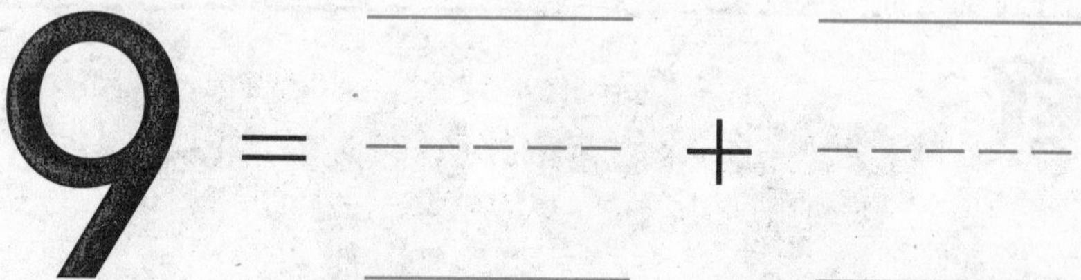

9 = ___ + ___

___ = ___ + ___

Directions 5 and 6 Have students use yellow and red counters to show how to break apart the 9 pumpkins, draw a circle around two groups of pumpkins to show a different number pair for 9, and then complete the equation to tell the way to break apart 9. 7 **Higher Order Thinking** Have students draw 9 carrots. Then have them draw a circle around two groups of carrots to show a different number pair for 9, and then complete the equation to tell the way to break apart 9.

Name ____________________

Help Tools Games

Homework & Practice 8-6

Decompose and Represent Numbers 8 and 9

HOME ACTIVITY Give your child pennies, and then count 8 or 9 pennies aloud. Then have your child separate the pennies into two groups and write an equation about the pennies.

Another Look!

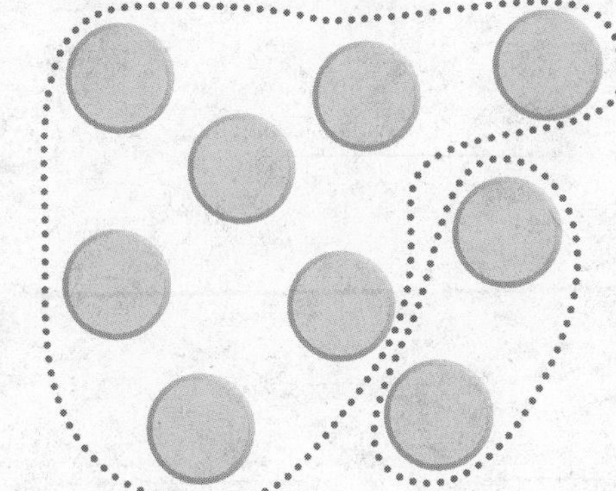

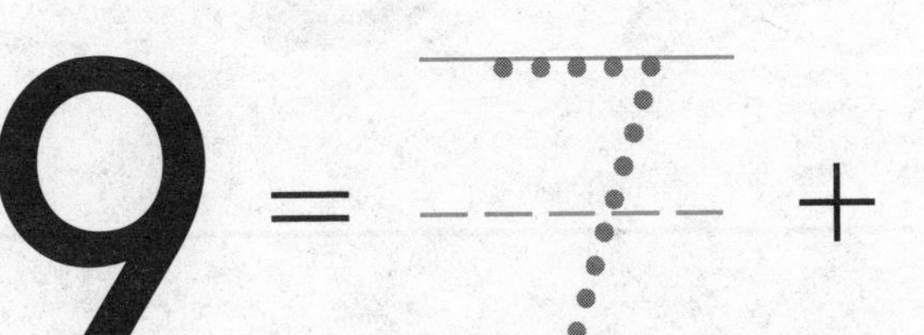

1

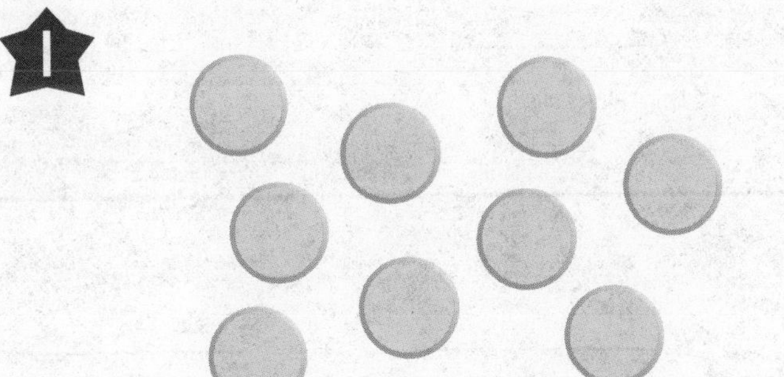

9 = ____ + ____

2

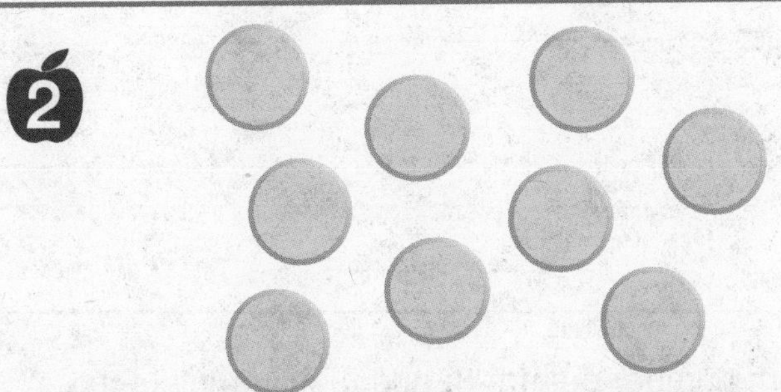

9 = ____ + ____

Directions Say: *You can break apart the counters to show number pairs for 9. Draw a circle around two groups of counters. You can also write an equation to tell the way to break apart 9:* 9 = 7 + 2. 1 and 2 Have students draw a circle around two groups of counters to show a different number pair for 9, and then complete the equation to tell the way to break apart 9.

3

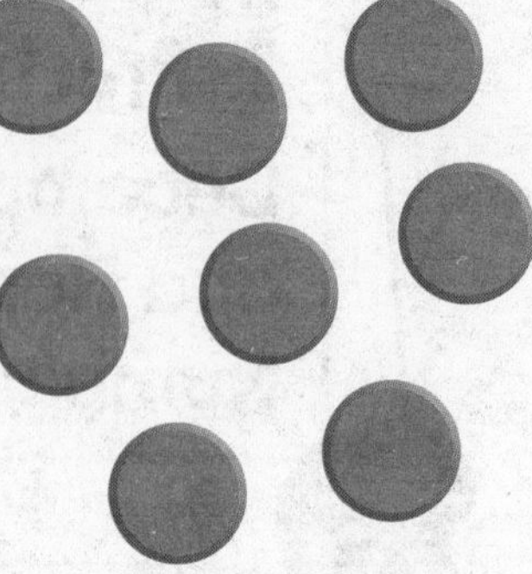

8 = ______ + ______

8 = ______ + ______

5

______ = ______ + ______

Directions 3 Have students draw a circle around two groups of counters to show a different number pair for 8, and then complete the equation to tell the way to break apart 8. 4 **Higher Order Thinking** Have students draw 8 counters. Then have them draw a circle around two groups of counters to show a different number pair for 8 than Item 3, and then complete the equation to tell the way to break apart 8. 5 **Higher Order Thinking** Have students draw 8 or 9 counters. Then have them draw a circle around two groups of counters to show a different number pair for the number of counters they drew, and then write an equation to tell the way to break apart the number they chose.

Solve & Share

Name ________________________

Lesson 8-7

Decompose and Represent 10

10 = ___ + ___

10 = ___ + ___

Directions Say: *Jada wants to write equations to describe ways to break 10 into two parts. Draw pictures of yellow and red counters, and then write equations to tell two different ways to break apart 10.*

I can ...
write equations to show the parts of 10.

I can also model with math.

10 = 7 + 3

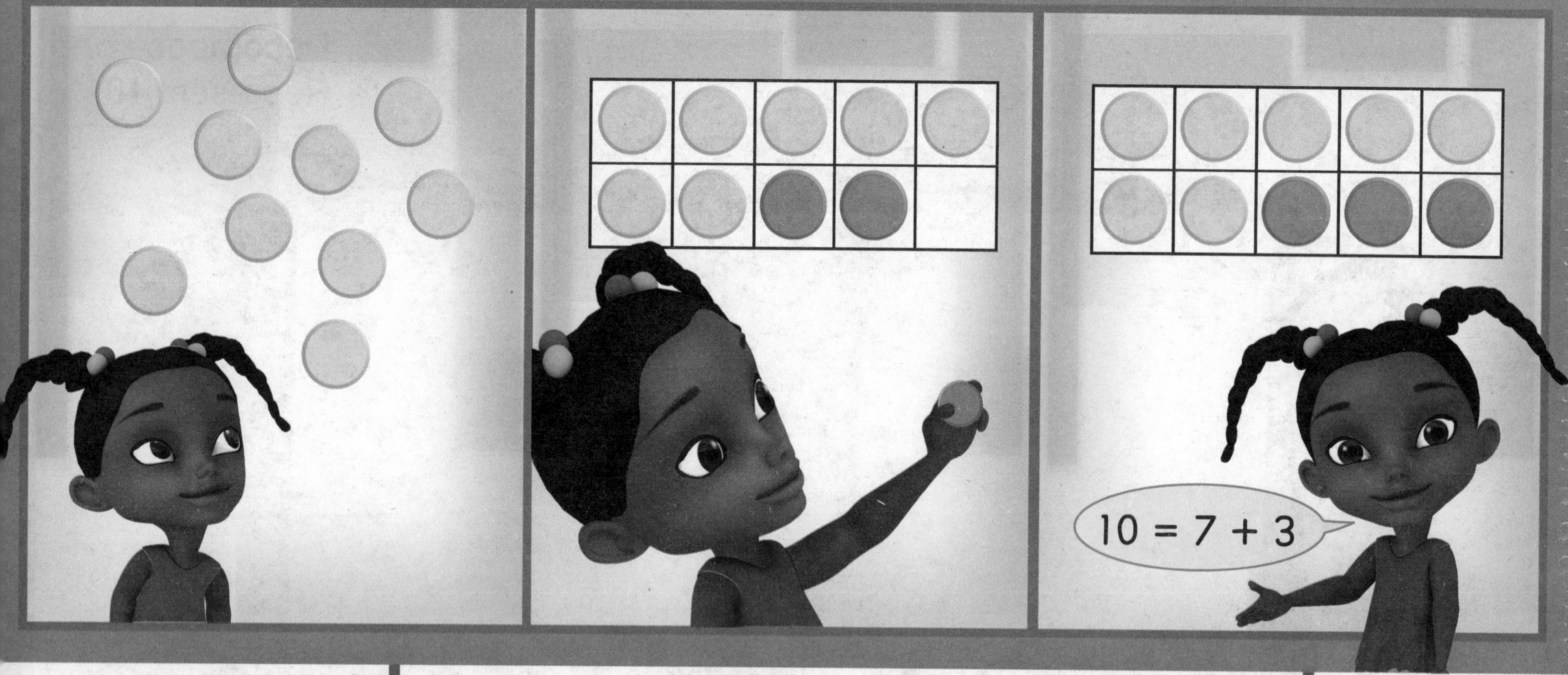

Guided Practice

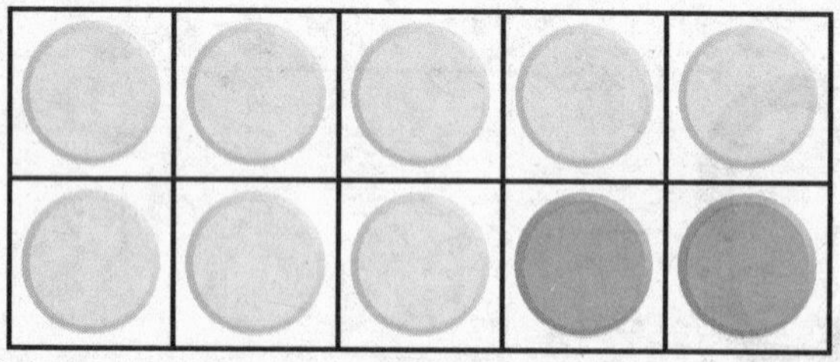

10 = 8 + 2

Directions 1 Have students color yellow and red counters in the ten-frame to show a number pair for 10, and then complete the equation to tell the way to break apart 10.

Name ______________________

2

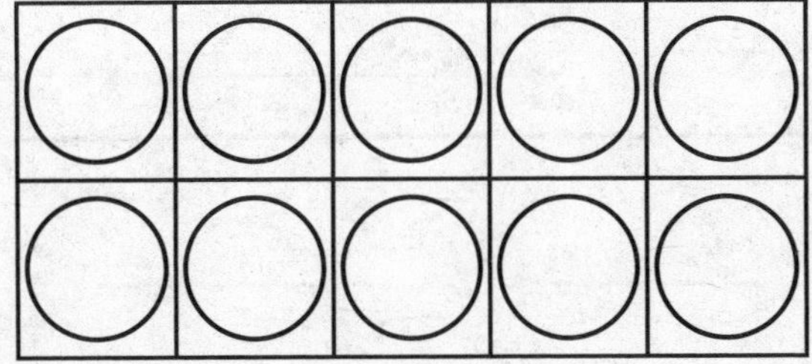

10 = ____ + ____

3

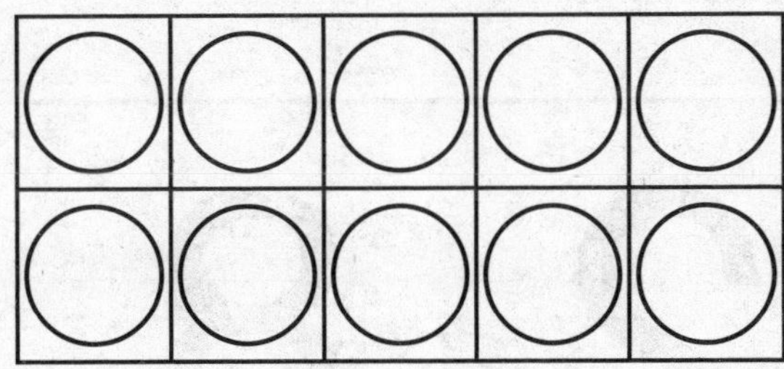

10 = ____ + ____

4

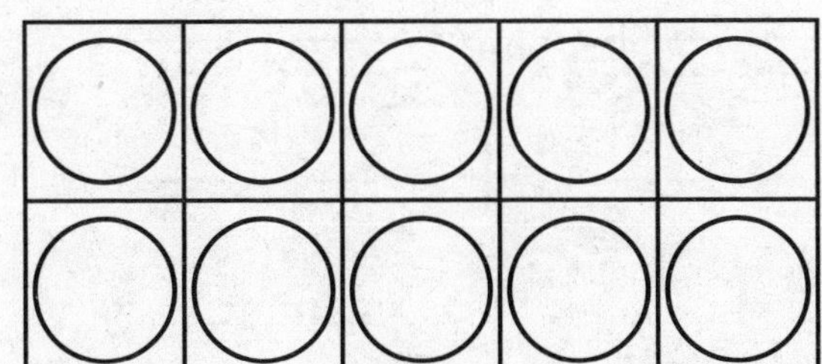

10 = ____ + ____

Directions 2–4 Have students color yellow and red counters in the ten-frame to show a different number pair for 10, and then complete the equation to tell the way to break apart 10.

Independent Practice

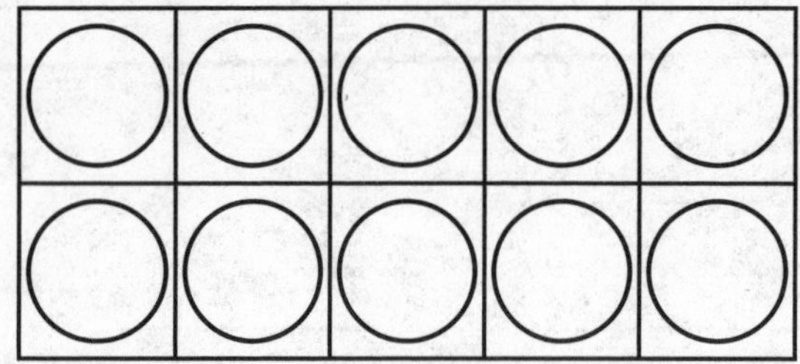

10 = ____ + ____

6

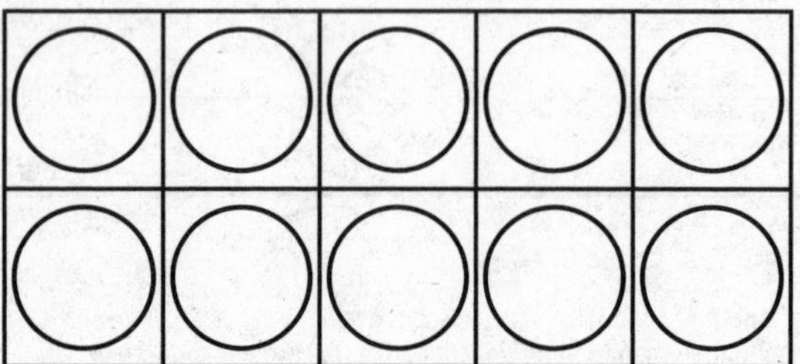

10 = ____ + ____

7

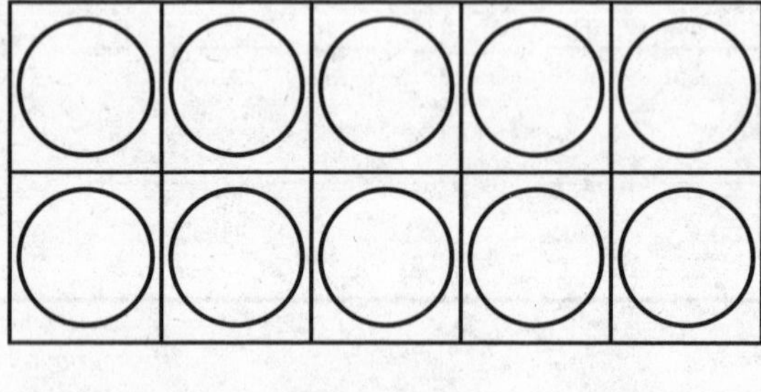

10 = 2 + 8

____ = ____ + ____

Directions 5 and 6 Have students color yellow and red counters in the ten-frame to show a different number pair for 10, and then complete the equation to tell the way to break apart 10. 7 **Higher Order Thinking** Have students color yellow and red counters in the top ten-frame to show the equation. Then have students write the related fact to the given equation, and then color yellow and red counters in the bottom ten-frame to match the equation they just wrote. Have students tell how the equations are both alike and different.

Name ____________________

Homework & Practice 8-7

Decompose and Represent 10

HOME ACTIVITY Draw 10 large circles on a piece of paper. Have your child count the number of circles. Then have him or her put household objects, such as pennies or paper clips, on some of the circles. Have your child write an equation that tells how many circles are empty and how many have objects. The equation should equal 10.

10 = 6 + 4

10 = ____ + ____

10 = ____ + ____

Directions Say: *You can break apart the cubes to show number pairs for 10. Color the cubes to show two groups of cubes. You can also write an equation to tell the way to break apart 10:* 10 = 6 + 4. 1 and 2 Have students color the cube train red and yellow to show a different number pair for 10, and then complete the equation to tell the way to break apart 10.

3

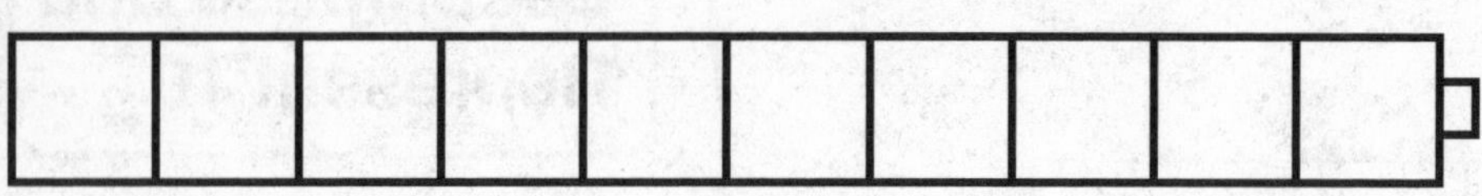

10 = ______ + ______

4

______ = ______ + ______

10 = 7 + 3

______ = ______ + ______

Directions 3 Have students color the cube train red and yellow to show a different number pair for 10, and then complete the equation to tell the way to break apart 10. 4 **Number Sense** Have students color the cube train red and yellow to show two different parts that add to 10, and then write an equation to tell the number pair. 5 **Higher Order Thinking** Have students color the cube train red and yellow to show the equation, and then write a different equation to match the counters in the frame. Have students tell how the equations are both alike and different.

Lesson 8-8

Solve Word Problems: Both Addends Unknown

Directions Say: *Jada has 6 books she wants to place on her book shelves. Draw one way she could put her books away, and then write the number to tell how many books you drew on each shelf. Write an equation to match what you drew. Explain why your answer is correct.*

I can ... write an addition equation to solve a word problem.

I can also make sense of problems.

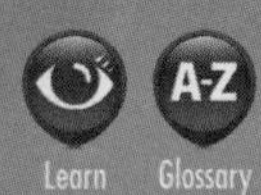

Guided Practice

Directions 1 Have students listen to the story, draw circles to show breaking apart, and then complete the equation to match the story. Have them explain how they know their answers are correct. *Jorge has 5 flowers. He wants to give some of them to Shelley and some of them to Lola. How can he break apart the group of flowers?*

Name ______________________________

4 = ___ + ___

3

9 = ___ + ___

4

6 = ___ + ___

Directions Have students listen to each story, draw circles to show breaking apart, and then complete the equation to match the story. Have them explain how they know their answers are correct. 2 *David has 4 marbles. He wants to give some marbles to John and some to Rob. How could he break apart the group of marbles?* 3 *Sarah has 9 seashells. She wants to give some to her brother and some to her grandfather. How can she break apart the group of shells?* 4 **Vocabulary** Say: *Nico has 6 toy owls. He wants to take some to school and leave some at home. How does he **break apart** the group of owls?* Complete the equation to match the story.

Independent Practice

10 = ____ + ____

6

3 = ____ + ____

6 = ____ + ____

Directions Have students listen to each story, draw circles to show breaking apart, and then complete the equation to match the story. Then have them explain how they know their answers are correct. 5 *Mia has 10 flowers. She wants to plant some in the garden and put some in the house. How can she take apart the group of flowers?* 6 *Krista has 3 beach balls. She wants to give some to Allison and some to Patrick. How can she take apart the group of balls?* 7 **Higher Order Thinking** Have students listen to the story, draw pictures to help solve the problem, and then complete the equation to match the story. Then have them explain how they know their answers are correct. *Larry has 6 coins. He wants to give some coins to Drew and some coins to Tom. If Larry gives Drew 6 coins, how many coins does Tom get?*

Name ____________________

Homework & Practice 8-8

Solve Word Problems: Both Addends Unknown

Another Look!

9 = 3 + 6

HOME ACTIVITY Read aloud the following problem: *A shirt has 8 buttons. The buttons are either black or white. How many buttons of each color are on the shirt?* Ask your child to draw a picture to solve the problem, and then complete the equation: ___ + ___ = 8. Repeat with different numbers of buttons.

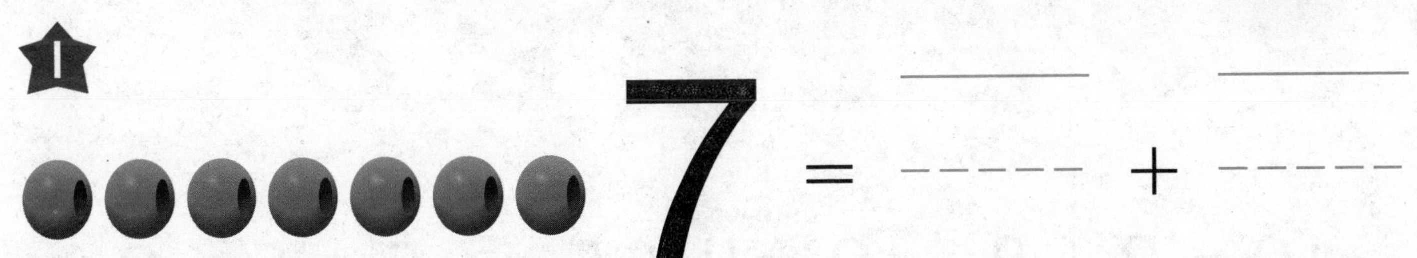

1. 7 = ___ + ___

2. 8 = ___ + ___

Directions Say: *Laura has 9 beads. She uses some to make a bracelet and some to make a necklace. How can she break apart the group of beads? Complete the equation to match the story.* Then have students discuss other ways to break apart the beads. Have students listen to the story, draw circles to show breaking apart, and then complete the equation to match the story. Then have them explain how they know their answers are correct. **1** *Dylan has 7 beads. He wants to give some to Amy and some to Laura. How can Dylan break apart the group of beads?* **2** *Sharon has 8 beads. She wants to give some to Kara and some to Emma. How can Sharon break apart the group of beads?*

3

$4 = \_\_\_ + \_\_\_$

4

$2 + 7 = 9$ $10 = 2 + 8$ $9 = 4 + 5$ $5 + 5 = 9$

$7 + 3 = 9$ $1 + 8 = 9$ $6 + 3 = 9$ $8 = 5 + 3$

Directions 3 Have students listen to the story, draw circles to show breaking apart, and then complete the equation to match the story. *Andrew has 4 sea stars. He gives some to Danny and some to Alisa. How can he break apart the group of sea stars?* 4 **Higher Order Thinking** Have students listen to the story, and then mark an X on the equations that are NOT answers to the story. Ask them to explain how they know which equations are answers and which are NOT answers. *Logan has 9 sea horse stickers. He wants to put some on his folder and some on his notebook. How can he break apart the group of stickers?*

Name ____________________

Lesson 8-9
Find the Missing Part of 10

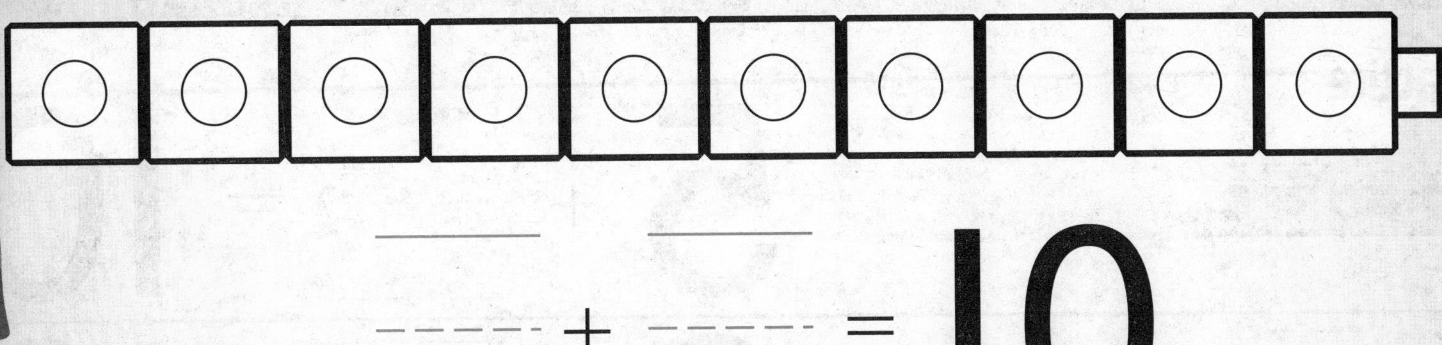

___ + ___ = 10

___ + ___ = 10

Directions Say: *Use red and blue cubes to make two different trains. Each train should have 10 cubes. Use blue and red crayons to color the cube trains you made. Then write the missing numbers in the equation for each cube train.*

I can …
find number partners for 10.

I can also model with math.

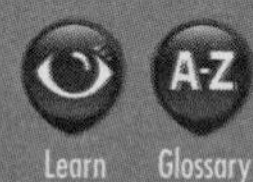

3 + ? = 10

10 in all

3 + 7 = 10

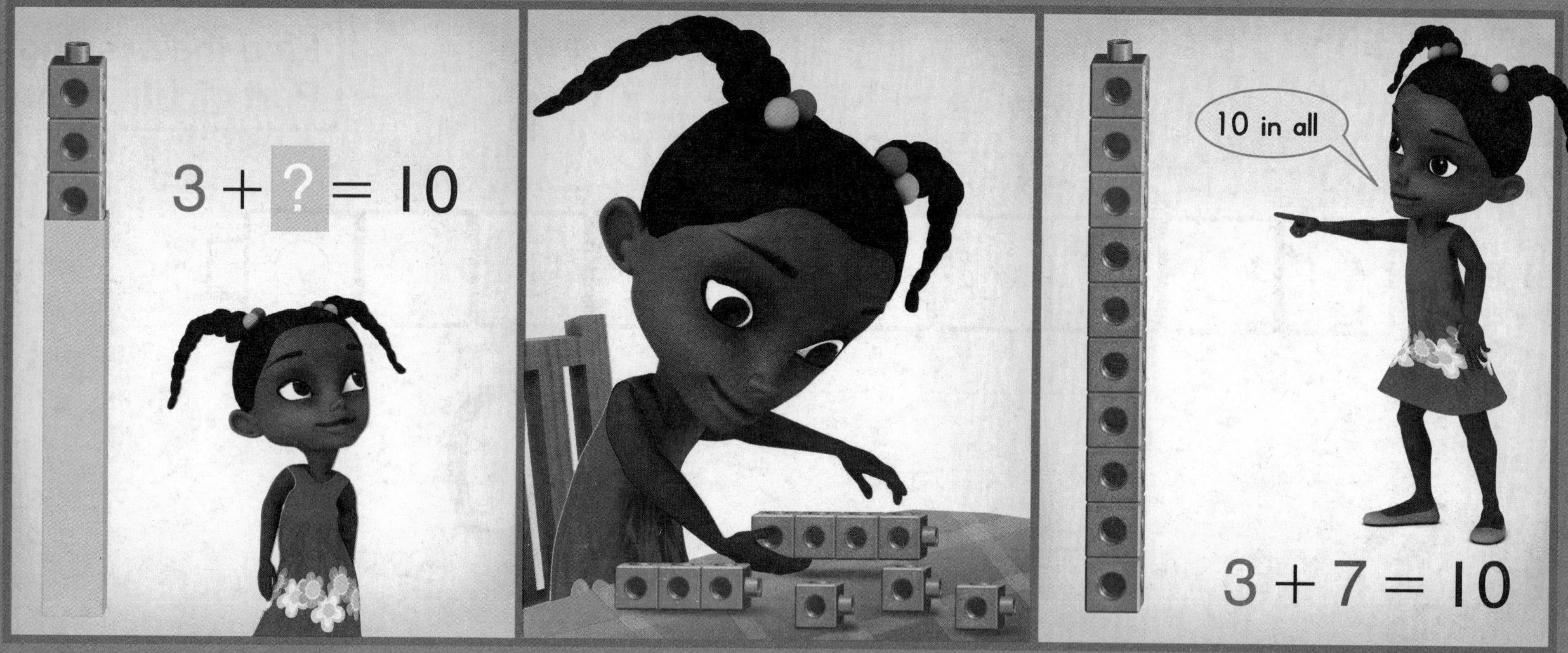

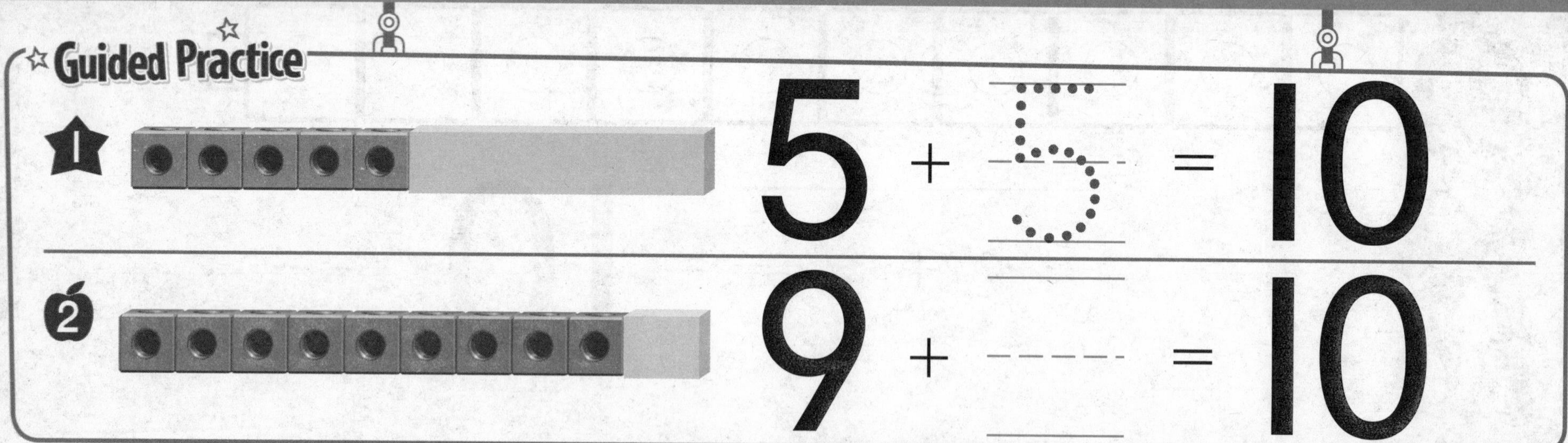

Directions Have students: 1 count the red cubes to find one part of 10, use blue cubes to find the number under the cover, and then write the missing number in the equation to tell the parts of 10; 2 count the blue cubes to find one part of 10, use red cubes to find the number under the cover, and then write the missing number in the equation to tell the parts of 10.

Name ______

3 $7 + \_\_\_ = 10$

4 $2 + \_\_\_ = 10$

5 $6 + \_\_\_ = 10$

6 $5 + \_\_\_ = 10$

Directions Have students: 3 count the red cubes to find one part of 10, use blue cubes to find the number under the cover, and then write the missing number in the equation to tell the parts of 10; 4 count the blue cubes to find one part of 10, use red cubes to find the number under the cover, and then write the missing number in the equation to tell the parts of 10; 5 and 6 count the straight fingers to find one part of 10, use their own fingers to find the other part, and then write the missing number in the equation to tell the parts of 10.

Independent Practice

7

$4 + \_\_\_ = 10$

8

$8 + \_\_\_ = 10$

9

$1 + \_\_\_ = 10$

10

$\_\_\_ + \_\_\_ = 10$

Directions 7–9 Have students draw a picture to show the parts of 10, and then write the missing number in the equation to tell the parts of 10. 10 **Higher Order Thinking** Say: *A child is holding up 3 fingers to show how old she is. What part of 10 is she showing? Use that number to write the missing numbers in the equation to tell the parts of 10.*

Name ______________________________

Help Tools Games

Homework & Practice 8-9

Find the Missing Part of 10

HOME ACTIVITY Hold up your hands in front of your child with 1 index finger straight and the rest of your fingers bent. Ask your child to tell you the parts of 10 that your fingers show (1 and 9). Then ask your child to write an equation for those parts of 10 (1 + 9 = 10). Repeat the activity with different combinations of straight and bent fingers.

Another Look!

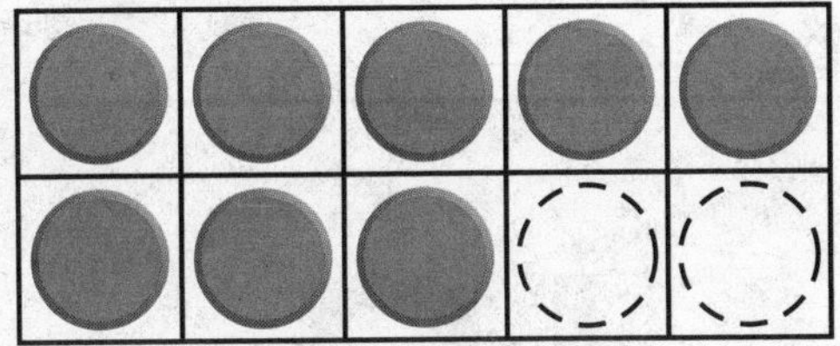

8 + 2 = 10

1

4 + ___ = 10

2

1 + ___ = 10

Directions Say: *You can show parts of 10 with counters and a ten-frame. Draw the missing part of 10, and then write the missing number in the equation to tell the parts of 10.* **1** and **2** Have students count the red counters to find one part of 10, draw the yellow counters to show the other part, and then write the missing number in the equation to tell the parts of 10.

3

5 + ____ = 10

4

7 + ____ = 10

5

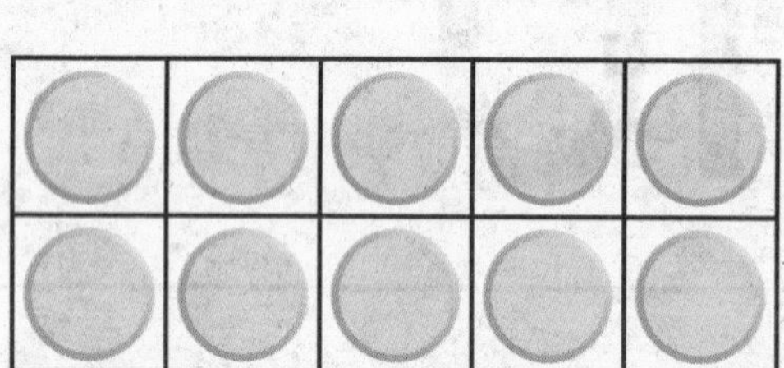

____ + ____ = 10

____ + ____ = 10

Directions 3 and 4 Have students use counters and a ten-frame to show the different parts of 10. Then have them draw the counters they use, and then write the missing number in the equation to tell the parts of 10. 5 **Higher Order Thinking** Say: *Nicholas has yellow and red counters to use to show parts of 10. Write the missing numbers in the two equations to show two different ways to tell the parts of 10 that Nicholas showed.*

Name ______________________

Lesson 8-10

Continue to Find the Missing Part of 10

Directions Say: *Jada visits a farm. The owner says there are 10 goats on the farm. Jada only sees 8 goats. How many are inside the barn? Draw pictures of the goats that are in the barn, and then tell how you know.*

I can ... find a missing part to make 10.

I can also model with math.

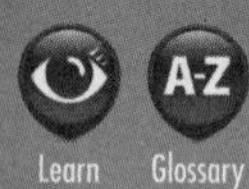

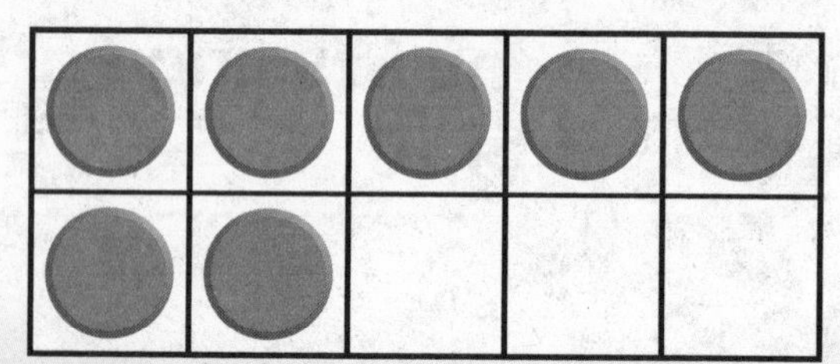

7 + ? = 10

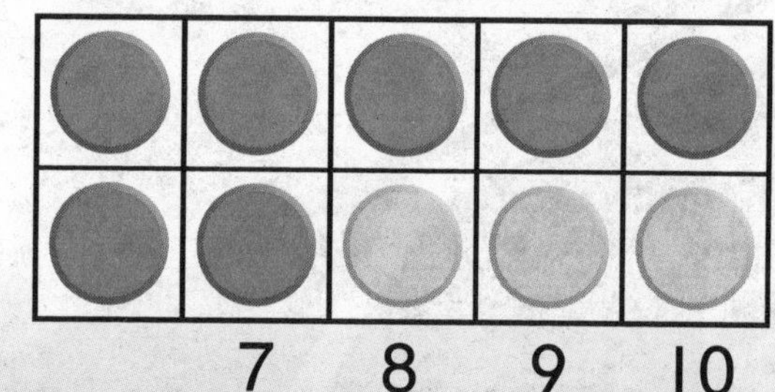

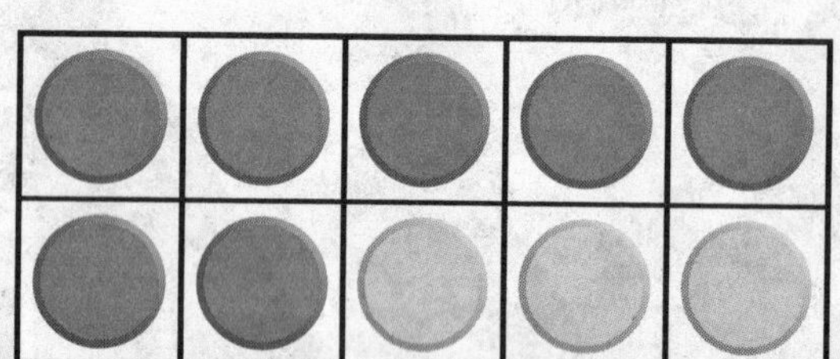

7 + 3 = 10

Guided Practice

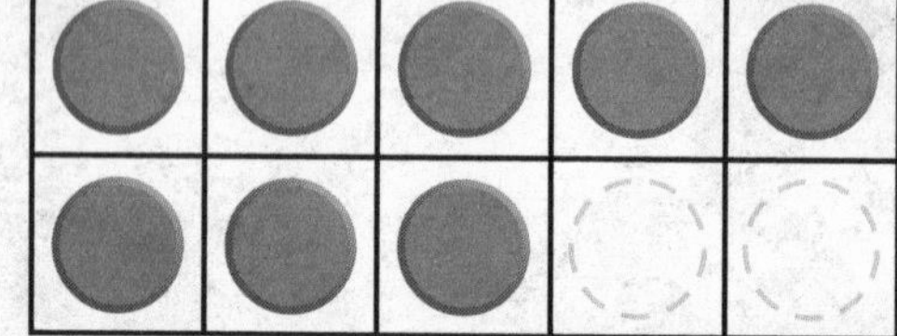

8 + 2 = 10

2

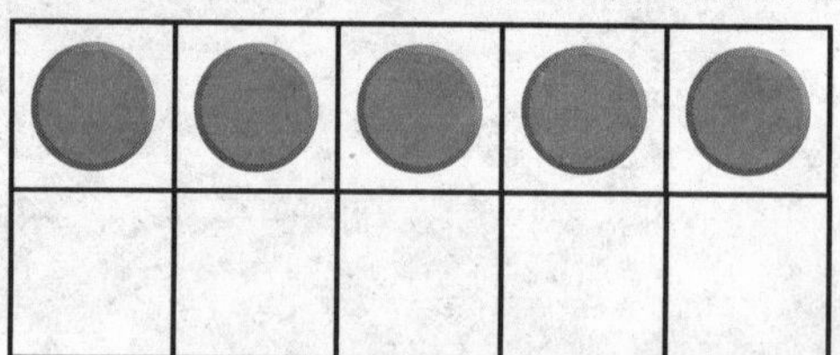

5 + ___ = 10

Directions 1–2 Have students draw yellow counters in the ten-frame to find the missing part of 10, and then write the missing number in the equation.

Name ______________________________

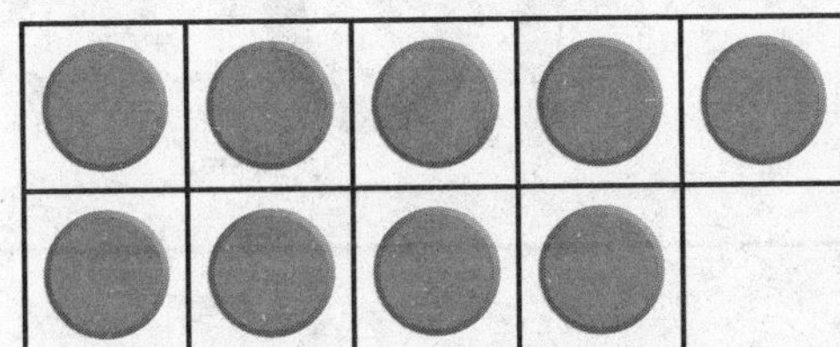

9 + ______ = 10

4

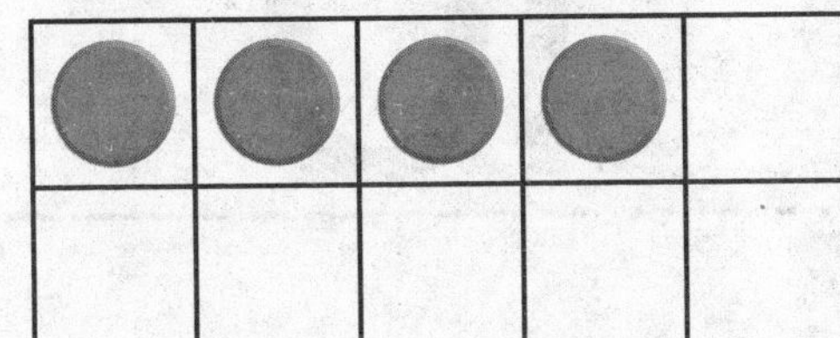

4 + ______ = 10

5

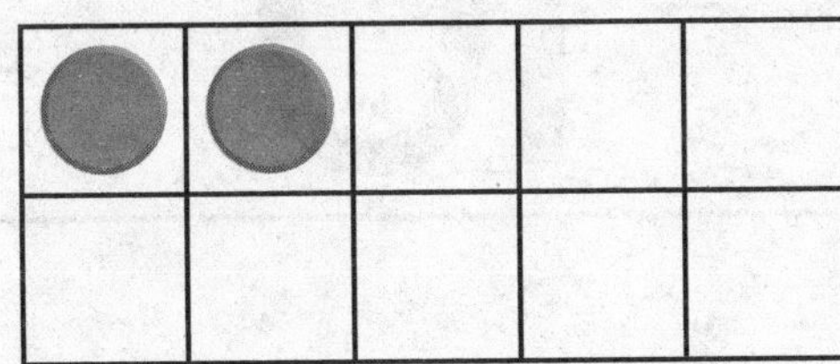

2 + ______ = 10

6

1 + ______ = 10

Directions 3–6 **Algebra** Have students draw yellow counters in the ten-frame to find the missing part of 10, and then write the missing number in the equation.

Independent Practice

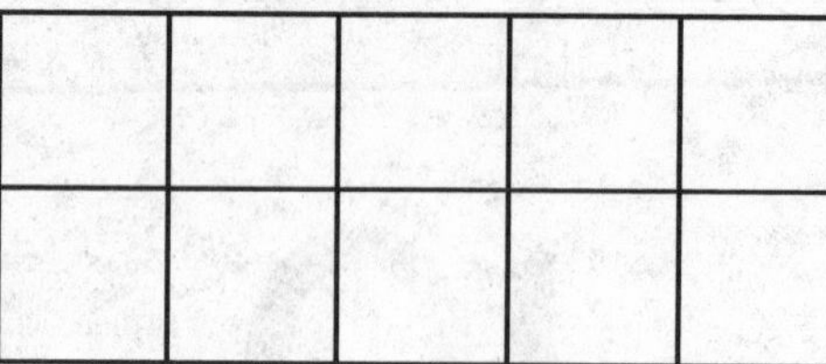

$3 + \_\_\_ = 10$

8

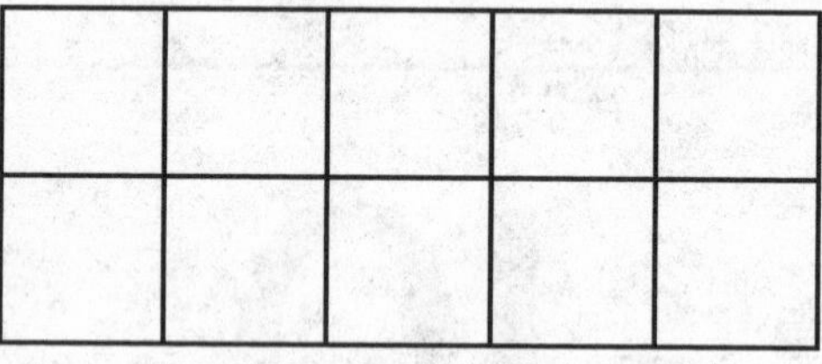

$5 + \_\_\_ = 10$

9

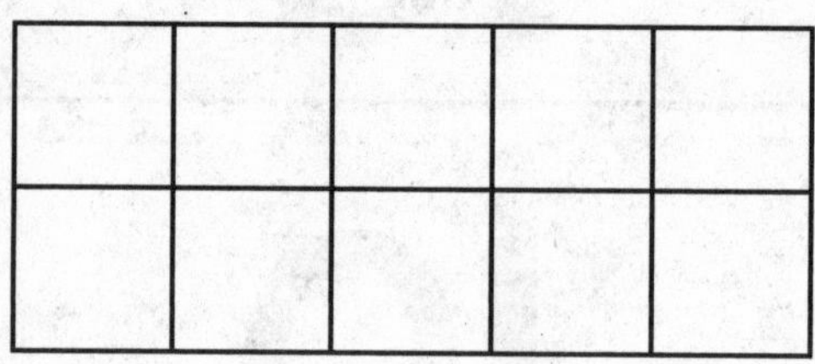

$0 + \_\_\_ = 10$

10

$5 + 5 = 10$ $5 + 6 = 10$ $9 + 2 = 10$ $9 + 1 = 10$

Directions 7–9 Have students draw counters in the ten-frame to show the part that they know, and then draw yellow counters in the empty spaces in the ten-frame and count to find the missing part of 10. Then have students write the missing number in the equation. 10 **Higher Order Thinking** Have students mark an X on the two equations that are NOT true. Then have them explain how they know which equations are true and which are NOT true.

Name ____________________

Help Tools Games

Homework & Practice 8-10

Continue to Find the Missing Part of 10

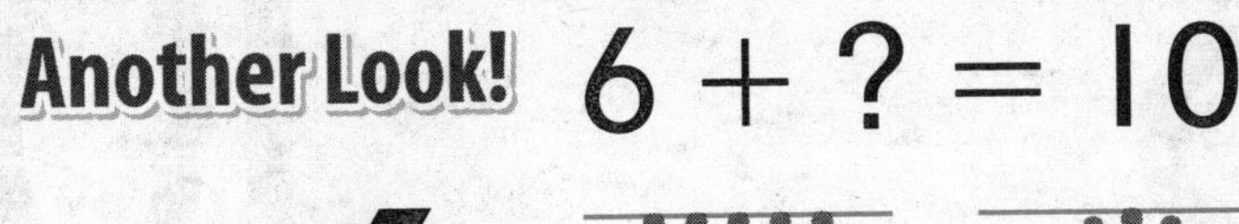

Another Look! 6 + ? = 10

6, 7, 8, 9, 10

6 + 4 = 10

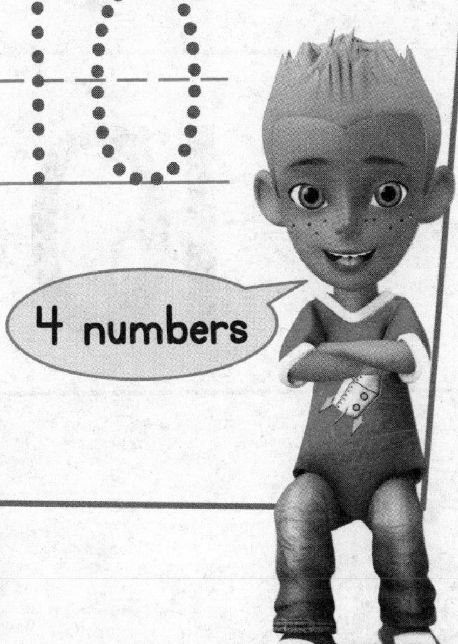

HOME ACTIVITY Give your child 7 small objects such as coins or beans. Ask your child to add objects until he or she has 10 objects. Then have your child fill in the missing number in this equation: 7 + ? = 10 (3). Repeat the activity by starting with groups of 5, 8, and 9 objects.

1

9 + ____ = 10

2

2 + ____ = 10

Directions Say: *You can count on to find the missing part of 10. Count on from 6 until you reach 10. How many numbers did you count? Write the missing number in the equation.* 1–2 Have students show how to count on to find the missing part of 10, and then write the missing number in the equation. Then have them explain how they know their answer is correct.

3 $7 + \_\_\_ = 10$

4 $5 + \_\_\_ = 10$

5 $1 + \_\_\_ = 10$

6 $10 + \_\_\_ = 10$

7

$\_\_\_ + \_\_\_ = 10$

8

$\_\_\_ + \_\_\_ = \_\_\_$

Directions 3–6 Have students count on to find the missing part of 10, and then write the missing number in the equation. Then have them tell how they know their answer is correct. 7 **Algebra** Say: *Roxy borrowed 10 colored pencils from Hannah. When she returned them, there were only 8 colored pencils in the box. How many colored pencils were missing?* Have students write the missing numbers in the equation, and then tell how they know their answers are correct. 8 **Higher Order Thinking** Have students draw counters to find the missing part of 10, and then write the equation to match the counters.

Show the Letter Name ______________________

TOPIC 8 **Fluency Practice Activity**

1

1 + 2	5 − 2	4 − 1	3 + 0	3 − 0
5 − 3	4 + 1	0 + 3	2 + 2	1 + 0
2 − 1	5 − 4	5 − 2	0 + 0	1 + 4
3 + 2	3 − 1	4 − 1	5 − 1	4 − 0
3 − 3	2 + 0	2 + 1	2 + 3	1 + 1

2

Directions Have students: 1 color each box that has a sum or difference that is equal to 3; 2 write the letter that they see.

I can …
add and subtract fluently to 5.

$10 - 5 = 5$

$6 + 3 = 9$

8 ◯ 7 = ____

 = ____ ◯ ____

Directions **Understand Vocabulary** Have students: 1 draw a circle around the **minus sign**; 2 draw a circle around the **sum**; 3 complete the number sentence and find the **difference**; 4 show a way to **break apart** the number by drawing one part in the box and one part outside the box. Then have them write an equation to tell how the whole was broken into two parts.

Name ____________________

Set A

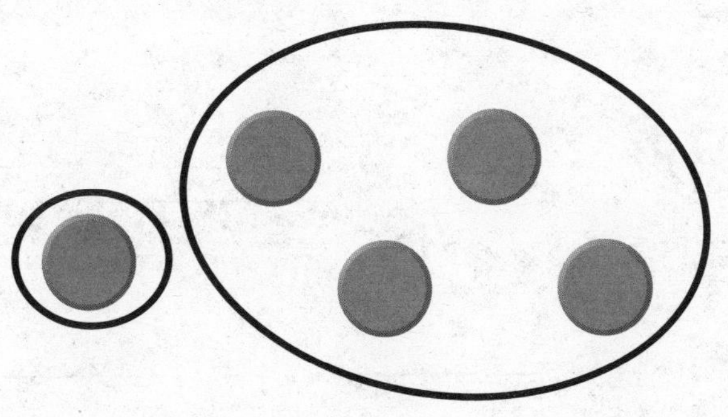

5 = 1 + 4

4 = ____ + ____

Set B

2 + 1 = 3

2

____ ◯ ____ = ____

Directions Have students: ★ use yellow and red counters to show how to break apart the 4 counters, draw a circle around two groups of counters to show a number pair for 4, and then complete the equation to show the way to break apart 4; 2 listen to the story, and then use connecting cubes to help act out the story to choose an operation. Then have students complete the equation to show the related fact for 2 + 1 = 3. *3 penguins are in a group. 1 leaves. How many penguins are left?*

Set C

4 + 1 = 5

3

Set D

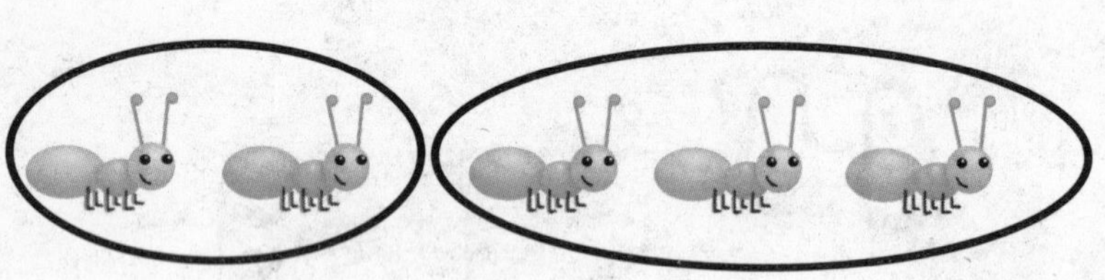

5 − 3 = 2

4

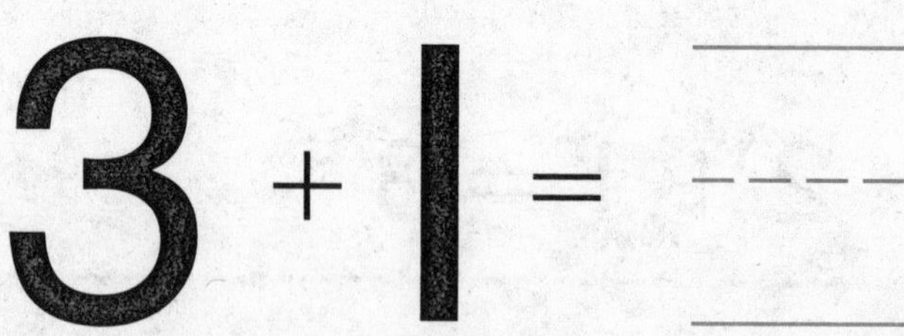

Directions Have students: 3 tell a story for 4 − 3. Then have them draw a picture to illustrate their story and write the equation. 4 solve the equation in any way they choose, and then tell how they solved the problem.

Name ________________________________

Set E

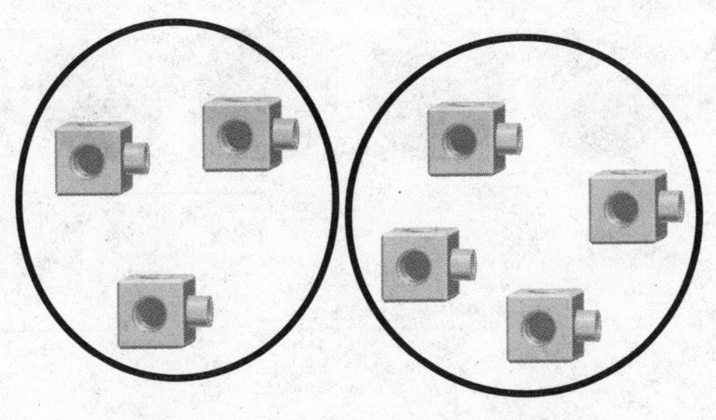

$7 = 3 + 4$

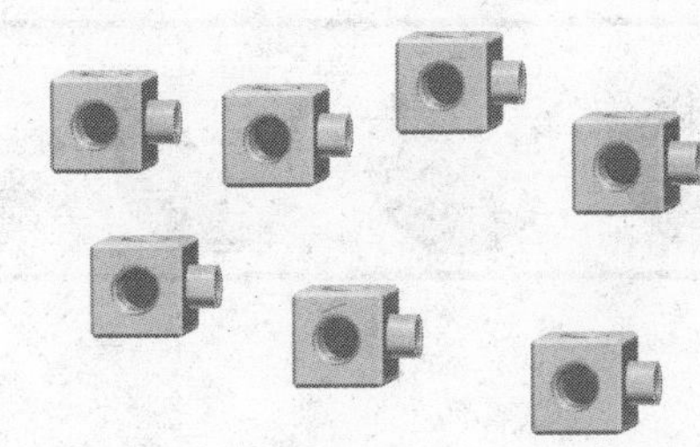

$7 =$ ____ $+$ ____

Set F

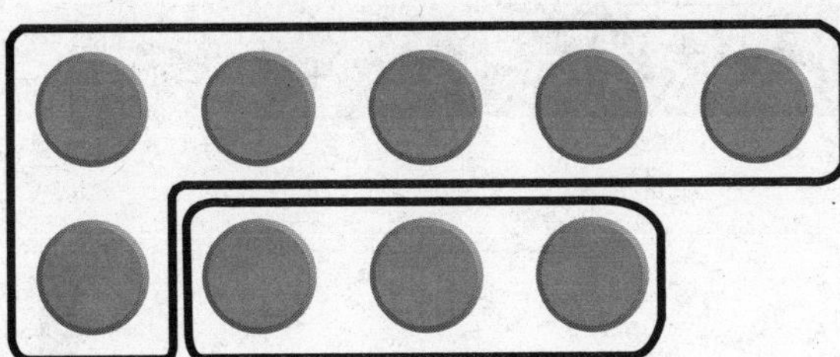

$9 = 6 + 3$

$9 =$ ____ $+$ ____

Directions Have students: 5 use yellow and red counters to show how to break apart the 7 cubes, draw a circle around two groups of cubes to show a number pair for 7, and then complete the equation to show the number pair; 6 use yellow and red counters to show how to break apart the 9 counters, draw a circle around two groups of counters to a show number pair for 9, and then complete the equation to show the number pair.

Set G

$5 = 1 + 4$

$6 = \_\_\_ + \_\_\_$

Set H

$1 + 9 = 10$

8

$6 + \_\_\_ = 10$

Directions Have students: 7 listen to the story, draw circles around each group to show breaking apart, and then complete the equation to match the story. *Bridget has 6 marbles. She gives some to Jessica and some to Christopher. How can she break apart the group of marbles?* 8 count the green cubes to find one part of 10, use yellow cubes to find the number under the cover, and then complete the equation to show the parts of 10.

Name ______________________________

A 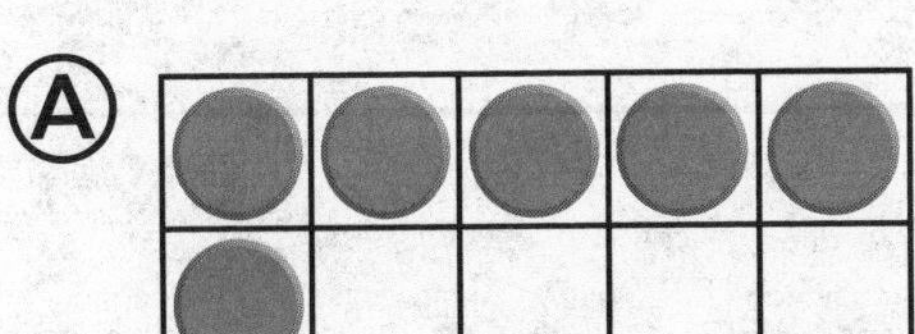

C 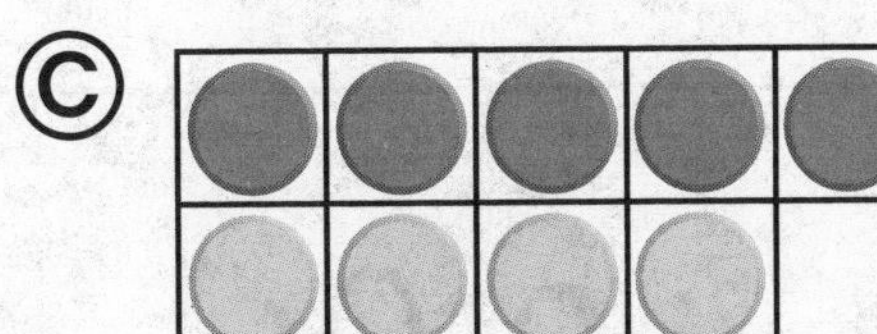

B 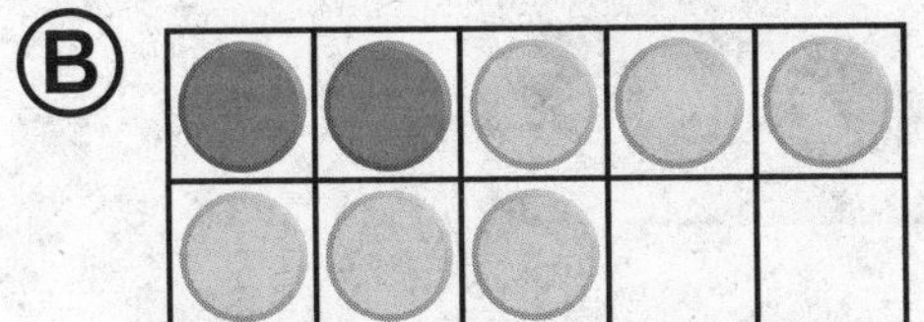

D 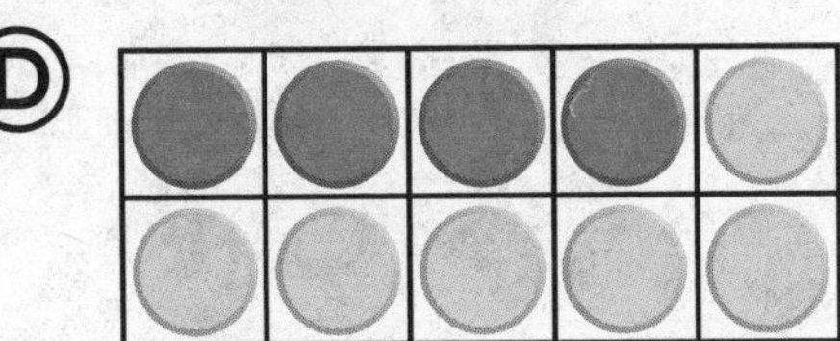

2

Ⓐ $7 = 2 + 5$

Ⓒ $7 = 6 + 1$

Ⓑ $7 = 3 + 4$

Ⓓ $8 = 3 + 5$

3

☐ $2 + 6 = 8$

☐ $4 + 4 = 8$

☐ $3 + 5 = 8$

☐ $5 + 3 = 8$

4

☐ $2 + 6 = 8$

☐ $2 + 7 = 9$

☐ $3 + 6 = 9$

☐ $6 + 3 = 9$

Directions Have students mark the best answer. 1 Which shows one way to break apart 10? 2 Which equation matches the picture? 3 Look at the picture. Mark all the equations that describe the picture. 4 Have students listen to the story, and then mark all the equations that show possible solutions. *Valentina buys 9 beads to make a bracelet. Some beads are blue and some are purple. How many blue beads and how many purple beads did she use so that there are exactly 9 beads in the bracelet?*

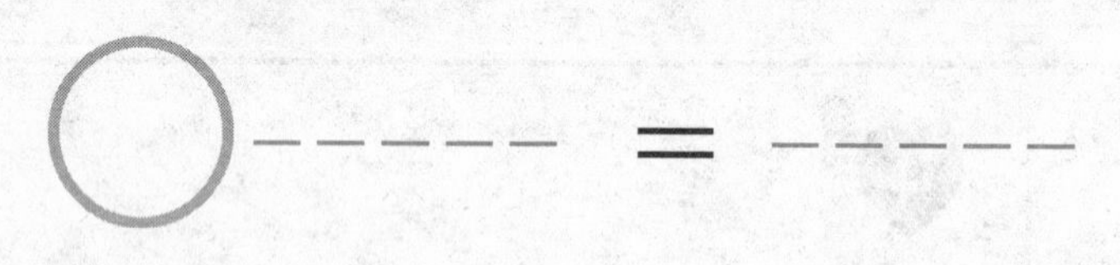

Directions Have students: use yellow and red counters to show how to break apart the 5 snails, draw a circle around the groups of snails to show a number pair for 5, and then complete the equation to show the way to break apart 5; listen to each story, use connecting cubes to help act out each story to choose an operation, and then write the equations to show the related facts. *2 penguins are in a group. 3 join them. How many penguins are there in all?* Then say: *5 penguins are in a group. 3 leave. How many penguins are left?* tell a story for 5 − 4. Then have them draw a picture to illustrate their story and write the equation.

Name ______________________________

8

$6 = \_\_\_ + \_\_\_$

9

$8 = \_\_\_ + \_\_\_$

10

$5 = \_\_\_ + \_\_\_$

Directions Have students: 8 draw a circle around two groups of cars to show number pairs for 6, and then complete the equation to show the number pair; 9 draw a circle around two groups of onions to show number pairs for 8, and then complete the equation to show the number pair; 10 listen to the story, draw circles to show breaking apart, and then write the numbers in the equation to match the groups they drew circles around. *Marco has 5 flowers. He gives some to his mom and some to his grandmother. How can he break apart the group of flowers?*

___ + ___ = 10

12

10 = ___ + ___

13

2 + ___ = 10

Directions Have students: 11 count the red cubes to find one part of 10, use blue cubes to find the number under the cover, and then complete the equation to show the parts of 10; 12 use red and blue crayons to color the cube train to break apart 10 cubes. Then have them complete the equation to show the number pair; 13 draw yellow counters in the ten-frame to show the missing part of 10. Then have them complete the equation.

Name ______________________________

TOPIC 8

Performance Assessment

1

7 = ___ + ___

7 = ___ + ___

2

___ = ___ + ___

3

___ + ___ = 5

___ + ___ = 5

5 − ___ = ___

5 − ___ = ___

Directions **Fern's Farmstand** Say: *Fern sells different fruits and vegetables at her farmstand.* Have students look at the: 1 carrots and cucumbers Fern has at her farmstand, and then write two equations to describe them; 2 lettuce and radishes Fern has at her farmstand, and then write an equation to describe them; 3 red and green peppers that Fern is selling at her farmstand. Have students tell a story about them, and then write the missing numbers in the equation for their story. Then have students write the missing numbers in the other three equations.

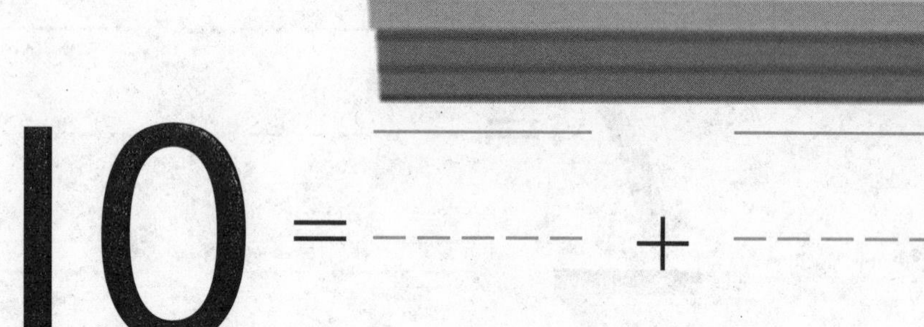

10 = ____ + ____ 10 = ____ + ____

9

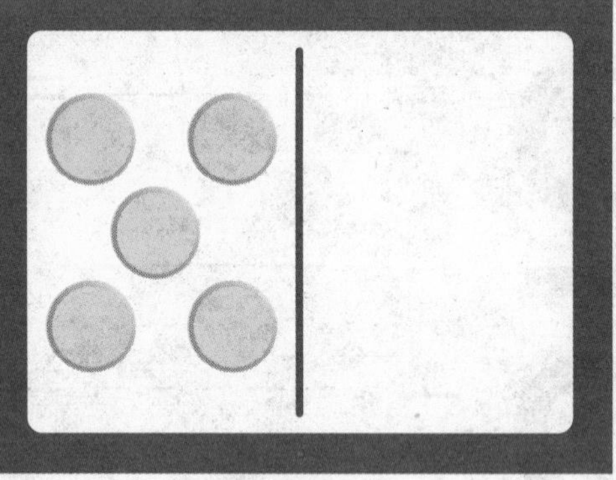

Directions Have students: listen to the story, draw pictures to show two ways to solve the problem, and then complete the equations. *Fern grows tomatoes for her farmstand. She grows red tomatoes and yellow tomatoes. How many tomatoes of each color should she put in her farmstand so that she has exactly 10 tomatoes in her farmstand?* listen to the story, draw counters to complete the model, and then write an equation to solve the problem. *Fern has 9 onions in her farmstand. Then she sells 5 of them. How many onions does she have now?*

Glossary

above

add

3 + 2 = 5

addition sentence

3 and 5 is 8.

attribute

B

balance scale

behind

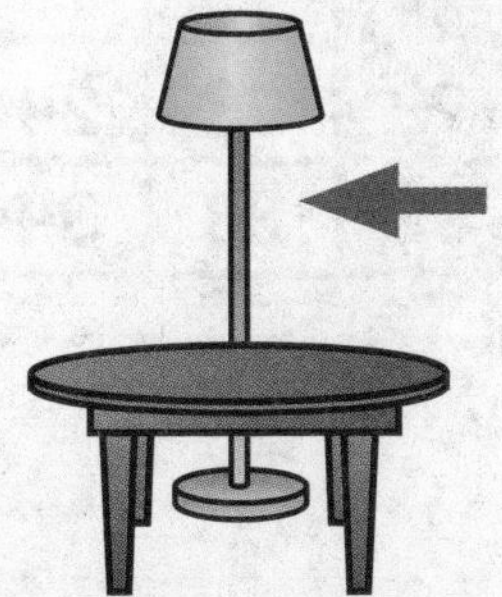

below

beside

break apart

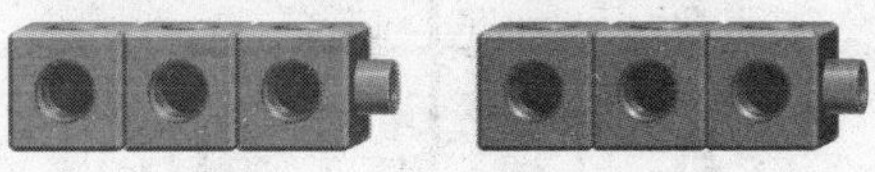

6 − 3 = 3

capacity

category

|| |||

chart

|| |||

circle

classify

column

1	2	3	4	5
11	12	13	14	15
21	22	23	24	25
31	32	33	34	35

compare

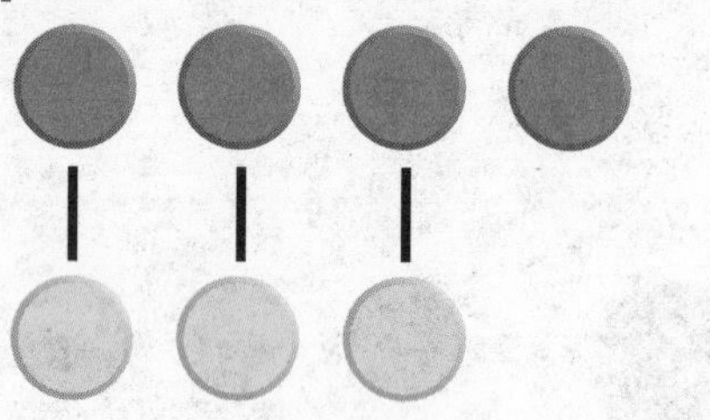

cone

count

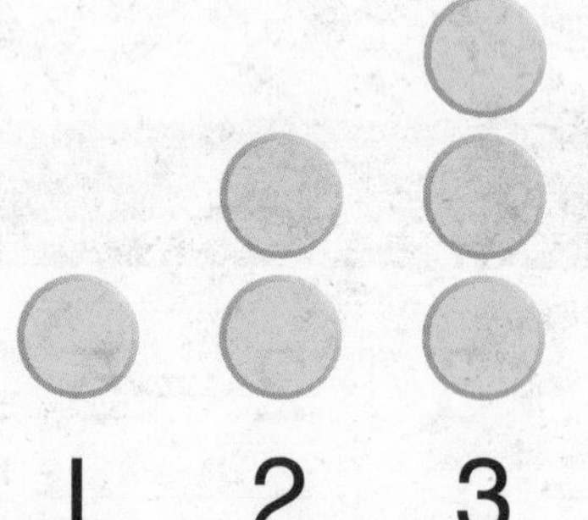

cube

cylinder

D

decade

1	2	3	4	5	6	7	8	9	10
11	12	13	14	15	16	17	18	19	20
21	22	23	24	25	26	27	28	29	30
31	32	33	34	35	36	37	38	39	40
41	42	43	44	45	46	47	48	49	50
51	52	53	54	55	56	57	58	59	60
61	62	63	64	65	66	67	68	69	70
71	72	73	74	75	76	77	78	79	80
81	82	83	84	85	86	87	88	89	90
91	92	93	94	95	96	97	98	99	100

difference

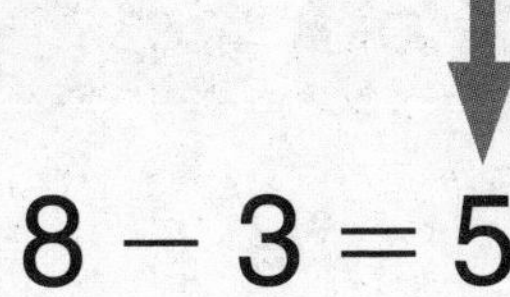

$8 - 3 = 5$

E

eight

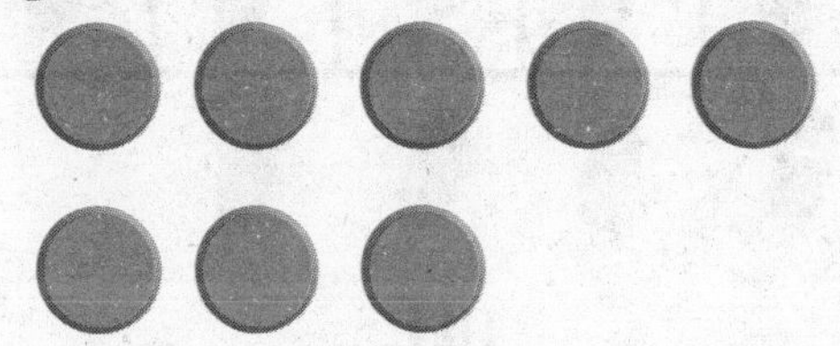

8

eighteen

18

eleven

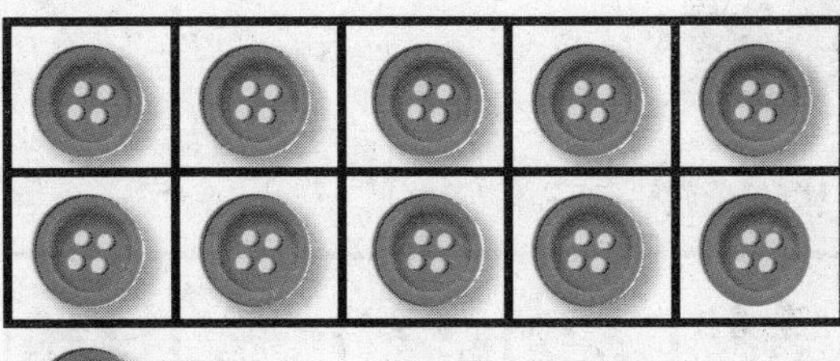

11

equal

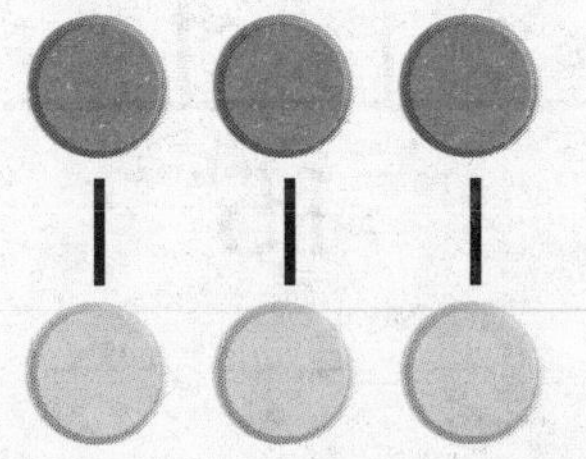

equal sign (=)

$4 + 3 = 7$

equation

$5 + 3 = 8$

$8 = 8$

fifteen

15

five

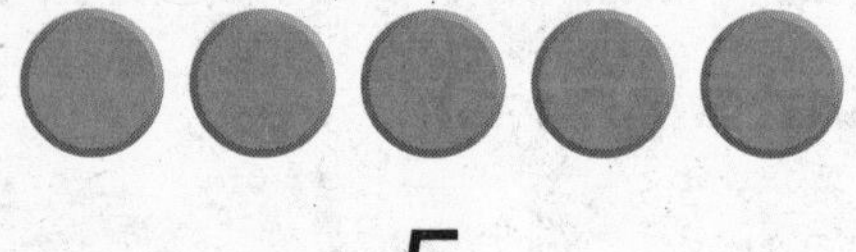

5

flat surface

four

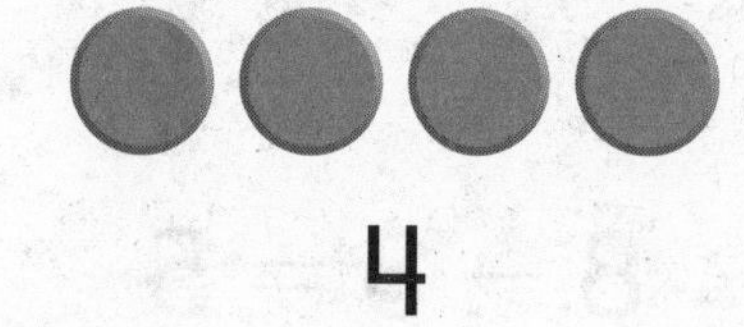

4

fourteen

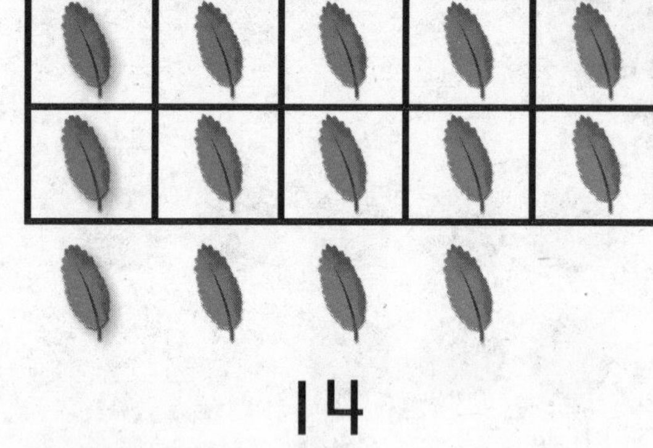

14

G

greater than

group

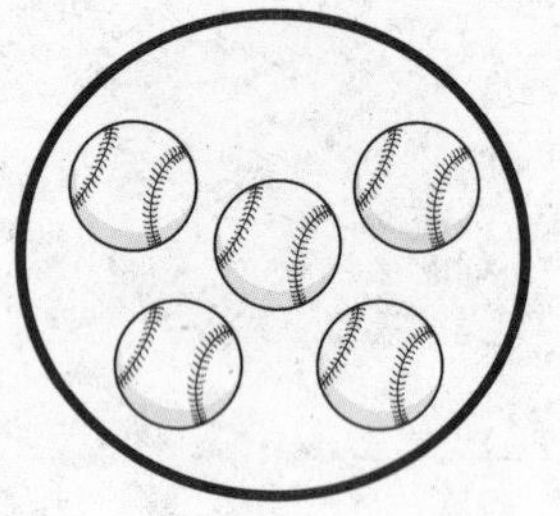

heavier

height

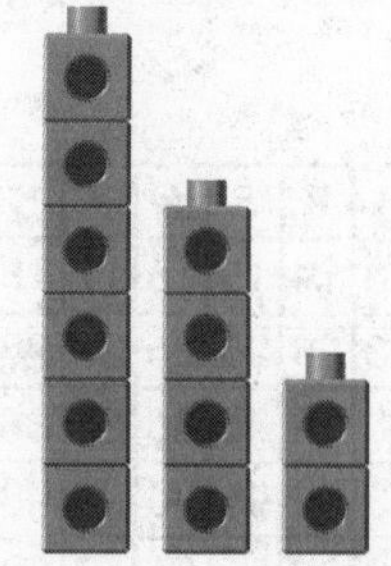

hexagon

How many more?

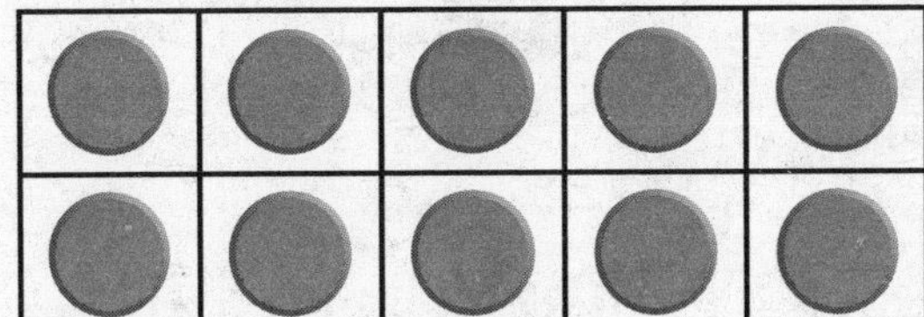

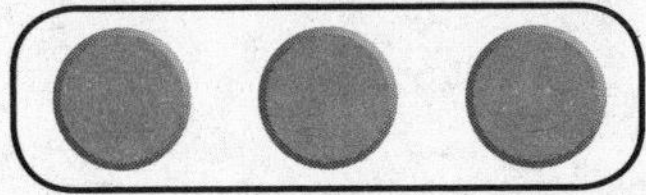

hundred chart

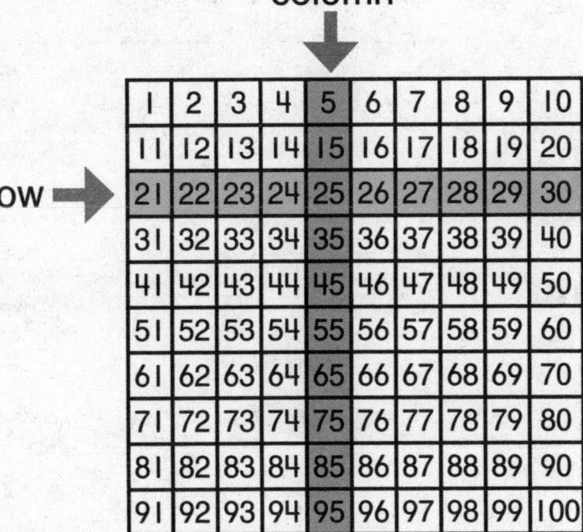

1	2	3	4	5	6	7	8	9	10
11	12	13	14	15	16	17	18	19	20
21	22	23	24	25	26	27	28	29	30
31	32	33	34	35	36	37	38	39	40
41	42	43	44	45	46	47	48	49	50
51	52	53	54	55	56	57	58	59	60
61	62	63	64	65	66	67	68	69	70
71	72	73	74	75	76	77	78	79	80
81	82	83	84	85	86	87	88	89	90
91	92	93	94	95	96	97	98	99	100

I

in all

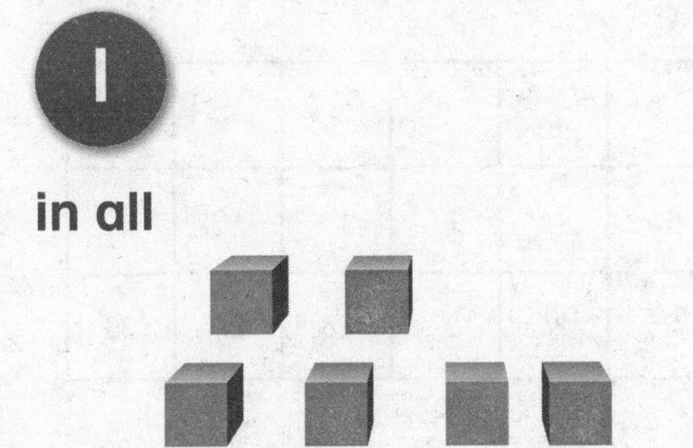

in front of

J

join

L

left

length

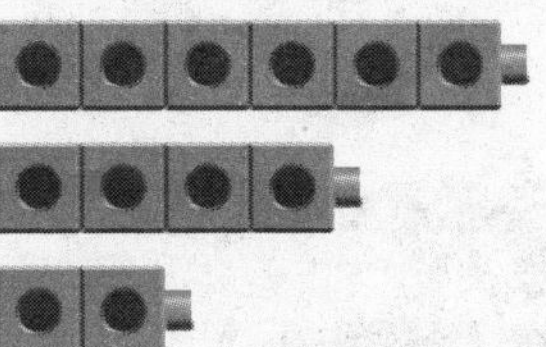

less than

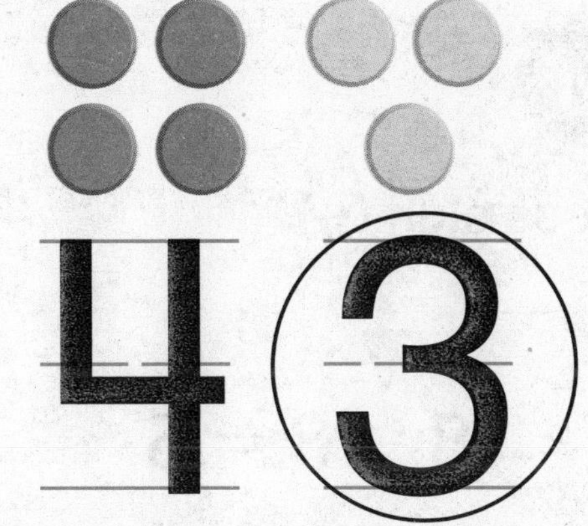

lighter

longer

M

minus sign (−)

$8 - 3 = 5$

model

N

next to

nine

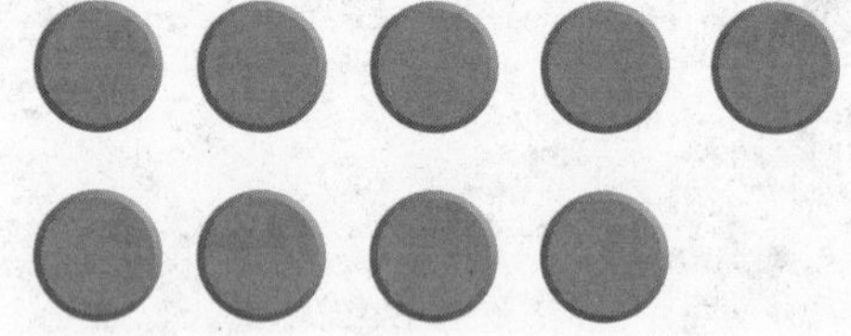

9

nineteen

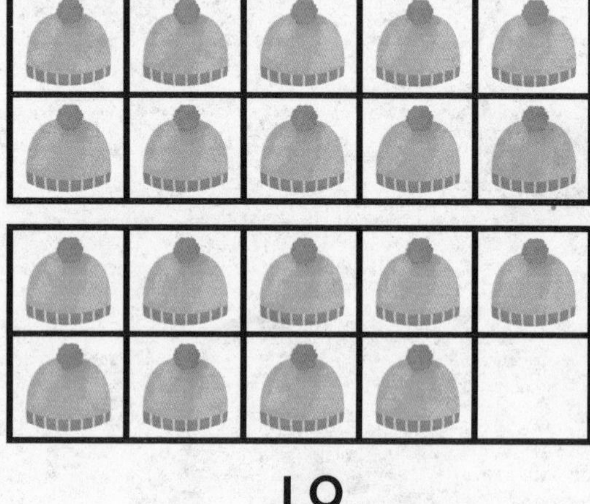

19

none

0

number

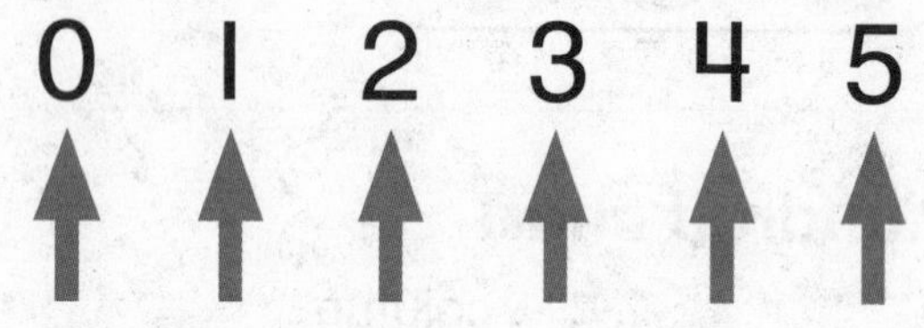

one

ones

5	6	7	8	9	10
15	16	17	18	19	20
25	26	27	28	29	30

operation

$4 + 2 = 6$
$4 - 2 = 2$

order

0 → 1 → 2 → 3 → 4 → 5

part

pattern

10 20 30 40 50

plus sign (+)

$3 + 1 = 4$

rectangle

roll

row

1	2	3	4	5
11	12	13	14	15
21	22	23	24	25
31	32	33	34	35

same number as

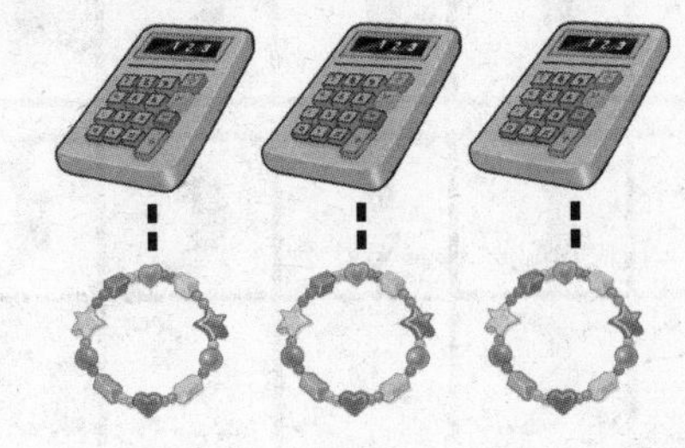

separate

seven

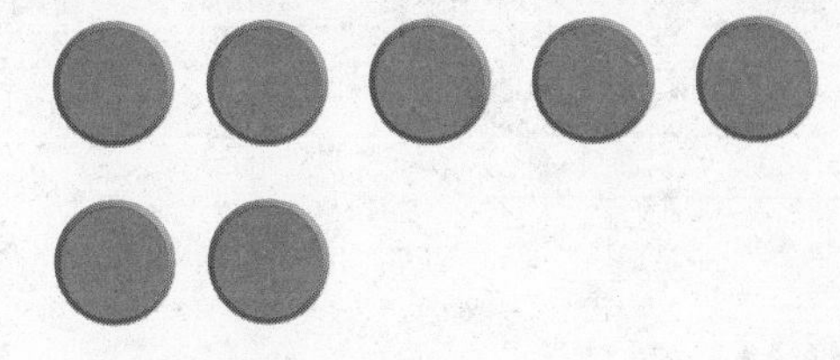

7

seventeen

17

shorter

side

six

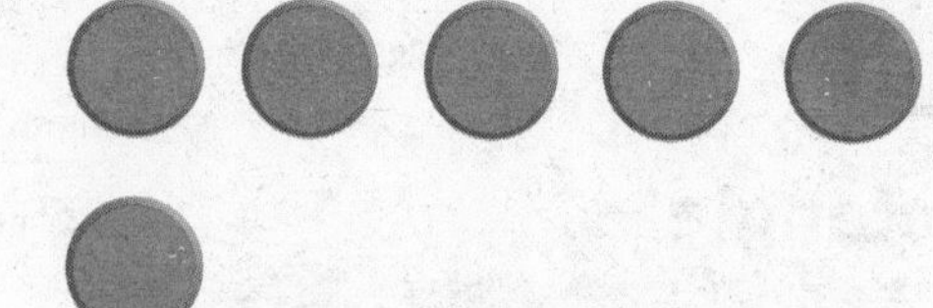

6

sixteen

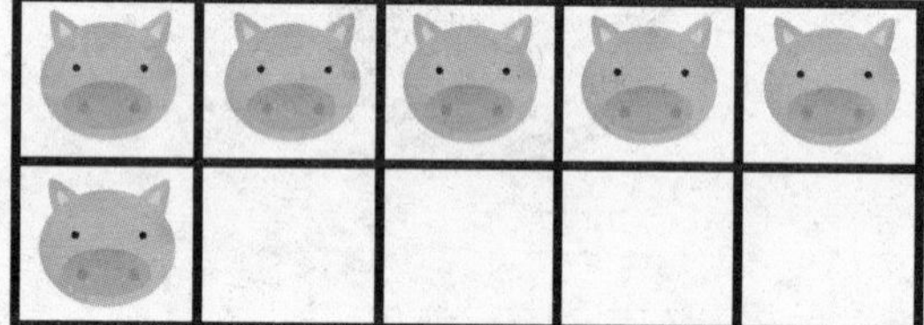

16

slide

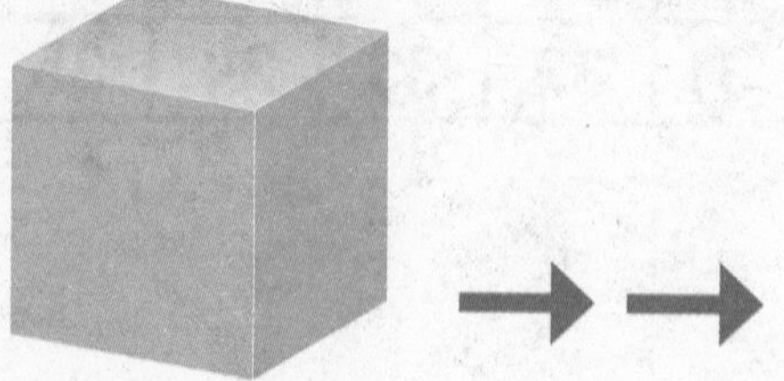

sort

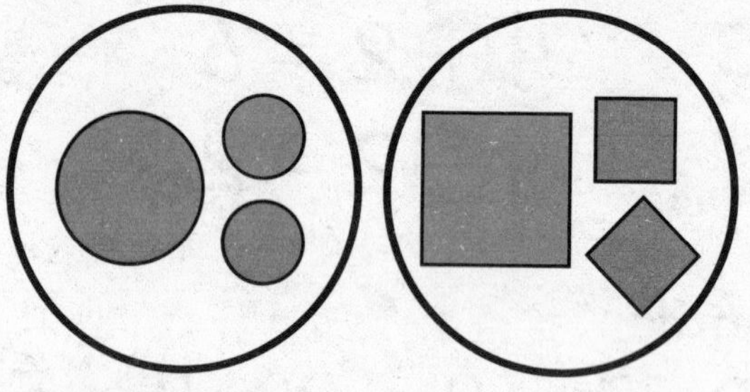

sphere

square

stack

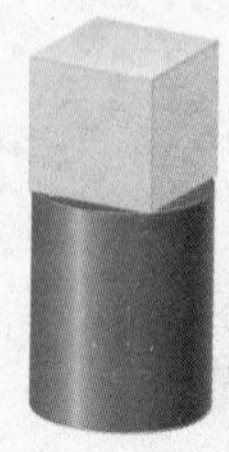

subtract

$3 - 1 = 2$

subtraction sentence

4 take away 3 is 1.

sum

$2 + 3 = 5$

take away

taller

tally mark

II	IIII

ten

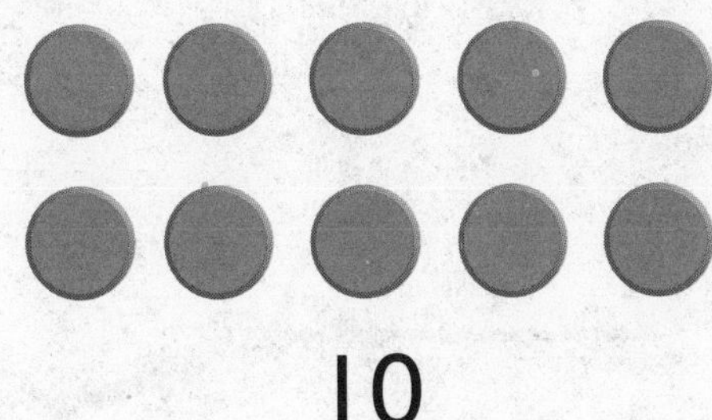

10

tens

5	6	7	8	9	10
15	16	17	18	19	20
25	26	27	28	29	30

thirteen

13

three

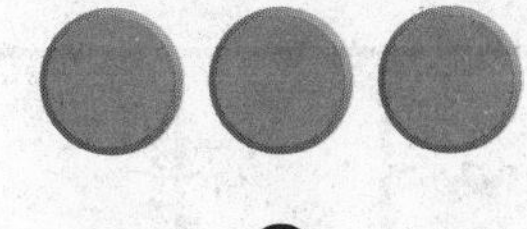

3

three-dimensional shape

triangle

twelve

12

twenty

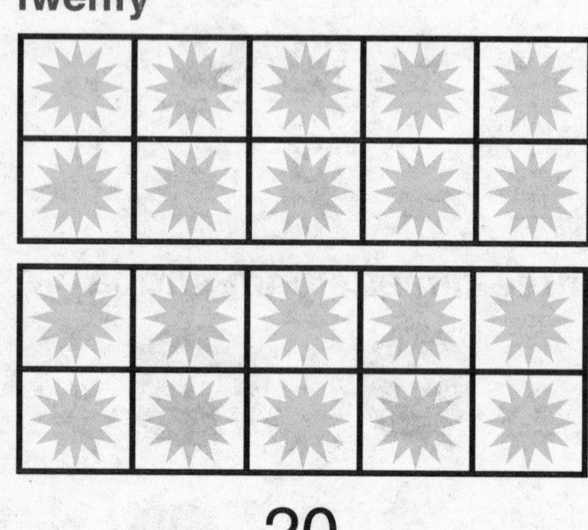

20

two

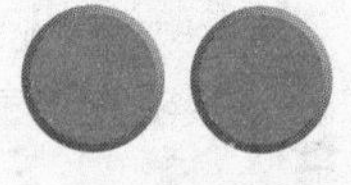

2

two-dimensional shape

V

vertex/vertices

W

weighs

weight

whole

Z

zero

0

Photographs

Every effort has been made to secure permission and provide appropriate credit for photographic material. The publisher deeply regrets any omission and pledges to correct errors called to its attention in subsequent editions.

Unless otherwise acknowledged, all photographs are the property of Pearson Education, Inc.

Photo locators denoted as follows: Top (T), Center (C), Bottom (B), Left (L), Right (R), Background (Bkgd)

001 Jorge Salcedo/Shutterstock;**085L** Evgeny Murtola/Shutterstock;**085R** 2rut/Shutterstock;**135** Michal Kolodziejczyk/Fotolia;**199** James Insogna/Fotolia;**245** Christopher Elwell/Shutterstock;**281** tankist276/Shutterstock;**359** Shutterstock;**431** Winai Tepsuttinun/Shutterstock;**507** Panda3800/Shutterstock;**563** Turbojet/Shutterstock;**621** Andrey Pavlov/Shutterstock;**675** Eugene Sergeev/Shutterstock;**745** Michael Flippo/Fotolia;**799** Singkham/Shutterstock.